Study Guide

to accompany

Discovering Psychology

Don H. Hockenbury
Sandra E. Hockenbury

Cornelius Rea
Douglas College

WORTH PUBLISHERS

Study Guide by Cornelius Rea
to accompany
Hockenbury & Hockenbury **Discovering Psychology**

ISBN: 1–57259–557–4

Printing: 5 4 3 2
Year: 02 01 00 99

Printed in the United States of America

Cover credit: *Survival Guide #1*, Collage, 24 by 48, 1995 by Phoebe Beasley

Worth Publishers
33 Irving Place
New York, NY 10003

Contents

To the Student

This study guide will enable you achieve your goals in your introductory psychology course: to study effectively and to learn the important concepts in Don and Sandy Hockenbury's textbook. Use this study guide in an active manner and as a complement to the textbook, not as a substitute for it. The approach taken here emphasizes guided learning and includes opportunities for self-testing and exam preparation. The learning phase of your guided study involves active interaction with the textbook material and this study guide will help you master the chapter concepts in a straightforward and enjoyable manner. The goal is to create independent, motivated students who enjoy learning for its own sake, who can think critically, and who have a deep conceptual understanding of the information presented in the textbook.

Advance Organizers and Learning Objectives

Don and Sandy Hockenbury have provided you with advance organizers at the beginning of each major section of each chapter. These will help you start thinking about the material and will give you an overview of what lies ahead. The learning objectives at the beginning of each main section in the study guide are derived from these advance organizers. So read these learning objectives before you read each section of the textbook chapter and before you start the exercises in the study guide. Both the advance organizers and the learning objectives are directly linked to the true/false tests, matching exercises, progress tests, and graphic organizers in the study guide. Successful completion of these activities will prepare you for tests, quizzes, exams and other evaluation procedures.

Skimming and Scanning

Skimming and scanning is another strategy that can facilitate learning. When you skim and scan a chapter you get a better idea of what lies ahead. So survey the chapter first. Spend some time looking at the graphics, and examine the special features, boxed inserts, and concept reviews; note the parts that look interesting to you. Pay attention to the pictures, cartoons, figures and tables. This preview will give you a clearer impression of what is going to be covered in the chapter. Don't worry about the details at this point; just try to get the big picture.

Getting a clear sense of what you are going to encounter before you actually read the chapter is very important and will make learning the material easier. For example, imagine trying to put together a big jigsaw puzzle. How much more difficult would this task be if you didn't know what the finished picture looked like? Do you think it would be easier if you had seen the finished picture? Of course it would! Likewise, when you skim and scan the chapter you will have some idea of the big picture and of how the various pieces of the chapter fit together.

Structured Note Taking   Good note taking is very important to learning. So we encourage you to take notes. The study guide structures your note taking by prompting you to write definitions, to paraphrase information, and to complete sentences. Simply highlighting sentences in the textbook is not sufficient. Highlighting does not involve active cognitive processing of the information, whereas writing, especially using your own words, does.

Graphic Organizers   The study guide emphasizes active learning and one aid to better understanding is the use of visualization. Completing the graphs, charts, and flow diagrams will provide a visual synopsis that will help you understand and remember the material. So be sure to complete all these exercises, and practice making your own graphic organizers.

Learning Checks: Matching Exercises, True/False Tests, and Progress Tests   The study guide contains learning checks in the form of conceptual questions, matching exercises, and true/false tests at the end of each section in every chapter. These exercises provide you with feedback as you progress through the chapter. Be sure to complete each of these before going on to the next section. Two progress tests containing multiple choice questions conclude each chapter. These are designed to help you assess your mastery of the material. If you don't know the answers to these questions, go back and study the parts of the textbook that you didn't understand.

Something To Think About   At the end of each chapter in the study guide there is a special feature called Something To Think About. This section contains thought-provoking questions about the chapter. We encourage you to think actively about what you have read in the chapter. Discuss these topics with friends and family members. This will help you remember the concepts and make learning more enjoyable. So, have fun!

Answers   Answers are found at the end of each chapter. Check your answers as you work your way through each chapter: getting immediate corrective feedback facilitates the learning process.

Chapter 1   Introducing Psychology

OVERVIEW   Chapter 1 starts by answering the question "What is psychology?" and then gives a brief history of the people and events that influenced the beginning of psychology. Included are the contributions made by philosophy and physiology and by the founder of psychology, Wilhelm Wundt. The two early schools, structuralism and functionalism, are discussed along with the emergence of the major perspectives in twentieth-century psychology. The state of psychology today is described as well as the major specialty areas that now exist in the discipline.

The four goals of psychology are listed, followed by an explanation of how these goals are achieved using the scientific method. Various research methods are outlined, and the advantages and disadvantages of each are discussed. The experimental method is explained in detail using a recently published study to illustrate important concepts such as dependent and independent variables, experimental and control groups, random assignment, and the double-blind technique.

Descriptive methods are explained next, and the advantages and disadvantages of using surveys, questionnaires, interviews, naturalistic observation, and case study research are discussed. Important issues such as the need for representative sampling and random selection are raised. Correlational studies and their uses and limitations are presented, and the concepts of correlation, the correlation coefficient, and negative and positive correlations are described and explained. Finally there is an important discussion about the ethical guidelines that regulate psychological research and the role played by the American Psychological Association.

Introduction: What Is Psychology
Learning Objective

When you have finished studying this section of the chapter, you should be able to:

1. Define psychology and state how the definition has changed over time.

*Read the section "Introduction: What Is Psychology?" and **write** your answers to the following:*

1. Psychology is the _____
   _____ .

2. The definition of psychology has _____
   _____ .

The Early History of Psychology
Learning Objectives

When you have finished studying this section of the chapter, you should be able to:

1. Name and list the contributions of the key people involved in the early history of psychology.

2. Describe the influence of philosophy and identify the key issues raised.

3. Define physiology and explain how it influenced the development of psychology.

4. Identify the two first schools of psychology and identify the founders.

5. State how the approaches of structuralism and functionalism differed and identify their common goal.

6. List the limitations of structuralism and explain why it no longer exists as a school of thought in contemporary psychology.

7. Specify functionalism's key themes and explain their influence on contemporary psychology

8. Name two of William James's students and list their contributions to the development of psychology.

Read the section "The Early History of Psychology" and write the answers to the following:

1. "What is the proper subject matter of psychology?" "What methods should psychologists use?" "What should the nature of psychology be?" These are questions that the first _____

_____ .

2. (a) Early philosophers such as Aristotle were interested in psychological topics like

_____ , _____ ,

_____ , and _____ .

(b) French philosopher _____ proposed that the mind and body are separate entities.

(c) Another issue raised by philosophers was the _____ issue, where _____ refers to the inborn characteristics of the individual and _____ refers to the environmental influences that shape the individual.

(d) The eventual emergence of psychology as a science hinged on advances in other sciences, particularly _____ .

(e) _____ is a branch of biology that studies the functions and parts of living organisms, including humans.

(f) Collectively, the early scientific discoveries made by physiologists established the foundation for an idea crucial to the development of psychology, that _____ could be applied to issues of

_____ .

3. (a) Wundt is credited with opening the first

_____

at the University of Leipzig in 1879.

(b) He described the connection between _____ and _____ but promoted the idea that psychology should be _____

_____ .

(c) Wundt stated that psychology should use _____ to study mental processes.

4. (a) Wundt's student _____ established structuralism, the first major school in psychology.

(b) Structuralism studied the _____

_____ .

(c) The structuralists used _____ to analyze conscious experience into its elemental _____ or components.

5. The main limitations of structuralism were that

(a) individual subjects _____ in their responses to the same stimulus from trial to trial,

(b) different subjects often provided very different _____ about the same stimulus, and

(c) _____ could not be used to study children or animals.

(d) Complex topics such as _____ , _____ , _____ , and _____ did not lend themselves to scientific investigation using introspection.

6. (a) _____ influenced the beginning of the functionalist school of psychology.

(b) Functionalism stressed the importance of how behavior _____ to allow organisms to _____ to their environment.

(c) Functionalism expanded psychology to include applications to _____ , _____ , and

_____ .

7. (a) The common goal of functionalism and structuralism is an emphasis on the study of

_____ .

(b) In contrast to the structuralists, William James saw _____ as an ongoing stream of mental activity.

(c) Functionalism's twin themes, the importance of the _____ role of behavior and the emphasis on

_____ psychology in enhancing human behavior, continue to be evident in many areas of modern psychology.

8. Two of James's students were:

(a) _____ established the

first _____

in the U.S. and founded the American Psychological Association.

(b) _____ conducted research in many areas, including

_____ , _____ , and

_____ , founded a psychological laboratory at Wellesley College in 1891, and became the first woman president of the American Psychological Association.

Review of Key Terms and Key Names 1

psychology	introspection
nature-nurture issue	William James
physiology	functionalism
Wilhelm Wundt	G. Stanley Hall
structuralism	Mary Whiton Calkins

Matching Exercise

Match the appropriate term / name with its definition or description.

1. _____ American psychologist who conducted research on memory, personality, and dreams; established one of the first U.S. psychology research laboratories; first woman president of the American Psychological Association.

2. _____ Looking inward in an attempt to reconstruct feelings and sensations experienced immediately after viewing a stimulus object.

3. _____ Early school of psychology that emphasized studying the purpose, or function, of behavior and mental experiences.

4. _____ The scientific study of behavior and mental processes.

5. _____ German physiologist who founded psychology as a formal science; opened first psychology research laboratory in 1879.

True/False Test

Indicate whether each statement is true or false by placing T or F in the blank space next to each item.

1. ___ G. Stanley Hall was an American psychologist who established the first psychology research laboratory in the United States and founded the American Psychological Association.

2. ___ Structuralism stresses the importance of how behavior functions to allow people and animals to adapt to their environment.

3. ___ The nature-nurture issue refers to the debate about whether the mind and body are separate entities.

4. ___ Physiology is a branch of biology that studies the functions and parts of living organisms, including human beings.

5. ___ William James was an American philosopher and psychologist who founded psychology in the United States and established the psychological school called functionalism.

Check your answers and review any areas of weakness before going on to the next section.

Leaders in Psychology
Learning Objectives

When you have finished studying this section of the chapter, you should be able to:

1. Identify the approach that dominated psychology until the 1960s.

2. Name the founders of behaviorism and list their respective contributions.

3. Specify the subject matter and methodology of behaviorism.

4. Name the founder of psychoanalysis and state the emphasis of this approach.

5. Identify the founder of Gestalt psychology and describe his approach.

6. Explain how the approach taken by humanistic psychology differs from behaviorism and psychoanalysis.

7. Identify the founders of humanistic psychology and list the aspects of human behavior they emphasize.

Read the section "Leaders in Psychology" and **write** *your answers to the following:*

1. (a) Behaviorism's focus was on the scientific study of _____ that could be objectively measured and verified.

   (b) Behaviorism rejected the emphasis on _____ promoted by the structuralists and functionalists.

   (c) _____ dominated psychology until the 1960s.

2. (a) _____ grew out of the pioneering work of Russian physiologist Ivan Pavlov.

   (b) Pavlov's work on salivation in dogs led him to believe that he had discovered the _____ by which all behaviors are _____ .

   (c) The American psychologist who championed behaviorism as a new school in psychology was _____ ; he rejected both _____ as a scientific methodology and _____ as the subject matter of psychology.

   (d) The person who followed in Watson's footsteps in championing a behavioral psychology was the American psychologist _____ .

   (e) The goal of the behaviorists was to discover the fundamental principles of _____ .

3. (a) The Austrian physician who emphasized unconscious processes rather than overt observable behavior was _____ .

   (b) _____ is a school of psychology that focuses on the role of unconscious conflicts in determining behavior and personality; these conflicts are almost always _____ in nature.

   (c) Freud's theory was based on the idea that past experiences, especially childhood experiences, are critical in the formation of adult _____ and _____ and that glimpses of unconscious impulses are revealed in _____ , _____ , _____ , and _____ .

4. (a) Gestalt psychology emphasizes the _____ rather than the individual elements of conscious experience stressed by the structuralists.

   (b) The founder of Gestalt psychology was _____ .

   (c) Gestalt psychology helped advance the study of _____ and _____ in American psychology.

   (d) Unlike behaviorism, Gestalt psychology assigns an important role to _____ in organizing sensations into meaningful perceptions.

5. (a) The school of psychology that emphasizes conscious experiences, including each person's unique potential for psychological growth and self-direction, is _____ psychology.

   (b) The person credited with founding humanistic psychology is _____ .

(c) Another humanistic psychologist who developed a theory of motivation that emphasizes personal growth was _____ .

(d) Unlike behaviorists, who stress the importance of _____ , and psychoanalysts, who emphasize _____ , humanistic psychologists believed that _____ , _____ , _____ , and the potential for personal psychological growth are the most important factors.

Psychology Today
Learning Objectives

When you have finished studying this section of the chapter, you should be able to:

1. Name the major approaches in contemporary psychology.

2. Describe what events led to the emergence of biological psychology and list its main areas of study today.

3. Explain what is meant by "the cognitive revolution" and state the focus of cognitive psychology.

4. Specify the scope of cross-cultural psychology and explain its importance.

5. List and differentiate between the major perspectives in contemporary psychology.

6. Explain the difference between a *perspective* and a *specialty* area.

7. List the specialty areas in contemporary psychology and describe the focus of each.

8. Distinguish between psychology and psychiatry and explain the role psychoanalysts play.

*Read the section "Psychology Today" and **write** your answers to the following:*

1. (a) Biological psychology emphasizes studying the _____ .

(b) Advances in _____ and _____ increased the influence of biological psychology.

2. (a) Because it represented a break from traditional behaviorism, the emergence of cognitive psychology in the 1960s is often called _____ .

(b) The focus of cognitive psychology is on the important role of _____ in how people process _____ , develop _____ , solve _____ , and think.

(c) One important factor in the cognitive revolution was the development of the first _____ , which gave psychologists a model for human mental processes.

3. (a) Psychologists who study the diversity of human behavior in different cultural settings and countries are called _____ psychologists.

(b) The phenomenon of social loafing in some countries and its opposite effect in others points to the enormous influence that _____ and _____ factors can have on behavior.

(c) Today's psychologists tend to characterize themselves according to the _____ they emphasize in investigating psychological topics and the _____ in which they practice.

4. There are six major perspectives in psychology:

(a) The _____ perspective emphasizes the physical bases of behavior.

(b) The _____ perspective emphasizes environmental influences on behavior.

(c) The _____ perspective emphasizes unconscious influences on behavior and personality.

(d) The _____ perspective emphasizes psychological growth and personal potential.

(e) The _____ perspective emphasizes mental processes.

(f) The _____ perspective emphasizes the influence of culture on behavior.

5. Which specialty area is represented by each of the following?

   (a) Dr. Matthews studies the relationship between behavior and such physical systems as the nervous system, the endocrine system, the immune system, and genetics. She would most likely be classified as a(n) _____ psychologist.

   (b) Michele wants to study physical, social, and psychological changes that occur over the lifespan when she attends graduate school. Michele is planning to be a(n) _____ psychologist.

   (c) Dr. Bowman studies the causes, treatment, and prevention of different types of mental disorders. Dr. Bowman is most likely a(n) _____ psychologist.

   (d) _____ psychologists explore how individuals are affected by people and situations and what factors influence conformity, obedience, persuasion, interpersonal attraction, helping behavior, prejudice, aggression, and many other phenomena.

   (e) Dr. Steinberg examines individual differences and the characteristics that make each person unique. He is most likely to be classified as a(n) _____ psychologist.

   (f) Ingrid is interested in investigating mental processes, reasoning, thinking, problem solving, memory, perception, mental imagery, and language. Ingrid is probably planning a career as a(n) _____ psychologist.

   (g) Dr. Whinney is a(n) _____ psychologist who develops instructional methods and materials used to train people in both educational and work settings, and she also studies how people of all ages learn, whereas her colleague, Dr. Marx, is a(n) _____ psychologist whose focus is on designing programs that promote the intellectual, social, and emotional development of children, including those with special needs.

   (h) Dr. Barton is concerned with stress and coping, the relationship between psychological factors and well-being, and ways of promoting health-enhancing behaviors. Dr. Barton is probably a(n) _____ psychologist.

   (i) Pitor, who just completed his Ph.D., applied for an advertised job that was concerned with the relationship between people and work and included the study of job satisfaction, worker productivity, personnel selection, and the interaction between people and equipment. Pitor has applied for a job as a(n) _____ psychologist.

6. (a) A(n) _____ has a medical degree and thus can prescribe drugs and perform medical procedures.

   (b) A(n) _____ has a doctorate in psychology and intensive training in treating people with psychological disorders.

Graphic Organizer 1

Below are statements representing some of the major perspectives and specialty areas in contemporary psychology. Which perspective is reflected by each statement and which specialty area is being described? Write your answers in the spaces provided.

Statement	Perspective	Specialty
1. My interest is in how different parenting styles and techniques influence each child's individual potential for growth and self-determination.		
2. I study the relationship between people and work and more specifically how to increase productivity. I believe that by changing environmental factors, increasing the use of rewards and praise for correct behavior, and providing corrective feedback, workers' overt behavior can be changed.		
3. How people of all ages learn, as well as developing instructional methods and materials to help the learning process, is the focus of my research. In particular, I stress the role played by thinking, problem solving, memory, and use of mental imagery.		
4. Mostly I work with people who suffer from mental disorders, and I believe that the main causes of mental illness are either genetic or due to some malfunction in the central nervous system or endocrine system. I often prescribe medications and order medical procedures.		
5. I often travel to different countries to research helping behavior, conformity, and obedience. My research tends to show that many behavioral patterns, for instance, the amount of personal space people require to feel comfortable, vary from one country to another.		
6. I believe that unconscious conflicts, early childhood experiences, and repressed sexual and aggressive feelings make us who we are, and I use this point of view in my work on individual differences and in trying to determine what characteristics make each of us unique.		
7. I focus on the relationship between psychological factors and health, in particular on how people cope with stress in their lives. It is not what happens to us that is important; rather, how we perceive and think about potentially stressful events determines our well-being.		
8. My research keeps me in the lab most of the time, and my main focus is on the principles and conditions of learning and motivation. Recently I have been investigating how quickly rats learn the layout of a maze as a function of either large or small amounts of reinforcement.		

Review of Key Terms and Key Names 2

behaviorism
Ivan Pavlov
John B. Watson
B. F. Skinner
Sigmund Freud
psychoanalysis
Gestalt psychology
Max Wertheimer
humanistic psychology
Carl Rogers
Abraham Maslow
biological psychology
cognitive psychology
cross-cultural
  psychology
perspective

specialty area
experimental psychology
developmental
  psychology
social psychology
personality psychology
health psychology
educational psychology
school psychology
industrial/organizational
  psychology
clinical psychologist
counseling psychology
psychiatrist
psychoanalyst

Matching Exercise

Match the appropriate term/name with its definition or description.

1. _____ A psychologist who has a doctorate in psychology and intensive training in diagnosing and treating people with mental disorders.

2. _____ German psychologist who founded the school of Gestalt psychology.

3. _____ The study of physical, social, and psychological changes over the lifespan, from conception to death.

4. _____ A school of psychology and theoretical viewpoint that emphasizes the study of observable behaviors, especially as they pertain to the process of learning.

5. _____ Austrian physician and founder of psychoanalysis.

6. _____ A mental health professional who has a medical degree plus years of specialized training in the diagnosis and treatment of mental disorders.

7. _____ A specialty area that helps develop the instructional methods and materials used to train people in both educational and work settings and studies how people of all ages learn.

8. _____ A general term that describes research focused on such basic topics as sensory processes, principles of learning, emotion, and motivation.

9. _____ A point of view or general framework that reflects the emphasis a psychologist may take in investigating psychological topics.

10. _____ American psychologist who founded the school of humanistic psychology.

11. _____ A specific area in psychology in which psychologists are trained and in which they work or practice.

12. _____ A specialty area that investigates mental processes, information processing, reasoning, thinking, problem solving, memory, perception, mental imagery, and language.

13. _____ An area of psychology that examines individual differences and the characteristics and traits that make each person unique.

True/False Test

Indicate whether each statement is true or false by placing T or F in the blank space next to each item.

1. ____ Ivan Pavlov was an Austrian physician whose work focused on the unconscious causes of behavior and personality formation and who founded psychoanalysis.

2. ____ Biological psychology studies the physical bases of human and animal behavior.

3. ____ B. F. Skinner was a famous American psychologist who championed behaviorism after its founding.

4. ____ Counseling psychology is concerned with the relationship between people and work, and it includes the study of job satisfaction, worker productivity, personnel selection, and the interaction between people and equipment.

5. ____ Abraham Maslow was a humanistic psychologist who developed a theory of motivation that emphasized psychological growth.

6. ____ Psychoanalysis studies environmental influences on behavior and personality without reference to mental processes and is concerned with understanding how we learn to become who we are.

7. ____ Gestalt psychology assigns an important role to the perception of whole figures and has advanced the study of perception and problem solving in American psychology.

8. ____ Cross-cultural psychology stresses the importance of cultural and ethnic influences on behavior.

9. ___ A school of psychology and theroetical view-point that emphasizes each person's unique potential for psychological growth and self-direction is called humanistic psychology.

10. ___ School psychology focuses on designing programs that promote the intellectual, social, and emotional development of children, including those with special needs.

11. ___ Psychologists who explore how individuals are affected by people and situations and what factors influence conformity, obedience, persuasion, interpersonal attraction, and other related phenomena are called social psychologists.

12. ___ Health psychology is concerned with stress and coping, the relationship between psychological factors and well-being, and ways of promoting health-enhancing behaviors.

13. ___ Industrial/organizational psychology aims to improve everyday functioning by helping people solve problems in daily living and cope more effectively with challenging situations in their lives through either one-to-one sessions or group therapy.

14. ___ John B. Watson was the American psychologist who founded behaviorism, emphasizing the study of observable behavior and rejecting the study of mental processes.

> Check your answers and review any areas of weakness before going on to the next section.

The Scientific Method
Learning Objectives

When you have finished studying this section of the chapter, you should be able to:

1. Define the scientific method.

2. List the four goals of psychology.

3. Explain the assumptions and attitudes of psychologists.

4. Summarize the four steps of the scientific method and define the term *empirical evidence*.

5. List and explain the key terms and concepts used in the scientific method.

6. Explain how the scientific method generates new knowledge and challenges established ways of thinking.

*Read the section "The Scientific Method" and **write** your answers to the following:*

1. The four basic goals of psychology are to:
   (a) _____ , (b) _____ ,
   (c) _____ , and
   (d) _____
   behavior and mental processes.

2. The scientific method refers to a set of
   _____ , _____ , and
   _____ that guide researchers in
   _____ ,
   _____ , and
   _____ .

3. (a) Psychologists are guided by the basic scientific assumption that all events are lawful, and this means that psychologists assume that _____
   _____ .

   (b) Psychologists share a set of attitudes in trying to achieve the goals of psychology, and these include being _____ ,
   having a healthy sense of
   _____ , and being
   _____ in the claims they make.

4. (a) Evidence that is a result of observation, measurement, and experimentation is called
   _____ .

   (b) As part of the overall process of producing scientific evidence, psychologists follow four steps:
   (1) _____
   (2) _____
   (3) _____
   (4) _____

5. (a) Once a researcher has identified a question or issue to be investigated, it must be posed in the form of a(n) _____ that can be tested empirically.

   (b) A(n) _____ is a tentative statement that describes the relationship between two or more variables.

(c) Factors that can change or vary and are capable of being observed, measured, and verified are called _____ .

(d) A(n) _____ is a precise description of how a variable in a study will be manipulated or measured.

(e) _____ are critical because many concepts that psychologists investigate can be measured in more than one way.

6. (a) In designing a study investigators must decide between two research methods: _____ and _____ .

(b) The _____ method provides evidence for cause-and-effect relationships, and the _____ method involves strategies for observing and describing behavior.

(c) Naturalistic observation, surveys, case studies, and correlational studies are commonly used _____ methods.

7. (a) _____ are mathematical methods used to summarize, analyze, and draw conclusions about data.

(b) If the results of research are not likely to have occurred by chance, they are called _____ .

(c) Meta-analysis is a statistical technique that involves the analysis of _____ on a specific topic in order to identify overall trends.

8. (a) Psychologists describe their methods and explain their procedures in detail so that other investigators may _____ , or repeat, the study.

(b) A tentative explanation that tries to account for the diverse findings on the same topic is called a(n) _____ or a model.

(c) A(n) _____ is a tentative statement about the relationship between two or more variables, whereas a(n) _____

is a tentative explanation that tries to integrate and account for the relationship among various findings and observations.

(d) When new results challenge the established way of thinking about a phenomenon, a(n) _____ is expanded, modified, and even replaced, and thus the _____ base of psychology is constantly evolving.

9. Read the following descriptions and provide the correct term in each case:

(a) Dr. Marlow is interested in drinking and driving behavior and wants to know the frequency with which people will drive after receiving feedback from a breathalyzer test. In one condition she sets up her equipment in a bar and administers the test to patrons who are leaving and planning to drive and then observes whether or not feedback on their level of intoxication influenced their decision to drive. Dr. Marlow is using

_____

research.

(b) In the above example Dr. Marlow makes this prediction: the majority of people who are told that they are over the legal limit will still drive, and the higher the level on the breathalyzer test, the more likely it is that they will drive. Dr. Marlow has formulated a(n) _____ .

(c) After collecting data over many weeks, Dr. Marlow performs calculations and mathematical tests to see if her prediction was correct. Dr. Marlow is using _____ to analyze her data.

(d) Dr. Marlow next writes a report describing the background of this research and details her research design, data collection methods, results, analyses, and conclusions. She submits her report to a respected psychology journal for peer review and publication. She is following step _____ of producing scientific evidence by

_____ .

Review of Key Terms 3

scientific method
empirical evidence
hypothesis
variable
operational definition
experimental method
descriptive method

cause-and-effect
  relationship
statistics
statistical significance
meta-analysis
replicate
theory

Matching Exercise

Match the appropriate term with its definition or description.

1. _____ A statistical technique that involves combining and analyzing the results of many research studies on a specific topic in order to identify overall trends.

2. _____ To repeat or duplicate a scientific study in order to increase confidence in the validity of the original findings.

3. _____ A set of assumptions, attitudes, and procedures that guide researchers in creating questions to investigate, generating evidence, and drawing conclusions.

4. _____ A tentative statement about the relationship between two or more variables.

5. _____ A precise description of how the variables in a study will be manipulated or measured.

6. _____ A method of investigation used to demonstrate cause-and-effect relationships by purposely manipulating a factor thought to produce change in a second factor.

7. _____ Mathematical methods used to summarize data and draw conclusions based on the data.

True/False Test

Indicate whether each statement is true or false by placing T or F in the blank space next to each item.

1. ___ A statistically significant finding is one that is not likely to have occurred by chance.

2. ___ Empirical evidence is evidence that is the result of observation, measurement, and experimentation.

3. ___ A variable is a tentative statement that

describes the relationship between two or more factors.

4. ___ Descriptive methods are research strategies for observing and describing behavior and include naturalistic observation, survey, case studies, and correlational studies.

5. ___ The cause-and-effect relationship demonstrated by the experimental method is one in which changes in one variable cause change in a second variable.

6. ___ A theory is a statistical technique that involves the analysis of many research studies on a specific topic in order to identify overall trends.

> Check your answers and review any areas of weakness before going on to the next section.

The Experimental Method
Learning Objectives

When you have finished studying this section of the chapter, you should be able to:

1. Describe the experimental method and state its main purpose.

2. Define the terms *independent* and *dependent* variable and provide examples that illustrate each.

3. Explain the purpose of random assignment and state why it is important.

4. List and describe the experimental conditions and explain the purpose of a control group.

5. Describe the variations in experimental design and explain why they vary.

6. State what is meant by expectancy effects and explain the purpose of the placebo control procedure.

7. List the limitations of the experimental method.

*Read the section "The Experimental Method" and **write** your answers to the following:*

1. (a) The _____ method is used to demonstrate a cause-and-effect relationship between _____ in one variable and the _____ on another variable.

(b) Conducting an experiment involves deliberately varying one factor, which is called the _____ variable, and measuring the effects on another factor, called the _____ variable.

(c) If all other factors are held constant, then any changes in the _____ variable can be attributed to the changes in the _____ variable, and that's why an experiment can demonstrate a _____ relationship between the two variables.

2. (a) Random assignment means that
_____
_____ .

(b) Random assignment is important because it ensures _____
_____
and also helps ensure that _____
_____ .

3. (a) A control group is the group in the experiment that _____
_____ .

(b) The control group serves several important functions. First, it serves as a _____ to which changes in the other experimental groups can be compared, and second, it can be used to check for changes that occur _____ or _____ over time.

(c) Because the control group is not exposed to the _____ variable, whatever changes occur in the _____ variable in the control group cannot have been caused by the _____ variable.

4. (a) The experimental group is the group in the experiment that _____
_____ .

(b) To ensure objectivity in rating videotaped behaviors, raters are _____ , or

unaware of the experimental condition that is being rated.

5. (a) The group exposed to a fake treatment or a substance with no known effects is called the _____ group and is used in experiments to help check for _____ .

(b) _____ refer to changes that may occur simply because subjects think changes are going to occur.

(c) A double-blind study is one in which neither the _____ nor the _____ are aware of the experimental condition to which participants have been assigned.

(d) The purpose of the double-blind technique is to guard against the possibility that the _____ will inadvertently display cues or signals about the purpose of the experiment to the _____ .

(e) A single-blind study is one in which the _____ but not the _____ are aware of the critical information about the experiment.

(f) The purpose of the double-blind technique is to guard against the possibility that the researcher will display
_____ ,
which are subtle cues or signals that communicate what is expected of particular subjects.

6. There are a number of limitations to the experimental method:

(a) The _____ conditions of some experiments may produce results that do not _____ well or do not _____ to real situations or populations beyond those of the study.

(b) Even experiments conducted in natural settings have disadvantages, such as a _____ in experimental control.

(c) Due to ethical concerns, it may not be feasible to _____ .

(d) It may be impossible to create experimentally the kinds of _____ that researchers want to study.

7. Dr. Denton studies the effects of marijuana on memory. He designs an ethically approved experiment that consists of two groups: group A gets the active ingredient in cannabis, THC, and group B gets a harmless inert substance, and neither the researcher nor the participants know who is getting the drug and who is not. Subjects are assigned to each group by chance, and all subjects are given a long list of word pairs to learn and are later given a memory test.

(a) The independent variable in this study is _____ .

(b) The dependent variable is the _____ .

(c) Group A is the _____ group, and group B is the _____ group.

(d) Dr. Denton has used a(n) _____ technique in designing the experiment, and this along with the control procedure used should help guard against _____ and _____ .

(e) Subjects ended up in group A or group B on the basis of _____ .

Graphic Organizer 2

Read the following and label each step appropriately:

	Step
1. Reports from people who experienced isolation from others indicate that being alone or socially isolated made people fearful or anxious. From this you speculate that anxiety might increase the desire to affiliate with others.	
2. You set up a situation where half the subjects are exposed to either a high-fear condition or a low-fear condition. Then you measure their desire to affiliate by giving them a questionnaire.	
3. You summarize the responses from each group, carry out the appropriate statistical analyses, and then decide what inferences can be made.	
4. You write a detailed account of the study and submit it to a journal for publication.	

Review of Key Terms 4

experimental method
independent variable
dependent variable
random assignment
control group
experimental group

placebo control
expectancy effects
double blind
single blind
demand characteristics

Matching Exercise

Match the appropriate term with its definition or description.

1. _____ An experimental technique in which the researchers, but not the subjects, are aware of the critical information about the experiment.

2. _____ A method of investigation used to demonstrate cause-and-effect relationships by purposely manipulating a factor thought to produce change in a second factor.

3. _____ The factor that is observed and measured for change in an experiment.

4. _____ A change in a subject's behavior produced by the subject's belief that change should happen.

5. _____ The group of subjects who are exposed to all experimental conditions except the independent variable.

6. _____ Subtle cues or signals that communicate what is expected of particular subjects.

True/False Test

Indicate whether each statement is true or false by placing T or F in the blank space next to each item.

1. ____ Random assignment means that all subjects have an equal chance of being assigned to any of the conditions or groups in the study.

2. ____ Subjects in the placebo control group receive all the experimental conditions except the dependent variable.

3. ____ Subjects in the experimental group receive all the experimental conditions including the independent variable.

4. ____ The independent variable in an experiment is purposely manipulated in order to effect a change in another variable.

5. ____ An experimental technique in which neither the participants nor the researcher is

aware of the experimental conditions to which each subject has been assigned is called the double-blind technique.

Check your answers and review any areas of weakness before going on to the next section.

Descriptive Methods
Learning Objectives

When you have finished studying this section of the chapter, you should be able to:

1. Define descriptive methods and list four types.

2. Distinguish between descriptive methods and experimental methods and list the advantages and disadvantages of each.

3. Describe naturalistic observation and provide an example that illustrates this technique.

4. Explain how case studies are used and specify the benefits of case study research.

5. Describe the difference between surveys and interviews and list the advantages and disadvantages of each.

6. Explain what a sample is and describe how representative sampling and random selection affect the validity and reliability of results.

7. Define *correlation* and specify what a correlational study involves and what its limitations are.

8. Explain what the correlation coefficient is and what it measures.

9. Define negative and positive correlation and provide examples that illustrate each.

10. List the five key provisions of the American Psychological Association (APA) ethical guidelines.

*Read the section "Descriptive Methods" and **write** your answers to the following:*

1. (a) Descriptive methods do not involve deliberately _____

    _____ ;

    instead they are research strategies for

    _____

    behavior.

(b) Using descriptive methods, researchers can answer important questions such as _____ certain behaviors take place, _____ they occur, and whether they are _____ _____ , such as a person's age, race, and educational level.

(c) Descriptive methods can provide a wealth of information about behavior that would be difficult or impossible to

_____ .

2. (a) The systematic observation and recording of behaviors as they occur in their natural setting is called _____ .

(b) Jane Goodall and her colleagues used _____ to study chimpanzee behavior in the wild.

(c) One advantage of _____ is that it can allow researchers to study human behaviors that could not be ethically manipulated in an experimental situation, and in addition results can often be _____ more confidently to real-life situations than can artificially or staged situations.

3. (a) A _____ is an intensive, in-depth investigation of an individual and can involve compiling data from a wide variety of different sources.

(b) Although _____ are most often used to investigate rare, unusual, or extreme conditions, they can provide psychologists with information about normal behavior.

4. (a) Surveys and questionnaires typically involve a _____ format in which subjects respond to a structured set of questions about their _____ , _____ , _____ , or _____ .

(b) An advantage offered by _____

is that investigators are able to gather information from a large group of people.

(c) A(n) _____ is a survey method that is conducted in person and where the participant's responses to a structured set of questions are recorded by the investigator.

5. (a) A(n) _____ is a segment of a larger group or population, and a _____ very closely parallels or matches the larger group on relevant characteristics such as age, sex, race, marital status, and educational level.

(b) Random selection means that _____ of the larger group has a(n) _____ chance of being selected for inclusion in the sample.

6. (a) A correlational study examines how _____ two variables are _____ each other.

(b) A(n) _____ is a numerical indicator of how strongly related two factors seem to be.

(c) A(n) _____ , even a very strong one, does not necessarily indicate _____ .

7. (a) A positive correlation indicates that two variables vary systematically in the _____ direction, either _____ or _____ together.

(b) A negative correlation indicates that two variables vary systematically in the _____ direction; as one _____ , the other _____ .

(c) That two variables may be strongly correlated (either positively or negatively) is not evidence of a(n) _____ relationship.

(d) Correlational research has two advantages: first, it can be used to _____ some factors and _____ others that merit more intensive study, and second, the results of correlational research can allow researchers to make _____ .

8. The five key provisions of the APA ethical guidelines regulating research with human participants are:

(a) _____

(b) _____

(c) _____

(d) _____

(e) _____

9. Read the following and decide which term applies in each case:

(a) If a researcher found a correlation efficiency of –0.85 between the amount of exercise people do and their weight, this would indicate that the _____ people exercise, the _____ they weigh.

(b) If an organization wants to find out more about the spending habits of high-income people, they would be advised to conduct a _____ using a representative _____ that would be _____ selected from this population.

(c) Dr. Klatz is interested in whether there is a difference in the way males and females carry objects such as textbooks, notepads, bags, and other large objects, so he sets up a hidden camera on the main concourse of a large university and videotapes people at various times throughout the day. Dr. Klatz is using _____ .

(d) A psychologist discovers that the more control people feel they have over what happens in their work environments, the more productive they are. The psychologist has discovered a(n) _____ correlation between perceived control and productivity.

(e) A psychologist who wants to find out more about the lives and experiences of some people who claim to have been abducted by aliens and also wants to know how these people are viewed by their families, friends, and co-workers would be advised to use the _____ method of research.

Graphic Organizer 3

The following diagram shows both positive and negative correlations between variables. In cells A through D the arrows indicate a relationship between the amount students study and their grade point average (GPA). Fill in the appropriate term in each space provided.

Amount of Study (X)

	High	Low
High GPA (Y)	Cell A ↑ ↑	Cell B ↓ ↑
Low	Cell C ↑ ↓	Cell D ↓ ↓

1. Cell A indicates a _____ correlation, and cell D indicates a _____ correlation.

2. Cell C indicates a _____ correlation, and cell B indicates a _____ correlation.

3. Cell A: _____ amounts of X are associated with _____ levels of Y

   Cell D: _____ amounts of X are associated with _____ levels of Y

4. Cell C: _____ amounts of X are associated with _____ levels of Y

   Cell B: _____ amounts of X are associated with _____ levels of Y

Review of Key Terms 5

descriptive method
naturalistic observation
case study
survey
questionnaire
interview
sample
representative sample
random selection
correlational study

correlation coefficient
positive correlation
negative correlation
culture
ethnocentrism
individualistic cultures
collectivistic cultures
pseudoscience
critical thinking

Matching Exercise

Match the appropriate term with its definition or description.

1. _____ A finding that two factors vary systematically in the same direction, increasing and decreasing together.

2. _____ A questionnaire or interview designed to investigate the opinions, behaviors, or characteristics of a particular group.

3. _____ Scientific procedures that involve systematically observing behavior in order to describe the relationships among behaviors and events.

4. _____ A selected segment of the population used to represent the group that is being studied.

5. _____ A selected segment that very closely parallels the larger population being studied on relevant characteristics.

6. _____ A research strategy that allows the precise calculation of how strongly related two factors are to one another.

7. _____ The systematic observation and recording of behaviors as they occur in their natural setting.

8. _____ The active process of trying to minimize the influence of preconceptions and biases while rationally evaluating evidence; determining what conclusions can be drawn from the evidence and considering alternative explanations.

9. _____ A broad term that refers to the attitudes, values, beliefs, and behaviors shared by a group of people and communicated from one generation to another.

10. _____ The tendency to use your own culture as the standard for judging other cultures.

True/False Test

Indicate whether each item is true or false by placing T or F in the blank space next to each item.

1. ____ A case study is an intensive, in-depth investigation of an individual.

2. ____ An interview is a survey method that is conducted in person using a structured set of questions in a predetermined order, with the interviewer recording the person's responses.

3. ____ Scientific research using the questionnaire method involves sending out thousands of paper-and-pencil tests on specific topics to people (using names on a catalogue mailing list, for example) and summarizing the data from those who reply and then generalizing to the whole population.

4. ____ If a negative correlation is found between two variables it means that the two factors in question are totally unrelated.

5. ____ A correlation coefficient is a numerical indicator of how strongly related two factors seem to be.

6. ____ Random selection means that every member of the larger group or population has an equal chance of being selected for inclusion in the sample.

7. ____ Individualistic cultures emphasize the needs and goals of the group over the needs and goals of the individual.

8. ____ A pseudoscience is a fake or a false science.

9. ____ Collectivistic cultures emphasize the needs and goals of the individual over the needs and goals of the group.

Check your answers and review any areas of weakness before going on to the next section.

Something to Think About

1. When family and friends find out you are taking a psychology course, someone typically makes some comment about "headshrinking"

and "psychoanalyzing," that "psychology is just plain old common sense," and so on. To prepare yourself for these remarks, think about how you would explain what psychology really is and how you might "educate" your family and friends about the difference among psychiatry, clinical psychology, and psychoanalysis.

2. If you are like most introductory psychology students, you were probably motivated to take this course, at least in part, because of a number of questions you had about human behavior and mental processes. For example, students often wonder if hypnosis can really help recover repressed memories and memories of past lives, if a lie detector really can detect lies, if "satanic messages" imbedded in the lyrics of rock music can cause people to commit suicide, if ESP really exists, or whether subliminal tapes can really improve memory, clear up acne, or improve self-esteem. Now that you know more about the science of psychology, take one of your questions and think about how a psychologist might go about answering it.

> Check your answers and review any areas of weakness before doing the following progress tests.

Progress Test 1

Review the complete chapter (including Concept Reviews 1.1–1.4 and the boxed inserts), review all your study notes, and then test yourself on the following progress test. Check your answers. If you make a mistake, review your notes, the appropriate section in the study guide, and, if necessary, the relevant part of the chapter in your textbook.

1. Two disciplines influenced the founding of psychology. The discipline that concerns itself with questions such as how the mind and body are related and the nature-nurture issue is _____ , and the discipline that is a branch of biology and studies functions and structures of living organisms is

   _____ .

   (a) chemistry; physics
   (b) neurology; sociology
   (c) physics; neurology
   (d) philosophy; physiology

2. A Japanese psychologist investigating the relationship between worker satisfaction and productivity was surprised to find that North American workers were less productive when working as part of a group than when working alone. In some Asian countries he had found the opposite to be true. This researcher probably has a _____ perspective and his specialty area is _____ psychology.
   (a) cross-cultural; developmental
   (b) humanistic; health
   (c) behavioral; developmental
   (d) cross-cultural; industrial/organizational

3. Dr. Hammersly focuses on the role of unconscious factors in his patients' behaviors and spends time analyzing their dreams and delving into their early childhood experiences. Dr. Finkleman is more concerned with the way her patients think and reason, and her psychotherapy involves teaching her patients how to recognize irrational thinking and helping them find different ways of thinking about their situation. Dr. Hammersly's perspective is _____ and Dr. Finkleman's perspective is _____ .
   (a) cognitive; behavioral
   (b) psychoanalytic; cognitive
   (c) humanistic; biological
   (d) cognitive; psychoanalytic

4. The Sam Stone study is discussed in the text. To state that the results of this study were statistically significant means that
   (a) they occured purely by chance
   (b) the subjects were all selected by chance
   (c) they are unlikely to have been due to chance
   (d) the experimenters used a double-blind procedure

5. A researcher who investigates individual differences and how people differ on such characteristics as shyness, assertiveness, self-esteem, etc., is most likely a _____ psychologist.
   (a) clinical
   (b) biological
   (c) developmental
   (d) personality

6. To ensure that differences among subjects are evenly distributed across all experimental conditions and that there is no bias in how they are put in their respective groups, a researcher studying the effects of violence on TV and its effect on children should
   (a) operationally define the role each subject is expected to play and assign them on the basis of how closely they fit the definition
   (b) make sure that the smartest people are assigned to the experimental conditions
   (c) make sure that there is an equal number of males and females, young and old, smart and stupid, short and tall, etc., in each group
   (d) randomly assign the subjects to each condition in the experiment

7. A researcher is very interested in how sleep deprivation affects performance and cognitive abilities. She proposes that there is a relationship between the amount of sleep deprivation and the ability to solve complex mental tasks; the more sleep-deprived people are, the more mistakes they are likely to make. She has
   (a) developed a theory
   (b) formulated a hypothesis
   (c) produced empirical evidence
   (d) merely stated the obvious

8. In a study investigating the effects of sleep deprivation and cognitive performance a researcher discovers a statistically significant difference between the cognitive scores of subjects who were sleep-deprived for one hour each night and those who were sleep-deprived for four hours per night. This finding indicates that
   (a) the differences between the groups were too small to be meaningful
   (b) sleep deprivation improves mental health
   (c) smarter people need less sleep than less intelligent people
   (d) the differences between the groups are not likely to have occurred by chance

9. An experimenter who decides to repeat the essence of an earlier study using different subjects is
   (a) replicating the previous study
   (b) wasting his time
   (c) doing a meta-analysis
   (d) doing a correlation

10. In an experiment designed to test the effects of alcohol on motor coordination, group 1 subjects are given a precise amount of alcohol in a mixed drink and group 2 participants are given a drink that smells and tastes exactly like the alcoholic drink but contains no alcohol.
    (a) Group 1 is the control group.
    (b) Group 2 is the experimental group.
    (c) Group 2 is the placebo control group.
    (d) Group 1 will have much more fun than group 2.

11. A researcher is interested in what people talk about when they are riding in elevators, so she and her research assistants spend many hours riding in elevators and unobtrusively recording the conversations they hear. This researcher is using
    (a) naturalistic observation
    (b) experimental research
    (c) correlational research
    (d) case study research

12. In an attempt to understand how traumatic brain injuries affect behavior, Dr. Nicolai extensively and carefully observes and questions three accident victims who had injuries to the backs of their heads. Which research method is Dr. Nicolai utilizing?
    (a) naturalistic observation
    (b) experimental research
    (c) correlational research
    (d) case study research

13. In order to find out students' opinions about the recent cut-backs at her university, Gira sent a questionnaire to every twentieth person on the list of currently enrolled students. Gira used the technique of
    (a) replication   (c) random sampling
    (b) meta-analysis   (d) interviewing

14. If research showed that the more students study, the higher is their grade point average (GPA), this would indicate that
    (a) there is a positive correlation between study behavior and GPA
    (b) there is a negative correlation between study behavior and GPA
    (c) high GPA causes good study behavior
    (d) because the two variables are related, it is possible to make predictions because correlation implies causality

15. Ethical principles developed by the American Psychological Association require psychologists to

    (a) always tell the participants the exact nature of the experiment and inform them of the hypothesis that will be tested
    (b) never, under any circumstances, use deception with potential participants
    (c) withhold all information about the nature, results, and conclusions of the study because of the confidentiality principle
    (d) obtain informed consent and voluntary participation of potential participants

16. Dr. Joyce supports the view that the goal of psychology should be to discover the fundamental principles of learning, and instead of mental processes, psychologists should focus exclusively on overt behavior. Dr. Joyce would be classified as a _____ psychologist.

    (a) behavioral   (c) psychoanalytic
    (b) cognitive   (d) humanistic

17. A psychologist who investigates the perception of whole figures rather than individual elements of conscious experience and studies the mental activity involved in problem solving and in organizing sensations into meaningful perceptions is probably a _____ psychologist.

    (a) behavioral   (c) Gestalt
    (b) psychoanalytic   (d) biological

18. According to the Box 1.1, Culture and Human Behavior, individualistic cultures emphasize the needs and goals of the _____ over the needs and goals of the _____ .

    (a) individual; group
    (b) country; company
    (c) group; individual
    (d) collective; group

19. Collectivistic cultures emphasize the needs and goals of the _____ over the needs and goals of the _____ .

    (a) individual; group
    (b) country; company
    (c) group; individual
    (d) collective; group

20. According to the Application section, which of the following is true of pseudoscience?

    (a) It is a legitimate science that uses both established and unorthodox methods in the search for the truth.

(b) It is a fake or false science.
(c) It is not accepted by most of the scientific establishment because pseudoscientists have discovered truths that threaten all the fundamental laws and principles of science.
(d) It does not use sophisticated jargon, impressive-looking statistical graphs, or elaborate theories, and virtually no pseudoscientist has impressive-sounding credentials.

Progress Test 2

After you have checked your understanding of the material in Progress Test 1 and have done a complete chapter review with special focus on any areas of weakness, you are ready to assess your knowledge on Progress Test 2. Check your answers. If you make a mistake, check your notes, check the relevant area in the study guide, and, if necessary, review the appropriate sections of your textbook.

1. "Psychology should study the purpose of behavior and mental processes and how they function to allow organisms to adapt to their environment." This is what a _____ might say.

    (a) functionalist   (c) behaviorist
    (b) structuralist   (d) psychoanalyst

2. Dr. Ames researches changes in children's intellectual abilities as they grow older. Dr. Ames's specialty area is _____ psychology.

    (a) social   (c) developmental
    (b) educational   (d) clinical

3. Which of the major perspectives in psychology today would Wilhelm Wundt say most resembled his point of view?

    (a) behavioral   (c) cognitive
    (b) psychoanalytic   (d) humanistic

4. Dr. Sandman investigates the relationship between sleep deprivation and cognitive abilities. He decides to test subjects in his sleep research lab under varying conditions. First he allows all his subjects to get a number of uninterrupted nights' sleep and records how long each subject sleeps on average. Next he decides that sleep deprivation would be either two, three, or four hours less than the average for each subject. Dr. Sandman

    (a) has operationally defined one of his variables
    (b) is using cruel and unusual punishment

(c) has empirically demonstrated a cause-and-effect relationship

(d) has proposed a theory

5. An educational psychologist is interested in whether student evaluations of instructors' performance is actually a good measure of teaching ability. A literature review showed some inconsistent findings across hundreds of different studies. To get a sense of the overall trends in this body of research, the investigator would be advised to use a technique called

(a) the correlation coefficient

(b) meta-analysis

(c) case study research

(d) replication

6. Compared to clinical psychologists, psychiatrists are more likely to

(a) prescribe drugs and other medical procedures for their clients

(b) assume that mental disorders are the result of unconscious conflicts

(c) use a cognitively based therapy rather than a biologically based therapy

(d) favor a humanistic perspective rather than a psychoanalytic perspective

7. In an experiment testing the effects of subliminal persuasion on memory and self-esteem, subjects were randomly assigned to one of four conditions. The reason for the random assignment is to

(a) increase the probability that the same number of subjects end up in each condition

(b) increase the likelihood that the subjects are representative of people in general

(c) decrease the probability of expectancy effects

(d) reduce the possibility of bias and ensure that differences among participants are spread out across all experimental conditions

8. In the above experiment group A participants listened to a memory tape and were told it would improve their memory, group B got the same tape but were told it would improve their self-esteem, group C participants listened to a self-esteem tape and were told it would improve their self-esteem, and group D got the same tape but were told it would enhance memory. All subjects were given a pretest and

posttest measure of self-esteem and memory. The dependent variable in the experiment was

(a) the random assignment to the four groups

(b) the scores on the pretest and posttest

(c) listening to either the self-esteem tapes or the memory tapes

(d) the level of deception used

9. Researchers and participants in a study examining the effects of cannabis on memory are both unaware of which subjects actually received the active ingredient and which were given a placebo. This study involves the use of

(a) replication

(b) the single-blind procedure

(c) the double-blind procedure

(d) correlational techniques

10. Researchers using a form of descriptive research have found that the bigger the line of credit people have at their bank, the more money they are likely to owe. The researchers have found _____ between the size of the line of credit and the amount of debt.

(a) a positive correlation

(b) a negative correlation

(c) a cause-and-effect relationship

(d) a zero correlation

11. An experimenter found that variable A and variable B had a correlation coefficient of +.55 and variable C and variable D had a correlation coefficient of −.75. She can conclude that

(a) variables A and B have a stronger correlation than variables C and D

(b) variable A causes variable B, but C and D are unrelated

(c) variable A and B have a weaker correlation than variables C and D

(d) variables A and B are strongly correlated but C and D have no relationship

12. If researchers wanted to discover the extent to which education level can be used to predict political preferences, they would most likely use

(a) correlational research

(b) naturalistic observation

(c) experimental research

(d) replication

13. In an experiment children were randomly assigned to either a group that watched a violent video or a group that watched a nonviolent video, and later the level of aggression in both groups was measured under controlled laboratory conditions. In this example the measure of the children's aggression was the
   (a) dependent variable
   (b) independent variable
   (c) control variable
   (d) naturalistic variable

14. Mary is given an in-depth interview, and her friends, family, and co-workers are contacted for further information. In addition, she is given a number of psychological tests and her behavior in various situations is observed. This is an example of _____ research.
   (a) survey
   (b) correlational
   (c) case study
   (d) experimental

15. In an attempt to predict the winner in the next election, The Kneed to Know Kompany contacts a randomly selected representative sample of the voting population and questions them about their voting plans. This is an example of _____ research.
   (a) correlational
   (b) survey
   (c) case study
   (d) experimental

16. Behaviorism and psychoanalysis dominated psychology for many decades early in the century, but in the 1950s a new school of thought emerged, _____ , which emphasized conscious experience, each person's unique potential for psychological growth, self-determination, and free will.
   (a) structuralism
   (b) functionalism
   (c) humanistic psychology
   (d) cross-cultural psychology

17. According to the In Focus Box 1.3, animal research is condoned by the American Psychological Association as long as the research
   (a) has an acceptable scientific purpose
   (b) will likely increase knowledge about behavior
   (c) will likely increase understanding of the species under study
   (d) produces results that benefit the health and welfare of humans or other animals
   (e) all of the above

18. According to the Culture and Human Behavior Box 1.1, ethnocentrism
   (a) is the tendency to use one's own culture as the standard for judging other cultures
   (b) refers to introspective self-centered analysis
   (c) is much more common in individualistic cultures than collectivistic cultures
   (d) is much more common in collectivistic cultures than in individualistic cultures

19. When evaluating claims made in the media about psychology-related topics, the Application section makes the point that
   (a) skepticism is the rule, not the exception, in science
   (b) there is no way to sort out true claims from false claims
   (c) testimonials are the most reliable source of information
   (d) pseudoscientific claims are legitimate scientific claims

20. According to the Critical Thinking Box 1.2, critical thinking involves
   (a) minimizing the influence of preconceptions and biases while rationally evaluating evidence
   (b) scrutinizing the evidence before drawing conclusions
   (c) being flexible while maintaining an attitude of healthy skecptisism
   (d) engaging in reflective thinking
   (e) all of the above

Answers

Introduction: What Is Psychology?

1. science of behavior and mental processes

2. changed and evolved over time

The Early History of Psychology

1. psychologists had to struggle with

2. (a) sleep, dreams, the senses; memory
   (b) René Descartes
   (c) nature-nurture; nature; nurture
   (d) physiology
   (e) physiology
   (f) scientific methods; human behavior and thinking

3. (a) working research laboratory in psychology
   (b) physiology; psychology; established as a separate scientific discipline
   (c) experimental methods

4. (a) Edward B. Titchener
   (b) components or structures of the conscious human mind
   (c) introspection; structures

5. (a) varied
   (b) introspective reports
   (c) introspection
   (d) learning, development, mental disorders; personality

6. (a) William James
   (b) functions; adapt
   (c) education, child rearing; the work environment

7. (a) conscious experiences
   (b) consciousness
   (c) adaptive; applying

8. (a) G. Stanley Hall; psychology research laboratory
   (b) Mary Whiton Calkins; dreams, memory; personality

Matching Exercise 1

1. Mary Whiton Calkins

2. introspection

3. functionalism

4. psychology

5. Wilhelm Wundt

True/False Test 1

1. T   4. T
2. F   5. T
3. F

Leaders in Psychology

1. (a) observable behavior
   (b) consciousness
   (c) behaviorism

2. (a) behaviorism
   (b) mechanism; learned
   (c) John B. Watson; introspection; consciousness or mental processes
   (d) B. F. Skinner
   (e) learning

3. (a) Sigmund Freud
   (b) psychoanalysis; sexual or aggressive
   (c) personality; behavior; dreams, memory blocks, slips of the tongue; spontaneous humor

4. (a) perception of whole figures
   (b) Max Wertheimer
   (c) perception; problem solving
   (d) mental activities

5. (a) humanistic
   (b) Carl Rogers
   (c) Abraham Maslow
   (d) environmental influences; unconscious processes; self-determination, free will, choice

Psychology Today

1. (a) physical bases of human and animal behavior
   (b) drug treatment; technology

2. (a) the cognitive revolution
   (b) mental processes; information; language; problems
   (c) computers

3. (a) cross-cultural
   (b) cultural; ethnic
   (c) perspective; specialty

4. (a) biological
   (b) behavioral
   (c) psychoanalytic
   (d) humanistic
   (e) cognitive
   (f) cross-cultural

5. (a) biological
   (b) developmental
   (c) clinical
   (d) social
   (e) personality
   (f) cognitive
   (g) educational; school
   (h) health
   (i) industrial/organizational
6. (a) psychiatrist
   (b) clinical psychologist

Graphic Organizer 1

Perspective	Specialty
1. humanistic	developmental
2. behavioral	industrial/organizational
3. cognitive	educational
4. biological	psychiatrist
5. cross-cultural	social
6. psychoanalytic	personality
7. cognitive	health
8. behavioral	experimental

Matching Exercise 2

1. clinical psychologist
2. Max Wertheimer
3. developmental psychology
4. behaviorism
5. Sigmund Freud
6. psychiatrist
7. educational psychology
8. experimental psychology
9. perspective
10. Carl Rogers
11. specialty area
12. cognitive psychology
13. personality psychology

True/False Test 2

1. F	6. F	11. T
2. T	7. T	12. T
3. T	8. T	13. F
4. F	9. T	14. T
5. T	10. T	

The Scientific Method

1. (a) describe
   (b) explain
   (c) predict
   (d) control or influence
2. assumptions, attitudes; procedures; creating questions to investigate, generating evidence; drawing conclusions
3. (a) behavior and mental processes follow consistent patterns
   (b) open-minded; scientific skepticism; cautious
4. (a) empirical evidence
   (b) (1) creating testable questions, (2) designing a study to collect data, (3) analyzing data to arrive at conclusions, (4) reporting the results
5. (a) hypothesis
   (b) hypothesis
   (c) variables
   (d) operational definition
   (e) operational definitions
6. (a) experimental; descriptive
   (b) experimental; descriptive
   (c) descriptive
7. (a) statistics
   (b) statistically significant
   (c) many research studies
8. (a) replicate
   (b) theory
   (c) hypothesis; theory
   (d) theory; knowledge
9. (a) experimental (in a natural setting)
   (b) hypothesis
   (c) statistics
   (d) 4; reporting her findings

Matching Exercise 3

1. meta-analysis
2. replicate
3. scientific method
4. hypothesis
5. operational definition
6. experimental method
7. statistics

True/False Test 3

1. T	3. F	5. T
2. T	4. T	6. F

The Experimental Method

1. (a) experimental; changes; effects
   (b) independent; dependent
   (c) dependent; independent; cause-and-effect

2. (a) all subjects have an equal chance of being assigned to any of the experimental conditions
   (b) that the differences among subjects are spread out across all experimental conditions; the assignment of subjects is done in an unbiased manner

3. (a) experiences all experimental conditions except the independent variable
   (b) baseline; naturally; spontaneously
   (c) independent; dependent; independent

4. (a) is exposed to all experimental conditions, including the independent variable
   (b) blind

5. (a) placebo control; expectancy effects
   (b) expectancy effects
   (c) experimenter; participants
   (d) experimenter; participants
   (e) experimenter; participants
   (f) demand characteristics

6. (a) artificial; generalize; apply
   (b) decrease
   (c) study some issues experimentally
   (d) conditions

7. (a) the drug and placebo conditions
   (b) participants' scores on the memory test
   (c) experimental; placebo control
   (d) double-blind; expectancy effects; demand characteristics
   (e) random assignment

Graphic Organizer 2

1. formulating the hypothesis

2. designing the experiment and collecting the data

3. analyzing the data and drawing conclusions

4. reporting the findings

Matching Exercise 4

1. single blind

2. experimental method

3. dependent variable

4. expectancy effects

5. control group

6. demand characteristics

True/False Test 4

1. T   3. T   5. T
2. F   4. T

Descriptive Methods

1. (a) manipulating the variables to which subjects are exposed; observing and describing
   (b) when; how often; related to other factors
   (c) study experimentally

2. (a) naturalistic observation
   (b) naturalistic observation
   (c) naturalistic observation; generalized

3. (a) case study
   (b) case studies

4. (a) paper-and-pencil; experiences, beliefs, behaviors; attitudes
   (b) surveys
   (c) interview

5. (a) sample; representative sample
   (b) every member; equal

6. (a) strongly; related to or associated with
   (b) correlation coefficient
   (c) correlation; causality

7. (a) same; increasing; decreasing
   (b) opposite; increases; decreases
   (c) cause-and-effect
   (d) rule out; include; predictions

8. (a) Informed consent and voluntary participation of subjects are required.
   (b) Students must be given the option of not participating in research involving credits without being penalized in any way.
   (c) Psychologists are restricted in their use of deception.
   (d) All records must be kept confidential.
   (e) Participants must be allowed the opportunity to obtain information about the study once it is completed and must be debriefed about the nature of their involvement in the study.

9. (a) more; less
   (b) survey; sample; randomly
   (c) naturalistic observation
   (d) positive
   (e) case study

Graphic Organizer 3

1. positive; positive

2. negative; negative

3. high; high; low; low

4. high; low; low; high

Matching Exercise 5

1. positive correlation

2. survey

3. descriptive method

4. sample

5. representative sample

6. correlational study

7. naturalistic observation

8. critical thinking

9. culture

10. ethnocentrism

True/False Test 5

1. T	4. F	7. F
2. T	5. T	8. T
3. F	6. T	9. F

Something to Think About

1. Psychology tackles questions that people have grappled with for thousands of years. Instead of using anecdotal evidence, intuition, philosophical discussion, and speculation, psychology uses the scientific method to answer questions that are amenable to empirical testing. It uses four steps in generating empirical evidence. First questions are formulated into testable hypotheses, next the study is designed and data are collected, then statistical analyses are used and conclusions are drawn, and finally the results are reported. Psychologists operationally define all variables and precisely specify the method of measurement or manipulation. Following this process, they can be confident in the reliability and validity of their results.

   The difference among clinical psychologists, psychiatrists, and psychoanalysts is training. Clinical psychologists have a doctorate in psychology and extensive training in dealing with people with mental disorders (assessment, diagnosis, and treatment). Psychiatrists, on the other hand, have an M.D. plus years of training in dealing with people with mental disorders and, because of their medical qualifications, can prescribe drugs and order medical procedures such as electroshock therapy. A psychoanalyst can be a psychologist, psychiatrist, or other mental health professional who has extensive training in Freudian psychotherapeutic methods.

2. Many of the questions that students have coming in to psychology can be tested empirically and quite a few have, in fact, been answered. For example, how would you test the claim that subliminal messages can influence our behavior? It turns out that psychologists have done just that.

   The essence of their experimental design was the use of two subliminal tapes, one claiming to improve self-esteem and the other claiming to improve memory. They randomly assigned subjects to one of four groups and gave them all pretests on measures of self-esteem and memory. Members of group 1 were given the memory tape to listen to for a set period of time and told it would help improve their memory; those in group 2 were given the same memory tape but were told it would improve their self-esteem. (Remember, on subliminal tapes you can't, by definition, hear the messages, only the surface music.) Group 3 was given the self-esteem tape and told it would improve self-esteem, and group 4 was given the same self-esteem tape but told that it would improve memory. All subjects listened to their respective tapes for exactly the same length of time, at the same times of the day, etc. Later they were given another test of self-esteem and memory. The pretest and posttest scores for all conditions were compared.

   What do you think the results showed? If you believe the claims of those who promote the power of subliminal tapes, then groups 1 and 3 should have shown significant improvement in memory and self-esteem scores, respectively. And, one would assume, if the results were not due to some placebo effect, then groups 2 and 4 should have shown some improvement—memory improvement for group 2 and self-esteem improvement for group 4—because that is what they were actually exposed to.

   The results were clear and unequivocal: there was no improvement in any of the groups between their pretest and posttest scores. In contrast to the claims of their promoters, subliminal tapes were shown to be of no value in improving memory or self-esteem.

   This is a good example of how useful the scientific method is in answering questions of a psychological nature. Can you apply what you know about scientific psychology to answer other questions you may have?

Progress Test 1

1. d	8. d	15. d
2. d	9. a	16. a
3. b	10. c	17. c
4. c	11. a	18. a
5. d	12. d	19. c
6. d	13. c	20. b
7. b	14. a	

Progress Test 2

1. a	8. b	15. b
2. c	9. c	16. c
3. c	10. a	17. e
4. a	11. c	18. a
5. b	12. a	19. a
6. a	13. a	20. e
7. d	14. c	

Chapter 2   The Biological Foundations of Behavior

OVERVIEW   Chapter 2 starts by outlining the scope and diversity of biological psychology and noting that biological psychologists investigate the physical processes underlying psychological experiences and behavior.

The first section describes the structure and functions of the neuron. Neuronal activation, synaptic transmission, and the role of neurotransmitters are outlined. The functions and effects of six neurotransmitters (acetylcholine, dopamine, serotonin, norepinephrine, GABA, and endorphins) are discussed.

The next section presents a discussion of the structure and function of the various divisions of the nervous system: (1) the central nervous system, which consists of the brain and spinal cord; (2) the peripheral nervous system, with its two main subdivisions, the somatic and autonomic nervous systems, and (3) the sympathetic and parasympathetic systems, which together make up the autonomic nervous system. This section ends by focusing on the endocrine system, its various glands, and its chemical messengers, called hormones.

The brain and how its complex operations are studied (e.g., case studies, EEG, MRI, CAT, and PET scans) are presented next, followed by a guided tour of the brain. Important brain regions (hindbrain, midbrain, and forebrain) and their various structures and functions are described. The different roles of the four lobes of the brain (temporal, occipital, parietal, and frontal) are explained, and finally, the functions of such subcortical structures as the thalamus, hypothalamus, hippocampus, and amygdala are described.

The chapter ends with a discussion of hemispheric specialization and the part played by split-brain patients in discovering the different roles played by each hemisphere of the brain.

Introduction: Biological Psychology

Learning Objectives

When you have finished studying this section of the chapter, you should be able to:

1. Define biological psychology and explain why psychologists are concerned with human biology.

2. Name some of the systems, structures, and functions that biological psychologists study.

*Read the section "Introduction: Biological Psychology" and **write** your answers to the following:*

1. (a) Biological psychology attempts to understand _____

that correspond with our

_____ .

(b) Biological psychology reflects not only the research findings of psychologists, but also the contributions of _____ ,

_____ , _____ , and

_____ .

2. Biological psychology studies

(a) the _____ system,

(b) the _____ and its specialized functions, such as language and vision,

(c) cells called _____ , and

(d) the _____ system.

The Neuron: The Basic Unit of Communication

Learning Objectives

When you have finished studying this section of the chapter, you should be able to:

1. Describe the function of neurons and glial cells in the brain and nervous system.

2. Name the three different types of neurons and state what each does.

3. Identify the basic components of the neuron and explain the processes that take place within the neuron when it is activated.

4. Explain how information is communicated between neurons.

5. Name six neurotransmitters and describe their effects on behavior and physiological functioning.

*Read the section "The Neuron: The Basic Unit of Communication" and **write** your answers to the following:*

1. (a) Neurons are cells that are highly specialized to _____ and _____ information from one part of the body to another.

   (b) _____ are the basic units of communication in the nervous system.

   (c) _____ help neurons by providing nutrition, removing waste products, and enhancing the speed of communication between neurons.

2. Name and describe the functions of the three different types of neurons:

   (a) _____
   _____
   _____

   (b) _____
   _____
   _____

   (c) _____
   _____
   _____

3. The three basic components of the neuron are the (a) _____ ,
   (b) _____ , and (c) _____ .

4. (a) Information is received by the _____ and transmitted to the _____ and then passed along the _____ to other cells in the body.

   (b) The myelin sheath is a _____
   _____
   that _____ the rate at which neural messages are sent.

5. (a) Within the neuron, information is communicated in the form of brief electrical messages called _____ .

   (b) The _____ is the minimum level of stimulation required to activate a particular neuron.

   (c) The resting potential is the state in which a neuron _____
   _____ .

   (d) The _____
   states that either a neuron is sufficiently stimulated and an action potential occurs or a neuron is not sufficiently stimulated and an action potential does not occur.

6. (a) The _____ and _____ neurons are separated by a tiny fluid-filled space called the _____ .

   (b) At the end of the axon are several small branches called _____ .

   (c) The synaptic vesicles contain chemicals called _____ .

   (d) Synaptic transmission refers to the process _____
   _____ .

   (e) _____ is the process by which neurotransmitter molecules detach from a postsynaptic neuron and are reabsorbed by the presynaptic neuron so they can be recycled and used again.

(f) A given neuron can communicate either a(n) _____ message that _____ the likelihood that the postsynaptic neuron will activate and generate an action potential or a(n) _____ message that _____ the likelihood that the postsynaptic neuron will activate and generate an action potential.

7. (a) Our ability to perceive, feel, think, move, act, and react depends on the delicate balance of _____ in the nervous system.

(b) Name and describe the function and effects of six neurotransmitters:

(1) _____ stimulates _____ and is involved in memory functions.

(2) _____ is involved in a number of different functions, including _____ , _____ , and _____ , and abnormal levels are involved in some mental disorders.

(3) _____ is involved in _____ , _____ , and emotional states, including depression.

(4) _____ has been implicated in some mental disorders and is involved in _____ and in the processes of _____ and _____ retrieval.

(5) _____ (gamma-aminobutyric acid) usually communicates _____ messages to other neurons and helps balance and offset _____ messages.

(6) _____ are neurotransmitters that regulate _____ , are chemically similar to the opiate drug _____ , and are involved in

positive emotions associated with aerobic exercise.

8. (a) Much of what is known about the different _____ comes from observing the effects of _____ and other substances.

(b) The venom of a black widow spider causes _____ to be released continuously by motor neurons, causing severe muscle spasms; curare works by mimicking _____ , thus blocking its receptor sites and causing almost instantaneous paralysis.

(c) Prozac works by inhibiting the reuptake of _____ , increasing the availability of this neurotransmitter in the brain; the drug cocaine produces its exhilarating "rush" by interfering with the reuptake of _____ .

Graphic Organizer

Identify the parts of the neuron in the figure below:

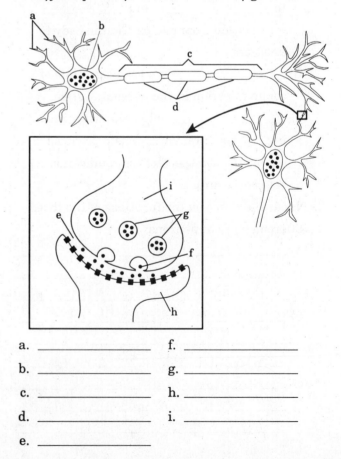

a. _____   f. _____

b. _____   g. _____

c. _____   h. _____

d. _____   i. _____

e. _____

9. Read the following and decide which neuro-transmitter is most likely involved:

(a) Mrs. Cartwright's memory functions have deteriorated and she has been diagnosed as suffering from Alzheimer's disease.

_____

(b) The relaxing effects of alcohol, Valium, and Xanax are believed to be the results of increeased activity of _____, which communicates inhibitory messages and slows brain activity.

(c) When Smita was diagnosed with schizophrenia, her doctor prescribed an antipsychotic drug that reduced the activity of _____ and blocked its receptor sites.

(d) Patients afflicted with Parkinson's disease suffer from rigidity, muscle tremors, and poor balance and have trouble initiating movements. It is believed that these symptoms are the result of diminished production of the neurotransmitter _____.

Review of Key Terms 1

biological psychology
neuron
glial cells
sensory neuron
motor neuron
interneuron
cell body
dendrites
axon
myelin sheath
action potential
stimulus threshold
resting potential
all-or-none law
synapse

synaptic gap
axon terminals
synaptic vesicles
neurotransmitter
synaptic transmission
reuptake
acetylcholine
dopamine
serotonin
norepinephrine
GABA (gamma-aminobutyric acid)
endorphins
nervous system

Matching Exercise

Match the appropriate term with its definition or description.

1. _____ A highly specialized cell that communicates information in electrical and chemical form.

2. _____ The primary internal communication network of the body; divided into the central nervous system and the peripheral nervous system.

3. _____ Neurotransmitters that regulate pain perception.

4. _____ A type of neuron that signals muscles to contract or relax.

5. _____ A neurotransmitter that is involved in sleep and emotions.

6. _____ The part of a neuron that contains the nucleus.

7. _____ A brief electrical impulse by which information is transmitted along the axon of a neuron.

8. _____ Chemical messenger manufactured by a neuron.

9. _____ The long, fluid-filled tube that carries a neuron's messages to other body areas.

10. _____ The point of communication between two neurons.

11. _____ Tiny pouches or sacs in the axon terminals that contain chemicals called neurotransmitters.

12. _____ A neurotransmitter that is involved in the regulation of bodily movements and thought processes.

13. _____ The minimum level of stimulation required to activate a particular neuron.

14. _____ A neurotransmitter that inhibits brain activity.

True/False Test

Indicate whether each statement is true or false by placing T or F in the blank space next to each item.

1. ____ Norepinephrine is a neurotransmitter involved in learning and memory; also a hormone manufactured by the adrenal glands.

2. ____ Biological psychology is the specialized branch of psychology concerned with the diagnosis and treatment of mental disorders.

3. ____ Reuptake is the process in which neurotransmitters are released by one neuron, cross the synaptic gap, and affect adjoining neurons.

4. ____ Glial cells assist neurons by providing structural support, nutrition, and removal of cell wastes; they manufacture myelin.

5. ____ Interneurons communicate information from one neuron to the next.

6. ____ Synaptic transmission is the process by which neurotransmitter molecules detach from a postsynaptic neuron and are reabsorbed by a presynaptic neuron so that they can be recycled and used again.

7. ____ Axon terminals are branches at the end of the axon that contain tiny pouches or sacs called synaptic vesicles.

8. ____ Sensory neurons communicate information to the muscles and glands of the body and signal muscles to contract or relax.

9. ____ Dendrites are the long, fluid-filled tubes that carry information *from* the neuron *to* other cells in the body, including other neurons, glands, and muscles.

10. ____ The myelin sheath is a white, fatty covering wrapped around the axons of some neurons that increases their speed of communication.

11. ____ The resting potential is a brief electrical impulse by which information is transmitted along the axon of a neuron.

12. ____ Acetylcholine is a neurotransmitter that produces muscle contractions and is involved in memory functions.

13. ____ The synaptic gap is a tiny space between the axon terminal of one neuron and the dendrite of an adjoining neuron.

14. ____ The all-or-none law states that either a neuron is sufficiently stimulated and an action potential occurs or a neuron is not sufficiently stimulated and an action potential does not occur.

> Check your answers and review any areas of weakness before going on to the next section.

The Nervous System and the Endocrine System: Communication Throughout the Body

Learning Objectives

When you have finished studying this section of the chapter, you should be able to:

1. Identify the two main divisions of the nervous system and describe the functions of each.

2. List the two major parts of the central nervous system and explain how spinal reflexes work.

3. Identify the first two divisions of the peripheral nervous system and describe their functions.

4. List the two branches of the autonomic nervous system and explain their different but complementary functions.

5. Describe the function of the endocrine system and explain the role hormones play.

6. Describe the roles of the hypothalamus, pituitary gland, adrenal glands, and the gonads, and name the male and female sex hormones.

Read the section "The Nervous System and the Endocrine System: Communication Throughout the Body" and **write** *your answers to the following:*

1. (a) The _____ system is the complex, organized communication network of neurons and nerves and has two main divisions, the _____ and the _____ .

   (b) The _____ is the most important transmitter of messages in the _____ nervous system and in the peripheral nervous system, communication occurs along _____ .

   (c) _____ are made up of large bundles of neuron axons.

2. (a) The central nervous system contains the _____ and the _____ .

   (b) _____ refer to simple, automatic behaviors that are produced by the spinal cord and occur without involvement of the brain.

   (c) The simplest spinal reflex involves a(n) _____ that communicates sensation to the spinal cord, a(n) _____ that relays information within the spinal cord, and a(n) _____ leading from the spinal cord that signals muscles to react.

3. (a) The peripheral nervous system has two subdivisions, the

   _____

   and the _____ .

   (b) The _____ nervous system communicates sensory information received by sense organ receptors to the central nervous system and carries messages from the central nervous system along motor nerves to the muscles.

   (c) The _____ nervous system regulates involuntary functions such as heartbeat, blood pressure, digestion, and breathing.

4. (a) The autonomic nervous system has two branches, the

   _____ and

   the _____ .

   (b) The _____ nervous system is the body's emergency system and produces rapid physical arousal in response to perceived threats or in response to emotions such as anger or anxiety.

   (c) The fight-or-flight response refers to

   _____

   _____

   _____ .

   (d) The _____ nervous system maintains normal body functions and conserves the body's physical resources.

Graphic Organizer 2

Below is a diagram of the nervous system. Write in the name of each division and choose the appropriate function of each from the list below (e.g., A is the appropriate choice for the nervous system).

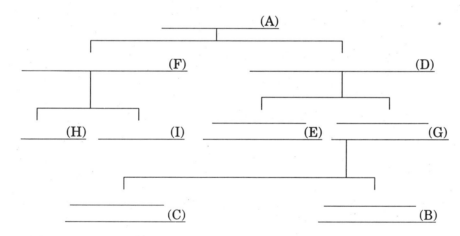

A. Complex, organized communication system of nerves and neurons.

B. Maintains normal body functions and conserves physical resources.

C. Produces rapid physical changes to perceived threats and emergencies.

D. Includes all nerves lying outside the central nervous system.

E. Communicates sensory and motor information.

F. Consists of the brain and spinal cord.

G. Regulates involuntary functions such as heartbeat and respiration.

H. Main organ of the nervous system and made up of billions of neurons.

I. A very busy transmission system handling both incoming and outgoing messages to and from the brain.

5. (a) The _____ system is made up of glands located throughout the body and uses chemical messengers called _____ to transmit information from one part of the body to another.

   (b) These chemical messengers influence many _____ and _____ processes and are secreted into the bloodstream by the _____ glands.

   (c) Metabolism, growth rate, digestion, blood pressure, and sexual development and reproduction are all processes regulated by _____ .

6. (a) The signals that trigger the secretion of hormones are regulated primarily by a brain structure called the _____ .

   (b) This structure serves as the main link between the _____ system and the _____ system.

   (c) The pituitary gland secretes hormones that _____ _____ .

7. Read the following and complete the sentence with the correct term:

   (a) Allison accidentally touched a hot stove top and immediately withdrew her hand before becoming consciously aware of the sensation or movement. She was able to do this because of her _____ .

   (b) Always a daredevil, Michael dove off the cliff into the river below. Unfortunately, he hit the water head first and is now paralyzed from the shoulders down. Apart from his paralysis, all his mental functions are intact and he is attempting to complete his college degree. His present inability to move the lower part of his body is a result of permanent damage to his _____ .

   (c) At home alone late at night, Jason had just finished watching the most frightening video he had ever seen when there was a sudden knocking on the door. His heart rate suddenly increased, his breathing accelerated, and he began to sweat. These physiological changes were most likely triggered by his _____ .

   (d) When Jason answered the door, he discovered it was only the pizza delivery and before long he calmed down and his blood pressure, heart rate, and breathing returned to their normal state. These physical reactions were most likely regulated by his _____ .

Review of Key Terms 2

nervous system	sympathetic nervous
central nervous system	system
nerve	parasympathetic
spinal reflexes	nervous system
peripheral nervous	fight-or-flight response
system	endocrine system
somatic nervous system	hormones
autonomic nervous	hypothalamus
system	pituitary gland

Matching Exercise

Match the appropriate term with its definition or description.

1. _____ Bundle of neuron axons that carries information in the peripheral nervous system.

2. _____ A communication system composed of glands located throughout the body that secrete hormones into the bloodstream.

3. _____ Simple, automatic behaviors that are processed in the spinal cord.

4. _____ The branch of the autonomic nervous system that maintains normal body functions and conserves the body's physical resources.

5. _____ A peanut-sized forebrain structure that is part of the limbic system and regulates behaviors related to survival, such as eating, drinking, and sexual activity.

6. _____ Division of the nervous system that includes all the nerves lying outside the central nervous system.

7. _____ Subdivision of the peripheral nervous system that regulates involuntary functions.

True/False Test

Indicate whether each statement is true or false by placing T or F in the blank space next to each item.

1. ___ The nervous system is the primary internal communication network of the body; divided into the central nervous system and the peripheral nervous systems.

2. ___ The central nervous system is a major division of the nervous system and consists of the brain and spinal cord.

3. ___ The pituitary gland is the inner portion of the adrenal medulla and secretes epinephrine and norepinephrine.

4. ___ The fight-or-flight response refers to physiological changes, such as increased heart rate, accelerated breathing, dry mouth, and perspiration, that occur in response to perceived threats or danger.

5. ___ The sympathetic nervous system maintains normal body functions and conserves physical resources.

6. ___ Hormones are chemical messengers that are secreted into the bloodstream by endocrine glands.

7. ___ The somatic nervous system regulates involuntary functions such as heartbeat, digestion, breathing, and blood pressure.

> Check your answers and review any areas of weakness before going on to the next section.

Studying the Brain: The Toughest Case to Crack

Learning Objectives

When you have finished studying this section of the chapter, you should be able to:

1. Explain how case studies of brain-damaged people have helped in unlocking some of the mysteries of the brain.

2. Define the term *lesion* and describe how animal research using this technique has helped in understanding brain functioning.

3. List the five main imaging techniques used to study the brain and specify what each attempts to accomplish.

*Read the section "Studying the Brain: The Toughest Case to Crack" and **write** your answers to the following:*

1. What is a case study? _____
   _____
   _____
   _____

2. (a) Lesions are produced by _____
   _____ .

   (b) After brain lesions have been done on the brains of humans and animals, experimenters observe _____
   _____ .

   (c) By electrically stimulating specific brain areas with electrodes, researchers can study the _____ .

3. Name the four methods used to study the living brain, completing a description of each:
   (a) The _____
   uses electrodes placed on the scalp to
   _____ .

   (b) The _____ produces two-dimensional pictures of brain structures using multiple _____
   _____ .

   (c) The _____ provides three-dimensional, highly detailed views of the brain using _____
   _____ .

   A new technique that takes a rapid series of brain images that are then put together by a computer to produce clear, sharp "movies" of brain activity is called _____ .

   (d) The _____ provides color-coded images of the brain's activity by measuring _____
   _____ .

A Guided Tour of the Brain

Learning Objectives

When you have finished studying this section of the chapter, you should be able to:

1. Name the three major divisions of the brain and list the two that make up the brainstem.

2. Name and describe the functions of the three structures that make up the hindbrain and explain the role of the reticular formation.

3. Describe the midbrain and list its major functions.

4. List the two most prominent structures of the forebrain.

5. Describe the cerebral cortex, name the four lobes, and explain the function of each.

6. Explain the role of the association areas.

7. Name the four subcortical structures of the forebrain and explain the function of each.

8. Describe the limbic system and list the responses and behaviors affected by it.

Read the section "A Guided Tour of the Brain" and **write** *your answers to the following:*

1. (a) The three major divisions of the brain are the _____ , the _____ , and the _____ .

   (b) The _____ includes the _____ and the _____ , which are located at the base of the brain.

2. (a) The _____ connects the spinal cord with the rest of the brain.

   (b) The three structures that make up the hindbrain are the _____ , the _____ , and the _____ .

   (c) The _____ controls vital life functions such as breathing, circulation, and muscle tone.

   (d) The _____ connects other regions of the brain to the _____ , which helps coordinate and integrate movements on each side of the body.

(e) The _____ is a large two-sided structure at the back of the brain responsible for muscle coordination, fine motor movements, and maintaining posture and equilibrium.

(f) At the core of the medulla and the pons is a network of neurons called the _____ , which plays an important role in regulating _____ , _____ , and _____ .

3. Decide which area of the brain is most likely involved in each of the following:

   (a) Marcel had a stroke on the *right* side of his brain in an area that controls motor movement and as a result he has trouble moving the *left* side of his body. The reason that he has trouble moving the *left* side of his body is because incoming sensory messages and outgoing motor messages cross over at the _____ level of the brain.

   (b) If this area of your brain was electrically stimulated while you were fast asleep, you would wake up instantly:

   _____

   (c) After being hit in the head by a baseball, Larry now has jerky, uncoordinated movements and can no longer type or play his guitar: _____

   (d) In the third round of a boxing match Bruno caught a right hook that snapped his head back, and when he hit the canvas his breathing stopped: _____

4. (a) The brain structure that is part of the brainstem and is an important relay station that helps coordinate auditory and visual information before sending it on to higher brain centers is called the _____ .

   (b) The substantia nigra is involved in _____ and contains a large concentration of neurons that produce _____ .

5. (a) The outer portion of the forebrain is called the _____ , which is divided into two _____ .

(b) A thick bundle of axons called the _____ connects the two hemispheres and serves as their primary communication link.

6. Name and complete the description of the functions of the four lobes of the cerebral cortex:

(a) The _____ lobe is near the temples and contains the

_____ ,

which receives _____ information.

(b) The _____ lobe is at the back of the brain and contains the

_____ and

is where _____ information is received.

(c) The _____ lobe is involved in processing _____ information, such as _____ ,

_____ , _____ , and

_____ .

(d) The _____ lobe processes _____ and is involved in anticipatory thinking, planning, and emotional expression and control.

7. (a) The _____ are involved in processing and integrating sensory and motor information, language, abstract reasoning, creative thought, and the integration of perceptions and memories.

(b) The prefrontal association cortex is involved in the _____ .

8. (a) The _____ consists of the hypothalamus, hippocampus, amygdala, and thalamus.

(b) The finding that rats and other animals would work hard to obtain electrical brain stimulation led researchers to speculate that there might be _____ in certain regions of the limbic system.

(c) The limbic system is involved in

_____ , _____ ,

_____ , and _____ .

9. There are four forebrain structures located beneath the cerebral cortex:

(a) The structure that identifies and integrates sensory information for all the senses except smell and relays it to higher brain centers is the _____ .

(b) The peanut-sized structure that is involved in diverse functions, including eating, drinking, frequency of sexual activity, fear, aggression, and exerting control over the secretion of endocrine hormones, is called the _____ .

(c) The curved structure that is involved in learning and forming new memories is the

_____ .

(d) The almond-shaped structure that is involved in controlling a variety of emotional response patterns, including fear, anger, and disgust, and in learning and memory formation is the _____ .

Graphic Organizer 3

Identify the four lobes of the brain in the diagram:

(a) _____

(b) _____

(c) _____

(d) _____

Review of Key Terms 3

electroencephalograph (EEG)
CAT (computerized axial tomography) scan
magnetic resonance imaging (MRI) scanner
PET (positron emission tomography) scan
brainstem
hindbrain
medulla
pons
cerebellum
reticular formation
midbrain
substantia nigra
forebrain
cerebral cortex
cerebral hemispheres
temporal lobe
primary auditory cortex
occipital lobe
primary visual cortex
parietal lobe
somatosensory cortex
frontal lobe
primary motor cortex
association areas
prefrontal association area
limbic system
thalamus
hypothalamus
suprachiasmatic nucleus (SCN)
hippocampus
amygdala

Matching Exercise

Match the appropriate term with its definition or description.

1. _____ An area of the hypothalamus that plays a key role in regulating daily sleep/wake cycles and other rhythms of the body.

2. _____ The nearly symmetrical left and right halves of the cerebral cortex.

3. _____ An area on each hemisphere of the cerebral cortex located above the temporal lobe that processes somatic sensations.

4. _____ A midbrain area involved in motor control and containing a large concentration of dopamine-producing neurons.

5. _____ The part of the temporal lobe that receives auditory information.

6. _____ A hindbrain structure that connects the medulla to the two sides of the cerebellum; helps coordinate and integrate movement on each side of the body.

7. _____ A forebrain structure that processes sensory information from all of the senses, except smell, and relays it to the cerebral cortex.

8. _____ A part of the occipital lobe where visual information is received.

9. _____ A curved forebrain structure that is part of the limbic system and is involved in learning and forming new memories.

10. _____ A region of the brain made up of the hindbrain and the midbrain.

11. _____ A band of tissue in the frontal lobe where the movements of different parts of the body are represented.

12. _____ A large association area of the brain, situated in front of the primary motor cortex, that is involved in the planning of voluntary movements.

13. _____ A hindbrain structure that controls vital life functions such as breathing, circulation, and muscle tone.

14. _____ An instrument that uses electrodes placed on the scalp to record the brain's electrical activity.

15. _____ A complex of nerve fibers located in the core of the medulla and pons that helps regulate attention, arousal, and sleep.

16. _____ An instrument that provides three-dimensional, highly detailed views of the brain using electrical signals generated by the brain in response to magnetic fields.

True/False Test

Indicate whether each statement is true or false by placing T or F in the blank space next to each item.

1. ____ The frontal lobe is the largest lobe of the cerebral cortex; processes voluntary muscle movement and is involved in thinking, planning, and emotional expression and control.

2. ____ The somatosensory cortex is a band of tissue on the parietal lobe that receives information from touch receptors in different parts of the body.

3. ____ The hindbrain is a region at the base of the brain that controls several structures that regulate basic life functions.

4. ____ The cerebellum is a hindbrain structure that controls vital life functions such as breathing, circulation, and muscle tone.

5. ____ The forebrain is the largest and most complex brain region, containing centers for complex behaviors and mental processes.

6. ____ The cerebral cortex is the wrinkled outer portion of the forebrain that contains the most sophisticated brain centers.

7. ____ The midbrain is the region at the base of the brain that contains several structures that regulate basic life functions.

8. ___ The occipital lobe is a region at the back of each cerebral cortex hemisphere that is the primary receiving area for visual information.

9. ___ The association areas are the regions of the cerebral cortex where information from different brain centers is combined and integrated.

10. ___ The temporal lobe is an area on each hemisphere that is the primary receiving area for auditory information.

11. ___ The amygdala is a hindbrain structure that connects the medulla to the two sides of the cerebellum.

12. ___ The CAT (computerized axial tomography) scanner is a sophisticated instrument that provides color-coded images of brain activity by measuring the amount of glucose used in different brain regions.

13. ___ The limbic system consists of forebrain structures that form a border around the brainstem and are involved in emotion, motivation, learning, and memory.

14. ___ The hypothalamus is a peanut-sized forebrain structure that is part of the limbic system and regulates behavior related to survival, such as eating, drinking, and sexual activity.

15. ___ The PET (positron emission tomography) scanner is an instrument that produces two-dimensional pictures of brain structures using multiple X-rays that are reassembled by a computer.

> Check your answers and review any areas of weakness before going on to the next section.

Specialization in the Cerebral Hemispheres

Learning Objectives

When you have finished studying this section of the chapter, you should be able to:

1. Identify the key people involved in this area of biological psychology and list their contributions.

2. Define *aphasia* and differentiate between Broca's aphasia and Wernicke's aphasia.

3. Describe the split-brain operation and explain why it was carried out.

4. Explain how and why research was conducted using split-brain patients and describe the procedure used for presenting visual stimuli separately to each hemisphere.

5. List the most important functions of each cerebral hemisphere.

*Read the section "Specialization in the Cerebral Hemispheres" and **write** your answers to the following:*

1. (a) Clinical evidence for specialized language ability in the lower left frontal lobes came from the work of _____ , who treated patients who had great difficulty speaking but could comprehend written or spoken language.

   (b) An area in the lower left frontal lobe, known to play a crucial role in speech production, is called _____ area.

2. (a) _____ discovered an area on the left temporal lobe that is involved in the ability to understand spoken and written communication.

   (b) Patients who have difficulty comprehending language and whose speech often makes little sense are most likely to have damage on the left _____ lobe in _____ area.

3. (a) Someone with either a partial or complete inability to articulate ideas or understand spoken or written language due to brain injury or brain damage is likely to be given the general diagnosis of _____ .

   (b) Victims of _____ aphasia find it difficult to produce speech, but their comprehension of verbal or written words is unaffected.

   (c) Victims of _____ aphasia can produce speech but often have difficulty finding the right words and have great difficulty understanding written or spoken communication.

4. (a) The procedure of surgically cutting the corpus callosum is called the _____ .

(b) In order to reduce _____ , patients underwent an operation in which the _____ was surgically severed.

(c) These patients are called _____ patients.

5. (a) The American psychologist who pioneered research on brain specialization in split-brain patients was _____ .

(b) A procedure for presenting stimuli to each hemisphere separately involves split-brain patients focusing on a midpoint while words or pictures are flashed to the _____ or _____ of the midpoint.

(c) Visual information presented to the right of the midpoint is projected to the person's _____ hemisphere, and visual information to the left of the midpoint is projected to the person's _____ hemisphere.

(d) A split-brain patient who is presented with a picture or a word to the left of the midpoint will _____ to state what was seen; if the stimulus is to the right of the midpoint, the patient will _____ to state what was seen.

6. (a) List the main areas of specialization of the left hemisphere: _____
_____
_____

(b) List the main areas of specialization of the right hemisphere: _____
_____
_____
_____
_____
_____

Review of Key Terms and Key Names 4

Pierre Paul Broca
Broca's area
Karl Wernicke
Wernicke's area
aphasia
Broca's aphasia
Wernicke's aphasia

corpus callosum
split-brain operation
Roger Sperry
split-brain patient
functional plasticity
structural plasticity

Matching Exercise

Match the appropriate term/name with its definition or description.

1. _____ The American psychologist who received the Nobel Prize in 1981 for his pioneering research on brain specialization in split-brain patients.

2. _____ The partial or complete inability to articulate ideas or understand spoken or written language due to brain damage or injury.

3. _____ A person who has had his or her corpus callosum surgically cut.

4. _____ A language area on the left temporal lobe concerned with speech comprehension.

5. _____ A thick band of over 200 million nerve fibers that connects the two cerebral hemispheres and acts as a communication link between them.

6. _____ The ability of the brain to gradually shift functions from damaged to undamaged areas.

7. _____ A phenomenon in which brain structures physically change in response to environmental influences.

True/False Test

Indicate whether each statement is true or false by placing T or F in the blank space next to each item.

1. ___ Karl Wernicke was a German neurologist who in 1874 discovered an area on the left temporal lobe that, when damaged, produces meaningless or nonsensical speech and difficulties in verbal or written comprehension.

2. ___ The split-brain operation was carried out on patients specifically so that psychologists could scientifically study hemispheric specialization in the cerebral cortex of humans.

3. ___ Broca's aphasia is a speech disorder that results from the surgical severing of the corpus callosum.

4. ___ Patients with Wernicke's aphasia can speak but may have problems finding the right words and typically have great difficulty understanding written or spoken communication.

5. ___ Broca's area is a language area on the lower left frontal lobe of the cerebral cortex.

6. ___ Pierre Paul Broca was a French surgeon and neuroanatomist who discovered an area on the lower left frontal lobe that, when damaged, produces speech disturbances but no loss of comprehension.

> Check your answers and review any areas of weakness before going on to the next section.

Something to Think About

1. A biological psychologist who specializes in the assessment and diagnosis of people with brain-related problems is faced with the following cases. Based on what you now know about biological psychology, the brain, and nervous system functioning, give some thought to what the specialist's assessment might be.
   (a) Fraser slipped on ice and hit the back of his head on the sidewalk, and now his vision is seriously affected. Which brain area is most likely affected?
   (b) Following an operation to remove a brain tumor, Yoko is able to read and understand written and spoken language but has difficulty speaking and expressing herself clearly. It is likely that she has damage in which part of the brain?
   (c) Ever since a brain lesion destroyed part of her limbic system, Vanessa has had trouble controlling her appetite and has had a constant urge to eat and drink. Which structure was most likely damaged?
   (d) Raphael is now twelve years old but is only four feet tall. His growth problem is most likely related to some malfunctioning of either of which two glands?

2. Family members and friends who know you are taking a psychology course may ask you some interesting and curious questions. One question that is often asked is, "I know that regular exercise helps keep me in shape physically, but is there anything I can do to prevent mental deterioration?" What advice would you give in response to that question?

Progress Test 1

Review the complete chapter (including Concept Reviews 2.1–2.4 and all boxed inserts), review all your study notes, and then test yourself on the following progress test. Check your answers. If you make a mistake, review your notes, the appropriate section in the study guide, and, if necessary, the relevant part of the chapter in your textbook.

1. A hunter in a South American jungle uses the poison curare on the tip of his arrow, and when the arrow strikes an animal, it becomes almost instantly limp and quickly suffocates because its respiratory system has become paralyzed. The curare has _____ the neurotransmitter_____ .
   (a) blocked the release of; acetylcholine
   (b) blocked the receptors for; acetylcholine
   (c) increased the release of; acetylcholine
   (d) increased the reuptake of; acetylcholine

2. Miguel has been diagnosed with schizophrenia. His psychologist believes that Miguel's hallucinations and perceptual distortions may, in part, be caused by _____ amounts of the neurotransmitter _____ .
   (a) diminished; dopamine
   (b) excessive; dopamine
   (c) diminished; serotonin
   (d) excessive; serotonin

3. Jenny has just finished running a very tough marathon (26.22 miles) but seems to be very happy and elated. One cause of her "runner's high" may be due to abnormally high levels of chemical substances in her brain called
   (a) acetylcholines   (c) endorphins
   (b) serotonins   (d) dopamines

4. Neural impulses or action potentials travel
   (a) from the axon to the cell body
   (b) from the cell body to the axon
   (c) from the cell body to the dendrite
   (d) from the axon to the dendrite

5. Following his final exam in statistics, Stewart was tense and anxious. However, after drinking a few beers he felt much more relaxed and less inhibited. On reason for his altered state may be because alcohol _____ GABA activity, which in turn _____ brain activity.

    (a) increases; reduces
    (b) decreases; inhibits
    (c) increases; increases
    (d) decreases; increases

6. When Dr. Maxwell electrically stimulated a specific area of the cortex in the right hemisphere, the patient's left hand twitched. The part of the cortex that was stimulated was

    (a) Broca's area
    (b) the primary motor cortex
    (c) Wernicke's area
    (d) the somatosensory cortex

7. The primary motor cortex is to the somatosensory cortex as the _____ is to the _____ .

    (a) frontal lobe; parietal lobe
    (b) occipital lobe; temporal lobe
    (c) temporal lobe; occipital lobe
    (d) parietal lobe; frontal lobe

8. Neurotransmitters are to hormones as _____ is to _____ .

    (a) the nervous system; the endocrine system
    (b) a nerve; a neuron
    (c) the hypothalamus; the pituitary gland
    (d) the brain; the spinal cord

9. If the picture of a hammer is flashed to the left of the midpoint during an experiment with a split-brain patient and he is asked to indicate what he saw,

    (a) the patient will verbally report what he saw
    (b) the patient will draw a picture of a hammer with his right hand
    (c) the patient will not be able to verbally report what he saw
    (d) the patient will draw the picture of an apple with his left hand

10. In order to determine which area of Drucilla's brain was most active when she read a passage from a book, neuroscientists radioactively tagged glucose and used a technique involving a(n)

    (a) PET scan   (c) MRI scan
    (b) CAT scan   (d) EEG

11. If researchers electrically stimulate the reticular formation in a sleeping cat, it is most likely that the cat will

    (a) aggressively attack the researchers
    (b) stop breathing
    (c) become paralyzed on both sides of the body
    (d) instantly wake up, fully alert

12. Sonny suffered brain damage when he was knocked down in a boxing match and can no longer hear in one ear. It is most probable that one of his _____ lobes was injured.

    (a) ear   (d) frontal
    (b) occipital   (e) parietal
    (c) temporal

13. If researchers destroy or lesion the amygdala of a timid cat, it is likely that the cat will

    (a) become even more fearful
    (b) lose its timidity and fearfulness
    (c) become a vicious predator and start attacking large dogs
    (d) stop breathing and die

14. As a result of a stroke, Mr. Nelson can no longer understand what he reads or what is being said to him, and he often has trouble finding the right words when he tries to speak. Mr. Nelson suffers from

    (a) Wernicke's aphasia
    (b) Broca's aphasia
    (c) Parkinson's disease
    (d) Alzheimer's disease

15. If a normal right-handed individual sustained damage to the right cerebral hemisphere, this would most likely reduce the ability to

    (a) manipulate blocks to match a particular design
    (b) recognize people's faces
    (c) appreciate art and music
    (d) decipher visual cues related to emotional expression
    (e) all of the above

16. The occipital lobe is to _____ as the temporal lobe is to _____ .

    (a) anticipatory thinking; seeing
    (b) seeing; anticipatory thinking
    (c) seeing; hearing
    (d) hearing; seeing

17. If someone taps you on the back, you sense the touch because the _____ cortex in the _____ lobe receives this tactile information.
    (a) primary motor; frontal
    (b) primary visual; occipital
    (c) primary somatosensory; parietal
    (d) primary auditory; temporal

18. According to the Critical Thinking section, which of the following statements about male versus female brains is false?
    (a) Male and female brains are much more different than they are alike
    (b) Sex differences in brain structure explain why women consistently outscore men on all tests of intellectual and creative ability
    (c) Sex differences in brain structure are large and consistent
    (d) all of the above are false

19. According to the Application section, psychologists studied 5,000 people as they aged in order to learn what happens to intellectual abilities over the lifespan. The results showed that
    (a) intellectual decline is not an inevitable result of aging
    (b) compared to women, men suffer greater intellectual decline over the lifespan
    (c) intellectual decline is an inevitable result of aging for all people
    (d) compared to men, women suffer greater intellectual decline over the lifespan

20. Structural plasticity refers to the capacity of some brain structures to
    (a) change in response to environmental stimulation
    (b) remain rigid or "hard-wired" for life
    (c) deteriorate with age and cause forgetfulness
    (d) wear out if they are used too much

Progress Test 2

After you have checked your understanding of the material in Progress Test 1 and have done a complete chapter review with special focus on any areas of weakness, you are ready to further assess your knowledge in Progress Test 2. Check your answers. If you make a mistake, review your notes, the appropriate parts of the study guide, and, if necessary, the relevant sections of your textbook.

1. A patient is suffering from a number of symptoms, including depression, sleep disturbances, mood fluctuations, and decreased sexual appetite, and has problems in learning and memory retrieval. Her doctor prescribes Prozac and some other drugs because it is likely that the patient's problems are due to abnormal levels of the neurotransmitters
    (a) dopamine and acetylcholine
    (b) serotonin and endorphins
    (c) acetylcholine and norepinephrine
    (d) serotonin and norepinephrine

2. Signal reception is to _____ as signal transmission is to _____ .
    (a) myelin sheath; cell body
    (b) dendrite; axon
    (c) action potential; resting potential
    (d) axon; dendrite

3. A brief electrical impulse by which information is transmitted along the axon is called the
    (a) action potential
    (b) stimulus threshold
    (c) resting potential
    (d) all-or-none response

4. Neurotransmitters are chemical messengers that
    (a) carry information in the endocrine system
    (b) travel from the cell body along the axon and create an action potential
    (c) assist neurons by providing physical support, nutrition, and waste removal
    (d) travel across the synaptic gap and affect adjoining neurons

5. While cooking dinner for a large family gathering, Mindy was so distracted by all the conversations going on around her that she attempted to pick up a very hot pan by the handle. She instantly withdrew her hand before becoming consciously aware of the sensation or her own hand movement until after it happened. Mindy was able to do this because of her
    (a) spinal reflexes
    (b) parasympathetic nervous system
    (c) high levels of endorphins
    (d) limbic system

6. If a patient suffers damage to the hippocampus, she is likely to have problems
    (a) learning and forming new memories
    (b) remembering events and things that happened before her brain injury
    (c) comprehending spoken and written language
    (d) controlling emotional drives such as aggression and pleasure

7. After Eduardo's serious ski accident, doctors detected damage to his cerebellum. Eduardo is most likely to have trouble
   (a) swallowing, coughing, and breathing
   (b) sleeping
   (c) staying awake
   (d) playing tennis, typing, and walking with a smooth gait

8. In a typical test situation with a split-brain patient, if a picture of an apple is briefly presented to the right of the center point and the patient is asked to name the object
   (a) she will be unable to say what she saw
   (b) she will be able to draw a picture of the object with her left hand
   (c) she will report that she saw nothing
   (d) she will say she saw an apple

9. Randy is left-handed. If he is like most left-handers,
   (a) his right hemisphere will be dominant for language
   (b) he will be slightly mentally retarded
   (c) his left hemisphere will be dominant for language
   (d) he will have significantly less artistic competence and musical ability than most right-handers

10. If a researcher anesthetizes the entire right hemisphere of a right-handed patient who is asked to recite the alphabet aloud while reclining on the operating table with both arms extended upward, it is most probable that the patient's
    (a) left arm will fall limp but she will continue saying the alphabet
    (b) right arm will fall limp but she will continue saying the alphabet
    (c) left arm will fall limp and she will become speechless
    (d) right arm will fall limp and she will become speechless

11. Dr. Sandhu conducts research on how behavior and mental processes are related to the brain, biochemistry, and other body systems. It is most likely that Dr. Sandhu is a
    (a) phrenologist
    (b) biological psychologist
    (c) humanistic psychologist
    (d) psychoanalyst

12. After a police car with flashing lights goes by him and pulls over another driver for speeding, Jerry's heartbeat soon slows down, his blood pressure decreases, and he stops sweating so much. These physical reactions are most directly regulated by his
    (a) sympathetic nervous system
    (b) parasympathetic nervous system
    (c) somatic nervous system
    (d) central nervous system

13. As a result of a stroke, 75-year-old Mrs. Yee suffered brain damage; and while she is no longer able to speak, she can understand what is being said to her. Mrs. Yee suffers from
    (a) Wernicke' aphasia
    (b) damage to her left occipital lobe
    (c) Broca's aphasia
    (d) damage to her left temporal lobe

14. Dr. Jones systematically observes and records the behavior of people whose brains have been damaged by illness or injury. He is using an investigative technique called
    (a) MRI scan   (c) PET scan
    (b) CAT scan   (d) case study

15. Nancy suffers from severe epilepsy that has not responded to any treatment her doctors have tried. As a final resort, they operate on her brain and surgically cut the
    (a) amygdala   (c) corpus callosum
    (b) hippocampus   (d) adrenal cortex

16. The parietal lobe is to _____ as the frontal lobe is to _____ .
    (a) anticipatory thinking; hearing
    (b) sensing touch; anticipatory thinking
    (c) seeing; hearing
    (d) tasting; smelling

17. When doctors removed a tumor from Andrew's occipital lobe, they also had to remove healthy brain tissue from the same area. When he recovers, Andrew is most likely to suffer some loss of
    (a) language comprehension
    (b) muscular coordination
    (c) visual perception
    (d) taste perception

18. The chapter prologue describes the story of Asha, who suffered a stroke. What Asha's story illustrates is that the brain has a remarkable ability to gradually shift functions from damaged to undamaged areas, a phenomenon called
    (a) neural regeneration
    (b) functional plasticity
    (c) synaptic transmission
    (d) structural plasticity

19. According to the Critical Thinking section, when male and female brains have been compared in anatomical studies
    (a) the findings have found been consistent, reliable, and valid
    (b) researchers have found clear differences in the brain structure of males and females that account for intellectual and cognitive differences between the sexes
    (c) the findings have been contradictory and inconsistent
    (d) there are more differences than similarities in male and female brains

20. According to the Application section, research has shown that compared to high school dropouts, university graduates had 40 percent more _____ .
    (a) synaptic connections
    (b) brain mass
    (c) neurons in their brains
    (d) axons in the corpus callosum

Answers

Introduction: Biological Psychology

1. (a) the internal physical events and processes; experiences and behavior
   (b) biologists, chemists, neurologists; psychiatrists

2. (a) nervous
   (b) brain
   (c) neurons
   (d) endocrine

The Neuron: The Basic Unit of Communication

1. (a) receive; transmit
   (b) neurons
   (c) glial cells

2. (a) Sensory neurons convey information to the brain from specialized receptor cells in the sense organs, the skin, and the internal organs.
   (b) Interneurons communicate information from one cell to the next and are the most common type of cell in the body.
   (c) Motor neurons communicate information to the muscles and glands of the body.

3. (a) cell body
   (b) dendrites
   (c) axon

4. (a) dentrites; cell body; axon
   (b) white, fatty covering made up of glial cells; increases

5. (a) action potentials
   (b) stimulus threshold
   (c) is prepared to activate and is polarized so that it is negative on the inside and positive on the outside
   (d) all-or-none law

6. (a) presynaptic (sending); postsynaptic (receiving); synaptic gap
   (b) axon terminals
   (c) neurotransmitters
   (d) in which neurotransmitters are released by one neuron, cross the synaptic gap, and affect adjoining neurons
   (e) reuptake
   (f) excitatory; increases; inhibitory; decreases

7. (a) neurotransmitters
   (b) (1) acetylcholine; muscle contractions
       (2) dopamine; movement, attention; learning
       (3) serotonin; sleep, moods
       (4) norepinephrine; activation of neurons throughout the brain; learning; memory
       (5) GABA; inhibitory; excitatory
       (6) endorphins; pain perception; sexuality, pregnancy, labor

8. (a) neurotransmitters; drugs
   (b) acetylcholine; acetylcholine
   (c) serotonin; dopamine

Graphic Organizer 1

a. dentrites, b. cell body, c. axon, d. myelin sheath, e. synaptic gap, f. neurotransmitter, g. synaptic vesicles, h. postsynaptic neuron, i. presynaptic neuron

9. (a) acetylcholine
   (b) GABA
   (c) dopamine
   (d) dopamine

Matching Exercise 1

1. neuron
2. nervous system
3. endorphins
4. motor neuron
5. serotonin
6. cell body
7. action potential
8. neurotransmitter
9. axon
10. synapse
11. synaptic vesicles
12. dopamine
13. stimulus threshold
14. GABA (gamma-aminobutyric acid)

True/False Test 1

1. T	6. F	11. F
2. F	7. T	12. T
3. F	8. F	13. T
4. T	9. F	14. T
5. T	10. T	

The Nervous System and the Endocrine System: Communication Throughout the Body

1. (a) nervous; central nervous system; peripheral nervous system

(b) neuron; central; nerves

(c) nerves

2. (a) brain; spinal cord

   (b) spinal reflexes

   (c) sensory neuron; interneuron; motor neuron

3. (a) somatic nervous system; autonomic nervous system

   (b) somatic

   (c) autonomic

4. (a) sympathetic nervous system; parasympathetic nervous system

   (b) sympathetic

   (c) physiological changes, such as increased heart rate, accelerated breathing, dry mouth, and perspiration, in response to perceived threat or danger

   (d) parasympathetic

Graphic Organizer 2

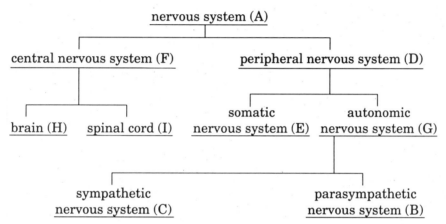

5. (a) endocrine; hormones

   (b) physical; behavioral; endocrine

   (c) endocrine hormones

6. (a) hypothalamus

   (b) endocrine; nervous

   (c) affect the functioning of other glands as well as hormones that act directly on physical processes

7. (a) spinal reflexes

   (b) spinal cord

   (c) sympathetic nervous system

   (d) parasympathetic nervous system

Matching Exercise 2

1. nerve

2. endocrine system

3. spinal reflexes

4. parasympathetic nervous system

5. hypothalamus

6. peripheral nervous system

7. autonomic nervous system

True/False Test 2

1. T		5. F	
2. T		6. T	
3. F		7. F	
4. T			

Studying the Brain: The Toughest Case to Crack

1. a research method that involves observing and giving a highly detailed description of a single individual or event.

2. (a) surgically altering or destroying specific portions of the brain

   (b) the subsequent effects on behavior

   (c) behavioral effects

3. (a) electroencephalograph (EEG); record the brain's electrical activity

   (b) CAT (computerized axial tomography) scan; X-rays that are reassembled by a computer

   (c) magnetic resonance imaging (MRI) scanner; electrical signals generated by the brain in response to magnetic fields; functional MRI

(d) PET (positron emission tomography) scan; the amount of glucose used in different brain regions

A Guided Tour of the Brain

1. (a) hindbrain; midbrain; forebrain
   (b) brainstem; hindbrain; midbrain

2. (a) hindbrain
   (b) medulla; pons; cerebellum
   (c) medulla
   (d) pons; cerebellum
   (e) cerebellum
   (f) reticular formation; attention, arousal; sleep

3. (a) hindbrain (more specifically, the medulla is the point at which neural messages cross over)
   (b) reticular formation
   (c) cerebellum
   (d) medulla

4. (a) midbrain
   (b) motor control; dopamine

5. (a) cerebral cortex; cerebral hemispheres
   (b) corpus callosum

6. (a) temporal; primary auditory cortex; auditory
   (b) occipital; primary visual cortex; visual
   (c) parietal; somatosensory; touch, temperature, pressure; body position
   (d) frontal; voluntary movement

7. (a) association areas
   (b) planning of voluntary movements

8. (a) limbic system
   (b) pleasure centers
   (c) emotions, motivation, learning; memory

9. (a) thalamus
   (b) hypothalamus
   (c) hippocampus
   (d) amygdala

Graphic Organizer 3

(a) temporal lobe
(b) occipital lobe
(c) parietal lobe
(d) frontal lobes

Matching Exercise 3

1. suprachiasmatic nucleus (SCN)
2. cerebral hemispheres
3. parietal lobe
4. substantia nigra

5. primary auditory cortex
6. pons
7. thalamus
8. primary visual cortex
9. hippocampus
10. brainstem
11. primary motor cortex
12. prefrontal association area
13. medulla
14. electroencephalograph (EEG)
15. reticular formation
16. magnetic resonance imaging (MRI) scanner

True/False Test 3

1. T	6. T	11. F
2. T	7. F	12. F
3. T	8. T	13. T
4. F	9. T	14. T
5. T	10. T	15. F

Specialization in the Cerebral Hemispheres

1. (a) Pierre Paul Broca
   (b) Broca's

2. (a) Karl Wernicke
   (b) temporal; Wernicke's

3. (a) aphasia
   (b) Broca's
   (c) Wernicke's

4. (a) split-brain operation
   (b) epileptic seizures; corpus callosum
   (c) split-brain

5. (a) Roger Sperry
   (b) left; right (right; left)
   (c) left; right
   (d) not be able; be able

6. (a) language abilities, speech, writing, and musical and artistic ability (but not appreciation)
   (b) nonverbal emotional expression, visual perception tasks such as completing a puzzle, face recognition, reading maps, copying designs, drawing, and musical and artistic appreciation (but not ability)

Matching Exercise 4

1. Roger Sperry
2. aphasia

3. split-brain patient

4. Wernicke's area

5. corpus callosum

6. functional plasticity

7. structural plasticity

True/False Test 4

1. T		3. F		5. T	
2. F		4. T		6. T	

Something to Think About

1. (a) The occipital lobe is most likely affected because it includes the primary visual cortex where visual information is received, so damage to this area could affect vision.

   (b) Yoko probably has damage to the left frontal lobe, Broca's area. Damage here would not affect comprehension but would influence speech production.

   (c) Vanessa's hypothalamus was most likely damaged. The hypothalamus is part of the limbic system and regulates appetite, along with other functions.

   (d) The hypothalamus exerts considerable control over the secretion of endocrine hormones by directly influencing the pituitary gland. The pituitary gland produces *growth hormone*, which, not surprisingly, stimulates growth. So we can guess that Raphael's short stature is the result of malfunction in this system.

2. In answer to this question, the news is good. Because of the brain's structural plasticity, some brain structures can change in response to environmental stimulation. Research with rats has demonstrated that, in addition to other changes, an enriched environment increases the number and length of dendrites, enlarges the size of neurons, and increases the number of neural connections. More importantly, there is an impressive amount of correlational research showing that the human brain also seems to benefit from enriched environments. Getting a good education, as long as the process is challenging, is one way to "exercise" the brain. Another piece of advice is to remain mentally active throughout the lifespan and get involved in complex and stimulating activities; and if you haven't done so already, marry a smart person.

It is important to point out that intellectual decline is not the inevitable result of aging. To increase the number of synaptic connections and dendritic growth, the best advice is to get involved in novel, challenging, and unfamiliar pursuits. Keep pumping those neurons and remember, "if you don't use it, you lose it!"

Progress Test 1

1. b		8. a		15. e	
2. b		9. c		16. c	
3. c		10. a		17. c	
4. b		11. d		18. d	
5. a		12. c		19. a	
6. b		13. b		20. a	
7. a		14. a			

Progress Test 2

1. d		8. d		15. c	
2. b		9. c		16. b	
3. a		10. a		17. c	
4. d		11. b		18. b	
5. a		12. b		19. c	
6. a		13. c		20. a	
7. d		14. d			

Chapter 3 Sensation and Perception

OVERVIEW Chapter 3 describes both sensation and perception. First the basic principles of sensation are discussed, including sensory threshold, Weber's Law, and sensory adaptation. Then the senses of vision, hearing, smell, taste, kinesthesis, and equilibrium are explained, followed by a discussion of pain, pain perception, and the gate-control theory of pain.

Perception is explored next, and the distinction between sensation and perception is made clear. How we perceive depth is explained, and both monocular and binocular cues are listed and described. The perception of motion and the perception of shape are both explained, along with the phenomenon of perceptual constancy. Next, how we misperceive objects and events in our world is illustrated through various illusions. That perception is a psychological process is made clear through a discussion of perceptual sets, expectations, learning experiences, cultural factors, and their influence on our interpretations.

The chapter ends with the Application section, which is devoted to how we can use various perceptual strategies and techniques in the control of pain.

Introduction: Sensation and Perception
Learning Objective

When you have finished studying this section of the chapter, you should be able to:

1. Define sensation and perception and give examples that illustrate their differences.

*Read the section "Introduction: Sensation and Perception" and **write** your answers to the following:*

1. (a) The primary function of the nervous system is _____ of information from one part of the body to another.

   (b) Being able to detect patches of color and edges of objects reflects _____ , and integrating and organizing them so that we interpret (identify) them reflects

   _____ .

Some Basic Principles of Sensation
Learning Objectives

When you have finished studying this section of the chapter, you should be able to:

1. Identify the basic principles of sensation.

2. Define *transduction* and explain how it works.

3. List the two types of sensory thresholds and provide an example that illustrates each.

4. Explain Weber's Law and specify its relationship to the just noticeable difference, or jnd.

5. Describe the process of sensory adaptation.

*Read the section "Some Basic Principles of Sensation" and **write** the answers to the following:*

1. (a) The vibrations of physical energy in the air are called _____ waves; the response to dissolvable chemicals in the mouth is _____ ;

the detection of airborne chemical molecules inhaled through the nose is _____ ; the response to pressure on the skin is called _____ ; and vision is the result of physical energy called _____ waves.

(b) _____ convert the different forms of physical energy into electrical impulses that are transmitted via neurons to the brain.

(c) The process by which a form of physical energy is converted into a coded neural signal that can be processed by the nervous system is called _____ .

2. (a) _____ refers to the point at which a stimulus is strong enough to be detected by activating sensory receptors.

(b) The _____ refers to the smallest possible strength of a stimulus that can be detected half of the time, and the _____ refers to the smallest possible difference between two stimuli that can be detected half of the time.

(c) The just noticeable difference (jnd) is another term for the _____ .

(d) A principle of sensation that holds that the jnd will vary depending on its relation to the original stimulus is called

_____ .

(e) _____ states that for each sense the size of the jnd is a constant proportion of the size of the initial stimulus. In other words, our psychological experience of sensation is _____ .

3. (a) After being exposed to a constant stimulus for a time, we become _____ of it.

(b) The gradual decline in sensitivity to a constant stimulus is called

_____ .

(c) Our experience of sensation is _____ to the duration of exposure.

4. Read the following and write the correct term in the space provided:

(a) When Anton went to have his hearing tested, he was presented with many different tones, and some were at such a low level of intensity he could hardly detect them. These sounds were below Anton's _____ threshold.

(b) If you detect a sequence of sounds as a series of different tones, this is _____ , and if you recognize the sequence of sounds as a melody, this is

_____ .

(c) Jan was exposed to a 100-watt light, and when its brightness was increased by 5 watts, she was not aware of the increase. However, when a 20-watt light was increased by 5 watts, she detected the increase immediately. Jan's experience illustrates _____ .

(d) The school bell rings at lunch time. The process by which our ears convert the sound waves from the bell into a coded neural signal that can be processed by the nervous system is called _____ .

(e) Not realizing how cold it is after you have been on the ski slope for a while is an example of _____ .

(f) Not being able to detect a sound because its level is too low is to the _____ threshold as being able to just barely notice that two sounds are not the same is to the _____ threshold.

Review of Key Terms 1

sensation	difference threshold
perception	just noticeable difference
sensory receptors	(jnd)
transduction	Weber's Law
sensory threshold	sensory adaptation
absolute threshold	

Matching Exercise

Match the appropriate term with its definition or description.

1. _____ The level at which a stimulus is strong enough to be detected by activating sensory receptors.

2. _____ The process by which a form of physical energy is converted into a coded neural signal that can be processed by the nervous system.

3. _____ The smallest possible strength of a stimulus that can be detected half the time.

4. _____ The process of integrating, organizing, and interpreting sensations.

5. _____ Specialized cells unique to each sense organ that respond to a particular form of sensory stimulation.

True/False Test

Indicate whether each statement is true or false by placing T or F in the blank space next to each item.

1. ____ Sensation refers to the process of detecting a physical stimulus, such as sound, light, heat, or pressure.

2. ____ Sensory adaptation refers to the decline in sensitivity to a constant stimulus.

3. ____ Weber's Law is a principle of sensation that holds that the size of the just noticeable difference will vary depending on its relation to the strength of the original stimulus.

4. ____ The smallest possible difference between two stimuli that can be detected half the time is called the just noticeable difference.

5. ____ The smallest possible difference between two stimuli that can be detected half the time is called the difference threshold.

Check your answers and review any areas of weakness before going on to the next section.

Vision: From Light to Sight
Learning Objectives

When you have finished studying this section of the chapter, you should be able to:

1. Explain how vision works and specify the functions of rods and cones.

2. Name the various parts of the eye and list their respective functions.

3. Label the appropriate parts of the eye on a diagram.

4. Describe how color vision works, name the two main theories of color vision, and explain how they differ.

Read the section "Vision: From Light to Sight" and **write** *your answers to the following:*

1. (a) The sense organ for vision is the _____ , which contains receptor cells that are sensitive to the physical energy changes of _____ .

   (b) X-rays, microwaves, ultraviolet rays, etc., are forms of _____ energy and they differ in terms of their _____ .

   (c) The difference from one wave peak to another is called a(n) _____ .

   (d) Humans are only capable of visually detecting a _____ portion of the electromagnetic spectrum range.

2. (a) The _____ is a clear membrane covering the visible part of the eye that helps gather and direct incoming light.

   (b) The black opening in the middle of your eye is called the _____ , and it is surrounded by the colored part of the eye called the _____ .

   (c) The _____ is actually a ring of muscles that expand or contract to precisely control the size of the _____ .

   (d) In dim light the iris _____ the pupil and in bright light it _____ the pupil.

   (e) The transparent structure located behind the pupil that actively focuses, or bends, light as it enters the eye is called the _____ , and this process is called _____ .

   (f) The _____ is a thin, light-sensitive membrane located at the back of the eye that contains the sensory receptors for vision.

(g) The two kinds of sensory receptors are the _____ and the _____ ; when exposed to light, they undergo a chemical reaction that results in a(n) _____ signal.

3. (a) The eye contains far _____ rods than cones, and the _____ are hundreds of times more sensitive to light than the _____ .

(b) We rely on the _____ for our vision in dim light and at night, and we rely on the _____ for vision in bright light, for sensing fine details, and for color vision.

(c) It takes about _____ minutes for rods to reach their maximum sensitivity to the available light compared to about _____ minutes for cones.

(d) _____ are more prevalent in the periphery, or outlying area, of the retina, and as a result, in dim light or at night, we are better off using our peripheral vision.

(e) The _____ is a region in the center of the retina where the cones are most concentrated and where visual information is most sharply focused.

4. (a) Most visual information is processed in the _____ , but it undergoes some preliminary processing in the _____ .

(b) Information from the sensory receptors, the rods and cones, is collected by specialized neurons called _____ cells, which in turn funnel information to other specialized neurons called _____ cells.

(c) For the most part a single ganglion cell receives information from _____ cones, but another

ganglion cell may receive information from _____ rods. Consequently the cones can send messages of much greater _____ to the brain, whereas the visual information transmitted by the rods is far less _____ .

(d) Cones are especially important in visual acuity, which refers to the _____ .

(e) Visual acuity is strongest when images are focused on the _____ because of the strong concentration of cones there.

5. (a) The _____ is a thick bundle of ganglion cell axons that exits from the back of the eye and carries visual information to the visual cortex of the brain.

(b) There are no rods or cones in the area where the _____ leaves the eye, and consequently there is a small gap in the field of vision called the _____ .

6. Our experience of color involves three properties of light waves:

(a) _____ is also known as color, with different wavelengths corresponding to our subjective experience of different colors.

(b) _____ is the property of color that corresponds to the purity of the light waves.

(c) _____ is the property of color that corresponds to the intensity or amplitude of the light wave.

7. (a) White light contains _____ and thus all colors, whereas black light _____ all wavelengths and reflects none.

(b) _____ is the perceptual experience of different wavelengths of light, involving hue, saturation (purity), and brightness (intensity).

8. There are two theories of color vision:

   (a) According to the _____ theory, cones in the retina are especially sensitive to red, green, or blue light, and colors other than these are the result of the stimulation of a combination of these cones.

   (b) According to the _____ theory, there are four basic colors that are divided into two pairs of color-sensitive neurons, red-green and blue-yellow, that oppose each other; when one member of a color pair is stimulated, the other is inhibited.

9. (a) _____ is an inherited form of color deficiency or weakness in which an individual cannot distinguish between certain colors.

   (b) A visual experience that occurs after the original stimulus is no longer present is called a(n) _____ .

   (c) Trichromatic theory provides the best explanation for _____ , and opponent-process theory best accounts for _____ .

   (d) Both theories of color vision are accurate because each theory correctly describes color vision at a(n) _____ level of visual processing.

10. Decide which term applies to the following:

    (a) According to the trichromatic theory, if Mr. Colorado's red-, green-, and blue-sensitive cones are stimulated simultaneously, then he should see _____ .

    (b) If you have normal vision and you stare at a red circle for a couple of minutes and then shift your eyes to a white surface, the after-image of the circle will be _____ .

    (c) Following an accident it was discovered that the fovea in Harbinder's right eye was destroyed. Although he can still see with this eye, it is likely that he will have trouble seeing _____ and _____ when his left eye is closed.

(d) Fido, like most dogs, lacks receptor cells for long wavelengths of about 700 nanometers. It is very probable that Fido cannot see the color _____ .

(e) According to the opponent-process theory, if certain cells in Dale's retina are stimulated by exposure to green light, they are likely to be inhibited by exposure to _____ light.

Graphic Organizer 1

Identify each part of the eye by writing the name on the appropriate line and then match its function by placing the corresponding number next to the name. [For example, "1. retina" is the first answer.]

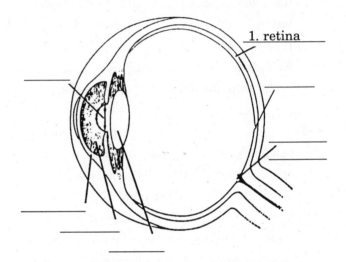

1. retina

1. A light-sensitive membrane located at the back of the eye that contains sensory receptors for vision.

2. The black opening in the middle of the eye that changes size to let in different amounts of light.

3. A clear membrane covering the visible part of the eye that helps gather and direct incoming light.

4. The colored part of the eye that is the muscle that controls the size of the pupil.

5. A transparent structure located behind the pupil that actively focuses, or bends, light as it enters the eye.

6. A small area in the center of the retina that contains cones but not rods.

7. The point where the optic nerve leaves the eye.

Review of Key Terms 2

wavelength
cornea
pupil
iris
iridology
lens
accommodation
retina
rods
cones
fovea
bipolar cells

ganglion cells
visual acuity
optic nerve
blind spot
color
hue
saturation
brightness
trichromatic theory
color blindness
afterimage
opponent-process theory

Matching Exercise

Match the appropriate term with its definition or description:

1. _____ The visual ability to see fine details.

2. _____ A visual experience that occurs after the original source of stimulation is no longer present.

3. _____ The distance from one wave peak to another.

4. _____ The process by which the lens changes shape to focus incoming light so that it falls on the retina.

5. _____ The perceived intensity of color that corresponds to the amplitude of the light wave.

6. _____ The thick nerve that exits from the back of the eye and carries visual information to the visual cortex in the brain.

7. _____ The theory that the sensation of color is due to cones in the retina that are especially sensitive to red, green, or blue light.

8. _____ The short, thick, pointed sensory receptors of the eye that detect color and are responsible for color vision and visual acuity.

9. _____ The property of wavelengths of light known as color, with different wavelengths corresponding to our subjective experience of different colors.

10. _____ The long, thin, blunt sensory receptors that are highly sensitive to light but not color and are primarily responsible for peripheral vision and night vision.

11. _____ The specialized neurons in the retina that collect sensory information from the rods and cones and then funnel it on to other specialized neurons before it is transmitted to the brain.

12. _____ The perceptual experience of different wavelengths of light, involving hue, saturation (purity), and brightness (intensity).

True/False Test

Indicate whether each statement is true or false by placing T or F in the blank space next to each item.

1. ____ The cornea is the transparent structure located behind the pupil that actively focuses, or bends, light as it enters the eye.

2. ____ The opponent-process theory states that color vision is the product of opposing pairs of color receptors, red-green, black-white, and blue-yellow; when one member of a color pair is stimulated, the other is inhibited.

3. ____ The lens is the clear membrane covering the visible part of the eye that helps gather and direct incoming light.

4. ____ A single ganglion cell may receive information from only one or two cones and another may receive information from a hundred or more rods.

5. ____ The retina is a small area in the center of the back of the eye that is composed entirely of cones and is where visual information is most sharply focused.

6. ____ The colored part of the eye, which is actually a ring of muscles that controls the size of the pupil, is called the iris.

7. ____ The pupil is the opening in the middle of the iris that changes size to let in different amounts of light.

8. ____ The fovea is a thin, light-sensitive membrane located at the back of the eye that contains two kinds of sensory receptors for light and vision.

9. ____ Iridology is based on the unproven notion that physical and psychological functioning are reflected in the iris, the colored part of your eye.

10. ____ Saturation is the property of color that corresponds to the purity of the light wave.

11. ___ Color blindness occurs because there are no receptor cells in the area where the optic nerve exits the eye.

12. ___ An inherited form of visual deficiency or weakness in which an individual cannot distinguish between certain wavelengths is referred to as the blind spot syndrome.

Check your answers and review any areas of weakness before going on to the next section.

Hearing: From Vibration to Sound
Learning Objectives

When you have finished studying this section of the chapter, you should be able to:

1. Define *audition* and explain the process of audition.
2. Describe the nature of sound and list the physical properties of sound waves.
3. Label the appropriate parts of a diagram of the ear.
4. Name and describe the functions of the various structures of the ear.
5. Distinguish between the place and frequency theories of audition and specify how each attempts to explain the phenomenon of pitch.

*Read the section "Hearing: From Vibration to Sound" and **write** your answers to the following:*

1. (a) _____ is the technical term for the sense of hearing.
   (b) The ability to sense and perceive very subtle differences in sound is important to
   _____ survival,
   _____ interactions, and
   _____ development.

2. (a) _____ are the physical stimuli that produce our sensory experience of sound.
   (b) Loudness is determined by the intensity, or _____ , of a sound wave and is measured in units called _____ .
   (c) The softest sound that a human can hear, or

the absolute threshold, is represented by _____ decibels.
   (d) Pitch refers to the relative _____ or _____ of a sound and is determined by the _____ of a sound wave.
   (e) _____ refers to the rate of vibration, or number of waves per second, and is measured in units called
   _____ .
   (f) The distinctive quality of a sound produced by the combination of several sound wave frequencies is called _____ .

3. (a) The human ear is made up of the _____ ear, where sound waves are collected; the _____ ear, where they are amplified; and the _____ ear, where they are transduced into neural messages.
   (b) The three structures of the outer ear are the
   _____ .
   (c) The _____ separates the outer ear from the middle ear, and the _____ separates the middle ear from the inner ear.
   (d) The middle ear contains three tiny bones called the _____
   _____ .
   (e) _____ deafness is hearing loss due to damage to the tiny bones of the middle ear. This type of deafness can often be helped by a(n) _____ , which amplifies sounds.
   (f) The cochlea is the main structure in the _____ ear and it contains the _____ and tiny projecting fibers called _____ , which are responsible for transducing, or transforming, the vibrations of sound waves into neural impulses.
   (g) _____ deafness is due to dam-

age to the hair cells or auditory nerve, which cannot be helped by a(n) _____ .

4. (a) The _____ is a key structure involved in the discrimination of pitch.

    (b) According to the _____ theory, the basilar membrane vibrates at the same _____ as the sound wave, and this theory can explain sounds up to about 1,000 hertz.

    (c) A child can typically hear pitches ranging from about _____ to _____ hertz, and this presents a problem for _____ theory.

    (d) The _____ theory suggests that different frequencies cause larger vibrations at different locations along the basilar membrane.

    (e) Higher-frequency sounds cause maximum vibration near the _____ end of the basilar membrane, and lower-frequency sounds cause maximum vibration at the _____ end.

    (f) Different pitches excite different _____ along the basilar membrane, and higher-pitched sounds are interpreted according to the _____ where the hair cells are most active.

    (g) _____ theory helps explain our discrimination of lower-frequency sounds, and _____ theory helps explain our discrimination of higher-pitched sounds; for midrange pitches, both _____ and _____ are involved.

5. Read the following and write the correct term in the space provided:

    (a) The retina in the eye performs a function that parallels the function of the _____ in the ear.

    (b) Rita has had her hearing tested and has been told by the experts that a hearing aid will help restore her hearing. Rita probably has _____ deafness.

    (c) After a small area of his basilar membrane was damaged, Hamish could no longer hear high-pitched sounds. This loss of hearing can best be explained by the _____ theory.

    (d) Mrs. Newbold is 75 years old and has had some hearing loss due to stiffness of the tiny bones in her middle ear. It is possible that her deafness can be helped by a(n) _____ .

    (e) Dr. Emison's research, which found that high-frequency sounds trigger activity near the stirrup end of the basilar membrane, supports the _____ theory of pitch.

Graphic Organizer 2

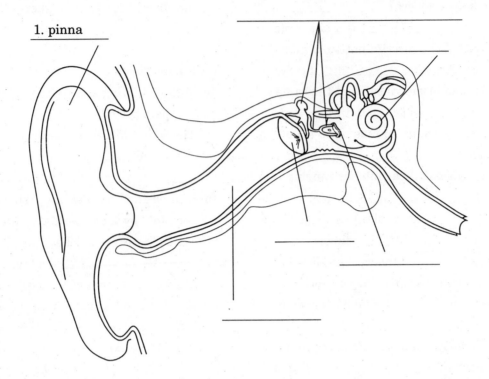

1. pinna

Identify each part of the ear by writing the name on the appropriate line and then match its function by placing the corresponding number next to the name. [For example, "1. pinna" is the first answer.]

1. The oddly shaped flap of skin and cartilage that's attached to each side of the head.

2. A tightly stretched membrane at the end of the ear canal that vibrates when sound waves hit it.

3. A fluid-filled coiled structure that contains the sensory receptors for sound.

4. The tunnel that the sound waves travel down to reach the eardrum.

5. The tightly stretched membrane that separates the middle ear from the inner ear.

6. The small structures of the middle ear whose joint action almost doubles the amplification of the sound.

Review of Key Terms 3

audition	decibels
sound waves	pitch
loudness	frequency
amplitude	hertz

timbre	oval window
outer ear	inner ear
pinna	cochlea
ear canal	basilar membrane
eardrum	hair cells
middle ear	nerve deafness
hammer, anvil, and	frequency theory
stirrup	place theory
conduction deafness	

Matching Exercise

Match the appropriate term with its definition or description.

1. _____ A type of deafness due to damage to the hair cells or auditory nerve.

2. _____ The technical term for the sense of hearing.

3. _____ The rate of vibration, or number of waves per second.

4. _____ The hairlike sensory receptors for sound found in the basilar membrane.

5. _____ The physical stimuli that produce our sensory experience of sound.

6. _____ The distinctive quality of a sound, determined by the complexity of the sound waves.

7. _____ The part of the ear that collects sound waves and consists of the pinna, the ear canal, and the eardrum.

8. _____ The relative highness or lowness of a sound, determined by the frequency of the sound wave.

9. _____ The view that different frequencies cause larger vibrations at different locations along the basilar membrane.

10. _____ The unit of measurement for loudness.

11. _____ The intensity or amount of energy of a wave, reflected in the height of the wave; determines a sound's loudness.

12. _____ The small, tightly stretched membrane that separates the middle ear from the inner ear.

True/False Test

Indicate whether each statement is true or false by placing T or F in the blank space next to each item.

1. ____ The intensity (or amplitude) of a sound, mesured in decibels, is called loudness.

2. ____ According to frequency theory, the basilar membrane vibrates at the same frequency as the sound wave, thereby enabling low-frequency sound to be transmitted to the brain.

3. ____ The eardrum is a tightly stretched membrane that separates the middle ear from the inner ear.

4. ____ Conduction deafness is the result of damage to the tiny bones in the middle ear.

5. ____ The hammer, anvil, and stirrup are important transduction structures in the inner ear.

6. ____ The cochlea is a coiled fluid-filled structure that contains the sensory receptors for sound.

7. ____ Hertz refers to the number of wave peaks per second.

8. ____ The ear canal is the fluid-filled section of the ear that contains the cochlea.

9. ____ The structure within the cochlea that contains the hair cells is called the basilar membrane

10. ____ The oval window is a tightly stretched membrane at the end of the ear canal that vibrates when sound waves hit it.

11. ____ The pinna is the oddly shaped flap of skin and cartilage that is attached to each side of your head.

12. ____ The inner ear is the part of the ear where sound is transduced into neural impulses; consists of the cochlea and semicircular canals.

> Check your answers and review any areas of weakness before going on to the next section.

The Chemical and Body Senses: Smell, Taste, Touch, and Position

Learning Objectives

When you have finished studying this section of the chapter, you should be able to:

1. Define *olfaction* and *gustation* and explain what is meant by the "chemical senses."

2. Describe the process of olfaction and the role played by the olfactory nerve, olfactory bulb, and olfactory cortex.

3. Explain how odors are recognized and how pheromones affect behavior.

4. Define *taste* and describe the role of the taste buds in gustation.

5. Identify the skin senses and list their respective functions.

6. Define pain and explain the processes involved in pain perception.

7. Describe the gate-control theory of pain and explain the role of substance P.

8. List the various types of pain, specify the conditions that influence the perception of pain, and explain the role of endorphins.

9. Explain how the kinesthetic sense works and describe the influence of proprioceptors, the vestibular sacs, and the semicircular canals.

*Read the section "The Chemical and Body Senses: Smell, Taste, Touch, and Position" and **write** your answers to the following:*

1. (a) _____ refers to our sense of
    smell and _____ refers to our
    sense of taste.

   (b) Sensory receptors for taste and smell
    respond to different types of
    _____ substances, and that is
    why they are sometimes called the
    _____ senses.

2. (a) The sensory stimuli that produce our sensa-
    tion of odor are _____ .

   (b) Airborne _____ encounter mil-
    lions of olfactory receptor cells high in the
    nasal cavity.

   (c) Stimulation of these receptor cells in the
    nose is converted into neural messages that
    travel along the axons that make up the
    _____ .

   (d) Hundreds of different odor receptors have
    been identified, but we can identify approxi-
    mately _____ different odors; it
    appears that a given smell activates a
    _____ of different receptors and
    that specific odors are identified by the
    brain when it interprets the pattern of
    receptors that are stimulated.

   (e) The _____ nerve connects to the
    olfactory bulb in the brain, which is actually
    the enlarged ending of the
    _____ cortex.

   (f) Axons from the olfactory bulb also project to
    structures in the _____ system
    of the brain.

   (g) The olfactory sense is the only sense with a
    direct connection to the brain (and to the
    outside world), and unlike the other senses,
    it does not pass through the
    _____ before being relayed to
    the higher brain centers of the cortex.

   (h) As with other senses, we experience sensory
    _____ to odors when exposed to
    them for a period of time, with maximum

    _____ occurring in less than a
    minute.

3. (a) Our sense of taste, or _____ ,
    results from stimulation of special receptors
    in the mouth.

   (b) The stimuli that produce the sensation of
    taste are _____ sub-
    stances in whatever you eat or drink, and
    these substances are dissolved by saliva,
    which allows them to activate the
    _____ .

   (c) The _____ are the spe-
    cialized receptors for taste that, when acti-
    vated, send neural messages to the
    _____ , which then directs the
    information to several higher brain regions
    in the cortex.

   (d) The four primary taste qualities are
    _____ , _____ ,
    _____ , and _____ ,
    and all others are a combination of these.

4. (a) The _____ senses provide
    essential information about your physical
    status and your physical interaction with
    objects in your environment.

   (b) The _____ is the largest and
    heaviest sense organ in the body.

   (c) There are many different kinds of receptors
    in the _____ and some are spe-
    cialized to respond to just one kind of stimu-
    lus, such as _____ ,
    _____ , or _____ .

   (d) One important receptor involved in the
    sense of touch is called the
    _____ , which is located
    beneath the skin; if pressure stimulation is
    constant, this receptor either reduces the
    number of signals sent or stops responding
    altogether.

5. (a) Pain is the sensation of _____
    or _____ , and virtually any

external (or internal) stimulus that can produce tissue damage can cause pain.

(b) Pain is important to our _____ because it provides us with information about our body and what is happening to it.

(c) The most influential theory for explaining how pain is processed is called the _____ theory; this model suggests that the sensation of pain is controlled by a series of _____ that open and close in the spinal cord.

(d) Pain begins when an intense stimulus activates small-diameter sensory fibers called _____ endings in the skin, muscles, or internal organs that carry messages to the spinal cord, releasing a neurotransmitter called _____.

(e) _____ causes other neurons to become activated, and they send their messages through open signal gates to the thalamus in the brain.

6. (a) Depending on how the brain interprets the experience of pain, the signals down the _____ either _____ or _____ the gates.

(b) Psychological and emotional factors that can _____ the experience of pain include anxiety, fear, and a sense of helplessness; factors that can _____ the experience of pain include positive emotions, a sense of control, distraction, and laughter.

(c) The pain experience is also influenced by _____ and _____ learning experiences about the meaning of pain and how one should react to pain.

(d) Psychological factors influence the release of _____, the body's natural painkillers, which are produced in many parts of the brain and body.

(e) In the brain, _____ can inhibit the transmission of pain signals, and in the

spinal cord they inhibit the release of substance _____.

(f) A person's _____ and _____ state can influence other bodily processes, such as muscle tension, blood flow, heart rate, and respiration.

7. (a) The _____ sense involves specialized sensory neurons called _____, which are located in the muscles and joints and communicate information to the brain about changes in body position and muscle tension.

(b) The _____ sense provides a sense of balance or equilibrium by responding to changes in gravity, motion, and body position.

(c) There are two sources of vestibular sensory information, both located in the ear: the _____ canals and the _____ sacs. These structures are filled with fluid and lined with hairlike receptor cells that shift in response to _____, changes in body _____, or changes in _____.

(d) Maintaining our equilibrium also involves information from other senses, particularly _____.

(e) When information from the _____ conflicts with information from the vestibular system, the result can be _____, _____, and _____.

8. Read the following and write in the correct term in the space provided:

(a) On the day of her final statistics exam, Nadia has a sore ankle. According to the gate-control theory, it is likely that Nadia's fear and anxiety about the exam will _____ her perception of the pain in her ankle.

(b) Mortimer goes fishing in a small boat, and the motion of the waves makes him nauseous. Mortimer's _____ and _____ are most likely responsible for making him feel ill.

(c) If you are blindfolded and asked to touch your chin, nose, and forehead with your index finger, you probably will have no trouble doing so. This ability is due to your _____ sense.

(d) Arleigh accidentally scrapes the skin off his knuckles while working on his car. The pain he feels following the injury is caused in part by the release of the neurotransmitter _____ .

(e) As a result of damage to her olfactory bulb, Danielle has lost the ability to sense the _____ of whatever she eats or drinks.

(f) If a person experiences damage to the thalamus, the sense that will be least affected is the sense of _____ .

Review of Key Terms 4

olfaction	pain
gustation	gate-control theory
chemical senses	free nerve endings
airborne molecules	substance P
olfactory nerve	endorphins
olfactory bulb	kinesthetic sense
pheromones	proprioceptors
taste buds	vestibular sense
skin senses	semicircular canals
Pacinian corpuscle	vestibular sacs

Matching Exercise

Match the appropriate term with its definition or description.

1. _____ The technical term for our sense of taste.

2. _____ The fluid-filled sacs that are lined with hairlike receptor cells that shift in response to motion, changes in body position, and gravity.

3. _____ The receptor for touch that is located beneath the skin and that when stimulated by pressure converts the stimulation into neural messages that are relayed to the brain.

4. _____ The name sometimes given to our sense of taste and sense of smell because they both involve sensory receptors for chemical substances.

5. _____ The small-diameter sensory fibers in the skin, muscles, or internal organs that when activated by an intense stimulus begin the process of pain perception.

6. _____ The enlarged ending of the olfactory cortex at the front of the brain where the sensation of smell is registered.

7. _____ The specialized sensory receptors for taste that are located on the tongue and inside the mouth and throat.

8. _____ Chemical signals used by animals to communicate territorial boundaries and sexual receptiveness.

9. _____ The technical term for the sense of balance or equilibrium.

10. _____ The body's natural painkillers that are produced in many parts of the brain and the body.

True/False Test

Indicate whether each item is true or false by placing T or F in the space next to each item.

1. ____ Pain is the unpleasant sensation of physical discomfort or suffering that can occur in varying degrees of intensity.

2. ____ Gate-control theory suggests that pain is the product of both physiological and psychological factors that cause spinal "gates" to open and relay patterns of intense stimulation to the brain, which perceives them as pain.

3. ____ Airborne chemical molecules are emitted by the substances we are smelling; we inhale them through the nose and through the opening in the palate at the back of the throat.

4. ____ The olfactory nerve connects directly to the olfactory bulb, and it is here that smells are perceived by the brain.

5. ____ Proprioceptors are sensory neurons in the spinal cord that regulate the release of endorphins.

6. ___ Olfaction is the technical term for our sense of smell.

7. ___ The semicircular canals are fluid-filled structures lined with hairlike receptors that shift in response to motion, changes in bodily position, and gravity and are a source of information for our vestibular sense.

8. ___ Substance P is one of the body's natural painkillers and is produced in many parts of the brain and body in response to intense stimulation.

9. ___ The kinesthetic sense is the technical name for the sense of location and position of body parts in relation to one another.

> Check your answers and review any areas of weakness before going on to the next section.

Perception

Learning Objectives

When you have finished studying this section of the chapter, you should be able to:

1. Define *perception* and contrast it with the definition of *sensation*.

2. Identify the three questions with which perceptual processing is concerned.

3. Describe the goals of Gestalt psychology.

*Read the section "Perception" and **write** your answers to the following:*

1. (a) Perception is the process of

   _____ , _____ , and

   _____ sensory information in a

   meaningful way.

   (b) Cognitive processes such as

   _____ and _____

   are involved in determining the meaning of

   an object.

2. Perceptual processes help us organize our sensations to answer three basic questions:

   (a) _____

   (b) _____

   (c) _____

3. (a) The German psychologists who investigated the basic rules of perceptual organization

were called _____ psychologists.

   (b) The German word _____ means a unified whole, and this perspective maintains that we perceive whole objects or figures rather than isolated bits and pieces of information.

Depth Perception: "How Far Away Is It?"

Learning Objectives

When you have finished studying this section of the chapter, you should be able to:

1. Define *depth perception* and state why it is important.

2. List and describe the various monocular cues used in depth perception.

3. Distinguish between pictorial cues and accommodation.

4. Name the various binocular cues and give examples that illustrate each.

*Read the section "Depth Perception: 'How Far Away Is It?'" and **write** your answers to the following:*

1. (a) The ability to perceive distance or the location of three-dimensional objects is called

   _____ .

   (b) The cues used to judge the distance of objects that require the use of only one eye are called _____ cues.

2. Identify the following monocular cues:

   (a) Two similar-sized objects are observed, and the object that appears larger is perceived as being closer: _____

   (b) One object partially blocks or obscures the view of another object and the partially blocked object is perceived as being farther away: _____

   (c) Faraway objects appear hazy or slightly blurred by the atmosphere:

   _____

   (d) The details of a distinct surface texture gradually become fuzzy or less clearly defined as distance increases: _____

(e) Parallel lines seem to meet in the distance: _____

(f) A moving person observes that nearby objects that are passed seem to move faster than objects that are far away:

_____

3. (a) Artists using monocular cues to create the perception of distance or depth in paintings are using _____ cues.

(b) A monocular cue that utilizes information about changes in the shape of the lens of the eye to help us estimate distance is called

_____ .

4. (a) In contrast to monocular cues, _____ cues for distance or depth perception require information from both eyes.

(b) A binocular cue based on the degree to which muscles rotate the eyes to focus on an object is called _____ .

(c) Focusing on an object held about six inches from the eyes will require a greater degree of _____ than if we focus on it at arm's length; the information provided by these signals from the eyes is used to judge distance.

(d) A distance cue that relies on information provided by the two slightly different images that result from having eyes a number of inches apart is called

_____ .

(e) When the two retinal images of an object are very different, we perceptually interpret the object as being _____ , and when they are almost identical, the object is perceived as being _____ .

(f) Stereograms use the binocular depth cue of

_____ .

The Perception of Motion: "Where Is It Going?"
Learning Objectives
When you have finished studying this section of the chapter, you should be able to:

1. Specify which sources of information influence the perception of motion.

2. Describe induced motion and explain its relevance for perception.

3. Explain how stroboscopic motion works and how it relates to the perception of motion.

4. Discuss how auditory cues influence our perception of distance and direction of sounds.

*Read the section "The Perception of Motion: 'Where Is It Going?'" and **write** your answers to the following:*

1. (a) When a moving object moves across the retina, our eye muscles make micro-fine _____ to keep the object in focus.

(b) We also compare the moving object to the _____ , which is usually stationary.

(c) We perceive movement when complex neural pathways combine information from _____ activity, the changing _____ image, and the contrast of the moving object with its stationary _____ .

(d) It is known that some neurons are highly specialized to detect motion in _____ direction but not in the _____ direction, whereas other neurons are specialized to detect motion of one particular _____ , but not faster or slower.

2. (a) We typically assume that the _____ we are observing moves while the background or frame remains stationary, and this sometimes leads to the illusion of motion called _____ motion.

(b) In Gestalt psychologist Karl Dunker's experiment on _____ motion, when the _____ slowly moved to the right, the subjects perceived the dot as moving to the left despite the fact that the dot never moved.

3. (a) _____ motion refers to the phenomenon whereby two lights spaced apart and flashing on and off in succession create the perception of one light moving back and forth in space.

(b) Although no actual movement takes place and the two flashing lights are detected at two different points on the retina, the brain's _____ combines this rapid sequence of visual information to arrive at the perceptual experience of motion.

4. (a) We also use _____ information to judge distance and direction.

(b) Using only one ear, the _____ the sound, the closer it is perceived to be, but using two ears allows more accurate location of the _____ as well as the distance of a sound.

(c) The _____ and _____ of a sound are calculated by the brain on the basis of differences in time lag and loudness detected by each ear; sounds to the left, for example, arrive at the left ear slightly sooner and slightly louder than at the right ear.

The Perception of Shape: "What Is It?"

Learning Objectives

When you have finished studying this section of the chapter, you should be able to:

1. Describe the process of shape perception and explain its relevance in determining what objects are.

2. Define the figure-ground relationship and specify the importance of this perceptual principle.

3. Explain how figure-ground relationships contribute to the perception of reversible figures and to the use of camouflage in the animal kingdom.

4. List the principles of perceptual grouping and give an example to illustrate each.

*Read the section "The Perception of Shape: 'What Is It?'" and **write** your answers to the following:*

1. (a) Although we rely to some degree on size, color, and texture to determine what an object might be, we rely primarily on an object's _____ to identify it.

(b) _____ refers to the fact that when we view a scene, we automatically separate the elements of that scene into the feature that clearly stands out and its less distinct background.

(c) Our ability to separate a scene into _____ and _____ is a psychological accomplishment, not a function of the actual elements of the scene we are looking at.

(d) The perception of an image in two different ways (as with the vase example in Figure 3.12) is called _____ , and this ability underscores the notion that our perception of figure is a(n) _____ phenomenon.

2. (a) We actively organize elements to try to produce the stable perception of well-defined, whole objects, according to a number of Gestalt _____ or laws.

(b) The law of Prägnanz is also called the _____ and states that when several perceptual organizations are possible, the perceptual interpretation that will occur will be the one that produces the _____ , _____ , and most stable shape.

(c) The law of Prägnanz encompasses all other _____ , including the figure-ground relationship.

(d) Our perceptual system works in an economical and efficient way to reveal "the essence of something," which is roughly what the German word _____ means.

3. Read the following and write the correct term in the space provided:

(a) Dr. Schwartz investigates the basic rules of perceptual organization, and he believes that we perceive whole objects or figures rather than isolated bits and pieces of sensory information. Dr. Schwartz is most likely a _____ psychologist.

(b) At a noisy party Ben's attention is focused on what his girlfriend is saying and he is able to tune out the conversations of others. Using a Gestalt perceptual principle to analyze this example, the noisy environment is the _____ and his girlfriend's voice is the _____ .

(c) After viewing the stereogram for a few minutes, Nina was surprised when very distinct three-dimensional objects appeared from the two-dimensional scene. The binocular cue responsible for this phenomenon is

_____ .

(d) Hernando knows that the red bicycle in the parking lot is closer to him than the green bicycle because the red one casts a larger retinal image than the green one. This illustrates the distance cue known as

_____ .

(e) Emily paints a long garden pathway bordered with flowers and depicts the parallel lines of flowers as getting smaller and eventually meeting at the horizon; Emily is using _____ to convey depth on the canvas.

(f) Ricardo uses sequentially flashing Christmas tree lights in front of his house to make it look as though Santa and his sleigh are moving from the garden to the roof. Ricardo is using the perceptual illusion of

_____ .

Review of Key Terms 5

perception	accommodation
Gestalt psychology	binocular cues
depth perception	convergence
monocular cues	binocular disparity
relative size	induced motion
overlap	stroboscopic motion
aerial perspective	auditory cues
texture gradient	figure-ground
linear perspective	relationship
motion parallax	figure-ground reversal
pictorial cues	law of Prägnanz

Matching Exercise

Match the appropriate term with its definition or description.

1. _____ A school of psychology founded in Germany in the early 1900s that maintained that our sensations are actively processed according to consistent perceptual rules that result in meaningful whole perceptions.

2. _____ The law that states that when several perceptual organizations are possible, the perceptual interpretation that will occur will be one that produces the best, simplest, and most staple shape.

3. _____ The monocular cue that suggests that faraway objects often appear hazy or slightly blurred by the atmosphere.

4. _____ The binocular cue that relies on the fact that our eyes are set a couple of inches apart and thus a slightly different image of an object is cast on the retina of each eye.

5. _____ A Gestalt principle of perceptual organization that states that we automatically separate the elements of a perception into the feature that clearly stands out from its less distinct background.

6. _____ A monocular cue that occurs when one object partially blocks or obscures the view of another object and the partially blocked object is perceived as being farther away.

7. _____ Distance or depth cues that require the use of both eyes.

8. _____ A monocular cue that utilizes information about changes in the shape of

the lens of the eye to help us gauge depth and distance.

9. _____ An illusion of movement that results when two separate, carefully timed flashing lights are perceived as one light moving back and forth.

10. _____ The use of visual cues (either monocular or binocular) to perceive the distance or three-dimensional characteristics of objects.

11. _____ The perception of an image in which the ground can be perceived as the figure and the figure as the ground; underscores that our perception of figure and ground is a psychological phenomenon.

True/False Test

Indicate whether each item is true or false by placing T or F in the space next to each item.

1. ____ Perception is defined as the process of integrating, organizing, and interpreting sensory information in a way that is meaningful.

2. ____ Induced motion occurs when a sound reaches one ear slightly before reaching the other and results in the perception of movement.

3. ____ Relative size refers to the monocular cue whereby one object partially blocks or obscures the view of another object and the partially blocked object appears farther away.

4. ____ Monocular cues for distance or depth information require information from both eyes.

5. ____ The depth cue that occurs when parallel lines seem to meet in the distance (and the closer together the lines appear to be, the greater the perception of depth) is called linear perspective.

6. ____ Convergence is a binocular cue that relies on the degree to which muscles rotate the eyes to focus on an object; the less convergence, the farther away the object appears to be.

7. ____ When we are in motion, we can use the speed of passing objects to estimate the distance of objects; nearby objects will appear to move much faster relative to distant objects. This monocular cue is called motion parallax.

8. ____ In addition to monocular and binocular visual cues, auditory cues can also be used to judge distance and direction.

9. ____ Texture gradient is a binocular cue for distance in which parallel lines seem to meet in the distance and their surface or texture become less clearly defined the farther away they are.

10. ____ Monocular cues that are used by artists to create the perception of distance or depth in paintings are called pictorial cues.

Check your answers and review any areas of weakness before going on to the next section.

Perceptual Constancies
Learning Objectives

When you have finished studying this section of the chapter, you should be able to:

1. Define perceptual constancy and specify the principles that guide our perceptions of constancy.

2. List and describe the three forms of constancy.

3. Explain how size constancy, shape constancy, and brightness constancy work and provide examples that illustrate each.

*Read the section "Perceptual Constancies" and **write** your answers to the following:*

1. (a) The tendency to perceive objects, especially familiar objects, as unchanging despite changes in sensory input is called

   _____ .

   (b) Without _____ our perception of reality would be in a constant state of flux instead of the stable view of the world we normally perceive.

2. (a) Size constancy is the perception that an object remains the same _____ despite its changing image on the

   _____ .

(b) An important principle of size constancy is that if the retinal image of an object does not change but the perception of its distance increases, we will perceive the object as _____ ; this principle is easily demonstrated with the phenomenon of the _____ .

3. (a) The tendency to perceive familiar objects as having a fixed shape regardless of the image they cast on our retinas is called _____ .

(b) If we observe a door opening toward us, the retinal image of its rectangular shape changes but our _____ of its shape remains constant.

4. (a) Brightness constancy is when the brightness of an object stays the _____ though the lighting conditions _____ .

(b) The perception of brightness constancy occurs because objects always reflect the same _____ of available light, even if the lighting conditions change dramatically.

Factors That Influence Perceptual Interpretations

Learning Objectives

When you have finished studying this section of the chapter, you should be able to:

1. Describe the effects of **educational, cultural,** and life experiences on **perceptual interpretations.**

2. Define *perceptual set* and **explain how it** accounts for various perceptual experiences.

3. Define *perceptual illusions* and state why psychologists are interested in these perceptual mistakes.

4. List three perceptual illusions, give an example that illustrates each, and provide the theoretical reasons for their occurrence.

*Read the section "Factors That Influence Perceptual Interpretations" and **write** your answers to the following:*

1. (a) In the broadest sense our _____ , _____ , and _____ experiences shape what we perceive.

(b) A _____ refers to the influence of prior assumptions and expectations on perceptual interpretations.

(c) People who have reported sightings of UFOs, the Loch Ness monster, mermaids, etc., have interpreted ambiguous stimuli in terms of the _____ they held in the situation, seeing what their expectations led them to see.

2. (a) When we misperceive the true characteristics of an object or image, we experience a(n) _____ .

(b) The perceptual contradictions of _____ not only are fascinating but also can shed light on how the _____ processes of perception guide us to perceptual conclusions.

3. (a) The Müller-Lyer illusion involves the misperception of the _____ of lines.

(b) Visual depth cues that promote the perception that a line with outward-pointing arrows is _____ from us and a line with inward-pointing arrows is _____ to us contribute to the Müller-Lyer illusion.

(c) _____ constancy plays an important role in the Müller-Lyer illusion.

(d) Although two lines produce _____ retinal images, one line is embedded in visual depth cues that make us perceive it as farther away and thus our brain interprets it as being _____ .

4. (a) The moon illusion is the misperception that a full moon is _____ when viewed on the horizon than in the overhead sky.

(b) The retinal image of a full moon is _____ when the moon is observed on the horizon compared to when it is seen in the overhead sky.

(c) A partial explanation of the moon illusion is that people perceive objects on the horizon as _____ than objects that are directly overhead in the sky.

(d) The depth perception cue of overlap adds to the perception that the horizon moon is _____ than the overhead moon.

(e) The moon illusion also involves the misapplication of _____ constancy, and even though the retinal image of the moon remains constant, we perceive the moon as _____ because it seems farther away on the horizon.

(f) If all distance cues are removed, the size of the moon on the horizon will look _____ as it does when directly overhead.

5. (a) Perceptual illusions underscore the fact that what we see is not merely a simple reflection of the world, but rather our subjective perceptual _____ of it.

(b) The various illusions, photographs, and other perceptual demonstrations presented in the text clearly illustrate the fundamental difference between _____ and perception.

(c) Through our _____ , we detect different forms of energy but it is our brain that _____ and _____ that information, giving it a meaning that is a reasonably accurate reflection of the physical world.

6. Read the following and write the correct term in the space provided:

(a) Stereotypes are mental conceptions that we have about individuals belonging to specific racial or ethnic groups and can influence how we interpret their behaviors. Stereotypes are most similar to _____ .

(b) William noticed that the full moon seemed to be much larger on the horizon than when it was overhead. His friend Jane, a psychology major, explained that the illusion results from distance cues that make the horizon moon seem _____ than when it is overhead.

(c) Your unopened introductory psychology textbook produces a trapezoidal retinal image, but you typically perceive the book as a rectangular object. The reason for this is due to _____ constancy.

(d) When asked to judge the length of two equal lines, people consistently report the one with outward-pointing arrows as being longer than the one with inward-pointing arrows. These people are experiencing the _____ illusion.

Review of Key Terms 6

perceptual set
perceptual constancy
size constancy
shape constancy
brightness constancy
perceptual illusion

Müller-Lyer illusion
moon illusion
extrasensory perception (ESP)
parapsychology

Matching Exercise

Match the appropriate term with its definition or description.

1. _____ The influence of prior assumptions and expectations on perceptual interpretations.

2. _____ The tendency to perceive objects, especially familiar objects, as constant and unchanging despite changes in sensory input.

3. _____ A famous visual illusion involving the misperception of the identical length of two lines, one with arrows pointed inward and one with arrows pointed outward.

4. _____ The perception of an object as maintaining the same size despite changing images on the retina.

5. _____ The term for the investigation of claims of various paranormal phenomena.

True/False Test

Indicate whether each item is true or false by placing T or F in the space next to each item.

1. ____ A perceptual illusion is the tendency to perceive objects as constant and unchanging despite changes in sensory input.

2. ____ The moon illusion involves the misperception that the moon is larger when it is on the horizon than when it is directly overhead.

3. ____ The perception of a familiar object as maintaining the same shape regardless of the image produced on the retina is called shape constancy.

4. ____ Brightness constancy is the perception that the brightness of an object remains the same even though the lighting conditions change.

5. ____ Extrasensory perception (ESP) is based on the idea that sensory information can be detected by some means other than through the normal processes of sensation.

Check your answers and review any areas of weakness before going on to the next section.

Something to Think About

1. It is not uncommon for people to have some strange experiences that they interpret as extrasensory perception, or ESP. Suppose that a friend or family member told you about such an experience. This person may feel quite convinced that something extraordinary has occurred. Based on what you have learned in this chapter, how would you go about explaining to them what has most likely taken place.

2. Imagine that you have decided to become a visual artist. You want to paint a picture that includes a variety of elements such as buildings, fields, a river, a mountain, and some people and animals. Using what you know about sensation and perception, think of all the monocular cues that you could use to give your masterpiece a sense of depth. In addition, can you think of any perceptual components that might add interest to your canvas?

Check your answers and review any areas of weakness before doing the progress tests.

Progress Test 1

Review the chapter (including Concept Reviews), review all your study notes, and then test yourself on the following progress test. Check your answers. If you make a mistake, review your notes and the relevant section of the study guide and, if necessary, go back and read the appropriate part of your textbook.

1. Dr. Kandola's research showed that with low-frequency sounds the vibrations of hair cells in the basilar membrane were at the same frequency as the sound waves that stimulated them. This research supports the _____ theory of pitch.
   - (a) place
   - (b) frequency
   - (c) timbre
   - (d) amplitude

2. Dr. Frankenstein's younger brother built a monster but omitted a very important part of his anatomy. As a result, the monster cannot transform sounds into neural messages. The missing part is the
   - (a) eardrum
   - (b) middle ear with its tiny bones
   - (c) vestibular sacs
   - (d) basilar membrane

3. A red pen is displayed in Roger's peripheral vision while he stares straight ahead. He correctly identifies the object but is unable to name the color. The reason for this is that
   - (a) there are many rods and very few cones in the periphery of the retina
   - (b) there are many cones but very few rods in the periphery of the retina
   - (c) there are no receptor cells for vision in the periphery of the retina
   - (d) the stimulus was below Roger's difference threshold

4. After staring at a blue light for a few minutes, Yoko shifts her gaze to a white wall and experiences an afterimage whose color is _____ ; Yoko's experience provides support for the _____ theory of color vision.
   - (a) red; opponent-process
   - (b) yellow; opponent-process
   - (c) red; trichromatic
   - (d) yellow; trichromatic

5. When looking carefully at a picture of a country scene we are able to detect fine visual details, especially when they are focused on the fovea. One reason for this visual acuity is that
   - (a) the fovea contains rods, which have many individual neural connections to the cortex
   - (b) the fovea contains cones, which have many individual neural connections to the cortex
   - (c) the fovea is the spot where the optic nerve leaves the eye
   - (d) there are only bipolar cells in the fovea and these are specialized for feature detection

6. After Jackson has been in the hot tub for a few minutes, he no longer notices how hot the water is. The reason for this is
   - (a) sensory adaptation
   - (b) the just noticeable difference
   - (c) Jackson's thick skin
   - (d) sensory saturation

7. Neville is color-blind and cannot see red or green, yet he can see yellow with no problem. Which theory of color vision can most easily explain this?
   - (a) trichromatic theory
   - (b) place theory
   - (c) opponent-process theory
   - (d) frequency theory

8. Ever since her operation Madame Burgundi can no longer experience the flavors of the gourmet foods and wines she serves in her restaurant. It is most likely that she has suffered damage to her
   - (a) kinesthetic sense
   - (b) sense of smell
   - (c) sense of humor
   - (d) vestibular sense

9. The dizziness and disorientation Shelly felt after she rolled down the hill are a function of her
   - (a) basilar membrane
   - (b) Pacinian corpuscles
   - (c) semicircular canals and vestibular sacs
   - (d) proprioceptors

10. As Pancho gazed down the railway tracks, it seemed to him that the two parallel rails actually met in the distance. Pancho is experiencing the monocular depth cue
    - (a) linear perspective
    - (b) aerial perspective
    - (c) motion parallax
    - (d) texture gradient

11. Many people have mistaken a floating log for Ogopogo, the alleged Okanagan Lake monster. The most likely reason for this misperception is
    - (a) a perceptual set
    - (b) monocular vision
    - (c) rye whisky
    - (d) extrasensory perception

12. If Fred holds a letter very close to his nose as he reads it and Charlie holds it at arm's length when he reads it, Fred will experience _____ Charlie.
    - (a) more convergence than
    - (b) the identical level of convergence as
    - (c) less convergence than
    - (d) more motion parallax than

13. You are in an experiment conducted in a darkened room and are shown a large lighted frame with a single dot of light inside it. The frame slowly moves to the left, and the dot remains stationary. It is probable that you will perceive
    - (a) induced motion
    - (b) the dot moving to the right
    - (c) the frame remaining stationary
    - (d) all of the above

14. As a result of an accident, Kevin can no longer see with his left eye, but his right eye was unaffected. Which of the following cues will Kevin *not* be able to use to judge distance?
    - (a) overlap
    - (b) linear perspective
    - (c) motion parallax
    - (d) binocular disparity

15. You have just arrived at the beach and the texture of the sand toward the water appears smooth, even, and perfectly flat, yet the sand beneath your feet is rough and uneven and you can see individual small stones, seashells, and other debris. You are experiencing the monocular distance cue of
    - (a) motion parallax
    - (b) aerial perspective
    - (c) linear perspective
    - (d) texture gradient

16. As Demi moves away from the camera, her image on the screen grows smaller and smaller, yet viewers do not perceive Demi as the incredible shrinking woman. This illustrates
    (a) convergence
    (b) retinal disparity
    (c) size constancy
    (d) motion parallax

17. Nedzad claims that by examining the color and markings of your iris he can tell a lot about you, including level of mental stress, presence of any mental disorders, personality characteristics, past history of disease and injuries, and much more. According to Science Versus Pseudoscience Box 3.1, Nedzad is probably
    (a) a psychic palm reader
    (b) an iridologist
    (c) mentally ill
    (d) a biological psychologist

18. There has been a longstanding debate on whether perceptual principles are universal and inborn (nativist position) or vary from culture to culture and are influenced by experience and learning (empiricist position). According to Culture and Human Behavior Box. 3.4, the evidence supports
    (a) the nativist position
    (b) the empiricist position
    (c) neither the nativist nor the empiricist position
    (d) the nativist position slightly more than the empiricist position

19. To reduce the experience of pain, Dexter looks away and focuses on a picture on the wall as a nurse sticks a hypodermic needle into his arm. Dexter is using the pain control technique of
    (a) counter-irritation
    (b) relaxation
    (c) biofeedback
    (d) distraction

20. Muriel claims to be able to sense at any given moment what important leaders and well-known personalities are thinking. Muriel is claiming to possess the power of
    (a) telepathy
    (b) clairvoyance
    (c) psychokinesis
    (d) precognition

Progress Test 2

After you have checked your understanding of the material in Progress Test 1 and have done a complete chapter review with special focus on any areas of weakness, you are ready to assess your knowledge in Progress Test 2. Check you answers. If you make a mistake, review your notes and the relevant section of the study guide and, if necessary, review the appropriate part of your textbook.

1. Detection of stimulus energy is to the interpretation of the information as _____ is to _____ .
   (a) transduction; accommodation
   (b) hue; saturation
   (c) hearing; vision
   (d) sensation; perceptions

2. When Julius returns from getting a drink of water, he resumes weightlifting a 150-pound free weight and doesn't notice that someone has added a five-pound ring to each end. For Julius the additional ten pounds
   (a) is not a just noticeable difference (jnd)
   (b) is below his absolute threshold
   (c) is not sensed because of sensory adaptation
   (d) is easy to lift because water releases endorphins

3. Patrick has blue irises and Christine has brown irises. It is most probable that Patrick's irises will be able to expand and contract his pupils _____ when compared to Christine's irises
   (a) much more quickly
   (b) much more slowly
   (c) at the same rate
   (d) faster in bright light and slower in dim light

4. Mario was born with a genetically inherited visual deficiency. It is most probable that Mario suffers from
   (a) red-green color blindness
   (b) blue-yellow color blindness
   (c) stroboscopic vision
   (d) binocular disparity

5. While carrying out a sensory demonstration that places the retinal image of the picture of a small object on the exact spot where her optic nerve exits the eye, Deidre should expect the image of the object to
   (a) change to its opposite color
   (b) look twice as large as it had before
   (c) produce an afterimage if she shifts her gaze to a white surface
   (d) disappear from sight

6. When Tony was painting a large landscape picture, he used many different-colored paints. The technical term for the different wavelengths of light that produce the subjective sensation of different colors in Tony's painting is
   (a) saturation
   (b) hue
   (c) brightness
   (d) timbre

7. As Rodney was setting up the equipment for the concert, he adjusted the amplitude of the speaker system. This is most likely to affect the _____ of the music.
   (a) pitch
   (b) frequency
   (c) timbre
   (d) loudness

8. Eight-year-old Sean can hear sounds close to 20,000 hertz. This sensory capacity is best explained by
   (a) extrasensory perception (ESP) theory
   (b) the opponent-process theory
   (c) the frequency theory
   (d) the place theory

9. While walking in the garden, Ayan suddenly noticed the beautiful odor of roses. Ayan is using her _____ sense, and the process by which the odor is converted into neural signals that her brain can understand is called _____ .
   (a) gustatory; saturation
   (b) olfactory; transduction
   (c) gustatory; convergence
   (d) olfactory; saturation

10. When Derrick removed all visual distance cues, he noticed that the moon on the horizon looked the same size as it was when directly overhead. Derrick concluded correctly that the distance cues make the horizon moon seem _____ when it is overhead.
    (a) farther away than
    (b) closer than
    (c) smaller than
    (d) the same size as

11. Whenever Robyn looks at her boyfriend, her pupils dilate. The eye structure responsible for this response is called the
    (a) retina
    (b) fovea
    (c) iris
    (d) cornea

12. On the day of an important job interview Madeline wakes up with a slight toothache. As the time for the stressful interview approaches, her anxiety increases and so does her perception of the pain from her tooth. When the interview is over, Madeline is elated because she feels it has gone well and, to her surprise, she feels hardly any pain from her tooth. Madeline's experience is best explained by the _____ theory and the contribution of her psychological and emotional state.
    (a) opponent-process
    (b) gate-control
    (c) place
    (d) frequency

13. Astrid holds a pencil quite close to her nose and opens and closes her left and right eyes a couple of times in succession and notices that the images are quite different. When she views the same pencil in a similar manner from across the room, the images are almost identical. Astrid has demonstrated the _____ cue of _____ .
    (a) binocular; retinal disparity
    (b) monocular; motion parallax
    (c) binocular; overlap
    (d) monocular; convergence

14. When blindfolded, most people are not able to accurately and consistently identify the location of an object that makes a sound directly above the precise midpoint of their heads. The reason for this is that
    (a) they cannot judge distance and direction from auditory cues
    (b) when deprived of one sense, all the other senses are adversely affected
    (c) the sound waves reach each ear at the same time and they need to detect a difference in time lag and loudness to pinpoint the location of a sound
    (d) the blindfold obscures all visual cues and without these they cannot judge location or distance

15. As dusk descends Avril thinks that the yellow tulips are just as yellow as they had been earlier when there was more daylight. Despite the changing lighting conditions, Avril's perception of the color of the flowers did not change and this is best explained by _____ constancy and the fact that objects always reflect the same _____ of available light.
    (a) brightness; amount
    (b) size; degree
    (c) brightness; proportion
    (d) shape; amount

16. Jose notices that when the moon is near the horizon, it appears larger than when it is overhead in the sky. The effect is mainly the result of
    (a) distance cues that make the horizon moon seem farther away
    (b) the retinal image of the horizon moon being larger than the retinal image of the moon when it is overhead
    (c) distance cues that make the horizon moon seem nearer
    (d) having to tilt your head upward when looking at the overhead moon

17. There were twelve people in the classroom when Dickson walked in—four in the front row, four in the middle row, and four in the back row. Dickson is likely to perceive these people as three groups of four because of the Gestalt principle of
    (a) similarity   (c) continuation
    (b) closure   (d) proximity

18. According to the Application section, the process of learning voluntary control over largely autonomic body functions such as heartbeat, blood pressure, and muscle tension by using specialized sensitive equipment is called
    (a) iridology   (c) biofeedback
    (b) psychokinesis   (d) acupuncture

19. Willard believes he can influence the mechanical systems within slot machines with the power of his mind alone. Willard is claiming to possess the power of
    (a) telepathy   (c) psychokinesis
    (b) clairvoyance   (d) precognition

20. Maxwell is a male pig and, like most male pigs, he releases a chemical substance in the sweat glands to communicate territorial boundaries and sexual receptiveness. Female pigs use their _____ sense to detect these airborne chemical scents called _____ .
    (a) gustatory; vestibulars
    (b) olfactory; pheromones
    (c) gustatory; pheromones
    (d) olfactory; vestibulars

Answers

Introduction: Sensation and Perception

1. (a) communication
   (b) sensation; perception

Some Basic Principles of Sensation

1. (a) sound; taste; smell; touch; light
   (b) sensory receptors
   (c) transduction

2. (a) sensory threshold
   (b) absolute threshold; difference threshold
   (c) difference threshold
   (d) Weber's Law
   (e) Weber's Law; relative

3. (a) less aware
   (b) sensory adaptation
   (c) relative

4. (a) absolute
   (b) sensation; perception
   (c) Weber's Law
   (d) transduction
   (e) sensory adaptation
   (f) absolute; difference

Matching Exercise 1

1. sensory threshold

2. transduction

3. absolute threshold

4. perception

5. sensory receptors

True/False Test 1

1. T   3. T   5. T
2. T   4. T

Vision: From Light to Sight

1. (a) eye; light
   (b) electromagnetic; wavelengths
   (c) wavelength
   (d) minuscule (very tiny)

2. (a) cornea
   (b) pupil; iris
   (c) iris; pupil
   (d) widens (expands); narrows (contracts)
   (e) lens; accommodation
   (f) retina
   (g) rods; cones; neural

3. (a) more; rods; cones
   (b) rods; cones
   (c) thirty; five
   (d) rods
   (e) fovea

4. (a) brain; retina
   (b) bipolar; ganglion
   (c) only one or two; hundreds of; visual detail; specific
   (d) ability to see fine detail
   (e) fovea

5. (a) optic nerve
   (b) optic nerve; blind spot

6. (a) hue
   (b) saturation
   (c) brightness

7. (a) all wavelengths; absorbs
   (b) color

8. (a) trichromatic
   (b) opponent-process

9. (a) color blindness
   (b) afterimage
   (c) color blindness; afterimages
   (d) different

10. (a) white
    (b) green
    (c) color; fine detail
    (d) red
    (e) red

Graphic Organizer 1

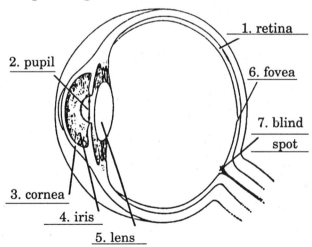

1. retina
2. pupil
3. cornea
4. iris
5. lens
6. fovea
7. blind spot

Matching Exercise 2

1. visual acuity

2. afterimage

3. wavelength

4. accommodation

5. brightness

6. optic nerve

7. trichromatic theory

8. cones

9. hue

10. rods

11. bipolar cells

12. color

True/False Test 2

1. F	5. F	9. T
2. T	6. T	10. T
3. F	7. T	11. F
4. T	8. F	12. F

Hearing: From Vibration to Sound

1. (a) audition
   (b) physical; social; language

2. (a) sound waves
   (b) amplitude; decibels
   (c) 0
   (d) "highness"; "lowness"; frequency
   (e) frequency; hertz
   (f) timbre

3. (a) outer; middle; inner
   (b) pinna, ear canal, and eardrum
   (c) eardrum; oval window
   (d) hammer, anvil, and stirrup
   (e) conduction; hearing aid
   (f) inner; basilar membrane; hair cells
   (g) nerve; hearing aid

4. (a) basilar membrane
   (b) frequency; frequency
   (c) 20; 20,000; frequency
   (d) place
   (e) stirrup; opposite
   (f) hair cells; place
   (g) frequency; place; frequency; place

6. (a) cochlea
   (b) conduction
   (c) place
   (d) hearing aid
   (e) place

Graphic Organizer 2

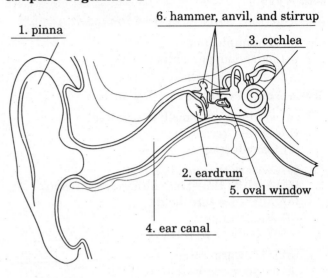

1. pinna
2. eardrum
3. cochlea
4. ear canal
5. oval window
6. hammer, anvil, and stirrup

Matching Exercise 3

1. nerve deafness
2. audition
3. frequency
4. hair cells
5. sound waves
6. timbre
7. outer ear
8. pitch
9. place theory
10. decibels
11. amplitude
12. oval window

True/False Test 3

1. T	5. F	9. T
2. T	6. T	10. F
3. F	7. T	11. T
4. T	8. F	12. T

The Chemical and Body Senses: Smell, Taste, Touch, and Position

1. (a) olfaction; gustation
   (b) chemical; chemical

2. (a) chemical substances
   (b) molecules
   (c) olfactory nerve
   (d) 10,000; group
   (e) olfactory; olfactory
   (f) limbic
   (g) thalamus
   (h) adaptation; adaptation

3. (a) gustation
   (b) chemical; taste buds
   (c) taste buds; thalamus
   (d) sweet, salty, sour; bitter

4. (a) skin
   (b) skin
   (c) skin; pressure; warmth; cold
   (d) Pacinian corpuscle

5. (a) discomfort; suffering
   (b) survival
   (c) gate-control; gates
   (d) free nerve; substance P
   (e) substance P

6. (a) spinal cord; open; close
   (b) intensify; reduce
   (c) social; cultural
   (d) endorphins
   (e) endorphins; P
   (f) mental (psychological); emotional

7. (a) kinesthetic; proprioceptors
   (b) vestibular
   (c) semicircular; vestibular; motion; position; gravity
   (d) vision
   (e) eye; dizziness, disorientation; nausea

8. (a) intensify
   (b) semicircular canals; vestibular sacs
   (c) kinesthetic
   (d) substance P
   (e) smell
   (f) smell (olfaction)

Matching Exercise 4

1. gustation
2. vestibular sacs
3. Pacinian corpuscle
4. chemical senses
5. free nerve endings
6. olfactory bulb
7. taste buds
8. pheromones

9. vestibular sense
10. endorphins

True/False Test 4

1. T	4. T	7. T
2. T	5. F	8. F
3. T	6. T	9. T

Perception

1. (a) integrating, organizing; interpreting
   (b) memory; learning

2 (a) How far away is the object?
   (b) Where is it going?
   (c) What is it?

3. (a) Gestalt
   (b) *Gestalt*

Depth Perception: "How Far Away Is It?"

1. (a) depth perception
   (b) monocular

2. (a) relative size
   (b) overlap
   (c) aerial perspective
   (d) texture gradient
   (e) linear perspective
   (f) motion parallax

3. (a) pictorial
   (b) accommodation

4. (a) binocular
   (b) convergence
   (c) convergence
   (d) binocular disparity
   (e) closer; father away
   (f) binocular disparity

The Perception of Motion: "Where Is It Going?"

1. (a) movements
   (b) background
   (c) eye muscle; retinal; background
   (d) one; opposite; speed

2. (a) object; induced
   (b) induced; frame

3. (a) stroboscopic
   (b) visual system

4. (a) auditory
   (b) louder; direction
   (c) direction; distance

The Perception of Shape: "What Is It?"

1. (a) shape
   (b) shape constancy
   (c) figure; ground
   (d) figure-ground relationship; psychological

2. (a) principles
   (b) law of simplicity; best, simplest
   (c) Gestalt principles
   (d) *Prägnanz*

3. (a) Gestalt
   (b) ground; figure
   (c) binocular disparity
   (d) relative size
   (e) linear perspective
   (f) stroboscopic motion

Matching Exercise 5

1. Gestalt psychology
2. law of Prägnanz
3. aerial perspective
4. binocular disparity
5. figure-ground relationship
6. overlap
7. binocular cues
8. accommodation
9. stroboscopic motion
10. depth perception
11. figure-ground reversal

True/False Test 5

1. T	5. T	9. F
2. F	6. T	10. T
3. F	7. T	
4. F	8. T	

Perceptual Constancies

1. (a) perceptual constancy
   (b) perceptual constancy

2. (a) size; retina
   (b) larger; afterimage

3. (a) shape constancy
   (b) perception

4. (a) same; change
   (b) proportion

Factors That Influence Perceptual Interpretations

1. (a) educational, cultural; life
   (b) perceptual set
   (c) perceptual sets

2. (a) perceptual illusion
   (b) illusions; normal

3. (a) length
   (b) farther away; closer
   (c) size
   (d) identical; longer

4. (a) bigger (larger)
   (b) the same
   (c) more distant (farther away)
   (d) farther away
   (e) size; larger
   (f) the same size

5. (a) interpretation
   (b) sensation
   (c) senses; integrates; interprets

6. (a) perceptual sets
   (b) farther away
   (c) shape
   (d) Müller-Lyer

Matching Exercise 6

1. perceptual set
2. perceptual constancy
3. Müller-Lyer illusion
4. size constancy
5. parapsychology

True/False Test 6

1. F	3. T	5. T
2. T	4. T	

Something to Think About

1. The first thing to understand is that these strange experiences happen to many people and there is nothing particularly unique about them. The problem arises when we interpret these situations. These experiences, of course, do not constitute proof of ESP, no matter how strongly someone believes that they do. Instead, there are two less extraordinary concepts that can explain these occurrences: coincidence and

the fallacy of positive instances. Coincidence is the term used to describe an event that occurs simply by chance, and this alone can account for many of the experiences reported by people. Combine coincidence with our tendency to remember coincidental events that seem to confirm our belief about unusual phenomena, i.e., the fallacy of positive instances, and the feeling that something unusual has happened can be very strong, even though there are no rational grounds for it. Finally, there is the lack of any strong scientific evidence for the existence of ESP, despite years of intensive study by psychologists interested in this topic. To date, there has not been a single replication of any parapsychology experiment that has claimed to show evidence of ESP. This, of course, does not prove conclusively that ESP does not exist, and while one should keep an open mind, there is not a shred of evidence or any rational reason to believe in its existence.

2. Some of the most common monocular or pictorial cues that are useful in conveying a sense of depth on the canvas are overlap, where "nearer" objects are depicted as blocking or obscuring more "distant" objects; linear perspective, where parallel lines are depicted as converging toward the top of the painting, for instance; and texture gradient, where one conveys depth by painting surfaces with distinct textures as being clearly defined where it is supposed to be close to the observer and gradually less and less clearly defined to depict distance. Relative size and aerial perspective are also useful devices to convey depth.

Progress Test 1

1. b	8. b	15. d
2. d	9. c	16. c
3. a	10. a	17. b
4. b	11. a	18. b
5. b	12. a	19. d
6. a	13. d	20. a
7. c	14. d	

Progress Test 2

1. d	8. d	15. c
2. a	9. b	16. a
3. c	10. a	17. d
4. a	11. c	18. c
5. d	12. b	19. c
6. b	13. a	20. b
7. d	14. c	

Chapter 4 Consciousness and Its Variations

OVERVIEW Chapter 4 examines the varieties of consciousness we experience and discusses how biological and environmental "clocks" regulate our circadian rhythms and sleep/wake cycles. The discovery of REM sleep and how the EEG is used to measure brain-wave activity are presented. The different stages of sleep and their associated brain-wave activity and behavioral patterns, including the various sleep disorders, are examined. This is followed by a discussion of dreams and mental activity during sleep, and two major theories of the meaning of dreams and their relevance to psychological and physiological functioning are presented.

Altered states of consciousness are introduced next, and both hypnosis and meditation are discussed in this context. Under hypnosis profound sensory and perceptual changes may be experienced, and this section of the chapter focuses on phenomena such as posthypnotic suggestion, hypnotic amnesia, hypermnesia, and the relationship between memory and hypnosis. Hilgard's notions of dissociation and the hidden observer are examined, and the controversy surrounding how to explain hypnosis is discussed. Finally, meditation is defined and techniques for inducing a meditative state are presented, along with research findings on transcendental meditation, or TM.

The final section of the chapter is concerned with using drugs to alter consciousness. The various psychoactive drugs are classified and listed, along with their various effects on brain activity and physiological and psychological functioning. Drug dependence, drug abuse, drug tolerance, and withdrawal symptoms are discussed. Depressant drugs include alcohol, barbiturates, tranquilizers, and inhalants; opiates include opium, morphine, heroin, and some prescription drugs; the most common stimulants are caffeine, nicotine, amphetamines, and cocaine; and finally the psychedelic drugs include mescaline, LSD, and marijuana.

Introduction: Consciousness: Experiencing the "Private I"

Learning Objectives

When you have finished studying this section of the chapter, you should be able to:

1. Define consciousness and explain what William James meant by *stream of consciousness.*

2. List the reasons why research on consciousness was abandoned for a time and why it has regained legitimacy.

*Read the section "Introduction: Consciousness: Experiencing the 'Private I'" and **write** your answers to the following:*

1. (a) Your immediate awareness of

   _____ , _____ ,

   _____ , and the world around you

   represents the experience of consciousness.

   (b) Even though your conscious experience is

   constantly _____ , you don't

   experience your personal consciousness as

   _____ .

2. (a) William James described consciousness as a

   _____ or _____ .

   (b) The subjective experience of consciousness has a feeling of _____ , which helps provide us with a sense of personal identity.

3. (a) In the late 1800s the first psychologists tried to capture the structure of conscious experience through the technique of _____ ; this approach was abandoned because such _____ reports were not objectively verifiable.

   (b) Psychologists at the turn of the century resisted the study of consciousness; instead they emphasized the scientific study of _____ , which could be directly observed, measured, and verified.

4. The reasons psychologists returned to the study of consciousness in the second half of the century were that:

   (a) It was becoming abundantly clear that a complete understanding of behavior was not possible until the role of

   _____ in

   behavior was considered.

   (b) New and more objective ways to study _____ were developed.

   (c) Technological advances in studying _____ activity were producing intriguing results.

The Biological and Environmental "Clocks" Regulating Consciousness
Learning Objectives

When you have finished studying this section of the chapter, you should be able to:

1. Define circadian rhythms and provide an example to illustrate the concept.

2. Explain the function of the suprachiasmatic nucleus (SCN) and the role of melatonin in the sleep/wake cycle.

3. Describe the research on "free-running" circadian rhythms and explain the role of sunlight in regulating the sleep/wake cycle.

4. Define jet lag, list the four common situations that can produce jet-lag symptoms, and explain how melatonin is involved in these symptoms.

*Read the section "The Biological and Environmental 'Clocks' Regulating Consciousness" and **write** the answers to the following:*

1. (a) The most obvious variation in consciousness that we experience is the daily

   _____ cycle.

   (b) The term *circadian rhythms* refers to

   _____ and _____ fluctuations that systematically vary over a period of about 24 hours and include _____ alertness and the

   _____ cycle.

   (c) Researchers have identified over 100

   _____ that ebb and flow over any given 24-hour period, such as blood pressure, the secretion of different hormones, and pain sensitivity.

2. (a) All your many _____ are controlled by a master biological clock—a tiny cluster of neurons in the _____ in the brain—called the suprachiasmatic nucleus (SCN).

   (b) The _____ is the internal pacemaker that governs the timing of circadian rhythms, including the sleep/wake cycle and the mental alertness cycle.

   (c) One of the most important environmental time cues that help keep the circadian rhythms synchronized to one another on a 24-hour schedule is _____ and especially _____ .

   (d) As the sun sets each day, the decrease in available light is detected by the

   _____ through its connections to the visual system, and this triggers an increase in the production of a hormone called _____ by the pineal gland.

(e) Increased blood levels of the hormone _____ make you sleepy, and at night the peak level of this hormone is between 1:00 and 3:00 a.m.; shortly before sunrise the _____ gland all but stops producing the hormone and you soon wake up.

(f) Sunlight _____ , or sets, the SCN so that it keeps circadian cycles synchronized and operating on a 24-hour schedule.

3. (a) Researchers have put volunteers in underground bunkers or caves for various periods of time in order to deprive them of all _____ and create "free-running" conditions.

   (b) Under free-running conditions, people tend to drift to the SCN's natural rhythm of roughly a(n) _____ .

   (c) When people leave the free-running condition and are once again exposed to normal daylight, sunlight _____ the biological clock, which resumes the _____ cycle.

4. (a) When environmental time cues are out of sync with our internal biological clock, we may experience _____ and _____ effects, such as unclear thinking, loss of concentration, memory problems, depression, irritability, disrupted sleep, and physical and mental fatigue, which collectively are called _____ .

   (b) The circadian cycle of the hormone _____ seems to play a key role in making you feel very sleepy, sluggish, and groggy after a long flight over many time zones.

   (c) Night-shift workers such as nurses, doctors, people who work in law enforcement, the military, broadcasting, and weather services, etc., can all experience the symptoms of _____ because their circadian rhythms are out of sync with daylight/darkness time cues.

   (d) After working a night shift people returning home are often exposed to bright morning light, which is a potent stimulus and can reset the person's _____ to a day schedule.

5. Read the following and write the correct term in the space provided:

   (a) Sheena works night shifts and has found that she can sleep quite well during the day now that she has hung heavy curtains in her bedroom that effectively block out any daylight. She is able to get restful sleep in the daytime because her _____ are staying in sync with her night work schedule, and she has prevented sunlight from resetting her _____ .

   (b) Although Marvin was very tired after pulling an "all-nighter" to finish a paper, he began to feel much less drowsy as the morning proceeded. His reaction is probably due to decreased levels of the hormone _____ .

   (c) Herman usually experiences a slump in his mental alertness in mid-afternoon but feels very energetic in the early evening. These daily fluctuations are an example of _____ .

   (d) During a history lecture Alfie is listening and taking notes but at times he is also thinking about his girlfriend and the argument they had last night, and he wonders what he will say to her when he phones her that afternoon; this gets him thinking about how often his parents fight and whether arguing is genetic, which reminds him about his biology exam next week. This description reflects Alfie's _____ .

   (e) Dr. Parizeau arranges for volunteers to spend several weeks in underground caves without exposure to sunlight, clocks, or other time cues. He is attempting to create

_____

in his research on circadian rhythms.

Review of Key Terms and Key Names 1

consciousness
William James
introspection
circadian rhythm
biological clock
suprachiasmatic nucleus
    (SCN)

melatonin
pineal gland
free-running condition
jet lag

Matching Exercise

Match the appropriate term/name with its definition or description:

1. _____ Personal awareness of mental activities, internal sensations, and the external environment.

2. _____ Subjective verbal reports that try to capture the structure of conscious experience through examining one's present mental state.

3. _____ A cluster of neurons in the hypothalamus in the brain that govern the timing of circadian rhythms.

4. _____ Symptoms such as physical and mental fatigue, depression, irritability, disrupted sleep, and fuzziness in concentration, thinking, and memory that result from circadian rhythms being out of sync with daylight/darkness cues.

5. _____ A cycle or rhythm that is roughly 24 hours long; refers to daily fluctuations in many biological and psychological processes.

True/False Test

Indicate whether each statement is true or false by placing T or F in the blank space next to each item.

1. ____ The "biological clock" is another name for the tiny cluster of neurons in the hypothalamus technically called the suprachiasmatic nucleus, or SCN.

2. ____ William James was the American psychologist who proposed that psychology should not study consciousness because it could not be objectively investigated; instead psychology should emphasize the scientific study of overt observable behavior.

3. ____ The pineal gland is a gland located in the brain that regulates the production of the hormone melatonin.

4. ____ Researchers have put volunteers in underground bunkers, depriving them of all environmental time cues for various periods of time, in order to create free-running conditions.

5. ____ Melatonin is a hormone manufactured by the pineal gland that produces sleepiness.

_____
| Check your answers and review any areas of weakness before going on to the next section. |

Sleep
Learning Objectives

When you have finished studying this section of the chapter, you should be able to:

1. Describe the invention of the electroencephalograph and explain its contribution to modern sleep research.

2. Define REM and NREM sleep and describe the characteristics of the various stages of sleep.

3. List the changes in sleep patterns over the lifespan.

4. Specify the functions of sleep and state what sleep deprivation studies have demonstrated.

5. Distinguish between the two theories of sleep and list the evidence that supports each.

*Read the section "Sleep" and **write** your answers to the following:*

1. (a) Traditionally, sleep was largely viewed as a period of restful _____ in which dreams sometimes occurred.

   (b) The electroencephalograph measures the rhythmic electrical activity of the brain called _____ .

   (c) The electroencephalograph produces a graphic record called a(n)

   _____ , or _____ .

(d) Along with brain activity, sleep researchers monitor a variety of other _____ functions during sleep, such as eye movements, muscle movements, body temperature, blood pressure, and breathing rate.

2. (a) Researchers found that particular brain-wave activity, as measured by the EEG, was often associated with rapid movements of the sleeper's eyes, and this heralded the discovery of _____ sleep, abbreviated as _____ .

(b) Today researchers distinguish between _____ sleep, often called active sleep or paradoxical sleep, and _____ sleep, or

_____

sleep, often called quiet sleep.

(c) Active sleep, or _____ sleep, is associated with heightened bodily and brain activity during which dreaming consistently occurs, and in quiet sleep, or

_____ sleep, the body's physiological functions and brain activity are slowed down.

3. (a) When you are awake and reasonably alert, your brain generates small, fast brain waves, called _____ brain waves, and when you relax and close your eyes, your brain's electrical activity slows down, generating _____ brain waves.

(b) During the drowsy transition from wakefulness to light sleep, you may experience odd but vividly realistic sensations called

_____ .

(c) Probably the most common

_____ is the

vivid sensation of falling, which is often accompanied by an involuntary muscle spasm of the whole body that can jolt the

person awake, called a

_____ .

4. (a) As people drift off to sleep, they initially enter NREM sleep and begin a progression through _____ stages of NREM sleep; each stage is characterized by corresponding _____ in brain and body activity, and progression through these NREM stages occupies the first

_____ to _____

minutes of sleep.

(b) When you enter the first stage of sleep, the _____ brain waves associated with drowsiness are replaced by even slower _____ brain waves.

(c) Stage 1 NREM sleep lasts only

_____ minutes, and a person can be easily awakened during this stage of sleep.

(d) Stage 2 represents the onset of true sleep and is marked by the appearance of bursts of brain activity called

_____ .

(e) Theta brain waves are predominant in stage 2, but large, slow brain waves called _____ brain waves also begin to emerge and gradually increase in frequency over the fifteen to twenty minutes spent in stage 2.

5. (a) Stages 3 and 4 of NREM sleep are physiologically very _____ (similar/different); both stages are defined by the amount of delta brain wave activity, and combined they are referred to as _____ sleep.

(b) When delta brain waves represent more than 20 percent of total brain activity, the sleeper is said to be in stage _____ NREM sleep, and when they exceed 50 percent, the sleeper is said to be in stage _____ NREM sleep.

(c) During the twenty to forty minutes spent in the night's first episode of stage 4 NREM sleep, delta waves eventually come to represent _____ percent of brain activity, and during this stage the person is very difficult to awaken.

(d) During stage 4 NREM sleep the sleeper's heart rate, blood pressure, and breathing rate drop to their lowest levels, but the muscles are still capable of movement; _____ occurs during this stage.

(e) When researchers briefly awaken people during stage _____ and ask them to perform some simple task, they can do so but they generally don't remember it the next morning.

(f) Approximately seventy minutes into a typical night's sleep, the sequence of stages reverses itself, and within minutes the sleeper cycles back from stage _____ to stage _____ to stage _____ and then enters a dramatic new phase, the night's first episode of _____ sleep.

6. (a) During _____ sleep the brain becomes more active, generating smaller and faster brain waves, and visual and motor neurons fire repeatedly, just as they do during wakefulness.

(b) _____ usually occur during REM sleep, and although the brain is very active, voluntary muscle activity is suppressed.

(c) REM sleep is accompanied by considerable _____ arousal; heart rate, blood pressure, and respiration can fluctuate up and down, muscles twitch, and in both sexes, sexual arousal may occur.

(d) Throughout the night the sleeping person cycles between NREM and REM sleep, with each cycle lasting about _____ minutes on the average, but the duration of cycles may vary from _____ to _____ minutes.

(e) As the night progresses, episodes of _____ sleep become increasingly longer and less time is spent in _____ sleep.

(f) Stage _____ and stage _____ slow-wave sleep usually occur only during the first two ninety-minute cycles, and during the last two ninety-minute cycles before awakening, periods of REM sleep can last as long as 40 minutes; NREM sleep is composed primarily of stage _____ sleep.

7. (a) Over the course of our lives the _____ and _____ of sleep change considerably.

(b) Four months before birth REM sleep constitutes _____ of fetal life; one month before birth the fetus demonstrates distinct wake/sleep cycles, spending _____ hours each day in REM sleep, and at birth the newborn sleeps about 16 hours a day, about _____ percent of which is in REM sleep.

(c) From birth onward the average amount of time spent sleeping gradually _____ ; the amount of time devoted to REM sleep and slow-wave NREM sleep also gradually _____ over the lifespan.

(d) As the amount of deep sleep and REM sleep _____ throughout adulthood, more time is spent in lighter stage ____ NREM sleep, and consequently sleep becomes more fitful and less satisfying as we age.

8. (a) _____ studies have demonstrated that we have a biological need for sleep, and with as little as one day's sleep deprivation research subjects will develop _____ , episodes of sleep lasting only a few seconds that occur during wakefulness.

(b) People who _____ for a day or more also experience disruptions in mood, mental abilities, reaction time, perceptual skills, and complex motor skills.

(c) If subjects in one group are selectively deprived of REM sleep and those in another group are selectively deprived of slow-wave NREM sleep, subjects in the first group will experience _____ whereas those in the second group will experience _____ when allowed to sleep uninterrupted.

9. (a) The _____ theory of sleep suggests that sleep and dreaming promote physiological processes that renew, repair, and rejuvenate the body and mind.

(b) Research suggests that NREM sleep is important for restoring the _____ , whereas REM sleep is important for restoring the _____ .

(c) The _____ theory of sleep suggests that the sleep patterns exhibited by different animals, including humans, reflect the survival value of being prevented from interacting with the environment when doing so is most hazardous.

(d) Animals with few natural predators, such as gorillas and lions, sleep _____ than grazing animals such as cattle and horses.

(e) While researchers still aren't sure exactly what functions are served by sleep, there is evidence to support the _____ theory of sleep _____ (and/but not) the _____ theory of sleep.

Sleep Disorders: Troubled Sleep
Learning Objectives

When you have finished studying this section of the chapter, you should be able to:

1. Define the term *sleep disorders* and list the most common symptoms associated with these disturbances.

2. List and describe the main characteristics of the various sleep disorders.

Read the section "Sleep Disorders: Troubled Sleep" and **write** *your answers to the following:*

1. (a) _____ are serious disturbances in the normal sleep pattern that interfere with daytime functioning and cause subjective distress.

(b) The most common sleep complaint among adults is _____ , which occurs when people repeatedly complain about the quality or duration of their sleep, when they experience difficulty going to sleep or staying asleep, or when they wake before it is time to get up.

(c) Alcohol, over-the-counter medications, and even sleep-inducing medications that physicians sometimes prescribe are generally not recommended for dealing with _____ .

2. (a) Unlike insomnia, sleepwalking and night terrors are sleep disturbances that are much more common in _____ than in adults.

(b) Sleepwalking and night terrors usually occur during stages _____ and _____ of NREM sleep.

(c) Children spend considerably more time each night in _____ sleep compared to adolescents or adults.

(d) About 25 percent of all children have at least one episode of _____ , or somnambulism, which typically occurs during the first three hours of sleep.

(e) Like sleepwalking, _____ , or _____ , typically occur during stage 3 or 4 of NREM sleep.

(f) The first sign of a(n) _____ in a child is sharply increased physiological arousal, restlessness, sweating, racing heart, and abruptly sitting up in bed and letting out a panic-stricken cry or scream and thrashing about in bed or even sleepwalking.

(g) Surprisingly, the child quickly goes back to sleep and wakes in the morning with _____ of the incident.

3. (a) The behavior of a person with _____ may involve leaping out of bed, running around the room, lashing out at imagined intruders, or grabbing furniture.

(b) It is believed that a person with _____ is acting out his dreams because of the brain's failure to suppress muscle movements during REM sleep.

(c) The disorder called _____ is one in which the sleeper repeatedly stops breathing during the night.

(d) A person with sleep apnea may stop breathing for as little as ten seconds or for so long that the sleeper's skin turns blue before waking up, and up to

_____

attacks can occur in a single night, even though the person may have no recollection of the repeated awakenings the next day.

(e) The most common symptom of _____ is excessive daytime sleepiness and brief lapses into sleep throughout the day, usually lasting an hour or less; some people with the disorder experience dramatic sudden daytime _____ that last up to several minutes.

(f) Laughter, anger, surprise, sexual arousal, and other intense emotional states can trigger _____ in which sufferers instantly enter REM sleep and experience _____ , that is, their muscle go limp and they collapse.

(g) Vivid and sometimes terrifying

_____ are common during sleep attacks.

4. Read the following and write the correct term in the space provided:

(a) James went to bed a short while ago and although his eyes are closed and he is very relaxed, he has not yet fallen asleep. If James's brain is relatively normal, it is probably generating _____ brain waves.

(b) Shortly after falling asleep, James gives a sudden jump with his whole body and is suddenly wide awake. James has most likely experienced the most common hypnagogic hallucination of _____ accompanied by a _____ .

(c) Roger has been under a lot of stress ever since he started college three months ago, and now that the final exam period is approaching, Roger is experiencing problems sleeping. He will most likely be diagnosed as suffering from

_____ .

(d) In an attempt to deal with his sleep disturbance, Roger decided to try over-the-counter
sleep medication combined with alcohol.
Roger's approach is most likely to make his
problem _____ (better/worse) in
the long run.

(e) After being asleep for about two hours,
eight-year-old Lilly suddenly sits up in bed
screaming incoherently, and her mother has
trouble waking her and calming her down.
Lilly is experiencing a(n)

_____ and is probably in

stage _____ or

_____ of NREM sleep.

(f) Ben is enjoying a night out with a bunch of
his college friends at Yuk Yuks comedy club
and is laughing heartily at a very funny act
when he suddenly goes limp and falls asleep

for a few minutes. It is very likely that Ben
is suffering an attack of _____
and has instantly entered REM sleep and
experienced _____ .

(g) Mrs. Eastman has just turned sixty-five and
is worried because she is waking up more
easily nowadays, sleeps less than seven
hours most nights, and feels less rested and
less satisfied after sleeping. A sleep specialist is most likely to say that she

_____

_____ .

(h) Debbie has been asleep for about ten minutes and she is now in stage 2 of sleep. Her
brain-wave activity is likely to be predomi-
nantly _____ waves and to be
marked by _____ .

Graphic Organizer 1

The diagram below shows the brain waves typical of each stage in a ninety-minute (approximately) sleep cycle. *Match the term or description with the correct brain wave pattern.*

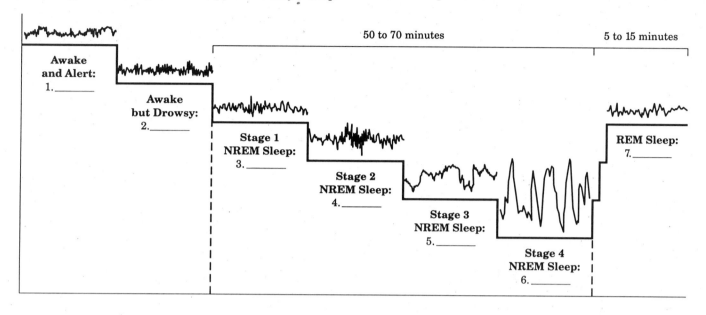

A. Brain waves associated with dreaming

B. Sleep spindles

C. Beta brain waves

D. Mixture of theta and delta brain waves

E. Alpha brain waves

F. Delta brain waves

G. Mixture of alpha and theta brain waves

Review of Key Terms 2

electroencephalograph	microsleeps
electroencephalogram (EEG)	REM rebound
REM sleep	restorative theory of sleep
NREM sleep	adaptive theory of sleep
active and paradoxical sleep	sleep disorders
quiet sleep	insomnia
beta brain waves	sleepwalking (somnambulism)
alpha brain waves	night terrors (sleep terrors)
hypnagogic hallucinations	REM sleep behavior disorder
myoclonic jerk	sleep apnea
sleep spindles	narcolepsy
theta brain waves	sleep paralysis
delta brain waves	
slow-wave sleep	

Matching Exercise

Match the appropriate term with its definition or description.

1. _____ A condition in which a person regularly experiences the inability to fall asleep, stay asleep, or feel adequately rested by sleep.

2. _____ Type of sleep during which rapid eye movements and dreaming occur.

3. _____ The view that sleep and dreaming are essential to normal physical and mental functioning.

4. _____ Brain-wave pattern associated with relaxed wakefulness and drowsiness.

5. _____ A sleep disorder in which the person repeatedly stops breathing during sleep.

6. _____ The graphic record of brain activity produced by an electroencephalograph.

7. _____ Short bursts of brain activity that characterize stage 2 NREM sleep.

8. _____ Vivid sensory phenomena that can occur during the onset of sleep.

9. _____ The term used to refer to the combination of stage 3 and stage 4 sleep.

10. _____ An involuntary muscle spasm of the whole body that jolts the person completely awake and often accompanies the hypnagogic hallucination of falling.

11. _____ The bodily state that occurs when narcoleptics are having a sleep attack and they instantly enter REM sleep; their muscles go limp and they collapse.

12. _____ A sleep disorder in which the sleeper acts out his or her dreams.

13. _____ A phenomenon in which a person who is deprived of REM sleep greatly increases the amount of time spent in REM sleep at the first opportunity to sleep uninterruptedly.

True/False Test

Indicate whether each statement is true or false by placing T or F in the blank space next to each item.

1. ____ *Active sleep* and/or *paradoxical sleep* are other terms for NREM sleep.

2. ____ The adaptive theory of sleep suggests that unique sleep patterns of different animals evolved over time to help promote survival and environmental adaptation.

3. ____ Sleep disorders are serious disturbances in the normal sleep pattern that interfere with daytime functioning and cause subjective distress.

4. ____ Narcolepsy is a sleep disorder in which the person repeatedly stops breathing during sleep and awakens momentarily.

5. ____ Sleepwalking is a sleep disorder, more common in children than adults, in which the child gets out of bed, moves around in a slow, poorly coordinated, automatic manner, usually with a blank, staring look on his or her face.

6. ____ Quiet sleep is another term for REM sleep.

7. ____ Beta brain waves are patterns of electrical activity that begin in stage 1 NREM sleep and predominate in stage 2 NREM sleep.

8. ____ Episodes of sleep lasting only a few seconds that occur during wakefulness are called microsleeps; they can occur after as little as one day's sleep deprivation.

9. ____ Night terrors are characterized by sharply increased physiological arousal; the sleeper will typically sit up in bed and let out a panic-stricken scream or cry, thrash around in bed, or even sleepwalk.

10. ____ NREM sleep is the nondreaming, quiet sleep that is divided into four stages.

11. ____ Theta brain waves are small, fast patterns of electrical activity of the brain that reflect an awake and reasonably alert state of consciousness.

12. ____ An electroencephalograph (EEG) is an instrument that uses electrodes placed on the scalp to measure and record the brain's electrical activity.

13. ____ Delta brain waves are the long slow waves associated with stage 3 and stage 4 of NREM sleep.

Check your answers and review any areas of weakness before going on to the next section.

Dreams and Mental Activity During Sleep

Learning Objectives

When you have finished studying this section of the chapter, you should be able to:

1. Define and contrast *sleep thinking* and *dreaming*.

2. Name the five characteristics of dreams and specify the most common themes in our dreams.

3. Explain why we don't remember our dreams, define *nightmare*, and give an example.

4. Describe Freud's dream theory and distinguish between manifest and latent content of dreams.

5. Explain how the activation-synthesis model accounts for the phenomenon of dreaming.

Read the section "Dreams and Mental Activity During Sleep" and **write** *your answers to the following:*

1. (a) On the average about _____ percent of a night's sleep is spent dreaming, or almost _____ hours every night.

   (b) More prevalent than dreams is

   _____ , which occurs during NREM sleep and consists of vague, uncreative, bland, and thoughtlike ruminations about real-life events.

(c) In contrast to _____ , a dream is an unfolding episode of mental images that is storylike, involving characters and events.

(d) Usually dreams occur during _____ sleep, but they can also occasionally occur during _____ sleep.

(e) There are usually _____ or _____ episodes of dreaming each night, with early morning dreams lasting as long as forty minutes.

2. The five basic characteristics of a dream are:

(a) _____ can be intense.

(b) _____ and _____ are usually illogical.

(c) _____ are sometimes bizarre.

(d) Even _____ details are uncritically accepted.

(e) The dream _____ are difficult to remember.

3. (a) The content of our dreams usually reflects the daily _____ of the dreamer and includes worry about exams, money, health, or troubled relationships.

(b) Certain themes such as _____ or being _____ or attacked are common across cultures.

(c) In sleep labs, researchers have successfully influenced dream _____ while the subjects were asleep and dreaming.

4. (a) There are individual differences in dream recall, but on average approximately _____ percent of our dreams are forgotten.

(b) You are much more likely to recall a dream if you _____ during it.

(c) The more vivid, bizarre, or emotionally intense a dream is, the more likely it is to be _____ the following morning.

(d) _____ upon waking interfere with our ability to recall dreams.

(e) It is difficult to remember _____ during sleep, not just dreams.

(f) During sleep it seems that the brain is largely _____ to forget most experiences; brain chemistry and functioning may not support _____ and _____ ; and the neurotransmitters needed to create new memories are not _____ .

5. (a) An unpleasant anxiety dream that occurs during REM sleep and has a frightening or unpleasant theme is called a _____ .

(b) In adults, an occasional _____ is a natural and relatively common experience and is not indicative of a psychological disorder or sleep disorder unless it frequently causes personal distress.

6. (a) Freud believed that _____ and _____ instincts are the motivating forces that dictate human behavior, but because they are consciously unacceptable, they are repressed.

(b) Freud proposed that _____ are the disguised fulfillments of repressed wishes and urges and function as a sort of psychological safety valve for the release of these unconscious and unacceptable desires.

(c) The _____ content of a dream is made up of the actual dream images themselves, and the _____ content of a dream represents its disguised psychological meaning.

(d) According to Freud, dreams can be analyzed and the _____ content is revealed by looking for symbolic expressions of repressed urges and wishes in the images of the _____ content.

7. (a) According to the _____ model, dreaming is our subjective awareness of the brain's internally generated signals during sleep.

(b) More specifically, this model maintains that the experience of dream sleep is due to the automatic activation of _____ circuits at the base of the brain that arouse more sophisticated brain areas, such as visual centers, that we normally use to assess the external world.

(c) The activated brain combines, or _____ , internally generated sensory signals and imposes meaning on them; the dream story itself is derived from a hodge-podge of memories and sensations.

(d) Different elements of dreams correspond to the _____ of particular brain areas; when the emotion centers are active, the result is _____ intense dreams, and when the brain's visual centers are active, there are _____ elements in the dream.

(e) To understand the psychology of dreaming, you must understand the _____ of the sleeping brain.

(f) The _____ of a dream is not to be found by decoding the dream symbols, but by _____ the way the dreamer makes sense out of the chaos of dream images.

8. Read the following and write the correct term in the space provided:

(a) Meredith recalls having a dream about dancing in a ballet with a very big, strong, muscled male dancer when suddenly the music switches to loud rock music and the man disappears. According to Freud, Meredith's account represents the _____ of the dream.

(b) The very sudden and surprising change in Meredith's dream could be the result of a burst of neural activity that spread upward from the brainstem and activated a different center of her brain. This interpretation is most consistent with the _____ model of dreaming.

(c) After falling asleep Ricardo finds that his mind keeps returning to the material he has been studying all day in preparation for his exam the next morning. Ricardo is experiencing the most common form of mental activity during sleep, called

_____ .

(d) Dr. Roach is a cross-cultural psychologist interested in investigating sleep and dreams. His cross-cultural data are likely to show that the dreams of people in various parts of the world have _____ (common/no common) themes.

(e) Maxwell claims that he has no recollection of any dream when he wakes up in the morning, and he is convinced that he never dreams. On way to demonstrate to Maxwell that he does dream is to wake him up after he has been asleep for about _____ minutes, when he is clearly in _____ sleep.

Review of Key Terms and Key Names 3

sleep thinking	manifest content
dream	latent content
nightmare	J. Allan Hobson
lucid dream	activation-synthesis
Sigmund Freud	model of dreaming

Matching Exercise

Match the appropriate term/name with its definition or description:

1. _____ The term for the actual images in the dreams.

2. _____ The Austrian physician who founded psychoanalysis and proposed the wish-fulfillment theory of dreams.

3. _____ Repetitive, bland, and uncreative ruminations about real-life events during sleep.

4. _____ Professor of psychiatry at the Harvard School of Medicine who extensively researched sleep and dreaming; proposed the activation-synthesis model of dreaming with co-researcher Robert McCarley.

5. _____ A dream in which the sleeper is aware that he or she is dreaming.

True/False Test

Indicate whether each item is true or false by placing T or F in the space next to each item

1. ___ A nightmare is a vivid frightening experience that occurs during slow-wave stages 3 and 4 NREM sleep and is characterized by physiological arousal, loud screaming, and sleepwalking.

2. ___ A dream is a storylike episode of unfolding mental imagery during sleep.

3. ___ The latent content of a dream refers to the disguised psychological content of a dream.

4. ___ The activation-synthesis model of dreaming states that brain activity during sleep produces dream images (*activation*), which are combined by the brain into a dream story (*synthesis*).

Check your answers and review any areas of weakness before going on to the next section.

Hypnosis
Learning Objectives

When you have finished studying this section of the chapter, you should be able to:

1. Define *hypnosis* and list the characteristics of the hypnotic state.

2. Describe the history of hypnosis and name the person most associated with its origin.

3. List the characteristics of people who are most responsive to hypnosis.

4. Specify the effects of hypnosis, describe posthypnotic suggestion, and explain the relationship between hypnosis and memory.

5. Name the psychologist who discovered the hidden observer phenomenon and explain the role of dissociation in hypnosis.

*Read the section "Hypnosis" and **write** your answers to the following:*

1. (a) _____ can be defined as a cooperative social interaction in which one person, the subject, responds to suggestions by another person, the hypnotist, which produces changes in perception, memory, and behavior.

(b) Hypnosis is characterized by highly focused _____ , increased responsiveness to _____ , vivid images and fantasies, and a willingness to accept _____ of logic or reality.

2. (a) Psychologists have found that about _____ percent of adults are highly susceptible to hypnosis, _____ percent are difficult or impossible to hypnotize, and most adults are somewhere in between.

(b) Children tend to be _____ (less/more) responsive to hypnosis than adults, and there is some evidence that the degree of hypnotic susceptibility may run in families.

(c) The best candidates for hypnosis are individuals who approach the hypnotic experience with positive, receptive _____ and _____ and who have the ability to become deeply absorbed in _____ and _____ while engaged in activities such as reading fiction, watching movies, and listening to music.

3. (a) Deeply hypnotized subjects sometimes experience feelings of _____ from their bodies, profound _____ , and sensations of _____ , but more often they can converse normally and remain fully aware of their surroundings.

(b) Sensory changes that can be induced through hypnosis include temporary _____ , temporary _____ , or a complete loss of _____ in some part of the body.

(c) Painful _____ and

_____ procedures, including

surgery, have been successfully performed

with hypnosis as the only anesthesia.

(d) People can also experience

_____ under hypnosis.

(e) When a _____ suggestion is

made during hypnosis, the subject will carry

out that specific suggestion after the hypnot-

ic session is over; these effects last only a

few hours or days before they wear off.

4. (a) In posthypnotic amnesia a subject is unable

to recall information or events that occurred

_____ or _____

hypnosis, whereas in hypermnesia a sub-

ject's memory is supposed to be enhanced for

_____ .

(b) Many studies have shown that efforts to

enhance memories hypnotically can lead to

_____ and _____ ;

false memories, or

_____ , can be inadver-

tently created when hypnosis is used to aid

recall.

(c) A person _____ (can/cannot) be

hypnotized against his or her will; hypnosis

_____ (can/cannot) make you

stronger than your physical capabilities or

induce talents that are not already present;

and, finally, hypnosis _____

(can/cannot) make you perform behaviors

that are contrary to your morals or values.

5. (a) Dissociation refers to the splitting of

_____ into two or more simulta-

neous streams of mental activity; one

stream responds to the hypnotist's sugges-

tions, whereas the other, dissociated stream

processes information that is unavailable to

the consciousness of the hypnotized subject.

(b) The second, dissociated stream of mental

activity is referred to as the

_____ , but this does not

mean that the hypnotized person has multi-

ple personalities.

(c) Hypnosis has been used in

_____ , _____ , and

_____ as well as in sports

and business in attempts to improve perfor-

mance and enhance motivation.

Meditation
Learning Objectives

*When you have finished studying this section of the
chapter, you should be able to:*

1. Define *meditation* and explain how it works.

2. List and describe the most common techniques
   used in meditation.

3. Specify the effects of meditation.

*Read the section "Meditation" and **write** your
answers to the following:*

1. (a) Meditation refers to a group of techniques

that induce an altered state of focused

_____ and heightened

_____ .

(b) Meditation takes many forms; it has been

used by most _____ as well as

by people for nonspiritual reasons and has

even been included as a component in some

forms of psychotherapy.

(c) Common to all forms of meditation are the

goals of controlling or retraining

_____ .

2. (a) _____ techniques involve focus-

ing awareness on a visual image, your

breathing, a word, or a phrase; when a

sound is used, it is typically a short word or

a religious phrase, called a

_____ , that is mentally

repeated.

(b) _____ techniques involve

a present-centered awareness of the passing

moment without mental judgment, a quiet awareness of the here and now without distracting thoughts.

(c) A meditation technique widely used in research is _____ , in which the subjects sit quietly with eyes closed, mentally repeat their mantra, and use a strategy for getting rid of distracting thoughts.

3. (a) Numerous studies have shown that even beginning meditators practicing _____ experience a state of lowered physiological arousal, including decreased blood pressure, decreased heart rate, and changes in brain waves.

(b) Meditators show EEG patterns that are dominated by _____ brain-wave activity, which is similar to the state of drowsiness that precedes stage 1 sleep.

(c) Many experienced meditators describe the meditative experience as simultaneously producing _____ and a state of _____ , whereas people who practice mental relaxation with their eyes closed often describe the experience as relaxing but _____ .

4. Read the following and write the correct term in the space provided:

(a) Janna quickly becomes deeply absorbed in fantasy and imagination while reading fiction or watching movies. It is very likely that Janna is among the 15 percent of adults who are _____ to hypnosis.

(b) While under hypnosis Karl describes a very frightening experience of being lost at the fairgrounds when he was 6 years old. When his therapist makes the suggestion that Karl will soon forget this traumatic event, he is attempting to induce

_____ .

(c) During every final exam period Declan gets very uptight and anxious. At the suggestion of a friend, he has tried using a meditation technique that focuses his awareness and attention by repeating a simple phrase over and over to himself. Declan is using the _____ technique of meditation.

(d) A researcher suggests to a hypnotized subject that the letter D does not exist. After being brought out of the trance, the subject is asked to recite the alphabet, and when she does, she skips the letter D. This example illustrates the use of

_____ .

(e) An eyewitness to a robbery (who couldn't remember much of the incident) was hypnotized. When the hypnotherapist suggested that there had been three white men and one black woman involved in the robbery, the subject agreed and described them in some detail. All the other five witnesses reported that there was only one white male robber involved. The hypnotherapist has created a(n) _____ .

Review of Key Terms and Key Names 4

hypnosis
posthypnotic suggestion
Ernest R. Hilgard
posthypnotic amnesia
hypermnesia
pseudomemory
dissociation

hidden observer
meditation
concentration techniques
opening-up techniques
transcendental
    meditation (TM)

Matching Exercise

Match the appropriate term / name with its definition or description.

1. _____ A meditative technique that has been widely used in research in which practitioners sit quietly with eyes closed, mentally repeat the mantra they have been given, and practice a strategy for getting rid of distracting thoughts.

2. _____ A cooperative social interaction in which one person, the subject, responds to suggestions by another person, the hypnotist, and that produces changes in the subject's perception, memory, and behavior.

3. _____ The splitting of consciousness into two or more simultaneous streams of mental activity.

4. _____ A suggestion made during hypnosis that the person carry out a specific instruction following the hypnotic session.

5. _____ A hypnotic suggestion to enhance the person's memory for past events.

6. _____ Hilgard's term for the hidden, or dissociated, stream of mental activity during hypnosis.

True/False Test

Indicate whether each item is true or false by placing T or F in the space next to each item.

1. ____ Ernest Hilgard is the contemporary American psychologist who extensively studied hypnosis and advanced the dissociation theory of hypnosis.

2. ____ A meditative technique that involves a present-centered awareness of the passing moment without mental judgment and does not involve concentrating on a mantra or object or activity is called a concentration technique.

3. ____ Posthypnotic amnesia is the result of a hypnotic suggestion that produces an inability in the subject to recall specific information or events that occurred before or during hypnosis.

4. ____ Pseudomemories are false memories (even though the person may be very confident that the memories are real) that result when suggestions are made during hypnosis that create distortions and inaccuracies in recall.

5. ____ The opening-up meditative techniques involve focusing awareness on a visual image or your breathing, or mentally repeating a sound called a mantra.

6. ____ Meditation is any of a number of sustained concentration techniques that focus attention and heighten awareness.

> Check your answers and review any areas of weakness before going on to the next section.

Psychoactive Drugs
Learning Objectives

When you have finished studying this section of the chapter, you should be able to:

1. Define the term *psychoactive drugs*, list their common properties, and specify what factors influence the effects, use, and abuse of psychoactive drugs.

2. Name and describe the characteristics of the most common depressants and list their various physical and psychological effects.

3. Describe the main effects of opiates and explain how they affect the brain and relieve pain.

4. List the main stimulants and describe how they affect the brain and psychological functioning.

5. Name the most common psychedelic drugs and describe how they affect the brain and influence perception, mood, and thinking.

*Read the section "Psychoactive Drugs" and **write** your answers to the following:*

1. (a) Psychoactive drugs are _____ substances that can alter arousal, mood, thinking, sensation, and perception.

   (b) The four broad categories of psychoactive drugs are _____ , _____ , _____ , and _____ .

2. (a) _____ is a broad term that refers to a condition in which a person feels psychologically and physically compelled to take a specific drug.

   (b) When an individual experiences _____ , his body and brain chemistries have physically adapted to the drug.

   (c) Many physically addictive drugs gradually produce _____ , which means that increasing amounts of the drug are needed to gain the original, desired effect.

   (d) When a person is physically dependent on a drug, abstaining from the drug produces

_____ , which are unpleasant physical reactions to the lack of the drug plus an intense craving for it.

(e) Withdrawal from stimulating drugs may produce depression and fatigue, whereas withdrawal from depressant drugs may produce excitability; the withdrawal symptoms are opposite to the drug's action, and this phenomenon is called the

_____ .

3. (a) Biologically, psychoactive drugs disrupt brain activity by interfering with _____ transmission among neurons.

(b) Drug effects can be influenced by the person's _____ , _____ . _____ , or _____ and whether the drug is taken alone or in combination with other drugs.

(c) Personality characteristics, mood, expectations, experience with the drug, and the _____ in which the drug is taken can also affect the drug response.

4. (a) The depressants are a class of drugs that _____ or _____ central nervous system activity and result in drowsiness, sedation, or sleep and are potentially physically addictive.

(b) Used in _____ (large/small) amounts, alcohol reduces tension, anxiety, and possibly the risk of heart disease, but it is also a _____ drug with a high potential for _____ .

(c) Factors such as body weight, gender, food consumption, and the rate of alcohol consumption also affect _____ levels.

(d) Alcohol depresses the activity of neurons throughout the brain and impairs cognitive abilities such as _____ , _____ , and _____ and physical abilities such as muscle coordi-

nation and balance; in excessive amounts, alcohol can cause death.

(e) Because alcohol is physically addictive, _____ can include disrupted sleep, anxiety, mild tremors, confusion, hallucinations, severe tremors, and seizures, depending on the level of dependence; the severest symptoms are collectively called _____ .

(f) Psychological effects of alcohol depend on the person's environment and expectations, but the variety of experiences produced are due to the fact that alcohol lessens _____ by depressing the brain centers responsible for judgment and self-control.

5. (a) _____ , also called "downers," are powerful drugs that reduce anxiety and promote sleep by depressing activity in the brain centers that control arousal, wakefulness, and alertness; they produce physical and psychological dependence.

(b) _____ are depressants that are prescribed to relieve anxiety and, although chemically different, produce effects similar to, though less powerful than, those produced by barbiturates.

6. (a) A group of addictive drugs that relieve pain and produce feelings of euphoria are called _____ or _____ .

(b) Natural opiates include _____ , which is derived from the opium poppy; _____ , the active ingredient in opium; and codeine, which can be derived from either _____ or _____ .

(c) Synthetic and semisynthetic opiates include _____ , methadone, and the prescription painkillers Percodan and Demerol.

(d) Opiates produce their powerful effects by mimicking the brain's own natural painkillers, called _____ .

(e) When used medically, opiates alter an individual's reaction to _____ by reducing the brain's perception of _____ , and people who take opiates for relief after surgery rarely develop drug tolerance or dependence.

(f) The most frequently abused opiate is _____ , which produces an intense "rush" of euphoria followed by feelings of contentment, peacefulness, and warmth; ceasing to take the drug produces unpleasant _____ symptoms.

7. (a) All _____ drugs are at least mildly addicting and all tend to increase brain activity.

(b) _____ is found in coffee, tea, cola drinks, and many over-the-counter medications and is the most widely used _____ drug in the world; it stimulates the cerebral cortex, resulting in increased mental alertness and wakefulness, and is physically addictive.

(c) Regular coffee, tea, or cola drinkers will experience _____ symptoms if they abruptly stop caffeine intake (headache, irritability, drowsiness, and fatigue); in high doses, caffeine can produce anxiety, restlessness, insomnia, and increased heart rate.

(d) _____ is another widely used, legal, and extremely addictive stimulant; it is found in all tobacco products and can increase mental alertness and reduce fatigue and drowsiness.

8. (a) Sometimes called "speed" or "uppers," _____ suppress appetite and can elevate mood and produce a sense of euphoria, but when abused, they can produce

severe psychological and physical problems.

(b) Cocaine is an illegal _____ that is derived from the leaves of the coca tree, found in South America; when "snorted" in purified form, it reaches the brain in seconds and provides intense euphoria, mental alertness, and self-confidence, which last for several minutes.

9. (a) The term _____ was coined in the 1950s to describe a group of drugs that create profound perceptual distortions, alter mood, and affect thinking.

(b) _____ , which is derived from the peyote cactus, and _____ , which is derived from the mushroom of the same name, have both been used for hundreds of years in religious rites in Latin America.

(c) In contrast to naturally occurring psychedelics, _____ is a much more potent and powerful synthetic psychedelic that can produce psychological effects with relatively few physiological changes.

(d) _____ and _____ are very similar chemically to the neurotransmitter serotonin, which is involved in regulating moods and sensations.

(e) The effects of a(n) _____ experience vary greatly, depending on an individual's personality, current emotional state, surroundings, and other people present; withdrawal symptoms occur and adverse reactions to _____ include "flashbacks," depression, long-term psychological instability, and prolonged psychotic reactions.

10. (a) One of the world's most widely used illegal drugs, _____ , is made from the dried and crushed leaves, stems, flowers, and seeds of the common plant *Cannabis sativa*; its active ingredient is the chemical _____ .

(b) Low to moderate doses of _____ produce a sense of well-being, mild euphoria, and a dreamy state of relaxation, with enhanced taste, touch, and smell, whereas higher doses can sometimes produce sensory distortions that resemble a mild psychedelic experience.

(c) _____ and its active ingredient _____ have been shown to be helpful in the treatment of pain, epilepsy, hypertension, asthma, and glaucoma, and in cancer patients it can prevent the nausea and vomiting caused by chemotherapy; its medical use, however, is very limited and politically controversial.

(d) Most _____ users do not develop tolerance or physical dependence, but heavy users may; some of the negative effects include interference with muscle coordination, perception, learning, memory, cognitive functions, and reproductive processes.

11. Read the following and write the correct term in the space provided:

(a) Sian regularly drinks five or six cups of strong coffee a day. If she is like most people, she would probably be surprised to find out that caffeine is a(n) _____ drug and is _____ addictive.

(b) Zachary has been using a mood-altering, euphoria-enhancing psychoactive drug, and with its continued use he now needs to take larger and larger doses in order to experience its original effects. Zachary is developing _____ for the drug.

(c) At a party where he has had too much to drink, the normally shy Darryl keeps people entertained for quite a while with his very silly antics. Darryl's unusual behavior is probably caused by the fact that alcohol _____ by depressing the brain centers responsible for judgment and self-control.

(d) It is very probable that if Darryl continues drinking at the party he will lose coordination and balance, and the next day he may _____ (remember/not remember) very clearly the events of the evening before.

(e) While undergoing chemotherapy for cancer, Brendan is given marijuana to help prevent nausea and vomiting. It is very likely that Brendan _____ (will/will not) develop tolerance and physical dependence.

(f) Dora has been suffering from severe anxiety, so her doctor prescribes a depressant drug called Valium, which is a commonly prescribed _____ .

(g) Shortly after "snorting" an illegal psychoactive drug, Samuel experiences intense euphoria, mental alertness, and self-confidence that lasts for several minutes. It is most likely that Samuel has inhaled the stimulant drug _____ .

Graphic Organizer 2

Read the following examples and decide the name of the drug involved and indicate what class of drug it represents:

Example	Drug Name	Drug Class
1. During a party Jordy becomes less and less inhibited as the night wears on, and by the time the party is nearly over, he is very unco-ordinated and unbalanced and has trouble walking.		
2. After taking her prescription drug for a number of weeks, Janet no longer feels the intense anxiety she used to suffer.		
3. Mrs. Smothers, who suffers from glaucoma, and Mr. Hartley, who has asthma, have both been given an ordinarily illegal drug at the university hospital.		
4. Harold has used a powerful synthetic drug for a number of years to create sensory and perceptual distortions and to alter his mood, but now he is experiencing "flashbacks," depression, and occasional psychotic reactions.		
5. Henrietta was a very heavy coffee drinker and now has quit cold turkey; she is experiencing headaches, irritability, drowsiness, and fatigue.		
6. Following surgery Gregory was given a common prescription drug under medical supervision in order to alleviate his pain.		
7. Just before his exam Juan smokes a couple of cigarettes and finds he is less tired, more mentally alert, and yet fairly relaxed.		

Review of Key Terms 5

psychoactive drug
physical dependence
tolerance
withdrawal symptoms
drug-rebound effect
depressants
delirium tremens (DTs)
barbiturates
tranquilizers
opiates
opium
morphine
stimulants

caffeine
nicotine
amphetamines
cocaine
psychedelic drugs
mescaline
LSD
psilocybin
marijuana
THC
hashish
sleep inertia

Matching Exercise

Match the appropriate term with its definition or description.

1. _____ The active ingredient of marijuana and other preparations derived from the hemp plant.

2. _____ A category of psychoactive drugs that depress or inhibit brain activity.

3. _____ A stimulant drug found in tobacco products.

4. _____ A drug that alters normal consciousness, perception, mood, and behavior.

5. _____ A psychedelic drug derived from the peyote cactus.

6. _____ A condition in which increasing amounts of a physically addictive drug are needed to produce the original, desired effect.

7. _____ A potent form of marijuana made from the resin of the hemp plant.

8. _____ Unpleasant physical reactions, combined with intense drug cravings, that occur when a person abstains from a drug on which he or she is physically dependent.

9. _____ A stimulant drug derived from the coca tree.

10. _____ Drugs that are chemically

similar to morphine and that relieve pain and produce euphoria.

11. _____ A class of stimulant drugs that arouse the central nervous system and suppress appetite.

12. _____ The collective term for withdrawal symptoms associated with high levels of dependence on alcohol; may involve confusion, hallucinations, severe tremors, or seizures.

13. _____ Sleepiness upon awakening that interferes with the ability to perform mental or physical tasks.

True/False Test

Indicate whether each item is true or false by placing T or F in the space next to each item.

1. ____ Marijuana is a psychoactive drug derived from the hemp plant.

2. ____ Barbiturates are a category of depressant drugs that reduce anxiety and produce sleepiness.

3. ____ When withdrawal symptoms occur that are the opposite of a physically addictive drug's action, this is referred to as the drug-rebound effect.

4. ____ Caffeine is the stimulant drug found in tobacco products.

5. ____ Opium is a natural opiate derived from the opium poppy.

6. ____ A person who is physically addicted to the depressant psychoactive drug alcohol is called an alcoholic.

7. ____ Psilocybin is a psychedelic drug derived from the psilocybe mushroom, which is sometimes called "magic mushroom."

8. ____ LSD is the active ingredient of marijuana and other preparations derived from the hemp plant.

9. ____ Morphine is the active ingredient of the natural opiate called opium.

10. ____ Tranquilizers, such as Valium, Librium, etc., are depressants that are prescribed to relieve anxiety.

11. ____ Psychedelic drugs are a category of psychoactive drugs that increase brain activity, as reflected in aroused behavior and increased mental alertness.

12. ____ Physical dependence is a condition in which a person has physically adapted to a drug so that the person must take the drug regularly in order to avoid withdrawal symptoms.

13. ____ Stimulants are a category of psychoactive drugs that create sensory and perceptual distortions, alter mood, and affect judgment by altering brain chemistry or activity.

Check your answers and review any areas of weakness before going on to the next section.

Something to Think About

1. We've all heard the complaint "there's so much to do, and so little time!" When people are busy and feel pressured, they often end up sleep-deprived, and sleep-deprived people are not as efficient or productive as well-rested people; more importantly, they are more likely to make potentially dangerous mistakes. Those most at risk are those on shift work or who suffer jet-lag symptoms for whatever reason.

   Imagine you are a consultant and have been asked to prepare a paper for an organization concerned with these problems among its employees. Based on what you have learned about the sleep/wake cycle, circadian rhythms, biological and environmental clocks, etc., what would you put in your report?

2. Almost everybody has some fascination with dreams and what they mean. Some people believe that dreams can foretell the future or are important in other mysterious ways. Suppose a friend tells you she has had a dream about taking a very important math exam, and in the dream she could not understand a single question on the exam! She just stared at the exam until the professor announced the exam was over and removed the paper from in front of her. At this point she woke up in a very anxious state. Now she is worried that when she takes the real exam next week, her dream will come true! What would you say to her about dreams and their meaning, lucid dreaming, theories of dreams, etc.?

Check your answers and review any areas of weakness before doing the progress tests.

Progress Test 1

Review the complete chapter (including Concept Reviews and the boxed inserts), review all your study notes, and then test yourself on the following progress test. Check your answers. If you make a mistake, review your notes, the relevant section of the study guide, and, if necessary, go back and read the appropriate part of your textbook.

1. Nightmares are to _____ as night terrors are to _____ .
   (a) sleep spindles; beta waves
   (b) alpha waves; beta waves
   (c) REM sleep; slow-wave NREM sleep
   (d) slow-wave NREM sleep; REM sleep

2. Justine believes that dreaming is simply our awareness of the brain's internally generated signals which activate different brain areas. Justine's views are most consistent with the
   (a) adaptive theory of sleep
   (b) activation-synthesis theory of dreams
   (c) restorative theory of sleep
   (d) wish-fulfillment theory of dreams

3. After ingesting a small dose of a psychoactive drug, Graham experiences vivid visual hallucinations and other perceptual distortions and feels as if he is floating above his body. Graham is most likely experiencing the effects of
   (a) cocaine   (d) LSD
   (b) barbiturates   (e) cappuccino
   (c) tranquilizers

4. "Consciousness is like a stream or river; it is continuous and cannot be divided or broken down into component parts." The person most likely to have made that statement is
   (a) Sigmund Freud   (c) Ernest Hilgard
   (b) J. Allan Hobson   (d) William James

5. After flying from San Diego to New York, Jasmine experiences a restless, sleepless night and the next day is irritable and cannot concentrate on the work she has to do. Jasmine's problems are likely due to
   (a) disruption in her circadian rhythms
   (b) high blood levels of melatonin
   (c) jet lag
   (d) all of the above

6. People have no problem staying up a little later each night on the weekend. The most likely explanation for this is that
   (a) the SCN naturally tends toward a 25-hour day
   (b) the SCN naturally tends toward a 23-hour day
   (c) there are no obvious environmental time cues on the weekend
   (d) there are much better late-night movies on TV on the weekend

7. Richard has just finished his fourth night shift and is driving home from work in the bright morning light. The most likely effect of this exposure is that
   (a) the bright light will reset his body clock to a day schedule
   (b) he will become very drowsy and sleepy
   (c) he will experience an increase in the production of melatonin
   (d) all of the above

8. Mrs. Caduggan complains that her somewhat overweight husband snores and snorts throughout the night and appears to be gasping for breath. She notes that this happens most often when he is sleeping on his back. Mr. Caduggan suffers from
   (a) sleep apnea
   (b) sleep inertia
   (c) narcolepsy
   (d) REM sleep behavior disorder

9. In order to find out what goes on in people's brains during a typical night's sleep, researchers are most likely to
   (a) ask people to try to remember as much as possible when they awake in the morning
   (b) watch subjects closely in the sleep research lab and observe what they do all night
   (c) wake people up every fifteen minutes and ask them what is going on in their mind
   (d) use an electroencephalograph to measure their brain-wave activity throughout the night

10. Just as you are about to fall asleep, you have the sudden feeling of falling and your body gives an involuntary spasm. You have experienced
    (a) a sleep spindle   (c) sleep apnea
    (b) a myoclonic jerk   (d) a microsleep

11. Stage 2 sleep is to _____ as stage 4 is to _____ .
    (a) beta waves; alpha waves
    (b) alpha waves; beta waves
    (c) sleep spindles; delta waves
    (d) dreams; nightmares

12. Harry has been asleep for about an hour or so, and his heart begins to beat faster, his breathing becomes irregular, and his closed eyes move rapidly back and forth. His brain waves are probably
    (a) like those of an awake, alert person
    (b) alpha waves
    (c) theta waves
    (d) delta waves

13. Eight-year-old Billy gets out of bed at 1 a.m. and starts to sleepwalk. He is most likely
    (a) in slow-wave stage 3 or 4 NREM sleep
    (b) suffering from narcolepsy
    (c) in REM sleep
    (d) suffering from sleep apnea

14. Mary is one year old, and if she is like most children that age, she will spend about _____ of her sleep in REM sleep
    (a) 50 percent   (c) one-third
    (b) 100 percent   (d) two-thirds

15. Dr. Gerhardt believes that sleep promotes physiological processes that repair and rejuvenate the body and mind. Dr. Gerhardt's view is consistent with the _____ theory of sleep.
    (a) adaptive
    (b) activation-synthesis
    (c) wish-fulfillment
    (d) restorative

16. Mr. Jensen repeatedly complains about the quality and duration of his sleep; he claims that he can't fall asleep and stay asleep and usually wakes up before it is time to get up. Mr. Jensen apparently suffers from
    (a) sleep apnea   (c) paradoxical sleep
    (b) narcolepsy   (d) insomnia

17. According to Science Versus Pseudoscience Box 4.1, biorhythms and circadian rhythms
    (a) are identical phenomena
    (b) are both supported by scientific evidence
    (c) have virtually nothing in common
    (d) both use date of birth to predict a person's personality and capabilities

18. According to the Application section, Improving Sleep and Mental Alertness, sleep inertia refers to
    (a) feelings of grogginess upon awakening from sleep that interfere with the ability to perform mental or physical tasks

    (b) a sleep disorder in which the person stops breathing during sleep and awakens momentarily
    (c) the paralysis that accompanies stage 3 and 4 deep sleep
    (d) the sudden involuntary spasm of the whole body during stage 1 sleep

19. According to Critical Thinking Box 4.4, there is _____ among psychologists about which explanation of hypnosis is correct.
    (a) total agreement
    (b) considerable disagreement
    (c) no common ground or complementary position
    (d) no debate

20. In Focus Box 4.2 presents information about sleep. Which of the following is (are) not true according to this section?
    (a) Deaf people who use sign language sometimes "sleep sign" during sleep.
    (b) It's difficult to wake sleepwalkers because they are in a deep sleep.
    (c) If you wake up during a REM period, you may experience a brief sleep paralysis.
    (d) It is possible to learn foreign languages, chemistry, etc., by listening to tape recordings while fast asleep.
    (e) All of the above.

Progress Test 2

After you have checked your understanding of the material in Progress Test 1 and have done a complete chapter review with special focus on any areas of weakness, you are now ready to assess your knowledge in Progress Test 2. Check your answers. If you make a mistake, review your notes, the relevant section of the study guide, and, if necessary, the appropriate part of your textbook.

1. Dr. Benjamin hypnotizes a client and suggests that she will no longer feel a craving for cigarettes. Dr. Benjamin is making use of
    (a) posthypnotic suggestion
    (b) hypermnesia
    (c) posthypnotic amnesia
    (d) meditation

2. Amber sits in a relaxed position, closes her eyes, and begins to recite her mantra. Amber is practicing
    (a) meditation   (c) sleep inertia
    (b) hypnosis   (d) dissociation

3. Researchers who have found evidence that subjects appear to have a "hidden observer" are likely to suggest that hypnosis involves
   (a) dissociation
   (b) social factors
   (c) stages 3 and 4 NREM sleep
   (d) experimenter bias

4. John drinks five or six cups of coffee every day; if he doesn't, he feels irritable, drowsy, and fatigued. John is _____ a(n) _____ drug.
   (a) addicted to; psychedelic
   (b) physically dependent on; opiate
   (c) addicted to; depressant
   (d) physically dependent on; stimulant

5. Nicotine is to alcohol as a _____ drug is to a _____ .
   (a) stimulant; depressant
   (b) psychedelic; stimulant
   (c) depressant; stimulant
   (d) depressant; psychedelic

6. Hugo is sixty-five years old and, according to his wife, he sometimes jumps out of bed during the night and appears to be acting out his dreams. It is very likely that Hugo suffers from a sleep disorder called
   (a) narcolepsy
   (b) sleep inertia
   (c) sleep apnea
   (d) REM sleep behavior disorder

7. Phelan has just had a very painful operation. His doctors are most likely to prescribe _____ for pain relief.
   (a) a tranquilizer
   (b) marijuana
   (c) morphine
   (d) alcohol

8. Mr. Godfrey has cancer and was given marijuana to counter the nausea and vomiting following chemotherapy. The active ingredient that makes this a useful drug in such cases is
   (a) psilocybin   (c) LSD
   (b) cannabis   (d) THC

9. After he abruptly stops taking a depressant psychoactive drug, Ernie suffers from sleep problems, excitability, and restlessness. Ernie is suffering from
   (a) drug-rebound effect (c) sleep inertia
   (b) tolerance   (d) sleep apnea

10. Dr. Garfield uses hypnosis on a patient while doing some dental work. When he asks her to raise her hand if some part of her can feel pain, she raises her hand. This illustrates
    (a) the hidden observer   (c) meditation
    (b) paradoxical sleep   (d) tolerance

11. Sleep researchers deprive subjects of REM sleep for a number of nights but allow them an otherwise normal sleep; the subjects are likely to experience _____ when next allowed to sleep uninterrupted.
    (a) narcolepsy
    (b) REM rebound
    (c) sleep inertia
    (d) hypnagogic hallucination rebound

12. Research indicates that the percentage of total sleep spent in REM sleep is higher in _____ than in _____ .
    (a) infants; adults   (c) old people; children
    (b) females; males   (d) cats; dogs

13. Harold has a dream in which he is on a train traveling through mountains in what he thinks is Switzerland. He can see the train very clearly going in and out of tunnels over and over again. Harold's therapist suggests that the dream is not about travel in a foreign country but really about Harold's concern with his sexual performance. The therapist is attempting to reveal the _____ of Harold's dream.
    (a) restorative aspects
    (b) manifest content
    (c) latent content
    (d) activation-synthesis aspects

14. In the above example the therapist is utilizing the _____ theory of _____ .
    (a) restorative; sleep
    (b) adaptive; sleep
    (c) activation-synthesis; dreams
    (d) wish-fulfillment; dreams

15. During a very intense game of pool Gary attempts a very difficult shot that will win him the game when he suddenly collapses and falls fast asleep on the pool table. Gary probably suffers from _____ and is experiencing _____ .
    (a) sleep apnea; sleep paralysis
    (b) narcolepsy; a sleep attack
    (c) insomnia; sleep inertia
    (d) REM sleep behavior disorder; sleep paralysis

16. According to In Focus Box 4.2, which of the following is true?

    (a) Some people never sleep.
    (b) Some people never dream.
    (c) It is extremely dangerous to awaken a sleepwalker.
    (d) If you dream you are falling and you hit the ground, you will wake up dead.
    (e) None of the above.

17. Kerry enjoys her nightly sleep very much because she is sometimes aware that she is dreaming and, while still asleep, can often determine the course and outcome of the dream. Kerry often says she feels like a movie director in these nighttime productions: Kerry is most probably a(n)

    (a) heavy drug user
    (b) myoclonic jerk
    (c) insomniac
    (d) lucid dreamer

18. According to Box 4.3, What You Really Want to Know About Dreams, which of the following is true?

    (a) People who have been blind all their lives don't dream.
    (b) Up until the widespread use of color TV, most people's dreams were in black and white.
    (c) Virtually all mammals experience sleep cycles in which REM sleep alternates with slow-wave NREM sleep, and it is reasonable to conclude that they may experience dreams.
    (d) Eating cheese before going to sleep is a good way to ensure you have interesting, juicy dreams.

19. According to the Application section, Improving Sleep and Mental Alertness, which of the following is true?

    (a) If you work rotating shifts, arrange it so that your shift changes progress from the morning to evening to night shifts and stay on the same shift as long as possible.
    (b) It is best to exercise vigorously just before you go to bed so you will feel tired.
    (c) Always go to bed on a full stomach to avoid night starvation and disrupted sleep.
    (d) Drink two or three stiff alcoholic beverages before retiring for the night.
    (e) You should do all of the above.

20. Biorhythms are discussed in Science Versus Pseudoscience Box 4.1. Which of the following point(s) is (are) made?

    (a) Biorhythms is a popular pseudoscience.
    (b) The notion that there are three "natural biorhythms" rigidly fixed from birth on is unproved.
    (c) Although "biorhythms" and "biological rhythms" sound very similar, they have virtually nothing in common.
    (d) The legitimate scientific study of biological rhythms examines the consistent but potentially varying cycles of living organisms over time.
    (e) All of the above.

Answers

Introduction: Consciousness: Experiencing the "Private I"

1. (a) thoughts, sensations, memories
   (b) changing; disjointed (discontinuous)

2. (a) stream; river
   (b) continuity

3. (a) introspection; subjective
   (b) behavior

4. (a) conscious mental processes
   (b) conscious experience
   (c) brain

The Biological and Environmental "Clocks" Regulating Consciousness

1. (a) sleep/wake
   (b) physiological (biological); psychological; mental; sleep/wake
   (c) bodily processes

2. (a) circadian rhythms; hypothalamus
   (b) SCN, or suprachiasmatic nucleus
   (c) bright light; sunlight
   (d) SCN; melatonin
   (e) melatonin; pineal
   (f) entrains

3. (a) environmental time cues
   (b) 25-hour
   (c) resets; 24-hour

4. (a) psychological; physiological; jet lag
   (b) melatonin
   (c) jet lag
   (d) body clock

5. (a) body clock/circadian rhythms; SCN
   (b) melatonin
   (c) a circadian rhythm
   (d) consciousness
   (e) free-running conditions

Matching Exercise 1

1. consciousness

2. introspection

3. suprachiasmatic nucleus (SCN)

4. jet lag

5. circadian rhythm

True/False Test 1

1. T   3. T   5. T
2. F   4. T

Sleep

1. (a) inactivity
   (b) brain waves
   (c) EEG; electroencephalogram
   (d) physical

2. (a) rapid-eye-movement; REM
   (b) REM; NREM; non-rapid-eye-movement
   (c) REM; NREM

3. (a) beta; alpha
   (b) hypnagogic hallucinations
   (c) hypnagogic hallucination; myoclonic jerk

4. (a) four; decreases; fifty; seventy
   (b) alpha; theta
   (c) a few
   (d) sleep spindles
   (e) delta

5. (a) similar; slow-wave
   (b) 3; 4
   (c) 100
   (d) sleepwalking
   (e) 4 NREM
   (f) 4; 3; 2; REM

6. (a) REM
   (b) dreams
   (c) physiological
   (d) 90; 70; 120
   (e) REM; slow-wave
   (f) 3; 4; 2

7. (a) quantity; quality
   (b) almost all; twelve; 50
   (c) decreases; decrease
   (d) decrease; 2

8. (a) sleep deprivation; microsleeps
   (b) are deprived of sleep
   (c) REM rebound; slow-wave NREM rebound

9. (a) restorative
   (b) body; mind
   (c) adaptive
   (d) more
   (e) restorative; and; adaptive

Sleep Disorders: Troubled Sleep

1. (a) sleep disorders
   (b) insomnia
   (c) insomnia

2. (a) children
   (b) 3; 4
   (c) deep
   (d) sleepwalking

(e) night terrors; sleep terrors
(f) night terror
(g) no recollection

3. (a) REM sleep behavior disorder
   (b) REM sleep behavior disorder
   (c) sleep apnea
   (d) 300
   (e) narcolepsy; sleep attacks
   (f) sleep attacks; sleep paralysis
   (g) hypnagogic hallucinations

4. (a) alpha
   (b) falling; myoclonic jerk
   (c) situational or transient insomnia
   (d) worse
   (e) night terror; 3; 4
   (f) narcolepsy; sleep paralysis
   (g) is experiencing sleep disturbances that are normal for her age
   (h) theta; sleep spindles

Graphic Organizer 1

1. C	4. B	6. F
2. E	5. D	7. A
3. G		

Matching Exercise 2

1. insomnia
2. REM sleep
3. restorative theory of sleep
4. alpha brain waves
5. sleep apnea
6. electroencephalogram (EEG)
7. sleep spindles
8. hypnagogic hallucinations
9. slow-wave sleep
10. myoclonic jerk
11. sleep paralysis
12. REM sleep behavior disorder
13. REM rebound

True/False Test 2

1. F	6. F	11. F
2. T	7. F	12. T
3. T	8. T	13. T
4. F	9. T	
5. T	10. T	

Dreams and Mental Activity During Sleep

1. (a) 25; two
   (b) sleep thinking
   (c) sleep thinking
   (d) REM; NREM
   (e) four; five

2. (a) emotions
   (b) content; organization
   (c) sensations
   (d) bizarre
   (e) images

3. (a) concerns
   (b) falling; chased
   (c) content

4. (a) 95
   (b) wake
   (c) remembered
   (d) distractions
   (e) any experience
   (f) programmed; information processing; storage; available

5. (a) nightmare
   (b) nightmare

6. (a) sexual; aggressive
   (b) dreams
   (c) manifest; latent
   (d) latent; manifest

7. (a) activation-synthesis
   (b) brainstem
   (c) synthesizes
   (d) activation; emotionally; visual
   (e) physiology
   (f) meaning; analyzing

8. (a) manifest
   (b) activation-synthesis
   (c) sleep thinking
   (d) common
   (e) seventy; REM

Matching Exercise 3

1. manifest content
2. Sigmund Freud
3. sleep thinking
4. J. Allan Hobson
5. lucid dream

True/False Test 3

1. F	3. T
2. T	4. T

Hypnosis

1. (a) hypnosis
   (b) attention; suggestions; distortions

2. (a) 15; 10
   (b) more
   (c) attitudes; expectations; imagination; fantasy

3. (a) detachment; relaxation; timeliness
   (b) blindness; deafness; sensations
   (c) medical; dental
   (d) hallucinations
   (e) posthypnotic

4. (a) before; during; past events
   (b) distortions; inaccuracies; pseudomemories
   (c) cannot; cannot; cannot

5. (a) consciousness
   (b) hidden observer
   (c) medicine, dentistry; psychotherapy

Meditation

1. (a) attention; awareness
   (b) religions
   (c) attention

2. (a) concentration; mantra
   (b) opening-up
   (c) transcendental meditation

3. (a) TM
   (b) alpha
   (c) relaxation; alertness; boring

4. (a) susceptible
   (b) posthypnotic amnesia
   (c) concentration
   (d) posthypnotic suggestion
   (e) pseudomemory

Matching Exercise 4

1. transcendental meditation (TM)
2. hypnosis
3. dissociation
4. posthypnotic suggestion
5. hypermnesia
6. hidden observer

True/False Test 4

1. T	3. T	5. F
2. F	4. T	6. T

Psychoactive Drugs

1. (a) chemical
   (b) depressants, stimulants, opiates; psychedelic drugs

2. (a) addiction
   (b) physical dependence
   (c) tolerance
   (d) withdrawal symptoms
   (e) drug-rebound effect

3. (a) synaptic
   (b) size, gender, age; metabolism
   (c) setting (context)

4. (a) depress; inhibit
   (b) small; dangerous; abuse
   (c) blood alcohol
   (d) concentration, memory; speech
   (e) withdrawal symptoms; delirium tremens, or DTs
   (f) inhibitions

5. (a) barbiturates
   (b) tranquilizers

6. (a) opiates; narcotics
   (b) opium; morphine; opium; morphine
   (c) heroin
   (d) endorphins
   (e) pain; pain
   (f) heroin; withdrawal

7. (a) stimulant
   (b) caffeine; psychoactive
   (c) withdrawal
   (d) nicotine

8. (a) amphetamines
   (b) stimulant drug

9. (a) *psychedelic drug*
   (b) mescaline; psilocybin
   (c) LSD
   (d) LSD; mescaline
   (e) psychedelic; LSD

10. (a) marijuana; THC
    (b) THC
    (c) marijuana; THC
    (d) marijuana

11. (a) psychoactive; physically
    (b) tolerance
    (c) lessens inhibitions
    (d) not remember
    (e) will not
    (f) tranquilizer
    (g) cocaine

Graphic Organizer 2

1. alcohol; depressant
2. tranquilizer; depressant
3. marijuana; psychedelic
4. LSD; psychedelic
5. caffeine; stimulant
6. morphine; opiate
7. nicotine; stimulant

Matching Exercise 5

1. THC
2. depressants
3. nicotine
4. psychoactive drug
5. mescaline
6. tolerance
7. hashish
8. withdrawal symptoms
9. cocaine
10. opiates
11. amphetamines
12. delirium tremens (DTs)
13. sleep inertia

True/False Test 5

1. T	6. T	11. F
2. T	7. T	12. T
3. T	8. F	13. F
4. F	9. T	
5. T	10. T	

Something to Think About

1. Generally speaking, humans are very adaptable and most people can adapt to shift work. We'll leave aside the issue of whether people want to work shifts or not and assume in this instance that it is part and parcel of the job. If shifts are scheduled to take into account our natural tendencies and utilize knowledge about sleep/wake cycles, circadian rhythms, and the role of the SCN, then they need not produce the usual jet-lag symptoms.

   The first thing to note in your report is our inclination to drift to longer days (the 25-hour day rather than the 24-hour day), as we often do on weekends. It would seem best, therefore, to rotate shifts forward: first shift, 8 a.m. to 4 p.m., second shift, 4 p.m. to 12 midnight, and then midnight to 8 a.m. for the third shift.

   The length of the shift is the next issue to address. Every shift change is going to take some time to get used to and will be accompanied by some jet-lag symptoms, so the less someone has to change, the better. It would probably be best to have people do the same shift for at least a month before changing to the next shift forward.

   Shift workers should be given as much information as possible about circadian rhythms, sleep/wake cycles, and the role of the SCN in the production of melatonin. People finishing a night shift, for example, could be told the value of black-out curtains to avoid having their biological clock reset by bright light, and those suffering from sleep inertia could be given the information presented in the Application section (Improving Sleep and Mental Alertness). For instance, for the midnight to 8 a.m. shift, having bright lights, especially in the early part of the shift, can help people adjust to the night shift.

2. This dream sounds like a real nightmare! The first thing to tell your friend is that dreams cannot predict the future. She is not likely to fail the exam because of her dream. Her dream reflects the fact that she is concerned and worried about the course. The best way to do well on the exam, and to deal with exam anxiety, is to become as well prepared as possible. There are two theories of dreams presented in the textbook. Freud's view is that the manifest content is relatively unimportant, and he would suggest looking for disguised symbolic meaning that reflects the latent content. The other view is the activation-synthesis idea, which suggests that if someone is worried and anxious, then these concerns are likely to show up in a dream if these well-worn neural pathways are activated. In other words, the brain produces dream images that are synthesized into a meaningful story using memories about daily events, past experiences, concerns, and worries.

   The person's interpretation of the dream may tell us more about the dreamer than anything else. If that is the case, then it would be fairly safe to assume that this dreamer is experiencing some perceived difficulty with the course (or some aspect of it) and/or the course material itself.

   One final suggestion you could make is related to the idea of lucid dreaming. If she is a lucid dreamer, it is quite possible that she could go to sleep and have the same dream again, but this time have a completely different and much more positive outcome!

Progress Test 1

1. c	8. a	15. d
2. b	9. d	16. d
3. d	10. b	17. c
4. d	11. c	18. a
5. d	12. a	19. b
6. a	13. a	20. d
7. a	14. c	

Progress Test 2

1. a	8. d	15. b
2. a	9. a	16. e
3. a	10. a	17. d
4. d	11. b	18. c
5. a	12. a	19. a
6. d	13. c	20. e
7. c	14. d	

Chapter 5   Learning

OVERVIEW   Chapter 5 asks the question "What is learning?" and covers the behavioral, cognitive, and ecological approaches to the study of learning.

The behavioral perspective, founded by Watson, involves classical conditioning (Pavlov) and operant conditioning (Skinner). The focus is on the relationship between environmental events and outwardly observable behavior and involves the scientific investigation of the formation of associations between stimuli, the effects of consequences on behavior, and the study of learning without reference to mental events.

The cognitive perspective stresses the important role played by mental events in learning. Rescorla's research demonstrated the importance of cognitive factors in classical conditioning, Tolman showed that operant conditioning can involve cognitive maps and latent learning, and Bandura pointed out the importance of observational learning.

The ecological perspective emphasizes the importance of natural behavior patterns and environmental influences in conditioning and learning. Garcia's research on taste aversion demonstrated that classical conditioning is constrained by biological preparedness, and other researchers showed that operant conditioning can be affected by natural behavior patterns such as instinctive drift.

Introduction: What Is Learning?
Learning Objectives

When you have finished studying this section of the chapter, you should be able to:

1. Define *learning* and *conditioning* and name the two forms of conditioning.
2. List the three perspectives in the scientific study of learning.

*Read the section "Introduction: What Is Learning?" and **write** your answers to the following:*

1. (a) Psychologists define learning as a relatively

   _____

   _____ .

   (b) The learning of new behavior often reflects some kind of

   _____ .

   (c) Conditioning is the process of _____

   _____ .

(d) The two types of conditioning are

   _____ and

   _____ .

(e) The three perspectives in the study of learning are _____ ,

   _____ , and _____ .

The Behavioral Perspective
Learning Objectives

When you have finished studying this section of the chapter, you should be able to:

1. Describe the approach taken by the behavioral perspective.
2. Identify the founder of behaviorism.
3. Identify the basic assumptions and beliefs of the behavioral perspective.

*Read the section "The Behavioral Perspective" and **write** your answers to the following:*

1. (a) Behaviorism is a broad approach to the study of _____ that emphasizes

   _____ .

   (b) The founder of behaviorism was

   _____ .

2. What are the basic assumptions of behaviorism?

   (a) Internal _____ are far too _____ to be included in the scientific study of human behavior.

   (b) _____ , _____ , and other conscious experiences are not appropriate _____ for psychology.

   (c) Psychology should study only

   _____—

   what the organism does or says.

   (d) Virtually all human behavior is the result of _____ , the result of past experience and environmental influences.

Classical Conditioning: Associating Stimuli

Learning Objectives

When you have finished studying this section of the chapter, you should be able to:

1. Define *classical conditioning*.
2. Identify the discoverer of classical conditioning and explain how he investigated it.
3. Explain how classical conditioning occurs and how classically conditioned responses can be weakened or eliminated.
4. Explain how conditioned emotional reactions form and how classical conditioning affects physiological reactions.

*Read the section "Classical Conditioning: Associating Stimuli" and **write** your answers to the following:*

1. (a) _____ discovered classical conditioning, which describes a process of _____ associations between stimuli.

2. Define each of the following terms:

   (a) The unconditioned stimulus (UCS) is

   _____

   _____ .

   (b) The unconditioned response (UCR) is

   _____

   _____ .

   (c) The conditioned stimulus (CS) is

   _____

   _____ .

   (d) The conditioned response (CR) is

   _____

   _____ .

3. (a) Pavlov discovered that the more _____ the conditioned stimulus and the unconditioned stimulus are paired, the stronger the association between the two.

   (b) Pavlov also discovered that the _____ of stimulus presentations affects the strength of the conditioned response; the conditioned stimulus should be presented shortly before the unconditioned stimulus.

   (c) _____ occurs when stimuli that are similar to the original conditioned stimulus also elicit the conditioned response, and _____ occurs when a particular conditioned response is made to one stimulus but not to the other stimuli.

   (d) If the conditioned stimulus is repeatedly presented without being paired with the unconditioned stimulus, the conditioned response will gradually _____ and _____ . Pavlov called this phenomenon _____ .

   (e) Following extinction, Pavlov found that if he allowed several hours to elapse and then introduced the tone (CS) again, the extinguished CR (salivation) would reappear. He called this _____ .

4. (a) Your textbook describes the classical conditioning of Little Albert by Watson and Rayner. What were the CS, the UCS, and the UCR, in their experiment?

CS	UCS	UCR

(b) What was the CR? _____

(c) This classical conditioning experiment demonstrated how

_____ form.

(d) Little Albert reacted with fear to other animals such as a rabbit, a dog, and a sealskin coat. What is this process called?

_____

(e) Why would this study not be allowed today?

_____

5. Sandy had a roommate named Elaine who turned out to be seriously disturbed. As a result of this experience, Sandy developed a conditioned emotional response to the name *Elaine*.

(a) The CS is _____ and the CR is _____

_____ .

(b) What advice could you give Sandy to help her deal with this phobia?

_____

_____

_____

_____

_____

_____

_____

6. (a) Caffeine-dependent people often feel alert after just a few sips of coffee in the morning even though it can take up to forty-five minutes for the caffeine to reach significant levels in the bloodstream. This illustrates the fact that _____ responses can be classically conditioned.

(b) The sight, taste, and smell of the coffee in the above example act as _____ stimuli to elicit the sense of increased alertness, which is the _____ response.

(c) Originally, when the caffeine in the coffee entered the bloodstream, it automatically elicited a natural reaction of increased alertness; in this case the caffeine is the _____ stimulus and the increased alertness to caffeine in the bloodstream is the _____ response.

Graphic Organizer 1

In his classic experiment Pavlov repeatedly presented a neutral stimulus, such as a tone, just before putting food in the dog's mouth, which automatically elicited salivation. After several repetitions the tone alone triggered the salivation. Label the following graph using the correct terms (UCS, UCR, CS, CR):

Before Conditioning

Food in the mouth is the ____ and the salivation is the ____ .	The neutral stimulus is the ___. It elicits no salivation before conditioning.

During Conditioning

The neutral stimulus is the ___.	+	Food in the mouth is the ____.	→	The salivation is the ____.

After Conditioning

The tone alone is the ___ .	→	The salivation is now the ___.

Review of Key Terms and Key Names 1

learning
behavioral perspective
cognitive perspective
ecological perspective
John B. Watson
Ivan Pavlov
classical conditioning
elicit

unconditioned stimulus
unconditioned response
conditioned stimulus
conditioned response
stimulus generalization
stimulus discrimination
extinction
spontaneous recovery

Matching Exercise

Match the appropriate term/name with its definition or description.

1. _____ The gradual weakening and disappearance of conditioned behavior; in classical conditioning, occurs when the conditioned stimulus is repeatedly presented without the unconditioned stimulus; in operant conditioning, occurs when an emitted behavior is no longer followed by a reinforcer.

2. _____ In learning theory, a general explanation of learning that emphasizes the relationship between outwardly observable behaviors and environmental events, rather than mental processes.

3. _____ A relatively permanent change in behavior as a result of past experience.

4. _____ The unlearned, reflexive response that is elicited by an unconditioned stimulus.

5. _____ American psychologist who founded behaviorism in the early 1900s, an approach that emphasizes the scientific study of outwardly observable behavior rather than subjective mental states.

6. _____ The learned, reflexive response to a conditioned stimulus.

7. _____ The occurrence of a learned response not only to the original stimulus but to other, similar stimuli as well.

8. _____ A formerly neutral stimulus that acquires the capacity to elicit a reflexive response.

True/False Test

Indicate whether each statement is true or false by placing T or F in the blank space next to each item.

1. ___ Classical conditioning is the basic learning process that involves primarily cognitive processes and ecological factors, rather than the formation of associations between stimuli.

2. ___ *Elicit* means to draw out or bring forth and causes an existing behavior to occur.

3. ___ The unconditioned stimulus is the natural stimulus that reflexively elicits a response without the necessity of prior learning.

4. ___ In addition to the behavioral perspective, the scientific study of learning involves two other approaches: the cognitive perspective and the ecological perspective.

5. ___ Spontaneous recovery happens when a learned response occurs not only to the original stimulus but to other, similar stimuli as well.

6. ___ Stimulus discrimination occurs when a learned response is made to a specific stimulus but not to other, similar stimuli.

7. ___ Ivan Pavlov was the Russian physiologist who first described the basic learning process of associating stimuli that is now called classical conditioning.

Check your answers and review any areas of weakness before going on to the next section.

Operant Conditioning: Associating Behaviors and Consequences

Learning Objectives

When you have finished studying this section of the chapter, you should be able to:

1. Define the Law of Effect and name the person who formulated it.

2. Describe the procedures used in operant conditioning as demonstrated by Skinner's experiments.

3. Explain the similarities and differences between positive and negative reinforcement.

4. Differentiate between punishment and negative reinforcement, providing examples of each.

5. Describe the shaping procedure used in operant conditioning.

6. Explain the difference between continuous and partial reinforcement, then name, describe, and give examples of each of the four schedules of reinforcement.

---

*Read the section "Operant Conditioning: Associating Behaviors and Consequences" and **write** your answers to the following:*

1. (a) Skinner believed that the most important form of learning was demonstrated by _____ behaviors that were actively _____ by the organism.

   (b) To study active behaviors Skinner drew upon the earlier work of _____ , who had proposed the Law of Effect.

   (c) The Law of Effect states that responses followed by a(n) _____ are strengthened and more likely to occur again in the same situation, and responses followed by a(n) _____ are less likely to occur again.

   (d) Skinner coined the term *operant* to describe active behavior that _____ upon the environment to produce _____ .

   (e) Skinner's operant conditioning model explains learning as a process in which _____ is shaped and maintained by its _____ .

2. (a) Reinforcement is a(n) _____ or _____ that follows an operant and increases the likelihood of the operant being repeated.

   (b) Reinforcement can take two forms, _____ or _____ .

   (c) How do positive and negative reinforcement differ?

   Positive reinforcement involves

   _____

   _____ .

Negative reinforcement involves

_____

_____

_____ .

(d) Reinforcement (positive and negative) always _____ the probability of behavior occurring in the future.

3. The following are examples of negative reinforcement. Decide which illustrates *escape* and which illustrates *avoidance*.

(a) You go to the dentist on a regular basis and as a result you don't experience problems such as toothaches.
This an example of _____ .

(b) Your partner is complaining about your messy habits, so you put on your running gear and go for a five-mile jog.
This is an example of _____ .

(c) You study hard all semester because you don't want to end up with a low grade point average.
This is an example of _____ .

(d) You turn the air conditioner on when the temperature in your room gets too hot and uncomfortable.
This is an example of _____ .

4. The difference between primary reinforcers and conditioned reinforcers is that

(a) primary reinforcers are _____

_____

_____ .

(b) conditioned reinforcers are _____

_____

_____

_____ .

5. (a) Punishment refers to the presentation of an event or stimulus following a behavior that acts to _____ the likelihood of the behavior being repeated.

(b) Negative reinforcement and punishment are often confused. Explain how they differ.

(1) Punishment always _____

_____ .

(2) Negative reinforcement always

_____

_____ .

6. For each of the following, decide whether the example illustrates negative reinforcement (N) or punishment (P):

(a) ____ In order not to get a ticket, Marco always wears his seatbelt whenever he drives his car.

(b) ____ Darryl has tried some new aftershave. "It smells like diesel oil!" comments his girlfriend. Darryl never uses that aftershave again.

(c) ____ Maria stops misbehaving at the dinner table because bad table manners means no dessert.

(d) ____ Greta's cigarette lighter ignites the hair spray she has just put on her hair and burns her bangs and eyebrows. Greta no longer smokes when she is doing her hair.

(e) ____ Jim no longer picks up hitchhikers after the last one robbed him at gun point.

(f) ____ Before pouring milk on her cereal, Carmelitta smells the carton to make sure the milk has not gone sour.

7. (a) Punishment is not always effective because it is often _____ ; to be effective, punishment should

_____ the response and must be consistently applied.

(b) The major drawbacks with using punishment to change behavior are that even though it may suppress a response it does not _____ the appropriate behavior; when it is intense, it may produce undesirable results, such as complete passivity, _____ , _____ , or hostility; and punished behavior is likely to _____ after the punitive consequences are withdrawn.

(c) A discriminative stimulus is a specific stimulus in the presence of which a particular _____ is more likely to be _____ .

Graphic Organizer 2

The following is a very useful way to organize the procedures used in operant conditioning. The arrow ↑ *or* ↓ *indicates whether the behavior increases or decreases. Fill in the blanks in cells 1, 2, 3, and 4.*

	Appetitive Stimuli (e.g., food, water)	Aversive Stimuli (e.g., shock)
The operant response is followed by	**Cell 1** FOOD ↑ This is called _____	**Cell 2** SHOCK ↓ This is called _____
The operant response precludes or prevents the delivery of	**Cell 3** FOOD ↓ This is called _____	**Cell 4** SHOCK ↑ This is called _____

8. (a) _____ involves reinforcing successively closer approximations to a behavior until the correct behavior is displayed.
   (b) Athletic coaches, teachers, parents, and child-care workers all use _____ techniques.

9. (a) The partial reinforcement effect states: Behaviors that are _____ reinforced tend to be much _____ resistant to extinction than behaviors conditioned using _____ reinforcement.
   (b) _____ reinforcement may increase the probability of the behavior it follows even though there is no actual relationship between the behavior and the consequence.

(c) When Skinner delivered food pellets to pigeons in an operant chamber every fifteen seconds independent of the birds' behavior, he observed _____ .

10. Complete each of the following sentences with the correct term: fixed ratio (FR), variable ratio (VR), fixed interval (FI), variable interval (VI).
    (a) With a(n) _____ schedule, reinforcement is made available for the first response following a set period of time.
    (b) When reinforcement is made available only after a set number of responses have been made, this is called a _____ schedule.
    (c) With a _____ schedule an unpredictable number of responses have to be made before reinforcement is available.

(d) When the first response after an unpredictable period of time is reinforced, this is
called a _____ schedule.

11. What type of schedule do each of these examples illustrate?

(a) Your instructor, Dr. Jones, decides to give
surprise quizzes throughout the semester.
Your studying will be reinforced on a
_____ schedule.

(b) Your instructor, Dr. Wong, schedules a quiz
every two weeks throughout the semester.
Your studying will be reinforced on a
_____ schedule.

(c) A rat gets a food pellet for every 20 responses. It is reinforced on a _____
schedule.

(d) Maria sells magazine subscriptions by
phone. She makes many calls but only gets

paid for making a sale. She is reinforced on
a _____ schedule.

(e) Juanita and her colleagues assemble TV
sets in a factory. They get paid a bonus for
every ten TVs they produce. They are being
rewarded on a(n) _____
schedule.

12. (a) The application of learning principles to
help people develop more effective or adaptive behaviors is called

_____ .

(b) _____ has
been used to train animals (e.g., seeing-eye
dogs) to help physically challenged people, to
increase cooperative behavior of young dental patients, and to increase social skills in
school children.

Graphic Organizer 3

*There are four types of partial reinforcement sched-
ules. Fill in each cell with the appropriate term:*

	Based on the number of responses made	Based on the elapsed time
Fixed	Cell 1 _____	Cell 2 _____
Variable	Cell 3 _____	Cell 4 _____

Revew of Key Terms and Key Names 2

B. F. Skinner
Law of Effect
operant
reinforcement
operant conditioning
positive reinforcement
negative reinforcement
primary reinforcer
conditioned reinforcer

punishment
discriminative stimulus
Skinner box
shaping
continuous
    reinforcement
partial reinforcement
extinction

partial reinforcement
    effect
accidental reinforcement
schedule of
    reinforcement

fixed ratio
variable ratio
fixed interval
variable interval
behavior modification

Matching Exercise

Match the appropriate term/name with its definition or description.

1. _____ The application of learning principles to help people develop more effective or adaptive behaviors.

2. _____ A schedule of reinforcement in which every occurrence of a particular response is reinforced.

3. _____ American psychologist who developed the operant conditioning model of learning and emphasized studying the relationship between environmental factors and observable actions, not mental processes, in trying to achieve a scientific explanation of behavior.

4. _____ The popular name for an operant conditioning chamber, the experimental apparatus invented by B. F. Skinner to study the relationship between environmental events and active behaviors.

5. _____ A situation in which a response results in the removal, avoidance, or escape of a punishing stimulus, increasing the likelihood of the response being repeated in similar situations.

6. _____ A reinforcement schedule in which a reinforcer is delivered after a fixed number of responses have occurred.

7. _____ The presentation of a stimulus or event following a behavior that acts to decrease the likelihood of the behavior being repeated.

8. _____ A stimulus or event that has acquired reinforcing value by being associated with a primary reinforcer; also called a secondary reinforcer.

9. _____ A term that describes what happens when it *appears* as if a particular response has resulted in reinforcement when in reality the consequence is just a coincidence.

10. _____ The operant conditioning procedure of selectively reinforcing successively closer approximations of a goal behavior until the goal behavior is displayed.

11. _____ A reinforcement schedule in which a reinforcer is delivered for the first response that occurs after a fixed time interval has elapsed.

12. _____ The delivery of a reinforcer according to a preset pattern based on the number of responses or the time interval between responses.

True/False Test

Indicate whether each statement is true or false by placing T or F in the blank space next to each item.

1. ____ Partial reinforcement refers to a situation in which the occurrence of a particular response is only sometimes followed by a reinforcer.

2. ____ A primary reinforcer is a stimulus or event that is naturally or inherently reinforcing for a given species, such as food, water, or other biological necessities.

3. ____ A variable-ratio schedule is one in which a reinforcer is delivered for the first response that occurs after an average time interval has elapsed but the time varies unpredictably from trial to trial.

4. ____ A discriminative stimulus is a specific stimulus in the presence of which a particular response is more likely to be reinforced and in the absence of which a particular response is not reinforced.

5. ____ A variable-interval schedule is one in which a reinforcer is delivered after an average number of responses but the number varies unpredictably from trial to trial.

6. ____ The partial reinforcement effect refers to the fact that continuously reinforced behaviors are more resistant to extinction than behaviors that are only sometimes reinforced.

7. ____ The occurrence of a stimulus or event following a response that increases the likelihood of the response being repeated is a definition of reinforcement.

8. ____ Positive reinforcement refers to a situation in which a response is followed by the addition of a reinforcing stimulus, increasing the likelihood of the response being repeated in a similar situation.

9. ____ Extinction refers to the gradual weakening and disappearance of conditioned behavior when it is no longer followed by a reinforcer.

10. ____ The Law of Effect states that responses followed by a satisfying effect become strengthened and are more likely to recur in a particular situation, whereas responses followed by a dissatisfying effect are weakened and less likely to recur in a particular situation.

11. ___ Operant conditioning is the basic learning process that involves changing the probability of a response being repeated by manipulating the consequences of that response.

12. ___ *Operant* is Skinner's term for an actively emitted (or voluntary) behavior that operates on the environment to produce consequences.

> Check your answers and review any areas of weakness before going on to the next section.

The Cognitive Perspective
Learning Objectives

When you have finished studying this section of the chapter, you should be able to:

1. Identify the key people in the cognitive perspective.

2. List the main cognitive factors involved in classical conditioning and operant conditioning.

3. Explain what is meant by latent learning and cognitive maps, give examples to illustrate each, and identify the person who developed these concepts.

4. Describe the process of observational learning as demonstrated by Bandura's experiments.

Read the section "The Cognitive Perspective" and **write** *your answers to the following:*

1. (a) According to the behavioral perspective, learning results from _____

   _____

   and there is no need to consider

   _____ or _____

   processes.

   (b) According to the cognitive perspective, learning involves _____

   as well as external events.

   (c) Cognition refers to _____

   _____

   _____ .

2. (a) According to Rescorla, classical conditioning

   _____

   _____ .

   (b) For learning to occur, the conditioned stimulus must be a(n) _____ of the unconditioned stimulus.

3. (a) Tolman believed that

   _____ are involved in learning complex behavior.

   (b) A cognitive map is a(n) _____

   _____ .

   (c) In contrast to the behaviorists, Tolman believed that _____ is not necessary for learning to occur.

4. (a) Learning that is not reflected in actual performance is called _____ learning.

5. (a) _____ is the psychologist most strongly identified with observational learning.

   (b) Almost all children who were promised reinforcement for imitating aggressive models of behavior did so despite the fact that this learning was not evident in their earlier behavior. How did Bandura explain this?

   _____

   _____

   _____

   _____

   _____

   (c) How are Bandura's results similar to Tolman's work with rats in mazes?

   _____

   _____

   _____

   _____

6. (a) Four cognitive processes that interact to determine whether imitation will occur are:

(1) You must pay _____ to the model's behavior.

(2) You must _____ the model's behavior.

(3) You must be able to transform the mental representations into

_____ .

(4) There must be some _____ to imitate the model's behavior.

(b) Motivation is crucial to the actual _____ of the learned behavior.

(c) Imitation is most likely to occur if it is expected to be followed by

_____ .

7. Read the following and write the correct term or word in the space provided:

(a) Maria watches the cooking show *Cucina Amore* on public TV on Saturday afternoon and quite often cooks one of the dishes she sees the chef prepare. Maria's culinary ability is the result of _____ learning.

(b) Dr. Bristow believes that reinforcement is not necessary for learning to occur but that the *expectation* of reinforcement can affect the performance of what has been learned. Dr. Bristow is emphasizing the importance of _____ factors in learning.

(c) If a rat has been allowed to explore a maze for a number of trials without ever getting a reinforcer, it is very _____ (likely/unlikely) that when food is made available in the goal box, the rat will find it very quickly with few errors.

(d) Mr. and Mrs. Delbrook both stopped smoking when they started a family because they wanted to model healthy behavior patterns for their children. They are apparently aware of the importance of

_____ learning in children's development.

Review of Key Terms and Key Names 3

cognitive perspective
Robert A. Rescorla
Edward C. Tolman
cognitive map

latent learning
observational learning
Albert Bandura

Matching Exercise

Match the appropriate term/name with its definition or description:

1. _____ Learning that occurs through observing the actions of others.

2. _____ Tolman's term used to describe learning that occurs in the absence of reinforcement but is not behaviorally demonstrated until a reinforcer becomes available.

3. _____ American psychologist who used the terms *cognitive map* and *latent learning* to describe experimental findings that strongly suggested that cognitive factors play a role in animal learning.

4. _____ Tolman's term used to describe the mental representation of the layout of a familiar environment.

5. _____ American psychologist who experimentally investigated observational learning, emphasizing the role of cognitive factors.

6. _____ In learning theory, a general approach to the study of learning that stresses the role of expectation, mental representation, and other mental processes in learning.

7. _____ American psychologist who experimentally demonstrated the involvement of cognitive processes in classical conditioning.

Check your answers and review any areas of weakness before going on to the next section.

The Ecological Perspective: Biological Predispositions to Learn

Learning Objectives

When you have finished studying this section of the chapter, you should be able to:

1. Identify the key people in the ecological perspective.
2. Describe the ecological perspective and explain how it challenged the traditional behavioral perspective.

Read the section "The Ecological Perspective: Biological Predispositions to Learn" and **write** *your answers to the following:*

1. (a) The traditional behaviorist view is that the general principles of learning apply to virtually all _____ and all _____ situations.

   (b) The ecological perspective stresses that the study of learning must consider the unique _____ patterns of different _____ that have evolved in relation to the species' natural environment.

   (c) According to the ecological perspective, an animal's _____ patterns and _____ can influence what it is capable of learning.

2. (a) Don got sick several hours after eating Sandy's spaghetti. Stomach flu was the actual cause of his illness, yet he now dislikes the taste, smell, or sight of spaghetti. Don has developed a _____ .

   (b) In taste aversion a(n) _____ pairing can result in classical conditioning, and the time span between the two stimuli (CS and UCS) can be _____ , not a matter of seconds; these findings violate two basic principles of _____ .

   (c) _____ was the researcher who demonstrated taste aversion experimentally in laboratory rats.

3. (a) Contrary to Pavlov's claim, research has shown that associations cannot be formed between just any stimulus and any response (e.g., rats did not form an association between taste and shock but did form an association between taste and illness). One explanation for this phenomenon is that

   _____

   _____ .

   (b) Biological preparedness is the idea that an organism is _____ to form associations between certain stimuli and responses.

4. (a) Psychologists studying operant conditioning found that an animal's

   _____ can interfere with learning.

   (b) The Brelands called the natural behavior patterns that prevented the animal they were training from making the learned responses _____ .

   (c) Instinctive drift demonstrates that learning through operant conditioning is constrained by _____ .

5. (a) The Hockenburys' answer to the question "Does the ecological perspective invalidate the principles of classical and operant conditioning?" would be _____ and they would conclude that

   _____

   _____

   _____

   _____ .

   (b) In the final analysis, the most important consequence of learning may be that it promotes _____ of many different species to their unique environments.

6. Read the following and write the correct term in the space provided:

   (a) Eddie had no problem training a pigeon to peck a disk and a rat to press a bar for food.

However, when he tried to get a pigeon to press a bar and a rat to peck a disk for food, he ran into some problems. Eddie's problem is most likely related to the animals'

_____ .

(b) Dr. Munchausen believes that the general principles of learning apply to virtually all species and all learning situations, whereas his colleague Dr. Milstein believes that an animal's natural behavioral patterns and unique characteristics can influence what it is capable of learning. Dr. Munchausen supports the _____ perspective, and Dr. Milstein believes in the _____ perspective.

(c) Dr. Wells decided to classically condition some rats. He used a tone (CS) followed by a shock (UCS) for group 1, and for group 2 he used a taste (CS) followed by a shock. It is very _____ (likely/unlikely) that the rats in group 1 will be classically conditioned, and it is very _____ (likely/unlikely) that the rats in group 2 will be classically conditioned.

Review of Key Terms and Key Names 4

ecological perspective   biological preparedness
taste aversion   instinctive drift
John Garcia

Matching Exercise

Match the appropriate term/name with its definition or description.

1. _____ In learning theory, the idea that an organism is innately predisposed to form associations between certain stimuli and responses.

2. _____ American psychologist who experimentally demonstrated the learning of taste aversions in animals, a finding that challenged several of the basic assumptions of classical conditioning.

3. _____ A learned tendency to avoid food that once made you sick.

4. _____ The tendency of an animal to revert to its instinctive behaviors that can interfere with the performance of an operantly conditioned response.

5. _____ In learning theory, a general approach that emphasizes that the study of learning must consider the unique behavior patterns of different species that have evolved in relation to the species' natural environment.

> Check your answers and review any areas of weakness before going on to the next section.

Something to Think About

1. Imagine that you are a behavioral therapist and a client comes to you with a fairly serious problem. He has a real fear of going to the dentist, and despite the need for some important dental work, he can't bring himself to make an appointment. Using what you know about classical conditioning, explain how his phobia might have come about and describe how to go about extinguishing the fear.

2. Mrs. Denton can't understand why scolding her ten-year-old son for misbehaving only seems to make the problem worse. Using what you know about operant conditioning techniques, what advice would you give Mrs. Denton about how she might (a) reduce the disruptive behavior and (b) increase more appropriate behavior.

3. Imagine your family has decided to get a new puppy dog. Using what you know about operant conditioning techniques, what advice would you give them about how they should train the dog to be obedient, obey commands, and do some neat pet tricks.

> Check your answers and review any areas of weakness before doing the progress tests.

Progress Test 1

Review the complete chapter (including Concept Reviews and all the boxed inserts), review all your study notes, and then test yourself on the following progress test. Check your answers. If you make a mistake, review your notes, review the relevant section of the study guide, and, if necessary, go back and read the appropriate part of your textbook.

1. Learning is best defined as
   (a) any change in the behavior of an organism
   (b) a relatively permanent change in behavior due to experience
   (c) a change in behavior due to education or schooling
   (d) a relatively permanent change in behavior due to maturation

2. A dog conditioned to salivate to the sound of a whistle may also salivate to the sound of a flute. Pavlov called this phenomenon
   (a) stimulus discrimination
   (b) stimulus generalization
   (c) extinction
   (d) spontaneous recovery

3. Watson and Rayner's study of Little Albert demonstrated how learning principles can be applied in
   (a) conditioning emotional reactions
   (b) operantly conditioning responses
   (c) negatively reinforcing responses
   (d) extinguishing conditioned responses

4. Some forms of radiation therapy make patients sick. A patient who has eaten vegetarian pizza just before the therapy (and is then sick) later feels ill when she sees or smells pizza. In this example of taste aversion learning, the conditioned stimulus is the
   (a) vegetarian pizza
   (b) radiation therapy
   (c) illness induced by the therapy
   (d) nausea felt at the sight or smell of pizza

5. When an event that follows an operant response increases the likelihood of that behavior's being repeated, the response has been
   (a) extinguished   (c) reinforced
   (b) punished   (d) generalized

6. Behaviors that are only occasionally reinforced are more resistant to extinction than behaviors conditioned using continuous reinforcement. This phenomenon is called
   (a) the Law of Effect
   (b) punishment
   (c) the partial reinforcement effect
   (d) the continuous reinforcement effect

7. People who put money in a gambling or slot machine are typically reinforced on a
   (a) fixed-interval schedule
   (b) fixed-ratio schedule
   (c) variable-interval schedule
   (d) variable-ratio schedule

8. Manny always uses his "lucky" pencil on multiple-choice computer answer sheets ever since he scored 90 percent the first time he used it on an exam. This is an example of
   (a) superstitious behavior
   (b) primary reinforcement
   (c) biological preparedness
   (d) instinctive drift

9. The fact that learning can occur without reinforcement and may not be reflected in actual performance is most clearly demonstrated by research on
   (a) escape and avoidance learning
   (b) generalization
   (c) spontaneous recovery
   (d) latent learning

10. Which of the following is true of the cognitive perspective?
    (a) Mental processes are an important component of learning.
    (b) The informational value of the CS as a reliable predictor of the UCS is the most important thing that is learned in classical conditioning.
    (c) Organisms use cognitive processes to draw inferences about the cues they encounter in their environment.
    (d) All of the above.

11. At the beginning of the semester many new students spend the first week or so exploring the campus. Later they can often easily locate places they have not been to before. Tolman would suggest that they have formed a(n)
    (a) biological predisposition
    (b) cognitive map
    (c) instinctive drift
    (d) sense of direction

12. Garcia's studies of taste aversion in rats demonstrated that classical conditioning is constrained by
    (a) cognitive processes
    (b) biological predispositions
    (c) observational learning
    (d) environmental factors

13. The Brelands had trouble operantly conditioning relatively simple responses in raccoons because of
    (a) instinctive drift
    (b) their inability to be trained using operant conditioning
    (c) cognitive constraints
    (d) delayed reinforcement

14. Eating delicious food is to receiving money as _____ is to _____ .
    (a) positive reinforcement; negative reinforcement
    (b) delayed reinforcement; immediate reinforcement
    (c) accidental reinforcement; superstitious behavior
    (d) primary reinforcement; conditioned reinforcement

15. Which of the following is true of Rescorla's cognitive interpretation of classical conditioning?
    (a) For learning to occur, the CS must be a reliable predictor of the UCS.
    (b) Biological preparedness is a major constraint in this type of learning.
    (c) The formation of cognitive maps is essential in learning.
    (d) Instinctive drift will always interfere with this type of learning.

16. When Guido is a passenger in a car, he suffers from motion sickness; when he is the driver, he feels fine. As a result, Guido always insists on doing the driving. This example illustrates the phenomenon of
    (a) stimulus generalization
    (b) extinction
    (c) stimulus discrimination
    (d) superstitious behavior

17. According to Critical Thinking Box 5.3, B. F. Skinner maintained that
    (a) human freedom is an illusion
    (b) all behavior arises from causes that are within the individual and environmental factors have little or no influence

    (c) cognitive factors are the crucial elements in all learning
    (d) the ecological perspective best explains animal behavior but can't be applied to human beings

18. According to the Application section, which of the following is true?
    (a) Observing good role models can be used to improve self-control.
    (b) Cognitive aspects of learning such as focusing on the delayed rather than the immediate reinforcer can play a role in making better choices.
    (c) Precommitment involves making an advance commitment to your long-term goal, one that will be difficult to change when a conflicting reinforcer becomes available.
    (d) All of the above.

19. Which of the following is a strategy for changing behavior that is recommended as an alternative to punishment?
    (a) Stop reinforcing the problem behavior.
    (b) Reinforce an incompatible behavior.
    (c) Reinforce the nonoccurrence of the problem behavior.
    (d) Remove the opportunity to obtain positive reinforcement.
    (e) All of the above.

20. According to In Focus Box 5.4, a phobia is
    (a) an extreme, irrational fear of a specific object, animal, or situation
    (b) a fear of heights that most people would feel if they were dangled off the roof of a very tall building
    (c) a desire to seek out and stand in small enclosed places, such as a broom closet
    (d) a form of schizophrenia characterized by hallucinations of small, creepy animals

Progress Test 2

After you have checked your understanding of the material in Progress Test 1 and have done a complete chapter review with special focus on any areas of weakness, you are now ready to assess your knowledge in Progress Test 2. Check your answers. If you make a mistake, review your notes, the relevant section of the study guide, and, if necessary, the appropriate part of your textbook.

1. Which of the following best illustrates classical conditioning?
   (a) Henry feels ill at the sight or smell of peanut butter because it once made him sick.
   (b) Annalee studies hard because she wants to get good grades.
   (c) Virginia goes shopping for new clothes fairly frequently because it makes her feel good.
   (d) Lyndle drives at the posted speed limit after getting a number of speeding tickets.

2. Erv developed a fear of attics after he was accidentally locked in his own attic by his wife. Erv's present fear and apprehension of the attic is a(n)
   (a) unconditioned response (UCR)
   (b) conditioned emotional response
   (c) unconditioned stimulus
   (d) conditioned stimulus

3. Which of the following best illustrates operant conditioning?
   (a) Jane always salivates at the sight or smell of pizza.
   (b) After two years at college, Michael feels fear and anxiety whenever he hears the word *exam*.
   (c) Jason makes as many subscription phone calls as he can because he gets paid 10 cents for each call.
   (d) Mary hates fried chicken after suffering food poisoning the last time she ate it.

4. Alcoholics who are given drinks containing a drug that makes them sick do not always come to associate alcohol with illness. The most likely explanation is that classical conditioning in humans is more complex than classical conditioning in rats and may involve more higher-level _____ processes.
   (a) cognitive   (c) environmental
   (b) biochemical   (d) ecological

5. In a classical conditioning experiment, the experimenter repeatedly pairs a bell with an electric shock for one group of subjects, and for a second group the bell is only occasionally paired with the shock. Based on Rescorla's cognitive analysis of classical conditioning, you would be most justified in predicting that
   (a) conditioning will be greater in the first group compared to the second
   (b) conditioning will be greater in the second group compared to the first
   (c) there will be no difference between the groups in strength of conditioning
   (d) the second group will exhibit the partial reinforcement effect

6. The _____ states that responses followed by a satisfying effect become strengthened and are more likely to recur in a particular situation, while responses followed by an unsatisfactory effect are less likely to recur in a particular situation.
   (a) partial reinforcement effect
   (b) Law of Effect
   (c) ecological perspective
   (d) cognitive perspective

7. An animal trainer wants to train a pigeon to turn in circles. Initially, she gives the pigeon a food pellet for a quarter-turn, then only for making a half-turn, and finally only after the pigeon has completed a full turn. She has used
   (a) discrimination training
   (b) negative reinforcement
   (c) punishment
   (d) shaping

8. Which one of the following behaviors is typically reinforced on a variable-ratio schedule?
   (a) studying for surprise or unexpected quizzes
   (b) checking the mailbox to see if the mail has arrived
   (c) inserting coins into a vending machine to get a candy bar
   (d) inserting coins into a gambling (slot) machine

9. Increased response rate is to decreased response rate as _____ is to _____ .
   (a) positive reinforcement; negative reinforcement
   (b) negative reinforcement; punishment
   (c) positive reinforcement; punishment
   (d) both (b) and (c)
   (e) all of the above

10. A negative reinforcer tends to _____ the behavior it follows.
    (a) strengthen
    (b) eliminate
    (c) decrease or weaken
    (d) have an unpredictable effect on

11. On the first day of class Professor Cameron tells her psychology students that surprise tests will be given many times throughout the term. Because students can never predict exactly when a test is going to be given, they need to study on a consistently regular basis if they want to do well in the course. Their studying is being reinforced on a
    (a) fixed-interval schedule
    (b) fixed-ratio schedule
    (c) variable-interval schedule
    (d) variable-ratio schedule

12. Which of the following is an example of negative reinforcement?
    (a) Mary closes her bedroom window because the street traffic is too loud.
    (b) Juanita eats all her vegetables because if she does her mother won't nag her.
    (c) In order to avoid getting another speeding ticket, Mario always drives at the posted speed limit.
    (d) All of the above.

13. Which of the following is an example of observational learning?
    (a) A rat presses a bar to obtain a pellet of food.
    (b) A dog salivates at the sound of an electric can opener because it has been associated with getting food.
    (c) Mary does not wear her new hat after seeing people laugh and point at another person wearing a similar hat.
    (d) John puts a great deal of money into a slot machine even though he only wins occasionally.

14. When Zahra first arrived on campus, she spent a lot of time simply exploring her new environment. Although she had never been there before, she had no problem finding the library a couple of weeks later after she got her first library research assignment. This example illustrates
    (a) latent learning
    (b) the development of a cognitive map
    (c) cognitive aspects of learning
    (d) all of the above

15. Sebastian has often had stir-fried yak with his girlfriend at their favorite Mongolian restaurant. On one occasion, he gets very sick a few hours later. In the future he will most likely avoid which of the following?
    (a) his girlfriend
    (b) Mongolians
    (c) stir-fried yak
    (d) all Asian restaurants

16. In terms of important contributions to the study of learning, _____ is to observational learning as _____ is to the ecological perspective.
    (a) Skinner; Pavlov
    (b) Bandura; Garcia
    (c) Rescorla; Tolman
    (d) Watson; Thorndike

17. According to the Application section, we often choose a short-term reinforcer over a more valuable long-term goal. Your textbook suggests that the reason we do this is because
    (a) the relative value of a reinforcer can shift over time
    (b) as the availability of a reinforcer gets closer, the subjective value of the reinforcer increases
    (c) when we make our decision, we'll choose whichever reinforcer has the greatest subjective value
    (d) all of the above

18. According to Seligman (In Focus Box 5.4), people are more likely to develop phobias of spiders, snakes, heights, etc., compared to doorknobs, knives, washing machines, ladders, etc., because
    (a) we are biologically prepared to do so
    (b) doorknobs, knives, and ladders are inherently safer than spiders, snakes, and heights
    (c) of instinctive drift
    (d) of latent learning

19. According to In Focus Box 5.1, John B. Watson
    (a) believed that punishment was the best and most desirable way to change behavior
    (b) vehemently opposed Skinner's idea that freedom is just an illusion
    (c) was a pioneer in the application of classical conditioning principles to advertising
    (d) postulated the Law of Effect

20. According to In Focus Box 5.2, which of the following is true?

    (a) The best and most effective way to change undesirable behavior is through the use of punishment.

    (b) Punishment works better than any other behavioral strategy in changing undesirable behavior.

    (c) There are no effective strategies for reducing undesirable behaviors.

    (d) There are a number of strategies other than punishment that can be used to change undesirable behavior.

Answers

Introduction: What Is Learning?

1. (a) permanent change in behavior due to past experience
   (b) adaptation to the environment
   (c) learning associations between environmental events and behavioral responses
   (d) classical conditioning; operant conditioning
   (e) the behavioral; the cognitive; the ecological

The Behavioral Perspective

1. (a) learning; changes in outwardly observable behavior
   (b) John B. Watson

2. (a) mental processes; subjective
   (b) thoughts, feelings; subject matter
   (c) outwardly observable behavior
   (d) learning

Classical Conditioning: Associating Stimuli

1. (a) Ivan Pavlov; learning

2. (a) the natural stimulus that reflexively elicits a response without the necessity of prior learning
   (b) the unlearned, reflexive response that is elicited by the unconditioned stimulus
   (c) a formerly neutral stimulus that acquires the capacity to elicit a learned, reflexive response
   (d) the learned, reflexive response to a conditioned stimulus

3. (a) frequently
   (b) timing
   (c) generalization; discrimination
   (d) weaken; disappear; extinction
   (e) spontaneous recovery

4. (a)

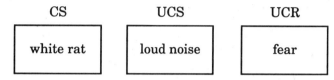

CS	UCS	UCR
white rat	loud noise	fear

   (b) fear
   (c) conditioned emotional reactions
   (d) generalization
   (e) ethical reasons

5. (a) the name *Elaine*; the anxiety that Sandy now feels when she hears the name *Elaine*
   (b) Sandy should try an extinction procedure in which she is exposed repeatedly to the name *Elaine* (the CS) without the UCS. She should also be cautioned that even if this procedure is successful, it is possible that after a time period without encountering any Elaines, the name *Elaine* may evoke a CR because of the phenomenon of spontaneous recovery.

6. (a) physiological
   (b) conditioned; conditioned
   (c) unconditioned; unconditioned

Graphic Organizer 1

Before Conditioning

Food in the mouth is the UCS and the salivation is the UCR.

The neutral stimulus is the CS. It elicits no salivation before conditioning.

During Conditioning

The neutral stimulus is the CS. + Food in the mouth is the UCS. → The salivation is the UCR.

After Conditioning

The tone alone is the CS. → The salivation is now the CR.

Matching Exercise 1

1. extinction
2. behavioral perspective
3. learning
4. unconditioned response
5. John B. Watson
6. conditioned response
7. stimulus generalization
8. conditioned stimulus

True/False Test 1

1. F
2. T
3. T
4. T
5. F
6. T
7. T

Operant Conditioning: Associating Behaviors and Consequences

1. (a) new; emitted
   (b) Edward L. Thorndike
   (c) satisfying effect; unsatisfactory effect
   (d) operates; consequences
   (e) behavior; consequences

2. (a) stimulus; event
   (b) positive; negative
   (c) the presentation or addition of a reinforcing stimulus following an operant; a situation in which the behavior results in the removal of, or avoidance or escape from, an unpleasant or aversive stimulus
   (d) strengthens or increases

3. (a) avoidance
   (b) escape
   (c) avoidance
   (d) escape

4. (a) naturally or inherently reinforcing for a given species, such as food, water, or other biological necessities
   (b) stimuli or events that have acquired their reinforcing properties by being associated with primary reinforcers (also called secondary reinforcers)

5. (a) decrease
   (b) (1) decreases the probability of a behavior's being repeated
       (2) increases the likelihood that the response will occur again

6. (a) N
   (b) P
   (c) P
   (d) P
   (e) P
   (f) N

7. (a) delayed; immediately follow
   (b) teach or promote; fear, anxiety; reappear
   (c) operant (response); reinforced

Graphic Organizer 2

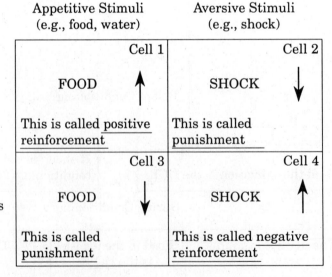

	Appetitive Stimuli (e.g., food, water)	Aversive Stimuli (e.g., shock)
The operant response is followed by	**Cell 1** FOOD ↑ This is called <u>positive</u> reinforcement	**Cell 2** SHOCK ↓ This is called punishment
The operant response precludes or prevents the delivery of	**Cell 3** FOOD ↓ This is called punishment	**Cell 4** SHOCK ↑ This is called <u>negative</u> reinforcement

8. (a) shaping
   (b) shaping

9. (a) only occasionally or intermittently; more;
       continuous
   (b) accidental
   (c) superstitious behavior

10. (a) FI
    (b) FR
    (c) VR
    (d) VI

11. (a) VI
    (b) FI
    (c) FR
    (d) VR
    (e) FR

12. (a) behavior modification
    (b) behavior modification

Graphic Organizer 3

	Based on the number of responses made	Based on the elapsed time
Fixed	Cell 1 Fixed ratio	Cell 2 Fixed interval
Variable	Cell 3 Variable ratio	Cell 4 Variable interval

Matching Exercise 2

1. behavior modification
2. continuous reinforcement
3. B. F. Skinner
4. Skinner box
5. negative reinforcement
6. fixed ratio
7. punishment
8. conditioned reinforcer
9. accidental reinforcement
10. shaping
11. fixed interval
12. schedule of reinforcement

True/False Test 2

1. T	6. F	11. T
2. T	7. T	12. T
3. F	8. T	
4. T	9. T	
5. F	10. T	

The Cognitive Perspective

1. (a) both classical and operant conditioning;
       mental; cognitive
   (b) mental processes
   (c) thoughts, expectations, information process-
       ing, mental representations, and other inter-
       nal mental processes

2. (a) depends upon the information the condi-
       tioned stimulus (CS) provides about the
       unconditioned stimulus (UCS)
   (b) reliable predictor

3. (a) cognitive processes
   (b) mental representation of the layout of a
       familiar environment
   (c) reinforcement

4. (a) latent

5. (a) Albert Bandura
   (b) Observational learning is the result of
       cognitive processes that are actively judg-
       mental and constructive and not just
       mechanical copying. Reinforcement is not
       necessary for learning to occur, but the
       expectation of reinforcement affected the
       performance of what the children had
       learned earlier.
   (c) Both demonstrated that reinforcement was
       not essential for learning to occur and that
       learning can take place in the absence of
       performance or observable behavior (i.e.,
       latent learning). Both stress the importance
       of cognitive variables in learning.

6. (a) (1) attention
       (2) remember
       (3) actions you are capable of reproducing
       (4) motivation
   (b) performance
   (c) rewards or reinforcers

7. (a) observational
   (b) cognitive

(c) likely

(d) observational

Matching Exercise 3

1. observational learning

2. latent learning

3. Edward C. Tolman

4. cognitive map

5. Albert Bandura

6. cognitive perspective

7. Robert A. Rescorla

The Ecological Perspective: Biological Predispositions to Learn

1. (a) species; learning
   (b) behavior; species
   (c) natural behavior; unique characteristics

2. (a) taste aversion
   (b) single; several hours; classical conditioning
   (c) John Garcia

3. (a) animals have a biological predisposition to learn some things and not others
   (b) innately predisposed

4. (a) natural behavior patterns
   (b) instinctive drift
   (c) inborn or instinctive behavior patterns

5. (a) no; thousands of laboratory experiments have shown that behavior can be reliably and predictably influenced by classical and operant conditioning procedures
   (b) adaptation

6. (a) biological preparedness
   (b) behavioral; ecological
   (c) likely; unlikely

Matching Exercise 4

1. biological preparedness

2. John Garcia

3. taste aversion

4. instinctive drift

5. ecological perspective

Something to Think About

1. The first assumption that someone who adheres to the behavioral perspective would make is that the irrational fear, or phobia, was the result of a classical conditioning process. In the past the client had a very unpleasant experience at a dentist's office. One could speculate that as a child he was taken to the dentist and experienced pain and fear as a result of having a hypodermic needle inserted into his gum or of the drill striking a nerve. If this were the case, the dentist (CS) has become associated with the needle or drill (UCS) which elicited pain and fear (UCR). The dentist (CS) now evokes a fear response (CR), and this fear may have generalized to all dentists.

   One way to get rid of the irrational fear would be to use an extinction procedure in which the CS (the dentist) is presented over and over without the UCS until the fear subsides. This might mean that the client will have to find a very understanding dentist who will allow him to make many visits to the office without having any work done. The behavioral perspective predicts that this would eventually result in a reduction of the irrational fear and therefore allow the client to get some much-needed dental work done. It would also be important to point out that following a prolonged absence from the dentist, spontaneous recovery may occur.

2. It is possible that Mrs. Denton's "scolding" may in fact be reinforcing the undesirable behavior. Attention, in almost any form, from an adult can be a powerful positive reinforcer for a child. If this is the case, then withholding reinforcement (scolding) will tend to extinguish the target behavior, but only if it is consistent. Inconsistent or intermittent reinforcement will make the behavior very resistant to extinction.

   In addition, it is important to encourage desirable behavior. Pay attention to any instance of good behavior, or any close approximation of the goal behavior, by giving praise or some other positive reinforcer. In other words, use a shaping procedure initially, and then use partial reinforcement to ensure that the desirable behavior becomes resistant to extinction. It is also important to model the appropriate behavior and avoid punishment.

3. Operant conditioning techniques can be used to train animals. Decide on the target behavior(s) and start by using a shaping procedure and continuous positive reinforcement. Pick one of the behaviors you want to train—for example having the dog sit at the command "sit"—and

use a reinforcer such as "good dog!" while patting the dog on the head or chest. The command "sit" should be followed with gentle pressure on the dog's rear end to make him sit and then he should be immediately reinforced. After just a few trials the dog will sit on command without the application of pressure to his back, and he should always be immediately reinforced. It is important to let the dog know who is in command at all times without using punishment. After the dog is obeying the commands regularly, then switch to a partial reinforcement schedule, and reinforce the dog for obeying only occasionally. This will ensure greater resistance to extinction. Dogs can be trained to do many neat tricks in this manner, but remember to work with the animal's natural repertoire of behaviors (biological predispositions). Some dogs can learn some behaviors more easily than others.

Progress Test 2

1. a	8. d	15. c
2. b	9. d	16. b
3. c	10. a	17. d
4. a	11. c	18. a
5. a	12. d	19. c
6. b	13. c	20. d
7. d	14. d	

Progress Test 1

1. b	8. a	15. a
2. b	9. d	16. c
3. a	10. d	17. a
4. a	11. b	18. d
5. c	12. b	19. e
6. c	13. a	20. a
7. d	14. d	

Chapter 6 Memory

OVERVIEW Chapter 6 examines memory and the mechanisms involved in remembering and forgetting. The fundamental processes of encoding, storage, and retrieval are presented along with the capacity, duration, and function of each of the three stages of memory: sensory memory, short-term memory, and long-term memory. The three basic categories of information stored in long-term memory and their organization are presented.

How retrieval works and the problems associated with retrieval failure are examined; also included are the tip-of-the-tongue phenomenon, the serial position effect, different forms of the encoding specificity principle, and flashbulb memories. How memories are constructed and reconstructed, the sources of potential problems (schema distortion, source confusion, the misinformation effect), and the influence of such problems on eyewitness testimony and false memories are all given consideration in this section.

Forgetting, theories of forgetting, and relevant research findings are explored next. Finally, the biological basis of memory is explained and the contributions of empirical research and case studies of brain-damaged patients are presented. The chapter ends with a discussion of the two forms of amnesia and includes an examination of the role played by brain structures such as the hippocampus and the amygdala.

Introduction: Memory Processes and Stages

Learning Objectives

When you have finished studying this section of the chapter, you should be able to:

1. Define *memory* and explain the processes of encoding, storage, and retrieval.

2. Describe the three-stage model of memory, differentiate among the three stages, and explain how they interact

3. Define *sensory memory* and list its functions, duration, and capacity.

4. Explain the role of short-term, working memory; specify its duration and capacity; and list various ways for overcoming its limitations.

5. Describe the function of long-term memory and specify the factors that increase the efficiency of long-term encoding.

6. List and differentiate between the basic categories of information stored in long-term memory and explain how this information is organized.

*Read the section "Introduction: Memory Processes and Stages" and **write** the answers to the following:*

1. (a) Memory refers to the mental processes that

   enable us to _____ ,

   _____ , and _____

   information.

   (b) Rather than being a single process, memory involves three fundamental processes:

   _____ refers to the process of

   transforming information into a form that

   can be entered and retained by the memory

system; _____ is the process of retaining information in memory so that it can be used at a later time; and _____ involves recovering the stored information so that we can be consciously aware of it.

2. (a) In the stage model of memory there are three distinct stages, _____ memory, _____ memory, and _____ memory, and information is transferred from one stage to another.

   (b) Each memory stage is thought to differ in terms of _____ (how much information can be stored), _____ (how long the information can be stored), and _____ (what is done with the stored information).

3. (a) _____ memory registers a great deal of information from the environment and holds it for a very brief period of time; after a few seconds or less, the information fades.

   (b) During this very brief period of time, if you select or pay _____ to some aspect of the environmental information that's being registered, it will be transferred to the second stage of memory, _____ memory.

   (c) _____ memory, also known as working memory, refers to the active, working memory system that can temporarily hold all current information that you are consciously aware of for up to about _____ seconds.

   (d) Imagining, remembering, and problem solving all take place in working, or _____ , memory; most of the vast amounts of information temporarily held in working memory fades and is forgotten in a matter of seconds, but some information that is actively processed may be encoded for storage in _____ memory.

   (e) _____ memory is the third stage of memory, and it represents the relatively longlasting storage of memories that may last for a lifetime.

   (f) Information flow requires an interaction between all three stages of memory; first, information is momentarily registered in _____ memory; if attention is paid to it, it is transferred to _____ memory, where information retrieved from _____ memory is used to interpret it.

4. (a) It was largely through the research of _____ in 1960 that the characteristics of visual sensory memory were first identified.

   (b) Visual sensory memory holds a great deal of information very briefly, for about _____ , just long enough for us to pay attention to specific elements that are significant to us at the moment, and it is this meaningful information that is transferred to _____ memory.

   (c) Visual sensory memory is sometimes referred to as _____ memory because it is the brief memory of an image, or _____ , and auditory sensory memory is sometimes referred to as _____ memory, meaning a brief memory that is like a(n) _____ .

   (d) The duration of visual sensory memory is about _____ to _____ a second, whereas auditory sensory memory holds information for up to _____ seconds.

(e) An important function of sensory memory is to very briefly _____ our sensory impressions so that they overlap slightly with one another; this gives rise to our perception of the world around us as _____ rather than a series of disconnected images or disjointed sounds.

5. (a) Short-term, or working, memory is the stage of memory in which information transferred from _____ memory and information retrieved from _____ memory become conscious.

(b) An important function of working memory is that it provides temporary _____ for information that is currently being used in some _____ cognitive activity.

(c) You can hold most types of information in short-term memory up to about _____ seconds before it's forgotten or decays, but if it is _____ , or repeated over and over again, it can be maintained in short-term memory much longer; this is called maintenance

_____ .

(d) The capacity of short-term memory is limited to about _____ items, or bits of information, at one time, and when filled to capacity, new information will _____ , or bump out, currently held information unless it is consciously and constantly repeated.

(e) One way to increase the amount of information that can be held in short-term memory is through _____ ; this is the process of grouping related items together into a single unit.

(f) Although overall capacity can be increased through _____ , short-term memory still has only about seven mental

slots available and each slot can hold either a simple or a complex message.

6. (a) Long-term memory refers to the _____ of information over extended periods of time; a long-term memory can involve recalling what you were doing just minutes ago or ten years ago.

(b) In terms of duration, some long-term memories can last a _____ , and the amount of information that can be held in long-term memory is _____ .

(c) One common method of getting information into long-term memory is to repeat the to-be-remembered information over and over again; this strategy, called _____ rehearsal, it is less effective than elaborative rehearsal, which involves focusing on the _____ of information to help encode and transfer it to long-term memory.

(d) Two additional factors that enhance encoding and improve memory are the _____ effect, in which you apply information to yourself, and the use of _____ , which involves trying to picture the information in a vivid manner.

7. There are three major categories of information stored in long-term memory:

(a) _____ information refers to the long-term memory of how to perform different skills, operations, and actions.

(b) _____ information refers to long-term memory of events or episodes that were personally experienced; it is also called autobiographical memory.

(c) _____ information is a general store of knowledge of facts, names, definitions, concepts, ideas, etc.

8. (a) Information in long-term memory is _____ , not just a random jumble of information, but the processes involved are not very well understood.

(b) The process whereby information is actively organized into related groups during recall from long-term memory is called _____ ; there is usually some logical _____ between bits of information stored in long-term memory.

(c) The _____ model accounts for the way information is organized in long-term memory by noting that concepts are logically linked, or associated, among different clusters of information.

(d) When one concept is activated in the _____ , it can spread in any number of directions, activating other associations, especially those with strong connections.

9. Read the following and write in the correct term in the space provided:

(a) During a math exam Trevor is desperately trying to think of the correct formula, which he knew when he was studying last week, but despite all his efforts, it just won't come to mind. Trevor is experiencing trouble with one of the three fundamental processes of memory, called _____ .

(b) To help learn the number of days in each month, eight-year-old Gloria has been reciting a short rhyme over and over: "Thirty days has September, April, June and November; all the rest have thirty-one except February." She is using the fundamental process of _____ to transform the information into a form that can be entered and retained by the memory system.

(c) In the above example Gloria is using a type of rehearsal that is giving some meaning to an otherwise hard-to-remember string of numbers; this is called _____ rehearsal.

(d) After looking up a phone number in the book, Alysha is able to remember it only long enough to press all the correct numbers on the key pad. The phone number is in her _____ memory and is briefly stored there by the use of _____ rehearsal.

(e) Vito is an excellent chess player and can easily recall the exact positions of most of the chess pieces after a brief glance at the board. He explains his ability by pointing out that he does not try to memorize where all the individual pieces are but instead focuses on the relatively few attack patterns the pieces make up. Vito is using _____ to improve the capacity of his short-term memory.

(f) When 55-year-old Mr. Adams put on roller skates for the first time in over forty years, he had no trouble remembering how to skate. He is making use of one of the three categories of information stored in long-term memory, called _____ information.

Review of Key Terms and Key Names 1

Elizabeth Loftus
memory
encoding
storage
retrieval
stage model of
   memory
sensory memory
short-term memory
   (working memory)
long-term memory
George Sperling
visual sensory memory
   (iconic memory)

auditory sensory
   memory
   (echoic memory)
maintenance rehearsal
chunking
elaborative rehearsal
self-reference effect
visual imagery
procedural information
episodic information
semantic information
clustering
association
semantic network model

Matching Exercise

Match the appropriate term / name with its definition or description.

1. _____ Rehearsal that involves focusing on the meaning of information to help encode and transfer it to long-term memory.

2. _____ A model that describes units of information in long-term memory as being organized in a complex network of associations.

3. _____ The process of recovering information stored in memory so that we are consciously aware of it.

4. _____ Organizing items into related groups during recall from long-term memory.

5. _____ American psychologist who has conducted extensive research on the memory distortions that can occur in eyewitness testimony.

6. _____ The mental representation, or pictures, especially vivid ones, used to enhance encoding.

7. _____ The active stage of memory in which information is stored for about thirty seconds.

8. _____ Long-term memory of personally experienced events; also called autobiographical memory.

9. _____ The process of transforming information into a form that can be entered and retained by the memory system.

10. _____ A model describing memory as consisting of three distinct stages: sensory memory, short-term memory, and long-term memory.

11. _____ The mental processes that enable us to retain and use information over time.

12. _____ Long-term memory of how to perform different skills, operations, and actions.

True/False Test

Indicate whether each statement is true or false by placing T or F in the blank space next to each item.

1. ____ George Sperling is the American psychologist who identified the duration of visual sensory memory in a series of classic experiments in 1960.

2. ____ Auditory sensory memory is sometimes referred to as iconic memory because it is a brief memory of an image, or icon.

3. ____ Creating a simple story to help remember information by applying information to oneself is called the self-reference effect.

4. ____ Semantic information is the general knowledge of facts, names, and concepts stored in long-term memory.

5. ____ When people are presented with the stimulus word *salt*, they frequently respond with the word *pepper*, and this suggests that there is some logical *association* between bits of information in long-term memory.

6. ____ Storage is the process of transforming information into a form that can be entered and retained by the memory system.

7. ____ Sensory memory is the stage of memory that registers information from the environment and holds it for a very brief period of time.

8. ____ Maintenance rehearsal involves focusing on the meaning of information to help people encode and transfer it to long-term memory.

9. ____ Chunking refers to the organization of items into related groups during recall from long-term memory.

10. ____ Visual sensory memory is sometimes referred to as echoic memory, meaning a brief memory that is like an echo.

11. ____ Long-term memory is the stage of memory that represents the long-term storage of information.

Check your answers and review any areas of weakness before going on to the next section.

Retrieval: Getting Information from Long-Term Memory
Learning Objectives

When you have finished studying this section of the chapter, you should be able to:

1. Define *retrieval* and describe how retrieval cues work.

2. Explain what the tip-of-the-tongue (TOT) experience tells us about the nature of memory.

3. Describe how retrieval is tested and explain what the serial position effect is.

4. List the different forms that the encoding specificity principle takes and give examples that illustrate each.

5. Specify the role distinctiveness plays in retrieval and evaluate the accuracy of flashbulb memories.

*Read the section "Retrieval: Getting Information from Long-Term Memory" and **write** your answers to the following:*

1. (a) Retrieval refers to the process of accessing, or retrieving, stored information, and in many instances, the ability to retrieve stored memories hinges on having an appropriate _____ .

   (b) The inability to recall long-term memories because of inadequate or missing retrieval cues is referred to as

   _____ .

2. The TOT experience refers to the inability to get at a bit of information that you're absolutely certain is stored in your memory; it illustrates several aspects of the retrieval process:

   (a) Retrieving information is not an

   _____ process.

   (b) In many instances, information is stored in memory but not accessible without the right

   _____ .

   (c) Information stored in memory is

   _____ and connected in relatively logical ways.

3. (a) _____ involves producing information using no retrieval cues and is the memory measure used on essay tests.

   (b) _____ involves remembering an item of information in response to a retrieval cue and is the memory measure used on matching questions and fill-in-the-blank tests.

   (c) _____ involves identifying the correct information out of several possible choices, and multiple-choice tests are one example of this type of retrieval .

   (d) From a student's point of view

   _____ and

   _____ tests are probably best because they provide retrieval cues that help access stored information.

4. (a) The serial position effect refers to the tendency to retrieve information more easily from the _____ and the _____ of a list rather than the

   _____ .

   (b) The serial position effect is especially prominent when you have to engage in

   _____ , that is, remembering a list of items in their original order.

   (c) The tendency to recall the first items in a list is called the _____ effect, whereas the tendency to recall the final items in a list is called the

   _____ effect.

5. The encoding specificity principle, which states that re-creating the original conditions improves retrieval effectiveness, can take several forms:

   (a) The _____ is the tendency to remember information more easily when the retrieval occurs in the same setting in which the information was originally learned.

   (b) _____

   involves better recall of information when the particular mental or pharmacological state of learning and retrieval match.

   (c) _____

   occurs when information encoded in a certain emotional state is most retrievable when in the same emotional state.

   (d) _____ refers to the idea that a given mood tends to evoke memories that are consistent with that mood; when in a _____ mood, you're more likely to recall positive memories; when in a _____ mood, you're more likely to recall negative or unpleasant memories.

6. (a) Encoded information representing a unique, different, or unusual event is easier to recall than routine events because such memories are said to be characterized by a high degree of _____ .

(b) The recall of very specific images or details surrounding a significant, rare, vivid, or personally meaningful event is called a(n) _____ memory, and although there is usually a high level of _____ in the accuracy of these memories, research suggests that they are no better recalled than everyday memories.

Reconstructing Memories: Sources of Potential Errors

Learning Objectives

When you have finished studying this section of the chapter, you should be able to:

1. Explain how retrieval involves the active reconstruction of memories.

2. Define the term *schemas* and describe how they contribute to memory distortions.

3. Describe the nature of false memories and explain how source confusion plays a part in their construction.

4. List the factors that can reduce the accuracy of eyewitness testimony and describe how the misinformation effect works in memory distortion.

5. State what can be concluded about the reliability of memory.

Read the section "Reconstructing Memories: Sources of Potential Errors" and **write** *your answers to the following:*

1. (a) Every new memory formed is not simply recorded, but actively _____ .

(b) To form a new memory, you actively organize and encode information; later, when retrieval is attempted, details from memory are actively _____ , or rebuilt.

(c) In the process of _____ and _____ a memory, two general factors can contribute to errors and distortions: the information stored before the memory occurs and the information acquired after the memory occurs.

2. (a) Organized clusters of knowledge and information about particular topics are called _____ ; these can be useful in forming new memories but can also contribute to memory distortions.

(b) Research shows how _____ we already hold can influence what we remember, that once a memory is formed it has the potential to be _____ by new information, and that it is very easy for memories to become _____ .

3. (a) A _____ memory is a distorted or inaccurate memory that feels completely real and is often accompanied by all the emotional impact of a real memory.

(b) Confusion occurs when the true source of a memory is forgotten, and this is a common cause of _____ memories.

(c) _____ refers to evidence given by people who were present and observed a crime or some other event taking place; this evidence is based on recall of what happened.

(d) Research clearly shows that _____ is subject to memory distortion, and this can have serious implications in real life.

(e) A phenomenon in which people's existing memories can be altered by exposing them to misleading information is called the _____ ; this can be a source of memory distortion when people are asked to recall the original events or information.

(f) According to one psychologist, the single largest factor leading to the conviction of innocent people in over 1,000 cases examined was _____ error.

4. (a) Despite the ways in which memory can be distorted, people's memories tend to be _____ for overall details; when memory distortions do occur, they usually involve _____ bits of information or specific details.

5. Read the following and write the correct term in the space provided:

   (a) When Cathy feels depressed, she remembers certain sad events in her childhood that she never thinks about otherwise. Cathy is experiencing the effects of _____ .

   (b) Hendrik has a vivid memory of exactly what he was doing when President Bush declared war on Iraq. This example illustrates a _____ memory.

   (c) Although elderly Mrs. Haggerty has been experiencing some memory problems recently, she always has complete answers to questions asked by her family but appears to be filling in blanks with logical, though often incorrect, information. This example illustrates the _____ nature of memory.

   (d) Jessie cannot remember the newer name of the small Central American country that was formerly called British Honduras until she is told it starts with the letter B. The letter B acts as a _____ for the name *Belize*.

   (e) The progress tests in this study guide utilize which test or measure of memory?

   _____

   (f) When Mr. Melvin questioned a witness, he deliberately kept referring to the murder weapon as large scissors instead of garden shears. When the witness was later asked to identify the garden shears as the murder weapon, he appeared slightly confused and said he believed the weapon was a large pair of scissors. Mr. Melvin has successfully used the _____ .

   (g) Researchers had a group of subjects memorize long lists of words in a room full of fresh flowers. Later half the subjects were tested in the same room and half were tested in a room with no flowers. Those tested in the same room recalled significantly more than those in the different room. This is one form of the _____ principle called the _____ .

Graphic Organizer 1

Read the definitions and fill in the correct term next to the appropriate number in the puzzle below (items 1–6). When you have finished, the letters in the boxes will spell a significant memory term. Write out the definition of this term (item 7).

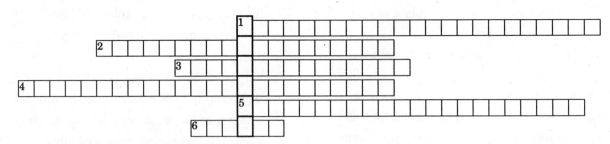

1. An encoding specificity phenomenon in which information that is learned in a particular mental state is more likely to be recalled while the person is in the same state.

2. The inability to recall long-term memories because of inadequate or missing retrieval cues.

3. The recall of very specific images or details surrounding a vivid, rare, or significant personal event.

4. A memory phenomenon that involves the sensation of knowing that specific information is stored in long-term memory but being temporarily unable to retrieve it.

5. An encoding specificity phenomenon in which information encoded in a certain emotional state is most retrievable when the person is in the same emotional state.

6. A test of long-term memory that involves retrieving information without the aid of retrieval cues.

7. Write out the definition of the memory term:

_____

_____

_____

Review of Key Terms 2

retrieval	primacy effect
retrieval cue	recency effect
retrieval cue failure	encoding specificity
tip-of-the-tongue (TOT)	principle
experience	context effect
recall	state-dependent
cued recall	retrieval
recognition	mood-dependent
serial position effect	retrieval
serial recall	mood congruence

distinctiveness	source confusion
flashbulb memory	eyewitness testimony
schema	misinformation effect
false memory	

Matching Exercise

Match the appropriate term with its definition or description.

1. _____ The tendency to recover information more easily when the retrieval occurs in the same setting as the original learning of the information.

2. _____ The process of accessing stored information.

3. _____ An organized cluster of information about a particular topic.

4. _____ The tendency to remember items at the beginning and end of a list better than items in the middle.

5. _____ A memory distortion that occurs when the true source of the memory is forgotten.

6. _____ A test of long-term memory that involves remembering an item of information in response to a retrieval cue.

7. _____ A memory distortion phenomenon in which people's existing memories can be altered by exposing them to misleading information.

8. _____ A clue, prompt, or hint that helps trigger recall of a given piece of information stored in long-term memory.

9. _____ An encoding specificity phenomenon in which a given mood tends to evoke memories that are consistent with that mood.

10. _____ The principle that when the conditions of information retrieval are similar to the conditions of information encoding, retrieval is more likely to be successful.

11. _____ The recall of very specific images or details surrounding a vivid, rare, or significant personal event.

12. _____ A distorted or inaccurate memory that feels completely real and is often accompanied by all the emotional impact of a real memory.

True/False Test

Indicate whether each statement is true or false by placing T or F in the blank space next to each item.

1. ____ The primacy effect refers to the tendency to recall the final items in a list during serial recall.

2. ____ Eyewitness testimony is the most reliable and accurate source of information about events that people have observed and almost always results in the conviction of only the guilty people.

3. ____ State-dependent retrieval is an encoding specificity phenomenon in which information that is learned in a particular mental state is more likely to be recalled while the person is in the same mental state.

4. ____ A test of long-term memory that involves retrieving information without the aid of retrieval cues is called recall, or free recall.

5. ____ The tip-of-the-tongue (TOT) experience involves the sensation of knowing that specific information is stored in long-term memory but being temporarily unable to retrieve it.

6. ____ Serial recall refers to remembering a list of items in their original order.

7. ____ When the encoded information represents a unique, different, or unusual memory, it is said to be characterized by a high degree of distinctiveness.

8. ____ Mood-dependent retrieval is an encoding specificity phenomenon in which a given mood tends to evoke memories that are consistent with that mood.

9. ____ The inability to recall long-term memories because of inadequate or missing retrieval cues is called retrieval cue failure.

10. ____ The recency effect refers to the tendency to recall the first items in a list during serial recall.

11. ____ Recognition refers to a test of long-term memory that involves identifying correct information out of several possible choices.

> Check your answers and review any areas of weakness before going on to the next section.

Forgetting: You *Forgot* the Plane Tickets?!

Learning Objectives

When you have finished studying this section of the chapter, you should be able to:

1. Define *forgetting* and describe its function in everyday life.

2. Name the psychologist who originated the scientific study of forgetting and explain the forgetting curve and why nonsense syllables were used.

3. Describe the role of encoding failure in forgetting and distinguish between proactive and retroactive interference.

4. Explain motivated forgetting and decay and list the mechanisms involved in each.

Read the section "Forgetting: You Forgot *the Plane Tickets?!" and* **write** *your answers to the following:*

1. (a) _____ is the inability to recall information that was previously available and is common in everyday life.

   (b) From the standpoint of a person's

   _____ , it is

   probably beneficial to _____ the

   details of unpleasant memories, such as past

   failures, social embarrassments, and unhap-

   py relationships.

2. (a) Hermann Ebbinghaus began the

   _____ of forgetting over a

   century ago.

(b) Ebbinghaus used _____
so that he could be sure that he was studying memory and forgetting of completely
new material, rather than information that
had preexisting associations in his memory.

(c) Ebbinghaus plotted his results on a line
graph, which he called the
_____ , and this reveals
two distinct patterns in the relationship
between _____ and the passage
of time.

(d) Much of what we _____ is lost
relatively soon after we learn it; if we learn
something in a matter of minutes on one
occasion, forgetting will occur in a
_____ ; if we spend many
sessions over many weeks or months, most
forgetting will be during the first
_____ after learning the
information.

(e) The amount of forgetting eventually
_____ , and information
that is not quickly forgotten seems to be
remarkably stable in memory over long
periods of time.

3. Researchers have identified four potential causes of forgetting:

(a) _____ refers to the inabil-
ity to recall specific information because of
insufficient encoding for storage in long-
term memory and explains why, for example, you forget a person's name five minutes
after being introduced.

(b) According to the _____ theory,
forgetting is caused by one memory compet-

ing with or replacing another memory, with
similarity between the two memories being
the critical factor.

(c) _____
occurs when a new memory
_____ with remembering an old
memory; the misinformation effect may be a
function of this type of forgetting.

(d) _____
occurs when an old memory
_____ with a new memory, for
example, when you refer to your current
partner by a previous partner's name.

(e) Motivated forgetting (a Freudian idea)
refers to the idea that we forget because we
are motivated to forget, usually because a
memory is _____ or
_____ .

(f) There are two forms of motivated forgetting:
_____ , in which a person
makes a deliberate, conscious effort to forget
information, and _____ , which
is forgetting that occurs unconsciously, with
all awareness of an event or experience
blocked from conscious awareness.

(g) According to _____ theory, we
forget memories because we don't use them
and they fade away over time as a matter of
normal brain processes; when a new memory is formed, it creates a
_____ , which is a change
in brain structure or chemistry that, if not
used, gets eroded by normal metabolic brain
processes.

Graphic Organizer 2

Use the following to review forgetting due to interference in the test phase. Write in the type of *interference that is responsible for forgetting in the test phase.*

Memorizing Phase	Test Phase	Type of Interference
1. Learn A first; later learn B	Test A	
2. Learn A first; later learn B	Test B	

The Search for the Biological Basis of Memory

Learning Objectives

When you have finished studying this section of the chapter, you should be able to:

1. Name the key people who speculated about and/or conducted research into the physical basis of memory.
2. Explain how memories are both localized and distributed in the brain.
3. Discuss the role of neurons in long-term memory.
4. Describe how case studies of people with amnesia, or severe memory loss, have provided important insights into the brain structures involved in memory.
5. Define both *retrograde* and *anterograde amnesia* and specify what has been learned from case studies of individuals with these memory disorders.
6. Explain what is meant by consolidation and describe the role played by the hippocampus and amygdala in normal memory.

Read the section "The Search for the Biological Basis of Memory" and **write** *your answers to the following:*

1. (a) _____ speculated that the memory involved in learning a classically conditioned response would ultimately be explained as a matter of changes in the brain, but it was _____

who set out in the 1920s to find experimental evidence to support this idea.

(b) The brain changes associated with the formation of a long-term memory and whose theoretical existence suggests localization of a memory in a specific brain area are called

_____ , or engrams.

(c) The search for the engram led to the conclusion that memories are not localized in specific locations but are _____ , or stored, throughout the brain, but recent research by _____ has shown that some memories seem to be localized at specific spots in the brain.

(d) Research on memory and the brain suggests that memories have the potential to be both

_____ and _____ , with very simple memories being the former and more complex memories the latter.

2. (a) The notion of a memory _____ suggests that some change must occur in the workings of the brain when a new long-term memory is stored.

(b) Research has shown that both the

_____ and _____ of the neurons in the brain change when a new memory is acquired and that these changes create a memory circuit.

(c) Each time a memory is recalled, the neurons in the circuit are activated, the communication links are strengthened, and the memory becomes established as a(n) _____ memory.

3. (a) Amnesia is the technical term for severe _____ and two types have been identified, retrograde and anterograde.

(b) People who suffer from retrograde amnesia are unable to remember some or all of their _____ , especially _____ memories for recent events.

(c) The process of setting a new memory permanently in the brain is called memory _____ , and if disrupted before the process is complete, a long-term memory is vulnerable and may be lost.

(d) Anterograde amnesia is the inability to _____ .

(e) Case studies of people with brain damage suggest the _____ is not involved in most short-term memory tasks or in the storage or retrieval of long-term memories, but instead the critical role it plays seems to be the encoding and transfer of new memories from short-term to long-term memory.

(f) Destruction of the _____ does not affect the formation of procedural memories but is critical in the formation of new episodic memories.

(g) The _____ seems to be responsible for associating memories that involve different senses and also for the encoding of emotional qualities associated with particular memories, such as fear or anger.

4. Read the following and write the correct term in the space provided:

(a) Adam could not remember his new phone number when he first moved and kept recalling his old phone number instead.

Adam's inability to remember his new number is due to _____ interference.

(b) At a recent orientation meeting Jeremy was introduced to five of the directors, and much to his embarrassment, after a short while he could not remember their names. Jeremy's memory lapse is probably due to _____ .

(c) Later that night Jeremy was thinking about his embarrassment at the meeting and decided that because it was normal to forget names under the circumstance, he was just not going to think about it any more. Jeremy is using a form of motivated forgetting called _____ .

(d) Bruno was knocked out in his last boxing match and he cannot remember anything about the fight or events that happened before the bout. Bruno is most likely suffering from a form of amnesia called _____ amnesia.

(e) Mr. Henry, who had his hippocampus removed during a recent brain operation, is most likely to have trouble forming _____ memories.

(f) Jackson has just finished a course in Spanish and is experiencing problems in remembering the Italian he learned last semester. Jackson's memory problem is a result of _____ .

Review of Key Terms and Key Names 3

forgetting
Hermann Ebbinghaus
nonsense syllable
forgetting curve
encoding failure
interference theory
retroactive interference
proactive interference
motivated forgetting
suppression
repression
decay theory

memory trace
engram
Karl Lashley
Richard F. Thompson
amnesia
retrograde amnesia
memory consolidation
anterograde amnesia
hippocampus
amygdala
cryptomnesia

Matching Exercise

Match the appropriate term/name with its definition or description.

1. _____ Motivated forgetting that occurs consciously.

2. _____ Loss of memory caused by the inability to store new memories.

3. _____ The brain changes associated with a particular stored memory.

4. _____ Severe memory loss.

5. _____ American psychologist and neuroscientist who conducted extensive research on the neurobiological foundations of learning and memory.

6. _____ The inability to recall information that was previously available.

7. _____ The view that forgetting is due to normal metabolic processes that occur in the brain over time.

8. _____ Motivated forgetting that occurs unconsciously.

9. _____ The theory that forgetting is caused by one memory competing with or replacing another.

10. _____ German psychologist who originated the scientific study of forgetting; plotted the first "forgetting curve," which describes the basic pattern of forgetting learned information over time.

11. _____ The inability to recall specific information because of insufficient encoding for storage in long-term memory.

12. _____ A memory distortion phenomenon in which "hidden," or unremembered, memory becomes the basis for a seemingly "new" memory.

True/False Test

Indicate whether each item is true or false by placing T or F in the space next to each item.

1. ____ Karl Lashley was the American physiological psychologist who attempted to find the specific brain location of particular memories.

2. ____ Retroactive interference is forgetting in which an old memory interferes with remembering a new memory.

3. ____ The theory that forgetting occurs because an undesired memory is held back from awareness is called motivated forgetting.

4. ____ Memory consolidation is the gradual, physical process of converting new long-term memories to stable, enduring long-term memory codes.

5. ____ Retrograde amnesia is a loss of memory caused by the inability to store new memories.

6. ____ Damage to or destruction of the hippocampus can affect the ability to transfer short-term memories into long-term memories.

7. ____ Hermann Ebbinghaus used nonsense syllables to study the memory and forgetting of completely new material rather than information that had preexisting associations in memory.

8. ____ The engram is the name given to the memory trace in the brain associated with the formation of long-term memories.

9. ____ Proactive interference is forgetting in which a new memory interferes with remembering an old memory.

10. ____ Damage to or destruction of the amygdala will make monkeys lose their normal fear of snakes and other natural predators.

11. ____ The forgetting curve reveals two distinct patterns in the relationship between forgetting and the passage of time; much of what is learned is forgotten relatively quickly and the amount of forgetting eventually levels off.

> Check your answers and review any areas of weakness before going on to the next section.

Something to Think About

1. You may have met that rare person who seems to have a perfect memory and rarely forgets anything. Most of us, however, are not like that, and we struggle to learn and retain at least some of the vast amount of material we are constantly exposed to in the "information age." If someone were to ask you what you have learned about memory and forgetting that could help them, what would you say?

2. Suppose a friend of yours is falsely identified as being the culprit in a grocery store hold-up and comes to you for help. Based on what you know about eyewitness testimony and related phenomena, what advice would you give him?

> Check your answers and review any areas of weakness before doing the progress tests.

Progress Test 1

Review the complete chapter (including Concept Reviews and the boxed inserts), review all your study notes, and then test yourself on the following progress test. Check your answers. If you make a mistake, review your notes and the relevant section of the study guide, and, if necessary, go back and read the appropriate part of your textbook.

1. In preparation for his biology exam, Lionel repeats the list of terms and their definitions over and over. Lionel's rehearsal strategy involves the fundamental memory process of
   (a) encoding   (c) retrieval
   (b) storage   (d) wasting his time

2. Michael's aggressive, arrogant behavior and indifferent attitude have resulted in the break-up of many relationships, and he is now contemplating getting married for the third time. Michael is confident that this time it will work and that his previous relationship problems were never his fault. Michael is either actively _____ or unconsciously _____ memory of his own behavior.
   (a) suppressing; repressing
   (b) repressing; suppressing
   (c) consolidating; schematizing
   (d) schematizing; consolidating

3. Five-year-old Betty can recite the alphabet perfectly every time she is asked to do so. Betty's ability to do this involves the fundamental memory process of
   (a) repression   (c) retrograde amnesia
   (b) retrieval   (d) encoding

4. Acquisition is to retention as _____ is to _____ .
   (a) retrograde; retroactive
   (b) procedural; episodic
   (c) encoding; storage
   (d) storage; retrieval

5. Dirk can remember in vivid detail where he was and what he was doing when he heard about the Space Shuttle *Challenger* exploding during take-off. Dirk's flashbulb memory is stored in his
   (a) iconic memory   (c) long-term memory
   (b) short-term memory (d) echoic memory

6. Whenever Killian is introduced to someone, he usually remembers the name by repeating it over and over to himself. Killian is using a memory strategy called
   (a) rehearsal
   (b) retroactive interference
   (c) repression
   (d) chunking

7. One conclusion that can be drawn from Ebbinghaus's work on forgetting is that
   (a) we can remember only about seven nonsense syllable at one time
   (b) most of what we forget when we memorize new information occurs relatively soon after we learn it
   (c) the duration of visual sensory memory is less than half a second
   (d) the capacity of long-term memory is large but fleeting

8. Mrs. Carson was very busy when she phoned her husband and quickly listed the 12 items she wanted him to pick up at the store. After she hung up, Mr. Carson attempted to write down the items. It is very likely that he will
   (a) forget the items in the middle
   (b) remember only the middle and the last items
   (c) remember only the first and middle items
   (d) forget the first and last items and remember the items in the middle

9. Iladana was given a list of twenty-five random words to remember. In recalling the words, she remembered groups of related words, such as apple, pear, banana, and orange. This pattern of recall illustrates
   (a) the serial position effect
   (b) clustering
   (c) repression
   (d) cryptomnesia

10. One reason Charlie finds it easier to remember a list of words that includes *automobile, cigarettes, encyclopedia, lampshade, geranium,* and *seashell* compared to a list of the same length that includes *philosophy, processes, justice, abstraction, fundamental,* and *inherent* is that with the first list it is easier to use
    (a) echoic processing
    (b) maintenance rehearsal
    (c) procedural memory
    (d) visual imagery

11. Karen can remember very clearly when and where she met Jim and how she felt when he first spoke to her. This information stored in Karen's long-term memory is called

    (a) procedural information
    (b) episodic information
    (c) semantic information
    (d) retroactive information

12. When Kirk was given a long list of items to memorize, he found it easier to remember them when he regrouped all the items according to whether they were vegetables, furniture, animals, etc. Kirk is using a memory aid called

    (a) the serial position effect
    (b) the self-referencing technique
    (c) the context effect
    (d) chunking

13. When she first transferred from a college to a university, Kelly had trouble remembering her new student number; she would always recall her old college student number instead. Kelly's memory problem is an example of

    (a) retrograde amnesia
    (b) proactive interference
    (c) anterograde amnesia
    (d) retroactive interference

14. Mrs. Kahn experienced no trouble skiing despite the fact that she had not been on the slopes for almost fifteen years. Mrs. Kahn's current skiing ability is probably due to _____ information stored in her long-term memory.

    (a) procedural
    (b) episodic
    (c) semantic
    (d) repressed

15. After his hippocampus was destroyed by a tumor, it is very likely that Mr. Locke will experience problems

    (a) forming procedural memories
    (b) recognizing common objects
    (c) correctly repeating items over and over
    (d) transferring short-term memories into long-term memory

16. Mr. Locke (in the above example) is likely to be classified as suffering from

    (a) retrograde amnesia
    (b) anterograde amnesia
    (c) retrieval cue failure
    (d) false-memory syndrome

17. Lisa took some strong painkillers while she was studying for her exam; the following week she took the same pills before the exam because she wanted to be in the same emotional state on both occasions. Lisa appears to believe in

    (a) maintenance rehearsal
    (b) elaborative rehearsal
    (c) mood-dependent retrieval
    (d) source confusion

18. According to the Application section, one way to improve memory is to learn the material over several sessions rather than cramming in one long session. This method of study is called

    (a) distributed practice
    (b) massed practice
    (c) maintenance rehearsal
    (d) serial position learning

19. According to the Culture and Human Behavior Box, declines in memory ability

    (a) are due entirely to a natural, biological aging process
    (b) may be influenced by cultural expectations about aging and memory abilities
    (c) are mainly the function of disease processes such as Alzheimer's disease
    (d) are most evident in members of the deaf culture who communicate with American Sign Language

20. According to the Critical Thinking Box, which of the following is true?

    (a) Physical and sexual abuse of children does happen.
    (b) Memories of childhood abuse can become repressed and surface later in life.
    (c) Repressed memories that have been recovered in therapy need to be regarded with caution.
    (d) The high level of confidence someone has in a memory is no guarantee that the memory is accurate.
    (e) All of the above.

Progress Test 2

After you have checked your understanding of the material in Progress Test 1 and have done a complete chapter review with special focus on any areas of weakness, you are ready to assess your knowledge in Progress Test 2. Check your answers. If you make a mistake, review your notes, the relevant section of the study guide, and, if necessary, the appropriate part of your textbook.

1. When Gary was preparing for an exam, he tried a number of different strategies to give the material meaning. Gary is using _____ to help him remember the information.
   (a) elaborative rehearsal
   (b) maintenance rehearsal
   (c) retroactive interference
   (d) proactive interference

2. Shortly after he finished reading an exciting novel, Sean fell down the stairs and suffered a concussion and now has no recall of ever having read the novel. Sean's memory problem is probably the result of
   (a) retrieval cue failure
   (b) encoding failure
   (c) disruption of memory consolidation
   (d) mood incongruence

3. Sean (in the above example) is most likely to be classified as suffering from
   (a) anterograde amnesia
   (b) proactive forgetting
   (c) retrograde amnesia
   (d) retroactive forgetting

4. Richard F. Thompson classically conditioned rabbits to eyeblink to a tone and later found that there was change in brain activity in the rabbits' cerebellums. This result suggests that long-term memories
   (a) are stored in a very localized region of the brain
   (b) are distributed and stored across multiple brain locations
   (c) have no biological or physical basis in the brain
   (d) are very vulnerable if they are not given enough time to consolidate

5. Dr. Dement believes that forgetting is due to normal metabolic processes in the brain eroding memory traces. Dr. Dement supports the
   (a) interference theory
   (b) motivated forgetting theory
   (c) semantic network model
   (d) decay theory

6. When Manfred, who used to be a compulsive gambler, is asked if he won much when he gambled, he recalls losing much less money than was actually the case. Manfred's memory failure best illustrates
   (a) motivated forgetting
   (b) retrieval cue failure
   (c) retroactive interference
   (d) proactive interference

7. Henry has memorized a new personal identity code he was given by security and now he can't remember his old personal identity code. Henry is experiencing the effects of
   (a) mood congruence
   (b) source confusion
   (c) proactive interference
   (d) retroactive interference

8. Jeffery, who was an eyewitness to a robbery, initially thought the robber looked like a female. When he was questioned by a police detective, it was suggested to him many times that the robber was probably a man with long hair. Later, when he was giving testimony on the witness stand, Jeffery was quite sure that it was a man who robbed the store. This example illustrates
   (a) state-dependent memory
   (b) mood congruence
   (c) a flashbulb memory
   (d) the misinformation effect

9. State-dependent memory is to _____ as mood-dependent memory is to
   _____ .
   (a) a pharmacological state; an emotional state
   (b) retroactive interference; proactive interference
   (c) an emotional state; a pharmacological state
   (d) proactive interference; retroactive interference

10. The smell of cherry blossoms awakened in Mrs. Yamomoto vivid memories of her childhood in Osaka. The aroma of the blossoms apparently acted as an effective
    (a) schema   (c) flashbulb cue
    (b) echoic cue   (d) retrieval cue

11. During a discussion about old movies, Grace could not bring to mind the name of the actor who played the sidekick of Sidney Greenstreet in *The Maltese Falcon*, despite the fact that she felt she knew the name and had, in fact, talked about his role in the movie on other occasions. Grace is experiencing

(a) the serial position effect
(b) encoding failure
(c) the tip-of-the-tongue (TOT) phenomenon
(d) anterograde amnesia

12. Multiple-choice exam questions measure
_____ ; short essay questions measure _____ .
(a) recall; recognition
(b) recognition; recall
(c) short-term memory; long-term memory
(d) long-term memory; short-term memory

13. Neddy cannot accurately remember the order of the numbers on the small calculator he has owned for ten years and uses quite frequently. Neddy's problem in recall is most likely a function of
(a) retrieval cue failure
(b) proactive interference
(c) encoding failure
(d) retroactive interference

14. Most subjects in an experiment responded with *sky* and *grass* to the stimulus words *blue* and *green*. Results such as these support
(a) the semantic network model
(b) decay theory
(c) motivated forgetting theory
(d) interference theory

15. Emelia can quite easily list all the fifty states of the United States and the ten provinces and two territories of Canada. This type of information in long-term memory is called _____ information.
(a) procedural   (c) semantic
(b) episodic   (d) state-dependent

16. Harold, who was in the kitchen, asked Jane, who was reading a book in the living room, whether she wanted a diet or a regular soft drink. Jane replied, "What did you say?" but before Harold could respond, Jane said, "Make it a regular Coke, please." This example illustrates
(a) iconic memory
(b) repression
(c) echoic memory
(d) a flashbulb memory

17. The _____ is to encoding the emotional aspects of memory as the _____ is to encoding and transferring new information from STM to LTM.
(a) hippocampus; amygdala
(b) serial position effect; context effect
(c) amygdala; hippocampus
(d) misinformation effect; TOT phenomenon

18. According to the Critical Thinking Box, cryptomnesia refers to
(a) memories of being buried in a mausoleum or crypt
(b) a memory distortion in which a seemingly "new" or "original" memory is actually based on an unrecalled previous memory
(c) loss of memory caused by the inability to store new memories
(d) severe memory loss following a near-death experience

19. The Application section lists a number of strategies that can be used to improve memory for important information. Which of the following is *not* one of those strategies?
(a) Use visual imagery.
(b) Organize the information.
(c) Counteract the serial position effect.
(d) Use contextual cues to jog memories.
(e) Always use massed practice, especially during all-night cramming sessions before a test.

20. According to the Critical Thinking Box, which of the following is true?
(a) There is ample scientific evidence that people can remember actual past lives.
(b) There is good reason to believe that many memories of past lives are examples of cryptomnesia.
(c) Most reincarnation memories can only be recovered by a skilled hypnotherapist.
(d) Most people cannot recall memories of past lives because of repression.

Answers

Introduction: Memory Processes and Stages

1. (a) acquire, retain; retrieve
   (b) encoding; storage; retrieval

2. (a) sensory; short-term; long-term
   (b) capacity; duration; function

3. (a) sensory
   (b) attention; short-term
   (c) short-term; thirty
   (d) short-term; long-term
   (e) long-term
   (f) sensory; short-term; long-term

4. (a) George Sperling
   (b) half a second; short-term
   (c) iconic; icon; echoic; echo
   (d) one-quarter; one-half; a few
   (e) store (register); continuous

5. (a) sensory; long-term
   (b) storage; conscious
   (c) thirty; rehearsed; rehearsal
   (d) seven; displace
   (e) chunking
   (f) chunking

6. (a) storage
   (b) lifetime; limitless
   (c) maintenance; meaning
   (d) self-reference; visual imagery

7. (a) procedural
   (b) episodic
   (c) semantic

8. (a) organized
   (b) clustering; association
   (c) semantic network
   (d) semantic network

9. (a) retrieval
   (b) encoding
   (c) elaborative
   (d) short-term; maintenance
   (e) chunking
   (f) procedural

Matching Exercise 1

1. elaborative rehearsal
2. semantic network model
3. retrieval
4. clustering
5. Elizabeth Loftus
6. visual imagery
7. short-term memory (working memory)

8. episodic information
9. encoding
10. stage model of memory
11. memory
12. procedural information

True/False Test 1

1. T	5. T	9. F
2. F	6. F	10. F
3. T	7. T	11. T
4. T	8. F	

Retrieval: Getting Information from Long-Term Memory

1. (a) retrieval cue
   (b) retrieval cue failure

2. (a) all-or-nothing
   (b) retrieval cue
   (c) organized

3. (a) recall
   (b) cued recall
   (c) recognition
   (d) cued-recall ; recognition

4. (a) beginning; end; middle
   (b) serial recall
   (c) primacy; recency

5. (a) context effect
   (b) state-dependent memory
   (c) mood-dependent memory
   (d) mood congruence; positive; blue (bad)

6. (a) distinctiveness
   (b) flashbulb; confidence

Reconstructing Memories: Sources of Potential Errors

1. (a) constructed
   (b) reconstructed
   (c) constructing; reconstructing

2. (a) schemas
   (b) schemas; changed; distorted

3. (a) false
   (b) false
   (c) eyewitness testimony
   (d) eyewitness testimony
   (e) misinformation effect
   (f) eyewitness

4. (a) accurate; limited

5. (a) mood congruence

(b) flashbulb
(c) reconstructive
(d) retrieval cue

(e) recognition
(f) misinformation effect
(g) encoding specificity; context effect

Graphic Organizer 1

¹S T A T E D E P E N D E N T R E T R I E V A L
²R E T R I E V A L C U E F A I L U R E
³F L A S H B U L B M E M O R Y .
⁴T I P O F T H E T O N G U E E X P E R I E N C E
⁵M O O D D E P E N D E N T R E T R I E V A L
⁶R E C A L L

7. Schema—an organized cluster of information about a particular topic

Matching Exercise 2

1. context effect
2. retrieval
3. schema
4. serial position effect
5. source confusion
6. cued recall
7. misinformation effect
8. retrieval cue
9. mood congruence
10. encoding specificity principle
11. flashbulb memory
12. false memory

True/False Test 2

1. F	5. T	9. T
2. F	6. T	10. F
3. T	7. T	11. T
4. T	8. F	

Forgetting: You *Forgot* the Plane Tickets?!

1. (a) forgetting
   (b) psychological well-being; forget
2. (a) scientific study
   (b) nonsense syllables
   (c) forgetting curve; forgetting
   (d) learn (memorize); matter of minutes; few months
   (e) levels off

3. (a) encoding failure
   (b) interference
   (c) retroactive interference; interferes
   (d) proactive interference; interferes
   (e) unpleasant; disturbing
   (f) suppression; repression
   (g) decay; memory trace

Graphic Organizer 2

1. retroactive interference
2. proactive interference

The Search for the Biological Basis of Memory

1. (a) Ivan Pavlov; Karl Lashley
   (b) memory traces
   (c) distributed; Richard F. Thompson
   (d) localized; distributed
2. (a) trace
   (b) structure; function
   (c) long-term
3. (a) memory loss
   (b) past memories; episodic
   (c) consolidation
   (d) form new memories
   (e) hippocampus
   (f) hippocampus
   (g) amygdala
4. (a) proactive
   (b) encoding failure
   (c) suppression
   (d) retrograde
   (e) long-term
   (f) retroactive interference

Matching Exercise 3

1. suppression
2. anterograde amnesia
3. memory trace
4. amnesia
5. Richard F. Thompson
6. forgetting
7. decay theory
8. repression
9. interference theory
10. Hermann Ebbinghaus
11. encoding failure
12. cryptomnesia

True/False Test 3

1. T	5. F	9. F
2. F	6. T	10. T
3. T	7. T	11. T
4. T	8. T	

Something to Think About

1. We are all vulnerable to forgetting and some- times the consequences can be serious. So what can we do to improve memory? Fortunately, there are a number of strategies that can help us remember important information. One of the things you might want to include in your answer, based on the material in the textbook, is a discussion of the fundamental processes of encoding, storage, and retrieval. The function, capacity, and duration of each of the three stages of memory are also relevant to your dis- cussion. Of course, no discussion of the topic of memory would be complete without mentioning Ebbinghaus's work on forgetting and the vari- ous theories of forgetting and what they have contributed to our understanding. Finally, the Application section lays out ten of the most important strategies that could help improve memory.

2. It is a real nightmare to contemplate the prospect of being falsely accused and having an eyewitness pointing at you and saying very con- fidently, "Yes, that is the person. There's no doubt about it, he did it!" What can be done in such a situation? If the defendant does not have an alibi, the jury is very likely to believe a con- fident eyewitness who stands up in court, under oath, and points a finger at the accused. The first thing to consider is getting an expert wit- ness, such as Elizabeth Loftus, to testify to the problems inherent in eyewitness testimony. Such testimony, based on scientific evidence, is difficult to refute. Other aspects of memory dis- tortion to be considered are source confusion, the personal schema of the eyewitness, the power of the misinformation effect, evidence related to the false-memory syndrome, and rele- vant aspects of the encoding specificity theory. If your friend cannot afford the testimony of an expert witness, then we suggest he try to edu- cate his defense lawyer about the relevant research findings in this important area of psy- chology.

Progress Test 1

1. a	8. a	15. d
2. a	9. b	16. b
3. b	10. d	17. c
4. c	11. b	18. a
5. c	12. d	19. c
6. a	13. b	20. e
7. b	14. a	

Progress Test 2

1. a	8. d	15. c
2. c	9. a	16. c
3. c	10. d	17. c
4. a	11. c	18. b
5. d	12. b	19. e
6. a	13. c	20. b
7. d	14. a	

Thinking, Language, and Intelligence

OVERVIEW Chapter 7 deals with thinking, language, and intelligence. Thinking involves manipulating internal, mental representations of information in order to draw inferences and conclusions. Research on concept formation, the different kinds of concepts, and mental imagery is presented. Problem solving is discussed and various problem-solving strategies and models are explored. Functional fixedness and mental sets are identified as two common obstacles to effective problem solving. Decision making is investigated next, and different decision-making models are discussed. The availability heuristic and the representativeness heuristic are often used to estimate the likelihood of events when making risky decisions,

Language is defined and various aspects of language and language use are presented. Animal communication and the controversial debate over whether or not animals are capable of language are explored. Recent studies indicate that bonobos and dolphins seem to have demonstrated an elementary grasp of the rules of syntax, but the issue is far from settled.

The issue of what intelligence is and how it is measured is discussed. The history of the development of the intelligence testing movement is explored, and the contributions of various psychologists are identified. The difference between aptitude tests and achievement tests is explained, and the requirements of standardization, reliability, and validity are described.

The debate over the nature of intelligence centers on two key issues: whether intelligence is a single factor or a cluster of different abilities and how narrowly intelligence should be defined. Four different psychologists are identified, and their respective views on these issues are presented. The question of what determines intelligence is addressed next, and the heredity-environment debate is examined in detail. How twin studies have been used to investigate the issue, the differences in average IQ scores between various groups, the implications of cross-cultural research, and the problem of culture bias in intelligence tests are all explored.

Introduction: Thinking, Language, and Intellegence

Learning Objectives

When you have finished studying this section of the chapter, you should be able to:

1. Define *cognition* and state how cognitive abilities are related to the concept of intelligence.

2. Define *thinking* and state how mental images and concepts are involved.

3. List some of the basic characteristics of mental images and explain how we manipulate them.

4. Define the term *concept* and differentiate between natural concepts and formal concepts.

5. Explain what a prototype is and describe the role prototypes play in concept formation.

*Read the section "Introduction: Thinking, Language, and Intelligence" and **write** your answers to the following:*

1. (a) Cognition is a general term that refers to the _____ activities involved in _____ , _____ , and _____ knowledge.

   (b) A key dimension of _____ is how we use our cognitive abilities and accumulated knowledge to think, solve problems, make decisions, and use language.

2. (a) In the most general sense, _____ is involved in all conscious _____ activity, such as acquiring new knowledge, remembering, planning ahead, or daydreaming.

   (b) More narrowly, thinking involves manipulating _____ of information in order to draw inferences and conclusions; it is often directed toward some goal, purpose, or conclusion.

3. (a) A mental representation of objects or events that are not physically present is called a(n) _____ .

   (b) Experiments on the cognitive ability to manipulate mental images by scanning them or rotating them seem to indicate that we treat them much like the _____ they represent, although they are not always exact duplicates of real images.

4. (a) A concept is a(n) _____ category formed to group objects, events, or situations that share similar features.

   (b) Using _____ makes it easier to communicate with others, remember information, and incorporate new information.

   (c) A mental category formed by learning the rules or features that define it is called a(n) _____ .

   (d) If the defining features, or _____ , are present, then the object _____ (is/is not) included as a member or example of that concept.

   (e) A _____ is one that is formed as a result of everyday experience rather than by logically determining whether an object or event fits a specific set of rules; these have "fuzzy boundaries" because the rules or attributes are not always sharply defined.

   (f) The best or most typical instance of a particular concept is called a(n) _____ ; the more closely an item matches the _____ , the more quickly it is identified as being an example of that concept.

Solving Problems and Making Decisions
Learning Objectives

When you have finished studying this section of the chapter, you should be able to:

1. Explain what is meant by problem solving and describe the strategies involved.

2. Define *trial and error, algorithms, heuristics,* and *insight* and provide examples that illustrate each.

3. List the advantages and disadvantages of each of the problem-solving strategies.

4. Explain how functional fixedness and a mental set interfere with problem solving.

5. List the various cognitive strategies used to make decisions.

6. Describe the single-feature model, the additive model, and the elimination by aspects model of decision making and provide examples that illustrate each.

7. Specify the conditions under which each strategy is most appropriate.

8. Explain how the availability and representative heuristics are used and list the potential problems associated with each.

*Read the section "Solving Problems and Making Decisions" and **write** your answers to the following:*

1. (a) Problem solving refers to _____ and _____ directed toward attaining a goal that is not readily available.

2. (a) The strategy of _____ involves actually trying a variety of solutions and eliminating those that don't work; this can be useful if there is a limited range of possible solutions.

(b) A(n) _____ is a procedure or method that, when followed step by step, always produces the correct solution; although guaranteed to eventually generate a solution, it is not always practical.

(c) A(n) _____ is a general rule-of-thumb strategy that may or may not work; although not guaranteed to solve a given problem, _____ can reduce the number of possible solutions so that a trial-and-error method can be employed to eventually arrive at the correct one.

(d) One common _____ that is often used to solve a problem such as writing a term paper is to break the problem down into a series of _____ ; a second is _____ from the end point and determining the steps necessary to reach the final goal.

(e) The solution to a problem may arrive as a sudden realization or flash of _____ that happens after you mull the problem over; this can occur when you recognize how the problem is similar to a previously solved problem or realize that an object can be used in a novel way.

(f) Increasingly, cognitive psychologists are investigating nonconscious mental processes, including unconscious problem solving, _____ and _____ .

(g) _____ refers to coming to a conclusion or making a judgment without conscious awareness of the thought processes involved and involves two stages, the _____ stage and the _____ stage.

3. (a) When we view objects as functioning only in the usual or customary way, we're engaging in a tendency called _____ , and this may prevent us from seeing the full range of ways in which an object can be used.

(b) Tendencies to persist in solving problems with solutions that have worked in the past are called _____ , and while these can sometimes suggest a useful heuristic, they can also prevent us from coming up with new, possibly simpler, more effective solutions.

4. (a) The decision-making process is often complicated by the fact that each option has several _____ or aspects that can be considered, and it is rare that one alternative is superior in every category.

(b) In order to simplify the choice among many alternatives, a decision-making strategy called the _____ model can be used; this is useful for minor decisions but can increase the riskiness of an important or complex decision.

(c) A better strategy for complex decisions is to systematically evaluate the important features of each option; one such decision-making model is called the _____ model.

(d) In the _____ model, you first generate a list of the important factors and rate each using an arbitrary scale; this strategy can often reveal the best overall choice.

(e) The _____ model proposes that we evaluate all alternatives, one characteristic at a time, starting with the most important feature and discarding each if it doesn't meet that criterion; as the range of possible choices is narrowed down, the remaining alternatives are compared, one feature at a time, until just one alternative is left.

(f) Good decision makers adapt their strategy to the demands of the specific situation; if there are just a few choices and features to compare, the _____ model is most appropriate, but if the decision is complex, with multiple features, begin by using the _____ model and use the _____ model to make the final decision.

5. Some decisions must be made under conditions of uncertainty in which we must estimate the probability of a particular event occurring; in such instances we tend to rely on two rule-of-thumb heuristics:

(a) The _____ heuristic is used to estimate the likelihood of an event based on how easily other instances of the event are available in memory; when readily recalled, we tend to consider the event more likely to occur.

(b) The _____ heuristic can produce inaccurate estimates; when a rare event makes a vivid impression on us, we may overestimate its likelihood.

(c) The key point is that the _____ (less/more) accurately our memory of an event reflects the actual frequency of the event, the _____ (less/more) accurate our estimate of the event's likelihood will be.

(d) When we estimate an event's likelihood by comparing how similar its essential features are to our prototype of the event, we are using the _____ heuristic.

(e) The _____ heuristic can produce faulty estimates if we fail to consider possible variations from the prototype or we fail to consider the approximate number of prototypes that actually exist.

6. Read the following and write in the correct term or word in the space provided:

(a) After a chimpanzee tries unsuccessfully to get bananas that are out of reach, she sits for a long time staring at them. Suddenly, she looks around the cage, picks up a stick, and uses it to pull the bananas to within her reach, something she has never done before. Her solution to the banana problem is probably the result of _____ .

(b) You learn that one of the Russell children is taking ballet classes and you immediately conclude that it is their one daughter rather than any of their three sons. You reached a possibly erroneous conclusion as a result of using the _____ .

(c) Dr. Mendleson studies how people manipulate mental representations to draw inferences and conclusions. Dr. Mendleson is most likely a(n) _____ psychologist interested in people's _____ ability.

(d) You are asked to decide which city is farther north, Edinburgh, Scotland, or Stockholm, Sweden, so you try to picture a map of Europe in your mind. You are using a(n) _____ .

(e) Marisa has learned the rules and features that define a square, a rectangle, and a right-angle triangle. Marisa has learned a(n) _____ concept.

(f) Henry had trouble recognizing that a seahorse was a fish because it did not closely resemble his _____ concept of fish.

(g) As eight-year old Natalie tries to answer the question "How many days are in the month of November?" she recites the rhyme "Thirty days hath September . . ." She is using a(n) _____ to arrive at the correct answer.

(h) Hilda is asked to complete the sequence "J, F, M, A, _, _, _, _, _, _, _, _." After trying a few different possibilities she comes up with the correct answer—M, J, J, A, S, O, N, D, (the first letter of the months of the year). It appears that Hilda is using a(n) _____ strategy to solve the problem.

(i) Andy is trying to decide which of two equally affordable and attractive cars to purchase, so he makes a list of the advantages and disadvantages of each using an arbitrary rating scale. Andy is using the _____ model to help him make a decision.

Review of Key Terms 1

cognition	working backward
thinking	insight
mental image	intuition
concepts	functional fixedness
formal concept	mental set
natural concept	single-feature model
prototype	additive model
problem solving	elimination by aspects
trial and error	model
algorithms	availability heuristic
heuristic	representativeness
subgoals	heuristic

Matching Exercise

Match the appropriate term with its definition or description.

1. _____ A decision-making model where all the alternatives are evaluated one characteristic at a time, starting with the most important feature and scratching each alternative off the list of possible choices if it fails to meet the criterion.

2. _____ The manipulation of mental representations of information in order to draw inferences or conclusions.

3. _____ The most typical instance of a particular concept.

4. _____ The sudden realization of how a problem can be solved.

5. _____ A decision-making strategy in which the choice among many alternatives is simplified by basing the decision on a single feature.

6. _____ A strategy in which the likelihood of an event is estimated by comparing how similar it is to the typical prototype of the event.

7. _____ Coming to a conclusion or making a judgment without conscious awareness of the thought processes involved.

8. _____ A mental category that is formed by learning the rules or features that define it.

9. _____ The mental activities involved in acquiring, retaining, and using knowledge.

10. _____ The mental categories of objects or ideas based on properties that they share.

11. _____ A problem-solving strategy that involves following a general rule of thumb to reduce the number of possible solutions.

True/False Test

Indicate whether each statement is true or false by placing T or F in the blank space next to each item.

1. ____ Working backward is a common heuristic used to break a problem down into a series of smaller problems, and as each subproblem is solved, you get closer to solving the larger problem.

2. ____ A mental representation of objects or events that are not physically present is called a mental image.

3. ____ Problem solving is thinking and behavior directed toward attaining a goal that is not readily available.

4. ____ The tendency to persist in solving problems with solutions that have worked in the past is called functional fixedness.

5. ____ The additive model of decision making involves generating a list of factors that are most important, then using an arbitrary rating scale to rate each alternative on each factor, and finally adding these together for comparison purposes.

6. ___ The availability heuristic is a strategy in which the likelihood of an event is estimated on the basis of how easily other instances of the event are available in memory.

7. ___ A natural concept is a mental category that is formed as a result of everyday experience.

8. ___ A useful heuristic in which you start at the end point and determine the steps necessary to reach your goal uses the analysis of subgoals.

9. ___ A mental set is a tendency to view objects as functioning only in their usual or customary manner.

10. ___ A problem-solving strategy that involves following a specific rule, procedure, or method that inevitably produces the correct solution is referred to as an algorithm.

11. ___ Trial and error is a problem-solving strategy that involves attempting different solutions and eliminating those that do not work.

> Check your answers and review any areas of weakness before going on to the next section.

Language and Thought
Learning Objectives

When you have finished studying this section of the chapter, you should be able to:

1. Define *language* and list the five most important characteristics of language.

2. Describe the relationship between language and thinking.

3. Present evidence for and against the proposition that animals can learn language.

Read the section "Language and Thought" and **write** *your answers to the following:*

1. (a) The primary function of language is to

    _____ .

   (b) Language is a system for combining arbitrary _____ to produce an infinite number of meaningful

    _____ .

2. (a) To express meaningful information in a way that can be understood by others, language

requires the use of _____ .

   (b) For the vast majority of words the connection between the symbols and the meanings is completely _____ ; as a result language is tremendously flexible.

   (c) An important characteristic of language is that the _____ of the symbols is shared by others who speak the same language.

   (d) Language is a system; it is highly structured and follows specific rules for combining words called _____ .

   (e) Language is creative or

    _____ ; an infinite number of new and different phrases and sentences can be created or

    _____ .

   (f) A characteristic of language, the ability to communicate meaningfully about ideas, objects, and activities that are not physically present, is called _____ .

3. (a) All your _____ abilities are involved in understanding and producing language.

   (b) Language can affect our thoughts by influencing what we _____ .

   (c) Another important way in which language can influence thought has to do with our

    _____ of others.

   (d) Language that promotes

    _____ thinking can encourage discrimination against women, the elderly, and minorities or members of ethnic groups.

4. (a) Animals communicate with each other, but the question psychologists have investigated is whether animals are capable of mastering language; this active area of psychological research is referred to as _____ cognition or _____ cognition.

(b) The results of several ongoing studies have produced some compelling demonstrations of animal _____ learning, but many psychologists caution against jumping to the conclusion that animals can think or that they possess self-awareness because such conclusions are far from proven.

Measuring Intelligence
Learning Objectives

When you have finished studying this section of the chapter, you should be able to:

1. Define *intelligence*, name the three main contributors to the development of intelligence tests, and describe the role played by each.

2. Specify how Binet, Terman, and Wechsler differ in their beliefs about intelligence and its measurement.

3. List the main principles of test construction and explain their importance in the development of scientifically acceptable tests.

4. Explain the role of norms in standardization and define the normal curve or normal distribution.

5. Describe how reliability and validity are determined and defined.

*Read the section "Measuring Intelligence" and **write** your answers to the following:*

1. (a) The use of mental images and concepts, problem solving and decision making, and language capabilities are cognitive abilities that are aspects of what is commonly called

_____ .

(b) Wechsler defined _____ as the global capacity to think rationally, act purposefully, and deal effectively with the environment.

(c) Intelligence tests attempt to measure general _____ , rather than accumulated knowledge or aptitude for a specific subject or area.

2. (a) In the early 1900s the French government commissioned psychologist Alfred Binet to develop procedures to identify students who might require _____ .

(b) Along with Théodore Simon, Binet devised a series of tests to measure different kinds of elementary _____ , such as memory, attention, and the ability to understand similarities and differences.

(c) Binet found that brighter children performed like _____ children, whereas less capable children performed like _____ children, and it was this observation that led him to the idea of a mental level or mental age that was different from a child's chronological age.

(d) Binet _____ (did/did not) believe that he was measuring an inborn or permanent level of intelligence; he also believed that intelligence was too complex a quality to describe with a(n) _____ ; finally, he noted that an individual's score could _____ (vary/not vary) over time.

3. (a) Binet's test was translated and adapted by American psychologist Lewis Terman and is called the _____ .

(b) The _____ , or _____ , is a number derived by dividing the individual's mental age by the chronological age and multiplying the result by 100.

(c) During World War I army psychologists developed two group intelligence tests; the _____ test, which was administered in writing, and the _____ test, which was administered orally to those who could not read, were later adapted for civilian use.

(d) Despite concerns about the misuse of _____ tests, they quickly became popular and were used in a wide variety of settings, not just to identify children who might benefit from special educational help; it soon came to be believed that the _____ score was a fixed, inborn characteristic resistant to change.

4. (a) David Wechsler designed a new intelligence test called the

_____ ,

or _____ for short.

(b) Wechsler's test was specifically designed for _____ rather than children and provided scores on 11 subtests measuring different abilities grouped to provide an overall _____ score and _____ score.

(c) The _____ score represented scores on subtests of vocabulary, comprehension, knowledge of general information, and other verbal tasks, whereas the _____ score reflected scores on largely nonverbal subtests, such as identifying the missing parts in incomplete pictures, arranging pictures to tell a story, or arranging blocks to match a given pattern.

(d) Because the _____ provided an individualized profile of the subject's strengths and weakness on specific tasks, it marked a return to the attidudes and goals of _____ .

(e) Wechsler calculated the _____ by comparing an individual's score to the scores of others in the same general age group whose average score was statistically fixed at 100; the range of scores is statistically defined so that _____ of all scores fall between 85 and 115, which is considered to indicate "normal" or "average" intelligence.

(f) Wechsler also developed two tests for children: the

_____ ,

or _____ , and the

_____ ,

or _____ .

5. (a) _____ tests are designed to measure a person's level of knowledge, skill, or accomplishment in a particular area, such as mathematics or a foreign language; in contrast, _____ tests are designed to assess a person's capacity to benefit from education or training.

(b) _____ means that the test is given to a large number of subjects who are representative of the group of people for whom the test is designed, and the scores of this group establish the _____ or standards against which an individual's score is compared and interpreted.

(c) For IQ tests these standards closely follow a bell-shaped pattern of individual differences called the _____ or _____ , with most scores clustering around the average.

(d) If a test consistently produces similar scores on different occasions, it is said to be

_____ .

(e) To determine a test's _____ , psychologists check whether test and retest scores using two different versions of the test or two different halves of the test are highly similar.

(f) If a test measures what it is supposed to measure, it is said to be _____ ; one test of this essential requirement is to demonstrate its predictive value.

6. Read the following and write the correct term in the space provided:

(a) A Norwegian visitor to England asks the hotel clerk, "Can you please my key to my room give me?" This visitor has apparently not yet mastered the _____ of the English language.

(b) When Elinore's husband refers to her psychiatrist as a "headshrinker" during discussions with friends or family, he may be influencing their _____ perceptions of her and her therapist.

(c) Ten-year-old Jean performed at the same level as most 12-year-olds on Binet's test. Her _____ age is different from her _____ age.

(d) Marcel took the Standard-Binet test and his mental age and chronological age were identical. Marcel's IQ score is likely to be _____ .

(e) When 25-year-old Dagmar applied for a position with the Department of Defense, she was given a test and scored slightly above the norm on overall verbal ability but was well above the norm in overall performance for her age group. The test Dagmar was given was a(n) _____ called the _____ .

(f) The new Zander jealousy scale had test and retest scores that were highly similar but lacked predictive value, and it was not clear exactly what human attribute it was measuring. The Zander test has high _____ but low _____ .

Review of Key Terms and Key Names 2

language
syntax
generative
displacement
animal cognition
  (comparative cognition)
linguistic relativity
  hypothesis
intelligence

Alfred Binet
mental age
Lewis Terman
Stanford-Binet
  Intelligence Scale
intelligence quotient
  (IQ)
David Wechsler

Wechsler Adult
  Intelligence Scale
  (WAIS)
verbal score
performance score

standardization
normal curve (normal
  distribution)
reliability
validity

Matching Exercise

Match the appropriate term/name with its definition or description.

1. _____ The unique rules that every language has for combining words.

2. _____ The French psychologist who, along with French psychiatrist Théodore Simon, developed the first widely used intelligence test.

3. _____ The ability to communicate meaningfully about ideas, objects, and activities that are not physically present.

4. _____ A measurement of intelligence in which an individual's mental level is expressed in terms of the average abilities of a given age group.

5. _____ The intelligence test developed by Lewis Terman that was based on his translation and revision of the Binet-Simon intelligence test.

6. _____ The ability of a test to measure what it is intended to measure.

7. _____ A creative characteristic of language that allows one to generate an infinite number of new and different phrases and sentences.

8. _____ An active area of psychology concerned with all aspects of animal language research.

9. _____ A bell-shaped distribution of individual differences in a normal population in which most scores cluster around the average score.

10. _____ The global capacity to think rationally, act purposefully, and deal effectively with the environment.

True/False Test

Indicate whether each item is true or false by placing T or F in the space next to each item.

1. ____ Lewis Terman was a French psychiatrist who, along with French psychologist Alfred Binet, developed the first widely used intelligence test, called the Binet-Terman IQ Test.

2. ____ David Wechsler was the American psychologist who developed the Wechsler Adult Intelligence Scale (WAIS), the most widely used intelligence scale.

3. ____ The notion that differences among languages causes differences in the thoughts of their speakers is called the linguistic relativity hypothesis (the Whorfian hypothesis).

4. ____ The intelligence quotient (IQ) is a global measure of intelligence derived by comparing an individual's score to that of others in the same age group.

5. ____ The *verbal score* on the WAIS reflects scores on subtests such as identifying missing parts in incomplete pictures, arranging pictures to tell a story, or arranging blocks to match a given pattern.

6. ____ Reliability refers to the ability of a test to produce consistent results when administered on repeated occasions under similar conditions.

7. ____ Standardization is the process of administering a test to a large, representative sample of people under uniform conditions for the purpose of establishing norms.

8. ____ Language is a system for combining arbitrary symbols to produce an infinite number of meaningful statements.

9. ____ The *performance score* on the WAIS represents scores on subtests of vocabulary, comprehension, knowledge of general information, and other similar tasks.

10. ____ The Wechsler Adult Intelligence Scale (WAIS) was designed specifically as an achievement test but is now widely used as an aptitude test.

> Check your answers and review any areas of weakness before going on to the next section.

Four Views on the Nature of Intelligence

Learning Objectives

When you have finished studying this section of the chapter, you should be able to:

1. Describe the two key issues that are central to the debate on the nature of intelligence.

2. State the position that Spearman, Thurstone, Gardner, and Sternberg take on these issues and explain how these psychologists differ in their views of intelligence.

*Read the section "Four Views on the Nature of Intelligence" and **write** your answers to the following:*

1. Much of the controversy over the definition and nature of intelligence centers on two key issues:

   (a) Is intelligence a(n) _____ , _____ ability or a(n) _____ of different abilities?

   (b) Should the definition of intelligence be _____ to the mental abilities measured by intelligence tests, or should intelligence be defined more _____ ?

2. (a) The belief that a common factor, or general mental capacity, is at the core of different mental abilities originated with British psychologist _____ .

   (b) Psychologists who follow the approach that a(n) _____ or _____ , is responsible for overall performance on mental ability tests think that intelligence can be described as a single measure of general cognitive ability.

   (c) Lewis Terman's approach to measuring and defining intelligence as a single, overall IQ score was in the tradition of British psychologist _____ .

3. (a) Psychologist L. L. Thurstone disagreed that intelligence is a single mental capacity and proposed that there were seven different _____ , each of which was a relatively independent element of intelligence.

   (b) To Thurstone, the _____ factor was simply an overall average score of such independent abilities and consequently was less important than an individual's _____ of mental abilities.

(c) The approach of American psychologist _____ to measuring and defining intelligence as a pattern of different abilities was very similar to Thurstone's approach.

4. (a) Howard Gardner, whose approach is also similar to _____ , believes that mental abilities are _____ and _____ and cannot be accurately reflected in a single measure of intelligence such as an IQ score.

   (b) Gardner believes there are _____ , and he defines _____ as the ability to solve problems or create products that are valued within one or more cultural settings.

   (c) Some abilities emphasized by Gardner may be tapped by a standard intelligence test, such as _____ intelligence, but other abilities, such as _____ intelligence, may not be, despite being recognized and highly valued in many different cultures, including our own.

5. (a) Robert Sternberg agrees with _____ that intelligence is a much broader quality than the narrow range of mental abilities tested by a conventional IQ test, but he believes that some of Gardner's _____ are specialized "talents" rather than the more general quality of intelligence.

   (b) Sternberg's _____ theory of intelligence emphasizes both the universal aspects of intelligent behavior and the importance of adapting to the individual's particular social and cultural environment.

   (c) Sternberg contends that there are three forms of intelligence:

(1) _____ intelligence refers to the mental processes used in learning how to solve problems, picking a problem-solving strategy, and solving problems.

(2) _____ intelligence is the ability to deal with novel situations by drawing on existing skills and knowledge.

(3) _____ intelligence, also called _____ intelligence, involves the ability to adapt to the environment and is loosely equivalent to "street smarts"; a person who has a high level of this ability functions effectively within a given cultural context.

6. (a) Despite _____ (agreement/disagreement) on the specific nature and definition of intelligence, psychologists generally _____ (agree/disagree) that mental abilities such as abstract thinking, problem solving, and the capacity to acquire knowledge (all typically assessed on standard IQ tests) are important elements of intelligence.

   (b) Other important aspects of intelligence that exist and are not measured in conventional intelligence tests include _____ and the ability to adapt to one's environment.

The Roles of Genetics and Environment in Determining Intelligence
Learning Objectives

When you have finished studying this section of the chapter, you should be able to:

1. Describe the heredity-and-environment issue.

2. Specify the factors that contribute to the complexity of the relationship between genetics and environment, especially with regard to intelligence.

3. Define *heritability* and explain how twin studies are use in studying the heredity-environment issue

4. Explain why it cannot be concluded that group differences in average IQ are genetic in origin.

5. Specify why it is possible to determine genetic differences within a given group but not between groups.

6. Explain how culture might affect intelligence test results and present the results of cross-cultural studies on the effect of social discrimination on IQ.

Read the section "The Roles of Genetics and Environment in Determining Intelligence" and **write** *your answers to the following:*

1. (a) The debate on the origins of intelligence involves two basic questions: (1) Do we essentially _____ our intellectual potential from our parents, grandparents, and great-grandparents? (2) Is our intellectual potential primarily determined by our _____ and upbringing?

   (b) Virtually all psychologists agree that both _____ and _____ are important in determining intelligence levels; how much each contributes is the crucial issue.

2. (a) Eye color is completely _____ determined but height is a function of the interplay between _____ and _____ ; you inherit a potential range for height but where your actual height falls within that range is influenced by environmental factors.

   (b) How people's intelligence and personalities are determined is extremely complex; the genetic range of intellectual potential is influenced by _____ (one/many) gene(s), and _____ factors are not stable but constantly changing.

   (c) To deal with the complexities involved in the study of the role of heredity and environment, psychologists have used

   _____ .

3. (a) Identical twins share exactly the same genes because they developed from a single fertilized egg that split into two; consequently any dissimilarities between them must be due to _____ factors rather than _____ differences.

   (b) Fraternal twins develop from two different fertilized eggs and are therefore like any other pair of siblings, but because they are the same age, their _____ experiences are likely to be more similar than those of siblings of different ages.

   (c) Both genetic and environmental influences are important:
   (1) Genetic influence is shown by the fact that identical twins raised together have very _____ IQ scores.
   (2) Environmental influences are shown when two identical twins who are raised in different homes have _____ IQ scores and when two genetically unrelated people raised in the same home have IQs much more _____ than unrelated people from randomly selected homes.

   (d) Using studies based on degree of genetic relatedness, researchers have scientifically estimated _____—the percentage of variation within a given population that is due to heredity.

   (e) It is estimated that approximately 50 percent (or possibly 65 percent) of the difference among IQ scores _____ a specific group of people, or a given population, is due to genetic factors; this figure does not apply to a single individual's IQ score.

4. (a) Much of the controversy over the role of _____ in intelligence is due to attempts to explain the differences in average IQ scores for different racial groups.

   (b) Although *group* differences in *average* IQ scores have been found, it is important to

note that they do not predict
_____ differences in IQ scores.

(c) The most fundamental problem related to
the controversy over genetics and IQ scores
is the inappropriate comparison of
_____ differences in IQ scores.

5. (a) Unless the environmental conditions of two
racial groups are virtually identical, it is
impossible to estimate the overall
_____ differences between the
two groups, and even if intelligence were
primarily determined by heredity, IQ differences between groups could still be due
entirely to the _____ .

(b) Scarr and Weinberg, who explored the relationship between racial IQ differences and
the environment, concluded that IQ differences are due not to race but rather to the
_____ conditions and
_____ values to which children
are exposed.

(c) Changes in average IQ scores in many countries in just one generation can be accounted
for only by _____ changes
because the amount of time is far too short
for _____ influenced changes to
have occurred.

6. (a) The effect of social discrimination on intelligence test scores has been shown in numerous _____ studies; in
many different societies, the average IQ is
lower for members of a discriminated-
against minority, even when that group is of
the same race as the dominant group.

(b) _____-group children score 10
to 15 IQ points lower, are often one or two
years behind in basic reading and math
skills, are overrepresented in remedial programs and the number of school dropouts,
and are underrepresented among students
in higher education, compared to
_____-group children.

(c) The impact of _____ on group
differences in IQ remains even when the
minority-group and dominant-group members are of similar socioeconomic backgrounds.

7. (a) Another approach to explaining group differences in IQ scores has been to look at
_____ in the tests them-
selves; if standardized intelligence tests
reflect white, middle-class knowledge and
values, minority-group members may do
poorly, not because of lower intelligence, but
because of unfamiliarity with white, middle-
class _____ .

(b) It is now generally recognized that it is virtually impossible to design a test that is
completely culture-free because
_____ itself is not free of cultural influences; a test will tend to favor the
people from the culture in which it was
developed.

(c) Cultural differences may also be involved in
_____ behavior; people
from different cultural backgrounds may use
different organizational and problem-solving
_____ than those required on
the standardized test, and factors like motivation, _____ toward test tak-
ing, and _____ experience with
test taking can all influence performance
and test scores.

(d) Being aware that you are not expected to do
well on a particular test can create anxiety
and apprehension about being evaluated
and can lower both the _____
and _____ of responses on standardized test questions.

8. On the basis of the discussion about influences
of heredity and environment in intelligence,
three broad conclusions can be drawn about the
debate surrounding intelligence and race:

(a) The IQ of any given individual, regardless of what racial group he or she may belong to, is the result of the complex interaction of _____ and _____ influences.

(b) The IQ differences between racial groups are influenced much more by _____ factors than by _____ factors.

(c) Within a given racial group, the differences among people are due at least as much to _____ influences as to _____ influences.

9. Read the following and write the correct term in the space provided:

(a) Although Dr. Bowman recognizes that particular individuals might excel in specific areas, she believes that a factor, called general intelligence, or the *g* factor, is responsible for overall performance on mental ability tests. Her belief about the nature of intelligence is most consistent with the approach taken by psychologist _____ .

(b) Jamal is a highly valued maintenance worker because of his almost uncanny ability to be able to fix almost any piece of equipment that breaks down. Jamal is demonstrating what Robert Sternberg would call _____ intelligence, or _____ intelligence.

(c) Selma is a very successful, highly motivated, goal-directed, creative graphic designer. These aspects of her intelligence are _____ (not likely/very likely) to be assessed and measured on a conventional intelligence test.

(d) Dicky and Ricky are identical twins and have almost identical IQ scores despite the fact that they were separated at birth and raised separately. Joel and Joanna are fraternal twins raised together and their IQ scores are much less similar than Dicky's and Ricky's scores. This example provides most support for the _____ side in the heredity-environment debate.

(e) When Joel and Joanna's IQ scores are compared to the scores of two randomly selected unrelated people of the same age, their scores are found to be much more similar. This finding provides most support for the _____ side in the heredity-environment debate.

(f) Dr. Yokomoto, like the majority of experts on intelligence testing, is most likely to attribute the finding that Japanese and Chinese children outperform American children on mathematics achievement test to _____ factors.

(g) When Dr. Parsei, an expert on intelligence testing, was asked if it was possible to design an intelligence test that was completely culture-free, he claimed that is was not, because _____ itself is not free of cultural influences.

Graphic Organizer

Read the following statements and decide which psychologist is most associated with each:

Statement	Psychologist
1. I define intelligence as the global capacity to think rationally, act purposefully, and deal effectively with the environment; a good IQ test should have both verbal and performance scores representing subtests that measure a variety of abilities.	
2. My theory of intelligence emphasizes both universal aspects of intelligent behavior and the importance of adapting to the individual's particular social and cultural environment; there are essentially three forms of intelligence: componential; experiential; and contextual, or practical, intelligence.	
3. I'm not sure I have a fully developed theory of intelligence, but I do believe that we can help children do better in school if we devise tests that can identify those who need help and then provide that help. There is a great deal of variation in intelligence in any age group of children.	
4. I am convinced that a factor called general intelligence, or the *g* factor, is responsible for the overall performance on mental ability tests. Furthermore, I would go so far as to say that intelligence can be accurately expressed as a single number that reflects an individual's intellectual abilities.	
5. My position is that those who say that intelligence is a single general mental capacity are wrong. On the basis of my observations of what is valued in different cultures, I've concluded that there are multiple intelligences (at least seven), each independent of the other, and these must be viewed in the context of a particular culture.	
6. I tend to agree with statement 4 above. In addition, I believe that intelligence can best be expressed by a number I call the intelligence quotient, or IQ, which is derived by dividing the mental age by the chronological age and multiplying the result by 100.	

Review of Key Terms and Key Names 3

Charles Spearman
g factor (general intelligence)
L. L. Thurstone
primary mental abilities
Howard Gardner
Robert Sternberg
triarchic theory of intelligence
componential intelligence

experiential intelligence
contextual (or practical) intelligence
heredity
environment
heritability
identical twins
fraternal twins
creativity

Matching Exercise

Match the appropriate term / name with its definition or description.

1. _____ A contemporary American psychologist whose triarchic theory of intelligence includes three forms of intelligence (componential, contextual, and experiential).

2. _____ The percentage of variation within a given population that is due to heredity.

3. _____ The notion of a general intelligence factor that is responsible for a person's overall performance on tests of mental ability.

4. _____ A group of cognitive processes used to generate useful, original, and novel ideas or solutions.

5. _____ American psychologist who advanced the theory that intelligence is composed of several primary mental abilities and cannot be accurately described by an overall general, or *g* factor, measure.

6. _____ A form of intelligence that involves the ability to adapt to the environment and is sometimes described as street smarts.

7. _____ British psychologist who advanced the theory that a general intelligence factor, called the *g* factor, is responsible for overall intellectual functioning.

8. _____ A form of intelligence that involves the ability to deal with novel situations by drawing on existing skills and knowledge.

True/False Test

Indicate whether each item is true or false by placing T or F in the space next to each item.

1. ____ Howard Gardner is a contemporary American psychologist whose theory of intelligence states that there is not one intelligence but multiple intelligences, the importance of each being determined by cultural values.

2. ____ Identical twins develop from two different fertilized eggs and are 50 percent genetically similar to each other.

3. ____ Heredity refers to the traits, capacities, and intellectual potential that we inherit from our parents, grandparents, and great-grandparents.

4. ____ Componential intelligence refers to the mental processes used in learning how to solve problems, picking a problem-solving strategy, and solving problems.

5. ____ In the debate over what determines intelligence, environment refers to factors such as type of upbringing, nutritional and health standards, social and cultural factors, and other influences that may have an impact on intellectual development.

6. ____ Fraternal twins share exactly the same genes because they developed from a single fertilized egg that split into two.

7. ____ Sternberg's theory that there are three forms of intelligence—componential, contextual, and experiential—is called the triarchic theory of intelligence.

8. ____ According to Thurstone, primary mental abilities are relatively independent elements of intelligence and include verbal comprehension, numerical ability, reasoning, and perceptual speed.

Check your answers and review any areas of weakness before going on to the next section.

Something to Think About

1. Many people mistakenly believe that creativity is restricted to a few gifted, genius-level, artistic people. What would you tell someone who wants to be creative but does not believe he or she possesses an artistic temperament.

2. People vary in their IQ test scores, but about 68 percent of scores on tests such as the WAIS-R are between 85 and 115, the range for normal intelligence. A friend comes up to you and says, "Wouldn't it be great if we all had above-average IQ scores? Just think how wonderful life would be and how happy and successful we'd be!" How might you enlighten your friend about IQ tests and IQ scores?

Check your answers and review any areas of weakness before doing the progress tests.

Progress Test 1

Review the complete chapter (including Concept Reviews and all the boxed inserts), review all your study notes, and then test yourself on the following progress test. Check your answers. If you make a mistake, review your notes, review the relevant section of the study guide, and, if necessary, go back and read the appropriate part of your textbook.

1. As part of her vocational assessment, Lynda is given a test to see if she is suited to be an air traffic controller. This is an example of _____ testing.
   (a) intelligence
   (b) achievement
   (c) aptitude
   (d) motivational

2. When Aaron is asked to define *weapon*, he responds that it is anything you could use to beat someone up. Aaron is using the word *weapon* as a
   (a) natural concept
   (b) prototype
   (c) formal concept
   (d) heuristic

3. When Michelle is asked the same question as Aaron, she replies that a weapon is one of a variety of instruments, or objects, that can be used to defend, attack, hurt, maim, or kill and the term *weapon* can even include words, as in "the pen is mightier than the sword." Michelle is using the word *weapon* as a
   (a) natural concept
   (b) prototype
   (c) formal concept
   (d) heuristic

4. When three-year-old Claudia is asked which letter of the alphabet comes before *G*, she recites the alphabet from the beginning until she arrives at the solution. Claudia is using _____ to solve the problem
   (a) trial and error
   (b) insight
   (c) an algorithm
   (d) a heuristic

5. Louis forgot to bring his pillow when he went camping for the weekend, so he spent a very uncomfortable night. It didn't occur to Louis that he could use his down-filled jacket as a pillow. This example best illustrates
   (a) functional fixedness
   (b) mental set
   (c) the availability heuristic
   (d) use of an algorithm

6. When Vasilis is faced with the decision of which of two equally attractive apartments to rent, he makes a list of what is most important and gives each factor a numerical rating. It appears that Vasilis is using the _____ model of decision making
   (a) elimination by aspects
   (b) additive
   (c) single-feature
   (d) heuristic

7. Jerome *recently* saw a TV special where most of the psychologists interviewed were middle-aged males, so when he took his first psychology class he was surprised to find that his professor was a young female rather than an older bearded male. Jerome's surprise is probably due to his use of the
   (a) availability heuristic
   (b) representativeness heuristic
   (c) single-feature model
   (d) additive model

8. When Heidi tells Hans that she is going to enter a foot race to raise funds to end the arms race, he has no trouble understanding that she is going to run in a race to generate support for an anti-weapons cause. Hans's correct interpretation best illustrates the importance of
   (a) syntax
   (b) displacement
   (c) generativity
   (d) prototypes

9. When asked what she does for a living, Krista always replies that she is a sanitary·engineer rather than a garbage collector. Krista is probably aware of the effect of language on
   (a) memory
   (b) gender bias
   (c) social perception
   (d) income level

10. Six-year-old Bruce's performance on an intelligence test is at a level characteristic of an average four-year-old. Bruce's mental age is
    (a) eight
    (b) four
    (c) six
    (d) five

11. Scott is a very bright ten-year-old with a mental age of thirteen. If tested on the Stanford-Binet Intelligence Scale, his IQ score would most likely be
    (a) 100
    (b) 77
    (c) 150
    (d) 130

12. Twenty-year-old Val has just taken a test that includes vocabulary, comprehension, general knowledge, object assembly, arranging pictures to tell a story, and other items. Val has completed the
    (a) WAIS-R
    (b) WPPSI
    (c) WISC-R
    (d) Stanford-Binet

13. Dr. Bishop assesses the correlation between scores obtained on two halves of his new abstract reasoning test in order to measure the _____ of her test
    (a) reliability
    (b) validity
    (c) norms
    (d) aptitude

14. Millie is extremely adept at learning how to solve problems, picking problem-solving strategies, and actually solving problems. Robert Sternberg would call this form of intelligence
    (a) componential intelligence
    (b) experiential intelligence
    (c) contextual intelligence
    (d) general intelligence, or the *g* factor

15. Dr. Welch believes that there are multiple independent intelligences that cannot be reflected in a single measure of mental ability, and each intelligence must be viewed within a cultural context. Dr. Welch's position is most consistent with views of
    (a) Charles Spearman
    (b) L. L. Thurstone
    (c) Howard Gardner
    (d) Robert Sternberg

16. When Allison goes to graduate school, she plans to investigate aspects of the heredity-environment debate as it relates to intelligence. She is most likely to
    (a) use animals, such as rats and pigeons, in her research
    (b) get involved in twin studies
    (c) study the language abilities of primates
    (d) explore creativity and intuition

17. In his research on very young black children adopted into white middle-class families, Dr. Wilson found that their IQ scores were several points above the average of both blacks and whites. Dr. Wilson, like most experts in this area, is most likely to conclude that
    (a) intelligence is primarily determined by heredity
    (b) IQ scores cannot be improved by environmental factors
    (c) improved diet and health standards are the crucial factor in improving IQ scores
    (d) socioeconomic conditions, cultural values, and similar environmental factors can affect IQ scores

18. According to the Application section, creativity
    (a) is something that only a few very gifted people possess
    (b) refers to a group of cognitive processes used to generate useful, novel, and original ideas and solutions
    (c) is only concerned with artistic expression, with little or no practical value

    (d) refers to the ability to arrive at conclusions or make judgments without conscious awareness of the thought processes involved

19. According to the textbook, intuition
    (a) involves two stages, the guiding stage and the integrative stage
    (b) is the process of coming to a conclusion or making a judgment without conscious awareness of the thought processes involved
    (c) may involve what are commonly called hunches
    (d) involves all of the above

20. Which of the following is *not* one of the obstacles to logical thinking that can account for much of the persistence of unwarranted beliefs in pseudosciences?
    (a) the belief bias effect
    (b) confirmation bias
    (c) the underestimation effect
    (d) the fallacy of positive instances
    (e) the overestimation effect

Progress Test 2

After you have checked your understanding of the material in Progress Test 1 and have done a complete chapter review with special focus on any areas of weakness, you are now ready to assess your knowledge in Progress Test 2. Check your answers. If you make a mistake, review your notes, the relevant section of the study guide, and, if necessary, the appropriate part of your textbook.

1. As part of his overall vocational assessment, Steven took a test that measured his level of knowledge, skills, and accomplishments in particular areas such as mathematics and writing ability. Steven took
   (a) an aptitude test
   (b) an achievement test
   (c) an intelligence test
   (d) a motivational test

2. When Kathy is asked to recite the letters of the alphabet that do not have curved lines, she tries to picture and inspect each letter in her mind as she completes the task. Kathy is using
   (a) mental imagery   (c) a formal concept
   (b) a natural concept   (d) a prototype

3. Allan is asked to memorize a map of an island that has a hut, a lake, a tree, a beach, and a grassy area all clearly marked at distinct locations. Later he is asked to imagine a specific location, such as the hut; then a second location, the tree, is named and he has to press a button when he reaches the tree on the visual image in his mind. The results of this experiment will most likely reveal that the _____ the distance between the two points, the _____ time it will take to scan the mental image of the map.

   (a) greater; more
   (b) greater; less
   (c) shorter; more
   (d) All of the above are false; there is no relationship between distance and time taken to mentally scan points on the map.

4. When Earl is asked what object or objects come to mind in response to the word *vegetable*, he answers "potatoes and carrots." For Earl potatoes and carrots are

   (a) formal concepts   (c) algorithms
   (b) prototypes   (d) heuristics

5. Adrian took the WAIS test. One aspect of his general cognitive ability that is not likely to have been measured is his

   (a) linguistic ability
   (b) problem-solving ability
   (c) creativity
   (d) general knowledgel

6. When Elizabeth got her new VCR, she spent hours trying different approaches to programming the machine rather than consulting the manual. Elizabeth is using the _____ approach to problem solving.

   (a) algorithm   (c) heuristic
   (b) trial-and-error (d) insight

7. After spending weeks studying a variety of sources and materials, Terry still couldn't decide on a topic for her seminar presentation. However, when she was out for her daily jog, she suddenly had a flash of inspiration about her topic. Terry solved her problem

   (a) through insight
   (b) by using an algorithm
   (c) through functional fixedness
   (d) by using the representativeness heuristic

8. Whenever his TV had fuzzy pictures, Lloyd would bang the top of the TV set and the pic-ture would clear. Recently when he was playing a video on his new VCR, there were tracking problems which created a fuzzy picture, so Lloyd banged the top of the TV over and over to no avail. Lloyd appears to be experiencing an obstacle to solving the problem called

   (a) functional fixedness
   (b) subgoal analysis
   (c) a mental set
   (d) confirmation bias
   (e) prototypical male stupidity

9. Cynthia always buys the brand of paper towels that is on sale despite the fact that there are many brands with varying prices to choose from. Cynthia makes her decision about which paper towel to purchase based on the _____ model of decision making.

   (a) single-feature   (c) elimination by aspects
   (b) additive   (d) heuristic

10. Jan is orderly, neat, quiet, and shy. She enjoys reading in her spare time and is an avid chess player. Given this description, most people would guess that she is a librarian rather than a real estate agent. This tendency to classify Jan as a librarian illustrates the influence of

    (a) the availability heuristic
    (b) belief perseverance
    (c) the representativeness heuristic
    (d) the elimination by aspects strategy

11. When writing term papers, assignments, exams, etc., Gary is very careful to use "he or she" rather than just the masculine pronoun, "people" instead of "man," etc. Gary is apparently aware of the relationship between language and

    (a) memory   (c) social perception
    (b) gender bias   (d) functional fixedness

12. Melody is writing a paper for her course in comparative cognition. After reviewing all the relevant research on animal language, Melody is likely to conclude that

    (a) only humans possess language capabilities
    (b) animals can communicate with each other but are not capable of mastering any aspect of language.
    (c) some species have demonstrated an elementary understanding of syntax and certain other limited aspects of language
    (d) many animal species can "think," can use language, and possess self-awareness

13. Martin has had some difficulties in school and has fallen behind in academic achievement. His chronological age is ten and his IQ score on the Stanford-Binet is 70. Martin's mental age is therefore
    (a) seven
    (b) ten
    (c) thirteen
    (d) five

14. Dr. Peerless has designed a test to measure the level of scientific knowledge in high school graduates. In order to establish a norm against which individual scores may be interpreted and compared, she is presently administering the test to a large representative sample of high school graduates. Dr. Peerless is in the process of
    (a) establishing the test's reliability
    (b) establishing the test's validity
    (c) standardizing the test
    (d) determining the test's aptitude

15. Following the above process, Dr. Peerless set out to check whether her test is good at measuring what it was designed to measure. She did this by comparing scores on her test with the scores and grades obtained by students in high school science courses. In this instance Dr. Peerless is in the process of
    (a) establishing the test's reliability
    (b) establishing the test's validity
    (c) standardizing the test
    (d) determining the test's aptitude

16. Arnie is very adept at dealing with novel situations by drawing on previous experience and can often find unusual ways to relate old information to solve new problems. Robert Sternberg would call this _____ intelligence.
    (a) componential
    (b) experiential
    (c) contextual
    (d) motivational

17. As part of a bizarre experiment in a science fiction story, Dr. Igor places 100 genetically identical individual infants in different homes. Because they are all identical, the heritability of intelligence (i.e., the percentage of variation within the group that is due to genetic factors) should be _____ percent.
    (a) 0
    (b) 50
    (c) 65
    (d) 100

18. According to Culture and Human Behavior Box 7.2, the linguistic relativity hypothesis (or Whorfian hypothesis)
    (a) proposes that the differences among languages cause differences in the thoughts of their speakers
    (b) has been supported by the results of dozens of cross-cultural studies
    (c) accounts for the fact that the English language has more than a dozen words for *snow* but Eskimos have only one or two
    (d) holds that language does not determine cultural differences but instead language reflects cultural differences

19. According to In Focus Box 7.3, which of the following is true?
    (a) IQ scores reliably predict academic success.
    (b) Academic success is no guarantee of success beyond school.
    (c) Many different personality factors are involved in achieving success, such as motivation, emotional maturity, commitment to goals, creativity, and a willingness to work hard.
    (d) All of the above are true.

20. According to the Application section, which of the following is *not* a way to increase your potential to be creative?
    (a) Focus almost exclusively on extrinsic motivation.
    (b) Choose the goal of creativity.
    (c) Try different approaches.
    (d) Acquire relevant knowledge.
    (e) Engage in problem finding.

Answers

Introduction: Thinking, Language, and Intelligence

1. (a) mental; acquiring, retaining; using
   (b) intelligence

2. (a) thinking; mental
   (b) mental representations

3. (a) mental image
   (b) actual objects

4. (a) mental
   (b) concepts
   (c) formal concept
   (d) attributes; is
   (e) natural concept
   (f) prototype; prototype

Solving Problems and Making Decisions

1. (a) thinking; behavior

2. (a) trial and error
   (b) algorithm
   (c) heuristic; heuristics
   (d) heuristic; subgoals; working backward
   (e) insight
   (f) insight; intuition
   (g) intuition; guiding; integrative

3. (a) functional fixedness
   (b) mental sets

4. (a) features
   (b) single-feature
   (c) additive
   (d) additive
   (e) elimination by aspects
   (f) additive; elimination by aspects; additive

5. (a) availability
   (b) availability
   (c) less; less
   (d) representativeness
   (e) representativeness

6. (a) insight
   (b) representativeness heuristic
   (c) cognitive; thinking
   (d) mental image
   (e) formal
   (f) natural
   (g) algorithm
   (h) trial-and-error
   (i) additive

Matching Exercise 1

1. elimination by aspects model

2. thinking
3. prototype
4. insight
5. single-feature model
6. representativeness heuristic
7. intuition
8. formal concept
9. cognition
10. concepts
11. heuristic

True/False Test 1

1. F	5. T	9. F
2. T	6. T	10. T
3. T	7. T	11. T
4. F	8. F	

Language and Thought

1. (a) communicate
   (b) symbols; statements

2. (a) symbols
   (b) arbitrary
   (c) meaning
   (d) syntax
   (e) generative; generated
   (f) displacement

3. (a) cognitive
   (b) remember
   (c) social perception
   (d) stereotypical

4. (a) animal; comparative
   (b) language

Measuring Intelligence

1. (a) intelligence
   (b) intelligence
   (c) mental abilities

2. (a) special help
   (b) mental abilities
   (c) older; younger
   (d) did not; single number; vary

3. (a) Stanford-Binet Intelligence Scale
   (b) intelligence quotient; IQ
   (c) Army Alpha; Army Beta
   (d) intelligence; IQ

4. (a) Wechsler Adult Intelligence Scale; WAIS
   (b) adults; verbal; performance

(c) verbal; performance

(d) WAIS; Alfred Binet

(e) IQ; 68 percent

(f) Wechsler Intelligence Scale for Children; WISC; Wechsler Preschool and Primary Scale of Intelligence; WPPSI

5. (a) achievement; aptitude

(b) standardization; norms

(c) normal curve; normal distribution

(d) reliable

(e) reliability

(f) valid

6. (a) syntax

(b) social

(c) mental; chronological

(d) 100

(e) IQ test; WAIS-R

(f) reliability; validity

Matching Exercise 2

1. syntax

2. Alfred Binet

3. displacement

4. mental age

5. Stanford-Binet Intelligence Scale

6. validity

7. generative

8. animal cognition (comparative cognition)

9. normal curve (normal distribution)

10. intelligence

True/False Test 2

1. F	5. F	9. F
2. T	6. T	10. F
3. T	7. T	
4. T	8. T	

Four Views on the Nature of Intelligence

1. (a) single, general; cluster

(b) restricted; broadly

2. (a) Charles Spearman

(b) general; *g* factor

(c) Charles Spearman

3. (a) primary mental abilities

(b) *g*; specific pattern

(c) David Wechsler

4. (a) Thurstone's; independent; distinct

(b) multiple intelligences; intelligence

(c) linguistic; bodily-kinesthetic

5. (a) Gardner; intelligences

(b) triarchic

(c) (1) componential

(2) experiential

(3) contextual; practical

6. (a) disagreement; agree

(b) creativity

The Roles of Genetics and Environment in Determining Intelligence

1. (a) inherit; environment

(b) heredity; environment

2. (a) genetically; heredity; environment

(b) many; environmental

(c) twin studies

3. (a) environmental; hereditary

(b) environmental

(c) (1) similar

(2) different; similar

(d) heritability

(e) within

4. (a) heredity

(b) individual

(c) group

5. (a) genetic; environment

(b) socioeconomic; cultural

(c) environmental; genetically

6. (a) cross-cultural

(b) minority; majority

(c) discrimination

7. (a) cultural bias; culture

(b) intelligence

(c) test-taking; strategies; attitude; previous

(d) speed; accuracy

8. (a) hereditary; environmental

(b) environmental; genetic

(c) environmental; genetic

9. (a) Charles Spearman

(b) contextual; practical

(c) not likely

(d) heredity

(e) environment

(f) environmental

(g) intelligence

Graphic Organizer

1. David Wechsler

2. Robert Sternberg

3. Alfred Binet

4. Charles Spearman

5. Howard Gardner

6. Lewis Terman

Matching Exercise 3

1. Robert Sternberg

2. heritability

3. *g* factor (general intelligence)

4. creativity

5. L. L. Thurstone

6. contextual (or practical) intelligence

7. Charles Spearman

8. experiential intelligence

True/False Test 3

1. T   4. T   7. T
2. F   5. T   8. T
3. T   6. F

Something to Think About

1. Many people would like to be more creative, and fortunately there are things that can be done to increase our potential to be more creative. The first thing to tell someone is that creativity is hard to define precisely but that most cognitive psychologists agree that creativity is a group of cognitive processes used to generate useful, original, and novel ideas and solutions.

   Creativity is not confined to artistic expression and from the definition above you can see usefulness along with originality is involved in judging creativity. Based on the information in the Application section, you could then conduct your own mini-workshop on creativity. You can summarize the workshop by using the letters of the word **CREATE** as an acronym: **C**hoose the goal of creativity; **R**einforce intrinsic motivation; **E**ngage in problem finding; **A**cquire relevant knowledge; **T**ry different approaches; **E**xpect effort and setbacks.

2. First you could tell your friend that we can't all be above average. The distribution for intelligence will follow a normal, or bell-shaped, curve, with about 50 percent above average and

50 percent below average. Next you could talk a little about the problems involved in defining intelligence. Not even the experts agree. Some think that performance on mental ability tests reflects a general intelligence, or *g* factor; others think there are three forms of intelligence; and some postulate multiple intelligences. Despite these disagreements, psychologists do agree that intelligence involves such elements as abstract thinking, problem solving, and the capacity to acquire knowledge. They also tend to agree that aspects of intelligent behavior such as creativity, motivation, goal-directed behavior, and adaptation to one's environment are not measured by conventional intelligence tests. Thus, IQ scores reflect the limitations of existing intelligence tests. Finally, according to In Focus Box 7.3, whereas IQ scores may predict academic success, success in school is no guarantee of success and happiness in life in general. Many different personality factors are involved in achieving success, such as motivation, emotional maturity, commitment to goals, creativity, and, perhaps most important of all, a willingness to work hard. None of these attributes are measured by traditional IQ tests.

Progress Test 1

1. c   8. a   15. c
2. a   9. c   16. b
3. c   10. b   17. d
4. c   11. d   18. b
5. a   12. a   19. d
6. b   13. a   20. c
7. a   14. a

Progress Test 2

1. b   8. c   15. b
2. a   9. a   16. b
3. a   10. c   17. a
4. b   11. b   18. a
5. c   12. c   19. d
6. b   13. a   20. a
7. a   14. c

Chapter 8 Motivation and Emotion

OVERVIEW

Chapter 8 is concerned with motivation and emotion. Motivation refers to the forces that act on or within an organism to initiate and direct behavior. Instinct theories, drive theories, incentive theories, and humanistic theories are introduced. Biological principles of homeostasis, Maslow's hierarchy of needs, and the concept of self-actualization are discussed. The point is made that the motivation of any behavior is determined by the interaction of multiple factors, including biological, behavioral, cognitive, and social components.

The motivation to eat is influenced by psychological, biological, social, and cultural factors. Several internal and external signals involved in hunger and satiation are explored, including oral sensations, stomach signals, hormones (CCK and insulin), and brain areas such as the ventromedial and lateral hypothalamus. Set-point theory and the rate at which the body uses energy (basal metabolic rate, or BMR) are discussed in relation to regulation of body weight. Factors influencing obesity, anorexia nervosa, and bulimia nervosa are examined, and it is concluded that much is yet to be discovered about these disorders.

Sexual motivation, curiosity, sensation seeking, and arousal motives are discussed next. Competence motivation and achievement motivation are compared, and the Thematic Apperception Test (TAT) is introduced. Achievement motivation is expressed differently in individualistic and collectivistic cultures. The concept of self-efficacy and its relationship to motivation are both examined.

Emotions serve many different functions in human behavior and relationships and have three basic components: subjective experience, physiological arousal, and a behavioral or expressive response. The issue of the number of basic emotions and whether there are two or three dimensions on which emotions can be classified is presented. Facial expressions for some basic emotions seem to be universal and innate, but expression is also influenced by cultural display rules.

Four key theories of emotion are compared and contrasted. The James-Lange theory suggests that emotion results from our perceptions of physical arousal; the Cannon-Bard theory proposes that subjective experience and physiological arousal take place simultaneously; the facial feedback hypothesis posits the notion that expressing an emotion causes us to subjectively experience that emotion but that body changes do not necessarily cause emotions; the two-factor theory of emotion, proposed by Schachter and Singer, holds that emotion results when we apply a cognitive label to physiological arousal; and Richard Lazarus's cognitive-mediational theory proposes that emotion results from the cognitive appraisal of emotion-causing stimuli. Finally, some synthesis is suggested by an interactive approach that emphasizes the idea that cognitive appraisals, physiological arousal, and behavioral expression all contribute to subjective emotional experiences.

Introduction: The Study of Motivation
Learning Objectives

When you have finished studying this section of the chapter, you should be able to:

1. Define *motivation* and state how the formal definition is similar to our everyday use of the term.
2. List and describe the three characteristics associated with motivation.
3. List and describe the main theories of motivation.
4. Explain how each theory accounts for motivation and specify the limitations of each.
5. Describe the concept of drive and explain how it is related to homeostasis.
6. Identify the stages in Maslow's hierarchy of needs and specify what characterizes the study of motivation today.

*Read the section "Introduction: The Study of Motivation" and **write** your answers to the following:*

1. (a) Motivation refers to the forces that act on or within an organism to _____ and _____ behavior.
   (b) In everyday conversation, people often use the word *motivation* when they try to _____ or _____ the behaviors of others.
   (c) There are three basic characteristics commonly associated with motivation: _____ is seen in the initiation or production of behavior; _____ is seen in continued efforts or determination to achieve a particular goal, often in the face of obstacles; and _____ is seen in the greater vigor of responding that usually accompanies motivated behavior.
2. (a) In the late 1800s the newly founded science of psychology initially embraced _____ theories to explain motivation; this position suggests that people are motivated to engage in certain behaviors because of genetic programming.
   (b) Based on the work of Charles Darwin and his scientifically based theory of evolution, psychologists devised lengthy lists of _____ to account for every conceivable human behavior.
   (c) The problem with the early _____ theories was that they merely described and labeled behaviors, rather than actually explaining them, and by the 1920s and 1930s they fell out of favor; however, the more general idea that some human behaviors are _____ and _____ programmed has remained an important element in the overall understanding of motivation.
3. (a) During the 1940s and 1950s _____ theories were replaced by _____ theories.
   (b) _____ theories assert that behavior is motivated by the desire to reduce internal tension caused by unmet biological needs, such as hunger and thirst.
   (c) Leading theorists like psychologists Clark Hull and Robert Woodworth believed that _____ are triggered by the internal mechanism of _____ .
   (d) The principle of _____ states that the body monitors and maintains relatively constant levels of internal states, such as body temperature, fluid levels, and energy supplies.
   (e) When an internal imbalance is detected by _____ mechanisms, a(n) _____ is produced that activates behavior to reduce the need and to reestablish the balance of internal conditions.
   (f) Today, the _____ concept remains useful in the explanation of some motivated behaviors that have biological components but may be inadequate for

explaining other behaviors, such as those directed at _____ (increasing/decreasing) tension and psychological arousal.

4. (a) _____ theories proposed that behavior is motivated by the "pull" of external goals such as rewards.

(b) _____ theories of motivation drew heavily from well-established learning principles such as reinforcement and the work of influential learning theorists such as Pavlov, Watson, Skinner, and Tolman.

(c) Tolman stressed the importance of cognitive factors in learning and motivation, especially the _____ that a particular behavior will lead to a particular goal.

(d) When combined, the _____ and _____ theories seem to account for a broad range of behaviors, but the most obvious shortcoming of _____ theory was the inability to explain behaviors that are not primarily motivated by any kind of external factors, such as playing, mastering a new task, or simply trying to satisfy curiosity.

5. (a) While not discounting biological and external motivators, _____ theories stressed the idea that we are innately motivated to strive for a positive self-concept and the realization of our personal potential.

(b) _____ motivational theories emphasized the importance of _____ and _____ components in human motivation, such as how we perceive the world, how we think about ourselves and others, and our beliefs about our abilities and skills.

(c) Although the motivation to strive for a positive self-concept and personal potential was thought to be _____ , this viewpoint also recognized the importance of the _____ ; without personal, social,

and cultural support, the motivation to strive toward one's highest potential could be jeopardized.

(d) One of the most famous models of motivation, devised by Abraham Maslow, is called the _____ .

(e) Maslow believed that people are motivated to satisfy the needs at each level of the hierarchy before moving to the next level; people progressively move up the hierarchy, striving to eventually reach _____ .

(f) The _____ levels of Maslow's hierarchy emphasize fundamental biological, safety, and social needs, and at the _____ levels the needs become more individualized and growth-oriented.

(g) _____ is defined by Maslow as the full use and exploitation of talents, capacities, potentialities, etc.

(h) Limitations of this model are related to the vagueness of some concepts, studies with limited samples and questionable reliability, and the fact that most people do not experience _____ despite the claim that it is an inborn goal toward which all people supposedly strive.

(i) The _____ model of motivation is not as influential as it once was, but it did help establish the important role played by _____ and _____ factors in human motivation.

6. (a) Today, motivation researchers assume that the motivation of any behavior is determined by multiple factors that include _____ , _____ , _____ , and social components.

(b) Exactly how these different factors interact to energize and motivate behavior is still the subject of much research; rather than continuing to search for a(n) _____ theory of motivation, the focus today is on the study of specific types of motivated behavior, such as eating, sexuality, curiosity, and achievement.

6. Read the following and write the correct term in the space provided:

(a) In graduate school Amber is interested in studying the various forces acting on or within organisms that initiate and direct behavior. Her area of research is

_____ .

(b) When Trevor is hungry, he eats. The consumption of food serves to maintain

_____ .

(c) Manuel is struggling to make enough money to feed and clothe himself and pay the rent. According to Maslow, it is

_____ (likely/unlikely) that Manuel is close to reaching the goal of self-actualization.

(d) Mrs. Lewis gives a gold star to any child in her class who gets 100 percent on the weekly spelling test. This example illustrates _____ theory.

(e) Bruno the bear hibernates every winter. This behavior is an example of a(n)

_____ .

Review of Key Terms and Key Names 1

motivation
activation
persistence
intensity
instinct theories
drive theories
homeostasis

drive
incentive theories
humanistic theories
hierarchy of needs
Abraham Maslow
self-actualization

Matching Exercise

Match the appropriate term / name with its definition or description.

1. _____ The view that we are innately motivated to strive for a positive self-concept and the realization of our personal potential.

2. _____ The forces that act on or within an organism to initiate and direct behavior.

3. _____ A basic characteristic commonly associated with motivation and seen in the continued efforts or determination to achieve a particular goal, often in the face of obstacles.

4. _____ The American psychologist who developed a hierarchical model of human motivation in which needs must first be satisfied before people can strive for self-actualization.

5. _____ An impulse that activates behavior to reduce a need and restore homeostasis.

6. _____ The view that some motives are innate and due to genetic programming.

7. _____ Maslow's hierarchical division of motivation into levels that progress from basic physical needs to psychological needs to self-fulfillment needs.

True/False Test

Indicate whether each statement is true or false by placing T or F in the blank space next to each item

1. ____ Incentive theories propose that behavior is motivated by the "pull" of external goals, such as rewards.

2. ____ *Self-actualization* is defined by Maslow as "the full use and exploitation of talents, capacities, and potentialities."

3. ____ Activation is one of the basic characteristics commonly associated with motivation and is seen in the greater vigor of responding that usually accompanies motivated behavior.

4. ____ Drive theories propose that behavior is motivated by the desire to reduce internal tension caused by unmet biological needs, such as hunger or thirst.

5. ____ Homeostasis refers to the notion that the body monitors and maintains internal states, such as body temperature and energy supplies, at relatively constant levels.

6. ____ Intensity is one of the basic characteristics commonly associated with motivation and is seen in the initiation or production of behavior.

Check your answers and review any areas of weakness before going on to the next section.

The Motivation to Eat

Learning Objectives

When you have finished studying this section of the chapter, you should be able to:

1. Specify the motivational factors that influence us to eat.
2. Explain how oral signals, stomach signals, CCK, insulin, and the hypothalamus seem to influence hunger and eating behavior.

Read the section "The Motivation to Eat" and **write** *your answers to the following:*

1. (a) What, when, and how much you eat are influenced by diverse _____ , _____ , _____ , and cultural factors.
   (b) Psychologically, eating can be related to _____ , such as depression, anxiety, or stress.
   (c) Interpersonally, eating is often used to foster _____ , as when you have friends over for dinner or take a potential customer to lunch; food and eating behavior permeate many different dimensions of our lives.

2. (a) The _____ sensations involved in tasting and chewing food contribute greatly to the subjective pleasure and satisfaction of eating; they _____ (do/do not) seem to be what causes us to start or stop eating.
   (b) The stomach has sensory _____ that detect the stretching of the stomach muscles; as the stomach stretches to accommodate food, signals from these _____ are relayed to the brain, helping to trigger feelings of satiation.
   (c) A(n) _____ called cholecystokinin, or CCK, seems to play a role in signaling satiation; as food moves from the stomach to the intestines, CCK is secreted into the

bloodstream and conveyed to the brain, where it acts as a(n) _____ .

   (d) CCK seems to magnify the satiety-producing effects of food in the stomach by _____ (slowing/speeding up) the rate at which the stomach empties and by heightening the sensitivity of _____ in the stomach.

3. (a) _____ is a hormone secreted by the pancreas which helps regulate the metabolism of carbohydrates, fats, and starches in the body; higher levels lead us to experience more hunger and eat more food.
   (b) Normally, _____ levels begin to rise shortly after we start eating, but research by Judith Rodin has shown that we can become classically conditioned to produce increased _____ levels before consuming food.
   (c) People who are highly responsive to food cues are called _____ , whereas people who are less responsive to food cues are called _____ .
   (d) When _____ are exposed to an environmental stimulus that they've learned to associate with food, they produce significantly more insulin in anticipation of eating than _____ do.

4. (a) In the 1940s, the _____ , a small structure buried deep within the brain, was first implicated in the regulation of eating behavior; if a particular area called the ventromedial _____ (VMH) was damaged, an experimental animal would eat until it became obese.
   (b) A decade later, it was discovered that damage to another area, called the lateral _____ (LH), caused an animal to stop eating, and if left to its own devices the animal would starve to death.

(c) On the basis of these initial findings, it became widely believed that the _____ and its surrounding regions contained the "start eating" and "stop eating" centers, but later research cast serious doubts on this simple model.

5. Psychologists have reached a number of conclusions about the factors that regulate eating behavior:

   (a) _____ signals such as oral sensations, stretch receptors, and chemical signals like CCK and insulin appear to be involved, each providing some form of feedback to the brain.

   (b) It appears that the _____ and its surrounding regions detect these varied signals and, in turn, initiate or suppress eating behavior.

   (c) Our _____ response to external signals may trigger physiological changes in responsive individuals, such as increased insulin production, that lead to increased feelings of hunger.

   (d) What motivates us to eat at a particular moment is governed by a complex system involving the _____ of physiological, behavioral, cognitive, and environmental factors.

The Regulation of Body Weight
Learning Objectives

When you have finished studying this section of the chapter, you should be able to:

1. Explain the role the basal metabolic rate (BMR) plays in weight regulation and specify the factors that influence the BMR.

2. Identify how set-point theory accounts for the regulation of body weight.

3. Identify the misconceptions about the causes of obesity.

4. Describe how obese individuals differ from nonobese individuals in their response to food.

5. Explain why it is difficult to maintain weight loss.

6. Define anorexia and bulimia and list the characteristic of each disorder.

Read the section "The Regulation of Body Weight" and **write** *your answers to the following:*

1. (a) About _____ (one-third/two-thirds) of your body's energy is used for routine physical activities; the remaining _____ (one-third/two-thirds) is used for continuous body functions that are essential for life.

   (b) The rate at which your body uses energy for vital body functions when at rest is referred to as your _____ , abbreviated _____ .

2. (a) The finding that matched pairs maintained the same weight despite the fact that one ate twice as much as the other demonstrates that a constant body weight depends on the critical balance between _____ and basal metabolic rate.

   (b) A variety of factors influence a person's basal metabolic rate; on the average women have a(n) _____ metabolic rate than men, heavy people have a(n) _____ metabolic rate than slender people, and the BMR _____ with age.

   (c) _____ can also play a role in determining a person's BMR; although there are exceptions, one can reliably predict a child's approximate adult weight by considering the adult weight of his or her biological parents.

3. (a) Set-point weight is the particular weight that the body is naturally set to maintain by increasing or decreasing _____ .

(b) Set-point theory is based on the well-established principle of _____ ; increases or decreases in body weight are followed by corresponding changes in the body's _____ .

(c) Research suggests that the _____ and _____ of fat cells are established very early in life (by about the age of two) and are at least partly determined by genetic factors.

(d) Environmental factors, such as what and how much you eat, also play an important role in the amount of fat stored; at first, overeating produces an increase in the _____ of the fat cells, and if continued there will be an increase in the _____ of fat cells.

(e) Once acquired, fat cells are with you for life; your body essentially becomes programmed to maintain a higher _____ weight, and if you reduce your weight, the _____ of fat cells does not decrease; fat cells simply decrease in _____ .

(f) One criticism of set-point theory is that it merely _____ what occurs rather than _____ the underlying mechanisms; set-point theory nevertheless remains a useful model in helping us understand many aspects of body weight regulation.

4. (a) A person whose weight is _____ percent or more above his or her optimal weight is said to be obese; there is some specific cause, such as a brain tumor or a hereditary disease, for about _____ percent of obese individuals, but for the vast majority a specific cause cannot be identified.

(b) Several studies have demonstrated that many obese individuals tend to be highly responsive to _____ cues associated with food, such as time of day, how appetizing the food is, and easy availability of food.

(c) Individuals who are highly responsive to food-related stimuli tend to react physiologically with greater _____ production and generally operate with higher body _____ .

(d) The more _____ that circulates throughout a person's body, the faster fat deposits build from glucose not used for energy, and the person gains more weight; the more weight gained, the easier it becomes to gain additional weight.

(e) When an obese person restricts food intake, the body vigorously defends against the loss by sharply reducing the rate of _____ ; far fewer calories are now needed to maintain the obese weight because the body's expenditure of energy is sharply reduced and fat requires _____ (less/more) energy to maintain than lean body tissue does.

(f) Another critical finding is that the _____ rate remains decreased for as long as the person's body weight remains below the obese set-point weight.

(g) To maintain their lower weight, people must modify their eating patterns and follow a regular _____ program.

5. (a) Anorexia nervosa is a life-threatening disorder that involves _____ and has three key symptoms: the individual (1) _____ to maintain a minimally normal body weight, (2) is extremely afraid of gaining _____ or becoming _____ , and (3) has a distorted perception about the size of his or her _____ .

(b) Approximately 90 percent of cases of anorexia nervosa occur in adolescent or young _____ , and while the characteristics of the disorder are very similar, it is less common among _____ .

(c) It's rare that people with anorexia completely lose their _____ ; rather they tend to place themselves on a very restricted _____ , exercise excessively, engage in fasting and self-induced vomiting, and misuse laxatives.

(d) Depression, social withdrawal, insomnia, and, in women, failure to menstruate, along with a distorted _____ , frequently accompany the disorder; despite an emaciated appearance, the person with anorexia looks in the mirror and sees herself as being overweight.

(e) Approximately _____ percent of people with anorexia nervosa die from starvation, suicide, or physical complications accompanying extreme weight loss.

6. (a) People suffering from bulimia nervosa are _____ their normal weight range and may even be slightly _____ .

(b) Bulimic people engage in _____ eating and then purge themselves of the excessive food consumption by self-induced vomiting and less often by use of laxatives or enemas.

(c) People suffering from bulimia usually conceal their eating problems from others; episodes of _____ eating typically occur in secrecy and usually include the consumption of high-caloric, sweet foods that can be swallowed quickly; as much as 50,000 calories may be consumed at one time.

(d) Diverse cultural, psychological, social, and _____ factors seem to be involved in both anorexia nervosa and bulimia nervosa; among female identical twins, when one develops anorexia, better than _____ percent of the time the other twin also develops anorexia, whereas with nonidentical twins the rate of co-occurrence is only 5 percent.

7. Read the following and write the correct term in the space provided:

(a) Farah skipped lunch and later in the afternoon, as she was walking by the cafeteria, the smell of french fries made her mouth water. At this time it is likely that her blood level of insulin is _____ (high/ low).

(b) Farah is very responsive to food-related environmental stimuli even when she hasn't skipped a meal. Judith Rodin would classify her as a(n) _____ (external/ nonexternal).

(c) While Dr. Fleming was investigating the relationship between the brain and eating behavior, he discovered that rats would stop eating if he destroyed an area of their brain called the _____ hypothalamus, or _____ .

(d) Although he leads a somewhat sedentary lifestyle, 35-year-old Joshua has been about the same weight, give or take a pound or two, since his late teens. His set-point weight is most likely maintained by his _____ , or _____ .

(e) Despite trying many different weight-loss approaches, Roger is still about 30 percent above his optimal weight. According to most definitions, Roger would be classified as _____ .

(f) Claire is a 15-year-old of average height but weighs only 85 pounds. She has lost 30 pounds over the past eight or nine months by eating very little and going to aerobics classes twice a day. Claire suffers from

_____ .

Review of Key Terms 2

satiation
oral signals
stomach signals
cholecystokinin (CCK)
insulin
externals/nonexternals
ventromedial
  hypothalamus (VMH)
lateral hypothalamus
  (LH)

basal metabolic rate
  (BMR)
set-point weight
set-point theory
obese
anorexia nervosa
bulimia nervosa

Matching Exercise

Match the appropriate term with its definition or description:

1. _____ A hormone that seems to play a role in signaling satiation, or fullness.

2. _____ The sensations involved in tasting and chewing food that contribute greatly to the subjective pleasure and satisfaction of eating.

3. _____ The rate at which the body uses energy for vital body functions when at rest.

4. _____ Judith Rodin's terms for people who are highly responsive to environmental food-related stimuli and those who are less responsive to food cues.

5. _____ A particular area of the hypothalamus that, when damaged, causes an experimental animal to eat until it became obese.

6. _____ The particular weight that is set and maintained by increases or decreases in basal metabolic rate.

7. _____ A hormone secreted by the pancreas that helps regulate the metabolism of carbohydrates, fats, and starches in the body.

8. _____ Weighing 20 percent or more above one's optimal body weight.

True/False Test

Indicate whether each statement is true or false by placing T or F in the blank space next to each item.

1. ____ Bulimia nervosa is an eating disorder in which the individual refuses to maintain a minimally normal body weight, is extremely afraid of gaining weight or becoming fat, and has a distorted body image about his or her body size.

2. ____ If the lateral hypothalamus (LH) is damaged, an experimental animal will stop eating.

3. ____ Satiation is the feeling of fullness and diminished desire to eat.

4. ____ The stomach has sensory neurons that detect the stretching of the stomach muscles as it accommodates food; these stomach signals are relayed to the brain, helping to trigger feelings of satiation.

5. ____ Anorexia nervosa is an eating disorder in which a person engages in binge eating and then purges the excessive food consumption by self-induced vomiting or, less often, by taking laxatives or enemas.

6. ____ Set-point theory is based on the well-established principle of homeostasis; increases or decreases in body weight are followed by corresponding changes in the body's basal metabolic rate.

Check your answers and review any areas of weakness before going on to the next section.

Sexual Motivation and Behavior
Learning Objectives

When you have finished studying this section of the chapter, you should be able to:

1. Identify the multiple factors that are involved in understanding human sexuality.

2. List and describe the four stages of the human sexual response.

3. Explain how sexual motivation differs for lower and higher animals and specify the biological factors that are involved in sexual motivation.

4. Explain what sexual orientation means and state why it is sometimes difficult to define.

5. Identify the factors that have been associated with sexual orientation.

6. Identify the factors that characterize the sexual behavior patterns of adults and list the important aspects of sexual relationships in late adulthood.

Read the section "Sexual Motivation and Behavior" and **write** *your answers to the following:*

1. (a) Psychologists consider the drive to have sex a basic human _____ .

   (b) In most animals, sexual behavior is _____ determined and triggered by hormonal changes in the female; during the cyclical period known as _____ , a female animal is fertile and receptive to male sexual advances.

   (c) As you go up the evolutionary scale, moving from relatively simple to more sophisticated animals, sexual behavior becomes less _____ determined and more subject to learning and _____ influences.

   (d) Sexual behavior also becomes less limited to the goal of _____ ; in some primate species, sexual interaction serves important _____ functions, defining and cementing relationships among members of the group.

2. (a) In humans, sexual behavior is not limited to the goal of _____ or to a female's fertile period; while a woman's fertility is regulated by monthly hormonal cycles, these hormonal changes seem to have little or no effect on a female's sexual motivation.

   (b) Even when a woman's ovaries, which produce the female sex hormone _____ , are surgically removed or stop functioning during menopause, there is little or no drop in sexual interest.

   (c) In many nonhuman female mammals, removal of the ovaries results in _____ interest in sexual activity.

   (d) In male animals, removal of the testes (castration) typically causes _____ in sexual activity and interest; castration causes a significant decrease in levels of _____ , the hormone responsible for male sexual development.

   (e) When human males experience lowered levels of _____ due to illness or castration, _____ in sexual interest tends to occur, although the effects vary among individuals.

   (f) _____ is also involved in female sexual motivation; when levels are abnormally low, sexual interest often _____ ; thus in both men and women, sexual motivation is biologically influenced by body levels of the hormone _____ .

3. (a) The human sexual response cycle was first mapped by sex researcher pioneers _____ and _____ , who, in the name of science, observed hundreds of people engage in more than 10,000 episodes of sexual activity in their laboratory; their findings indicated that the human sexual response can be described as a cycle with four stages.

   (b) The _____ phase marks the beginning of sexual arousal, which can occur in response to sexual fantasies or other sexually arousing stimuli, physical contact with another person, or masturbation; this stage is accompanied by a variety of bodily changes in anticipation of sexual interaction.

   (c) In the second phase, the _____

phase, physical arousal builds as pulse and breathing rates continue to increase; during the first and second stages the degree of arousal may fluctuate up and down.

(d) _____ is the third and shortest phase of the sexual response cycle, during which blood pressure and heart rate reach their peak; both men (many of whom experience one intense _____) and women (many of whom are capable of multiple _____) describe the subjective experience of _____ in similar and very positive terms.

(e) During the _____ phase, arousal slowly subsides and returns to normal levels; males experience a(n) _____ period, during which they are incapable of having another erection or orgasm, and this period varies in length but tends to increase with age.

4. (a) Sexual orientation refers to whether a person is sexually aroused by members of the same sex, the opposite sex, or both sexes; a(n) _____ is sexually attracted to individuals of the other sex, a(n) _____ to individuals of the same sex, and a(n) _____ to individuals of both sexes.

(b) Technically, the term _____ can be applied to either males or females; however, females usually use the term *lesbian* and males use the term *gay* to describe their sexual orientation.

(c) Some people are exclusively _____ or _____, but others are less easy to classify; the key point is that there is not always a perfect correspondence between a particular person's sexual identity, sexual desires, and sexual behaviors.

(d) Although estimates vary, approximately _____ to _____ million American men and women are gay or lesbian.

5. (a) Psychologists and other researchers cannot say with certainty why people are homosexual or bisexual; evidence from twin studies suggests that _____ plays a role in determining a homosexual orientation.

(b) While studying gay twins, researchers found that the closer the degree of _____ relationship, the more likely it was that both brothers would be homosexual; both brothers were homosexual in _____ percent of identical twins, _____ percent of fraternal twins, and _____ percent of adoptive brothers.

(c) In twin studies of lesbians, both sisters were lesbian in _____ percent of identical twins, _____ percent of fraternal twins, and _____ percent of adoptive sisters.

(d) Since only about _____ of both identical twins were homosexual, it's clear that _____ alone cannot explain sexual orientation; nevertheless, these studies and others support the notion that sexual orientation is at least partly influenced by _____ .

6. (a) Neurobiologist Simon LeVay discovered a small but significant difference between heterosexuals and homosexuals in a tiny cluster of neurons in the _____ , which is known to be involved in sexual behavior; in male homosexuals and female heterosexuals, the cluster was only half the size as in heterosexual men.

(b) LeVay speculates that this tiny cluster of neurons in the _____ may be involved in determining sexual orientation, but there is no way of knowing if this difference in brain structure causes homosexual behavior in men.

(c) In general, the only conclusion we can draw from these studies is that some _____ and _____ factors are correlated with a homosexual orientation, but more definitive research is needed before causality can be determined.

7. Researchers investigating the effects of early life experience on sexual orientation concluded that:

(a) Homosexuality is _____ (due to/not due to) an unpleasant early heterosexual experience, such as being sexually abused during childhood by a member of the opposite sex.

(b) Homosexuals _____ (are/ are not) more likely than heterosexuals to report a first sexual encounter with a member of the same sex, such as being seduced by an older member of the same sex.

(c) Homosexuality _____ (is/is not) the result of an abnormal relationship between the parents and the child, such as having a father who is an inadequate male role model or having an overly dominant mother.

(d) Research suggests that there _____ (are/are no) consistent differences between homosexual and heterosexual adults in their patterns of early experiences; sexual orientation appears to be determined before adolescence and long before the beginning of sexual activity.

(e) Both homosexuals and heterosexuals typically become aware of their sexual feelings and orientation long before they express them in some form of sexual behavior; some researchers now believe that sexual orientation is established as early as age _____ and, once established, is highly resistant to change.

8. (a) _____ ,

_____ , _____ , and cultural factors are undoubtedly involved in determining sexual orientation; however, researchers are still unable to pinpoint exactly what those factors are and how they interact.

(b) Homosexuality in itself _____ (is still/is no longer) considered a sexual disorder by clinical psychologists and psychiatrists.

(c) Like heterosexuals, gays and lesbians can be found in every _____ and at every _____ level, and many are involved in long-term, committed, and caring relationships.

(d) Children who are raised by gay or lesbian parents _____ (are/are not) as well adjusted as children who are raised by heterosexual parents; also, they _____ (are/are not) more likely to be gay or lesbian in adulthood than are children who are raised by heterosexual parents.

9. (a) The notion that people today, especially younger people, have more sex partners than people did twenty or thirty years ago is basically _____ (false/accurate).

(b) Among people aged _____ to _____ , about half have had five or more sexual partners; in contrast, only about a third of those over age _____ have had five or more sexual partners.

(c) The vast majority of adults in the _____ to _____ age range had their first sexual experience in the context of marriage, compared to only about a third of today's young adults.

(d) Young adults today tend to become sexually active at a(n) _____ age and are marrying at a(n) _____ age; hence, younger people today tend to have more sexual partners than members of older generations.

(e) The vast majority of people (about 80 percent) had either _____ sexual partner or _____ in the previous year; by the age of _____ , about 90 percent of Americans have married and, once married or cohabiting, have a strong commitment to being faithful to each other.

10. (a) One-third of American adults have sex with a partner _____ or more times per week; one-third have sex _____ times per month; one-third have sex _____ times a year or not at all; for adults between eighteen and fifty-nine, men have sex an average of about _____ times per month and women about _____ times per month.

(b) Married or cohabiting couples have the _____ (least/most) active sex lives.

(c) About _____ percent of people reported that they were physically and emotionally satisfied with their sexual relationships.

11. (a) _____ is nearly universal as the most practiced sexual activity among heterosexual couples; more than two-thirds of Americans have either given or received _____ sex at some point in their lives; and about 26 percent of men and 20 percent of women have engaged in _____ sex.

(b) The most preferred sexual activities, in descending order for both sexes, are as follows: (1) having _____ intercourse; (2) watching the partner _____ ; (3) receiving _____ sex; and (4) giving _____ sex.

(c) Regardless of age, at least 90 percent of women found no appeal in the following sexual practices: (1) being _____ to do something sexual; (2) _____ someone to do something sexual; (3) receiving _____ intercourse; (4) having a(n) _____ sex partner; and (5) having sex with a(n) _____ .

(d) With the exception of having sex with a(n) _____ , at least 90 percent of men also found these sexual practices unappealing; other sexual practices that the majority of people do not find appealing include having _____ sex, using a(n) _____ or _____ , and watching other people engage in sexual activity.

(e) For the most part, Americans are fundamentally _____ (happy/unhappy) with the relationsips they have with their sexual partner and tend to be rather _____ and _____ in their sexual practices and preferences.

12. Read the following and write the correct term in the space provided:

(a) Mary and her husband James have just shared a fulfilling sexual experience. Unlike Mary, James is not likely to be able to experience another orgasm for a period of time; this is called the _____ period.

(b) Mrs. Jacobson had her ovaries removed because of cancer and is now in perfect health. As a result of the operation, the level of the female sex hormone will _____ ; the level of her interest in sexual activity will _____ .

(c) Dr. Jamison surgically removed the testes of an experimental laboratory rat. It is very probable that the rat will experience a(n) _____ in sexual activity and interest.

(d) Hamish, a twenty-five-year-old medical student, is heterosexual; his brother Stuart, a twenty-one-year-old philosophy major, is homosexual. The two brothers differ in their

_____ .

(e) According to the National Health and Social Life Survey, _____ is nearly universal as the most practiced sexual activity among heterosexual couples.

Review of Key Terms and Key Names 3

estrus	orgasm
estrogen	resolution phase
testosterone	refractory period
William H. Masters	sexual orientation
Virginia E. Johnson	heterosexual
excitement phase	homosexual
plateau phase	bisexual

Matching Exercise

Match the appropriate term / name with its definition or description.

1. _____ American behavioral scientist who, along with William H. Masters, conducted pioneering research in the field of human sexuality and sex therapy.

2. _____ The second stage in the human sexual response cycle in which physical arousal builds as pulse and breathing rates continue to rise; the penis becomes fully erect, the testes enlarge, the clitoris withdraws but remains sensitive, the vaginal entrance tightens, and vaginal lubrication continues.

3. _____ The term for a person who is sexually attracted to individuals of the other sex.

4. _____ For a male, a period of time following orgasm during which he is incapable of having another erection or orgasm.

5. _____ The term for a person who is attracted to individuals of the same sex.

6. _____ American physician who, along with Virginia E. Johnson, conducted pioneering research in the field of human sexuality and sex therapy.

7. _____ The first stage in the human sexual response cycle that marks the beginning

of sexual arousal and can occur in response to sexual fantasies or other sexually arousing stimuli, physical contact with another person, or masturbation.

True/False Test

Indicate whether each statement is true or false by placing T or F in the blank space next to each item.

1. ____ Estrus refers to the cyclical period during which a female animal is fertile and receptive to male sexual advances.

2. ____ The fourth stage of the sexual response cycle, during which both sexes tend to experience a warm physical glow and sense of well-being and arousal returns to normal, is called the resolution phase.

3. ____ A bisexual is sexually attracted to individuals of both sexes.

4. ____ Testosterone is the female sex hormone produced by the ovaries and influences a woman's monthly reproductive cycle.

5. ____ Orgasm is the third and shortest phase of the sexual response cycle, during which blood pressure and heart rate reach their peak and muscles in the vaginal walls and uterus contract rhythmically, as do the muscles in and around the penis as the male ejaculates.

6. ____ Estrogen is the male sex hormone produced by the testes and is responsible for male sexual development.

7. ____ Sexual orientation refers to the cultural, social, and psychological meanings that are associated with masculinity or femininity.

> Check your answers and review any areas of weakness before going on to the next section.

Arousal Motives: Curiosity and Sensation Seeking

Learning Objectives

When you have finished studying this section of the chapter, you should be able to:

1. Describe how arousal theory accounts for people's motivation to maintain an optimal level of arousal.

2. Identify the factors that influence curiosity and

exploratory behavior and explain how arousal theory deals with the pacing of curious behavior.

3. Specify what is meant by sensation-seeking behavior and list the characteristics of people who are sensation seekers.

Read the section "Arousal Motives: Curiosity and Sensation Seeking" and **write** *your answers to the following:*

1. (a) Arousal theory is based on the observation that people find both very _____ and very _____ levels of arousal quite _____ .

   (b) When arousal is too _____ , we experience boredom and try to _____ arousal by seeking out stimulating experiences; when arousal is too _____ , we seek to _____ arousal in a less stimulating environment.

   (c) According to arousal theory, people are motivated to maintain a(n) _____ level of arousal, one that is neither too _____ nor too _____ ; this level can vary from person to person, from time to time, and from one situation to another.

2. (a) One purpose of curiosity and exploratory behavior is to become familiar with and understand our world; in pursuit of this goal, we _____ the rate at which we gradually expose ourselves to increasing complexity and novelty.

   (b) As we become familiar with a stimulus, we _____ move toward stimuli that are slightly more complex, and this _____ produces the optimal level of physical and cognitive arousal that helps motivate curiosity.

   (c) If a stimulus is more complex than we can

process at the _____ that we can tolerate, uncomfortable levels of physical or cognitive arousal can occur; if this happens, the curiosity drive becomes _____ and we withdraw from the stimulus and may even experience intense anxiety and fear.

3. (a) What is considered _____ or _____ is relative to each individual's life experiences; as an individual becomes more familiar with his or her environment through exploratory behavior, the complexity or novelty of the objects or situations that inspire curiosity progressively _____ .

   (b) Some children respond positively to novel stimuli and easily adjust to changes in their environment, whereas other children do not; these _____ differences seem to be based on a genetic predisposition and are often remarkably consistent throughout a person's life.

4. (a) People who are highly motivated to try risky or exciting activities are called _____ ; those high in _____ are innately motivated to experience the high levels of arousal that are associated with varied and novel activities that often involve some degree of physical or social risk.

   (b) _____ are not attracted to danger per se but view themselves as independent, open-minded, and unconventional people who like feeling uninhibited, especially in relaxed social situations; they are _____ (flexible/ inflexible) in their style of thinking, are _____ (tolerant/intolerant) of uncertainty, and enjoy the discovery of new knowledge.

Competence and Achievement Motivation

Learning Objectives

When you have finished studying this section of the chapter, you should be able to:

1. Define *competence motivation* and *achievement motivation* and differentiate between the two.

2. Describe how achievement motivation is measured and explain how it is affected by culture.

3. Explain how the belief in self-efficacy relates to achievement and competence.

Read the section "Competence and Achievement Motivation" and **write** *your answers to the following:*

1. (a) When you strive to use your cognitive, social, and behavioral skills to be capable and exercise control in a situation, you are displaying _____ motivation.

    (b) _____ motivation is the drive to excel, succeed, or outperform others at some task.

    (c) Henry Murray first defined the _____ as the tendency to overcome obstacles, exercise power, and strive to do something difficult as well as as quickly as possible.

    (d) _____ motivation has been most commonly measured by a test called the Thematic Apperception Test, or TAT.

    (e) The TAT consists of a series of ambiguous pictures and the person being tested is asked to make up a story about each picture; the story is then coded in terms of its _____ themes and imagery. The TAT is relatively valid and reliable.

2. (a) When it is broadly defined as the desire for excellence, achievement motivation is found in many, if not all, cultures; in _____ cultures the need to achieve emphasizes personal, individual success rather than the success of the group; in _____ cultures achievement motivation tends to be more socially, family, or group oriented.

    (b) Competence and achievement motivation are closely linked to _____ .

    (c) _____ is the degree to which a person is subjectively convinced of his or her own capabilities, effectiveness, or efficiency in meeting the demands of a situation.

    (d) People with strong _____ exert greater motivational effort in trying to master a situation and will persist longer in the face of obstacles; those with low _____ exert little motivational effort and often settle for solutions that don't reflect their capabilities or they may abandon their efforts altogether.

    (e) If you have a high degree of _____ in your _____ , you may excel in a situation even though your skills are below average; if you _____ your _____ , you may underachieve or behave less competently, even though you may know full well what to do and objectively possess the needed skills.

3. Read the following and write the correct term in the space provided:

    (a) Young Alec practices at the golf range for one or two hours most days because he wants to be the best golfer he can possibly be and plans to become a professional golfer. His goal and behavior suggest that Alec has a high level of _____ motivation.

(b) Jasmine was very excited when she went to the zoo for the first time, and she was particularly curious and a little nervous about what she would find in the reptile house when they got there. As Jasmine and her parents entered the reptile facility, she got more and more anxious, and when she saw the lizards and snakes, she burst into tears. It appears that the situation was moving faster than Jasmine's curiosity and exploratory _____ .

(c) There is nothing Roland likes better than the quiet routine of his life. He goes to work at the same time every day, he meets his friends for bridge every Tuesday and Thursday evening, and he works out at the gym on Monday, Wednesday, and Friday. He takes his annual vacation at the same holi-day resort each year and usually stays at the same inn. Roland is likely to score very _____ (high/low) on Zukerman's Sensation Seeking Scale.

(d) Charmaine is a very confident about her ability to deal effectively and efficiently with any situation that might arise in her job as an air traffic controller. Albert Bandura would probably classify Charmaine as a person with a high level of

_____ .

(e) Allison wants to prove to herself that she is capable of mastering basic mathematical concepts, so she enrolls in an algebra course and an introductory statistics course. Allison is demonstrating _____ motivation.

Graphic Organizer 1

Identify the theory associated with each of the following statements:

Statement	Theory
1. I believe that behavior is motivated by the desire to reduce internal tension caused by unmet biological needs that "push" us to behave in certain ways.	
2. I emphasize the importance of psychological and cognitive components in human motivation and believe that we are innately driven to strive for a positive self-concept and the realization of our personal potential.	
3. I take my lead from Charles Darwin, and although it may not be popular today, I strongly believe that we are motivated to engage in certain behaviors because of genetic programming.	
4. We do what we do because of the "pull" of external goals, such as rewards. I think that learning theorists have it right when they say reinforcement is a key factor in motivation.	
5. How do we explain curiosity and exploratory behavior? I believe that we are motivated to maintain an optimal level of arousal, and when it is too low, we try to increase it by seeking out stimulating experiences. When arousal is too high, we seek to reduce arousal in a less stimulating environment.	

Review of Key Terms 4

arousal theory
sensation seeking
competence motivation
achievement motivation
Thematic Apperception
    Test (TAT)

individualistic cultures
collectivistic cultures
self-efficacy

Matching Exercise

Match the appropriate term with its definition or description:

1. _____ Cultures, such as those that characterize North American and European countries, in which the need to achieve emphasizes personal, individual success rather than the success of the group.

2. _____ The degree to which a person is subjectively convinced of his or her ability to effectively meet the demands of a situation.

3. _____ The view that people are motivated to maintain an optimal level of arousal which is neither too high nor too low.

4. _____ Motivated behavior directed toward demonstrating competence and exercising control in a situation.

5. _____ Cultures, like those of many Asian countries, in which achievement motivation is more socially oriented than individually oriented.

6. _____ The degree to which an individual is motivated to experience high levels of arousal associated with varied and novel activities.

7. _____ Motivated behavior directed toward excelling, succeeding, or outperforming others at some task.

8. _____ A test that consists of a series of ambiguous pictures; the person being tested is asked to make up a story about each picture, and the story is then coded in terms of its achievement themes and imagery.

Check your answers and review any areas of weakness before going on to the next section.

Emotion

Learning Objectives

When you have finished studying this section of the chapter, you should be able to:

1. Define *emotion* and specify the many functions emotions serve in human behavior and relationships.

2. List the three components of emotion and describe what basic emotions are.

3. Explain how culture and individual differences influence emotional experience.

4. Describe the physical changes associated with different emotions.

5. Identify the evidence that supports the idea that facial expressions of basic emotions are innate.

6. Explain how facial expressions are affected by cultural display rules.

*Read the section "Emotion" and **write** your answers to the following:*

1. (a) We are motivated to seek out experiences that produce _____ emotions and to avoid experiences that produce _____ emotions.

   (b) _____ are intense but short-lived and are more likely to have a specific cause, to be directed toward some particular object, and to motivate a person to take some sort of action; in contrast, a(n) _____ involves a milder emotional state that is more general and pervasive, such as gloominess or contentment, that lasts for a few hours or days.

   (c) Emotion is defined as a distinct psychological state involving three distinct components: _____ experience, _____ arousal, and a(n) _____ expression or response.

2. (a) Considerable _____ (agreement/disagreement) exists among psychologists regarding the definition and classification of emotions.

   (b) Some psychologists assert that there are a limited number of universal _____ emotions that are biologically determined products of evolution; these include anger, happiness, sadness, fear, disgust, surprise, anxiety, shame, and interest.

   (c) Some emotion theorists suggest that more complex emotions are produced by various combinations of _____ emotions; combining anger and disgust yields _____ , sadness plus surprise equals _____ , and _____ is the result of combining joy and acceptance.

   (d) Other theorists reject the idea of _____ emotions and instead believe that a large number of qualitatively different emotions exist.

   (e) People often experience a(n) _____ of emotions rather than a "pure" form of any single given emotion; in more complex situations people may experience _____ emotions in which different emotions are experienced simultaneously or in rapid succession.

   (f) When emotions are compared, they tend to be arranged along two dimensions, how _____ or _____ the emotion is and how much arousal is present; joy and rage involve _____ levels of arousal or intensity, whereas contentment and resentment involve relatively _____ levels of arousal.

3. (a) People from different cultures experience emotions in _____ way as Americans; there is general _____ among cultures regarding the subjective experience of different basic emotions such as joy, anger, fear, disgust, and sadness.

   (b) Researchers have also found some key _____ in cultural descriptions of emotion; for example, the Japanese perceive an additional dimension to Americans' two basic dimensions of pleasantness and arousal, called interpersonal engagement.

   (c) People vary greatly in the _____ of the emotions they experience; that is, some people are "more emotional" than others.

   (d) Regardless of their sex, people who experience very _____ positive emotions also tend to experience very _____ negative emotions.

   (e) People also differ in their _____ of emotions; emotionally _____ people tend to be better liked than people who are more inhibited in their display of emotions.

   (f) Less emotionally _____ people may experience emotions as intensely as more emotionally _____ people but they simply don't express their emotions as freely.

4. (a) The _____ or _____ component of emotions is especially evident when you experience an intense emotion such as anger or extreme fear.

   (b) _____ arousal involves the activation of the autonomic nervous system; arousal of the _____ nervous system gears you up for action, affecting heartbeat, blood pressure, respiration, perspiration, and other body systems.

(c) In contrast to emotions like anger or fear, other emotions, such as contentment, are characterized by a(n) _____ of body arousal, and research has shown that there are distinct differences in the pattern of physiological responses for different emotions.

(d) Surveys of many different cultures have suggested that distinct patterns of _____ experience may well be universal across cultures, at least for basic emotions like joy, fear, anger, sadness, and disgust but perhaps not for every emotion.

5. (a) In addition to their subjective and physiological components, emotions usually involve a(n) _____ or _____ component; we also show our emotions by our _____ , such as our gestures, changes in posture, and, most important, our facial expressions.

(b) Paul Ekman has estimated that the human face is capable of creating over _____ different expressions; a facial expression can display a single intense emotion, such as joy, anger, or disgust, but can also communicate the subtleties involved in mixed or complex emotions.

(c) Ekman and his colleagues have coded different facial expressions by carefully analyzing which facial _____ are involved in producing each expression; they have been able to precisely classify the facial expressions that characterize happiness, disgust, surprise, sadness, anger, and fear.

(d) Facial expressions for basic emotions seem to be _____ , or _____ , rather than learned.

(e) Psychologist Carroll Izzard found that facial expressions of pain, interest, and disgust are present at birth; the social smile emerges by or _____ weeks of age; by _____ months, sadness and anger are evident; and by _____ or _____ months of age, fear is displayed.

6. (a) Studies have shown that people from many different cultures accurately recognize the emotions expressed in photographs of facial expressions, even when the facial expressions display _____ of emotion.

(b) The social context, as well as culture, can influence the expression of emotion; cultural differences in the management of facial expressions are called _____ and can vary greatly from culture to culture.

Graphic Organizer 2

Identify the emotion (relaxation, alarm, annoyance, boredom, astonishment) associated with each of the following descriptions and indicate where it should go on the matrix provided below.

1. Much to her surprise Natasha receives an A+ in her third-year history course and can hardly believe it. _____

2. In the middle of the night Harry, who lives alone, is startled out of a deep sleep by strange noises coming from the basement.

   _____

3. During his three o'clock calculus class Nathan finds the topic totally uninteresting and starts losing his concentration. _____

4. On Saturday Dawn sleeps in and spends most of the morning propped up on comfortable pillows reading a romantic novel.

   _____

5. Five minutes after the meter has expired Dhillon arrives at his car only to find he has been given a $20 ticket. _____

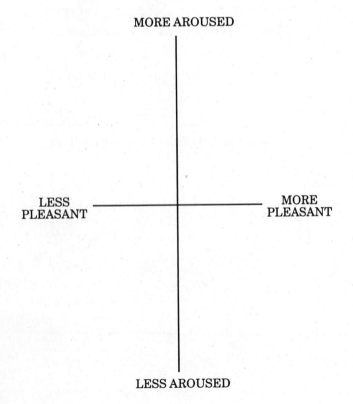

MORE AROUSED

LESS PLEASANT

MORE PLEASANT

LESS AROUSED

Explaining Emotions: Four Key Theories
Learning Objectives

When you have finished studying this section of the chapter, you should be able to:

1. Explain how theories of emotion differ in terms of which component of emotion they emphasize.

2. Describe the James-Lange and Cannon-Bard theories of emotion and explain how Cannon refuted the James-Lange theory.

3. Specify the main features of the facial feedback hypothesis and provide examples to illustrate it.

4. Explain how the two-factor theory accounts for emotions and specify what aspects of the theory have been supported by research.

5. Describe the cognitive-mediational theory of emotion and state how it differs from the two-factor theory.

*Read the section "Explaining Emotions: Four Key Theories" and **write** your answers to the following:*

1. (a) Theories of emotion tend to differ in terms of which component of emotion—

   _____ responses, expressive

   _____ , or _____

   experience—receives the most emphasis.

   (b) The James-Lange theory proposes that emotions follow this sequence: we

   _____ a stimulus,

   _____ and behavioral changes

   occur, and we _____

   these reactions as a particular emotion.

2. Walter Cannon challenged the James-Lange theory, criticizing it on a number of grounds:

   (a) Body reactions are similar for many emotions, yet our _____ experience of various emotions is very different.

   (b) Our emotional reaction to a stimulus is often faster than our _____ reaction; it takes several seconds for the

   _____ changes caused by activation of the sympathetic nervous system to take effect, but the subjective experi-

ence of emotion is often virtually instantaneous.

(c) When physiological changes are artificially
induced, as by drugs, people

_____

(always/do not necessarily) report feeling a
related emotion.

(d) People cut off from feeling body changes
(i.e., through spinal cord injuries)
_____ (do/do not) experience
true emotions; although physiological
arousal can amplify emotional feelings, the
perception of physical arousal
_____ (does/does not) seem to
be essential to the experience of emotion.

3. (a) According to the facial feedback hypothesis,
_____ a specific emotion, espe-
cially facially, causes us to _____
experience that emotion.

(b) Physical posture as well as facial
_____ can also affect the subjective influence of emotion.

(c) Our body responses, including feedback from
our muscles, can affect our _____
experience; _____ behavior
helps to activate and regulate emotional
experience, intensifying or lessening
emotion.

4. (a) The Cannon-Bard theory suggests that
when an emotion-arousing stimulus is perceived, information is relayed
_____ to the sympathetic
nervous system and to the cortex in the
brain.

(b) When the sympathetic nervous system is
activated, it causes the _____
response, and the activation of the cortex
causes the _____ experience of
emotion; they occur
_____ , and
neither causes the other.

5. (a) According to Schachter and Singer's two-factor theory (also called the cognitive arousal
theory), emotion is a result of the
_____ of physiological arousal
and the cognitive label we attach to explain
the stirred-up state; if one of these
_____ is absent, emotion will
not be experienced.

(b) Research has suggested that there is little
evidence for the two-factor theory's claim
that arousal is a(n) _____ (nec-
essary/unnecessary) condition for an emotional state or the idea that emotional states
can result from _____ unex-
plained arousal, but some aspects of the theory have been supported.

6. (a) Richard Lazarus's cognitive-mediational theory emphasizes that the most important
aspect of emotional experience is our
_____ interpretation, or
appraisal, of the emotion-causing stimulus,
event, or situation.

(b) For Lazarus, _____ (only
some/all) emotions are the result of
_____ appraisals of the personal meaning of events and experiences.

(c) Which process in emotion is *most* important
is the subject of continuous debate, but an
interactive approach, which conceptualizes
emotion as a dynamic system, might
acknowledge that _____
appraisals, _____
arousal, and _____ expression
all contribute to subjective emotional experience.

7. Read the following and write the correct term
in the space provided:

(a) Since the end of the semester, Ellen had
been feeling very contented and relaxed.
When she received her transcript in the
mail and discovered that she had got an A+

grade in her statistics class, she was over-joyed. Ellen's two different states (content-ment and joy) illustrate the difference between _____ and

_____ .

(b) Walking to the parking lot late at night, Camellia suddenly hears footsteps behind her. Her heartbeat and blood pressure increase, her muscles tense, her mouth goes dry, and she begins to perspire. These physi-ological reactions were activated by her

_____ nervous system.

(c) Mr. Hashimoto is very careful to hide his true feelings and control his facial expres-sions when he is in the presence of the chief executive officers of the company. This example illustrates the

_____ of his culture.

(d) Whenever she feels a bit gloomy, Danica sings the song "Pretend You're Happy When You're Blue," and if she follows the advice of the song, she actually experiences an eleva-tion in her mood. This example is consistent with the _____

of emotion.

(e) When Harbinder took his first ride on the High Peak ski lift, he looked down at the steep slopes beneath him and became aware of his high level of physiological arousal. Suddenly he felt fearful. Harbinder's experi-ence is best explained by the

_____ of

emotion.

Review of Key Terms and Key Names 5

emotion	nonverbal behavior
mood	display rules
basic emotions	William James
mixed emotions	James-Lange theory of
interpersonal	emotion
engagement	Walter B. Cannon
sympathetic nervous	Cannon-Bard theory of
system	emotion

facial feedback	cognitive-mediational
hypothesis	theory of emotion
two-factor theory of	interactive approach to
emotion	emotion
Richard Lazarus	

Matching Exercise

Match the appropriate term/name with its definition or description:

1. _____ The view that expressing a specific emotion, especially facially, causes the subjective experience of that emotion.

2. _____ The American psychologist who promoted the cognitive perspective in the study of emoting; proposed the cognitive-media-tional theory of emotion.

3. _____ A distinct psychological state that involves subjective experience, physical arousal, and a behavioral expression or response.

4. _____ Schachter and Singer's theo-ry that emotion is a result of the interaction of physiological arousal and the cognitive label that we apply to explain the arousal.

5. _____ Universal emotions that are biologically determined products of evolution and include anger, happiness, sadness, fear, dis-gust, surprise, anxiety, shame, and interest.

6. _____ A third cultural dimension, added to the two basic dimensions of emotion (pleasantness and arousal), that describes the degree to which each emotion involves relation-ships with others.

7. _____ Emotional expressions such as gestures, changes in posture, and facial expressions that don't rely on language or spo-ken communication.

8. _____ An approach to emotion that emphasizes the notion that cognitive appraisals, physiological arousal, and behav-ioral expression all contribute to subjective emotional expression.

9. _____ Social and cultural rules that regulate the expression of emotions, partic-ularly facial expressions.

True/False Test

Indicate whether each item is true or false by placing T or F in the space next to each item.

1. ___ Walter B. Cannon was an American psychologist who developed an influential theory of emotion called the two-factor theory of emotion.

2. ___ The cognitive-mediational theory of emotion is Lazarus's theory that emotions result from the cognitive appraisal of the effect a situation has on personal well-being.

3. ___ The James-Lange theory suggests that emotions arise from the perception and interpretation of bodily changes.

4. ___ Arousal of the sympathetic nervous system gears you up for action, affecting many body systems such as heartbeat, blood pressure, respiration, perspiration, and blood sugar levels.

5. ___ The Cannon-Bard theory proposes that emotions arise from simultaneous activation of the nervous system, which causes arousal, and the cortex, which causes the subjective experience of that emotion.

6. ___ In more complex situations we may experience mixed emotions, and these very different emotions are experienced simultaneously or in rapid succession.

7. ___ William James was an American psychologist who developed an influential theory of emotion called the facial feedback hypothesis.

8. ___ A mood is intense but rather short lived, is likely to have a specific cause, tends to be directed toward some particular object, and will motivate a person to take some sort of action.

Check your answers and review any areas of weakness before going on to the next section.

Something to Think About

Many Americans are obsessed with achieving, or at least getting closer to, the socially desirable goal of thinness. Approximately one-third of all American women and one-fifth of all American males are trying to lose weight, and the weight-loss industry is a $30 billion dollar a year enterprise. Based on what you have read in your textbook, what advice would you give a friend who is trying to lose weight?

Check your answers and review any areas of weakness before doing the progress tests.

Progress Test 1

Review the complete chapter (including Concept Reviews and the boxed inserts), review all your study notes, and then test yourself on the following progress test. Check your answers. If you make a mistake, review your notes, review the relevant section of the study guide, and, if necessary, go back and read the appropriate part of your textbook.

1. It is an innate characteristic of the European cuckoo to lay her eggs in other birds' nests. This behavior is an example of
   (a) an instinct
   (b) a drive
   (c) incentive motivation
   (d) homeostasis

2. Mrs. Kim talks proudly about her daughter Koko's ability to study hard and earn good grades in college and how Koko intends to go to medical school and become a brain surgeon. Mrs. Kim is referring to Koko's
   (a) motivation   (c) instincts
   (b) extrinsic desires (d) drive

3. About ten or fifteen minutes into his weightlifting routine, Scott usually begins to perspire heavily. His body's tendency to maintain a steady temperature through the cooling action of sweating is a function of
   (a) instinct
   (b) incentive motivation
   (c) homeostasis
   (d) self-actualization

4. Tim buys a lottery ticket every Friday with the expectation that he is going to win some money. His behavior illustrates
   (a) instinct
   (b) incentive motivation
   (c) drive
   (d) self-actualization

5. Nicole feels that she has all the material possessions she needs in life and is now determined to devote all her energy to her art. According to Maslow's hierarchy of needs, Nicole is probably striving
   (a) to fulfill her fundamental biological need to paint
   (b) to fulfill her basic safety needs
   (c) toward the realization of her personal potential
   (d) toward the realization of her social needs

6. Dr. Dorfman destroys the lateral hypothalamus of a laboratory rat. This procedure is likely to
   (a) permanently lower the rat's set point
   (b) decrease the rat's rate of metabolism
   (c) cause the rat to eat until it becomes obese
   (d) cause the rat to stop eating

7. After her fourth piece of pizza, Mary feels quite full. Her satiation is due, at least in part, to increased levels of the hormone
   (a) insulin
   (b) testosterone
   (c) cholecystokinin (CCK)
   (d) estrogen

8. Whenever he sees Amanda, Richard's heart beats faster and he gets a trembling feeling inside. Richard now thinks that he must be in love with Amanda. Which theory of emotion is represented in this example?
   (a) James-Lange theory
   (b) Cannon-Bard theory
   (c) two-factor theory
   (d) cognitive-mediational theory

9. Mr. Jackson is about thirty-five pounds overweight. Compared to people who are not overweight, Mr. Jackson is likely to have
   (a) higher metabolism
   (b) lower metabolism
   (c) the same metabolism
   (d) all of the above; there is no relationship between weight and metabolism

10. If Mr. Jackson is like most obese people, he probably differs from nonobese people in the daily regulation of his eating behavior by
    (a) being highly responsive to external cues associated with food
    (b) physiologically reacting to food-related stimuli with greater insulin production
    (c) having a generally higher body level of insulin
    (d) all of the above

11. Barney and Bailey are identical twins. Barney is gay. Therefore, there is
    (a) about a 50 percent chance that Bailey will also be homosexual
    (b) almost 100 percent chance that Bailey will also be homosexual
    (c) about a 20 percent chance that Bailey will also be homosexual
    (d) no way to predict Bailey's sexual orientation because there is no correlation between genetic factors and sexual behavior

12. Erin has been diagnosed with bulimia nervosa. The main characteristic of her eating disorder is
    (a) being 15 to 20 percent below the ideal body weight
    (b) a distorted self-perception about body shape and body weight
    (c) binge eating and purging by self-induced vomiting and occasionally by using laxatives or enemas
    (d) an obsession with food and a denial of being hungry

13. Jill is independent, openminded, and unconventional; loves the outdoors; and includes among her many interests skydiving, downhill skiing, white water kayaking, and hang-gliding. Jill is likely to be classified as
    (a) a sensation seeker
    (b) shy and timid
    (c) an external
    (d) a nonexternal

14. As part of his overall vocational assessment, Bertram took the Thematic Apperception Test (TAT). His score on this test is most likely to reveal his level of
    (a) competence motivation
    (b) achievement motivation
    (c) self-efficacy
    (d) emotionality

15. When Willard's romantic relationship ended, he felt pretty confused and experienced a combination of relief, sadness, nostalgia, anger, and jealousy. Willard's experience illustrates
    (a) basic emotions
    (b) mixed emotions
    (c) mood fluctuations
    (d) interpersonal engagement

16. When Moira was preparing for her first solo landing in a single-engine plane, she experienced a number of physiological reactions such as a racing heart, sweaty palms, and tension in her muscles. These physiological reactions were activated by her _____ nervous system.
    (a) central
    (b) sympathetic
    (c) skeletal
    (d) parasympathetic

17. Wilda is a diplomat and was trained in the customs, language, and religions of Slakia, where she is now posted. It is very unlikely that Wilda needed special training to correctly interpret her hosts' expressions of emotion as revealed by their
    (a) songs
    (b) dancing
    (c) facial expressions
    (d) eating etiquette

18. According to In Focus Box 8.1, which of the following is true?
    (a) Sexual fantasies are psychologically unhealthy.
    (b) Male and female sexual fantasies are almost identical in content and frequency.
    (c) Sexual fantasies are a sign of sexual frustration and dissatisfaction in a relationship.
    (d) All of the above are true.
    (e) None of the above are true.

19. It is claimed that subliminal self-help tapes will quickly and easily produce changes in our motivation, learning ability, attitudes, and other behaviors. According to Box 8.2,
    (a) all these claims have been supported by empirical evidence
    (b) subliminal self-help tapes are effective but only for highly suggestible people
    (c) because university and college bookstores sell subliminal self-help tapes, they probably work for improving study habits and passing exams
    (d) there is no scientific support for the claims made for self-help tapes

20. People often have strong opinions about which sex is more emotional. According to Culture and Human Behavior Box 8.3,
    (a) males are much more emotionally expressive than females in every culture studied
    (b) in the American culture, women tend to be more emotionally expressive than men
    (c) there is no evidence that males and females differ in emotional expressiveness in any culture
    (d) it's clear from the scientific evidence that women are naturally more emotional than men and their emotional expressiveness is not due to learning or cultural influences

Progress Test 2

After you have checked your understanding of the material in Progress Test 1 and reviewed the chapter with special focus on any areas of weakness, you are ready to assess your knowledge in Progress Test 2. Check your answers. If you make a mistake, review your notes, the relevant section of the study guide, and, if necessary, the appropriate part of your textbook.

1. Wayne would be embarrassed to cry in public and Dorothy would never express anger outside the privacy of her home. These examples illustrate American
   (a) cultural display rules
   (b) machismo
   (c) nonverbal behavior
   (d) interpersonal engagement rules

2. Dr. Spearpoint believes that emotions arise from the perception and interpretation of bodily changes. His views are most consistent with the
   (a) James-Lange theory
   (b) Cannon-Bard theory
   (c) facial feedback hypothesis
   (d) two-factor theory

3. Whenever he's feeling sad or unhappy, Milton "puts on a happy face" and often experiences an elevation in his mood when he does so. This result is best predicted by the
   (a) cognitive-mediational theory
   (b) two-factor theory
   (c) Cannon-Bard theory
   (d) facial feedback hypothesis

4. Javid and Jamal both got a 10 percent pay raise to their base salary of $15 an hour. Javid is very happy but Jamal is disappointed. Their different emotional reactions to the same pay raise reflect their different interpretations of the event. This example illustrates the _____ theory of emotion.
   (a) James-Lange
   (b) Cannon-Bard
   (c) two-factor
   (d) cognitive-mediational

5. When an irate customer yells at Cam and calls him a stupid idiot, Cam simultaneously experiences embarrassment, anger, fear, shame, and anxiety. Cam is experiencing
   (a) basic emotions only
   (b) a blend of emotions
   (c) mixed emotions
   (d) mood fluctuations

6. Jasbir has a term paper to write so she heads for the library to do the necessary research. Despite an initial failure to locate material related to her topic, Jasbir continues her catalogue search for many hours until she comes up with sufficient relevant information. She writes, rewrites, and edits her paper until she feels it is almost perfect. Jasbir is demonstrating which basic characteristic commonly associated with emotion?

   (a) activation   (c) intensity
   (b) persistence   (d) all of the above

7. After working in the garden all afternoon on a hot day, Mrs. Ulman is very thirsty and drinks a big glass of iced tea. Her motivation to drink to reduce her feeling of thirst can best be explained by

   (a) instinct theory
   (b) drive theory
   (c) incentive motivation
   (d) humanistic theory

8. Dr. Zascow thinks that emotion is best conceptualized as a dynamic system in which cognitive appraisals, physiological arousal, and behavioral expression all contribute to subjective emotional experience. Dr. Zascow's view is most consistent with the

   (a) integrative approach to emotion
   (b) cognitive-mediational theory of emotion
   (c) two-factor theory of emotion
   (d) James-Lange theory of emotion

9. While writing a term paper for her motivation course, Cara notes that the majority of people do not experience or achieve self-actualization, despite the claim that it is an innate goal all people are supposed to strive for. She decides that this is an important limitation of

   (a) instinct theories
   (b) drive theories
   (c) incentive theories
   (d) humanistic theories

10. Raymond has just eaten a very big meal, but when he smells his neighbor's barbecue, he gets the urge to eat again. Psychologists would most likely consider Raymond to be

    (a) an external
    (b) an internal
    (c) a nonexternal
    (d) suffering from bulimia nervosa

11. About six months ago, fifteen-year-old Kirsten went on a drastic weight-loss diet that caused her to drop from 115 to 85 pounds. Although she is dangerously underweight and undernourished, she continues to think she looks fat. Kirsten suffers from

    (a) obesity
    (b) a very high metabolic rate
    (c) bulimia nervosa
    (d) anorexia nervosa

12. Shortly after having his lunch, Marty is daydreaming in class. He imagines the taste and smell of his favorite pizza and he starts feeling hungry. In this instance, his feelings of hunger are probably caused by

    (a) increased levels of insulin
    (b) decreased levels of insulin
    (c) increased levels of cholecystokinin (CCK)
    (d) satiation

13. Dr. Gilbert destroyed the ventromedial hypothalamus of a laboratory rat. This procedure is most likely to

    (a) cause the animal to eat until it becomes obese
    (b) cause the animal to stop eating
    (c) lower the animal's set point for body weight
    (d) raise the animal's set point for body weight

14. Irfan's weight increased seven pounds above his normal set-point body weight. According to set-point theory, Irfan is likely to experience a(n) _____ in hunger and a(n) _____ in his metabolic rate.

    (a) increase; increase
    (b) decrease; decrease
    (c) increase; decrease
    (d) decrease; increase

15. The desire to drink when thirsty is to _____ theory as the desire to avoid boredom is to _____ theory.

    (a) humanistic; drive
    (b) arousal; incentive
    (c) self-actualization; homeostasis
    (d) drive; arousal

16. Merv is in his early twenties. If he is typical of people his age, his basic metabolic rate (BMR) has _____ compared to when he was a child.

    (a) decreased
    (b) increased
    (c) remained relatively the same
    (d) All of the above may be true because there is no relationship between age and BMR

17. In the human sexual response cycle, the first phase is to _____ as the last phase is to _____
    (a) plateau; resolution
    (b) excitement; orgasm
    (c) orgasm; plateau
    (d) excitement; resolution

18. Because of illness thirty-year-old Manjit had her ovaries surgically removed. As a result of this operation, Manjit is likely to experience
    (a) homosexual feelings and urges
    (b) an increase in her production of estrogen
    (c) a steep drop in sexual activity and interest
    (d) little or no change in sexual motivation

19. Laureen is a homosexual. It is very probable that
    (a) her sexual orientation was determined before adolescence and before any sexual activity occurred
    (b) she experienced some early childhood sexual abuse by a member of the opposite sex
    (c) her father was overly domineering and her mother was ineffectual and provided her with a poor feminine role model
    (d) her first sexual experience occurred in childhood with a member of the same sex

20. In order to break the vicious circle of flooding-stonewalling-flooding, the Application section suggests that couples should
    (a) become aware of the gender differences in handling emotion
    (b) call a time-out whenever either one begins to feel overwhelmed or in danger of flooding
    (c) spend the time-out period thinking about ways to resolve the conflict, not about ways to mount a more effective counterattack
    (d) recognize that males need to try to stop avoiding conflict and females should try to raise issues in need of resolution in a calm manner and without personal attacks
    (e) do all of the above

Answers

Introduction: The Study of Motivation

1. (a) initiate; direct
   (b) understand; explain
   (c) activation; persistence; intensity

2. (a) instinct
   (b) instincts
   (c) instinct; innate; genetically

3. (a) instinct; drive
   (b) drive
   (c) drives; homeostasis
   (d) homeostasis
   (e) homeostatic; drive
   (f) drive; increasing

4. (a) incentive
   (b) incentive
   (c) expectations
   (d) drive; incentive; incentive

5. (a) humanistic
   (b) humanistic; psychological; cognitive
   (c) inborn; environment
   (d) hierarchy of needs
   (e) self-actualization
   (f) lowest; highest
   (g) self-actualization
   (h) self-actualization
   (i) humanistic; psychological; cognitive

6. (a) biological, behavioral, cognitive
   (b) grand

7. (a) motivation
   (b) homeostasis
   (c) unlikely
   (d) incentive
   (e) instinct

Matching Exercise 1

1. humanistic theories
2. motivation
3. persistence
4. Abraham Maslow
5. drive
6. instinct theories
7. hierarchy of needs

True/False Test 1

1. T	3. F	5. T
2. T	4. T	6. F

The Motivation to Eat

1. (a) psychological, biological, social
   (b) emotional states
   (c) relationships

2. (a) oral; do not
   (b) neurons; neurons
   (c) hormone; neurotransmitter
   (d) slowing; stretch receptors

3. (a) insulin
   (b) insulin; insulin
   (c) externals; nonexternals
   (d) externals; nonexternals

4. (a) hypothalamus; hypothalamus
   (b) hypothalamus
   (c) hypothalamus

5. (a) multiple
   (b) hypothalamus
   (c) psychological
   (d) interaction

The Regulation of Body Weight

1. (a) one-third; two-thirds
   (b) basal metabolic rate; BMR

2. (a) food intake
   (b) lower; higher; decreases
   (c) genetics

3. (a) BMR
   (b) homeostasis; basal metabolic rate
   (c) number; size
   (d) size; number
   (e) set-point; number; size
   (f) describes; explaining

4. (a) 20; 5
   (b) external
   (c) insulin; metabolic rate
   (d) insulin
   (e) metabolism; less
   (f) metabolic
   (g) exercise

5. (a) self-starvation; refuses; weight; fat; body
   (b) females; males
   (c) appetites; diet
   (d) self-perception
   (e) 10

6. (a) within; overweight
   (b) binge
   (c) binge
   (d) genetic; 50

7. (a) high
   (b) external
   (c) lateral; LH
   (d) basal metabolic rate; BMR
   (e) obese
   (f) anorexia nervosa

Matching Exercise 2

1. cholecystokinin (CCK)
2. oral signals
3. basal metabolic rate (BMR)
4. externals/nonexternals
5. ventromedial hypothalamus (VMH)
6. set-point weight
7. insulin
8. obese

True/False Test 2

1. F   3. T   5. F
2. T   4. T   6. T

Sexual Motivation and Behavior

1. (a) motive
   (b) biologically; estrus
   (c) biologically; environmental
   (d) reproduction; social

2. (a) reproduction
   (b) estrogen
   (c) a complete loss of
   (d) a steep drop; testosterone
   (e) testosterone; a similar drop
   (f) testosterone; wanes (diminishes); testosterone

3. (a) William Masters; Virginia Johnson
   (b) excitement
   (c) plateau
   (d) orgasm; orgasm; orgasms; orgasm
   (e) resolution; refractory

4. (a) heterosexual; homosexual; bisexual
   (b) *homosexual*
   (c) heterosexual; homosexual
   (d) 7; 15

5. (a) genetics
   (b) genetic; 52; 22; 11
   (c) 48; 16; 6
   (d) half; genetics; genetics

6. (a) hypothalamus
   (b) hypothalamus
   (c) biological; genetic

7. (a) not due to
   (b) are not
   (c) is not
   (d) are no
   (e) six

8. (a) psychological, biological, social
   (b) is no longer
   (c) occupation; socioeconomic
   (d) are; are not

9. (a) accurate
   (b) thirty; fifty; fifty
   (c) fifty; fifty-nine
   (d) earlier; later
   (e) one; none; thirty

10. (a) two; a few; a few; seven; six
    (b) most
    (c) 85

11. (a) vaginal intercourse; oral; anal
    (b) vaginal; undress; oral; oral
    (c) forced; forcing; anal; same-gender; stranger
    (d) stranger; group; vibrator; dildo
    (e) happy; conservative; traditional

12. (a) refractory
    (b) decrease; not be affected
    (c) decrease
    (d) sexual orientation
    (e) vaginal intercourse

Matching Exercise 3

1. Virginia E. Johnson
2. plateau phase
3. heterosexual
4. refractory period
5. homosexual
6. William H. Masters
7. excitement phase

True/False Test 3

1. T   4. F   6. F
2. T   5. T   7. F
3. T

Arousal Motives: Curiosity and Sensation Seeking

1. (a) high; low; unpleasant
   (b) low; increase; high; reduce
   (c) optimal; high; low

2. (a) pace

(b) gradually; pacing
(c) pace; inhibited

3. (a) novel; complex; increases
(b) temperamental

4. (a) sensation seekers; sensation seeking
(b) sensation seekers; flexible; tolerant

Competence and Achievement Motivation

1. (a) competence
(b) achievement
(c) need to achieve
(d) achievement
(e) achievement

2. (a) individualistic; collectivistic
(b) self-efficacy
(c) self-efficacy
(d) self-efficacy; self-efficacy
(e) confidence; abilities; doubt; abilities

3. (a) achievement
(b) pace
(c) low
(d) self-efficacy
(e) competence

Graphic Organizer 1

1. drive theory

2. humanistic theory

3. instinct theory

4. incentive theory

5. arousal theory

Matching Exercise 4

1. individualistic cultures

2. self-efficacy

3. arousal theory

4. competence motivation

5. collectivistic cultures

6. sensation seeking

7. achievement motivation

8. Thematic Apperception Test (TAT)

Emotion

1. (a) pleasurable; unpleasant
(b) emotions; mood
(c) subjective; physical; behavioral

2. (a) disagreement
(b) basic
(c) basic; contempt; disappointment; love
(d) basic
(e) blend; mixed
(f) pleasant; unpleasant; high; low

3. (a) much the same; agreement
(b) differences
(c) intensity
(d) intense; intense
(e) expression; expressive
(f) expressive; expressive

4. (a) physiological; physical
(b) physiological; sympathetic
(c) lowering
(d) physiological

5. (a) expressive; behavioral; nonverbal behavior
(b) 7,000
(c) muscles
(d) inborn; innate
(e) three; four; two; six; seven

6. (a) blends
(b) display rules

Graphic Organizer 2

1. astonishment
2. alarm
3. boredom
4. relaxation
5. annoyance

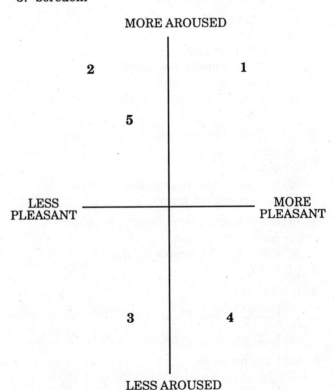

Explaining Emotions: Four Key Theories

1. (a) physical; behavior; subjective
   (b) perceive; physiological; interpret

2. (a) subjective
   (b) physiological; physiological
   (c) do not necessarily
   (d) do; does not

3. (a) expressing; subjectively
   (b) expression
   (c) subjective; expressive

4. (a) simultaneously
   (b) physical; subjective; at the same time

5. (a) interaction; factors
   (b) necessary; labeling

6. (a) cognitive
   (b) all; cognitive
   (c) cognitive; physiological; behavioral

7. (a) mood; emotion
   (b) sympathetic
   (c) display rules
   (d) facial feedback hypothesis
   (e) James-Lange theory

Matching Exercise 5

1. facial feedback hypothesis

2. Richard Lazarus

3. emotion

4. two-factor theory of emotion

5. basic emotions

6. interpersonal engagement

7. nonverbal behavior

8. interactive approach to emotion

9. display rules

True/False Test 4

1. F	4. T	7. F
2. T	5. T	8. F
3. T	6. T	

Something to Think About

Losing weight and keeping it off is a big problem for many people. Some things to consider in any discussion of our motivation to eat are psychological, biological, social, and cultural factors that can influence eating behavior. There are several internal and external signals involved in hunger and satiation (oral sensations, stomach signals, the roles of CCK and insulin, and the fact that some people are externals and some are nonexternals). The energy balance model and the role of BMR can explain regulation of body weight. In addition, set-point theory and the principle of homeostasis are useful for understanding why some people keep a relatively constant weight and in understanding obesity.

Obese people do not necessarily eat more than nonobese people. Instead, they may be highly responsive to external cues associated with food, have greater insulin production, and operate with higher body levels of insulin. Moreover, obese people gain weight more easily than nonobese people, and dieting may sharply reduce the rate of metabolism and keep it low for long periods of time.

The best advice to someone trying to lose weight is to modify their eating patterns and follow a regular exercise program. It's an uphill battle, and despite the gloomy statistics, many people have been successful following this advice and keeping weight off.

Discrimination against obese people in our society is not uncommon. They are often condemned, criticized, and blamed for the way they look. Informed discussion of the problem and an acceptance and tolerance of individual difference are good advise for everybody!

Progress Test 1

1. a	8. c	15. b
2. a	9. a	16. b
3. c	10. d	17. c
4. b	11. a	18. b
5. c	12. c	19. d
6. d	13. a	20. b
7. c	14. b	

Progress Test 2

1. a	8. a	15. d
2. a	9. d	16. a
3. d	10. a	17. d
4. d	11. d	18. d
5. c	12. a	19. a
6. d	13. a	20. e
7. b	14. d	

Chapter 9 Lifespan Development

OVERVIEW Chapter 9 examines the scope of developmental psychology and key themes such as the stages of lifespan development, the nature of change, and the interaction between heredity and environment. Genetic contributions to development are discussed and the stages of prenatal development are described.

Development during infancy and childhood and the capacities and capabilities of the newborn are explored. Aspects of social and personality development in infancy and childhood, including the nature of temperament and the concept of attachment, are discussed. Infants seem to be biologically predisposed to learn language and come in to the world with the ability to distinguish the sounds present in any language. The stages of language development and the child's comprehension and production abilities at each stage are described. Gender-role development and two theoretical approaches, social learning theory and gender schema theory, are discussed next.

Piaget's theory of cognitive development is presented next, and the various stages and their associated cognitive abilities are described. Criticisms of Piaget's theory are examined, and Vygotsky's theory, which emphasized the impact of social and cultural factors on cognitive development, is presented.

Adolescence is defined as a distinctive stage of development, and physical and sexual development, along with adolescent–parent relationships during this period, are examined. Erik Erikson's theory of psychosocial development stresses that each of the eight stages of life is marked by a particular psychosocial conflict; identity versus identity diffusion is presented as the main conflict associated with adolescence. Lawrence Kohlberg's theory of the development of moral reasoning and its various levels and stages are discussed next. Some researchers believe moral reasoning is affected by both gender and culture.

The three phases of adult development are described, and the contributions of genetics, environment, and the individual's lifestyle are explored. Love and work are the two key themes that dominate adult development; friendships, intimate love relationships, children, work, and marital satisfaction are discussed Late adulthood does not necessarily involve a steep decline in physical and cognitive functioning. Declines in mental ability can be minimized or eliminated with an active and mentally stimulating life, according to the activity theory of aging, and life satisfaction is highest when people maintain their previous levels of activity. Erikson identified the task of ego integrity as the key psychosocial task of old age. Finally, death, which can occur at any point in the lifespan, and Kübler-Ross's five-stage model of dying are examined.

Introduction: Your Life Story
Learning Objectives

When you have finished studying this section of the chapter, you should be able to:

1. Define *developmental psychology* and specify the scope of this specialty area.
2. Identify the key themes in developmental psychology.

Read the section "Introduction: Your Life Story" and ***write*** *your answers to the following:*

1. (a) At every age and every stage of life, developmental psychologists investigate the influence of multiple factors on development, including _____ , _____ , _____ , _____ , and behavioral factors.

   (b) The impact of these factors on development is greatly influenced by our _____ , _____ , and_____ characteristics; we are influenced by the events we experience, but we also shape the meaning and consequences of life events.

   (c) Along with studying common patterns of growth and change, developmental psychologists look at the ways that people _____ in their development and life stories.

2. (a) Developmental psychologists often conceptualize the lifespan in terms of basic _____ of development, usually defined by age and age-related changes; however, most of our physical, mental, and social changes occur _____ .

   (b) Another important theme in developmental psychology is the interaction between _____ and _____ , traditionally called the _____ issue.

   (c) Although we are born with a specific _____ potential that we inherit from our biological parents, our _____ influences and shapes how that potential is expressed; in turn, our _____ inheritance influences the ways in which we experience and interact with the _____ .

Genetic Contributions to Your Life Story
Learning Objectives

When you have finished studying this section of the chapter, you should be able to:

1. Describe how genetic makeup results from the pairing of one set of chromosomes from each biological parent and specify what DNA and genes do.
2. Define *genotype* and *phenotype* and explain the role environmental factors play in their relationship.
3. Compare the function of dominant and recessive genes and explain why males are more likely to display sex-linked recessive traits.

Read the section "Genetic Contributions to Your Life Story" and ***write*** *your answers to the following:*

1. (a) Each chromosome is a long, threadlike structure composed of twisted parallel strands of _____ , or _____ , which is the chemical basis of all heredity; _____ contains the chemical genetic code that has directed the growth and development of many of your unique characteristics.

   (b) The _____ code carried on each chromosome is arranged in thousands of segments called genes; each gene is a unit of _____ instructions pertaining to some characteristic, such as eye or hair color, height, or handedness.

   (c) At conception, _____ chromosomes from your biological mother's ovum were paired with _____ chromosomes from your biological father's sperm, resulting in _____ *pairs* of chromosomes.

2. (a) When a _____ combines conflicting genetic information (one gene for and one gene not for a certain trait), the _____ gene will influence the trait you actually display.

(b) Traits such as freckles, dark eyes, dark hair, and dimples are referred to as _____ characteristics because they require only one member of a gene pair to be _____ in order for the trait to be displayed.

(c) If both members of the gene pair happen to be _____ , the genes will simply act in harmony and your phenotype will express the _____ characteristic.

(d) In order to get a nondominant characteristic, like light hair, light eyes, etc., each gene in a gene pair must be a(n) _____ gene, whose instructions are not expressed if combined with a dominant gene; _____ genes are expressed only if paired with an identical _____ gene.

(e) Traits whose expression requires two identical _____ genes, like light hair and being dimple-free, are called _____ characteristics.

(f) What we really inherit from our biological parents is a genetic _____ that can be influenced by environmental conditions; the phenotype *expression* of that genetic programming may be influenced by the environment.

3. (a) Some _____ characteristics, such as color blindness and hemophilia, are much more common in men than women,

and that has to do with the _____ chromosome, the 23rd pair of chromosomes—the ones that determine biological sex.

(b) There are two types of _____ chromosomes, the large X chromosome and the smaller Y chromosome.

(c) In _____ , the 23rd pair of chromosomes is made up of two large X chromosomes, and in _____ , it is made up of a large X chromosome and a smaller Y chromosome.

(d) Following the normal pattern, _____ require the presence of two recessive genes, one on each X chromosome, in order for recessive characteristics associated with the 23rd chromosome pair to be displayed.

(e) For _____ , however, the smaller Y chromosome often does not contain a corresponding gene segment to match the one on their X chromosome; this means that _____ can display certain recessive characteristics as a result of only one recessive gene carried on the X chromosome of their XY pair.

(f) Traits determined by recessive genes on the X chromosomes are referred to as _____ characteristics.

(g) Because _____ require only one recessive gene on their X chromosome to display these traits, they are more common in _____ than in _____ ; thus, there is a gender difference in the heritability of recessive characteristics that are communicated on the sex chromosome.

Graphic Organizer 1

There is a dominant gene (D) for "dimples" and a recessive gene (r) for "no dimples." The matrix below shows the four possible combinations. Decide which combinations (genotype) will result in "dimples" or "no dimples" (phenotype).

	Dominant (D)	Recessive (r)
Dominant (D)	Cell 1 DD	Cell 2 Dr
Recessive (r)	Cell 3 Dr	Cell 4 rr

Cell 1: The genotype DD results in the phenotype of

_____

Cell 2: The genotype Dr results in the phenotype of

_____

Cell 3: The genotype Dr results in the phenotype of

_____

Cell 4: The genotype rr results in the phenotype of

_____

Prenatal Development
Learning Objectives

When you have finished studying this section of the chapter, you should be able to:

1. Describe how the single zygote develops into a full-term fetus.
2. Identify the three stages of prenatal development.
3. Define the term *teratogens* and explain what general principles seem to govern their impact on the fetus.

*Read the section "Prenatal Development" and **write** your answers to the following:*

1. (a) During the germinal period, also called the _____ period, the fertilized egg undergoes rapid cell division before becoming implanted on the mother's uterine wall.
   (b) Some of the _____ cells will eventually form the structures that house and protect the developing fetus and provide nourishment from the mother; by the end of the _____-week germinal period, the single cell has developed into a cluster of cells called the embryo.

2. (a) The embryonic period begins with week _____ and extends through week _____ ; during this time of rapid growth and intensive cell differentiation, the organs and major systems of the body form.
   (b) Protectively housed in the fluid-filled _____ sac, the embryo has as a lifeline the umbilical cord, which supplies nutrients, oxygen, and water and gets rid of carbon monoxide and other wastes.
   (c) The umbilical cord attaches the embryo to the _____ , a disk-shaped tissue on the mother's uterine wall; the _____ prevents the mother's blood from mingling with that of the developing embryo, acting as a filter to prevent harmful substances that might be present in the mother's blood from reaching the embryo.
   (d) Harmful agents or substances that can cause abnormal development or birth defects are called _____ and include exposure to radiation, toxic industrial chemicals, a number of diseases, and drugs such as alcohol, cocaine, and heroin.

3. (a) The _____ month marks the beginning of the fetal period, the final and longest stage of prenatal development; the main task of this period is for the body systems to grow and reach maturity in preparation for life outside the mother's body.
   (b) By the end of the _____ month, the fetus can move its arms, legs, mouth, and head; it becomes capable of reflexive

responses, such as fanning its toes and squinting its eyes.

(c) During the _____ month, the mother experiences quickening; she can feel the fetus moving. By the _____ month, essentially all the brain cells the person will ever have are present, though they will continue to develop long after birth.

(d) The fetus has distinct sleep/wake cycles, and during the _____ month, the fetus's brain activity becomes similar to that of a newborn baby's.

(e) During the final _____ months, the fetus will double its weight, gaining an additional three to four pounds of body fat, which helps the newborn adjust to changing temperatures outside the womb.

4. Read the following and write the correct term in the space provided:

(a) Dr. Dalliwhal is concerned with how people change over the lifespan, and his particular research focus is on the relationship between various teratogens and birth defects. Dr. Dalliwhal is most likely a _____ psychologist.

(b) From the day he was born, people have always responded very positively to Franco's good looks. Now that he is growing older, it is clear that he is developing a socially confident and outgoing personality. This best illustrates the interaction of _____ and _____ .

(c) Paul and Paula are newborn fraternal twins; in terms of chromosomes Paul received a(n) _____ from one parent and a(n) _____ from the other, and Paula received a(n) _____ from one parent and a(n) _____ from the other.

(d) It is now six weeks since Jennifer conceived.

The human organism she is carrying is called a(n) _____ ; from the eighth week on it will be called a(n)

_____ .

Review of Key Terms 1

developmental
  psychology
critical period
nature/nurture issue
chromosome
deoxyribonucleic acid
  (DNA)
gene
genotype
phenotype
dominant gene
dominant characteristics
recessive gene

recessive characteristics
sex chromosomes
sex-linked recessive
  characteristics
prenatal stage
germinal period
  (zygotic period)
zygote
embryonic period
embryo
teratogens
fetal period
fetus

Matching Exercise

Match the appropriate term with its definition or description.

1. _____ The stage of development before birth; divided into the germinal, embryonic, and fetal periods.

2. _____ The basic unit of heredity that directs the development of a particular characteristic; the individual unit of DNA instructions on a chromosome.

3. _____ The branch of psychology that studies how people change over the lifespan.

4. _____ Traits determined by recessive genes located on the X chromosome; in males, these characteristics require only one recessive gene to be expressed.

5. _____ Harmful agents or substances that can cause malformations or defects in an embryo or fetus.

6. _____ A long, threadlike structure composed of twisted parallel strands of DNA; found in the nucleus of the cell.

7. _____ In a pair of genes, the gene containing genetic instructions that will not be expressed unless paired with another recessive gene.

8. _____ The first two weeks of pre-natal development.

9. _____ The cluster of cells that the single-celled zygote has developed into by the end of the two-week germinal period.

10. _____ Traits whose expression requires two identical recessive genes, like those for light hair and being dimple-free.

11. _____ Chromosomes designated as X or Y that determine biological sex; the 23rd pair of chromosomes in humans.

True/False Test

Indicate whether each statement is true or false by placing T or F in the blank space next to each item.

1. ____ The fetus is the name given to the growing organism at the beginning of the third month.

2. ____ A critical period during development is a time during which the child is maximally sensitive to environmental influences.

3. ____ Deoxyribonucleic acid (DNA) is the chemical basis of heredity; carries genetic instructions in the cell.

4. ____ The fetal period is the second period of prenatal development, extending from the third week through the eight week.

5. ____ At conception, chromosomes from the biological mother and father combine to form a single cell called the fertilized egg, or zygote.

6. ____ In a pair of genes, the gene containing genetic instructions that will be expressed whether paired with another dominant gene or with a recessive gene is called the dominant gene.

7. ____ The embryonic period is the third and longest period of prenatal development, extending from the eight week until birth.

9. ____ An important theme in developmental psychology is the interaction between heredity and environment; traditionally called the nature/nurture issue.

9. ____ The genotype refers to observable traits or characteristics of an organism determined by the interaction of genetics and environmental factors.

10. ____ Traits such as freckles, dark eyes, dark hair, and dimples are referred to as dominant characteristics because they require only one

member of a gene pair to be dominant in order for the trait to be displayed.

11. ____ Phenotype refers to the underlying genetic makeup of a particular organism, including the genetic instructions for traits that are not actually displayed.

Check your answers and review any areas of weakness before going on to the next section.

Development During Infancy and Childhood

Learning Objectives

When you have finished studying this section of the chapter, you should be able to:

1. Identify the sensory capabilities and reflexes that physically helpless newborn infants are equipped with that enhance their chances for survival.

2. Explain how the sensory capabilities of the newborn promote the development of relationships with caregivers.

3. Describe how the brain develops after birth.

Read the section "Development During Infancy and Childhood" and write your answers to the following:

1. (a) The newly born infant enters the world with an impressive array of _____ and _____ capabilities, mostly reflexive in nature, that enhance the chances of survival.

   (b) The newborn's senses are keenly attuned to _____ , which helps the infant to quickly differentiate between his mother and other humans.

2. (a) Vision is the _____ (most/least) developed sense at birth; the optimal viewing distance for the newborn is about _____ to _____ inches, the perfect distance for a nursing baby to easily focus on his mother's face and make eye contact.

(b) When adults interact with very young infants, they almost always position themselves so that their face is about _____ to _____ inches from the baby's face; this, along with exaggerated head movements and facial expressions, makes it _____ (harder/easier) for the baby to see them.

(c) At birth an infant can distinguish between his mother's _____ and that of another woman.

(d) Especially if breast-fed, the newborn quickly becomes sensitized to the _____ of his mother's body and the mother becomes keenly attuned to her infant's characteristic appearance, _____ , and _____ texture.

3. (a) By the time she begins crawling, at around _____ to _____ months of age, the infant's view of the world, including distant objects, will be as clear as that of her parents.

(b) At birth, her brain is an impressive _____ percent of its adult weight, while her birth weight is only about 5 percent of her eventual adult weight; during infancy her brain will grow to about _____ percent of its adult weight, while her body weight will reach only about 20 percent of her adult weight.

(c) The newborn enters the world with essentially _____ the neurons her brain will ever have, an estimated 100 billion; after birth, however, the brain continues to develop rapidly.

(d) The number of _____ increases dramatically during the first two years of life, and the axons of many neurons acquire _____ , the white, fatty covering that increases a neuron's communication speed.

(e) The basic _____ of motor skill development is universal, but the _____ can vary greatly; each infant has her own genetically programmed timetable for physical maturation and developmental readiness to master different motor skills.

Social and Personality Development
Learning Objectives

When you have finished studying this section of the chapter, you should be able to:

1. Define *temperament* and *attachment* and differentiate between them.
2. Identify the main temperamental patterns that have been investigated.
3. Specify the basic premise of attachment theory.

Read the section "Social and Personality Development" and **write** *your answers to the following:*

1. (a) From birth, forming close social and emotional relationships with caregivers is essential to the infant's _____ and _____ well-being; the young infant _____ (does/does not) play a passive role in forming these relationships.

(b) Infants come into the world with very distinct and consistent _____ styles; some babies are fussy, some active and outgoing, and others shy.

2. (a) Research by Thomas and Chess has shown that about two-thirds of babies can be classified into one of three broad temperamental patterns: _____

(b) About one-third of infants can be characterized as _____ babies because they do not fit neatly into one of the three categories.

(c) These broad patterns of temperamental qualities are remarkably _____ (stable/unstable) from infancy through childhood.

(d) Virtually all temperament researchers agree that individual differences in temperament have a _____ and _____ basis, but they also agree that environmental experiences can modify a child's basic temperament.

3. (a) During the first year of life, the _____ that forms between the infant and his caregivers, especially his mother, is called attachment; according to attachment theory, an infant's ability to thrive _____ and _____ depends in part on the quality of attachment.

(b) In homes where both parents are present, infants tend to form attachments to both parents at about the same time. An infant is also capable of forming attachments to other consistent caregivers in his life, such as relatives or workers at a day-care center; thus, an infant is capable of forming _____ attachments.

4. (a) Psychologists assess _____ by observing the infant's behavior toward his or her mother.

(b) When his mother is present, the _____ attached infant will use her as a secure base from which to explore the new environment, periodically returning to her side; he will show distress when his mother leaves the room and will greet her warmly when she returns and is easily soothed.

(c) A(n) _____ attached infant is less likely to explore the environment even when his mother is present; he may appear either very anxious or completely indifferent and will tend to _____ or _____ his mother when she is present; in addition, these infants become extremely distressed when their mothers leave the room, and when reunited with their mothers, they are hard to soothe and comfort.

(d) Preschoolers with a history of being _____ attached tend to be more prosocial, empathetic, and socially competent than preschoolers with a history of _____ attachment; adolescents who were _____ attached in infancy have fewer problems, do better in school, and have more successful relationships with their peers than do adolescents who were _____ attached in infancy.

Languare Development
Learning Objectives

When you have finished studying this section of the chapter, you should be able to:

1. Explain how a biological predisposition functions in language acquisition.

2. Describe how language development is encouraged by caregivers.

3. Identify the stages of language development.

*Read the section "Language Development" and **write** your answers to the following:*

1. (a) By the time a child is three years old he will have learned approximately _____ words and the complex rules of his language.

(b) According to linguist _____ , every child is born with a biological predisposition to learn language, any language; each child possesses a universal grammar, a basic understanding of the common principles of language organization.

(c) At birth, infants _____ (can/cannot) distinguish among the speech sounds of all the world's languages, but by ten months of age, however, infants have _____ (gained/lost) this ability and can distinguish only among the speech sounds that are present in the language to which they have been exposed.

2. (a) Parents also seem to be biologically programmed to encourage language development by the way they speak to infants and toddlers; people in every culture, especially parents, use a style of speech called _____ , or infant-directed speech, with babies.

   (b) The content of _____ tends to be restricted to topics that are familiar to the child, and _____ is often used.

   (c) The adult use of

   _____

   seems to be instinctive; as infants mature and become more sophisticated in language skills, the speech patterns of parents change to fit the child's developing language abilities.

3. The stages of language development appear to be universal, and in virtually every culture, infants follow the same sequence of language development at roughly similar ages:

   (a) At about three months of age infants begin the _____ stage and at about five months of age infants start to _____ ; at about nine months of age, babies begin to _____ more in the sounds specific to their language.

   (b) Somewhere around their first birthday, infants produce their first real _____ , but before this infants' _____ vocabulary (the words they understand) is much larger than

their _____ vocabulary (the words they can say).

   (c) During the _____ stage, babies use a single word and vocal intonation to stand for an entire sentence.

   (d) Around their second birthday, during the _____ stage, infants begin putting words together to construct simple "sentences," such as "Mama go" and "No potty!"

   (e) The _____ stage reflects the first understanding of grammar; infants use the correct syntactical pattern of their language.

   (f) At around _____ years of age, children begin to rapidly increase the length and grammatical complexity of their sentences; there is a dramatic increase in the number of words that they can comprehend and produce, and by _____ age a child may have a production capacity of over 10,000 words.

4. Read the following and write the correct term in the space provided:

   (a) Dr. Snow is interested in the abilities of newborn children. While testing visual perception, she is likely to find that newborns will look longer at the image of a(n) _____ compared to other visual patterns.

   (b) Kathy gave birth to a normal, healthy, eight-and-half-pound baby. In terms of brain development, the baby has _____ (50 percent/75 percent/100 percent) of the brain cells she will ever have.

   (c) As Kathy's baby develops, it becomes apparent that she readily adapts to new experiences, displays positive moods and emotions, and has regular sleeping and eating patterns. She is likely to be classified as a temperamentally _____ baby.

(d) Kathy and her husband are consistently warm, responsive, and sensitive to their infant's needs, and the baby has developed the expectation that her needs will be met. It is very probable that the baby will form a(n) _____ attachment to her parents.

Review of Key Terms and Key Names 2

rooting reflex
sucking reflex
grasping reflex
temperament
easy temperament
difficult temperament
slow-to-warm-up
  temperament
attachment
secure attachment
insecure attachment

Noam Chomsky
motherese (infant-
  directed speech)
cooing and babbling
  stage
one-word stage
comprehension
  vocabulary
production vocabulary
two-word stage

Matching Exercise

Match the appropriate term / name with its definition or description.

1. _____ The automatic response elicited by touching a newborn's lips.

2. _____ A temperamental category for babies who have a low activity level, who withdraw from new situations and people, and who adapt to new experiences very gradually.

3. _____ A universal style of speech used with babies characterized by very distinct pronunciation, a simplified vocabulary, short sentences, a high pitch, and exaggerated intonation and expression.

4. _____ A biologically programmed stage in language development that occurs between about three months of age and nine months of age.

5. _____ The emotional bond that forms between an infant and her caretaker(s), especially her parents.

6. _____ The words that are understood by an infant or child.

7. _____ A form of attachment that may develop when an infant's parents are neglectful, inconsistent, or insensitive to his moods or behaviors and reflects an ambivalent or detached emotional relationship between an infant and his mother.

8. _____ A universal stage in language development, starting around two years of age, in which infants combine two words to construct simple "sentences" that reflect the first understanding of grammar.

True/False Test

Indicate whether each statement is true or false by placing T or F in the blank space next to each item.

1. ____ Production vocabulary refers to the words that an infant or child understands and can speak.

2. ____ The response that is displayed when an infant's palms are touched is called the rooting reflex.

3. ____ Babies with a difficult temperament tend to be intensely emotional, are irritable and fussy, cry a lot, and have irregular sleeping and eating patterns.

4. ____ During the one-word stage, babies use a single word and vocal intonation to stand for an entire sentence.

5. ____ Secure attachment is likely to develop when parents are consistently warm, responsive, and sensitive to their infant's needs.

6. ____ Noam Chomsky is the American linguist who proposed that people have an innate understanding of the basic principles of language, which is called a universal grammar.

7. ____ Babies with an easy temperament readily adapt to new experiences, generally display positive moods and emotions, and have regular sleeping and eating patterns.

8. ____ Touching the newborn's cheek elicits the grasping reflex; the infant turns toward the source of the touch and opens his mouth.

9. ____ Temperament is the inborn predisposition to consistently behave and react in a certain way.

Check your answers and review any areas of weakness before going on to the next section.

Gender-Role Development
Learning Objectives

When you have finished studying this section of the chapter, you should be able to:

1. Distinguish between the terms *gender, gender roles,* and *gender identity*.
2. Specify the important role gender plays in our culture.
3. Identify how boys and girls are treated differently and list the gender differences that develop during childhood.
4. Describe how social learning theory and gender schema theory deal with the development of gender roles.

Read the section "Gender-Role Development" and **write** *your answers to the following:*

1. (a) _____ refers to the cultural and social meanings that are associated with maleness and femaleness;

   _____ consist of the behaviors, attitudes, and personality traits that a given culture designates as either "masculine" or "feminine"; and

   _____ refers to a person's psychological sense of being either male or female.

   (b) Roughly between the ages of

   _____ and _____ , children can identify themselves and other children as boys or girls without understanding that sex is determined by physical characteristics; they tend, instead, to use attributes, such as hair style, clothing, and activities to identify the sexes.

   (c) From about the age of eighteen months to two years, sex differences in

   _____ begin to emerge, and they become more pronounced throughout early childhood; from about the age of

   _____ , there are consistent gender differences in preferred toys and play activities.

   (d) Throughout the remainder of childhood, boys and girls play primarily with members of their own sex; boys learn to

   _____ themselves within a group of male friends whereas girls tend to establish and maintain close friendships with one or two friends through

   _____ , _____ , and verbal conflict resolution.

2. (a) Based on the principles of learning, social learning theory contends that gender roles and gender-appropriate behavior are learned through _____ ,

   _____ , and modeling by parents and caregivers.

   (b) Research findings suggest that the effects of parental socialization in many areas of gender differences are relatively _____ (large/small); for the most part, parents treat their male and female children rather _____ (differently/similarly).

   (c) Children also learn gender differences through _____ , in which they observe and then imitate the sex-typed behavior of significant adults, older children, people on television, characters in children's book, etc.; they come to understand that certain _____ and _____ are considered appropriate for one sex or the other.

3. (a) In contrast to the relatively passive role played by children in social learning theory, gender schema theory contends that children _____ develop mental categories (or schemas) for _____ and _____ .

   (b) According to gender schema theory, children, like many adults, look at the world through "gender lenses"; gender schemas influence how people pay attention to,

   _____ , _____ , and _____ gender-relevant behavior.

Cognitive Development
Learning Objectives

When you have finished studying this section of the chapter, you should be able to:

1. Describe Jean Piaget's stage theory of cognitive development and list the various stages that children are assumed to pass through.
2. Explain the characteristics of each of the four cognitive stages in Piaget's theory.
3. Identify the criticisms of Piaget's theory.

Read the section "Cognitive Development" and **write** *your answers to the following:*

1. (a) The development of _____ is one reflection of the child's increasing sophistication in _____ processes such as thinking, remembering, and information processing.

   (b) The most influential theory of cognitive development is that of Swiss psychologist Jean Piaget, who believed that children _____ try to make sense out of their environment rather than _____ soaking up information about the world.

   (c) According to Piaget, children progress through four distinct biologically programmed cognitive stages: the sensorimotor stage, from _____ to age _____ ; the preoperational stage, from age _____ to age _____ ; the concrete operational stage, from age _____ to age _____ ; and the formal operational stage, which begins during _____ and continues into _____ .

   (d) As a child advances to a new stage, his thinking is _____ different from that used in the previous stage; this progression is assumed to be a continuous, gradual process, common to all cultures, but there can be individual variation in the rate of progress.

   (e) Children develop new understanding of the world in each progressive stage, building on the understanding acquired in the previous stage; as the child _____ new information and experiences, he eventually changes his way of thinking to _____ new knowledge.

2. (a) During the sensorimotor stage the infant acquires knowledge about the world through motor _____ that allow her to directly experience and manipulate objects; she expands this practical knowledge by reaching, grasping, pushing, pulling, and pouring, in the process gaining a basic understanding of the effects that her own _____ can produce.

   (b) At the beginning of the sensorimotor stage an object exists for the infant only if she can directly sense it; by the end of this stage, the child acquires a new cognitive understanding, called _____ , which is the realization that an object continues to exist even if it can't be seen.

   (c) Infants gradually acquire an understanding of _____ as they gain experience with objects, as their memory abilities improve, and as they develop mental representations of the world , which Piaget called _____ .

3. (a) In Piaget's theory _____ refer to logical, mental activities; thus the preoperational stage is a prelogical stage.

(b) The hallmark of preoperational thought is the child's capacity to engage in _____ thought, which refers to the ability to use words, images, and symbols to represent the world.

(c) Indications of the expanding capacity for _____ thought are the child's impressive gains in language and her use of fantasy and imagination while playing.

(d) The preoperational child's thought is characterized by _____ , _____ , and _____ .

(e) The preoperational child is unable to understand _____ , which holds that two equal physical quantities remain equal even if the appearance of one is changed as long as nothing is added or subtracted.

4. (a) With the beginning of the concrete operational stage the child becomes capable of true logical thought, is much less _____ in his thinking, can _____ mental operations, and can focus simultaneously on two aspects of a problem; in short, he understands the principle of _____ .

(b) The child's thinking and use of logic tends to be limited to tangible objects and events; he often has difficulty thinking logically about _____ situations or _____ ideas unless they are related to his personal experiences or actual events.

5. (a) The formal operational stage is characterized by the gradual emergence of the ability to think logically even when dealing with _____ concepts or _____ situations; this ability continues to increase in sophistication throughout adolescence and adulthood.

(b) While an adolescent may deal effectively with _____ ideas in one domain of knowledge, her thinking may not reflect the same degree of sophistication in other areas; even among many _____ , formal operational thinking is often limited to areas in which they have developed expertise or a special interest.

6. (a) While scientific research _____ (has/has not) supported Piaget's most fundamental idea that infants, young children, and older children use distinctly different cognitive abilities to construct their understanding of the world, there are three important criticisms of his theory.

(b) Piaget often _____ the cognitive abilities of infants and children; many researchers believe that Piaget confused _____ limitations with _____ limitations in assessing object permanence during infancy.

(c) Psychologist Renée Baillargeon used _____ tasks, rather than _____ tasks, in several studies to assess an infant's understanding of object permanence; she concluded that infants have much more sophisticated cognitive abilities than Piaget believed.

7. (a) Piaget's stages are not as _____ as he believed; studies have shown that many adults only display _____ thought in limited areas of knowledge, and some adults never display formal operational thought processes.

(b) Piaget later suggested that formal operational thinking may not be _____ and biologically programmed, but instead may be the product of an individual's expertise in a specific area.

(c) Many developmental psychologists reject the Piagetian notion of distinct stages, emphasizing instead the _____ model of cognitive development, which focuses on investigating the development of fundamental mental processes like attention, memory, and problem solving; in this approach cognitive development is viewed as a process of _____ change over the lifespan.

8. (a) Another criticism is that Piaget underestimated the impact of the _____ and _____ environment on cognitive development.

(b) Unlike Piaget, Russian psychologist Lev Vygotsky believed that cognitive development is strongly influenced by _____ and _____ factors such as the support and guidance that children receive from parents, other adults, and older children; research has supported this position.

(c) How these supportive _____ interactions are displayed varies from culture to culture; cross-cultural research has shown that cognitive development is strongly influenced by the _____ that are valued and encouraged in a particular environment.

(d) Despite these criticisms, Piaget's documentation of the many _____ changes that occur during infancy and childhood ranks as one of the most outstanding contributions to developmental psychology.

9. Read the following and write the correct term in the space provided:

(a) During a sex education talk, the teacher describes the differences in genetic composition and reproductive anatomy that are biologically determined characteristics that define a person as being male or female. The teacher is describing _____ .

(b) Sheila contends that children actively develop cognitive categories for masculinity and femininity and believes that these mental representations influence how children perceive, interpret, and remember relevant aspects of what is appropriate for boys and girls. Sheila's views are most consistent with _____ theory.

(c) Liam describes his girlfriend as gentle, caring, empathetic, and very feminine. Liam is referring to his girlfriend's _____ .

(d) Four-year-old Tiborg is not completely egocentric and five-year-old Natasha exhibits some understanding of conservation. Observations such as these suggest that Piaget may have _____ (overestimated/underestimated) the cognitive abilities of infants and children.

(e) Eight-year-old Nadia has the ability to think logically about visible and tangible objects and situations. She is in the _____ stage of cognitive development.

(f) Young Adrienne attempts to retrieve her toy bear after her father hides it under a blanket. This suggests that Adrienne has developed a sense of _____ .

(g) When Mrs. Goodley cut Janet's hot dog into eight pieces and Simon's into six pieces, Simon started to cry and complained that he wasn't getting as much hot dog as Janet. Piaget would say that Simon doesn't understand the principle of _____ .

(h) Three-year-old Rita calls all unfamiliar four-legged animals "doggies." She appears to be _____ these new experiences into her existing concept of a dog.

(i) Piaget would call Rita's mental representation or concept of dog a(n) _____ .

(j) During a tutorial devoted to the pros and cons of genetic engineering, Vasilis raised some important issues about the ownership of fertilized eggs and whether destroying them constitutes taking life. Piaget would say that Vasilis is in the _____ operational stage of cognitive development.

Review of Key Terms and Key Names 3

gender
gender roles
gender identity
social learning theory of
  gender-role
  development
gender schema theory
cognitive processes
Jean Piaget
qualitative difference in
  thinking
sensorimotor stage
object permanence
schemas

preoperational stage
operations
symbolic thought
egocentrism
irreversibility
centration
conservation
concrete operational
  stage
formal operational stage
information-processing
  model of cognitive
  development
Lev Vygotsky

Matching Exercise

Match the appropriate term/name with its definition or description.

1. _____ The ability to use words, images, and symbols to represent the world.

2. _____ The mental functions used in thinking, remembering, and processing information.

3. _____ The understanding that an object continues to exist even when it can no longer be seen.

4. _____ In Piaget's theory, the fourth stage of cognitive development, which lasts from adolescence through adulthood; characterized by the ability to think logically about abstract principles and hypothetical situations.

5. _____ Swiss child psychologist whose influential theory proposed that children progress through distinct stages of cognitive development.

6. _____ The model that views cognitive development as a continuous process over the lifespan and that studies the development of basic mental processes like attention, memory, and problem solving.

7. _____ Piaget's term for the mental representations of the world that children acquire as their memories improve and as they gain an understanding of object permanence.

8. _____ In Piaget's theory, the first stage of cognitive development, from birth to about age two; the period during which the infant explores the environment and acquires knowledge through sensing and manipulating objects.

9. _____ In Piaget's theory, the inability to take another person's perspective or point of view.

10. _____ The cultural, social, and psychological meanings that are associated with masculinity and femininity.

11. _____ The theory that gender-role development is influenced by the formation of schemas, or mental representations, of masculinity and femininity.

True/False Test

Indicate whether each statement is true or false by placing T or F in the blank space next to each item.

1. ____ In Piaget's theory, the word *operations* refers to logical, mental activities.

2. ____ Lev Vygotsky was the Russian psychologist who stressed the importance of social and cultural influences in cognitive development .

3. ____ In Piaget's theory, the concrete operational stage is the second stage of cognitive development, which lasts from about age two to age seven; characterized by increasing use of symbols and prelogical thought processes.

4. ____ In Piaget's theory, irreversibility is the inability to mentally reverse a sequence of events or logical operations.

5. ____ In Piaget's theory, centration refers to the understanding that two equal quantities remain equal even though the form or appearance is rearranged, as long as nothing is added or subtracted.

6. ____ According to Piaget, as a child advances to a new stage, his thinking is qualitatively different from that used in the previous stage; each new stage represents a fundamental shift in *how* the child thinks and understands the world.

7. ____ In Piaget's theory, the tendency to focus on only one aspect of a situation and ignore other important aspects of the situation is called conservation.

8. ____ Social learning theory of gender-role development is the theory that gender roles are acquired through the basic processes of learning, including reinforcement, punishment, and modeling.

9. ___ In Piaget's theory, the preoperational stage is the third stage of cognitive development, which lasts from about age seven to adolescence; characterized by the ability to think logically about concrete objects and situations.

10. ___ Gender identity refers to the behaviors, attitudes, and personality traits that are designated as either masculine or feminine in a given culture.

11. ___ Gender roles refer to people's psychological sense of being male or female.

> Check your answers and review any areas of weakness before going on to the next section.

Adolescence

Learning Objectives

When you have finished studying this section of the chapter, you should be able to:

1. Define *adolescence* and list the characteristics that accompany this stage of development.

2. Describe the physical and sexual changes that occur during adolescence, and explain how these affect the emergence of sexual relationships.

3. Identify the main aspects of relationships with parents and peers in adolescence and explain how adolescents begin the process of identity formation.

4. Describe Erikson's psychosocial theory of life-span development.

5. Describe Kohlberg's theory of moral development, and identify its various stages and levels.

6. Explain how moral reasoning is influenced by gender and culture.

*Read the section "Adolescence" and **write** your answers to the following:*

1. (a) Adolescence begins around age _____ and lasts until the individual assumes _____ roles and responsibilities.

(b) Puberty is the physical process of attaining _____ maturation and _____ capacity that begins during early adolescent years.

(c) Internally, puberty involves the development of the _____ sex characteristics, which involve the sex organs that are directly involved in reproduction (the uterus in females and the testes in males).

(d) Externally, development of the _____ sex characteristics, which are not directly involved in reproduction, signals increasing sexual maturity; these include changes in height, weight, and body shape, appearance of body hair, voice changes, and, in girls, breast development.

(e) The period of marked acceleration in weight and height gains, commonly called the _____, along with sexual maturation, occurs about two years earlier in females than in males.

(f) A female's first menstrual period, which is termed _____, typically occurs around age twelve or thirteen but may take place as early as age nine or ten or as late as age sixteen or seventeen; for boys, the _____ typically begin enlarging around age eleven or twelve, but the process can begin before age nine or after age fourteen.

(g) During early and middle adolescence, the physical changes of puberty prime the adolescent's interest in sexuality, but _____ and _____ factors significantly influence when, why, and how sexual behavior is initiated.

(h) With increasing age, there is a corresponding increase in the number of adolescents who have engaged in such sexual activities as kissing or petting; between the ages of _____ and_____, there is a sharp increase in the cumulative percentage of those who have had sexual intercourse, and by age _____ approximately 70 percent of females and 80 percent of males have lost their virginity.

2. (a) Parent–adolescent relationships are usually _____ ; most teenagers report that they _____ their parents and _____ (turn/never turn) to them for advice; if the relationships have been good before adolescence, they continue to be relatively smooth during adolescence.

   (b) Although parents remain _____ throughout adolescence, relationships with friends and peers become increasingly important; although peer influence can lead to undesirable behaviors in some instances, peers can influence one another in positive ways.

3. (a) Identity refers to the _____ , _____ , and ideals that guide an individual's behavior, and identity formation is a process that continues throughout the lifespan.

   (b) For the first time in the lifespan, the adolescent possesses the _____ skills necessary to deal with identity issues in a meaningful way.

   (c) Some aspects of personal identity involve characteristics over which the adolescent has no control, such as gender, race, ethnic background, and socioeconomic level; these identity characteristics are _____ and already _____ by the time an individual reaches the adolescent years.

   (d) Adolescents begin to _____ themselves on several different dimensions; social acceptance by peers, academic and athletic abilities, work abilities, personal appearance, and romantic appeal are some aspects of _____ .

   (e) Another challenge facing the adolescent is to develop a(n) _____ that is independent of her parents while retaining a sense of connection to her family; the adoles-

cent has several _____ that she must integrate into a coherent and unified whole to answer the question, "Who am I?"

4. (a) The adolescent's task of achieving an integrated identity is one important aspect of psychoanalyst Erik Erikson's influential theory of _____ development.

   (b) Erikson proposed that each of eight stages of life is associated with a particular _____ conflict that can be resolved in either a positive or negative direction; relationships with others play an important role in determining the outcome of each conflict.

   (c) The key _____ conflict facing the adolescent is identity versus identity diffusion.

   (d) Psychological research has generally _____ (supported/not supported) Erikson's description of the process of identity formation.

   (e) The process of identity formation only begins to take on serious meaning during _____ ; for most people, a stable and fully integrated identity probably does not occur until well in to the _____ years.

5. (a) An important aspect of _____ development during adolescence is a change in moral reasoning, that is, in how an individual thinks about moral decisions.

   (b) The most influential theory of moral development was proposed by psychologist Lawrence Kohlberg, who used _____ to investigate moral reasoning; he concluded that there are distinct _____ of moral development that unfold in an age-related, step-by-step fashion.

(c) Kohlberg proposed three distinct
_____ of moral reasoning, each
of which is based on the degree to which a
person conforms to the conventional standards of society; each _____ has
two _____ that represent different
degrees of sophistication in moral reasoning.

(d) Research has shown that only a few excep-
tional individuals display the philosophical
ideals associated with
_____ moral reasoning;
the normal course of changes in moral reasoning for most people seems to be captured
by Kohlberg's first four _____ ,
and by adulthood, the prominent form of
moral reasoning is _____ moral
reasoning.

6. (a) Kohlberg's theory is not without its critics;
psychologist Carol Gilligan points out that
Kohlberg's model reflects a
_____ perspective that may not
accurately depict the development of moral
reasoning in _____ .

(b) To Gilligan, Kohlberg's model is based on an
ethic of _____ rights and jus-
tice, which is a more common perspective for
_____ ; Gilligan's model is
based on an ethic of care and responsibility.

(c) In her studies of _____ moral
reasoning, Gilligan found that
_____ tended to stress the
importance of maintaining interpersonal
relationships and responding to the needs of
others, rather than focusing primarily on
individual rights.

(d) _____ also seems to have an
effect on moral reasoning; it has been
argued that Kohlberg's stories and scoring
system reflect a Western emphasis on individual rights, harm, and justice that is not
shared in many _____ .

(e) For example, Kohlberg's moral stages do not
reflect the sense of interdependence and the
concern for the overall welfare of the
_____ that is more common in
collectivistic _____ .

Graphic Organizer 2

Compare Piaget's and Kohlberg's theories. Read the following and decide which stage/level of development in each theory is being illustrated:

Statement	Theory	Stage/Level
1. Jeremy refuses to pay taxes and risks going to jail because he does not believe in supporting a government that spends so many tax dollars on weapons of mass destruction. Jeremy enjoys discussing his position and is very articulate in developing logical and coherent arguments.	Piaget	
	Kohlberg	
2. Mary is quite convinced that her older sister Natalie got more soft drink than she after her mother poured Natalie's can of soda into a long, thin glass and hers into a short, fat one. Despite being tempted to take a big drink out of Natalie's glass when she is in the washroom, Mary refrains because she thinks she might get punished.	Piaget	
	Kohlberg	
3. While playing a game of cards with his friends, Mark insists that everyone should have a chance to be dealer because that is the fair thing to do. Mark is also able to explain the rules to everyone by dealing a couple of practice hands, but he has difficulty later when he is trying to tell his Dad about the game without the cards.	Piaget	
	Kohlberg	
4. During a discussion with her therapist, Mrs. Bradshaw is asked to describe her husband. Among the things she notes is that he is very law abiding, always drives with extreme care, and frequently boasts that he has never received a ticket. He never completed high school because he couldn't handle all that abstract, hypothetical stuff and is fairly content working as a custodian in an office building.	Piaget	
	Kohlberg	

Adult Development
Learning Objectives

When you have finished studying this section of the chapter, you should be able to:

1. Explain how development continues throughout adulthood.

2. Describe the physical changes that take place in adulthood and identify some of the general patterns of social development that occur.

3. Explain how the transition to parenthood affects adults.

4. Describe K. Warner Shaie's longitudinal research on the effects of aging on physical and cognitive abilities.

5. Identify the cognitive changes that take place in late adulthood and list the factors that can influence social development during this stage of development.

6. Describe Kübler-Ross's stage theory of dying and assess its validity.

Read the section "Adult Development" and **write** *your answers to the following:*

1. (a) Your unique _____ blueprint greatly influences the unfolding of certain physical changes during adulthood, such as when your hair begins to thin, lose its color, and turn gray.

   (b) These influences can vary significantly from one person to another; for example, _____ , the cessation of menstruation that signals the end of reproductive capacity in women, may occur anywhere from the late thirties to the early fifties.

   (c) One key _____ factor that can influence the aging process is a person's lifestyle; staying mentally and physically active and eating a proper diet can both slow and minimize the degree of physical decline associated with aging.

2. (a) According to Erikson, the primary psychosocial task of _____ adulthood is to form a committed, mutually enhancing, intimate relationship with another person; during _____ adulthood the primary psychosocial task becomes one of generativity—to contribute to future generations through children, career, and other meaningful activities.

   (b) _____ friends tend to confide in one another about their feelings, problems, and interpersonal relationships; _____ friends typically minimize discussions about relationships or personal feelings or problems and instead tend to do things together, such as activities related to sports or hobbies.

   (c) Getting married and starting a family are the traditional tasks of _____ adulthood; in contrast to their parents, today's young adults are marrying at _____ (an earlier/a later) average age.

   (d) We tend to be attracted to and marry people who are _____ (different from/similar to) us on a variety of dimensions, including physical attractiveness, social and educational status, ethnic background, attitudes, values, and beliefs.

3. (a) Although it is commonly believed that children _____ the marital bond, marital satisfaction tends to _____ after the birth of the first child.

   (b) With the birth or adoption of your first child, you take on a commitment to nurture the physical, emotional, social, and intellectual well-being of the next generation; this can fundamentally alter your _____ as an adult.

   (c) The hassles and headaches of child rearing can be minimized if the marital relationship is _____ and _____ and if both husband and wife share household and child-care responsibilities.

   (d) Although marital satisfaction often

_____ when people first become parents, it _____ again after children leave home.

4. (a) There is much diversity in adult relationships; for example, the number of unmarried couples living together has _____ dramatically in the last twenty years; currently, better than _____ percent of all children are being raised by a single parent.

   (b) More than _____ of all first marriages end in divorce, and the phenomenon of remarrying and having a second family later in life is not unusual.

   (c) As divorce has become more _____ , the number of single parents and stepfamilies has _____ ; among married couples, an increasing number are opting for a _____ life together, and there are also gay and lesbian couples committed to long-term relationships.

   (d) Such diversity in adult relationships reflects the fact that adult _____ development does not always follow a predictable pattern; in the final analysis, any relationship that promotes the overall sense of happiness and well-being of the people involved is a successful one.

5. (a) Most people explore different career options, narrow down their options, and tentatively commit to a particular job in a particular field in _____ ; close to a _____ of people in their late twenties and early thirties do not change jobs in a particular field but completely switch occupational fields.

   (b) Dual-career families have become increasingly _____ , but the career tracks of men and women often differ if they have children; married women with children

are much _____ (more/less) likely than single women or childless women to interrupt their careers, leave their jobs, or switch to part-time work because of child-rearing responsibilities.

   (c) Generally, _____ roles seem to provide both men and women with a greater potential for increased feelings of self-esteem, happiness, and competence; the critical factor is not so much the _____ of roles that people take on, but the _____ of their experiences on the job, in marriage, and as a parent.

6. (a) The average life expectancy for men is about _____ years, and for women _____ years; the stage of late adulthood can easily last for _____ years or more, and the majority of older adults live healthy, active, and self-sufficient lives.

   (b) The stereotypical image that most of the elderly live in nursing homes is a myth; only about _____ percent of people over age sixty-five live in nursing homes, and among those aged eighty-five and older, less than _____ percent live in nursing homes.

   (c) Although they have _____ chronic medical conditions, the elderly tend to see themselves as relatively healthy, partly because they have _____ acute illnesses, such as colds and the flu, than younger people; even during the final years of life, the majority of older adults enjoy relatively good health, mental alertness, and self-sufficiency.

7. (a) In his longitudinal studies, K. Warner Schaie has found that general intellectual abilities gradually _____ until one's early forties and then become relative-

ly stable; after age sixty, a small but steadily increasing percentage of older adults experience _____ (sharp/slight) declines on tests of general intellectual abilities, but most remain unaffected.

(b) When declines in _____ abilities occur during old age, the explanation is often simply a lack of practice or experience with the kinds of tasks on _____ ability tests; even just a few hours of training can improve test scores for most older adults.

(c) Schaie found that those who were better educated and engaged in physical and mental activities throughout older adulthood showed the _____ declines in mental abilities; the _____ intellectual declines tended to occur in older adults with unstimulating lifestyles, such as people who lived alone, were dissatisfied with their lives, and engaged in few activities.

8. (a) According to the _____ theory of aging, life satisfaction in late adulthood is highest when you maintain your previous level of activity, either by continuing old activities or finding new ones; the optimal level of activity varies from person to person.

(b) Along with satisfying social relationships, the prescription for psychological well-being in old age includes achieving what Erikson called _____ , the feeling that one's life has been meaningful.

(c) Older adults experience _____ _____ when they look back on their lives and feel satisfied with their accomplishments, accepting whatever mistakes or missteps they may have made; those filled with regrets or bitterness about past mistakes, missed opportunities, or bad

decisions experience _____ , a sense of disappointment in life.

(d) Often the themes of _____ or _____ emerge as older adults engage in a life review, thinking about or retelling their life story to others.

9. (a) Attitudes toward death in old age _____ (lack/show) the same diversity that is reflected in other aspects of adult development; _____ (all/not all) older adults are resigned to death, even when poor health has severely restricted their activities.

(b) In general, anxiety about death tends to peak in _____ adulthood and to _____ in late adulthood; at any age, people respond with a wide variety of emotions when faced with the prospect of imminent death, such as when they are diagnosed with a terminal illness.

(c) Elizabeth Kübler-Ross proposed that the dying go through five stages; first, they _____ that death is imminent; second, they feel and express _____ ; third, they _____ ; fourth, they become _____ ; and finally they _____ their fate.

(d) Although Kübler-Ross's research did much to sensitize the public and the medical community to the emotional experience of dying, it now seems clear that the dying individual in fact _____ (does/does not) progress through a predictable series of stages.

(e) Faced with impending death, some older adults react with passive _____ , others with _____ and _____ ; some plunge into activity and focus their attention on _____ matters whereas others turn _____ , searching for the meaning of their life's story as the close of the final chapter draws near.

10. Read the following and write the correct term in the space provided:

(a) Delbert resists stealing cookies from the cookie jar because he is afraid his mother will punish him if he does. According to Kohlberg's theory, Delbert is demonstrating level _____ and stage _____ of moral reasoning.

(b) Compared to their grandparents, Mr. and Mrs. Belmont's children are likely to marry for the first time at _____ (an earlier/a later) age.

(c) David, a sixty-five-year-old retired civil servant, feels that his life has been unproductive and ultimately meaningless. According to Erikson, David has failed to achieve a sense of _____ .

(d) Andrew, a forty-five-year-old accountant, has just learned he has a terminal illness. According to Kübler-Ross, as soon as Andrew gets over his initial denial, he will experience _____ .

(e) Seventeen-year-old Brendan questions his parent's values but is not sure that his peer group's standards are totally correct either. His confusion about what is really important in life suggests that Brendan is struggling with the problem of _____ .

(f) Sarah is a twenty-five-year-old, white, middle class, well-educated, moderately religious person. If she is typical, she will marry someone very _____ (different from/similar to) herself.

(g) The last of the Sandwells' four children has just left home to pursue a career with NASA. If the Sandwells are like most parents whose children have left home, they are likely to experience a steady _____ (decline/increase) in marital satisfaction.

Graphic Organizer 3

Match the following statements with the correct theorist:

Statement	Theorist
1. I believe that social and cultural influences are the most important factors in cognitive development.	
2. In my view people have an innate understanding of the basic principles of language, which I call a "universal grammar."	
3. As a result of my research on cognitive development in infants using visual rather than manual tasks, I have concluded that Piaget was wrong about the age at which object permanence first appears.	
4. I believe that development continues throughout the lifespan and that individuals pass through eight distinct stages during which they are faced with resolving important psychosocial conflicts.	
5. As a result of my longitudinal research on lifespan development, I believe that intellectual decline is not a natural and inevitable result of the biological aging process.	
6. My primary interest is in how children develop intellectually and cognitively, and my theory proposes that children progress through four distinct stages in succession, each stage characterized by a qualitatively different way of thinking from the previous stage.	
7. The primary goal of my research has been to map out the development of moral reasoning in humans; it is my view that there are three levels, each consisting of two stages, and humans progress through these stages in sequence, until reaching the highest level.	

Review of Key Terms and Key Names 4

adolescence
identity
Erik Erikson
identity diffusion
moratorium period
integrated identity
moral reasoning
Lawrence Kohlberg
preconventional level
conventional level
postconventional level
ethic of individual rights
    and justice
ethic of care and
    responsibility

menopause
early adulthood
middle adulthood
late adulthood
generativity
activity theory of aging
authoritarian parenting
    style
permissive parenting
    style
authoritative parents
induction

Matching Exercise

Match the appropriate term/name with its definition or description.

1. _____ A descriptive technique that combines parental control with explaining why a behavior is prohibited.

2. _____ The natural cessation of menstruation and the end of reproductive capacity in women.

3. _____ Carol Gilligan's categorization of women's moral development and reasoning, based on her research that showed women tended to stress the importance of maintaining interpersonal relationships and responding to the needs of others, rather than focusing primarily on individual rights.

4. _____ Baumrind's term for a parenting style in which parents are extremely tolerant and not demanding; permissive-indulgent parents are responsive to their children, whereas permissive-indifferent parents are not.

5. _____ In Erikson's theory, the period following identity diffusion during which the adolescent experiments with different roles, values, and beliefs.

6. _____ The transitional stage between late childhood and the beginning of adulthood, during which sexual maturity is reached.

7. _____ A level in Kohlberg's theory that begins in late childhood and continues through adolescence and adulthood; characterized by moral reasoning that emphasizes social roles, rules, and obligations.

8. _____ A stage of adulthood, roughly from the forties to mid-sixties, when physical strength and endurance gradually decline.

9. _____ A person's definition or description of himself or herself, including the values, beliefs, and ideals that guide the individual's behavior.

10. _____ The psychosocial theory that life satisfaction in late adulthood is highest when people maintain the level of activity they displayed earlier in life.

11. _____ In Erikson's theory, the primary psychosocial task of middle adulthood in which the person contributes to future generations through children, career, and other meaningful activity.

True/False Test

Indicate whether each item is true or false by placing T or F in the space next to each item.

1. ____ Moral reasoning refers to the aspect of cognitive development that has to do with the way an individual reasons about moral decisions.

2. ____ Lawrence Kohlberg was the German-born American psychoanalyst who proposed an influential theory of psychosocial development throughout the lifespan.

3. ____ Early adulthood refers to the stage of development during the twenties and thirties when physical strength typically peaks.

4. ____ *Authoritarian parenting style* is Baumrind's term for parents who set clear standards for their children's behavior but are also responsive to the children's needs and wishes.

5. ____ Late adulthood refers to the stage of development from the mid-sixties on, when physical stamina and reaction time tend to decline further and faster.

6. ____ In Erikson's theory the adolescent's path to successful identity achievement begins with identity diffusion, which is characterized by little sense of commitment to the various issues he or she has to grapple with and social demands made on him or her.

7. ____ The ethic of individual rights and justice is Carol Gilligan's term for the ethic that she believes Kohlberg's theory is based on and that she suggests is a more common perspective for males.

8. ____ Following the moratorium period, during which the adolescent experiments with different roles, values, and beliefs, he or she may then choose among alternatives and make commitments and gradually arrive at an integrated identity.

9. ____ Kohlberg and his colleagues found that responses of children under age ten reflect postconventional moral reasoning based on self-interest and the tendency to avoid punishment and maximize personal gain.

10. ____ Erik Erikson was the American psychologist who proposed an influential theory of moral development.

11. ____ According to Baumrind, authoritative parents are demanding and unresponsive toward their children's needs or wishes.

12. ____ In Kohlberg's theory the preconventional level is characterized by moral reasoning that reflects self-chosen ethical principles that are universally applied.

> Check your answers and review any areas of weakness before going on to the next section.

Something to Think About

1. A topic that often crops up in discussions about raising children is whether putting children in day care is detrimental to their development.

Discussions like this can become quite heated, with people holding strong views on both sides of the debate. Based on what you have discovered in this chapter, what light could you shed on this controversial topic?

2. You may be planning to have a family one day if you haven't done so already. For most people this is quite a responsibility and a lot of work. Unlike many other areas in life where you have to take courses and pass exams, there is no formal training required for the job of parent. You, however, are fortunate because you are taking an introductory psychology course and have learned a few things about child development. What advice would you give people who are planning to have a family?

Check your answers and review any areas of weakness before doing the progress tests.

Progress Test 1

Review the complete chapter (including Concept Reviews and the boxed inserts), review all your study notes, and then test yourself on the following progress test. Check your answers. If you make a mistake, review your notes, review the relevant section of the study guide, and, if necessary, go back and read the appropriate part of your textbook.

1. When Thomas was conceived, he was a single fertilized egg called a(n)
   (a) zygote   (c) fetus
   (b) embryo   (d) infant

2. When Thomas was growing up, it became apparent that he was red-green color-blind. This disorder
   (a) is probably a sex-linked recessive characteristic
   (b) is more common in males than females
   (c) has to do with the 23rd pair of chromosomes
   (d) is all of the above

3. In her research, Dr. Joacim found that a pregnant mother's use of a certain chemical substance caused harm to the fetus. The chemical substance could be classified as
   (a) deoxyribonucleic acid
   (b) a chromosome
   (c) a narcotic
   (d) a teratogen

4. Keith is going to be twenty-one years old next month. If he is like most young people his age,
   (a) he is still a virgin
   (b) he had sexual intercourse for the first time before he was fourteen
   (c) he has been married for about a year
   (d) he has already lost his virginity

5. When Mrs. Euland touched her newborn's lips, he produced an automatic response called the _____ reflex.
   (a) rooting   (c) grasping
   (b) sucking   (d) greedy

6. It has become apparent to Mr. and Mrs. Euland that their baby has a low activity level, tends to withdraw from new situations and people, and adapts to new experiences very gradually. The baby would be classified as a(n) _____ baby.
   (a) easy
   (b) difficult
   (c) slow-to-warm-up
   (d) uninhibited

7. Aldred believes that gender roles develop as a result of young children observing others modeling particular gender-appropriate behaviors and that children are rewarded when they behave accordingly and are punished when they don't. Aldred's view is most consistent with
   (a) gender schema theory of gender-role development
   (b) Kohlberg's theory of gender-role development
   (c) social learning theory of gender-role development
   (d) Chomsky's theory of gender-role development

8. When she was almost eleven months old, Jessica said "ba ba" when she pointed at her bottle and "ma ma" when she pointed at her Mom. Jessica is in the _____ stage of language development.
   (a) cooing   (c) one-word
   (b) babbling   (d) two-word

9. Piaget is to cognitive development as Erikson is to _____ development.
   (a) moral
   (b) physical
   (c) emotional
   (d) psychosocial

10. When Neil's mother hides his favorite toy under a blanket, Neil acts as though it no longer exists and makes no attempt to retrieve it. Neil is in Piaget's _____ stage.
    (a) sensorimotor
    (b) preoperational
    (c) concrete operational
    (d) formal operational

11. In the above example Neil's behavior suggests that he
    (a) has developed object permanence
    (b) has not developed object permanence
    (c) is capable of reversible thinking
    (d) understands the principle of conservation

12. Nine-year-old Adam has acquired the mental operations to comprehend such things as conservation and reversibility and can solve tangible problems in a logical manner. Adam is in Piaget's _____ stage of development.
    (a) sensorimotor   (c) concrete operational
    (b) preoperational   (d) formal operational

13. Piaget is to cognitive development as Kohlberg is to _____ development.
    (a) moral   (c) emotional
    (b) physical   (d) psychosocial

14. Danielle has switched college majors four times and does not know what she wants to do after she gets her degree. Erikson would suggest that Danielle has not achieved a(n)
    (a) integrated identity
    (b) sense of generativity
    (c) conventional level of moral reasoning
    (d) concrete operational stage of development

15. Preconventional morality is to postconventional morality as _____ is to _____.
    (a) social approval; ethical principle
    (b) self-interest; social approval
    (c) self-interest; ethical principle
    (d) social approval; self-interest

16. Seventy-year-old Redner feels that his life has been full, interesting, and meaningful. According to Erikson, Redner has achieved a sense of
    (a) generativity   (c) identity
    (b) ego integrity   (d) initiative

17. Gordon, a fifty-year-old lawyer, has just learned from his physician that he has only one year to live. According to Kübler-Ross, his first reaction to hearing the news is likely to be

    (a) "No, it's not possible, there's obviously been some mix-up, some terrible mistake."
    (b) "Life is not worth living anymore."
    (c) "Why me? This is very unfair and makes me mad."
    (d) "Well, that's the way it goes, I guess."

18. Between the age of fifteen and sixteen Sean grew almost five inches. Sean experienced _____ during this year.
    (a) the development of primary sex characteristics
    (b) the adolescent growth spurt
    (c) the development of mammary glands
    (d) menarche

19. According to the Application section, a parenting style in which parents set clear standards for their children's behavior but are also responsive to the children's needs and wishes is called
    (a) authoritarian
    (b) permissive-indulgent
    (c) permissive-indifferent
    (d) authoritative

20. According to Culture and Human Behavior Box 9.1, infants typically sleep in their own bed and usually in a separate room from their parents in
    (a) all cultures   (c) the United States
    (b) all Western cultures (d) all Latin cultures

Progress Test 2

After you have checked your understanding of the material in Progress Test 1 and have done a complete chapter review with special focus on any areas of weakness, you are ready to assess your knowledge in Progress Test 2. Check your answers. If you make a mistake, review your notes, the relevant section of the study guide, and, if necessary, the appropriate part of your textbook.

1. Dr. Strayer is conducting longitudinal research on factors that correlate with getting older. She is likely to find that
    (a) intellectual abilities decline sharply with age
    (b) there is severe memory impairment as people reach late adulthood
    (c) most people maintain their intellectual abilities as they age
    (d) no matter how much practice older people have on mental skills, they still do very poorly on intellectual tasks

2. Mr. Danzig is a sixty-eight-year-old retired accountant. If he is typical of people his age, he is probably living
   (a) in his own home
   (b) in a nursing home
   (c) with his grown-up children
   (d) in a mental health facility

3. Darlene and Mike have been married for two years and have a nine-month-old infant. If they are like most young married couples, their level of marital satisfaction is probably
   (a) increasing dramatically
   (b) increasing slightly
   (c) declining
   (d) the same as it was when they first got married

4. Miguel is a twenty-five-year old, college-educated middle-class engineer. Like his Mexican parents, he is a devout Catholic. If Miguel is like most people, he will probably marry someone who is
   (a) completely different from him in every way as long as she is Catholic
   (b) very much like he is
   (c) much older than he is
   (d) much richer than he is

5. Mrs. Grant is forty-nine years old and has recently ceased to menstruate. Mrs. Grant has experienced
   (a) moratorium   (c) induction
   (b) menopause   (d) centration

6. Noreen is almost thirteen and has just had her first menstrual period. Noreen has experienced
   (a) menopause
   (b) menarche
   (c) induction
   (d) a refractory period

7. Mr. Gates believes in law and order, obeys all rules and regulations, and has respect for authorities just because they are authorities. Mr. Gates is likely at Kohlberg's _____ level of moral reasoning.
   (a) conventional   (c) concrete operational
   (b) preconventional   (d) formal operational

8. Sixteen-year-old Jade is reading books about different religions and philosophies and is trying out different approaches to how one should live one's life. Jade is in Erikson's
   (a) moratorium period
   (b) generativity stage

   (c) ego integrity period
   (d) formal operational stage

9. The Atwells have two teenage children. If they are like most parents, their relationship with their kids
   (a) is very negative and getting worse
   (b) is full of fights, arguments, anger, and hostility
   (c) is just about as positive as it was when the children were younger
   (d) was positive at first but has deteriorated as the children aged

10. Marcel is researching a paper for his child developmental course and discovers the work of Lev Vygotsky. In summarizing his contribution to developmental psychology, Marcel is likely to note that Vygotsky emphasized
    (a) genetic factors
    (b) clearly defined biological stages of cognitive development
    (c) clearly defined biological stages of moral development
    (d) social and cultural factors in cognitive development

11. Fourteen-year-old Jason has the ability to reason abstractly and think logically even about hypothetical situations. Jason is in Piaget's _____ stage of cognitive development.
    (a) sensorimotor
    (b) preoperational
    (c) concrete operational
    (d) formal operational

12. Kelly is five years old and uses her imagination and fantasy whenever she plays. Recently, for example, she used a discarded box as a make-believe castle and made up a very interesting dialogue between the "king" and "queen" of her castle. This illustrates
    (a) centration   (c) symbolic thought
    (b) conservation   (d) object permanence

13. Mrs. Hoff uses very distinct pronunciation, a simplified vocabulary, short sentences, a high pitch, and exaggerated intonation and expression whenever she interacts with her baby. This is an example of
    (a) motherese, or infant-directed speech
    (b) induction
    (c) fetal alcohol syndrome
    (d) cooing and babbling

14. In a situation designed to assess attachment, little Anthony used his mother as a safe base from which to explore the environment, showed distress when she left the room, and greeted her warmly when she returned. Anthony would be classified as
    (a) an inhibited baby
    (b) a securely attached baby
    (c) an insecurely attached baby
    (d) a slow-to-warm-up baby

15. Tasha is a newborn healthy infant. She has
    (a) all the neural connections she will ever have
    (b) all the dendrites she will ever have
    (c) all the myelin she will ever have
    (d) all the brain cells she will ever have
    (e) all of the above

16. Nine months after conception, baby Tracy is born. The stages of prenatal development she went through from first to last were
    (a) embryonic, fetal, germinal
    (b) fetal, embryonic, germinal
    (c) germinal, embryonic, fetal
    (d) germinal, fetal, embryonic

17. According to Critical Thinking Box 9.2, putting young children in a high-quality day-care facility
    (a) is detrimental to their physical health
    (b) severely disrupts the attachment process
    (c) has no detrimental effect on the children
    (d) is detrimental to their psychological health

18. According to the Application section, which of the following is *not* recommended for raising psychologically healthy children?
    (a) Work with your children's temperamental qualities.
    (b) Use instruction to teach as you discipline.
    (c) Let your children know that you love them.
    (d) Strive to be an authoritarian parent.
    (e) Listen to your children.

19. Psychologist Diana Baumrind has described a number of basic parenting styles. In her research she found that children of _____ parents were likely to be moody, unhappy, fearful, withdrawn, unspontaneous, and irritable.
    (a) permissive-indulgent
    (b) permissive-indifferent
    (c) authoritative
    (d) authoritarian

20. Baumrind also found that children of _____ parents were likely to be cheerful, socially competent, energetic, and friendly, with high levels of self-esteem, self-reliance, and self-control.
    (a) permissive-indulgent
    (b) permissive-indifferent
    (c) authoritative
    (d) authoritarian

Answers

Introduction: Your Life Story

1. (a) biological, environmental, social, cultural
   (b) attitudes, perceptions; personality
   (c) differ

2. (a) stages; gradually
   (b) heredity; environment; nature/nurture
   (c) genetic; environment; genetic; environment

Genetic Contributions to Your Life Story

1. (a) deoxyribonucleic acid; DNA; DNA
   (b) DNA; DNA
   (c) 23; 23; 23

2. (a) genotype; dominant
   (b) dominant; dominant
   (c) dominant; dominant
   (d) recessive; recessive; recessive
   (e) recessive; recessive
   (f) potential

3. (a) recessive; sex
   (b) sex
   (c) females; males
   (d) females
   (e) males; males
   (f) sex-linked recessive
   (g) males; males; females

Graphic Organizer 1

Cell 1: dimples

Cell 2: dimples

Cell 3: dimples

Cell 4: no dimples

Prenatal Development

1. (a) zygotic
   (b) zygote's; two

2. (a) three; eight
   (b) amniotic
   (c) placenta; placenta
   (d) teratogens

3. (a) third
   (b) third
   (c) fourth; fifth
   (d) sixth
   (e) two

4. (a) developmental
   (b) nature; nurture
   (c) X; Y; X; X
   (d) embryo; fetus

Matching Exercise 1

1. prenatal stage
2. gene
3. developmental psychology
4. sex-linked recessive characteristics
5. teratogens
6. chromosome
7. recessive gene
8. germinal period (zygotic period)
9. embryo
10. recessive characteristics
11. sex chromosomes

True/False Test 1

1. T	5. T	9. F
2. T	6. T	10. T
3. T	7. F	11. F
4. F	8. T	

Development During Infancy and Childhood

1. (a) physical; sensory
   (b) people

2. (a) least; 6; 12
   (b) 8; 12; easier
   (c) scent (smell)
   (d) smell; smell; skin

3. (a) seven; eight
   (b) 25; 75
   (c) all
   (d) dendrites; myelin
   (e) sequence; average age

Social and Personality Development

1. (a) physical; psychological; does not
   (b) behavioral

2. (a) easy, difficult, and slow to warm up
   (b) average
   (c) stable
   (d) genetic; biological

3. (a) emotional bond; physically; psychologically
   (b) multiple

4. (a) attachment
   (b) securely
   (c) insecurely; ignore; avoid
   (d) securely; insecure; securely; insecurely

Language Development

1. (a) 3,000
   (b) Noam Chomsky
   (c) can; lost

2. (a) motherese
   (b) motherese, "baby talk"
   (c) infant-directed speech (motherese)

3. (a) cooing; babble; babble
   (b) words; comprehension; production
   (c) one-word
   (d) two-word
   (e) two-word
   (f) two and a half; school

4. (a) human face
   (b) 100 percent
   (c) easy
   (d) secure

Matching Exercise 2

1. sucking reflex
2. slow-to-warm-up temperament
3. motherese (infant-directed speech)
4. cooing and babbling stage
5. attachment
6. comprehension vocabulary
7. insecure attachment
8. two-word stage

True/False Test 2

1. T	4. T	7. T
2. F	5. T	8. F
3. T	6. T	9. T

Gender-Role Development

1. (a) gender; gender roles; gender identity
   (b) two; three
   (c) behavior; three
   (d) assert; compromise, conciliation

2. (a) reinforcement, punishment
   (b) small; similarly
   (c) modeling; activities; attributes

3. (a) actively; masculinity; femininity
   (b) perceive, interpret; remember

Cognitive Development

1. (a) gender schemas; cognitive
   (b) actively; passively

   (c) birth; two; two; seven; seven; eleven; adolescence; adulthood
   (d) qualitatively
   (e) assimilates; accommodate

2. (a) actions; actions
   (b) object permanence
   (c) object permanence; schemas

3. (a) operations
   (b) symbolic
   (c) symbolic
   (d) egocentrism, irreversibility; centration
   (e) conservation

4. (a) egocentric; reverse; conservation
   (b) hypothetical; abstract

5. (a) abstract; hypothetical
   (b) abstract; adults

6. (a) has
   (b) underestimated; motor skill; cognitive
   (c) visual; manual

7. (a) universal; abstract-hypothetical
   (b) universal
   (c) information-processing; continuous

8. (a) social; cultural
   (b) social; cultural
   (c) social; skills
   (d) cognitive

9. (a) sex
   (b) gender schema
   (c) gender role
   (d) underestimated
   (e) concrete operational
   (f) object permanence
   (g) conservation
   (h) assimilating
   (i) schema
   (j) formal

Matching Exercise 3

1. symbolic thought
2. cognitive processes
3. object permanence
4. formal operational stage
5. Jean Piaget
6. information-processing model of cognitive development
7. schemas
8. sensorimotor stage
9. egocentrism

10. gender
11. gender schema theory

True/False Test 3

1. T	5. F	9. F
2. T	6. T	10. F
3. F	7. F	11. F
4. T	8. T	

Adolescence

1. (a) twelve; adult
   (b) sexual; reproductive
   (c) primary
   (d) secondary
   (e) adolescent growth spurt
   (f) menarche; testes
   (g) social; cultural
   (h) fifteen; eighteen; nineteen
2. (a) positive; admire; turn
   (b) influential
3. (a) values, beliefs
   (b) cognitive
   (c) fixed; internalized
   (d) evaluate; self-definition
   (e) identity; self-concepts
4. (a) psychosocial
   (b) psychosocial
   (c) psychosocial
   (d) supported
   (e) adolescence; adult
5. (a) cognitive
   (b) short stories; stages
   (c) levels; level; stages
   (d) postconventional; stages; conventional
6. (a) male; women
   (b) individual; males
   (c) women's; women
   (d) culture; cultures
   (e) group; cultures

Graphic Organizer 2

1. Piaget: formal operational stage; Kohlberg: postconventional level, stage 6
2. Piaget: preoperational stage; Kohlberg: preconventional level, stage 1
3. Piaget: concrete operational stage; Kohlberg: preconventional level, stage 2
4. Piaget: concrete operational stage; Kohlberg: conventional level, stage 4

Adult Development

1. (a) genetic
   (b) menopause
   (c) environmental
2. (a) early; middle
   (b) female; male
   (c) early; a later
   (d) similar to
3. (a) strengthen; decline
   (b) identity
   (c) warm; positive
   (d) declines; rises
4. (a) increased; 30
   (b) half
   (c) common; risen; child-free
   (d) social
5. (a) young adulthood; third
   (b) common; more
   (c) multiple; number; quality
6. (a) 72; 79; twenty
   (b) 5; 25
   (c) more; fewer
7. (a) increase; slight
   (b) mental; mental
   (c) smallest; greatest
8. (a) activity
   (b) ego integrity
   (c) ego integrity; despair
   (d) ego integrity; despair
9. (a) show; not all
   (b) middle; decrease
   (c) deny; anger; bargain; depressed; accept
   (d) does not
   (e) resignation; bitterness; anger; external; inward
10. (a) 1; 1
    (b) a later
    (c) ego integrity
    (d) anger
    (e) identity
    (f) similar to
    (g) increase

Graphic Organizer 3

1. Lev Vygotsky
2. Noam Chomsky
3. Renée Baillargeon
4. Erik Erikson
5. K. Warner Schaie

6. Jean Piaget

7. Lawrence Kohlberg

Matching Exercise 4

1. induction

2. menopause

3. ethic of care and responsibility

4. permissive parenting style

5. moratorium period

6. adolescence

7. conventional level

8. middle adulthood

9. identity

10. activity theory of aging

11. generativity

True/False Test 4

1. T	5. T	9. F
2. F	6. T	10. F
3. T	7. T	11. F
4. F	8. T	12. F

Something to Think About

1. Most psychologists today agree that *quality* of the child-care arrangements is the key factor in promoting secure attachment in early childhood and preventing problems in later childhood. In fact, many studies have found that children who experience high-quality day care tend to be more sociable, better adjusted, and more academically competent than children who experience poor-quality day care. In addition, some researchers have found that grade school children enrolled in high-quality day care from infancy experience no negative effects of their day care experience. Research in Sweden has supported these findings.

   It is clear that day care in itself does not necessarily lead to undesirable outcomes. The key factor is the quality of day care. High-quality day care is characterized by a number of key factors; caregivers should be warm and responsive, developmentally appropriate activities and a variety of play materials should be available, caregivers should have some training and education in child development, low staff turnover is important, and the ratio of caregivers to children should be low.

2. A short discussion of the various stages of cognitive, psychosocial, and moral development would be appropriate. Raising psychologically healthy children is possible if parents adopt some of the strategies that the experts suggest. Psychologist Diana Baumrind has described three basic parenting styles: authoritarian, permissive, and authoritative. Research has shown that the authoritative style produces the best results. Can parents learn to be authoritative in their parenting style? The Application section has a number of practical suggestions: let your children know that you love them, listen to your children, use induction to teach as you discipline, work with your children's temperamental qualities, and understand your child's age-related cognitive abilities and limitations.

   Although all children inherit genetic predispositions from both parents, research has shown that environmental factors, such as the social and cultural influences, educational experiences, and parenting style that children are exposed to have very powerful effects on development.

Progress Test 1

1. a	8. c	15. c
2. d	9. d	16. b
3. d	10. a	17. a
4. d	11. b	18. b
5. b	12. c	19. d
6. c	13. a	20. c
7. c	14. a	

Progress Test 2

1. c	8. a	15. d
2. a	9. c	16. c
3. c	10. d	17. c
4. b	11. d	18. d
5. b	12. c	19. d
6. b	13. a	20. c
7. a	14. b	

Chapter 10   Personality

OVERVIEW   Chapter 10 introduces the topic of personality by defining the term, describing a personality theory, and listing the four major theoretical perspectives in personality.

The psychoanalytic perspective was founded by Sigmund Freud, and the major components and assumptions of his theory are discussed. Psychoanalysis stresses the unconscious, the importance of sex and aggression, and the influences of early childhood experiences. Access to the unconscious may be gained through free association, dreams, slips of the tongue, and apparent accidents. The psychological processes of personality are presented, and the major defense mechanisms are discussed. The psychosexual stages of development, the various conflicts associated with each, and how the resolution of these conflicts affects the development of the adult personality are examined. The contributions made by the early followers of Freud, the neo-Freudians, are explored, and criticisms of Freud's theory and psychoanalysis are discussed.

The psychoanalytic perspective is compared and contrasted with the humanistic perspective. The theory of personality of Carl Rogers and his optimistic view of human nature are discussed. The self-concept, unconditional positive regard, the actualizing tendency, and the fully functioning person are examined, along with criticisms of the humanistic perspective.

The social cognitive perspective stresses the role of conscious thought processes, goals, self-regulation, and reciprocal determinism. The influence of self-efficacy on behavior, performance, motivation, and persistence is explored. The limitations of an empirically based approach to personality and the problems of ignoring unconscious conflicts and emotions are presented as criticisms of the social cognitive approach.

The trait perspective focuses on measuring and describing individual differences, and both surface and source traits are defined. Cattell believed there are sixteen basic personality factors, Eysenck proposed three, and the five-factor model suggested that there are five. It is concluded that traits are generally stable across time and across situations, but situations do influence how and whether traits will be expressed. Behavioral genetics research uses twin and adoption studies to measure the relative influence of genetics and environment.

The trait perspective is useful in describing individual differences and predicting behavior but has been criticized for its failure to explain human personality and the development of individual differences.

The final section of the chapter examines the area of personality assessment. Two basic types of personality tests are projective tests and self-report inventories. The two most common types of projective tests are examined, and their strengths and weaknesses are presented. The three most widely used self-report inventories are described, and their value in assessing both normal and abnormal populations is discussed.

The reliability, validity, and predictive value of self-report inventories are high, but they are criticized on a number of grounds.

Introduction: What Is Personality?

Learning Objectives

When you have finished studying this section of the chapter, you should be able to:

1. Define *personality* and state what a personality theory is.

2. List the four basic theoretical perspectives in personality and identify what each approach emphasizes.

*Read the section "Introduction: What Is Personality?" and **write** your answers to the following:*

1. (a) Personality is defined as an individual's _____

    _____ .

    (b) A personality theory is an attempt to

    _____ and _____

    how people are _____ , how

    they are _____ , and why every

    individual is unique; in short, a personality

    theory ambitiously tries to explain the

    _____ person, but no single the-

    ory can explain all aspects of human person-

    ality.

2. There are many personality theories, but they can be roughly grouped under four basic perspectives:

    (a) The psychoanalytic perspective emphasizes

    the importance of _____

    processes and the influence of

    _____ experience.

    (b) The humanistic perspective represents a(n)

    _____ look at human

    nature, emphasizing the _____

    and the fulfillment of a person's

    _____ .

    (c) The social cognitive perspective emphasizes

    _____ and conscious

    _____ processes, including the

importance of _____ about the

self, goal setting, and self-regulation.

    (d) The trait perspective emphasizes the

    _____ and

    _____ of specific person-

    ality differences among individuals.

The Psychoanalytic Perspective on Personality

Learning Objectives

When you have finished studying this section of the chapter, you should be able to:

1. Name the founder of the psychoanalytic perspective and describe the main influences on personality development according to this point of view.

2. Identify some of the key influences on Freud's thinking.

3. Explain how we get access to unconscious mental processes.

4. Describe the three basic structures of personality and identify their functions.

5. List the main defense mechanisms and specify the role played by each.

*Read the section "The Psychoanalytic Perspective on Personality" and **write** your answers to the following:*

1. (a) Freud was trained in _____ and

    _____ and was among

    the first to investigate the anesthetic and

    mood-altering properties of

    _____ ; his initial enthusiasm

    for its medical potential faded when he

    finally recognized that the drug is

    _____ .

    (b) Freud gave up _____

    research for a private practice in

    _____ : his theory gradually

    evolved during his first twenty years of private practice based on observations of his

_____ as well as self-analysis.

(c) Joseph Breuer, an early mentor of Freud, described a case in which the free expression of pent-up _____ associated with memories that only emerged under hypnosis resulted in the disappearance of psychological and physical symptoms. Breuer called this phenomenon

_____ .

(d) Because hypnosis did not work with many of his patients, Freud developed his own technique of _____ to help his patients uncover forgotten memories; patients would spontaneously report their uncensored _____ ,

_____ , and

_____ as they came to mind.

2. (a) Freud and Breuer described several of their case studies in their landmark book _Studies in Hysteria_; its publication in 1895 marks the beginning of _____ .

(b) By the early 1900s Freud had developed the basic tenets of his _____ theory; he was gaining _____ recognition and developing a following.

(c) For the next thirty years Freud continued to refine his theory; during this period he added ___ _____ to

_____ as a fundamental instinctual human motive.

(d) In 1930 Freud published _Civilization and Its Discontents_, in which he applied his psychoanalytic perspective to _____ as a whole; he argued that

_____ and

_____ are in basic conflict, a conflict that cannot be resolved.

(e) Freud died in 1939 in London, at the age of eight-three; today Freud's legacy continues to influence psychology, _____ ,

_____ , and art.

Freud's Dynamic Theory of Personality

Read the section "Freud's Dynamic Theory of Personality" and **write** your answers to the following:

1. (a) Freud saw personality and behavior as the constant interplay of conflicting psychological forces that operate at three different levels of awareness: the _____ ,

_____ , and _____

levels.

(b) The bulk of your thoughts, feeling, wishes, and drives are submerged in the

_____ , which exerts an enormous influence on your _____

thoughts and behavior.

2. (a) Although it is not directly accessible, Freud believed that _____ material often seeps through to the _____ level in distorted, disguised, or symbolic forms.

(b) Freud carefully analyzed his patients' reports of dreams and free associations for evidence of _____ wishes, fantasies, and conflicts.

(c) Dream analysis was particularly important to Freud; beneath the surface images, or _____ content, of a dream lay its _____ content, or the true, hidden, _____ meaning of the dream symbols.

(d) Freud believed that the _____ could also be revealed in

_____ actions, such as accidents, mistakes, instances of forgetting, and inadvertent slips of the tongue, which are often referred to as " _____ slips."

3. (a) The psychological energy that each person possesses evolves to form the three basic _____ of personality.

(b) The Id, the most primitive part of the personality, is entirely _____ , is present at birth, and is completely immune

to _____ , _____ ,

_____ , _____ , and

the demands of the external world.

(c) The Id's reservoir of psychological energy is derived from two conflicting instinctual drives, the life instinct, called _____ , which consists of biological urges that perpetuate the existence of the individual and the species, and the death instinct, called _____ , which is a destructive energy reflected in aggressive, reckless, and life-threatening behaviors.

(d) The Id is ruled by the _____ principle—the relentless drive toward immediate satisfaction of the instinctual urges, especially sexual urges; Freud used the word _____ to refer specifically to sexual energy or motivation.

(e) The Id strives to increase _____ , reduce _____ , and avoid

_____ .

4. (a) The Ego is _____ (completely/partly) conscious and develops from part of the Id's psychological energy; it represents the _____ , _____ , and planning dimensions of personality.

(b) As the mediator between the Id's instinctual demands and the restrictions of the outer world, the Ego operates on the _____ principle, which is the capacity to postpone _____ until the appropriate time or circumstances exist in the external world.

(c) The Ego is the _____ part of the personality that learns various compromises to reduce the tension of the Id's instinctual urges; if the Ego can't identify an acceptable compromise to satisfy an instinctual urge, it can _____ the

impulse, or remove it from conscious awareness.

(d) The Ego must deal with _____ demands and limitations, such as the parents' values and morals (their ideas of right or wrong ways to think, act, and feel) and society's values as advocated by teachers and religious and legal authorities; gradually these social values move from being _____ imposed demands to being _____ rules and values.

5. (a) The Superego is the _____ representation of parental and societal values, and it evaluates the acceptability of behavior; put simply, your Superego represents your _____ and judges your own behavior as right or wrong, good or bad, acceptable or unacceptable.

(b) If you fail to live up to these moral ideals, the Superego can be harshly punitive, imposing feelings of inferiority, _____ , _____ , _____ , and _____ .

6. (a) The Ego must be strong, flexible, and resourceful to successfully mediate conflicts between the _____ demands of the Id, the _____ authority of the Superego, and _____ restrictions; according to Freud, everyone experiences an ongoing daily battle among these warring personality processes.

(b) When Id or Superego demands threaten to overwhelm the Ego, _____ results; if Id impulses overpower the Ego, a person may act _____ and perhaps _____ ; if Superego demands overwhelm the Ego, an individual may suffer from _____ , _____ , or even suicidal impulses for failing to live up to the Superego's _____ standards.

(c) If a realistic solution or compromise is not possible, the Ego may temporarily reduce _____ by _____ thoughts or perceptions of reality through processes that Freud called Ego defense mechanisms; these largely unconscious self-deceptions help maintain an integrated sense of self.

(d) The most fundamental Ego defense mechanism is _____ , which in simple terms is _____ forgetting; to some degree, it occurs in every Ego defense mechanism.

(e) Unknown to the person, anxiety-producing thoughts, feelings, or impulses are pushed out of _____ awareness into the _____ ; however, if you encounter a situation similar to the one you've _____ , bits and pieces of memories of the previous situation may begin to surface; as a result other defense mechanisms may be deployed.

7. (a) _____ occurs when emotional impulses are redirected to a substitute object or person, usually one that is less _____ or _____ than the original source of conflict.

(b) The main drawback to any defense mechanism is that maintaining self-deceptions requires _____ , which is needed to cope effectively with the demands of daily life.

(c) Many psychologically _____ people use ego defense mechanisms on a short-term, limited basis to deal with stressful events; but when their use _____ or _____ with the use of more constructive coping strategies, these mechanisms can be counterproductive.

Personality Development
Learning Objectives

When you have finished studying this section of the chapter, you should be able to:

1. List and describe each of the psychosexual stages of development.

2. Identify the core conflicts of the oral, anal, and phallic stages and explain the consequences of fixation.

3. Explain the role the Oedipus complex plays in personality development.

Read the section "Personality Development" and ***write*** *your answers to the following:*

1. (a) According to Freud, people progress through five _____ stages of development; the foundations of adult personality development are established during the first five years of life, as the child progresses through the _____ , _____ , and _____ stages; the _____ stage occurs during late childhood; and the _____ stage begins in adolescence.

(b) Freud believed that the child expresses primitive _____ urges by seeking sensual pleasure from different body areas; thus the _____ stages are age-related developmental periods in which _____ impulses are focused on different body zones and are expressed through activities associated with these body areas.

(c) Over the first five years of life, the expression of primitive _____ urges progresses from one bodily zone to another in a distinct order. The first year of life is characterized by the _____ stage; during this time the infant derives pleasure through the _____ activities of sucking, chewing, and biting; during the next two years, the _____ stage, pleasure is derived through elimination and acquiring control over elimination; in the _____ stage, the child's pleasure seeking is focused on his or her

_____ .

2. (a) At each _____ stage, Freud believed that the infant or young child is faced with a developmental _____ that must be successfully resolved in order to move on to the next stage.

(b) The heart of this _____ is the degree to which parents either _____ or _____ the child's expression of pleasurable feelings through activities pertaining to different bodily zones.

(c) If _____ , the child will be left with feelings of unmet needs characteristic of that stage; if _____ , the child may be reluctant to move on to the next stage; in either case, the result of an unresolved developmental _____ is _____ at a particular stage; the person continues to seek pleasure through behaviors that are similar to those associated with that stage.

3. (a) The most critical conflict that the child must successfully resolve for healthy personality and sexual development occurs during the _____ stage.

(b) As the child becomes more aware of pleasure derived from the _____ area, Freud believed that the child develops a sexual attraction to the _____ parent and hostility toward the _____ parent; this is the famous Oedipus complex.

4. (a) For boys, the Oedipus complex unfolds as a confrontation with the _____ for the affections of the _____ ; the little boy experiences _____

anxiety when he realizes that his adversary is more physically powerful and may punish him by cutting off his genitals.

(b) To resolve the Oedipus complex and these anxieties, the little boy ultimately joins forces with his former enemy by resorting to the defense mechanism of _____ ; that is, he imitates and internalizes his _____ _____ values, attitudes, and mannerisms.

(c) There is one strict limitation in imitating and identifying with the _____ : only the father can enjoy the sexual affections of the mother; this limitation becomes internalized as a taboo against _____ urges in the boy's developing Superego.

5. (a) A girl also ultimately resolves the Oedipus complex by _____ with the same-sex parent and developing a strong Superego taboo against _____ urges, but the underlying sexual drama in a girl follows different themes.

(b) She feels contempt and resentment toward her mother, and in her attempt to take her mother's place with the father, she also _____ with her mother and _____ the attributes of the same-sex parent.

(c) Freud's views on female sexuality, particularly the concept of _____ , are among his most severely criticized ideas.

6. (a) Freud felt that because of the intense anxiety associated with the Oedipus complex, the sexual urges of male and female children become _____ during the _____ stage in late childhood.

(b) Outwardly, children in the _____ stage express a strong desire to associate with _____ peers, a preference that strengthens the child's sexual identity.

(c) The final resolution of the Oedipus complex occurs in adolescence, during the _____ stage; as _____ urges start to resurface, they are prohibited by the moral ideals of the Superego as well as by societal restrictions; instead, the person directs sexual urges toward socially acceptable substitutes, who often resemble the person's _____ parent.

(d) In Freud's theory, a healthy personality and sense of sexuality result when the _____ are successfully resolved at each _____ stage of development; this results not only in the person's capacity to _____ but also in expressions of productive living through one's life work, child rearing, and other accomplishments.

7. Read the following and write the correct term in the space provided:

(a) Wilma typically responds to stress and stressful situations in a very agitated, panic-stricken manner. Gloria, on the other hand, usually stays calm and handles things in a careful and thoughtful manner. The reactions of Wilma and Gloria indicate that each has a distinctive _____ .

(b) Colleen, who is suffering from some puzzling physical and psychological symptoms that don't appear to have any physiological cause, has decided to seek help from a Freudian psychoanalyst. The therapist is most likely to use _____ in an attempt to explore Colleen's unconscious.

(c) During a heated argument David inadvertently called his wife Joanne by his mother's name. From the psychoanalytic perspective, this "Freudian slip" reveals something about

David's _____ (conscious/pre-conscious/unconscious) motivation.

(d) Amelia had a very strange dream in which she was with a very handsome man on a train traveling through the Swiss Alps. The train kept going in and out of tunnels and going faster and faster as it made its way through the mountains. According to Freudian theory, the _____ (manifest/latent) content of the dream should give some clue as to what is going on in Amelia's unconscious.

(e) When two-year-old Tyler was told that he would get no dessert unless he finished eating all his vegetables, he turned the plate upside down and said he hated his Mom and Dad. Freud would have said that Tyler was responding to the demands of the

_____ .

(f) Kato found a wallet containing $200 in cash. For just a moment he was tempted to keep the money, but the thought of doing so made him feel guilty and anxious and he immediately took the wallet to the lost-and-found office. According to Freud, Kato's good deed was motivated by his _____ .

(g) Leslie sometimes thinks that the real reason her husband became a psychotherapist was to provide himself with a socially acceptable way to indulge his excessive inquisitiveness about other people's private lives. Leslie is suggesting that her husband is using an ego defense mechanism called

_____ .

(h) Nine-year-old Danny looks up to his father and wants to be an engineer just like him when he grows up. Freud would suggest that Danny is exhibiting signs of the process of _____ .

Graphic Organizer 1

Read the following and match each one with the appropriate stage of psychosexual development:

Description	Stage
1. Sixteen-year-old Graham has started going steady with Julie and is experiencing all the sensations of being in love.	
2. Five-year-old Annette has become very competitive with her mother for her father's affections and quite defiantly states that she is "Going to marry Daddy when I grow up!"	
3. Vivian is eight years old and does not like boys very much. In fact, she plays with her girlfriends almost exclusively.	
4. It seems that no matter what Marie gives her baby to play with, she immediately puts it in her mouth.	
5. Darcy is not quite two but seems to take great pleasure in refusing to obey his parents and by asserting his control and independence. His favorite word is "No!"	

Review of Key Terms and Key Names 1

personality
personality theory
Sigmund Freud
psychoanalysis
catharsis
free association
conscious
preconscious
unconscious
Id
Eros
libido
Thanatos
pleasure principle
Ego
reality principle

Superego
Ego defense mechanisms
repression
displacement
sublimation
psychosexual stages
oral stage
anal stage
phallic stage
fixation
Oedipus complex
castration anxiety
identification
penis envy
latency stage
genital stage

Matching Exercise

Match the appropriate term/name with its definition or description.

1. _____ In Freud's theory, the psychological and emotional energy associated with expressions of sexuality; the sex drive.

2. _____ An individual's unique and relatively consistent patterns of thinking, feeling, and behaving.

3. _____ In Freud's theory, the partly conscious self-evaluative, moralistic component of personality that is formed through the internalization of parental and societal rules.

4. _____ In Freud's theory, a child's unconscious sexual desire for the opposite-sex parent, usually accompanied by hostile feelings toward the same-sex parent.

5. _____ Latin for *I;* in Freud's theory, the partly conscious rational component of personality that regulates thoughts and behavior and is most in touch with the demands of the external world.

6. _____ A term used to describe a level of awareness that contains information that is not currently in conscious awareness but is easily accessible.

7. _____ The first psychosexual stage of development, during which the infant derives pleasure through the activities of sucking, chewing, and biting.

8. _____ In psychoanalytic theory, the Ego defense mechanism that involves unconsciously shifting the target of an emotional urge to a substitute target that is less threatening or dangerous.

9. _____ Austrian neurologist who founded psychoanalysis, which is both a com-

prehensive theory of personality and a form of psychotherapy; emphasized the role of unconscious determinants of behavior and early childhood experiences in the development of personality and psychological problems; key ideas include Id, Ego, and Superego; the psychosexual stages of development; and the Ego defense mechanisms.

10. _____ The second psychosexual stage of development, during which the infant derives pleasure through elimination and acquiring control of elimination.

11. _____ A theory that attempts to describe and explain individual similarities and differences.

12. _____ Latin for *the it*; in Freud's theory, the completely unconscious, irrational component of personality that seeks immediate satisfaction of instinctual urges and drives; ruled by the pleasure principle.

13. _____ The fourth psychosexual stage of development, during which the sexual urges of male and female children become repressed; outwardly, children express a strong desire to associate with same-sex peers, a preference that strengthens the child's sexual identity.

14. _____ Sigmund Freud's theory of personality, which emphasizes unconscious determinants of behavior, sexual and aggressive instinctual drives, and the enduring effects of early childhood experiences on later personality development.

15. _____ In psychoanalytic theory, largely unconscious distortions of thought or perception that act to reduce anxiety.

16. _____ In Freud's theory, age-related developmental periods in which the child's sexual urges are expressed through different body areas and the activities associated with those body areas.

True/False Test

Indicate whether each statement is true or false by placing T or F in the blank space next to each item.

1. ____ The final psychosexual stage of development, during which the person directs sexual urges toward socially acceptable substitutes and away from morally and societally prohibited ones, is called the phallic stage.

2. ____ As the Oedipus complex unfolds, the little boy feels affection for his mother and hostility and jealousy toward his father but realizes that his father is more physically powerful than he is; the boy experiences castration anxiety, or the fear that his father will punish him by castrating him.

3. ____ Fixation occurs if the child is frustrated or overindulged in his or her attempts to resolve the conflict associated with a stage, and the individual will continue to seek pleasure through behaviors that are similar to those associated with that psychosexual stage.

4. ____ In Freud's theory, the death instinct, reflected in aggressive, destructive, and self-destructive actions, is called Eros.

5. ____ In psychoanalytic theory, sublimation refers to the unconscious exclusion of anxiety-provoking thoughts, feelings, and memories from conscious awareness; the most fundamental Ego defense mechanism.

6. ____ The *unconscious* is a term used in Freud's theory to describe thoughts, feelings, wishes, and drives that are operating below the level of conscious awareness.

7. ____ Catharsis is a phenomenon that occurs when puzzling physical and psychological problems disappear after a person expresses pent-up emotions associated with traumatic events that may have been related to his or her problems.

8. ____ In psychoanalytic theory, an Ego defense mechanism that involves redirecting sexual urges toward productive, socially acceptable, nonsexual activities is called repression.

9. ____ As part of the resolution of her Oedipus complex, the little girl discovers that little boys have a penis and that she does not; she experiences a sense of loss, or deprivation, that Freud termed penis envy.

10. ____ The genital stage is the third psychosexual stage of development; during this stage the child's pleasure seeking is focused on his or her genitals.

11. ____ In psychoanalytic theory, identification is an Ego defense mechanism that involves reducing anxiety by modeling the behavior and characteristics of another person.

12. ____ The reality principle refers to the awareness of environmental demands and the capacity to accommodate them by postponing gratification until the appropriate time or circumstances exist.

13. ____ In Freud's theory, Thanatos refers to the self-preservation, or life, instinct, reflected in the expression of basic psychological urges that perpetuate the existence of the individual as well as the species.

14. ____ Free association is a psychoanalytic technique in which the patient spontaneously reports all thoughts, feelings, and mental images as they come to mind.

15. ____ All thoughts, feelings, and sensations that a person is aware of at any given moment represent the conscious level of awareness.

16. ____ The pleasure principle refers to the motive to obtain pleasure and avoid tension or discomfort; the most fundamental human motive and the guiding principle of the Id.

Check your answers and review any areas of weakness before going on to the next section.

The Neo-Freudians
Learning Objectives

When you have finished studying this section of the chapter, you should be able to:

1. Describe the similarities and differences in the approaches taken by Freud and the neo-Freudians.

2. List and describe the key ideas of Jung, Horney, and Adler.

3. Specify what influence the psychoanalytic perspective has had on Western culture and psychology.

4. Identify three criticisms of Freud's theory and, more generally, the psychoanalytic perspective.

*Read the section "The Neo-Freudians" and **write** your answers to the following:*

1. In general, the neo-Freudians disagreed with Freud on three key points:

   (a) Freud's belief that the primary motivation behind behavior is _____ urges.

   (b) Freud's contention that personality is fundamentally determined by _____ experiences; the neo-Freudians believed that personality can also be influenced by experiences throughout the lifespan.

   (c) Freud generally had a(n) _____ (optimistic/pessimistic) view of human nature.

2. (a) Carl Jung rejected Freud's belief that human behavior is fueled by the instinctual drives of _____ and _____ ; instead, he believed that people are motivated by a more general psychological energy that pushes them to achieve psychological _____ , self-_____ , and psychic wholeness and harmony.

   (b) Jung believed that the deepest part of the individual psyche is the _____ unconscious, which is shared by all people and reflects humanity's _____ evolutionary history.

   (c) Contained in the _____ unconscious are the _____ , the mental images of universal human instincts, themes, and preoccupations.

   (d) Two important archetypes that Jung described are the _____—the representations of _____ and _____ qualities; to achieve psychological harmony, it is important for men to recognize and accept their _____ aspects and for women to recognize and accept the _____ side of their nature.

   (e) Jung's ideas make more sense if you think of the _____ unconscious as reflecting shared human experiences and _____ as symbols that represent the common, universal themes of the human life cycle, such as birth, achieving a sense of self, parenthood, the spiritual search, and death.

(f) Jung was the first to describe two basic personality types: the _____ and the _____ ; Jung's emphasis on the drive toward psychological _____ and self-_____ anticipated some of the basic ideas of the humanistic perspective on personality.

3. (a) In contrast to Freud, Karen Horney stressed the importance of _____ and _____ factors; specifically, she emphasized the importance of _____ relationships, especially the parent–child relationship, in the development of personality.

(b) Horney believed that disturbances in _____ relationships, not sexual conflicts, are the cause of psychological problems; such problems arise from the attempt to deal with _____ , which Horney described as the feeling a child has of being isolated and helpless in a potentially hostile world.

(c) Horney disagreed with Freud's notion of _____ envy and instead proposed that men suffer from _____ envy.

4. (a) Striving toward_____ arises from universal feelings of _____ that are experienced during infancy and childhood, when the child is helpless and dependent on others.

(b) These feelings motivate people to _____ for their real or imagined weaknesses by emphasizing their talents and abilities and by working hard to improve themselves; Adler saw the universal feelings of _____ as ultimately being constructive and valuable.

(c) When people are unable to_____ for specific weaknesses or when their feelings of _____ are excessive, they can develop a(n) _____ complex.

Evaluating Freud and the Psychoanalytic Perspective on Personality

Read the section "Evaluating Freud and the Psychoanalytic Perspective on Personality" and ***write*** *your answers to the following:*

1. Although Sigmund Freud's ideas have had a profound and lasting effect on psychology, society, and culture, there are several valid criticisms of Freud's theory and psychoanalysis:

(a) First, Freud's theory relies wholly on data derived from a relatively _____ sample of patients and his own self-analysis; he did not take notes during his private therapy sessions, and it is only Freud's interpretations of the cases that are encountered.

(b) It is very difficult to scientifically _____ many psychoanalytic concepts because they are so vague and ambiguous; in addition, psychoanalytic concepts are often impossible to _____ , because even seemingly contradictory information can be used to support Freud's theory and psychoanalysis is better at explaining past behavior than predicting future behavior.

(c) Many people feel that Freud's theories reflect a(n) _____ view of women; Freud's theory uses _____ psychology as a prototype, and women are essentially viewed as a deviation from the norm of masculinity.

(d) Freud's theory made _____ (no/some) significant contributions to modern psychological thinking: he drew attention to the existence and importance of mental processes that occur outside of _____ awareness; it has been demonstrated that much of mental life is _____ ; early _____ experiences have a critical influence on interpersonal relationships and psychological adjustment in adulthood; and people differ significantly in the degree to which they are able to _____ their impulses, emotions, and thoughts toward adaptive and socially acceptable ends.

2. Read the following and write the correct term in the space provided:

(a) Wilfred suffered a lot of physical hardship and abuse as a child; as an adult he lacks confidence, can't hold down a job for long, and feels that nothing is really worth striving for. Adler would have said that Wilfred suffers from feelings of _____ .

(b) In a class discussion Louanne disputed Freud's assumption that women are inferior to men and that they suffer from penis envy; instead, she suggested that men suffer from womb envy and feel inadequate because they are incapable of bearing children. Louanne's views are most consistent with those of personality theorist

_____ .

(c) Adrian's therapist suggested that, to achieve psychological harmony, Adrian has to recognize and accept his feminine side, or anima. The therapist is referring to an important archetype in the _____ theory of personality.

(d) Dr. Preston, a Jungian psychologist, believes that the deepest part of the individual psyche is shared by all people and reflects humanity's common evolutionary history. Dr.

Preston is referring to Jung's notion of the

_____ .

(e) Frank is very sociable, is outgoing, and has a keen interest in sports and outdoor activities. Jung would probably describe Frank as a(n) _____ personality type.

Review of Key Terms and Key Names 2

neo-Freudians	Karen Horney
Carl Jung	basic anxiety
collective unconscious	womb envy
archetypes	Alfred Adler
anima	striving for superiority
animus	feelings of inferiority
introvert	inferiority complex
extravert	

Matching Exercise

Match the appropriate term / name with its definition or description.

1. _____ German-born American psychoanalyst who emphasized the role of social relationships and culture in personality; sharply disagreed with Freud's characterization of female psychological development, especially his notion that women suffer from penis envy; key ideas included basic anxiety.

2. _____ In Jung's theory, the inherited mental images of universal human instincts, themes, and preoccupations that are the main components of the collective unconscious.

3. _____ In Adler's theory, the desire to improve oneself, master challenges, and move toward self-perfection and self-realization, considered to be the most fundamental human motive.

4. _____ A fundamental emotion that Horney described as the feeling a child has of being isolated and helpless in a potentially hostile world.

5. _____ Adler's term for the personality characteristic that people who are unable to compensate for specific weaknesses develop; a general sense of inadequacy, weakness, and helplessness.

6. _____ In Jung's theory, the basic personality type that focuses attention and energy toward the outside world.

7. _____ An important archetype that, according to Jung, represents the feminine side in every man.

8. _____ In Jung's theory, the hypothesized part of the unconscious mind that is inherited from previous generations and that contains universally shared ancestral experiences and ideas.

True/False Test

Indicate whether each statement is true or false by placing T or F in the blank space next to each item.

1. ____ The term *neo-Freudians* was given to the early followers of Freud who developed their own theories yet still recognized the importance of many of Freud's basic notions, such as the influence of unconscious processes and early childhood experiences.

2. ____ Carl Jung was an Austrian physician who broke with Freud and developed his own psychoanalytic theory of personality, which emphasized social factors and motivation toward self-improvement and self-realization; key ideas included the inferiority complex and the superiority complex.

3. ____ The animus is the archetype in Jung's theory that represents the masculine side of every female.

4. ____ Horney used the term *womb envy* to describe the envy that men feel about women's capacity to bear children.

5. ____ In Jung's theory, the introvert is a basic personality type that focuses attention inward.

6. ____ Alfred Adler was the Swiss psychiatrist who broke with Freud to develop his own psychoanalytic theory of personality, which stressed striving toward psychological harmony; key ideas included the collective unconscious and archetypes.

7. ____ According to Adler's theory, striving for superiority arises from universal feelings of inferiority that are experienced during infancy and childhood, when the child is helpless and dependent on others.

Check your answers and review any areas of weakness before going on to the next section.

The Humanistic Perspective on Personality

Learning Objectives

When you have finished studying this section of the chapter, you should be able to:

1. Describe the main components that the humanistic perspective emphasizes.

2. Explain what role the self-concept, the actualizing tendency, and unconditional positive regard play in Rogers's personality theory.

3. Identify the key strengths and weaknesses of the humanistic perspective.

Read the section "The Humanistic Perspective on Personality" and **write** *your answers to the following:*

1. (a) In contrast to _____ pessimistic view of people as being motivated by unconscious sexual and destructive instincts, humanistic psychologists saw people as being innately _____ and their focus was on the _____ personality.

   (b) In contrast to the _____ view that human and animal behavior is due largely to environmental reinforcement and punishment, the humanistic psychologists emphasized human _____ and such uniquely human characteristics as _____ ; they contended that the most important factor in personality is the individual's _____ _____ , _____ perception of his or her self.

   (c) The two most important contributors to the humanistic perspective were Carl Rogers and Abraham Maslow; Maslow is famous for his _____ of needs, and his research identified several qualities of _____ people.

2. (a) Like _____ , Rogers's personality theory developed out of his clinical experi-

ences with his patients, whom he referred to as "clients" to emphasize their active and voluntary participation in therapy; in contrast to _____ , Rogers was continually impressed by his clients' drive to _____ and _____ their potential.

(b) These observations convinced Rogers that the most basic human motive is the

_____ .

3. (a) The cornerstone of Rogers's personality theory is the idea of the _____ .

(b) People are highly motivated to act in accordance with their _____ and will deny or distort experiences that create contradictions.

(c) Because they are motivated by the _____ tendency, infants and young children naturally gravitate toward self-enhancing experiences; as they become more self-aware, there is an increasing need for _____ regard, which is the sense of being loved and valued by other people, especially one's parents.

4. (a) Rogers maintained that most parents provide their children with

_____

regard, the sense that the child is valued and loved only when she or he behaves in a way that is acceptable to others; this may cause the child to deny or distort genuine feelings.

(b) People are said to be in a state of incongruence when their _____ conflicts with their actual experience.

(c) As people continually defend against genuine feelings and experiences that are inconsistent with their _____ , they become progressively more out of touch with their true feelings and essential self, often experiencing psychological problems as a result.

(d) _____

regard refers to the child's sense of being unconditionally loved and valued, even if he or she doesn't conform to the standards and expectations of others; in this way the child's _____ tendency is allowed its fullest expression.

(e) Rogers did not advocate _____ parenting; he thought that parents were responsible for controlling their children's behavior and for teaching them acceptable standards; parents can discipline their child's specific _____ without undermining the child's

_____ .

5. (a) Rogers believed that it is through consistent experiences of _____ regard that one becomes a psychologically healthy, fully functioning person.

(b) Fully functioning persons have a flexible, constantly evolving _____ ; they are _____ , _____ to new experiences, capable of _____ in response to new experiences, and likely to be creative and spontaneous and to enjoy harmonious relationships with others.

(c) Rather than defending against or distorting their own thoughts or feelings, these persons experiences _____ ; their sense of self is consistent with their emotions and experiences, and the _____ tendency is fully operational in them; and they make conscious choices that move them in the direction of greater _____ and fulfillment of potential.

6. The humanistic perspective has been criticized on two particular points.

(a) First, humanistic theories are hard to _____ or _____ scientifically; they tend to be based on philosophical assumptions or clinical observations rather than on _____ research; some humanistic concepts are difficult to define or measure objectively.

(b) Second, many psychologists believe that humanistic psychology's view of human nature is too _____ (pessimistic/optimistic); for example, if self-actualization is a universal human motive, why are self-actualized people so hard to find?

(c) The influence of humanistic psychology has _____ (increased/decreased) since the 1960s and 1970s; humanistic psychology promoted the scientific study of such topics as the healthy personality and creativity and focused attention on the importance of _____ experience and the _____ .

The Social Cognitive Perspective on Personality

Learning Objectives

When you have finished studying this section of the chapter, you should be able to:

1. Describe the focus of the social cognitive perspective.

2. Explain the principle of reciprocal determinism and identify the role of self-efficacy beliefs in personality.

3. Specify the strengths and weaknesses of the social cognitive perspective.

*Read the section "The Social Cognitive Perspective on Personality" and **write** your answers to the following:*

1. (a) The idea that a person's _____ thought processes in different _____ strongly influences his or her actions is one important characteristic of the social cognitive perspective on personality.

(b) People are seen as actively processing information from their _____ experiences; this information influences their _____ , _____ , _____ , and behavior as well as the specific environments they choose.

(c) The social cognitive perspective differs from _____ and _____ perspectives in several ways.

(d) First, rather than basing their approach on _____ or _____ derived from psychotherapy, social cognitive theorists rely heavily on _____ findings.

(e) Second, the social cognitive perspective emphasizes _____ , self-regulated behavior rather than _____ mental influences and instinctual drives.

(f) Third, social cognitive theory emphasizes that our sense of self can vary, depending on our _____ , _____ , and behaviors in a given situation.

2. (a) While several contemporary personality theorists have embraced the social cognitive approach, probably the most influential is _____ .

(b) Both _____ learning and self-efficacy play key roles in Bandura's approach to personality.

(c) Social cognitive theory emphasizes the social origins of _____ and _____ but also stresses active _____ processes and the human capacity for _____ .

3. (a) Bandura's research has shown that we attend not only to the actions of others, but also to the _____ that follow the actions, to the rules and _____ that apply to behavior in specific situations, and to the ways in which people _____ their own behavior.

(b) Bandura's process of

_____ oper-

ates in a circular fashion; the environment influences our thoughts and actions, our thoughts influence our actions and the environments we choose, and our actions influence our thoughts and the environments we choose.

4. (a) Collectively, a person's cognitive skills, abilities, attitudes, and especially beliefs of self-efficacy represent the person's

_____ ; and it is this that guides how we perceive, evaluate, and control our behavior in different situations.

(b) _____ refers to the degree to which you are subjectively convinced of your own capabilities and effectiveness in meeting the demands of a particular situation.

(c) Our _____ is very flexible; how we regard ourselves and our abilities varies, depending on the situations or tasks we're facing; in turn, our

_____ influence the tasks we are willing to try and how persistent we'll be in the face of obstacles.

(d) When we perform a task successfully, our sense of _____ becomes stronger; when we fail to deal effectively with a particular task or situation, our sense of _____ is undermined.

(e) From very early in life, children develop feelings of _____ from experiences in dealing with different tasks and situations, such as athletics and social and academic activities, and this is a life-long process.

5. (a) A key strength of the social cognitive perspective on personality is its grounding in empirical, laboratory research; it is built on research in _____ ,

_____ psychology, and

_____ psychology rather than on clinical impressions.

(b) Unlike the vague _____ and _____ concepts, the concepts of social cognitive theory are scientifically testable; they can be objectively defined and measured.

(c) Some psychologists believe that real-life, everyday situations are very

_____ , with _____ factors converging to affect behavior and personality; these influences are not adequately captured in the typical laboratory research situation, and it has been argued that _____ data may, in fact, be more reflective of the whole person.

(d) Other psychologists argue that the social cognitive perspective ignores

_____ influences, emotions, and conflicts; it lacks the richness of

_____ or

_____ theories, which strive to explain the whole person, including

_____ , irrational, and emotional aspects of personality.

(e) By emphasizing the reciprocal interaction of

_____ , _____ , and

_____ factors, the social cognitive perspective recognizes the complex combination of factors that influence our everyday behavior.

(f) By emphasizing the important role of

_____ , especially observational

_____ , the social cognitive perspective offers a developmental explanation of human functioning that persists throughout our lifetime.

(g) Finally, by emphasizing the

_____ of behavior, the social cognitive perspective places most of the responsibility for our behavior and the consequences that we experience squarely on our shoulders.

The Trait Perspective on Personality
Learning Objectives

When you have finished studying this section of the chapter, you should be able to:

1. Describe the main focus of trait theories of personality.
2. Define the term *trait* and specify how surface and source traits differ.
3. Identify the three influential trait theories.
4. Explain how the expression of personality traits is affected by situational demands.
5. Describe the focus of behavioral genetics.
6. List the key strengths and weaknesses of the trait perspective.

Read the section "The Trait Perspective on Personality" and **write** *your answers to the following:*

1. (a) The psychoanalytic, humanistic, and social cognitive theories emphasize the _____ among people, whereas the trait approach to personality focuses primarily on describing individual _____ ; trait theorists view the person as being a unique combination of personality _____ or _____ called traits.

    (b) People possess traits to different _____ ; traits are typically described in terms of a range from one extreme to its opposite, with most people falling in the middle of the range and fewer people falling at opposite poles.

2. (a) Surface traits lie on the surface and can be easily inferred from observable _____ (e.g., gloomy, cheerful, anxious, forgetful).

    (b) Source traits are thought to be more _____ than surface traits and

can give rise to a vast number of them; one goal of trait theorists has been to identify the most basic set of universal source traits that can be used to describe all individual _____ .

    (c) Pioneer trait theorist Raymond Cattell used a statistical technique called _____ to identify the traits that were most closely related to one another; he eventually reduced the number of source traits to _____ key personality factors.

3. Hans Eysenck's conception of personality includes just three dimensions:

    (a) The first dimension, _____ , is the degree to which a person directs his energies outward toward the environment and other people versus inward toward inner and self-focused experiences.

    (b) The second major dimension is _____ .

    (c) Surface traits associated with _____ are anxiety, tension, depression, and guilt; at the opposite end, _____ is associated with surface traits of being calm, relaxed, and even-tempered.

    (d) Eysenck believed that by combining these two dimensions people could be classified into four basic types:
    _____ ,
    _____ ,
    _____ , and
    _____ ;
    each type is associated with a different combination of surface traits.

    (e) In later research, Eysenck identified a third personality dimension, called _____ ; a person high on _____ is antisocial, cold, hostile, and unconcerned about others, whereas a person low on this trait is warm and caring toward others.

4. (a) Eysenck believes that individual differences in personality are due to _____ differences among people and that a(n) _____ nervous system is more easily aroused than a(n) _____ nervous system.

(b) Assuming that people tend to seek out an optimal level of arousal, _____ would seek stimulation from their environment more than _____ would; because _____ would be more uncomfortable than _____ in a highly stimulating environment, they would be much less likely to seek out stimulation.

(c) Research has shown that _____ preferred to study in a relatively noisy, open area with ample opportunities for socializing, whereas _____ preferred to study in a quiet section of the library; other research gives some tentative support to Eysenck's contention that there are physiological differences between _____ and _____ .

5. (a) Today, the consensus among many trait researchers is that the essential building blocks of personality can be described in terms of _____ basic personality dimensions, which are sometimes called the Big _____ ; these dimensions represent the structural organization of personality traits.

(b) The most commonly accepted factors according to the _____ model of personality traits are _____ , _____ , _____ , _____ , and _____ to experience; these appear to be universal.

(c) Research has shown that traits are remarkably _____ (stable/unstable) across time; today, most psychologists generally agree that personality traits are basically _____ (consistent/inconsistent) in different situations.

(d) Human behavior, however, is the result of a complex _____ between traits and situations; the situations that people choose and the characteristic way that they respond to similar situations are likely to be _____ (consistent/inconsistent) with their individual personality dispositions.

6. (a) The field of behavioral genetics studies the effects of genes and heredity on behavior; research involves measuring _____ and _____ among members of a large group of people who are genetically related to different degrees.

(b) Such studies may involve comparisons between _____ and _____ , or comparisons between _____ reared apart and _____ reared together.

(c) Adoption studies, in which adopted children are compared to their _____ and _____ families, are also used in behavioral genetics.

(d) Heredity seems to play a significant role in four personality traits: _____ , _____ , _____ to experience, and _____ ; however, the influence of environmental factors is at least equal to the influence of genetics.

7. (a) Psychologists _____ (agree/disagree) on how many basic traits exist; psychologists _____ (agree/disagree) that people can be described and compared in terms of basic personality traits.

(b) One criticism is that trait theories don't really _____ human personality; instead, they simply _____ general predispositions to behave in a certain way.

(c) A second criticism is that trait theorists don't attempt to _____ how or why individual differences develop.

(d) A third criticism is that trait approaches generally fail to address other important personality issues, such as the basic _____ that drive human personality, the role of _____ mental processes, how beliefs about the _____ influence personality, or how psychological _____ and _____ occur.

(e) Conspicuously absent are the grand conclusions about the essence of human nature that characterize the _____ and _____ theories.

8. Read the following and write the correct term in the space provided:

(a) Dunja is quite confident in her ability to service her own car but is less sure of her ability to bake cakes and cookies. Bandura would have called Dunja's different beliefs about her own abilities _____ beliefs.

(b) Eileen is consistently cheerful, optimistic, talkative, and impulsive. These traits, which are inferred from her observable behavior, are referred to as _____ traits.

(c) Navi is viewed by her family and friends as a flexible, creative, spontaneous, open, car-

ing person who likes, and is liked by, most people she interacts with. Carl Rogers would probably describe her as a(n)

_____

person.

(d) Alfred believes that from an early age we develop a set of perceptions and beliefs about ourselves, our nature, and our personal qualities and are motivated to act in accordance with these perceptions. Alfred's belief about personality development is most consistent with

_____

theory.

(e) Dr. Bhatt is concerned with describing, classifying, and measuring the numerous ways in which individuals may differ from one another. Her approach is most characteristic of the _____ perspective theory on personality.

(f) Whenever her son misbehaves, Rochelle's disciplinary strategy is to make sure he clearly understands that his behavior is not acceptable while taking care to reassure him that he is loved and valued. Rachel is using

_____ .

(g) Dr. Lavalle studies the effects of genes and heredity on behavior. His research has involved identical and fraternal twins who were separated at birth, identical and fraternal twins raised together, and the similarities and differences between adopted children and their adopted and biological parents. Dr. Lavalle works in the field of

_____ .

Graphic Organizer 2

*Read the following statements and match the
personality theorist and theory/perspective associated
with each:*

Statement	Theorist	Theory/ Perspective
1. I believe that people can be classified into four basic types: introverted-neurotic, introverted-stable, extraverted-neurotic, and extraverted-stable.		
2. It is my belief that people have an innate drive to maintain and enhance the human organism. This actualizing tendency is the most basic human motive, and all other motives, whether biological or social, are secondary.		
3. Using factor analysis, I came up with 16 personality factors that represent the essential source of human personality.		
4. My theory of personality stresses the influence of unconscious mental processes, the importance of sexual and aggressive instincts, and the enduring effects of early childhood experiences on personality.		
5. For me the most fundamental human motive is striving for superiority, which arises from universal feelings of inferiority. Depending on how people deal with these feelings, they may develop an inferiority complex.		
6. My research suggests that human functioning is caused by the interaction of behavioral, cognitive, and environmental factors, a process I call reciprocal determinism.		
7. For me the impact of social relationships and the nature of the parent–child interaction are the main determinants of personality. Different patterns of behavior develop as people try to deal with their basic anxiety. Males have an additional problem to deal with, womb envy.		
8. I am most well known for my theory of motivation and the notion of a hierarchy of needs. I also identified the qualities most associated with self-actualized people.		
9. It is apparent to me, from my observations of different cultures and my own patients, that the deepest part of the individual psyche is the collective unconscious, which contains the archetypes. Personality can be described on two basic dimensions, introversion and extraversion.		

Review of Key Terms and Key Names 3

humanistic psychology
Abraham Maslow
Carl Rogers
actualizing tendency
self-concept
positive regard
conditional positive
    regard
incongruence
unconditional positive
    regard
fully functioning person
congruence
Albert Bandura
self-efficacy
social cognitive theory

reciprocal determinism
self-system
trait
trait theory
surface trait
source traits
Raymond Cattell
Hans Eysenck
introversion
extraversion
neuroticism
emotional stability
psychoticism
five-factor model of
    personality
behavioral genetics

Matching Exercise

Match the appropriate term/name with its definition or description.

1. _____ A relatively stable, enduring predisposition to consistently behave in a certain way.

2. _____ The beliefs that people have about their ability to meet the demands of a specific situation; feelings of self-confidence or self-doubt.

3. _____ Contemporary American psychologist who is best known for his research on observational learning and his social cognitive theory of personality; key ideas include self-efficacy beliefs and reciprocal determinism.

4. _____ In Rogers's theory, the innate drive to maintain and enhance the human organism.

5. _____ A trait theory of personality that identifies five basic source traits (extraversion, neuroticism, agreeableness, conscientiousness, and openness to experience) as the fundamental building blocks of personality.

6. _____ American psychologist who was one of the founders of humanistic psychology and emphasized the study of healthy personality development; developed a hierarchical theory of motivation based on the idea that people will strive for self-actualization, the highest motive, only after more basic needs have been met; key ideas included the hierarchy of needs and self-actualization.

7. _____ In Eysenck's theory, a third dimension of personality; a person high on this trait is antisocial, cold, hostile, and unconcerned about others, whereas a person low on this trait is warm and caring toward others.

8. _____ In Rogers's theory, the term for the sense of being loved and valued by other people, especially one's parents.

9. _____ Bandura's theory of personality, which emphasizes the importance of observational learning, conscious cognitive processes, social experiences, self-efficacy beliefs, and reciprocal determinism.

10. _____ A theory of personality that focuses on identifying, describing, and measuring individual differences in traits.

11. _____ In Eysenck's theory, the dimension of personality that describes people who direct their energies outward toward the environment and other people; a person high on this dimension would be outgoing and sociable, enjoying new experiences and stimulating environments.

12. _____ American psychologist who was one of the founders of humanistic psychology; developed a theory of personality and form of psychotherapy that emphasized the inherent worth of people, the innate tendency to strive toward one's potential, and the importance of the self-concept in personality development; key ideas included the actualizing tendency and unconditional positive regard.

13. _____ The theoretical viewpoint on personality that generally emphasizes the inherent goodness of people, human potential, self-actualization, the self-concept, and healthy personality development.

14. _____ A model proposed by psychologist Albert Bandura that explains human functioning and personality as caused by the interaction of behavioral, cognitive, and environmental factors.

True/False Test

Indicate whether each statement is true or false by placing T or F in the blank space next to each item.

1. ____ Behavioral genetics is an interdisciplinary field that studies the effects of genes and heredity on behavior.

2. ____ In Rogers's theory, people are in a state of congruence when their feelings and experiences

are denied and distorted because they contradict or conflict with their self-concept.

3. ____ Hans Eysenck was a British-born American psychologist who developed a trait theory that identifies 16 essential source traits or personality factors; also developed the widely used self-report personality test, the Sixteen Personality Factor Questionnaire (16PF).

4. ____ Personality characteristics or attributes that can easily be inferred from observable behavior are called source traits.

5. ____ In Rogers's theory, the sense that you will be valued and loved only if you behave in a way that is acceptable to others is called conditional positive regard.

6. ____ Self-concept is the set of perceptions and beliefs that you hold about yourself.

7. ____ In Eysenck's theory, neuroticism refers to a person's predisposition to become emotionally upset.

8. ____ In Rogers's theory, the fully functioning person has a flexible, constantly evolving self-concept, is realistic, is open to new experiences, and is capable of changing in response to new experiences.

9. ____ Unconditional positive regard, in Rogers's theory, is the sense that you will be valued and loved even if you don't conform to the standards and expectations of others.

10. ____ A surface trait is the most fundamental dimension of personality; these broad basic traits are hypothesized to be universal and relatively few in number.

11. ____ In Rogers's theory, people are in a state of incongruence when their sense of self, or self-concept, is consistent with their emotions and experiences.

12. ____ Raymond Cattell was a German-born British psychologist who developed a trait theory of personality that identifies the three basic dimensions of personality as neuroticism, extraversion, and psychoticism.

13. ____ In Eysenck's theory, emotional stability reflects a person's predisposition to be emotionally even.

14. ____ Cognitive skills, abilities, and attitudes that emerge through developmental experiences involving the interaction of behavioral, cognitive, and environmental factors represent the person's self-system.

15. ____ In Eysenck's theory, introversion is a personality dimension in which the person directs his energies inward, toward his inner, self-focused experiences; a person high on this dimension might be quiet, solitary, and reserved, avoiding new experiences.

Check your answers and review any areas of weakness before going on to the next section.

Assessing Personality: Psychological Tests

Learning Objectives

When you have finished studying this section of the chapter, you should be able to:

1. Describe how self-report inventories and projective tests are used to measure personality.

2. Identify the basic goals of psychological tests.

3. Specify how projective tests and self-report inventories are administered and scored.

4. Identify the key strengths and weaknesses of projective tests and self-report inventories.

*Read the section "Assessing Personality: Psychological Tests" and **write** your answers to the following:*

1. (a) There are literally hundreds of psychological tests that can be used to assess abilities, aptitudes, interest, and personality; they are useful insofar as they accurately and consistently reflect a person's

   _____ on some dimension and can predict a person's future

   _____ functioning or

   _____ .

   (b) _____ tests developed out of the

   _____ approaches to personality; a person's responses to a vague image, such as an inkblot or ambiguous scene, is thought to be a(n) _____ of his unconscious conflicts, motives, psychological defenses, and personality traits.

   (c) The first _____ test was the famous Rorschach Inkblot Test; it consists of ten cards, five that show black and white inkblots and five that depict colored inkblots, and as the person describes what he sees in each, his responses are recorded verbatim and his behavior, gestures, and reactions are observed.

(d) Numerous scoring systems exist for the Rorschach; interpretation is based on such criteria as whether the person reports see-ing _____ or _____ objects, _____ or _____ figures, and movement and whether the person deals with the whole blot or just part of it.

2. (a) A more structured _____ test is the Thematic Apperception Test (TAT); the person is asked to look at a series of cards, each depicting an ambiguous scene, and cre-ate a story about the scene, including what the characters are feeling and how the story turns out.

(b) The stories are scored for the _____ , _____ , _____ , and conflicts of the main character and how conflicts are resolved; as with the Rorschach, interpret-ing the TAT involves the subjective judg-ment of the examiner.

3. (a) _____ tests are mainly used to help assess emotionally disturbed individu-als; their primary strength is that they pro-vide a wealth of _____ informa-tion about an individual's psychological functioning that can be explored further in psychotherapy.

(b) There are several drawbacks to _____ tests: the _____ situation or the examin-er's _____ can influence a per-son's responses; the scoring of these tests is highly _____ , with low inter-rater reliability; they often fail to produce

_____ results, with the same person achieving different results on sepa-rate occasions; and finally, they are poor at predicting future behavior.

(c) Despite their widespread use, especially among clinical psychologists, hundreds of studies of _____ tests seriously question their _____ (that the tests measure what they purport to mea-sure) and their _____ (the con-sistency of test results).

4. (a) _____ inventories typically use a paper-and-pencil format and take a direct, structured approach to assessing personali-ty; the person answers specific questions or rates herself on various dimensions of behavior and psychological functioning.

(b) Often called objective personality tests, _____ inventories contain items that have been shown by previous research to differentiate between people on a particu-lar personality characteristic; they are _____ (objectively/subjectively) scored against standardized norms.

(c) The most widely used _____ inventory is the Minnesota Multiphasic Personality Inventory (MMPI), which con-sists of 500 statements that the subject responds to as "True," "False," or "Cannot say"; topics include social, political, reli-gious, and _____ attitudes, physical and _____ health, interpersonal relationships, and _____ thoughts and behaviors.

(d) Designed to help in the diagnosis of psycho-logical disorders, the MMPI is widely used by _____ psychologists and _____ to assess patients; it is also used to evaluate the _____ health of candidates for such occupations as police officers, doctors, nurses, and professional pilots.

(e) Like many other _____ inventories, the MMPI has special scales to detect whether a person is answering honestly and consistently.

5. (a) In contrast to the MMPI, the California Personality Inventory (CPI) and the Sixteen Personality Factor Questionnaire (16PF) are inventories that are designed to assess _____ populations.

(b) The CPI provides measures on such characteristics as _____ effectiveness, self- _____ , independence, and empathy; profiles generated are used to predict such things as high school and college grades, delinquency, and _____ performance.

(c) The 16PF was originally developed by _____ and is based on his trait theory; it uses a forced-choice format in which the person must respond to each item by choosing one of three alternatives.

(d) The results generate a profile on _____ 16 personality factors; each factor represents a range, with a person's score falling somewhere along the continuum between two extremes; the 16PF is widely used for _____ counseling, _____ counseling, and evaluating employees and executives.

6. (a) The two most important strengths of self-report inventories are _____ and the use of established _____ ; the results of self-report inventories are _____ (subjectively/objectively) scored (by hand or computer) and compared to _____ established by previous research.

(b) The _____ and _____ of self-report inventories are far greater than those of projective tests; research has demonstrated that the MMPI, the CPI, and the 16PF provide accurate, consistent results that can be used to generally _____ behavior.

(c) Weaknesses of self-report inventories include the fact that people can successfully _____ responses and answer in _____ desirable ways; some people are prone to responding in a(n) _____ , such as answering "True" to all items; finally, people are not always accurate _____ of their own behavior, attitudes, attributes, and true feelings.

(d) Personality tests are generally useful strategies that can provide insights about the _____ makeup of people but are unlikely to provide a definitive description of a given individual; people can and often do change over time, so projective tests and self-report inventories provide a barometer of _____ and _____ functioning only at the time of the test.

7. Read the following and write the correct term in the space provided:

(a) Michelle was given a psychological test in which she was asked to look at a series of cards with ambiguous scenes and make up stories for each one. She was told to give as much detail as possible about what the characters are feeling and how the story ends. Michelle was given a(n) _____ test called the

_____ .

(b) When Roger was assessed for his suitability to be a police officer, he was given a 500-item test that was used to evaluate his mental health. The test he was given was most likely the _____ .

(c) Mr. and Mrs. Sheldrake want to get some idea of how their son is going to do in high school. The test that is best at predicting their son's high school grade is the

_____ .

(d) In his psychoanalytic practice Dr. Coles tries to understand his client's unconscious conflicts, motives, psychological defenses, and personality traits. It is very probable that Dr. Coles uses a(n) _____ test called the _____ .

(e) Dr. Cera sees a lot of married couples in his counseling practice. In an effort to help them resolve their conflicts, he frequently administers a test to each partner that generates a profile of their personality characteristics. Dr. Cera is most likely to use the

_____ .

Review of Key Terms 4

psychological test
projective test
Rorschach Inkblot Test
Thematic Apperception
 Test (TAT)
self-report inventory
Minnesota Multiphasic
 Personality Inventory
 (MMPI)

California Personality
 Inventory (CPI)
Sixteen Personality
 Factor Questionnaire
 (16PF)
possible selves

Matching Exercise

Match the appropriate term with its definition or description.

1. _____ A type of psychological test in which a person's responses to standardized questions are compared to established norms.

2. _____ A projective test using inkblots, developed by Swiss psychiatrist Hermann Rorschach in 1921.

3. _____ A self-report inventory that assesses personality characteristics in normal populations.

4. _____ A test that assesses a person's abilities, aptitudes, interests, or personality, based on a systematically obtained sample of behavior.

5. _____ A self-report inventory developed by Raymond Cattell that generates a

personality profile with ratings on 16 trait dimensions.

True/False Test

Indicate whether each statement is true or false by placing T or F in the blank space next to each item.

1. ____ A projective test is a type of personality test that involves a person's interpreting an ambiguous image and is used to assess unconscious motives, conflicts, psychological defenses, and personality traits.

2. ____ Possible selves refers to an aspect of the self-concept that includes images of the selves that you hope, fear, or expect to become in the future.

3. ____ The Minnesota Multiphasic Personality Inventory (MMPI) is a projective personality test that involves creating stories about each of a series of ambiguous scenes.

4. ____ The Thematic Apperception Test (TAT) is a self-report inventory that assesses personality characteristics and psychological disorders; used to assess both normal and disturbed populations.

Check your answers and review any areas of weakness before going on to the next section.

Something to Think About

1. Psychological tests and psychological testing continue to be a topic of discussion. Almost everyone has heard of the famous inkblot test, but not everyone knows what the test was designed to do and what its limitations are. Based on what you have learned about psychological tests in this chapter, what could you tell someone about the inkblot test and psychological tests in general?

2. The history of astrology can be traced back over 4,000 years. Astrology's basic premise is that the positions of the planets and stars at the time and place of your birth determine your personality and destiny. Today, belief in astrological predictions remains widespread, and you probably know a number of people who, even if they are not true believers, at least read their daily horoscope in the paper. How might you enlighten these people about scientific research on astrology?

> Check your answers and review any areas of weakness before doing the progress tests.

Progress Test 1

Review the complete chapter (including Concept Reviews and the boxed inserts), review all your study notes, and then test yourself on the following progress test. Check your answers. If you make a mistake, review your notes, review the relevant section of the study guide, and, if necessary, go back and read the appropriate part of your textbook.

1. Marvin is angry and upset after an argument with his boss. At home that evening he is harshly and unreasonably critical of his son for not getting all his homework assignments completed. According to Freud, Marvin is using an Ego defense mechanism called
   - (a) identification
   - (b) repression
   - (c) rationalization
   - (d) displacement

2. Seven-year old Salvatore prefers to play with his male friends and does not like playing with girls very much. Salvatore is probably in the _____ stage of psychosexual development
   - (a) anal
   - (b) phallic
   - (c) latency
   - (d) genital

3. Although Tim can recall many of the fun experiences he had when he left home and went to college, he has only vague memories of the girl he was engaged to but who left him suddenly for some other guy. Tim's unconscious forgetting is an Ego defense mechanism called
   - (a) identification
   - (b) sublimation
   - (c) displacement
   - (d) repression

4. Every time two-year-old Kate is given a bath, she plays with her genitals. If her parents chastise or punish her, she is likely to experience frustration, which could lead to an unresolved developmental conflict called
   - (a) fixation
   - (b) sublimation
   - (c) displacement
   - (d) denial

5. Zachary considers himself to be an outgoing, fun-loving type of person, and so he frequently goes to social gatherings, parties, etc. Sondra, on the other hand, thinks of herself as fairly quiet and shy, so she seeks out solitude when she can and enjoys quietly reading a book and listening to classical music. In Jung's theory, Zachary' and Sondra's different behaviors reflect
   - (a) the two basic personality type, the extravert and the introvert
   - (b) the two important archetypes, the anima and the animus
   - (c) a superiority complex and an inferiority complex
   - (d) penis envy and womb envy

6. Read the example in question 5 again. According to social cognitive theory, the different personalities of Zachary and Sondra reflect the interaction of behavioral, cognitive, and environmental factors, a process Bandura called
   - (a) identification
   - (b) displacement
   - (c) the actualizing tendency
   - (d) reciprocal determinism

7. Dr. Sharma stresses the importance of identifying, measuring, and describing individual differences in terms of various personality characteristics. His views are most representative of the _____ perspective on personality.
   - (a) psychoanalytic
   - (b) humanistic
   - (c) social cognitive
   - (d) trait

8. As part of a research project, Jasbinder was given the same psychological test three times at two-month intervals by three different therapists. She obtained very different results each time she took the test. It is most probable that she was given the
   - (a) MMPI
   - (b) 16PF
   - (c) CPI
   - (d) TAT

9. Dr. Welch is a clinical psychologist who uses the MMPI and the 16PF on a regular basis in his practice. If asked what the key strength of these tests is, he is most likely to note that
   - (a) they provide a wealth of qualitative information about the individual
   - (b) scoring relies on the examiner's subjective judgment and clinical experience and expertise
   - (c) they accurately measure the individual's unconscious motives and conflicts
   - (d) they are standardized and objectively scored

10. When asked to describe her son, Mrs. Reid notes that he often avoids trying or learning new tasks and that he appears to perceive himself as inadequate, weak, and helpless. Alfred

Adler would probably suggest that Mrs. Reid's son has developed _____ that keeps him from striving for mastery and self-improvement.

(a) an archetype
(b) a low level of self-efficacy
(c) an inferiority complex
(d) a fixation

11. Dr. Briston works in the field of behavioral genetics. His research most likely involves

(a) describing, classifying, and measuring individual differences
(b) comparisons between identical twins, fraternal twins, and between adopted children and their biological and adoptive parents
(c) investigating why some people achieve self-actualization and why others do not
(d) studying how unconscious conflicts influence motivation and behavior

12. Sheldon has frequently been rebellious, inconsiderate, and self-centered. His parents are consistent in disciplining him for his inappropriate behaviors while communicating to him that they value and love him. The person most likely to agree with their parenting approach and use of unconditional positive regard is

(a) Sigmund Freud   (c) Joseph Breuer
(b) Carl Rogers   (d) Carl Jung

13. Katrina thinks of herself as fairly laid back, easygoing, and relatively calm. She believes she is above average academically and intellectually and sees herself as very conscientious at work and caring and loving with her family. Carl Rogers would term this set of perceptions and beliefs that Katrina has about herself her

(a) self-efficacy   (c) self-system
(b) self-concept   (d) possible selves

14. Miguel is giving a presentation in his tutorial on the five-factor model of personality. Which of the following personality dimensions is *not* likely to be included in his talk?

(a) anal retentiveness
(b) extraversion
(c) neuroticism
(d) agreeableness
(e) openness to experience

15. Dr. Markowitz studies the effects of genes and heredity on behavior. One strategy he uses is to look for similarities and differences in identical twins who were separated at birth or early infancy and raised by different families. Dr. Markowitz is most probably a(n)

(a) psychoanalyst
(b) humanistic psychologist
(c) social cognitive psychologist
(d) behavioral geneticist

16. Raffi is shown a series of cards with ambiguous scenes and is told to make up a story about each one and to state what the characters are feeling and what motivates them. Raffi has been given the

(a) Thematic Apperception Test (TAT)
(b) Rorschach Inkblot Test
(c) California Personality Inventory (CPI)
(d) Minnesota Multiphasic Personality Inventory (MMPI)

17. Zintyre was very impressed when told by an astrologer that "You are gregarious, outgoing, and fond of travel. You tend to react negatively to authority figures and you have had a number of confrontations as a result. You enjoy good food and good wine and you don't suffer fools gladly." According to Science Versus Pseudoscience Box 10.4, which of the following is true?

(a) The astrologer probably has an extraordinary gift for accurately assessing personality.
(b) The astrologer is probably operating at chance level in assessing personality.
(c) The astrologer is using a proven scientific method in his personality assessment of Zintyre.
(d) Zintyre is probably extremely accurate in assessing the accuracy of the astrologer's personality description.

18. According to the Application section, the term *possible selves* refers to

(a) the unconscious part of the mind that motivates our behavior
(b) the main aspect of multiple personality disorder
(c) the aspect of the self-concept that includes images of the selves that you hope, fear, or expect to become in the future
(d) delusional thought processes

19. Science Versus Pseudoscience Box 10.4 discusses astrology and personality. It was concluded that

(a) the position of the planets and stars at the time and place of your birth determines your personality and destiny

(b) today, virtually nobody believes in astrological interpretations and predictions

(c) science has not been able to refute the claims, predictions, and interpretations of astrology

(d) neither popular nor serious astrology has any reliable basis in scientific fact

20. According to Critical Thinking Box 10.1, which of the following is true?

(a) Freud's view of human nature was deeply pessimistic.

(b) Rogers's view of human nature was deeply pessimistic.

(c) Freud believed that humans are positive, forward-moving, constructive, realistic, and trustworthy.

(d) Rogers believed that the essence of human nature is destructive but that societal, religious, and cultural restraints make people behave in good and moral ways.

Progress Test 2

After you have checked your understanding of the material in Progress Test 1 and have done a complete chapter review with special focus on any areas of weakness, you are ready to assess your knowledge in Progress Test 2. Check your answers. If you make a mistake, review your notes, the relevant section of the study guide, and, if necessary, the appropriate part of your textbook.

1. Nathan chews the end of his pen, bites his nails, overeats, smokes cigarettes, and talks incessantly. According to Freud, Nathan has probably fixated at the _____ stage of psychosexual development due to some unresolved conflict.

(a) oral   (c) phallic

(b) anal   (d) genital

2. Inferiority complex is to _____ as self-efficacy is to _____ .

(a) Freud; Jung

(b) Eysenck; Cattell

(c) Maslow; Rogers

(d) Adler; Bandura

3. Shelly was often rejected by her parents and as a result she mistrusts other people and treats them with hostility, which leads to their rejection of her. This cycle of rejection, mistrust, hostility, and further rejection illustrates what Bandura called

(a) self-efficacy

(b) identification

(c) displacement

(d) reciprocal determinism

4. During a class discussion of various perspectives on personality, Sasha notes that there is ample evidence that human beings are destructive and aggressive. He points to the millions who died in two world wars and the ongoing killings and massacres that continue in many parts of the world today. Sasha's observation about basic human nature supports the _____ perspective and is a criticism of the _____ perspective.

(a) humanistic; psychoanalytic

(b) trait; social cognitive

(c) social cognitive; trait

(d) psychoanalytic; humanistic

5. Dr. Sheenan is a clinical psychologist who wants to assess the extent to which a client is suffering from depression, delusions, and other mental health problems. Dr. Sheenan is most likely to use the

(a) 16PF   (c) MMPI

(b) CPI   (d) TAT

6. When Cindy was given the Rorschach Inkblot Test, she reported seeing a number of inanimate objects and some animal figures and tended to concentrate on very small details in each inkblot. Her therapist observed her behavior, gestures, and reactions as she responded to each card. Her therapist is most probably

(a) interested in her unconscious conflicts, motives, and psychological defenses

(b) assessing her suitability for a particular occupation, such as police officer or pilot

(c) trying to generate a personality profile based on a number of personality traits

(d) trying to predict how she will perform academically when she goes to college

7. Dr. Splotsky is a Jungian psychologist and believes that feminine and masculine are represented in two archetypes. Jung called these archetypes

(a) the introvert and the extrovert

(b) Eros and Thanatos

(c) the Id and the Ego

(d) the anima and the animus

8. Dr. Selnick believes in the importance of unconscious psychological conflicts, sexual and aggressive drives, and the formative influence of early childhood experiences. Dr. Selnick's views are most consistent with the _____ perspective.
   (a) psychoanalytic   (c) social cognitive
   (b) humanistic   (d) trait

9. Five-year-old Dunstan has recently become very possessive of his mother and appears to be jealous of his father. He is sometimes openly hostile, telling his father, "Don't kiss my Mommy!" According to Freud, Dunstan is in the _____ stage of psychosexual development and showing manifestations of _____ .
   (a) oral; fixation
   (b) anal; fixation
   (c) phallic; the Oedipus complex
   (d) latency; the Oedipus complex

10. Wendy believes that the most fundamental human motive is striving for superiority. She thinks that this drive arises from global feelings of inferiority and that human personality and behavior reflect our attempts to compensate for or overcome our perceived weaknesses. Which personality theorist is most likely to agree with Wendy's views?
    (a) Freud   (c) Horney
    (b) Jung   (d) Adler

11. David is very quiet, pessimistic, anxious, and moody and becomes emotionally upset very easily. In terms of Eysenck's four basic personality types, he would be classified as
    (a) introverted-neurotic
    (b) introverted-stable
    (c) extraverted-neurotic
    (d) extraverted-stable

12. During a class discussion, Cheryal challenged the Freudian assumption of female inferiority and the notion of penis envy. She suggested that Karen Horney's position that men suffer from _____ and feel inadequate because they are incapable of bearing children made much more sense.
    (a) an inferiority complex
    (b) fixation
    (c) low self-efficacy
    (d) womb envy

13. While writing a term paper on Carl Jung's theory of personality, Justin quoted Jung as saying

that the _____ contains "the whole spiritual heritage of mankind's evolution, born anew in the brain structure of every individual."
    (a) personal preconscious
    (b) collective conscious
    (c) personal unconscious
    (d) collective unconscious

14. Ursula's therapist instructs her to relax, close her eyes, and state aloud whatever thoughts come to mind no matter how trivial or absurd. The therapist is using a technique called
    (a) free association   (c) sublimation
    (b) displacement   (d) repression

15. The pleasure principle is to _____ as the reality principle is to _____ .
    (a) the oral stage; the anal stage
    (b) Thanatos; Eros
    (c) the Id; the Ego
    (d) the Ego; the Superego

16. Leanne studies very hard, but no matter how much time she puts in, she always feels that she hasn't studied enough. If she takes a break to socialize with her friends, she starts feeling guilty and anxious. Freud would say that Leanne has a
    (a) strong Superego
    (b) strong Id
    (c) weak Superego
    (d) strong Id

17. When Professor Mainprize was going through a very painful divorce, he tended to mark student papers very harshly and to make the exams difficult. A psychoanalyst would be most likely to view the professor's treatment of his students as an example of
    (a) identification   (c) displacement
    (b) repression   (d) sublimation

18. According to In Focus Box 10.3, which of the following is true?
    (a) Any two randomly chosen people of the same age, sex, and culture will likely have absolutely no similarities.
    (b) Some similarities between separated identical twins may be genetically influenced.
    (c) Personality is almost completely determined by genes.
    (d) Personality is almost completely determined by environmental factors.

19. According to the Application section, which of the following is false?
    (a) A person's self-concept is a multifaceted system of related images and ideas.
    (b) Possible selves influence our behavior in important ways.
    (c) We're often unaware of how possible selves we've mentally constructed influence our beliefs, actions, and self-evaluations.
    (d) A person's self-concept is a singular mental self-image.

20. Research investigating the effectiveness of astrology found that
    (a) astrologers performed at a level significantly better than chance
    (b) astrologers failed to perform at a level better than chance
    (c) astrologers performed much better than the control subjects in all conditions
    (d) the control subjects performed much better than the astrologers in all conditions

Answers

Introduction: What Is Personality?

. 1. (a) unique and relatively consistent patterns of
thinking, feeling, and behaving
(b) describe; explain; different; similar; whole

2. (a) unconscious; early childhood
(b) optimistic; self; unique potential
(c) learning; cognitive; beliefs
(d) description; measurement

The Psychoanalytic Perspective on Personality

1. (a) medicine; physiology; cocaine; addictive
(b) physiological; neurology; clients
(c) emotions; catharsis
(d) free association; thoughts, mental images;
feelings

2. (a) psychoanalysis
(b) psychoanalytic; international
(c) aggression; sexuality
(d) civilization; human nature; civilization
(e) literature, philosophy

Freud's Dynamic Theory of Personality

1. (a) conscious, preconscious; unconscious
(b) unconscious; conscious

2. (a) unconscious; conscious
(b) unconscious
(c) manifest; latent; unconscious
(d) unconscious; unintentional; Freudian

3. (a) structures
(b) unconscious; logic, values, morality, danger
(c) Eros; Thanatos
(d) pleasure; *libido*
(e) pleasure; tension; pain

4. (a) partly; organized, rational
(b) reality; gratification
(c) pragmatic; repress
(d) external; externally; internalized

5. (a) conscious; conscience
(b) guilt, shame, self-doubt; anxiety

6. (a) instinctual; moral; external
(b) anxiety; impulsively; destructively; guilt,
self-reproach; moral
(c) anxiety; distorting
(d) repression; unconscious
(e) conscious; unconscious; repressed

7. (a) displacement; threatening; dangerous
(b) psychological energy
(c) healthy; delays; interferes

Personality Development

1. (a) psychosexual; oral, anal; phallic; latency;
genital
(b) sexual; psychosexual; sexual
(c) sexual; oral; oral; anal; phallic; genitals

2. (a) psychosexual; conflict
(b) conflict; frustrate; overindulge
(c) frustrated; overindulged; conflict; fixation

3. (a) phallic
(b) genital; opposite-sex; same-sex

4. (a) father; mother; castration
(b) identification; father's
(c) father; incestuous

5. (a) identifying; incestuous
(b) identifies; internalizes
(c) penis envy

6. (a) repressed; latency
(b) latency; same-sex
(c) genital; incestuous; opposite-sex
(d) conflicts; psychosexual; love

7. (a) personality
(b) free association
(c) unconscious
(d) latent
(e) Id
(f) Superego
(g) sublimation
(h) identification

Graphic Organizer 1

1. genital
2. phallic
3. latency
4. oral
5. anal

Matching Exercise 1

1. libido
2. personality
3. Superego
4. Oedipus complex
5. Ego
6. preconscious
7. oral stage
8. displacement
9. Sigmund Freud

10. anal stage

11. personality theory

12. Id

13. latency stage

14. psychoanalysis

15. Ego defense mechanisms

16. psychosexual stages

True/False Test 1

1. F	7. T	13. F
2. T	8. F	14. T
3. T	9. T	15. T
4. F	10. F	16. T
5. F	11. T	
6. T	12. T	

Matching Exercise 2

1. Karen Horney

2. archetypes

3. striving for superiority

4. basic anxiety

5. inferiority complex

6. extravert

7. anima

8. collective unconscious

True/False Test 2

1. T	5. T
2. F	6. F
3. T	7. T
4. T	

The Neo-Freudians

1. (a) sexual
   (b) early childhood
   (c) pessimistic

2. (a) sex; aggression; growth; realization
   (b) collective; collective
   (c) collective; archetypes
   (d) anima and animus; feminine; masculine; feminine; masculine
   (e) collective; archetypes
   (f) introvert; extravert; growth; realization

3. (a) social; cultural; social
   (b) human; basic anxiety
   (c) penis; womb

4. (a) superiority; inferiority
   (b) compensate; inferiority
   (c) compensate; inferiority; inferiority

Evaluating Freud and the Psychoanalytic Perspective on Personality

1. (a) small and skewed
   (b) test; disprove
   (c) sexist; male
   (d) some; conscious; unconscious; childhood; regulate

2. (a) inferiority
   (b) Karen Horney
   (c) Jungian
   (d) collective unconscious
   (e) extravert

The Humanistic Perspective on Personality

1. (a) Freud's; good; healthy
   (b) behaviorist; growth; self-awareness; conscious, subjective
   (c) hierarchy; self-actualized

2. (a) Freud'; Freud; grow; develop
   (b) actualizing tendency

3. (a) self-concept
   (b) self-concept
   (c) actualizing; positive

4. (a) conditional positive
   (b) self-concept
   (c) self-concept
   (d) unconditional positive; actualizing
   (e) permissive; behavior; self-worth

5. (a) unconditional positive
   (b) self-concept; realistic, open; changing
   (c) congruence; actualizing; growth

6. (a) validate; test; empirical
   (b) optimistic
   (c) decreased; subjective; self-concept

The Social Cognitive Perspective on Personality

1. (a) conscious; situations
   (b) social; goals, expectation, beliefs
   (c) psychoanalytic; humanistic
   (d) self-analysis; insight; experimental
   (e) conscious; unconscious
   (f) thoughts, feelings

2. (a) Albert Bandura
   (b) observational
   (c) thoughts; actions; cognitive; self-regulation

3. (a) consequences; standards; regulate
   (b) reciprocal determinism

4. (a) self-system
   (b) self-efficacy
   (c) self-system; beliefs
   (d) self-efficacy; self-efficacy
   (e) self-efficacy

5. (a) learning, cognitive; social
   (b) psychoanalytic; humanistic
   (c) complex; multiple; clinical
   (d) unconscious; psychoanalytic; humanistic; unconscious
   (e) mental, behavioral; situational
   (f) learning; learning
   (g) self-regulation

The Trait Perspective on Personality

1. (a) similarities; differences; characteristics; attributes
   (b) degrees

2. (a) behavior
   (b) basic; differences
   (c) factor analysis; 16

3. (a) introversion-extraversion
   (b) neuroticism-emotional stability
   (c) neuroticism; stability
   (d) introverted-neurotic, introverted-stable, extraverted-neurotic; extraverted-stable
   (e) psychoticism; psychoticism

4. (a) biological; introvert's; extravert's
   (b) extraverts; introverts; introverts; extraverts
   (c) extraverts; introverts; introverts; extraverts

5. (a) five; Five
   (b) five-factor; extraversion, neuroticism, agreeableness, conscientiousness; openness
   (c) stable; consistent
   (d) interaction; consistent

6. (a) similarities; differences
   (b) identical twins; fraternal twins; identical twins; identical twins
   (c) biological; adoptive
   (d) extraversion, neuroticism, openness; conscientiousness

7. (a) disagree; agree
   (b) explain; label
   (c) explain

(d) motives; unconscious; self; change; growth
(e) psychoanalytic; humanistic

8. (a) self-efficacy
   (b) surface
   (c) fully functioning
   (d) social cognitive
   (e) trait
   (f) unconditional positive regard
   (g) behavioral genetics

Graphic Organizer 2

1. Hans Eysenck; trait
2. Carl Rogers; humanistic
3. Raymond Cattell; trait
4. Sigmund Freud; psychoanalytic
5. Alfred Adler; psychoanalytic (neo-Freudian)
6. Albert Bandura; social cognitive
7. Karen Horney; psychoanalytic (neo-Freudian)
8. Abraham Maslow; humanistic
9. Carl Jung; psychoanalytic (neo-Freudian)

Matching Excercise 3

1. trait
2. self-efficacy
3. Albert Bandura
4. actualizing tendency
5. five-factor model of personality
6. Abraham Maslow
7. psychoticism
8. positive regard
9. social cognitive theory
10. trait theory
11. extraversion
12. Carl Rogers
13. humanistic psychology
14. reciprocal determinism

True/False Test 3

1. T	6. T	11. F
2. F	7. T	12. F
3. F	8. T	13. T
4. F	9. T	14. T
5. T	10. F	15. T

Assessing Personality: Psychological Tests

1. (a) characteristics; psychological; behavior
   (b) projective; psychoanalytic; projection
   (c) projective
   (d) animate; inanimate; human; animal

2. (a) projective
   (b) motives, needs, anxieties

3. (a) projective; qualitative
   (b) projective; testing; behavior; subjective; consistent
   (c) projective; validity; reliability

4. (a) self-report
   (b) self-report; objectively
   (c) self-report; sexual; psychological; abnormal
   (d) clinical; psychiatrists; mental
   (e) self-report

5. (a) normal
   (b) interpersonal; control; job
   (c) Raymond Cattell
   (d) Cattell's; career; marital

6. (a) standardization; norms; objectively; norms
   (b) reliability; validity; predict
   (c) fake; socially; set way; judges
   (d) psychological; personality; psychological

7. (a) projective; Thematic Apperception Test (TAT)
   (b) MMPI
   (c) CPI
   (d) projective; Rorschach Inkblot Test
   (e) 16PF

Matching Exercise 4

1. self-report inventory

2. Rorschach Inkblot Test

3. California Personality Inventory (CPI)

4. psychological test

5. Sixteen Personality Factor Questionnaire (16PF)

True/False Test 4

1. T   3. F
2. T   4. F

Something to Think About

1. In any discussion of psychometric testing it is always a good idea to point out the important characteristics of a good test, namely, reliability and validity. In terms of personality testing there are basically two categories of tests, projective tests and self-report inventories.

   The famous Rorschach Inkblot Test is, of course, a projective test. In other words, it is assumed that people will project their unconscious feeling, motives, drives, thoughts, etc. in their responses to the series of inkblots. Similarly, the Thematic Apperception Test (TAT) gives subjects an opportunity to project unconscious information in the stories they make up about ambiguous scenes. Both tests developed out of the psychoanalytic approaches to personality, and scoring involves the subjective interpretations of the examiner. A brief discussion of Freud's theory as it relates to personality would probably be in order. A review of the most damaging criticisms of psychoanalysis may shed light on the topic, and the issue of the validity and reliability of projective tests should not be overlooked. Despite the criticisms, projective tests are widely used and can provide a wealth of qualitative data about an individual.

   Self-report inventories are used by clinical psychologists with both normal and abnormal populations in a variety of settings and for a variety of purposes. The most common are the MMPI, the CPI, and the 16PF. These are often called objective personality tests because they are standardized and objectively scored and measured against established norms. The reliability and validity of self-report inventories are far greater than those of projective tests. Some of the problems with these tests include a person's ability to fake responses and answer in a socially desirable manner, some people's tendency to answer in a set way to all questions, and the fact that people are not always the best judges of their own behavior.

   Personality tests are generally useful strategies that can provide insights about the psychological makeup of people. However, no personality test, by itself, is likely to provide a definitive description of a given individual. In addition, because people can and often do change over time, any personality test provides a profile of the person only at the time of the test.

2. Many people believe in astrology, and a large number consult professional astrologers to find out what they should do and what lies ahead for them in the future. Belief in astrology is not restricted to any class or group of individuals. People from all walks of life, from senior managers to assembly line workers, from government leaders to junior clerks, consult their

horoscopes on a regular basis. As is the case with many strongly held beliefs, it is often difficult to get true believers in astrology to listen to any information that might contradict what they feel is a valid point of view. It is always important to be aware of this and to respect their right to believe whatever they wish. However, if the opportunity does arise to have an open-minded discussion, presenting the results of Shawn Carlson's (1985) carefully designed study could be useful. Remember, the study involved 30 of the top American and European astrologers, and a panel of astrological advisers were involved in helping Carlson design the study. All the participating astrologers agreed beforehand that Carlson's study was a fair test of astrological claims, and the astrologers who approved the design predicted that 50 percent was the minimum effect they would expect to see. The results showed that astrologers performed at a chance level. In other words, anybody simply guessing would have done equally as well as the astrologers. Carlson's results are consistent with those of many other researchers. A careful review of the scientific research on astrology came to the conclusion that astrology has absolutely no reliable basis in scientific fact and cannot stand up to any valid statistical test that can be applied. Of course, if the astrologers had any real insight from their reading of the planets, they could easily have foreseen the outcome of Carlson's study!

Progress Test 1

1. d	8. d	15. d
2. c	9. d	16. a
3. d	10. c	17. b
4. a	11. b	18. c
5. a	12. b	19. d
6. d	13. b	20. a
7. d	14. a	

Progress Test 2

1. a	8. a	15. c
2. d	9. c	16. a
3. d	10. d	17. c
4. d	11. a	18. b
5. c	12. d	19. d
6. a	13. d	20. b
7. d	14. a	

Chapter 11 Social Psychology

OVERVIEW   Chapter 11 introduces the area of social psychology, which is the scientific study of the way individuals think, feel, and behave in social situations. Social cognition and social influence are two important areas of research in social psychology. Person perception, or forming impressions of other people, and the factors that influence our perceptions of others are explored. The process of attribution is discussed, and a number of important attributional biases are presented. The influence of culture on attributional processes is noted.

The social psychology of attitudes is examined, and the conditions under which attitudes determine behavior are identified. The role of cognitive dissonance in behavior and cognition is explored. The topic of prejudice is discussed along with the influence of stereotypes, in-groups, out-groups, the out-group homogeneity effect, in-group bias, and ethnocentrism. The origins of intergroup conflict and how such conflict can be reduced were researched by Sherif. It is suggested that cooperative learning is one way to reduce prejudice in classrooms.

Conformity occurs when people change their behavior, attitudes, or beliefs in response to real or imagined group pressure. Research by Asch, along with the conditions under which conformity is most likely to occur, is presented. Normative and informational social influences both contribute to conformity. Cultural differences in conformity are examined. A type of conformity called obedience was studied most extensively by Milgram. His original experimental design and the results of his research are presented in detail. Conditions that influence people to obey and to resist obeying authority figures are identified.

Latané and Darley's research on helping behavior, bystander intervention, and diffusion of responsibility is discussed, along with their model, which identifies the factors that increase and decrease the likelihood of bystander intervention. The Application section discusses the various techniques professional persuaders use to try to manipulate people's attitudes and behaviors.

Introduction: Social Psychology
Learning Objectives

When you have finished studying this section of the chapter, you should be able to:

1. Define *social psychology*.

2. Explain what is meant by *social cognition* and *social influence*.

*Read the section "Introduction: Social Psychology" and **write** your answers to the following:*

1. (a) Social psychology is the scientific study of

   the way individuals _____ ,

   _____ , and _____

   in social situations.

(b) Social cognition refers to how we form _____ of other people, how we _____ the meaning of other people's behavior, and how our behavior is affected by our _____ .

(c) Social influence focuses on how our behavior is affected by _____ factors and other people; it includes such questions as why we _____ to group norms, what compels us to _____ an authority figure, and when people will _____ a stranger.

Person Perception

Learning Objectives

When you have finished studying this section of the chapter, you should be able to:

1. Define *person perception* and list the four principles that this process follows.

2. Explain how social categories, implicit personality theories, and physical attractiveness affect person perception.

Read the section "Person Perception" and ***write*** *your answers to the following:*

1. (a) Person perception refers to the _____ processes we use to form _____ and draw _____ about the characteristics of others; it is an active and subjective process that always occurs in some interpersonal context.

   (b) Every interpersonal context has three key components: the _____ of the individual you are attempting to size up, your own _____ as the perceiver, and the specific _____ in which the process occurs; each component influences the conclusions you reach about other people.

2. Person perception follows four basic principles:

   (a) Your reactions to others are determined by your _____ of them, not by who or what they really are.

   (b) Your goals in a particular situation determine the amount and kind of _____ you collect about others.

   (c) In every situation, you _____ people partly in terms of how you expect them to act in that situation; you make reference to the _____ for the appropriate behavior in a particular social situation.

   (d) Your _____ also influences how you perceive others and how you act on your perceptions.

   (e) In combination, these four basic principles underscore that person perception is not a(n) _____ process in which we objectively survey other people, then add up their characteristic; instead, the _____ , our _____ , and the perception we have of others all interact.

3. (a) Social categorization is the _____ process of classifying people into _____ on the basis of common characteristics; this is mostly automatic and spontaneous and occurs outside of conscious awareness.

   (b) With limited time to form impressions, we rely on very _____ social categories; when we know more about a particular person, more _____ subcategories are likely to be used.

   (c) Using social categories has both disadvantages and advantages; relegating someone to a social category on the basis of _____ information ignores that person's _____ qualities; on the other hand, relying on social categories is a natural, adaptive _____ process that is efficient and effective for mentally organizing information about others.

   (d) When it is important to your goals to perceive another person as accurately as possible, you're less likely to rely on

_____ categorization; instead

you _____ and

_____ exert mental effort to

understand the other person better and to

form a more accurate impression.

4. (a) An implicit personality theory is a network

of assumptions or beliefs about the relation-

ship among various types of

_____ , _____ , and

_____ ; through our previous

social experiences, each of us has formed

cognitive _____ about the traits

and behaviors associated with different

types of people and we expect them to

behave accordingly.

(b) Like social categories, implicit personality

theories can be _____ as mental

shortcuts in perceiving other people; howev-

er, they are not always _____

and in some instances can be dangerously

misleading.

(c) Although they can lead to _____

conclusions, implicit personality theories

represent another important

_____ cognition strategy in our

efforts to make sense of other people; they

provide a mental framework that helps us

organize our _____ ,

_____ , and beliefs about

people.

Attribution: Explaining Behavior
Learning Objectives

*When you have finished studying this section of the
chapter, you should be able to:*

1. Define *attribution* and explain the role played
   by the fundamental attribution error, the actor–
   observer discrepancy, and the self-serving bias.

2. Describe how these biases shape the attributions we make.

*Read the section "Attribution: Explaining Behavior"
and **write** your answers to the following:*

1. (a) The process of _____ the cause,

   or the why, behind someone's behavior,

   including your own, is called attribution;

   psychologists also use the word to refer to

   the _____ you make for a par-

   ticular behavior, and the attributions we

   make have a strong influence on our

   thoughts and feeling about others.

   (b) The fundamental attribution error is the

   tendency to spontaneously attribute the

   behavior of others to _____ ,

   _____ characteristics while

   downplaying or underestimating the effects

   of _____ , _____

   factors.

   (c) The fundamental attribution error plays a

   role in a common explanatory pattern called

   _____ ; the

   _____ of a crime, disas-

   ter, or serious illness is blamed for having

   somehow caused the problem or for not hav-

   ing taken steps to avoid or present it.

   (d) The assumption that the world is fair and

   that we get what we deserve and deserve

   what we get is called the

   _____ .

2. (a) The exception to the fundamental attribu-

   tion error is when we explain our own

   behavior; in those instances we're more like-

   ly to use a(n) _____ ,

   _____ attribution than a(n)

   _____ , _____

   attribution.

   (b) This common attributional bias is called the

   _____ discrepancy

   because there is a discrepancy between the

   attributions you make when you are the

   _____ in a given situation and

   those you make when you are the

_____ of other people's behavior.

(c) One explanation for this bias is that we have more _____ about the potential causes of our own behavior than we do about the causes of other people's behavior; when we're more aware of the possible situational influences on the behavior, such as with people we know well, we are less susceptible to the _____ discrepancy and are better at seeing situations from their point of view.

3. (a) The tendency to attribute _____ outcomes of our own behavior to internal causes and _____ outcomes to external, situational causes is called the self-serving bias.

(b) In a wide range of situations, people tend to credit themselves for their _____ and to blame their _____ on external circumstances; psychologists explain the self-serving bias as being partly due to an attempt to save face and protect self-esteem in the face of _____ .

4. Read the following and write the correct term in the space provided:

(a) Adam got an A in his philosophy class and concluded that he had quite a talent for writing coherently and thinking logically. When he got a C in his sociology class, he expressed dissatisfaction with the course content, the teaching ability of the professor, and the quality and clarity of the exams. This best illustrates the

_____ .

(b) Rachel has just learned that her neighbor's teenage son, Brad, was involved in an automobile accident at a nearby intersection. She said to her husband, "Well, Brad's recklessness has finally got him into trouble!" Rachel's comment suggests that she has made the _____ .

(c) When Allen observed Mark miss what looked to him like an easy point, Allen concluded that Mark lacked skill in the game. Later, when Allen was in an identical position, he too failed to score. On this occasion, however, he concluded that it was the strong opposition team that prevented him from scoring. It would appear that Allen is committing the _____ .

(d) When Cheryl first met Charles, who is an archivist in the university library, she concluded that he was probably very quiet, introverted, and introspective. Later she was surprised when she went to a local club to find he was the lead singer in a heavy metal band. Cheryl's surprise is probably the result of using a(n)

_____

to make judgments about the traits and characteristics associated with certain types of people.

(e) After learning about some interesting social psychology phenomena in his introductory class, Patrick decided he would like to try a little experiment. He thought it would be interesting to see what would happen if he faced the back instead of the front while riding the elevator. Much to his surprise, however, he found that he could not carry out his plan. After a second or two he was overcome with embarrassment and ended up facing the front like everyone else. Patrick's behavior was governed by the

_____ of the situation.

(f) Grover does not support any charities because he believes that if people are poor, hungry, or homeless, it's because they did something to deserve the situation they are in. Grover's explanatory pattern is called _____ , and this may reflect his strong need to believe that the world is fair, an assumption called the

_____ .

Graphic Organizer 1

The following represent attributional processes. Decide which is (A) the fundamental attribution error, (B) the actor--observer discrepancy, or (C) the self-serving bias and decide whether the attribution is to the self or to others and whether it is internal (INT) or external (EXT).

Statement	Process	Attribution
1. I got an A in biology because I'm smart; I got a C in chemistry because the professor was disorganized, couldn't teach, and gave exams that were grossly unfair.		
2. My sister had a fender-bender because she is a typical female driver; when I had a fender-bender, it was because the other driver was an idiot.		
3. I don't care what he said about his car breaking down; he was fifteen minutes late for the first class so he must be one of those inconsiderate professors who is more concerned with his research than with his students.		

Review of Key Terms 1

social psychology
social cognition
social influence
person perception
social norms
social categorization
implicit personality
    theory
attribution

fundamental attribution
    error
blaming the victim
just-world hypothesis
actor–observer
    discrepancy
self-serving bias
self-effacing bias
    (modesty bias)

Matching Exercise

Match the appropriate term with its definition or description.

1. _____ The "rules," or expectations, for appropriate behavior in a particular social situation.

2. _____ The mental process of inferring the causes of people's behavior, including one's own. Also used to refer to the explanation made for a particular behavior.

3. _____ The tendency to attribute successful outcomes of one's own behavior to internal causes and unsuccessful outcomes to external, situational causes.

4. _____ The branch of psychology that studies how people think, feel, and behave in social situations.

5. _____ A network of assumptions or beliefs about the relationships among various types of people, traits, and behaviors.

6. _____ The tendency to attribute one's own behavior to external, situational causes while attributing the behavior of others to internal, personal causes; especially likely to occur with regard to behaviors that lead to negative outcomes.

7. _____ The assumption that the world is fair and we get what we deserve and deserve what we get.

True/False Test

Indicate whether each statement is true or false by placing T or F in the blank space next to each item.

1. ___ The effect that situational factors and other people have on an individual's behavior is called social cognition.

2. ___ The fundamental attribution error refers to the tendency to attribute the behavior of others to internal, personal characteristics while ignoring or underestimating the effects of external, situational factors; an attributional bias that is common in individualistic cultures.

3. ___ The mental processes we use to form judgments and draw conclusions about the characteristics and motives of others are called person perception.

4. ___ Social categorization refers to the mental process of classifying people into groups (or categories) on the basis of their shared characteristics.

5. ___ Social influence is the study of the mental processes people use to make sense of their social environment and includes the study of person perception, attribution, attitudes, and prejudice.

6. ___ The blaming-the-victim phenomenon occurs when the innocent victim of a tragedy, crime, disaster, or serious illness is held responsible for having somehow caused the misfortune or for not having taken steps to prevent or avoid it.

7. ___ The self-effacing bias (modesty bias) involves blaming failure on internal, personal factors while attributing success to external, situational factors; more common in collectivistic cultures than individualistic cultures.

> Check your answers and review any areas of weakness before going on to the next section.

Attitudes and Behavior
Learning Objectives

When you have finished studying this section of the chapter, you should be able to:

1. Define the term *attitude* and list the components of an attitude.

2. Identify the conditions under which attitudes are most likely to determine behavior.

3. Describe the process of cognitive dissonance and explain how it affects attitudes.

Read the section "Attitudes and Behavior" and **write** *your answers to the following:*

1. (a) Psychologists formally define an attitude as a(n) _____ tendency to evaluate some _____ , _____ , or _____ in a particular way; attitudes are typically positive or negative, but they can also be _____ , as when you have mixed feelings about an issue or a person.

   (b) Attitudes can be made up of several related components: (1) an attitude may have a(n) _____ component (your thoughts and conclusions about a given topic or object); (2) an attitude may have a(n) _____ , or _____ , component; and (3) an attitude can have a(n) _____ component, in which your attitude is reflected in your actions.

2. (a) Psychologists have found that people _____ (always/don't always) act in accordance with their attitudes.

   (b) You are most likely to behave in accordance with your attitudes when (1) your attitudes are _____ or are _____ expressed; (2) your attitudes have been formed through direct _____ ; (3) you are very _____ about the subject; (4) you have a vested _____ in the subject; and (4) you anticipate a(n) _____ outcome or response from others.

3. (a) Cognitive dissonance is an unpleasant state of _____ tension (dissonance) that occurs when there is _____ (consistency/an inconsistency) between two thoughts or perceptions; the state of dissonance is so unpleasant that we are strongly motivated to reduce it.

   (b) Cognitive dissonance commonly occurs in situations in which you become uncomfortably aware that your behavior and attitudes _____ (are/are not) in conflict; you are simultaneously holding two _____ cognitions, your original attitude and the way you have behaved.

   (c) If you can easily _____ your behavior to make it _____ with your attitude, then any dissonance can be quickly and easily resolved; but when your behavior cannot be easily _____ , you will tend to change your attitude to make it _____ with your behavior.

(d) Cognitive dissonance can also change the
_____ of an attitude so that it is
_____ with some behavior we've
already performed.

(e) Cognitive dissonance also operates when
choosing between two basically equal alternatives; each choice has _____
and _____ features, creating
dissonance, but once the choice is made, you
immediately bring your attitudes more
closely into line with that commitment,
reducing the dissonance; you emphasize the
_____ features of the choice you
rejected and the _____ features
of the choice you made.

Graphic Organizer 2

*The following statements reflect attitudes about
certain topics. Decide which component—cognitive,
affective, or behavioral—is represented by each statement.*

Statement	Component
1. I believe the automobile is the single most destructive element on this planet.	
2. I consistently recycle paper, plastic, pop cans, glass, and other waste.	
3. I vote for anti–gun control advocates and give them my full support.	
4. I get really angry when I see people carelessly throwing their litter on the ground.	
5. I don't want to contribute to the pollution of our city so I ride my bicycle or take public transport.	
6. I am very happy when I see women doing well in what used to be male-dominated occupations.	
7. In my opinion a woman's place is in the home, raising the kids and doing housework.	
8. I get really upset when motorists are rude and inconsiderate.	
9. I believe that the automobile is the greatest invention ever, and we need to elect politicians who will promise to build more roads and freeways.	

Understanding Prejudice
Learning Objectives

When you have finished studying this section of the chapter, you should be able to:

1. Define *prejudice* and explain what is meant by *stereotypes.*

2. Describe the function of stereotypes and identify the problems associated with the use of stereotypes.

3. Define the terms *in-group* and *out-group*, and list the effects that in-group/out-group thinking have on our social judgment, including prejudice and stereotypes.

4. Identify the biases that are associated with in-group/out-group thinking, and define *ethnocentrism.*

5. Describe Sherif's research on overcoming prejudice and explain how his findings can be applied in educational settings.

6. Specify the conditions that are essential for reducing tensions between groups, and explain how we can overcome prejudice at the individual level.

Read the section "Understanding Prejudice" and ***write*** *your answers to the following:*

1. (a) Prejudice is a(n)

   _____

   toward people who belong to a specific social group.

   (b) Prejudice is ultimately based on the exaggerated notion that members of "other" social groups are different from members of our own social group; however, racial and ethnic groups are far more

   _____ than they are

   _____ , and any differences that may exist between members of racial and ethnic groups are _____ (smaller/larger) than differences among various members of the same group.

2. (a) A specific kind of social category is a stereotype, which is defined as a cluster of

   _____ that are attributed to

members of a specific social group or category; in other words, stereotypes are based on the assumption that people have certain

_____ because of their membership in a particular group.

(b) Once formed, stereotypes are

_____ (easy/hard) to shake; when stereotypic beliefs become

_____ that are applied to all members of a given group, stereotypes can be very misleading, or even damaging, and may result in prejudice.

3. (a) People have a very strong tendency to perceive others in terms of two very basic social categories: the _____ ("us") refers to the group or groups to which we belong, whereas _____ ("them") refer to groups of which we are not a member.

   (b) _____ and _____ aren't necessarily limited to racial, ethnic, or religious boundaries but can include virtually any characteristic that can create a distinction.

   (c) We typically describe members of our _____ as being quite varied and diverse, whereas we tend to see members of the _____ as much more similar to one another; this tendency is called the

   _____

   effect.

   (d) _____ bias refers to our tendency to make more favorable, positive attributions for behaviors by members of our _____ and unfavorable, negative attributions for members of

   _____ .

   (e) One form of _____ bias is ethnocentrism, which is the belief that one's culture or ethnic group is superior to others; ethnocentric thinking contributes to the formation of _____ stereotypes about cultures whose customs differ from our own.

4. (a) In combination, stereotypes and in-group/out-group bias form the _____ basis for prejudicial attitudes; but prejudice also has a strong _____ component that is characterized by being intensely negative.

(b) Behaviorally, prejudice can be displayed in the form of _____ , behaviors ranging from privately sneering at another group to physically attacking members of the out-group; no matter where or when it occurs, _____ and violence occur against men, women, and children just because they are members of a particular out-group.

5. (a) Muzafer Sherif's research helped clarify the _____ that produce intergroup conflict and harmony; his research showed how conflict can be _____ and that intergroup conflict can be decreased when groups engage in a(n) _____ effort to achieve a common goal.

(b) Other researchers showed that _____ learning using the jigsaw classroom technique is one way of reducing prejudice in the classroom; this technique requires each student in a small, ethnically diverse group to become an expert in one aspect of their overall project and teach it to the other members of the group; _____ and _____ replaced competition.

(c) Children in the jigsaw classrooms had _____ self-esteem, a _____ liking for children in other ethnic groups, decreased use of negative stereotypes and prejudice, and a reduc-

tion of intergroup hostility, compared to children in traditional classrooms.

6. Read the following and write the correct term in the space provided:

(a) In Zeegland, where Majib grew up, women manage all the household finances, make all the major decisions regarding the family, and earn most of the family income. The men, on the other hand, tend to spend a lot of time hanging around together and trying to impress each other with the way they dress. Majib's belief that all women are naturally more assertive and domineering than men reflects her _____ about gender.

(b) In a discussion about gun control laws, Jerrilee said, "In my opinion easy access to guns is the major contributing factor to the high homicide rate in the U.S." This statement reflects the _____ component of Jerrilee's attitude about gun control.

(c) When a group of fine arts majors were having lunch together, they happened to sit next to a group of engineering students. During a discussion after lunch, one of the fine arts students remarked, "Boy, those engineering students are all alike. They are so loud, pushy, and aggressive, and, unlike us, they haven't got a scrap of creativity between them!" This statement reflects the

_____

effect.

(d) During a sociology class, the instructor described the types of foods the Heckawe tribe considers delicacies. The list included chopped up earthworms, sheep's eyeballs, water buffalo testicles, and live caterpillars. Later, while having a hamburger and fries for lunch, one of the students remarked that the Heckawe diet was disgusting and repulsive. Another suggested that one day they will become civilized and maybe even start eating good food just like us. These remarks illustrate a form of in-group bias called

_____ .

(e) When going to buy his first computer, Sylvester was having a tough time deciding on the model Z5000 Spartan or its equivalent in every way, the LX5000 MBI. With a toss of a coin he bought the Z5000 Spartan. Initially he was worried about his choice but since buying the PC he has sought out and talked to many enthusiastic owners of Z5000 Spartans and is now very pleased that he chose the better of the two options. It is very likely that Sylvester experienced

_____ when he purchased his PC, and his subsequent behavior was an attempt to _____ this unpleasant state of psychological tension.

Review of Key Terms and Key Names 2

attitude	in-group bias
cognitive dissonance	ethnocentrism
prejudice	discrimination
stereotype	Muzafer Sherif
in-group	jigsaw classroom
out-group	technique
out-group homogeneity effect	

Matching Exercise

Match the appropriate term/name with its definition or description.

1. _____ American social psychologist who is best known for his "Robert's Cave" experiments to study prejudice, conflict resolution, and group processes.

2. _____ The belief that one's own culture or ethnic group is superior to all others and the related tendency to use one's own culture as a standard by which to judge other cultures.

3. _____ A learned tendency to evaluate some object, person, or issue in a particular

way; such evaluations may be positive, negative, or ambivalent.

4. _____ A social group to which one belongs.

5. _____ An unpleasant state of psychological tension or arousal (dissonance) that occurs when two thoughts or perceptions (cognitions) are inconsistent; typically results from awareness that attitudes and behavior are in conflict.

6. _____ A social group to which one does not belong.

True/False Test

Indicate whether each statement is true or false by placing T or F in the blank space next to each item.

1. ____ Prejudice is a negative attitude toward people who belong to a specific social group.

2. ____ When prejudice is displayed behaviorally, it is called discrimination.

3. ____ The out-group homogeneity effect refers to the tendency to judge the behavior of in-group members favorably and out-group members unfavorably.

4. ____ A stereotype is a cluster of characteristics that are associated with all members of a specific social group, often including qualities that are unrelated to the objective criteria that define the group.

5. ____ The jigsaw classroom technique is a teaching technique that stresses cooperative, rather than competitive, learning situations.

6. ____ The in-group bias refers to the tendency to see members of out-groups as very similar to one another.

> Check your answers and review any areas of weakness before going on to the next section.

Conformity: Following the Crowd
Learning Objectives

When you have finished studying this section of the chapter, you should be able to:

1. Describe how Solomon Asch investigated conformity and list the factors that influence the degree to which people will conform.

2. Explain why people conform and how culture affects conformity.

*Read the section "Conformity: Following the Crowd" and **write** your answers to the following:*

1. (a) Conformity occurs when we change our

   _____ , _____ , or

   _____ in response to real or

   imagined group pressure.

   (b) _____ studied the degree

   to which people would conform to the group

   even when the group opinion was clearly

   wrong; he found that

   _____ (very few/the vast

   majority) conformed with the group judg-

   ment on at least one of the critical trials.

   (c) There are two basic reasons why we conform

   to the larger group: (1) our desire to be liked

   and accepted by the group, which is referred

   to as _____ social influence,

   and (2) our desire to be right. When we're

   uncertain or doubt our own judgment, we

   may look to the group as a source of accu-

   rate information, which is called

   _____ social influence.

   (d) Conformity _____ (increases/

   decreases) under the following circum-

   stances: subjects are more likely to go

   _____ (along with/against) the

   majority if one other participant dissents;

   any dissent _____ (increases/

   decreases) resistance to the majority opin-

   ion, even if the other person's dissenting

   opinion is wrong.

2. (a) In a wide-ranging meta-analysis British psy-

   chologists found that conformity is generally

   higher in _____ cultures than

   in _____ cultures.

   (b) Because _____ cultures

   tend to emphasize independence, self-

   expression, and standing out from the

crowd, the whole notion of conformity tends

to carry a negative connotation; in

_____ cultures, publicly con-

forming while privately disagreeing tends to

be regarded as socially appropriate tact or

sensitivity, whereas publicly challenging the

judgments of others is considered rude, tact-

less, and insensitive.

Obedience: Following Orders
Learning Objectives

When you have finished studying this section of the chapter, you should be able to:

1. Define *obedience*, describe the basic design of Milgram's obedience experience, and present the results.

2. List the factors that Milgram and other researchers identified as contributing to the subjects' obedience.

3. Identify the aspects of the experimental situa-tion that increase the likelihood of obedience.

4. Identify the factors that Milgram, in later stud-ies, found decreased the level of obedience.

*Read the section "Obedience: Following Orders" and **write** your answers to the following:*

1. (a) Stanley Milgram is best known for his stud-

   ies of obedience, which is defined as the

   _____ of an action in response

   to the _____ of an

   authority or person of higher status, like a

   teacher or supervisor.

   (b) Milgram wanted to find out if a person could

   be _____ by others into commit-

   ting a(n) _____ act, some action

   that violated his or her own conscience, such

   as hurting a stranger.

   (c) To answer that, Milgram embarked on one

   of the most systematic and controversial

   investigations in the history of psychology:

   how and why people _____ the

   destructive _____ of an

   authority figure.

2. (a) Milgram's subjects were fairly _____ of the population in terms of educational background and occupation, and the experiment was rigged so that the subjects were always in the role of the _____ in the experiment; the other subject, who was an accomplice, was always the _____ .

(b) The role of the _____ was to shock the _____ , who was strapped to a chair in a separate room; every time he made a mistake on the memorization task, a realistic but nonfunctioning shock generator with increments of 15 to 450 volts was used to deliver the "punishment."

(c) Each time the _____ made an error, the _____ was told to progress to the next level on the shock generator and announce the voltage before delivering the shock; the _____ followed a set, scripted series of responses as the voltage increased until he eventually stopped responding altogether.

(d) If the _____ protested that he wished to stop or that he was worried about the _____ safety, the experimenter would use one of two prompts to encourage the _____ to continue.

(e) According to the script, the experiment would be halted when the _____ refused to obey the experimenter's orders to continue or when the voltage reached the maximum level of 450 volts.

3. (a) The results showed that all estimates of the level of shock that people would give in this experimental situation were wrong; _____ of Milgram's subjects went to the full 450-volt level, and of those who defied the experimenter, _____ stopped before the 300-volt level.

(b) Milgram's subjects appeared genuinely _____ about hurting another person, and yet _____ of them continued to administer stronger and stronger shocks, obediently following the experimenter's commands.

4. Milgram and other researchers identified several aspects of the experimental situation that had a strong impact on the subjects' willingness to continue obeying the experimenter's orders:

(a) A previously well-established _____ framework to obey. When they arrived in the lab, they had the _____ that they would obediently follow the directions of the person in charge—the experimenter.

(b) The _____ , or _____ , in which the obedience occurred. They believed the experiment would advance scientific knowledge of learning and memory.

(c) The gradual, repetitive _____ of the task. At the beginning of the experiment, the subject administered a very low level of shock (15 volts), and like the learner's protests, the shocks _____ very gradually, 15 volts at a time.

(d) The experimenter's _____ and _____ . The experimenter took responsibility for the learner's well-being; thus, the subjects could believe that they were not responsible for the _____ of their actions.

(e) The _____ and _____ separation from the learner. First, the learner was not _____ . Second, punishment was _____ ; the subject simply pushed a switch on the shock generator. Finally, the learner never appealed directly to the teacher to stop the shocks.

5. (a) By varying his experiments, Milgram identified several conditions that _____ (increase/decrease) the likelihood of destructive obedience.

   (b) Willingness to obey _____ sharply when the buffers that separate the teacher from the learner are lessened or removed, as when both of them are put in the same room.

   (c) When subjects (teachers) were allowed to act as their own authority and freely choose the shock level, _____ percent of them did not venture beyond 150 volts, the first point at which the learner protested; clearly they were not responding to their own aggressive or sadistic impulses but rather to orders from an authority figure.

   (d) Milgram found that people are _____ (more/less) likely to muster up the courage to defy an authority when they see others do so; when they observed what they thought were two other subjects disobeying the experimenter, the real subject followed their lead _____ percent of the time and refused to continue.

6. The scientific study of conformity and obedience has produced some important insights:

   (a) _____ factors are very important; it is psychologically uncomfortable to be at odds with the majority or the authority, enough so that our judgment and perceptions can be distorted and we may act in ways that violate our conscience.

   (b) Each of us _____ (does/does not) have the capacity to resist group or authority pressures; _____ subjects refused to conform or obey despite considerable social and situational pressure.

   (c) No specific personality trait consistently _____ conformity or obedience in experimental situations, like the ones Asch and Milgram created.

   (d) Conformity and obedience are not completely bad in and of themselves; they are necessary for an orderly society; the critical issue is whether the norms we conform to or the orders we obey reflect values that respect the _____ , _____ , and _____ of others.

Helping Behavior: Coming to the Aid of Strangers

Learning Objectives

When you have finished studying this section of the chapter, you should be able to:

1. Identify the components of Latané and Darley's model of helping behavior.

2. List the factors that increase and decrease the likelihood that people will help others.

*Read the section "Helping Behavior: Coming to the Aid of Strangers" and **write** your answers to the following:*

1. (a) Beginning in the 1960s Bibb Latané and John Darley pioneered the study of _____ by conducting ingenious experiments in which people appeared to need help.

2. Latané, Darley, and other researchers identified specific factors that influence the decision to help or not to help. Which factors *increase* the likelihood of helping behavior?

   (a) The "feel _____ , do _____" effect. People who feel _____ , successful, _____ , or fortunate are more likely to help others.

(b) Feeling _____ .We tend to be more helpful when we're feeling _____ , such as after telling a lie or inadvertently causing an accident.

(c) Seeing others who are _____ to help. We are more likely to help if we see others helping.

(d) Perceiving the other person as _____ help. We're more likely to help people who are in need through no fault of their own.

(e) Knowing _____ to help. Simply knowing what to do contributes to the decision to help someone else.

(f) A _____ relationship. Any sort of _____ relationship, even the most minimal social interaction, such as making eye contact or engaging in small talk, increases the likelihood that one person will help another.

3. Which factors *decrease* the likelihood of helping behavior?

(a) The _____ of other people. People are much more likely to help when they are _____ ; if other people are present, helping behavior _____ , a phenomenon called the bystander effect.

(b) There appear to be two reasons for the bystander effect: (1) the _____ of other people creates a diffusion of responsibility; the responsibility to intervene is _____ (or diffused) among the other onlookers, and because no one person feels all the pressure to respond, each bystander becomes _____ likely to help; (2) each of us is motivated to some extent by the desire to behave in a socially acceptable way (_____ social influence) and to appear correct (_____ social influence); we

often rely on the reactions of others to help us define the situation and guide our responses.

(c) Being in a big city or a very small town. People are _____ (more/less) likely to help a stranger in very big cities (300,000 people or more) or in very small towns (5,000 people or less); people are _____ (more/less) likely to help a stranger in towns with populations in between these two extremes.

(d) _____ or _____ situations. When situations are _____ and people are not certain that help is needed, such as in domestic disputes or a lovers' quarrel, they're less likely to help.

(e) When the personal _____ for helping outweigh the _____ . As a general rule we tend to weigh the _____ as well as the _____ of helping in deciding whether to act.

4. Read the following and write the correct term in the space provided:

(a) Trent hates to wear ties but wears one to his sister's wedding to avoid the disapproval of his family. Trent's behavior illustrates the importance of _____ social influence.

(b) Harold is a subject in a replication of Milgram's obedience experiment. If he is like most of the subjects in the experiment, he _____ (will/will not) administer high levels of shock to the learner.

(c) If Harold was allowed to act as his own authority and freely choose the shock level, it is very _____ (likely/unlikely) that he will use a shock over 150 volts, the first point at which the learner is likely to protest.

(d) At the end of a music concert featuring his favorite group, Jamal joined everyone else in giving them a standing ovation. Jamal's behavior _____ (is/is not) an example of conformity.

(e) Carmichael was elated when he won $1,000 in the lottery. Later that day he was asked if he could volunteer a few hours on the weekend to help collect food for the local food bank and he readily agreed. This illustrates the _____ effect.

(f) While about twenty subjects were filling out a questionnaire in a classroom, an odorless vapor started seeping into the room from one of the heating vents. The room slowly began to fill with the vapor, yet nobody stopped what they were doing and nobody went to report the incident. One reason this bystander effect occurs is that the presence of other people creates a(n)

_____ .

Graphic Organizer 3

Describe the main effect investigated by each of the following social psychologists. (For example, Zimbardo's grasshopper study showed how behavior can change attitude through the process of cognitive dissonance.)

Researcher	Main Effect Investigated
1. Asch	
2. Sherif	
3. Milgram	
4. Latané and Darley	

Review of Key Terms and Key Names 3

conformity
Solomon Asch
normative social
   influence
informational social
   influence
Stanley Milgram
obedience
Bibb Latané

John M. Darley
"feel good, do good"
   effect
bystander effect
diffusion of
   responsibility
persuasion

Matching Exercise

Match the appropriate term/name with its definition or description.

1. _____ Contemporary American social psychologist who, along with co-researcher Bibb Latané, is best known for his pioneering studies of bystander intervention in emergency situations.

2. _____ The deliberate attempt to influence the attitudes or behavior of another person in a situation where that person has some freedom of choice.

3. _____ The phenomenon in which the greater the number of people present, the less likely each individual is to help someone in distress.

4. _____ Contemporary American social psychologist who, along with co-researcher John M. Darley, is best known for his pioneering studies of bystander intervention in emergency situations.

5. _____ The phenomenon in which the presence of other people makes it less likely that any individual will help someone in distress because the obligation to intervene is shared among all the onlookers.

6. _____ Source of behavior that is motivated by the desire to be correct.

True/False Test

Indicate whether each item is true or false by placing T or F in the space next to each item.

1. ____ Solomon Asch is the American social psychologist who is best known for his controversial series of studies investigating destructive obedience to an authority.

2. ____ Conformity is the tendency to adjust one's behavior, attitudes, or beliefs to group norms in response to real or imagined group pressure.

3. ____ A source of behavior that is motivated by the desire to gain social acceptance and approval is called normative social influence.

4. ____ Obedience is the performance of an action in response to the direct orders of an authority or person of higher status.

5. ____ Stanley Milgram is the American social psychologist who is best known for his pioneering studies of conformity.

6. ____ The "feel good, do good" effect refers to the fact that when people feel good, successful, happy, or fortunate, they are more likely to help others.

> Check your answers and review any areas of weakness before going on to the next section.

Something to Think About

1. A question that is often asked is "Why are so many people reluctant to help others who are in distress and need help?" The most usual responses are that people suffer from apathy and big cities alienate and depersonalize people. What would you say if someone asked you that question?

2. We are subjected to a wide variety of situations and stimuli that are designed to influence our attitudes or behavior. The most obvious of these are advertisements in the media, but many other sources that are more subtle are often encountered on a regular basis in our lives. What all these attempts to influence us have in common is the use of techniques of persuasion. Imagine you are hired by a company and they want you to write a brief summary of the factors that are most powerful in changing people's attitudes or behaviors. What would you put in your report?

> Check your answers and review any areas of weakness before doing the progress tests.

Progress Test 1

Review the complete chapter (including Concept Reviews and the boxed inserts), review all your study notes, and then test yourself on the following progress test. Check your answers. If you make a mistake, review your notes, review the relevant section of the study guide, and, if necessary, go back and read the appropriate part of your textbook.

1. Dr. Lopez is a social psychologist who studies the mental processes people use to make sense of their social environment, including the study of person perception, attribution, attitudes, and prejudice. His specific area of research is called
   (a) social cognition
   (b) abnormal psychology
   (c) social influence
   (d) personality

2. When Maryjane steps into the elevator, she quickly looks at the other passengers and decides that the gray-haired man with the beard must be a professor at the college. Maryjane has engaged in the process of
   (a) prejudicial thinking
   (b) discrimination
   (c) social categorization
   (d) ethnocentrism

3. Michael is an accountant, and he often wonders why people are surprised when they find out that he is also a skydiving instructor on the weekends. The most obvious explanation is that people form cognitive schemas about traits and behaviors that are associated with different types of people and occupations. The use of these types of assumptions is called
   (a) ethnocentrism
   (b) the actor–observer discrepancy
   (c) the self-serving bias
   (d) implicit personality theory

4. In her research, Dr. Chuang tries to answer such questions as why we conform to group norms, what compels us to obey authority figures, and when people will help strangers. Dr. Chuang's area of research is
   (a) social influence
   (b) learning and memory
   (c) social cognition
   (d) social categorization

5. Vince suggests that his sister's aggressive behavior results from her insecurity. Vince's explanation for his sister's behavior is an example of
   (a) the out-group homogeneity effect
   (b) the bystander effect
   (c) an attribution
   (d) cognitive dissonance

6. Sally did very poorly on her last math test. If her fifth-grade teacher concludes that Sally did poorly because she is not motivated to do well in school, the teacher is committing the
   (a) fundamental attribution error
   (b) actor–observer discrepancy
   (c) self-serving bias
   (d) social categorization error

7. While riding the ski lift, Jenny made fun of someone who wiped out on a steep section of the run: "A klutz like that shouldn't be allowed on the slopes!" Later, when Jenny wiped out in the same place, she blamed the icy conditions. This is an example of
   (a) the self-serving bias
   (b) the actor–observer discrepancy
   (c) prejudice
   (d) self-effacing (modesty) bias

8. When Allison landed a big contract for her firm, she accepted the credit for the hard work and her smart wheeler-dealing. When she failed to get the contract in another situation, she blamed the sneaky and dishonest tactics of the competition. This illustrates the
   (a) just-world hypothesis
   (b) self-serving bias
   (c) "feel-good, do-good" effect
   (d) actor–observer discrepancy

9. During a discussion on fast food and fast-food outlets, Reginald stated, "Fast food is great. I just love southern fried chicken, fries, coleslaw, and milkshakes." Reginald has a positive attitude toward fast-food restaurants, and this statement represents the _____ component.
   (a) cognitive   (c) behavioral
   (b) affective   (d) ambivalent

10. Faced with the equally attractive choice of either a baconburger or a cheeseburger, Jill finally decided on the cheeseburger. Shortly after she made her choice, she decided that the cheeseburger was a healthier choice and probably had fewer calories than the baconburger.

Her tendency to emphasize the positive aspects of her choice and the negative aspects of the choice she rejected is an example of

(a) conformity
(b) diffusion of responsibility
(c) prejudice
(d) cognitive dissonance

11. Manfred's classmate in university was from Turkey and he loved turkey sandwiches, turkey pizza, turkey burgers, and turkey sausages. Manfred now believes that the main diet of all people from Turkey is centered around meals made from turkey meat, and he has little doubt why the country is called Turkey. Manfred's beliefs about the culture of Turkey reflect

(a) ethnic stereotyping
(b) ethnocentrism
(c) the rule of reciprocity
(d) in-group bias

12. Jackson joined the Alpine cross-country ski club because he couldn't afford the cost of downhill skiing. Many members of his club think that downhill skiing is destroying the natural environment, and they often make derogatory remarks about downhillers. Since joining the club, Jackson has changed his attitude about downhill skiing, and he now promotes the benefits of cross-country skiing and joins his new buddies in categorizing all downhill skiers as self-centered, uncaring destroyers of the environment. This example illustrates

(a) the out-group homogeneity effect
(b) in-group bias
(c) stereotyping
(d) all of the above

13. Greg, who is a new faculty member, is on a college committee concerned with student evaluation. Greg disagrees with the proposal to institute a collegewide percentage system for grading. The other five members have already stated that they are in favor of the proposal. Which of the following is most likely to persuade Greg in his decision about how to vote?

(a) normative social influence
(b) informational social influence
(c) neither (a) nor (b); Greg may stick with his own view and vote against the proposal
(d) all of the above

14. Solomon Asch is to _____ as Stanley Milgram is to _____ .

(a) the just-world hypothesis; blaming the victim
(b) the rule of commitment; the rule of reciprocity
(c) conformity; obedience
(d) implicit personality theory; the bystander effect

15. Kyle is in sixth grade and, like most children in his school, he believes that his school is better than all the other schools in town. This best illustrates

(a) in-group bias
(b) ethnic stereotyping
(c) cognitive dissonance
(d) the fundamental attribution error

16. Just moments after dozens of people get off a crowded bus on their way to work, a badly dressed man stumbles and falls on the sidewalk near the bus stop. Research on bystander intervention would suggest that

(a) he will get immediate help from many people
(b) if one person stops to help him, other people are likely to help as well
(c) the presence of others will decrease the diffusion of responsibility
(d) no one in the crowd will perceive that he may need help

17. Which of the following is true of the just-world hypothesis?

(a) It suggests that perceiving victims in a negative light reduces fear of vulnerability and psychologically defends us against the threatening thought that tragedy could just as easily happen to us.
(b) It refers to the belief that we get what we deserve and deserve what we get.
(c) It contributes to the tendency to blame the innocent victim of a tragedy, crime, disaster, or some other misfortune.
(d) All of the above are true.

18. According to Critical Thinking Box 11.2, which of the following is true?

(a) Two-thirds of the subjects completely obeyed the experimenter's destructive demands and progressed to the full 450-volt level.
(b) Milgram was criticized because he failed to debrief the subjects after the experiment was over.

(c) Less than 1 percent of the subjects obeyed the experimenter's destructive demands and progressed to the full 450-volt level.

(d) The vast majority of Milgram's subjects experienced long-term traumatic reactions, such as depression, decreased self-esteem, and psychotic episodes.

19. According to the Application section, which of the following is correct?

(a) Persuasion refers to the deliberate attempt to influence the attitudes or behavior of another person in a situation where the person has some freedom of choice.

(b) Persuasion techniques are not effective in manipulating people in any way.

(c) Professional persuaders can easily manipulate and change the attitudes and behaviors of the vast majority of people.

(d) Because of the flexible nature of social norms, the vast majority of people can resist conforming to any societal standards.

20. According to Culture and Human Behavior Box 11.1, which of the following is true of the self-effacing bias (modesty bias)?

(a) It refers to the tendency to expend less effort on collective tasks than on the same task performed alone.

(b) It involves blaming failure on internal, personal factors while attributing success to external, situational factors.

(c) It refers to the tendency to work harder on collective tasks than on the same task performed alone.

(d) It involves attributing successful outcomes of one's own behavior to internal causes and unsuccessful outcomes to external, situational causes.

Progress Test 2

After you have checked your understanding of the material in Progress Test 1 and have done a complete chapter review with special focus on any areas of weakness, you are ready to assess your knowledge in Progress Test 2. Check your answers. If you make a mistake, review your notes, the relevant section of the study guide, and, if necessary, the appropriate part of your textbook.

1. Jake lost his job two months ago when the company he worked for downsized its operations, and despite his efforts, he has not found another job yet. One of his neighbors stated that Jake is just like most unemployed people—irresponsible, unmotivated, and basically lazy. The neighbor has committed the

(a) self-serving bias

(b) actor–observer discrepancy

(c) social categorization error

(d) fundament attribution error

2. When their town was threatened by a flood, two families who had been enemies for years ended up working together to try to save the town from the overflowing river. Generalizing from Sherif's findings, it is probable that this act of cooperative behavior may lead to

(a) increased antagonism once the danger has passed

(b) an increase in blaming the victims

(c) reduced conflict and increased harmony between the two families

(d) diffusion of responsibility

3. When people first hear about Milgram's obedience research, they are usually surprised by the results because

(a) the subjects were willing to take part in the experiment for so little money

(b) the learners willingly accepted high levels of shock for their mistakes

(c) the subjects were much more obedient than almost everyone would have predicted

(d) the learners performed significantly better when they were given electric shock

4. While Lyle was alone in a classroom filling out a questionnaire, an odorless vapor started seeping slowly into the room from one of the heating vents. In this situation it is very likely that Lyle will leave the room and report the strange odor to someone. If Lyle was in the room with a large group of other people who were also filling out questionnaires, it is much less likely that he would report the vapor. The difference in Lyle's behavior is best explained by

(a) the bystander effect

(b) the rule of reciprocity

(c) informational social influence

(d) cognitive dissonance

5. When Rachel found out that she had straight A's in all her courses, she was elated. Later that day, when she was asked if she could donate some money to the restore-the-church fund, she readily made a donation even though she is nonreligious and does not go to church. This illustrates

(a) cognitive dissonance·
(b) the "feel-good, do-good" effect
(c) conformity
(d) informational social influence

6. A researcher replicates Solomon Asch's classic experiment of conformity to group pressure. If her results are consistent with those of the original research, she will probably find that
(a) approximately one-third of the subjects are likely to conform on the critical trials
(b) about 90 percent of the subjects will shock the learner at the highest shock level
(c) approximately 90 percent of the subjects are likely to conform on the critical trials
(d) only about 10 percent of the subjects will shock the learner at the highest shock level

7. Fraser loves wearing sandals or thongs and hates wearing shoes. However, when he went to dinner with his girlfriend's family he wore shoes because he did not want to evoke their disapproval. Fraser's behavior best illustrates the importance of
(a) informational social influence
(b) normative social influence
(c) the bystander effect
(d) obedience

8. When Inge first joined the student society she was on a committee that was making a decision on some important financial matter with which she was not familiar. All the other members of the committee stated that they were going to vote against the proposal. Inge voted with the group because she assumed that they must have the correct information. This example illustrates
(a) the just-world hypothesis
(b) normative social influence
(c) informational social influence
(d) obedience

9. Tonya researches the topics of conformity, obedience, and helping behavior for a term paper. She is likely to conclude that
(a) people are inherently cruel, aggressive, and selfish
(b) social and situational factors, especially the behavior of others in the same situation, can have powerful effects on how people behave
(c) people get what they deserve and deserve what they get

(d) situational and social factors have little or no effect on how we behave and how we perceive others

10. If Marty is similar to the majority of subjects in Milgram's original obedience experiments, it is very probable that, when asked to administer high levels of shock to the learner, he will
(a) thoroughly enjoy inflicting pain on the learner
(b) immediately leave the experimental situation
(c) obey the instructions, but with some reluctance and discomfort
(d) demand to be paid more money

11. Quincy has reviewed the literature on conformity and obedience for a term paper. He is most likely to conclude that
(a) virtually nobody is capable of resisting group or authority pressure
(b) all people are innately predisposed to be cruel and aggressive
(c) conformity and obedience are not necessarily bad in and of themselves and are important for an orderly society
(d) all of the above are true

12. When Jorge was approaching the ticket window to place his bet on the next race, he thought that either horse, Con Brio or White Lightening, had an equal chance of winning and was debating which one to pick. After he placed his money on Con Brio, however, he felt very confident that he had backed the winner. This example illustrates the effect of
(a) cognitive dissonance
(b) the self-serving bias
(c) conformity
(d) social influence

13. Jenny got 90 percent on her biology midterm exam, Jean got 60 percent, and Jackie got 75 percent. On the basis of their scores on the exam, Jackie thinks to herself that Jenny must be really intelligent and that Jean must be a little slow. Which of the following is true?
(a) Jackie has made an attribution.
(b) Jackie's assessment of her classmates' intelligence is accurate.
(c) Jackie's evaluation reflects the in-group bias.
(d) Jackie's assessment of her classmates' intelligence reflects her prejudice.

14. During a discussion about gun control laws, Marylou said, "I believe it is every American's fundamental right to own a gun and the government has no right to pass laws banning the ownership of guns under any circumstances." This statement reflects the _____ component of Marylou's attitude about guns and gun control laws.

    (a) cognitive
    (b) affective
    (c) behavioral
    (d) dissonant

15. Pietro notices that when there are empty seats on the bus, nobody ever sits beside a stranger, but when the bus is crowded, people sit beside strangers all the time. He noticed that the same thing happens in movie theaters, the cafeteria, and even the classroom. Pietro's observation suggests that people's behavior in these situations is governed by

    (a) prejudice
    (b) social categorization
    (c) stereotypes
    (d) social norms

16. Yoko was late for work because the traffic was particularly heavy. When she arrived in the office, she apologized to her boss and insisted it was her own fault for being late; if she were less lazy, it wouldn't have happened. This example of blaming an accidental occurrence on an internal, personal disposition rather than situational factors is called the

    (a) self-serving bias
    (b) fundamental attribution error
    (c) actor–observer discrepancy
    (d) self-effacing bias (modesty bias)

17. Blaming the victim is less likely to occur when

    (a) we're able to help the victim in some way
    (b) we have empathy and can imagine how the innocent victim feels
    (c) we realistically acknowledge that we may also be threatened by the same misfortunes that others have experienced
    (d) all of the above

18. Attributional biases differ in collectivistic versus individualistic cultures. According to Culture and Human Behavior Box 11.1, in general, members of collectivistic cultures are _____ to commit the fundamental attribution error than members of individualistic cultures.

    (a) more likely
    (b) less likely
    (c) just as likely
    (d) All of the above are equally likely.

19. According to Critical Thinking Box 11.2, which of the following is true of Milgram's research?

    (a) It created a controversy that led to the establishment of ethical safeguards by the American Psychological Association and the federal government regarding experiments involving human subjects.
    (b) It was criticized for causing his subjects emotional stress, tension, and loss of dignity.
    (c) It demonstrated, much to everyone's surprise, that the majority of subjects would obey an authority figure even if it apparently meant hurting another person.
    (d) All of the above are true.

20. There are a number of techniques that professional persuasion experts use. According to the Application section, which of the following is *not* one of those techniques?

    (a) the rule of commitment
    (b) the that's-not-all technique
    (c) the foot-in-the-mouth technique
    (d) the low-ball technique
    (e) the rule of reciprocity

Answers

Introduction: Social Psychology

1. (a) think, feel; behave
   (b) impressions; interpret; attitudes
   (c) situational; conform; obey; help

Person Perception

1. (a) mental; judgments; conclusions
   (b) characteristics; characteristics; situation

2. (a) perceptions
   (b) information
   (c) evaluate; social norms
   (d) self-perception
   (e) one-way; context; self-perceptions

3. (a) mental; groups
   (b) broad; precise
   (c) superficial; unique; cognitive
   (d) automatic; consciously; deliberately

4. (a) people, traits; behaviors; schemas
   (b) useful; accurate
   (c) inaccurate; social; observations, memories

Attribution: Explaining Behavior

1. (a) inferring; explanation
   (b) internal, personal; external, situational
   (c) blaming the victim; innocent victim
   (d) just-world hypothesis

2. (a) external, situational; internal, personal
   (b) actor–observer; actor; observer
   (c) information; actor–observer

3. (a) successful; unsuccessful
   (b) successes; failures; failure

4. (a) self-serving bias
   (b) fundamental attribution error
   (c) actor–observer discrepancy
   (d) implicit personality theory
   (e) social norms
   (f) blaming the victim; just-world hypothesis

Graphic Organizer 1

1. C; INT for own success; EXT for own failure
2. B; EXT for self; INT for other
3. A; INT for other

Matching Exercise 1

1. social norms
2. attribution

3. self-serving bias
4. social psychology
5. implicit personality theory
6. actor–observer discrepancy
7. just-world hypothesis

True/False Test 1

1. F	4. T	6. T
2. T	5. F	7. T
3. T		

Attitudes and Behavior

1. (a) learned; object, person; issue; ambivalent
   (b) cognitive; emotional; affective; behavioral

2. (a) don't always
   (b) extreme; frequently; experience; knowledgeable; interest; favorable

3. (a) psychological; an inconsistency
   (b) are; conflicting
   (c) rationalize; consistent; justified; consistent
   (d) strength; consistent
   (e) desirable; undesirable; negative; positive

Graphic Organizer 2

1. cognitive
2. behavioral
3. behavioral
4. affective
5. behavioral
6. affective
7. cognitive
8. affective
9. cognitive

Understanding Prejudice

1. (a) negative attitude;
   (b) similar; different; smaller

2. (a) characteristics; characteristics
   (b) hard; expectations

3. (a) in-group; out-groups
   (b) in-groups; out-groups
   (c) in-group; out-group; out-group homogeneity
   (d) in-group; in-group; out-groups
   (e) in-group; negative

4. (a) cognitive; emotional
    (b) discrimination; discrimination
5. (a) conditions; created; cooperative
    (b) cooperative; interdependence; cooperation
    (c) high; greater
6. (a) stereotype
    (b) cognitive
    (c) out-group homogeneity
    (d) ethnocentrism
    (e) cognitive dissonance; reduce

Matching Exercise 2

1. Muzafer Sherif
2. ethnocentrism
3. attitude
4. in-group
5. cognitive dissonance
6. out-group

True/False Test 2

1.	T	3.	F	5.	T
2.	T	4.	T	6.	F

Conformity: Following the Crowd

1. (a) behavior, attitudes; beliefs
    (b) Solomon Asch; the vast majority
    (c) normative; informational
    (d) decreases; against; increases
2. (a) collectivistic; individualistic
    (b) individualistic; collectivistic

Obedience: Following Orders

1. (a) performance; direct orders
    (b) pressured; immoral
    (c) obey; orders
2. (a) representative; teacher; learner
    (b) teacher; learner
    (c) learner; teacher; learner
    (d) teacher; learner's; teacher
    (e) teacher
3. (a) two-thirds; not one
    (b) upset; the majority
4. (a) mental; expectation
    (b) situation, context
    (c) escalation; escalated
    (d) behavior; reassurances; consequences
    (e) physical; psychological; visible;
        depersonalized

5. (a) decrease
    (b) diminishes
    (c) 95
    (d) more; 90
6. (a) situational
    (b) does; some
    (c) predicts
    (d) rights, well-being; human dignity

Helping Behavior: Comng to the Aid of Strangers

1. (a) bystander intervention
2. (a) good; good; good; happy
    (b) guilty; guilty
    (c) willing
    (d) deserving
    (e) how
    (f) personalized; personalized
3. (a) presence; alone; declines
    (b) presence; shared; less; normative; informational
    (c) less; more
    (d) vague; ambiguous; ambiguous
    (e) costs; benefits; costs; benefits
4. (a) normative
    (b) will
    (c) unlikely
    (d) is not
    (e) "feel good, do good"
    (f) diffusion of responsibility

Graphic Organizer 3

1. Naive subjects yielded to group pressure in the line-judging task even though the group opinion was wrong.
2. The Robbers Cave study helped clarify the conditions that produce intergroup conflict and harmony and led to the use of the jigsaw classroom technique to promote cooperative behavior.
3. Dramatic illustration of the pressure to obey an authority figure's request to shock another person in a mock learning experiment.
4. Showed the conditions under which people are more likely to help a stranger in distress and also the factors that decrease helping behavior.

Matching Exercise 3

1. John M. Darley
2. persuasion

3. bystander effect

4. Bibb Latané

5. diffusion of responsibility

6. informational social influence

True/False Test 3

1.	F	4.	T
2.	T	5.	F
3.	T	6.	T

Something to Think About

1. There are instances, such as the Kitty Genovese case, where people could easily help someone by simply making a phone call and they don't. Latané and Darley have developed a model that addresses the question of why people don't intervene. For intervention to occur, people have to notice the event or incident, believe it is a situation in which help is needed, feel some sense of responsibility to help, and, finally, know how to deal with the situation.

   The final model identifies six specific factors that increase the likelihood that bystanders will help: (1) the "feel good, do good" effect, (2) feeling guilty, (3) seeing others who are willing to help, (4) perceiving others as deserving help, (5) knowing how to help, and (6) a personalized relationship with the person who needs help.

   In addition, a number of other factors that decrease the likelihood of bystanders helping were identified: (1) the presence of others, called the bystander effect, and the resulting diffusion of responsibility; (2) being in a big city or a very small town; (3) vague or ambiguous situations; and (4) when the personal costs for helping outweigh the benefits. In a discussion of this issue it is important to be able to explain and give examples of each of these factors.

2. Fortunately, you have a very good summary in the Application section: The Persuasion Game. Start by defining persuasion and then paraphrase the main strategies that professional persuaders use to manipulate people's attitudes and behaviors. These include the role of reciprocity, the that's-not-all technique, the rule of commitment, and the low-ball technique. You might also want to integrate material from the chapter, such as the role of cognitive dissonance in changing cognitions and behavior, and aspects of conformity and obedience research. Finally, you should discuss the ways people can defend themselves against professional persuasion techniques (e.g., sleeping on it, playing the devil's advocate, and paying attention to gut feelings).

Progress Test 1

1.	a	8.	b	15.	a
2.	c	9.	b	16.	b
3.	d	10.	d	17.	d
4.	a	11.	a	18.	a
5.	c	12.	d	19.	a
6.	a	13.	d	20.	b
7.	b	14.	c		

Progress Test 2

1.	d	8.	c	15.	d
2.	c	9.	b	16.	d
3.	c	10.	c	17.	d
4.	a	11.	c	18.	b
5.	b	12.	a	19.	d
6.	a	13.	a	20.	c
7.	b	14.	a		

Chapter 12 Stress, Health, and Coping

OVERVIEW

Chapter 12 is about stress, health, and coping. *Stress* is defined as a negative emotional state that occurs in response to events that are appraised as taxing or exceeding a person's resources. It is pointed out that health psychologists study stress and other psychological factors that influence health, illness, and treatment and are guided by the biopsychosocial model.

The life events approach to stress and the Social Readjustment Rating Scale are critically examined, and the influence of the person's subjective appraisal of an event is emphasized. Daily hassles are another important source of stress and can also contribute to the stress produced by major life events. It is noted that stress can be caused by approach-approach, avoidance-avoidance, and approach-avoidance conflicts as well as social factors such as unemployment, crime, racism, and different cultural values.

The physical effects of stress are discussed. Walter Cannon's fight-or-flight response and the bodily systems involved are presented. These include an endocrine pathway involving the sympathetic nervous system, the adrenal medulla, and the release of catecholamines. Hans Selye identified the three-stage general adaptation syndrome, which includes the alarm, resistance, and exhaustion stages. It is pointed out that Selye discovered a second endocrine pathway, which includes the hypothalamus, the pituitary gland, the adrenal cortex, and the release of corticosteroids. Ader and Cohen's research and its influence on the foundation of psychoneuroimmunology are presented, along with research findings on the effects of stress on the immune system.

Psychological factors can also influence our response to stress, and it is pointed out that the impact of stressors is reduced when people feel a realistic sense of control over the stressful situation. The way people explain negative events often determines whether they will persist or give up after failure, and two explanatory styles, optimistic and pessimistic, are identified. It is noted that chronic negative emotions are related to the development of some chronic diseases and that Type A behavior patterns can predict the development of heart disease, with the most critical component being hostility.

The role played by social support in dealing with stressful situations is explored, and the advantages and disadvantages of social support are examined. Women are more likely to be the providers of social support than men and tend to be more vulnerable to the stress contagion effect, whereas men are less likely to be upset by negative events that happen to people outside their immediate family.

Coping refers to the way that people try to change either their circumstances or their interpretations of circumstances in order to make them more favorable and less threatening, and a number of coping strategies are identified. Problem-focused coping involves efforts primarily aimed at directly changing or managing a threatening or harmful stressor. Emotion-focused coping involves efforts primarily aimed at relieving or regulating the emotional impact of a stressful situation. It is pointed out that these two coping strategies can involve a number of different methods for dealing with problems and that people tend to rely on multiple coping strategies in stressful situations. Men and women use similar coping styles, but culture affects the choice of coping strategies; individualistic and collectivistic coping strategies are compared and contrasted.

Introduction: What Is Stress?
Learning Objectives

When you have finished studying this section of the chapter, you should be able to:

1. Define the term *stress.*
2. Identify the main focus of health psychology and explain how health psychologists are guided by the biopsychosocial model

Read the section "Introduction: What Is Stress?" and **write** *your answers to the following:*

1. (a) Stress is widely defined as a negative

    _____ state occurring in

    response to events that are perceived as tax-

    ing or _____ a person's

    resources or ability to cope.

   (b) Whether or not we experience stress largely

    depends on our _____ of

    an event and the _____ we have

    to deal with the event.

   (c) Health psychology is one of the most rapidly

    growing specialty areas in psychology, and

    along with the study of _____ ,

    it focuses on how psychological factors influ-

    ence _____ , _____ ,

    _____ , and health-related

    behaviors.

   (d) Health psychologists are guided by the

    biopsychosocial model, according to which

    health and illness are determined by the

    complex interaction of _____ ,

    _____ , and _____

    factors.

Sources of Stress
Learning Objectives

When you have finished studying this section of the chapter, you should be able to:

1. Identify the most important sources of stress and explain how life events, daily hassles, conflict, and social and cultural factors contribute to stress.
2. Specify the problems that are associated with the life events approach

Read the section "Sources of Stress" and **write** *your answers to the following:*

1. (a) Stressors are _____ or

    _____ that are perceived as

    harmful, threatening, or challenging.

   (b) Early stress researchers Holmes and Rahe

    believed that any _____ that

    required you to adjust your _____

    and _____ would cause stress;

    they developed the Social Readjustment

    Rating Scale in an attempt to measure the

    amount of stress people experienced.

   (c) The scale includes 43 life events (both posi-

    tive and negative), each of which is assigned

    a numerical rating that estimates its rela-

    tive impact in terms of

    _____ ,

    which range from 11 for the least stress-

    producing to 100 for the most stress-

    producing.

   (d) Any change, whether positive or negative, is

    inherently stress-producing; researchers

    found that people who had more than

    _____ life change units within a

year had a(n) _____
rate of physical or psychological illness.

2. Several problems with the life events approach
have been pointed out:

(a) The link between scores on the Social
Readjustment Rating Scale and the development of physical and psychological problems
is relatively _____ ; most people
_____ (do/don't) develop physi-
cal or mental problems as a result of major
life events.

(b) The Social Readjustment Rating Scale does
not take into account a person's
_____ appraisal of an event,
response to that event, or ability to cope
with the event; it is assumed that a given
life event will have _____ (the
same/a different) impact on virtually everyone.

(c) The life events approach assumes
_____ in itself, whether good or
bad, produces stress; research has shown
that _____ life events have the
greatest adverse effects on health, especially
when they are unexpected or uncontrollable,
and _____ events are much less
likely to affect health adversely.

(d) It is generally agreed that
_____ events are significant
sources of stress, but _____ in
itself is not necessarily stressful.

3. (a) Stress researcher _____
and his colleagues developed a scale to measure daily hassles—everyday occurrences
that annoy and upset people; they believed
that these might be an important source of
stress.

(b) The frequency of daily hassles
_____ (is/is not) linked to psychological distress and physical symptoms;
in fact, the number of daily hassles people

experience is a _____ (worse/
better) predictor of physical illness and
symptoms than the number of major life
events experienced.

(c) One explanation is that minor stressors are
_____ ; each hassle may be rel-
atively unimportant in itself, but after a day
filled with minor hassles, the effects add up.

(d) Daily hassles also contribute to the stress
produced by
_____ ;
whether positive or negative, any
_____ can
create a ripple effect, generating a host of
new daily hassles.

4. (a) Another common source of stress is
_____—feeling pulled between
two opposing desires, motives, or goals; an
individual is motivated to _____
desirable or pleasant outcomes and to
_____ undesirable or unpleasant outcomes.

(b) A(n) _____
conflict represents a win-win situation—
being faced with a choice between two equally appealing outcomes; as a rule, these conflicts are usually easy to resolve and don't
produce much stress.

(c) More stressful are
_____ con-
flicts—having to choose between two unappealing or undesirable outcomes; a natural
response to this conflict is to avoid both outcomes by delaying the decision.

(d) Most stressful are
_____ con-
flicts; here, a single goal has both desirable
and undesirable aspects and people often
vacillate, or repeatedly go back and forth in
their minds, unable to make a decision; the
result is significant increase in feelings of
stress and anxiety.

5. (a) _____ conditions can also be an important source of stress; crowding, crime, unemployment, poverty, racism, inadequate health care, and substandard housing are all associated with increased stress; when people live in an environment that is inherently stressful, they often experience ongoing, or _____ , stress.

(b) People in the _____ socioeconomic levels of society tend to have the highest levels of psychological distress, illness, and death; in _____ neighborhoods, people are likely to be exposed to more negative life events, including daily hassles, and to have _____ resources available to cope with those events.

(c) Stress can also result when _____ clash; for refugees, immigrants, and their children, adapting to a new _____ can be extremely stress-producing.

6. Read the following and write the correct term in the space provided:

(a) Dr. Woodworth studies stress and how psychological factors influence health, illness, treatment, and health-related behaviors. Dr. Woodworth is a(n) _____ psychologist.

(b) If Dr. Woodworth is like most psychologists in his specialty area, he adheres to the theory that health and illness are determined by the complex interaction of biological, psychological, and social factors. In other words, he is guided by the _____ model.

(c) In the past year, Frank has gotten divorced, moved twice, and started a new relationship. In addition, he has gotten a promotion and a big raise at work but now has many more responsibilities. His score on the Social Readjustment Rating scale is likely to be _____ , and according to its developers, Homes and Rahe, Frank has _____ (an increased/a decreased) likelihood of developing serious physical or psychological problems.

(d) According to Richard Lazarus, Frank's major life events may create a ripple effect and generate a host of _____ that may accumulate to cause even greater stress.

(e) Janet can only take one course this semester because of work commitments. She is torn between two courses she really wants to take, each of which fits her work schedule. Janet is probably experiencing a(n)

_____

conflict.

Graphic Organizer 1

Read the following descriptions and decide which type of stress-producing conflict is involved: approach-approach, avoidance-avoidance, or approach-avoidance. In addition, label each one as producing either a high, medium, or low level of stress.

Description	Type of Conflict/ Level of Stress
1. Lyndle wants to maintain a high grade point average and needs to study hard before his exam tomorrow but has been asked by his girlfriend to go with her to a party this evening.	
2. A rat in the start box of a Y-shaped maze with two separate goal boxes at the end of each prong will receive an equally desirable food pellet in each one.	
3. Annalee is very happy to be doing well on her diet but now has to decide whether to go for lunch with her friends at her favorite Greek taverna or stay in the lunchroom and eat her low-calorie snack.	
4. In order to be able to borrow the family car for the evening, Jason has to decide between doing two equally unappealing chores, the family laundry or washing and waxing the bathroom and kitchen floors.	
5. Virginia entered her name in a contest and was overwhelmed when she won a seven-day Caribbean cruise. She has to decide between a seven-day eastern Caribbean cruise or a seven-day western Caribbean cruise.	
6. Melvin is overweight and out of shape and is given a choice of two daily exercise regimens by his doctor, one involving 40 minutes of running, exercise bike, and weightlifting and the other involving 40 minutes of running, step-up machine, and weightlifting.	

Review of Key Terms and Key Names 1

stress
health psychology
stressors
biopsychosocial model
Social Readjustment
  Rating Scale
Richard Lazarus
daily hassles

conflict
approach-approach
  conflict
avoidance-avoidance
  conflict
approach-avoidance
  conflict
acculturative stress

Matching Exercise

Match the appropriate term/name with its definition or description.

1. _____ American psychologist who helped promote the cognitive perspective in the study of stress and coping and, with his colleagues, developed the Daily Hassles Scale.

2. _____ A basic type of conflict where you're faced with a choice between two equally appealing outcomes; as a rule these conflicts are usually easy to resolve and don't produce much stress.

3. _____ A situation in which a person feels pulled between two or more opposing desires, motives, or goals.

4. _____ Everyday, minor events that annoy and upset people.

5. _____ The branch of psychology that studies how psychological factors influence health, illness, medical treatment, and health-related behaviors.

6. _____ A model that health psychologists are guided by and according to which health and illness are determined by the complex interaction of biological, psychological, and social factors.

True/False Test

Indicate whether each statement is true or false by placing T or F in the blank space next to each item.

1. ____ Stress refers to events or situations that are perceived as harmful, threatening, or challenging.

2. ____ The Social Readjustment Rating Scale was developed by Thomas Holmes and Richard Rahe in an attempt to measure the amount of stress people experienced as a function of life events that are likely to require some level of adaptation.

3. ____ An approach-avoidance conflict has a single goal with both desirable and undesirable aspects; when faced with this conflict, people often vacillate, or repeatedly go back and forth in their minds, unable to decide to approach or avoid the goal.

4. ____ Stressors refer to negative emotional states that occur in response to events that are perceived as taxing or exceeding a person's resources or ability to cope.

5. ____ An avoidance-avoidance conflict involves choosing between two unappealing or undesirable outcomes; people often delay making a decision when faced with this conflict, or they may bail out altogether.

6. ____ Acculturative stress describes the stress that results from the pressure of adapting to a new culture.

Check your answers and review any areas of weakness before going on to the next section.

Physical Effects of Stress: The Mind–Body Connection

Learning Objectives

When you have finished studying this section of the chapter, you should be able to:

1. Specify how stress can contribute to health problems both directly and indirectly.

2. Explain how the work of Cannon and Selye contributed to the early understanding of stress.

3. Identify the endocrine pathways that are involved in the flight-or-fight response and the general adaptation syndrome.

*Read the section "Physical Effects of Stress: The Mind–Body Connection" and **write** your answers to the following:*

1. (a) Stress can _____ affect a person's health by promoting behavior that jeopardizes physical well-being; people under chronic stress are more likely to use alcohol, coffee, and cigarettes than people under less stress.

   (b) High levels of stress can also interfere with _____ abilities, like attention, concentration, and memory; in turn, such _____ disruptions can increase the likelihood of accidents and injuries.

   (c) Stress can _____ affect physical health by altering body functions, leading to symptoms, illness, or disease; for example, stress can cause neck and head muscles to contract and tighten, resulting in stress-induced headaches.

2. (a) To explain the connection between stress and health, researchers have focused on how the _____ system, including the _____ , interacts with two other important body systems: the _____ and _____ systems.

(b) The rapidly occurring chain of internal physical reactions that prepare people either to _____ or to take _____ from an immediate threat is called the fight-or-flight response.

(c) The fight-or-flight response was first described by American physiologist _____ , one of the earliest contributors to stress research; he discovered that the fight-or-flight response involved both the _____ system and the _____ system.

(d) With the perception of a threat, the _____ system stimulates the adrenal medulla to secrete hormones called catecholamines, including _____ and _____ .

(e) Circulating through the blood, catecholamines _____ the rapid and intense bodily changes associated with the fight-or-flight response; once the threat is removed, the high level of bodily arousal tends to gradually subside, and within _____ to _____ minutes, a normal level is usually reestablished.

(f) As a(n) _____ reaction, the fight-or-flight response helps ensure _____ by swiftly mobilizing internal physical resources to defensively attack or flee an immediate threat; however, when exposure to an unavoidable threat is _____ , the intense arousal of the fight-or-flight response can also become _____ and can prove _____ to physical health.

3. (a) Hans Selye was the Canadian endocrinologist whose pioneering scientific investigations confirmed _____ suggestion that _____ stress can be physically harmful.

(b) Regardless of the condition that Selye used to produce _____ stress, he found the same pattern of physical changes in the experimental rats; first, the _____ glands became enlarged; second, _____ ulcers and loss of weight occurred; and third, there was shrinkage of the _____ gland and _____ glands, two key components of the immune system.

(c) Selye believed that these distinct _____ changes represented the essential effects of stress—the body's response to any demands placed on it; if stress continues, the effects became evident in three progressive stages Selye called the _____ syndrome.

4. (a) During the initial _____ stage, intense arousal occurs as the body mobilizes internal physical resources to meet the demands of the stress-producing event; Selye found that the rapidly occurring changes during the _____ stage are the result of the release of catecholamines by the _____ .

(b) In the _____ stage, the body actively tries to resist or adjust to the continuing stressful situation; the intense arousal of the _____ stage diminishes, but physiological arousal remains above normal and _____ to new stressors is impaired.

(c) If the stress-producing event persists, the _____ stage may occur; the symptoms of the _____ stage reappear, only this time irreversibly, and as the body's energy reserves become depleted, adaptation begins to break down, leading to _____ , physical disorders, and, potentially, death.

5. (a) Selye found that prolonged stress activates a second _____ pathway that involves the _____ , the _____ gland, and the _____ cortex, which is the outer portion of the adrenal gland.

(b) In response to a stressor, the _____ signals the _____ gland to secrete a hormone called adrenocorticotropic hormone (ACTH), which in turn stimulates the _____ cortex to release stress-related hormones called corticosteroids, the most important being cortisol.

(c) In the short run, the corticosteroids provide several benefits, helping the body against the harm caused by stressors; they _____ inflammation of body tissues and _____ muscle tone in the heart and blood vessels; however, continued high levels of corticosteroids can weaken important body systems, lowering immunity and increasing susceptibility to physical symptoms and illness.

Stress and the Immune System
Learning Objectives

When you have finished studying this section of the chapter, you should be able to:

1. Explain how stress can undermine health by impairing the immune system.
2. Describe how the work of Ader and Cohen challenged the existing view of the immune system.
3. Define *psychoneuroimmunology* and explain how the immune system interacts with the nervous system.
4. Identify the kinds of stressors that affect immune system functioning.

*Read the section "Stress and the Immune System" and **write** your answers to the following:*

1. (a) The immune system is the body's _____ system; it detects and battles foreign invaders, such as bacteria, viruses, and tumor cells, and its effectiveness can be diminished by stress.

(b) The most important elements of the immune system are _____ , the specialized white blood cells that fight bacteria, viruses, and other foreign invaders.

(c) _____ are initially manufactured in the bone marrow and then migrate to other immune system organs, such as the thymus and spleen, where they develop more fully and are stored until needed.

2. (a) The notion that the immune system operates _____ from the nervous system, the endocrine system, and psychological processes was challenged in the mid-1970s, when psychologist Robert Ader teamed up with immunologist Nicholas Cohen; they demonstrated that the immune system response in rats could be _____ conditioned.

(b) Ader and Cohen's research helped establish a new interdisciplinary field called _____ , which is the scientific study of the interconnections among psychological processes (_____), the nervous and endocrine systems (_____), and the immune system (_____).

(c) _____ has revealed that (1) the central nervous system and the immune system are directly linked via _____ nervous system fibers, which influence the production and functioning of lymphocytes; (2) the surfaces of lymphocytes contain receptor sites for _____ and _____ , including catecholamines and cortisol; and (3) lymphocytes themselves produce _____ and _____ , which in turn influence the nervous and endocrine systems.

(d) There is ongoing interaction and communication among the _____ system, the _____ system, and the _____ system; each system influences and is influenced by the other systems.

3. (a) Extremely stressful events _____ immune system functioning; furthermore, more common negative life events, such as the end or disruption of important interpersonal relationships and chronic stressors that continue for years, can _____ immune system functioning.

(b) Psychologist Janice Kiecolt-Glaser and her husband, immunologist Ronald Glaser, found that even the rather commonplace stress of exams _____ affects the immune system; a brief exposure to a psychological stressor, such as performing a frustrating task for thirty minutes or less, can temporarily _____ immune system responses.

(c) While stress-related immune system decreases may _____ our susceptibility to health problems, exposure to stressors _____ (does not translate/translates) automatically into poorer health.

(d) Your physical health is affected by the interaction of many factors, such as your unique _____ makeup, _____ , _____ , personal habits, and access to medical care; also required, of course, is exposure to _____ , _____ , and other disease-causing agents.

(e) It's important to keep in mind that the stress-induced decreases in immune functioning that have been demonstrated experi-

mentally are often _____ ; as psychoneuroimmunology researchers are careful to point out, these _____ decreases in immune function _____ (may/may not) translate into an added health risk for most people.

4. Read the following and write the correct term in the space provided:

(a) When Hans was hiking on a trail in a wilderness area he unexpectedly encountered a large brown bear and her two cubs. Hans froze in his tracks, and his heartbeat, blood pressure, and pulse increased dramatically. Fortunately, the bear and the cubs took off into the bush. The rapidly occurring chain of internal physical reactions that Hans experienced was described by Walter Cannon and called the _____ response.

(b) When Hans was startled and experienced a number of physiological changes, it is very likely that his sympathetic nervous system stimulated the adrenal medulla to secrete hormones called _____ .

(c) After overcoming the initial shock when she finds her new car has been badly damaged by a hit-and-run driver, Wilma phones the police and becomes actively involved in seeking witnesses to the incident. At this point it is most likely that Wilma is in the _____ stage of the general adaptation syndrome.

(d) Dr. Laslo believes that there is an interaction among psychological processes, the nervous and endocrine systems, and the immune system and that each system influences and is influenced by the other systems. It is very likely that Dr. Laslo works in the new interdisciplinary field called _____ .

(e) When Georgia was under a lot of stress, she became ill due to a viral infection. In response to this infection, the most important elements in her immune system, called _____ , will try to defend against the foreign invader.

Review of Key Terms and Key Names 2

fight-or-flight response	exhaustion stage
Walter Cannon	corticosteroids
catecholamines	immune system
Hans Selye	lymphocytes
general adaptation	Robert Ader
syndrome	psychoneuroimmunology
alarm stage	Janice Kiecolt-Glaser
resistance stage	

Matching Exercise

Match the appropriate term/name with its definition or description.

1. _____ American psychologist who made several important contributions to psychology, especially in the study of emotions; described the fight-or-flight response, which involves the sympathetic nervous system and the endocrine system.

2. _____ Specialized white blood cells that are responsible for immune defenses.

3. _____ Hormones secreted by the adrenal medulla that cause rapid physiological arousal; include adrenaline and noradrenaline.

4. _____ Canadian endocrinologist who was a pioneer in stress research; defined stress as "the nonspecific response of the body to any demand placed on it" and described a three-stage response to prolonged stress that he termed the *general adaptation syndrome.*

5. _____ Hormones released by the adrenal cortex that play a key role in the body's response to long-term stressors.

6. _____ The first stage of the general adaptation syndrome, during which intense arousal occurs as the body mobilizes internal physical resources to meet the demands of the stress-producing event.

7. _____ Body system that produces specialized white blood cells that protect the body from viruses, bacteria, and tumor cells.

True/False Test

Indicate whether each statement is true or false by placing T or F in the blank space next to each item.

1. ____ Robert Ader is the American psychologist who, with immunologist Nicholas Cohen, first demonstrated that immune system responses could be classically conditioned; helped establish the new interdisciplinary field of psychoneuroimmunology.

2. ____ The rapidly occurring chain of internal physical reactions that prepare people to either fight or take flight from an immediate threat is called the general adaptation syndrome.

3. ____ In the resistance stage of the general adaptation syndrome, the body actively tries to resist or adjust to the continuing stressful situation.

4. ____ Janice Kiecolt-Glaser is the American psychologist who, with immunologist Ronald Glaser, conducted extensive research on the effect of stress on the immune system.

5. ____ The fight-or-flight response is Hans Selye's term for the three-stage progression of physical changes that occur when an organism is exposed to intense and prolonged stress.

6. ____ Psychoneuroimmunology is an interdisciplinary field that studies the interconnections among psychological processes, nervous and endocrine system functions, and the immune system.

7. ____ In the exhaustion stage of the general adaptation syndrome, the symptoms of the alarm stage reappear, only this time irreversibly; as the body's energy reserves become depleted, adaptation begins to break down, leading to exhaustion, physical disorders, and, potentially, death.

Check your answers and review any areas of weakness before going on to the next section.

Individual Factors That Influence the Response to Stress

Learning Objectives

When you have finished studying this section of the chapter, you should be able to:

1. Identify the psychological factors that can affect our response to stress.

2. Explain how feelings of control, explanatory style, and chronic negative emotions influence stress and health.

3. Describe Type A behavior and specify the role that hostility plays in its relationship to health.

4. Define what is meant by social support and explain how it benefits health.

5. Explain how social support can sometimes increase stress.

6. Identify the gender differences that have been found in social support.

*Read the section "Individual Factors That Influence the Response to Stress" and **write** your answers to the following:*

1. (a) Psychological research has consistently shown that having a sense of

   _____ over a stressful situation _____ (increases/reduces) the impact of stressors and _____ feelings of anxiety and depression.

   (b) Those who can _____ a stress-producing situation often show _____ (no more/more) psychological distress or physical arousal than people not exposed to the stressor.

   (c) Researchers Rodin and Langer found that having _____ over even minor aspects of their environment had powerful effects on the health of nursing home residents.

2. (a) If you feel that you can _____ a stressor by taking steps to minimize or avoid it, you will experience _____ (more/less) stress, both subjectively and physiologically.

   (b) Having a sense of personal _____ also works by _____ (decreasing/enhancing) positive emotions, such as feelings of self-confidence, self-efficacy, autonomy, and self-reliance.

   (c) In contrast, feeling a lack of _____ over events produces all the landmarks of the stress response: levels of catecholamines and corticosteroids _____ and the effectiveness of immune system functioning _____ .

3. (a) According to psychologist _____ , how people characteristically explain their failures and defeats makes the difference; people who have an optimistic explanatory style tend to use _____ , _____ , and _____ explanations for negative events; people who have a pessimistic explanatory style use _____ , _____ , and _____ explanations for negative events.

   (b) Pessimists are also inclined to believe that _____ (a large amount/no amount) of personal effort will improve their situation; pessimists tend to experience _____ (more/less) stress than optimists.

   (c) _____ (Very few/Most) people fall somewhere along the spectrum of optimism and pessimism and are neither completely optimistic nor completely pessimistic in all areas of their lives.

   (d) Although a person's characteristic explanatory style, particularly for negative events, is relatively _____ across the lifespan, it may vary somewhat in different situations.

4. (a) Research has shown that people who are habitually _____ ,

_____ , _____ , and _____ are more likely to develop a chronic disease such as arthritis or heart disease.

(b) People who are tense, angry, and unhappy experience _____ stress than happier people; they also report _____ frequent and _____ intense daily hassles, and they react much _____ intensely and with _____ distress to the stressful event.

(c) _____ negative moods may also be associated with health risks; research shows that immune system functioning _____ on days when people experience negative events and bad moods and _____ on days when people experience positive events and good moods.

5. (a) The original formulation of the Type A behavior pattern included a cluster of three characteristics: (1) an exaggerated sense of _____ urgency, with the person often trying to do more and more in less and less time; (2) a general sense of _____ , with the person frequently displaying _____ and _____ ; and (3) intense _____ and _____ ; in contrast, people who were more _____ and _____ were classified as displaying the Type B behavior pattern.

(b) Initial research showed that Type A men were _____ (half/twice) as likely to develop heart disease as Type B men; later research suggested that some components of the Type A behavior pattern—time urgency and achievement striving— _____ (were/were not) associated with the development of heart disease.

(c) The critical component that emerged as the strongest predictor of cardiac disease was _____ , which refers to the tendency to feel _____ , annoyance, _____ , and contempt and to hold negative beliefs about human nature in general.

(d) _____ men and women are also prone to believing that the disagreeable behavior of others is intentionally directed against them; thus, they tend to be _____ , _____ , cynical, and pessimistic; they are much more likely than other people to develop heart disease.

(e) High levels of _____ increase the likelihood of dying from all natural causes, including cancer.

(f) _____ Type A people experience _____ (smaller/larger) increases in blood pressure, heart rate, and production of stress-related hormones; are prone to get angry _____ (less/more) often; experience stress _____ (more/less) frequently; and have _____ (less/more) severe negative life events and daily hassles than other people do.

6. (a) Psychologists have become increasingly aware of the importance that close relationships play in our ability to deal with stressors and, ultimately, in our physical health; research has shown that socially isolated people have _____ health and _____ death rates than people who have many social contacts or relationships.

(b) To investigate the role played by personal relationships in stress and health, psychologists measure the level of _____ support, which refers to the resources provided by other people in times of need.

7. (a) _____ support of friends and relatives can modify our _____ of a stressor's significance, including the degree to which we perceive it as threatening or harmful; simply knowing that support and assistance are readily available may make the situation seem less threatening.

(b) The presence of supportive others seems to _____ (increase/decrease) the intensity of physical reactions to a stressor.

(c) _____ support can influence our health by making us _____ (more/less) likely to experience negative emotions; in contrast, loneliness and depression are unpleasant emotional states that _____ levels of stress hormones and _____ affect immune system functioning.

(d) Relationships with others can also be a significant _____ of stress; negative interactions with other people are _____ (less/more) effective in creating psychological distress than positive interactions are in improving well-being.

(e) When people are perceived as being judgmental, their presence may _____ the individual's physical reaction to a stressor; in one study the presence of a favorite dog was more effective than the presence of a friend in _____ reactivity to a stressor.

8. (a) Women are _____ (less/more) likely than men to serve as providers of support, which can be a very stressful role; women may be more likely to suffer from the _____ effect, becoming upset about negative life events that happen to other people whom they care about.

(b) Women are _____ likely than men to be upset about negative events that happen to their relatives, friends, and others who are close to them; in contrast, men are _____ likely to be distressed only by negative events that happen to their immediate family—their wives and children.

(c) In general, men tend to rely heavily on a close relationship with their spouse, placing _____ importance on relationships with other people; women, in contrast, are _____ likely to list close friends along with their spouse as confidants.

(d) Having a strong network of social support is generally _____ in your ability to cope with stressors and maintain health.

Coping: How People Deal with Stress
Learning Objectives

When you have finished studying this section of the chapter, you should be able to:

1. Define *coping*, identify the two basic forms of coping, and specify when each form is typically used.

2. Describe the most common coping strategies and explain how culture affects coping style.

*Read the section "Coping: How People Deal with Stress" and **write** your answers to the following:*

1. (a) The _____ that you use to deal with distressing events are examples of coping, which refers to the ways in which we try to change circumstances, or our interpretations of circumstances, to make them more favorable and less threatening; coping tends to be a(n) _____ , ongoing process.

(b) When coping is effective, we _____ to the situation and stress is reduced; on the other hand, _____ coping can involve thoughts and behaviors that intensify or prolong distress or that produce self-defeating outcomes.

(c) _____ coping serves many functions: (1) it involves realistically _____ the situation and determining what can be done to minimize the impact of the stressor; (2) it often includes developing _____ tolerance for negative life events, maintaining self-esteem, and keeping emotions in balance; and (3) _____ coping efforts are directed toward _____ important relationships during stressful experiences.

2. (a) _____ coping is aimed at managing or changing a threatening or harmful stressor; we are likely to use this strategy if we think something can be done to change the situation.

(b) When using _____ coping, we direct our efforts toward relieving or regulating the _____ impact of a stressful situation; although this strategy doesn't change the problem, it can help you feel better about the situation.

3. (a) When people rely on aggressive or risky efforts to change the situation, they are engaging in _____ coping; ideally this type of coping is direct and assertive, but when it is hostile or aggressive, _____ coping may well generate negative emotions in the people being confronted, damaging future relations with them.

(b) In contrast, _____ involves efforts to rationally analyze the situation, identify potential solutions, and then implement them.

(c) When you shift your attention away from the stressor and toward other activities, you're engaging in the _____ coping strategy

called _____ ; the basic goal is to escape or avoid the stressor and neutralize distressing emotions.

(d) Examples of the _____ strategy to deal with a stressful situation might include escaping into fantasy (also called wishful thinking), exercising, etc.; maladaptive forms include drug use or excessive sleeping.

(e) In the long run _____ tactics are associated with poor adjustment and symptoms of depression and anxiety.

4. (a) Seeking social support is the coping strategy that involves turning to friends, relatives, or other people for _____ , _____ , or _____ support.

(b) When you acknowledge the stressor but attempt to minimize or eliminate its emotional impact, you're engaging in the coping strategy called _____ ; in certain high-stress occupations, this strategy can help people cope with painful human problems.

(c) _____ is the refusal to acknowledge that the problem even exists; like escape-avoidance strategies, _____ can compound problems in situations that require immediate attention.

(d) Perhaps the most constructive emotion-focused coping strategy is _____ , in which the person not only tries to minimize the _____ emotional aspects of the situation but also tries to create _____ meaning by focusing on personal growth; this strategy is sometimes used to help make sense of tragic events or catastrophic loss.

(e) Most people use multiple coping strategies in stressful situations, often combining

_____ and

_____ forms of coping; different coping strategies may be used at different stages of dealing with a stressful encounter.

5. (a) Culture _____ (does/does not) seem to play an important role in the choice of coping strategy.

(b) Members of individualistic cultures tend to emphasize personal _____ and personal _____ in dealing with problems; thus they are _____ likely to seek social support in stressful situations than are members of collectivistic cultures; members of collectivistic cultures tend to be _____ oriented toward their social group, family, or community and to seek help with their problems.

(c) Individualists tend to favor _____ strategies, like _____ coping and _____, which involve directly changing the situation to achieve a better fit with their wishes or goals.

(d) In collectivistic cultures, a _____ (lesser/greater) emphasis is placed on controlling your personal reactions to a stressful situation rather than trying to control the situation itself; this _____ coping style emphasizes gaining control over inner feelings by accepting and accommodating yourself to existing realities.

6. Read the following and write the correct term in the space provided:

(a) When Marie turned down Massimo's offer to go out for dinner on Friday night, he was very disappointed. Upon reflection, however, he decided that Marie was really not his type anyway, and he'd be better off going out with someone else. Massimo's rationaliza-

tion of the situation reflects a(n) _____ explanatory style.

(b) When asked by her therapist to describe her husband, Cheryl said that he was very competitive and ambitious, he was always very busy, and any demands made on his time angered and irritated him. Cheryl's description suggests that her husband may have a(n) _____ behavior pattern.

(c) Irene constantly complains about her health, her job, and how hard her life is. She tends to dislike most of the people she meets and always seems to be in a grouchy mood. It appears that Irene suffers from _____ emotions.

(d) Masa is a member of a group of engineers in a large industrial plant in Tokyo. Whenever things get stressful, Masa tries to control the outward expression of his emotions and endeavors to accept the situation with maturity, sereniity, and flexibility. Masa's _____ coping style is more characteristic of _____ cultures than of _____ cultures.

(e) Shortly after he lost his job and his relationship with his girlfriend ended, Jim went to visit his family. Unfortunately, being with his family made him feel worse. The only time he felt better was when he was with the family dog. It is possible that Jim perceived his family as being _____ and the dog as being _____ and unconditionally supportive.

(f) Although Lambert was very disappointed when he didn't even come close to winning his first mountain bike race, he concluded that all the training he did and the knowledge he gained from the experience were very beneficial experiences. Lambert is using a very constructive emotion-focused strategy called _____ .

Graphic Organizer 2

Read the following statements and decide which researcher(s)
is (are) most likely to have expressed these views:

Statement	Researcher(s)
1. I believe that when we are faced with danger or any threatening or stress-producing situation we have an immediate physical reaction that involves the sympathetic nervous system and the endocrine system and the release of catecholamines. I call these internal physical changes the fight-or-flight response.	
2. When we published the results of our research, we realized that we were challenging the prevailing scientific view that the immune system operates independently of the brain and psychological processes. However, our results, which demonstrated that the immune response in rats could be classically conditioned, have been replicated by many other researchers.	
3. We were some of the earliest researchers to study stress, and in an attempt to measure the amount of stress people experienced, we developed the Social Readjustment Rating Scale. Our view at the time was that any changes, either positive or negative, would cause stress and high levels of stress, as measured by life change units, would lead to the development of serious physical and psychological problems.	
4. My research on stress, which I define as the nonspecific response of the body to any demand, led me to postulate a three-stage model to prolonged stress, called the general adaptation syndrome. I believe that the stress response involves the hypothalamus, pituitary gland, adrenal cortex, and release of hormones such as ACTH and corticosteroids.	
5. My view is that what causes us problems in the long run is not so much the major life events, which do cause stress, but the cumulative effect of everyday occurrences that annoy, irritate, and upset people. I call these *daily hassles* and have developed a scale to measure them. The number of daily hassles is a better predictor of physical illness and symptoms than the number of major life events experienced.	
6. In my view it is the way people characteristically explain their failures and defeats that determines who will persist and who will not. I think there are two basic types of explanatory style, an optimistic explanatory style and a pessimistic explanatory style. Those who use a pessimistic explanatory style experience more stress than those who use an optimistic explanatory style.	
7. We are a husband-and-wife team who collected immunological and psychological data from medical students, who face three-day exam periods several times each academic year. We have consistently found that even the rather commonplace stress of exams adversely affects the immune system.	

Review of Key Terms and Key Names 3

Martin Seligman
optimistic explanatory style
pessimistic explanatory style
Type A behavior pattern
Type B behavior pattern
social support
stress contagion effect
coping
problem-focused coping
emotion-focused coping
confrontive coping
planful problem solving
escape-avoidance
seeking social support
distancing
denial
positive reappraisal
emotional support
tangible support
informational support

Matching Exercise

Match the appropriate term/name with its definition or description.

1. _____ Behavioral and cognitive responses used to contend with stressors; involves efforts to change circumstances, or one's interpretations of circumstances, to make them more favorable and less threatening.

2. _____ A problem-focused coping strategy in which the person relies on aggressive or risky efforts to change the situation.

3. _____ American psychologist who conducted research on explanatory style and the role it plays in stress, health, and illness; also developed the learned helplessness model.

4. _____ An emotion-focused coping strategy in which the person shifts his or her attention away from the stressor and toward other activities.

5. _____ A behavioral and emotional style characterized by a sense of time urgency, hostility, and competitiveness.

6. _____ A category of social support that includes the expression of concern, empathy, and positive regard.

7. _____ A gender difference in the effects of social support that results from women becoming upset about negative life events that happen to other people.

8. _____ The resources provided by other people in times of need, including emotional support, tangible support, and informational support.

9. _____ An emotion-focused coping strategy that involves turning to friends, relatives, or other people for emotional, tangible, or informational support.

10. _____ An emotion-focused coping strategy that involves the refusal to acknowledge that the problem exists.

True/False Test

Indicate whether each item is true or false by placing T or F in the space next to each item.

1. ____ An optimistic explanatory style involves accounting for negative events or situations with internal, stable, and global explanations.

2. ____ Type B behavior pattern is a behavioral and emotional style characterized by a relatively relaxed and laid-back approach to situations and problems.

3. ____ Informational social support involves direct assistance, such as providing transportation, lending money, or helping with meals, child care, or household tasks.

4. ____ Emotion-focused coping efforts are primarily aimed at relieving or regulating the emotional impact of a stressful situation.

5. ____ The most constructive emotion-focused coping strategy is positive reappraisal, which involves not only minimizing the negative emotional aspects of the situation but also trying to create positive meaning by focusing on personal growth.

6. ____ A pessimistic explanatory style involves accounting for negative events or situations with external, unstable, and specific explanations.

7. ____ An emotion-focused coping strategy in which the individual acknowledges the stressor but attempts to minimize or eliminate its emotional impact is called distancing.

8. ____ Problem-focused coping efforts are primarily aimed at directly changing or managing a threatening or harmful stressor.

9. ____ A problem-focused coping strategy that involves efforts to rationally analyze the situation, identify potential solutions, and then implement them is called planful problem solving.

10. ____ Tangible social support involves offering helpful suggestions and advice to a person in distress.

Check your answers and review any areas of weakness before going on to the next section.

Something to Think About

It sometimes seems that everyone you meet is stressed out. There are things to be done, deadlines to be met, social and family obligations, financial pressures, work-related problems, and so on. How can we cope with all this stress? Is there anything that can be done? Fortunately, there are some strategies that we can adopt that may help. What advice would you give someone who is experiencing stress?

Check your answers and review any areas of weakness before doing the progress tests.

Progress Test 1

Review the complete chapter (including Concept Reviews and the boxed inserts), review all your study notes, and then test yourself on the following progress test. Check your answers. If you make a mistake, review your notes, review the relevant section of the study guide, and, if necessary, go back and read the appropriate part of your textbook.

1. Natasha experienced a great deal of anxiety when she had three exams on the same day. In this situation the exams are _____ and her response is called _____ .
   (a) stress; stressors
   (b) the biological component; the cognitive component
   (c) stressors; stress
   (d) the social component; the biological component

2. Dr. Turnbull uses the biopsychosocial model to guide his research into how psychological factors influence health, illness, and treatment. Dr. Turnbull is most likely a
   (a) developmental psychologist
   (b) health psychologist
   (c) psychoneuroimmunologist
   (d) psychiatrist

3. When Donald filled out the Social Readjustment Rating Scale, his score was over 300 points.
   (a) It is absolutely certain that Donald will develop physical and psychological problems.
   (b) It is impossible to accurately predict whether Donald will develop physical and psychological problems.

   (c) Donald has probably experienced very few daily hassles during the past year.
   (d) Donald's subjective appraisal of the events in his life during the previous year will have no bearing on his health and well-being.

4. Del got up late and nicked himself in three places when he was shaving. When he poured his coffee, he found that there was no cream in the fridge, and as he was tying his shoe laces, one of them broke. Richard Lazarus would call these incidents
   (a) major life events   (c) minor life events
   (b) daily hassles   (d) life change units

5. To get the money for a ticket to a rock concert, Ken has to either wash and wax the two family cars or wash and wax the kitchen and bathroom floors. In trying to decide between these two equally unappealing choices, Ken is likely to experience an _____ conflict.
   (a) approach-avoidance
   (b) approach-approach
   (c) avoidance-avoidance
   (d) escape-avoidance

6. Yui is leaving Japan to work and live in the United States and is very excited about the move. When Yui arrives and starts work in the United States, she is likely to
   (a) be much more relaxed and laid back than she was in Japan
   (b) experience increased levels of stress due to the acculturation process
   (c) become physically and psychologically ill within weeks
   (d) adapt to the new environment without experiencing any stress whatsoever

7. During icy driving conditions, a car in the opposite lane spun out of control and almost sideswiped Lynda's car. Lynda's muscles tensed, and her blood pressure, heartbeat, and pulse rose dramatically. This rapidly occurring chain of internal physical reactions is called the
   (a) startle-freeze response
   (b) general adaptation syndrome
   (c) fight-or-flight response
   (d) slip-and-slide response

8. Dr. Andrews and his colleagues replicated Ader and Cohen's original research and found that the suppression of the immune system was influenced by
   (a) Type A behavior

(b) the general adaptation syndrome
(c) classical conditioning
(d) aerobic exercise

9. Anders, a fifty-two-year-old insurance sales-man, is unexpectedly called into the sales man-ager's office and told that he is going to be laid off because the company is downsizing. Which stage of the general adaptation syndrome is Anders likely experiencing?

(a) alarm stage   (c) exhaustion stage
(b) resistance stage   (d) denial stage

10. After overcoming the initial shock of having his house broken into and many of his personal possessions stolen, Vincent calls the police for help and starts thinking of ways to help catch the burglar and retrieve his belongings. At this point, Vincent is most likely in the _____ stage of the general adapta-tion syndrome.

(a) alarm   (c) exhaustion
(b) resistance (d) denial

11. When Claudia became ill because of a viral infection, her immune system kicked into high gear to defend her by producing

(a) lymphocytes   (c) catecholamines
(b) corticosteroids (d) noradrenaline

12. Dr. Blackman studies the interconnections among psychological processes, the nervous and endocrine systems, and the immune system. Like other specialists in the field of psychoneu-roimmunology, Dr. Blackman is aware that researchers have discovered that

(a) the central nervous system and the immune system are directly linked
(b) the surfaces of lymphocytes contain recep-tor sites for neurotransmitters and hor-mones, including catecholamines and corti-sol
(c) lymphocytes themselves produce neuro-transmitters and hormones
(d) all of the above are true

13. When Darcy was taking his statistics exam, he was very anxious and nervous. According to researchers such as Janice Kiecolt-Glaser, the stress of exams

(a) adversely affects the immune system
(b) has no effect on the immune system
(c) has a beneficial effect on the immune system
(d) none of the above

14. Whenever anything goes wrong in his life, Dean typically feels that it must be something about him that causes the problem, and he believes that no amount of personal effort will improve his situation. Martin Seligman would say that Dean has

(a) a Type A behavior pattern
(b) an optimistic explanatory style
(c) a Type B behavior pattern
(d) a pessimistic explanatory style

15. Dr. Chambers has a very busy clinical practice. To clear his mind of all the problems he has to deal with in the course of a day and to cope with the high level of stress, he goes to the gym for a workout four or five times a week. Dr. Chambers is using a(n) _____ coping strategy called _____ .

(a) emotion-focused; escape-avoidance
(b) problem-focused; denial
(c) emotion-focused; denial
(d) problem-focused; confrontive coping

16. After his third month of low sales, Allen is called into the sales manager's office and told that he had better start meeting his quota or he will be laid off. The manager appears to be cop-ing with the problem of low sales by using a(n) _____ strategy called

_____ .

(a) problem-focused; confrontive coping
(b) emotion-focused; escape-avoidance
(c) problem-focused; planful problem solving
(d) emotion-focused; confrontive coping

17. When Argento encountered a large bear on the hiking trail, he experienced acute stress. Which of the following would Walter Cannon consider to be the correct sequence involved in Argento's fight-or-flight response?

(a) pituitary, hypothalamus, ACTH release, sympathetic nervous system
(b) secretion of corticosteroids, ACTH release, perspiration, cognitive appraisal
(c) hypothalamus, sympathetic nervous sys-tem, adrenal medulla, secretion of cate-cholamines
(d) alarm, resistance, exhaustion

18. When Lester was having personal and academ-ic problems while attending college, he went to see one of the counselors, who provided him with some helpful suggestions to improve his study habits and advised him to enroll in a remedial course to improve his writing skills.

The type of social support that Lester received is called _____ support.

(a) emotional   (c) informational
(b) tangible   (d) confrontive

19. According to Culture and Human Behavior Box 12.1, which of the following is not a pattern of acculturation?

(a) integration   (d) marginalization
(b) assimilation   (e) disembarkation
(c) separation

20. Critical Thinking Box 12.2 discusses personality and disease. It is pointed out that psychologists and other scientists are cautious in the statements they make about the connection between personality and health for which of the following reasons?

(a) Many studies investigating the role of psychological factors in disease are correlational.
(b) Personality factors might indirectly lead to disease via poor health habits.
(c) It may be that the disease influences a person's emotions, rather than the other way around.
(d) All of the above are true.

Progress Test 2

After you have checked your understanding of the material in Progress Test 1 and have done a complete chapter review with special focus on any areas of weakness, you are ready to assess your knowledge in Progress Test 2. Check your answers. If you make a mistake, review your notes, the relevant section of the study guide, and, if necessary, the appropriate part of your textbook.

1. When Janeen was caught in a large traffic jam, she experienced a severe headache. In this case the traffic jam is to _____ as her headache is to _____ .

(a) fight; flight
(b) stressor; stress reaction
(c) flight; fight
(d) stress reaction; stressor

2. For his birthday Liam has to decide between a pair of skis and a mountain bike. In trying to decide between these two equally attractive alternatives, Liam is likely to experience an _____ conflict.

(a) approach-avoidance

(b) approach-approach
(c) avoidance-avoidance
(d) escape-avoidance

3. Fifty-five-year-old Maxwell is a very impatient and competitive defense lawyer who often becomes angry over insignificant matters; he has a reputation for being hostile toward judges and prosecuting attorneys. Maxwell is likely to be classified as having a(n)

(a) Type A behavior pattern
(b) pessimistic explanatory style
(c) Type B behavior pattern
(d) optimistic explanatory style

4. In the above example it is very likely that Maxwell is at high risk for developing heart disease. The main component of his behavior that is most likely to contribute to health problems is his

(a) impatience   (c) anger
(b) competitiveness (d) hostility

5. Heloise is an emergency room nurse. Whenever she has a particularly hectic and stressful shift, she and some of the other nurses find themselves making jokes and facetious remarks about the patients and the doctors. Heloise is using an emotion-focused coping strategy called

(a) confrontive coping
(b) denial
(c) distancing
(d) positive reappraisal

6. Madge wants advice on how to cope with the stress of returning to college after being out of school for a number of years. She would be best advised to approach college

(a) with a sense of personal control and optimism
(b) with a realistic but pessimistic attitude
(c) using an emotion-focused coping strategy called distancing
(d) using an emotion-focused coping strategy called denial

7. Whenever Beth experiences problems in her relationship with her fiancee she typically goes to see her family to talk about her troubles. Beth is using a(n) _____ strategy called _____ .

(a) problem-focused; confrontive coping
(b) emotion-focused; distancing
(c) problem-focused; planful problem solving
(d) emotion-focused; seeking social support

8. Robert Ader is to _____ as Hans Selye is to _____ .
   (a) classically conditioning the immune system response; general adaptation syndrome
   (b) fight-or-flight response; the cognitive reappraisal model
   (c) daily hassles; life event units
   (d) Type A behavior pattern; Type B behavior pattern

9. Kari is a very laid-back, easygoing mail carrier. She loves her job because it allows her to meet people and get daily exercise at the same time. Kari is likely to be classified as having
   (a) a Type A behavior pattern
   (b) a high risk of heart disease
   (c) a Type B behavior pattern
   (d) stress contagion syndrome

10. Jacob was one of the unsuccessful candidates for a job, and naturally he was disappointed. However, in his habitual manner, he thought that he would have better luck next time, especially if he took some additional training to make him more qualified for the position. Martin Seligman would say that Jacob has a(n)
    (a) Type A behavior pattern
    (b) optimistic explanatory style
    (c) problem-focused coping style
    (d) pessimistic explanatory style

11. While researching a paper for her psychology class, Joyce came across the research of Ader and Cohen on conditioning and immune system functioning. She is likely to conclude that their work was important for which of the following reasons?
    (a) It challenged the prevailing scientific view that the immune system operates independently of the brain and psychological processes.
    (b) It demonstrated that humans could be conditioned to salivate just like Pavlov's dogs.
    (c) Before their research was published, everyone believed that there was a strong interconnectedness among psychological processes, nervous and endocrine system functions, and the immune system.
    (d) It proved conclusively that the immune system could not be classically conditioned.

12. After a bank was robbed, the bank tellers and the customers got up off the floor, where they had been held at gunpoint. Because it was such a frightening experience, they are likely to have experienced a rapidly occurring chain of internal physical reactions called
    (a) daily hassles
    (b) the fight-or-flight response
    (c) the general adaptation syndrome
    (d) the stress contagion effect

13. Following the bank robbery it is very likely that the people who were very frightened experienced increased sympathetic nervous system functioning, stimulation of the adrenal medulla, and release of hormones called
    (a) lymphocytes   (c) testosterone
    (b) catecholamines   (d) estrogen

14. During her final year of medical training, Lissette was under constant pressure; she never seemed to get enough sleep, was anxious and nervous most of the time, and experienced many physical symptoms and disorders. As a result of this prolonged stress, it is likely that her hypothalamus, pituitary gland, and adrenal cortex will work together to release stress-related hormones called
    (a) lymphocytes   (c) corticosteroids
    (b) catecholamines   (d) acetylcholine

15. Helga, a college student, was offered a new job. On the plus side the higher salary and increased benefits are appealing, but on the down side she will have to work longer hours, take on extra responsibilities, and have a longer commute to work. She needs the extra money but she also needs to keep her high GPA at college. Helga is likely experiencing a type of conflict called _____ conflict.
    (a) approach-approach
    (b) avoidance-avoidance
    (c) escape-avoidance
    (d) approach-avoidance

16. Gregory was very disappointed when he didn't get accepted in the graduate program at State University. Upon reflection, however, he decided that the preparations he made in putting his application together and the knowledge he gained from the interview were very beneficial experiences. Gregory is using a(n) _____ strategy called _____ .
    (a) problem-focused; confrontive coping
    (b) emotion-focused; positive reappraisal
    (c) problem-focused; planful problem solving
    (d) emotion-focused; downward comparison

17. Having moved to the United States from China two years ago, Mi-Ling feels equally comfortable with her new American friends and her Chinese relatives. According to Culture and Human Behavior Box 12.1, Mi-Ling has adopted the acculturation pattern of
    (a) assimilation
    (b) separation
    (c) marginalization
    (d) integration

18. According to the Application section, which of the following is *not* recommended for helping someone in distress?
    (a) Give advice that the person has not asked for.
    (b) Be a good listener and show concern and interest.
    (c) Ask questions that encourage the person under stress to express his or her feelings and emotions.
    (d) Express affection for the person whether by a warm hug or simply a pat on the arm.
    (e) Be willing to invest time and attention in helping.

19. Critical Thinking Box 12.2 discusses personality factors and disease and concludes that
    (a) personality factors are the major cause of disease
    (b) a person's health at any given time is influenced by the complex interaction of biological, psychological, and social factors
    (c) the results of research on this topic are not valid because experimental rather than correlational techniques were used
    (d) poor health habits rather than personality factors are the major cause of disease

20. According to In Focus Box 12.3, which of the following strategies is recommended to minimize stress?
    (a) Exercise regularly.
    (b) Avoid or minimize stimulants.
    (c) Regularly practice a relaxation technique.
    (d) All of the above are recommended.

Answers
Introduction: What Is Stress?

1. (a) emotional; exceeding
   (b) cognitive appraisal; resources
   (c) stress; health, illness, treatment
   (d) biological, psychological; social

Sources of Stress

1. (a) events; situations
   (b) change; behavior; lifestyle
   (c) life change units
   (d) 150; increased/greater

2. (a) weak; don't
   (b) subjective; the same
   (c) change; negative; positive or desirable
   (d) undesirable; change

3. (a) Richard Lazarus
   (b) is; better
   (c) cumulative
   (d) major life events; major life event

4. (a) conflict; approach; avoid
   (b) approach-approach
   (c) avoidance-avoidance
   (d) approach-avoidance

5. (a) social; chronic
   (b) lowest; poverty-stricken; fewer
   (c) cultures; culture

6. (a) health
   (b) biopsychosocial
   (c) high; an increased
   (d) daily hassles
   (e) approach-approach

Graphic Organizer 1

1. approach-avoidance; high
2. approach-approach; low
3. approach-avoidance; high
4. avoidance-avoidance; medium
5. approach-approach; low
6. avoidance-avoidance; medium

Matching Exercise 1

1. Richard Lazarus
2. approach-approach conflict
3. conflict
4. daily hassles
5. health psychology
6. biopsychosocial model

True/False Test 1

1. F	3. T	5. T
2. T	4. F	6. T

Physical Effects of Stress: The Mind–Body Connection

1. (a) indirectly
   (b) cognitive; cognitive
   (c) directly

2. (a) nervous; brain; endocrine; immune
   (b) fight; flight
   (c) Walter Cannon; sympathetic nervous; endocrine
   (d) sympathetic nervous; adrenaline; noradrenaline
   (e) trigger; twenty; sixty
   (f) short-term; survival; prolonged; prolonged; harmful

3. (a) Cannon's; prolonged
   (b) prolonged; adrenal; stomach; thymus; lymph
   (c) physical; general adaptation

4. (a) alarm; alarm; adrenal medulla
   (b) resistance; alarm; resistance
   (c) exhaustion; alarm; exhaustion

5. (a) endocrine; hypothalamus; pituitary; adrenal
   (b) hypothalamus; pituitary; adrenal
   (c) reduce; enhance

Stress and the Immune System

1. (a) surveillance
   (b) lymphocytes
   (c) Lymphocytes

2. (a) independently; classically
   (b) psychoneuroimmunology; psycho-; -neuro-; -immunology
   (c) psychoneuroimmunology; sympathetic; neurotransmitters; hormones; neurotransmitters; hormones
   (d) nervous; endocrine; immune

3. (a) reduce; diminish
   (b) adversely; impair
   (c) heighten; does not translate
   (d) genetic; nutrition, exercise; bacteria, viruses
   (e) small; small; may not

4. (a) fight-or-flight
   (b) catecholamines
   (c) resistance
   (d) psychoneuroimmunology
   (e) lymphocytes

Matching Exercise 2

1. Walter Cannon
2. lymphocytes
3. catecholamines
4. Hans Selye
5. corticosteroids
6. alarm stage
7. immune system

True/False Test 2

1. T	5. F
2. F	6. T
3. T	7. T
4. T	

Individual Factors That Influence the Response to Stress

1. (a) control; reduces; decreases
   (b) control; no more
   (c) a sense of control
2. (a) control; less
   (b) control; enhancing
   (c) control; increase; decreases
3. (a) Martin Seligman; external, unstable; specific; internal, stable; global
   (b) no amount; more
   (c) most
   (d) stable
4. (a) anxious, depressed, angry; hostile
   (b) more; more; more; more; far greater
   (c) transient; decreases; improves
5. (a) time; hostility; anger; irritation; ambition; competitiveness; relaxed; laid back
   (b) twice; were not
   (c) hostility; anger; resentment
   (d) hostile; suspicious, mistrustful
   (e) hostility
   (f) hostile; larger; more; more; more
6. (a) poorer; higher
   (b) social
7. (a) social; appraisal
   (b) decrease
   (c) social; less; increase; adversely
   (d) source; more
   (e) increase; lowering
8. (a) more; stress contagion
   (b) more; more
   (c) less; more
   (d) advantageous

Coping: How People Deal with Stress

1. (a) strategies; dynamic
   (b) adapt; maladaptive
   (c) adaptive; evaluating; emotional; adaptive; preserving
2. (a) problem-focused
   (b) emotion-focused; emotional
3. (a) confrontive; confrontive
   (b) planful problem solving
   (c) emotion-focused; escape-avoidance
   (d) escape-avoidance
   (e) escape-avoidance
4. (a) emotional, tangible; informational
   (b) distancing
   (c) denial; denial
   (d) positive reappraisal; negative; positive
   (e) problem-focused; emotion-focused
5. (a) does
   (b) autonomy; responsibility; less; more
   (c) problem-focused; confrontive; planful problem solving
   (d) greater; emotion-focused
6. (a) optimistic
   (b) Type A
   (c) chronic negative
   (d) emotion-focused; collectivistic; individualistic
   (e) judgmental; nonjudgmental
   (f) positive reappraisal

Graphic Organizer 2

1. Walter Cannon
2. Robert Ader and Nicholas Cohen
3. Thomas Holmes and Richard Rahe
4. Hans Selye
5. Richard Lazarus
6. Martin Seligman
7. Janice Kiecolt-Glaser and Ronald Glaser

Matching Exercise 3

1. coping
2. confrontive coping
3. Martin Seligman
4. escape-avoidance
5. Type A behavior pattern
6. emotional support
7. stress contagion effect
8. social support

9. seeking social support

10. denial

True/False Test 3

1. F	5. T	9. T
2. T	6. F	10. F
3. F	7. T	
4. T	8. T	

Something to Think About

Chapter 12 contains a lot of information about stress, health, and coping. The more we know about these topics, the better we can understand what happens when we are placed in stressful situations. A good place to start in giving advice to someone is to explain what stressors are and what the stress reaction is. Identifying potential sources of stress, from major life events to daily hassles, is useful, and noting how our subjective cognitive appraisal of stressors influences our reactions is also important. There are physical reactions and psychological and social factors that influence our response to stress, and it is helpful to know about these, too. There are many different coping strategies that can be used, some of which are more adaptive than others.

Progress Test 1

1. c	8. c	15. a
2. b	9. a	16. a
3. b	10. b	17. c
4. b	11. a	18. c
5. c	12. d	19. e
6. b	13. a	20. d
7. c	14. d	

Progress Test 2

1. b	8. a	15. d
2. b	9. c	16. b
3. a	10. b	17. d
4. d	11. a	18. a
5. c	12. b	19. b
6. a	13. b	20. d
7. d	14. c	

Chapter 13　Psychological Disorders

OVERVIEW　Chapter 13 explores psychological disorders. The distinction between normal and abnormal behavior is addressed, and the criteria for diagnosing psychological disorders, according to DSM-IV, are presented. The prevalence of psychological disorders is examined, and it is pointed out that these disorders are much more common than previously thought.

The anxiety disorders, including generalized anxiety disorder, panic disorder, phobias, posttraumatic stress disorder, and obsessive-compulsive disorder, are discussed. The prevalence, course, and possible causes of these psychological disorders are identified.

Mood disorders involve serious, persistent disturbances in emotions that cause psychological discomfort and/or impair the ability to function. The symptoms of major depression and bipolar disorder are identified, and the course and potential causes of these mood disorders are discussed.

Dissociative experiences involve a disruption in awareness, memory, and personal identity. The different types of dissociative disorders, including dissociative amnesia, dissociative fugue, and dissociative identity disorder (DID), are examined, and the main symptoms of each are presented. The DID controversy is discussed, and theories of causation are explored.

Schizophrenia is defined, and the main symptoms are identified. The positive symptoms represent excesses in normal functioning and include delusions, hallucinations, and severely disorganized thought processes, speech, and behavior. The negative symptoms reflect deficits or decreases in normal functioning and include flat affect, alogia, and avolition. Three subtypes of schizophrenia are discussed, and the course and prevalence of the disorder are presented. Various theories of the causes of schizophrenia are explored, and the conclusion is reached that no single factor has emerged as causing this psychological disorder.

Introduction: Understanding Psychological Disorders

Learning Objectives

When you have finished studying this section of the chapter, you should be able to:

1. Define *psychopathology* and specify what characterizes abnormal behavior.

2. Provide the formal definition of a psychological disorder.

3. Explain what DSM-IV is and describe how it was developed.

4. Identify the prevalence of psychological disorders.

*Read the section "Introduction: Understanding Psychological Disorders" and **write** your answers to the following:*

1. (a) The line that divides normal and crazy behavior _____ (is/is not) sharply defined; in many instances, the difference between normal and abnormal behavior is a matter of _____ and is often determined by the social or cultural context in which a particular behavior occurs.

   (b) Psychopathology is defined as the scientific study of the _____ , _____ , and development of psychological disorders.

   (c) There is still a

      _____

      attached to suffering from a mental disorder; people are _____ to seek the help of a mental health professional.

2. (a) Although the terms are interchangeable, _____ generally prefer the term *psychological disorder*, whereas _____ tend to prefer the term *mental disorder*.

   (b) A psychological, or mental, disorder can be defined as a pattern of _____ or _____ symptoms that cause significant personal _____ , impair the ability to _____ in one or more important areas of life, or both; these symptoms must represent a serious departure from prevailing social and cultural norms.

   (c) DSM-IV stands for the _____ and _____ *Manual of Mental Disorders*, fourth edition; it was published by the American Psychiatric Association in 1994 and represents the consensus of a wide range of mental health professionals and organizations.

   (d) DSM-IV is a book that describes approximately _____ specific psycho-

logical disorders, including their _____ , the exact _____ that must be met to make a _____ , and the typical course of a particular mental disorder.

   (e) DSM-IV provides mental health professionals with (1) a common _____ to label mental disorders and (2) comprehensive _____ to diagnose mental disorders.

3. (a) The National Comorbidity Survey (NCS) surveyed a representative sample of Americans aged fifteen to fifty-four and asked them about symptoms of psychological disorder that they had experienced (1) at

      _____

      and (2) within

      _____ .

   (b) Almost one out of two adults (48 percent) had experienced the symptoms of a psychological disorder at some point during _____ ; 30 percent of the people had experienced the symptoms of a psychological disorder during

      _____ .

   (c) About 80 percent of those who had suffered from the symptoms of a mental disorder during _____ had not sought any type of treatment or help for their symptoms.

   (d) It is clear that many people who could potentially benefit from mental health treatment do not seek it; this may reflect lack of _____ about psychological disorders, or the fact that a(n) _____ still exists when it comes to seeking treatment for psychological symptoms, or lack of services or resources.

   (e) Even though the incidence of mental disorders is much higher than previously believed, _____ (very few/most) people weather the symptoms without becoming completely debilitated and without professional intervention; really serious conditions that demanded immediate treatment affected _____ to _____ percent of the people surveyed.

(f) The NCS also found that the prevalence of certain mental disorders _____ (were the same/differed) for men and women; women had a(n) _____ prevalence of anxiety and depression, whereas men had a(n) _____ prevalence of substance abuse disorders.

(g) DSM-IV has four categories of mental disorders that are some of the most common ones that mental health professionals encounter; these are _____ disorders, _____ disorders, _____ disorders, and _____ .

Anxiety Disorders
Learning Objectives

When you have finished studying this section of the chapter, you should be able to:

1. Describe the main symptoms of the anxiety disorders.
2. Differentiate between pathological anxiety and normal anxiety.
3. Identify the symptoms that characterize generalized anxiety disorder and panic disorder.
4. Describe the phobias and how they have been explained.

*Read the section "Anxiety Disorders" and **write** your answers to the following:*

1. (a) Anxiety is defined as an unpleasant emotional state characterized by _____ arousal and feelings of _____ , _____ , and worry that often hit during personal

crises and everyday conflicts; when it alerts you to a realistic threat, anxiety is _____ and _____ .

(b) As your internal alarm system, anxiety puts you on _____ alert, preparing you to defensively fight or flee potential dangers; it also puts you on _____ alert, making you focus your attention squarely on the threatening situation and become extremely vigilant.

(c) In the anxiety disorders, however, the anxiety is _____ .

(d) Three features distinguish normal anxiety from pathological anxiety: (1) pathological anxiety is _____ ; it is provoked by perceived threats that are _____ or _____ , and the anxiety response is out of proportion to the actual importance of the situation; (2) pathological anxiety is _____ ; the person can't shut off the alarm reaction, even when he or she knows it's _____ ; and (3) pathological anxiety is _____ ; it _____ with relationships, job or academic performance, or everyday activity.

2. (a) As a symptom, anxiety occurs in many different mental disorders; in anxiety disorder, however, anxiety is the _____ symptom and is manifested differently in each of the anxiety disorders.

(b) In _____ anxiety disorder and _____ disorder, the main symptom is intense anxiety that often does not seem to be triggered by anything specific.

(c) In the _____ , severe anxiety occurs in response to a specific object or situation.

(d) In _____ disorder, anxiety is triggered by memories of a traumatic experience.

(e) In _____ disorder, patho-
logical anxiety occurs in response to uncontrollable thoughts or urges to perform certain actions.

3. (a) _____ , _____ ,
_____ , and excessive apprehen-
sion is the main feature of generalized anxiety disorder; people with this disorder are
constantly tense and anxious, and their anxiety is pervasive.

(b) Normally, our anxiety quickly
_____ when a threatening situ-
ation is resolved; in generalized anxiety disorder, however, when one source of worry is
removed, another quickly moves in to take
its place, and because of this, generalized
anxiety disorder is sometimes referred to as
_____ anxiety.

4. (a) A panic attack is a(n) _____
episode of _____ anxiety that
rapidly escalates in intensity; the most common symptoms are a(n) _____
heart, _____ breathing, breathlessness, and a choking sensation; these are
often accompanied by sweating, trembling,
light-headedness, chills, or hot flashes.

(b) Along with these symptoms are feelings of
_____ and the belief that one is
about to die, go crazy, or completely lose control; a panic attack typically peaks within
_____ minutes of onset and
then gradually subsides.

(c) When panic attacks occur _____
and _____ , the person is said
to be suffering from panic disorder; the
_____ of panic attacks is
highly variable and quite unpredictable;
understandably, people with panic disorder
are quite apprehensive about when and
where the next panic attack will hit.

5. (a) Both _____ and

_____ causes seem to be
implicated in panic disorder; on the
_____ side, family and twin
studies have found that panic disorder tends
to run in families, but _____ alone
does not provide a complete explanation.

(b) _____ , people with
panic disorder are unusually sensitive to the
signs of physical arousal and they may be
_____ ; for example,
when normal subjects and panic disorder
patients are given a substance, like caffeine,
that triggers _____
arousal, only the panic disorder patients
react with a full-blown panic attack.

(c) According to the

_____

theory of panic disorder, people with panic
disorder tend to misinterpret the physical
signs of arousal as catastrophic and dangerous; after a frightening initial attack, the
person becomes extremely _____
about suffering another attack; in turn, he
or she becomes sensitized to physical
changes that might signal the onset of
another frightening episode.

(d) After a series of panic attacks, the person
becomes behaviorally _____ to
respond with fear to the physical symptoms
of arousal, and once established, such a
_____ response, combined with
catastrophic thoughts, can act as a spring-
board for repeated panic attacks, leading to
panic disorder.

6. (a) A phobia is a(n) _____ ,
_____ fear that is triggered by a
specific object or situation; encountering the
feared situation or object can provoke a full-
fledged _____ in some
people.

(b) People with a(n) _____ phobia are terrified of a particular object or situation and go to great lengths to avoid that object or situation, even though they know the fear is _____ .

(c) In the general population _____ phobias, such as fear of dogs or snakes, are extremely common; in comparison, severe phobias are characterized by incapacitating _____ and _____ that significantly interfere with daily life.

(d) About _____ percent of the population will experience a(n) _____ phobia at some point in their lives; more than _____ as many women as men suffer from a(n) _____ phobia.

7. The objects or situations that produce specific phobias tend to fall into four broad categories:

(a) Fear of particular _____ , such as flying; driving; or being in tunnels, bridges, elevators, or enclosed places.

(b) Fear of _____ of the natural _____ , such as heights, water, thunderstorms, or lightning.

(c) Fear of _____ or _____ , including fear of injections, needles, and medical or dental procedures.

(d) Fear of _____ and _____ , such as snakes, spiders, dogs, cats, slugs, or bats.

8. (a) People with agoraphobia fear having a(n) _____ in a public place from which it might be difficult to escape or get help; consequently, they tend to avoid situations that they think might provoke a(n) _____ and situations from which they would be unable to escape or get help if they did suffer a(n) _____ .

(b) Many agoraphobics become prisoners in their own homes, unable to go beyond their front doors; not surprisingly, then, agoraphobia is the phobia for which people _____ (least/most) often seek professional help.

9. (a) A person with _____ phobia is paralyzed by fear of _____ situations, especially if the situation involves performing even routine behaviors in front of others; the core of _____ phobia seems to be an irrational fear of being embarrassed, judged, or critically evaluated by others.

(b) People with _____ phobia recognize that their fear is excessive and unreasonable, but they still approach _____ situations with tremendous anxiety; in severe cases, they may even suffer a(n) _____ in _____ situations.

(c) When the fear of being embarrassed or failing in public significantly interferes with daily life, it qualifies as a(n) _____ phobia.

(d) Because of the avoidance of _____ situations, people with _____ phobia often have very low self-esteem, poor social skills, and few friends; they may also suffer from occupational or academic underachievement, have intense test anxiety, and have a fear of asking questions or making comments.

10. (a) _____ conditioning may well be involved if a specific phobia can be traced back to some sort of traumatic event; the feared object is the _____ stimulus and the learned fear is the _____ response.

(b) _____ conditioning is involved in helping to maintain the avoidance behaviors that accompany many phobias; taking steps to avoid the feared object is an example of _____ reinforcement.

(c) _____ learning is involved in the development of phobias that are the result of _____ others.

11. (a) Humans seem to be _____ prepared to acquire fears of certain animals and situations that were important survival threats in human evolutionary history; people also seem predisposed to develop phobias toward creatures that arouse _____ , like slugs, maggots, or cockroaches.

(b) Instinctively, it seems, many people find these creatures _____ , possibly because they are associated with disease, infection, or filth. Such phobias may reflect a fear of _____ or infection that is also based on human evolutionary history.

Posttraumatic Stress Disorder: Re-Experiencing the Trauma

Learning Objectives

When you have finished studying this section of the chapter, you should be able to:

1. Define *posttraumatic stress disorder (PTSD)* and *obsessive-compulsive disorder* and state what they have in common.

2. List the main characteristics of PTSD and state what causes it.

3. Identify the main symptoms of obsessive-compulsive disorder and list the most common types of obsessions and compulsions.

*Read the section "Posttraumatic Stress Disorder: Re-Experiencing the Trauma" and **write** your answers to the following:*

1. (a) Posttraumatic stress disorder (PTSD) is a longlasting anxiety disorder that develops in response to an extreme _____ or _____ trauma; extreme

traumas are events that produce intense feelings of _____ and _____ , such as a serious physical injury or threat of injury to yourself or to loved ones.

(b) Originally, PTSD was primarily associated with direct experiences of _____ ; it's now known that PTSD can also develop in survivors (as well as witnesses) of other sorts of extreme traumas, such as _____ , physical or sexual _____ , and random shooting sprees and can be experienced by children as well as adults.

(c) Three core symptoms characterize PTSD: (1) the person _____ recalls the event, replaying it in his or her mind, it is often unwanted or intrusive, and it interferes with normal thought processes; (2) the person avoids _____ or _____ that tend to trigger memories of the experience and undergoes a general numbing of _____ responsiveness; and (3) the person experiences the increased physical _____ associated with anxiety; he or she may be easily _____ , experience _____ disturbances, have problems concentrating and remembering, and be prone to irritability or angry outbursts.

(d) Several factors influence the likelihood of developing posttraumatic stress disorder: (1) people with a personal or family history of psychological disorders are _____ (more/less) likely to develop PTSD when exposed to extreme trauma; (2) the magnitude of the trauma plays _____ (a small/an important) role—_____ (less/more) extreme stressors are more likely to produce PTSD; and (3) when people undergo _____ , the incidence of PTSD can be quite high.

2. (a) Obsessive-compulsive disorder is an anxiety disorder in which a person's life is dominated by _____ thoughts (_____) and behaviors (_____).

   (b) Obsessions are _____ , _____ , _____ thoughts or mental images that cause the person great anxiety and distress; they have little basis in reality and are often extremely farfetched.

   (c) A compulsion is a(n) _____ behavior that the person feels driven to perform; typically, compulsions are _____ behaviors that must be carried out in a certain pattern or sequence.

   (d) Compulsions may be _____ physical behaviors, such as repeatedly washing the hands, or they may be _____ mental behaviors, such as counting or reciting certain phrases to oneself; when the person tries to resist performing the behavior, unbearable _____ , _____ , and distress result.

3. (a) People may experience _____ obsessions or compulsions, but, more commonly, they are _____ present; obsessions and compulsions are often linked in some way, even if the behaviors bear little logical relationship to the feared consequences; in all cases, obsessive-compulsives feel that something _____ will happen if the compulsive action is left undone.

   (b) Obsessions and compulsions take a(n) _____ (different/similar) shape in different countries; the _____ of the obsessions and compulsions tends to mirror the particular culture's concerns and beliefs.

   (c) Although researchers are far from fully understanding the causes of obsessive-compulsive disorder, _____ factors seem to be involved; a deficiency in the neurotransmitter _____ has been implicated in the disorder.

   (d) In addition, obsessive-compulsive disorder has been linked with dysfunction in specific brain areas, such as the _____ lobes, which play a key role in our ability to think and plan ahead, and the caudate nucleus, which is involved in regulating _____ .

4. Read the following and write the correct term in the space provided:

   (a) Dr. Janz is a psychiatrist who assesses and treats patients in a mental institution. Dr. Sloane is a clinical psychologist who works with a similar population of patients in a mental health clinic. Dr. Janz is likely to describe his patients as suffering from _____ disorders, whereas Dr. Sloane is more likely to use the term _____ disorder when referring to his patients' problems.

   (b) Seventeen-year-old Brad has a shaven head; his nose, ears, and navel are pierced; and each contain numerous rings. Shortly after purchasing a new pair of jeans, he cut and tore horizontal slits across the thigh and knee areas of each leg. Brad would be classified as _____ .

   (c) Mr. and Mrs. Jefferson want to hire a new housecleaner. Mr. Jefferson suggests that the best person would be someone who has an excessive dislike and fear of dirt, germs, and insects and who deals with anxiety about contamination by using a very thorough cleaning, washing, and disinfecting routine. Mrs. Jefferson thinks that any person fitting that description might have a problem called _____ disorder.

(d) Mr. Alviro suffers from intense anxiety most of the time. He is nervous and worried and is overly concerned about a wide range of life circumstances with little or no justification. Mr. Alviro probably suffers from _____ disorder.

(e) Maurice is very quiet and introverted. He is painfully shy in the presence of other people and has dropped many courses at college simply because they involved oral presentations. He has not managed to get a job because he has intense fear and anxiety about being interviewed. Maurice would probably be classified as having

_____ .

(f) Mr. Ng frequently recalls the horrors he and his family experienced in his native Cambodia. He suffers from sleep disturbances and is often awakened by terrifying nightmares. Mr. Ng is experiencing _____ disorder.

(g) Ever since the sudden death of her husband, Mrs. Baxter has experienced a number of terrifying and unexpected episodes in which her heart suddenly starts to pound for no apparent reason; she typically feels a choking sensation, has trouble breathing, and starts to sweat and tremble. Mrs. Baxter is probably experiencing

_____ .

Graphic Organizer 1

List the main symptoms of each of the following anxiety disorders:

General Anxiety Disorder	Panic Disorder	Phobias
1.	1.	1.
2.		2.

Obsessive-Compulsive Disorder	Posttraumatic Stress Disorder
1.	1.
2.	

Review of Key Terms 1

psychopathology
psychological disorder
  (mental disorder)
DSM-IV
anxiety
anxiety disorders
generalized anxiety
  disorder
panic attack
panic disorder

phobia
specific phobia
agoraphobia
social phobia
posttraumatic stress
  disorder (PTSD)
obsessive-compulsive
  disorder
obsessions
compulsions

Matching Exercise

Match the appropriate term with its definition or description.

1. _____ The scientific study of the origins, symptoms, and development of psychological disorders.

2. _____ Abbreviation for the *Diagnostic and Statistical Manual of Mental Disorders*, fourth edition; the book published by the American Psychiatric Association that describes the specific symptoms and diagnostic guidelines for different psychological disorders.

3. _____ An anxiety disorder in which the symptoms of anxiety are triggered by intrusive, repetitive thoughts and urges to perform certain actions.

4. _____ An unpleasant emotional state characterized by physical arousal and feelings of tension, apprehension, and worry.

5. _____ An irrational fear triggered by a specific object or situation.

6. _____ An anxiety disorder in which chronic and persistent symptoms of anxiety develop in response to an extreme physical or psychological trauma.

7. _____ An anxiety disorder involving the extreme and irrational fear of experiencing a panic attack in a public situation and being unable to escape or get help.

8. _____ An anxiety disorder characterized by an extreme or irrational fear of a specific object or situation that interferes with the ability to function in daily life.

True/False Test

Indicate whether each statement is true or false by placing T or F in the blank space next to each item.

1. ____ Compulsions refer to repeated, intrusive, and uncontrollable irrational thoughts or mental images that cause extreme anxiety and distress.

2. ____ A pattern of behavioral and psychological symptoms that cause significant personal distress, impair the ability to function in one or more important areas of daily life, or both is called a psychological (or mental) disorder.

3. ____ Generalized anxiety disorder is characterized by excessive, global, and persistent symptoms of anxiety; also called free-floating anxiety.

4. ____ Panic disorder is an anxiety disorder in which the person experiences frequent and unexpected panic attacks.

5. ____ Obsessions refer to repetitive behaviors or mental acts that are performed to prevent or reduce anxiety.

6. ____ Social phobia is an anxiety disorder involving the extreme and irrational fear of being embarrassed, judged, or scrutinized by others in social situations.

7. ____ Anxiety disorders are a category of psychological disorders in which extreme anxiety is the main diagnostic feature and causes significant disruptions in the person's cognitive, behavioral, and interpersonal functioning.

8. ____ A panic attack is a sudden episode of extreme anxiety that rapidly escalates in intensity.

> Check your answers and review any areas of weakness before going on to the next section.

Mood Disorders: Emotions Gone Awry
Learning Objectives

When you have finished studying this section of the chapter, you should be able to:

1. Explain what is meant by mood disorders, and describe how disturbed emotions cause psychological distress and impair daily functioning.

2. Identify the symptoms of major depression and explain what dysthymic disorder is.

3. Describe the course of depression and state how prevalent it is.

*Read the section "Mood Disorders: Emotions Gone Awry" and **write** your answers to the following:*

1. (a) In mood disorders, emotions violate the _____ of normal moods in quality, intensity, and duration; mood changes persist much longer than the normal fluctuations in moods that we all experience.

   (b) DSM-IV formally defines a mood disorder as a(n) _____ , _____ disturbance in a person's emotions that causes _____ discomfort, impairs the ability to _____ , or both.

2. (a) To be diagnosed with major depression, a person must display most of these symptoms for _____ weeks or longer; in many cases, there doesn't seem to be any _____ reason for the persistent feeling of depression; in other cases, a person's downward emotional spiral has been triggered by some _____ event or _____ situation.

   (b) If a family member or close friend dies, it is completely _____ to feel despondent and sad for _____ months as part of the mourning or bereavement process; as a general rule, if a person's ability to function after the death of a loved one is still seriously impaired after _____ months, major depression is suspected.

   (c) _____ is always a potential risk in major depression; pervasive negativity and pessimism are manifested in

_____ thoughts or a preoccupation with _____ .

(d) Abnormal _____ patterns are another hallmark of major depression; the amount of time spent in nondreaming, deeply relaxed sleep is greatly _____ , the person experiences sporadic REM periods of varying lengths, and episodes of sleeplessness are common; less commonly, some depressed people sleep excessively, sometimes as much as eighteen hours a day.

3. (a) In contrast to major depression, which significantly impairs a person's ability to function, some people experience a less severe form of depression called _____ disorder; this mood disorder is a(n) _____ , low-grade depression that is characterized by many of the symptoms of depression, but the symptoms are less intense.

(b) Usually, _____ disorder develops in response to some stressful event or trauma; although the person functions adequately, the negative mood can persist indefinitely, creating a chronic case of the blues.

(c) Some people with _____ disorder experience _____ depression; that is, they experience one or more episodes of major depression on top of their ongoing _____ disorder; as they recover from the episode of major depression, they return to the less intense depressed symptoms of _____ disorder.

4. (a) Depression is the _____ (least/most) common of all the psychological disorders; in any given year about _____ million Americans are affected by major depression.

(b) Women are about _____ as likely as men to be diagnosed with major depression; the lifetime odds of experiencing major depression are approximately 1 out of _____ for females and 1 out _____ for males.

(c) Most people who experience major depression try to cope with the symptoms _____ (by/without) seeking professional help; when depression _____ (is/is not) treated, it may become a recurring mental disorder that progressively becomes more severe.

(d) Better than _____ of all people who have been through one episode of major depression can expect a relapse, usually within two years; with each recurrence, the symptoms _____ (decrease/increase) in severity and the time between major depression episodes _____ (decreases/increases).

(e) For millions of people with seasonal affective disorder (SAD), repeated episodes of depression are as predictable as the changing _____ , especially the onset of _____ and _____ ; in its most common form, episodes of depression recur in the _____ and _____ months, when there is the least amount of sunlight; it is more common among _____ and those who live in the northern latitudes.

Bipolar Disorder: An Emotional Roller Coaster
Learning Objectives

When you have finished studying this section of the chapter, you should be able to:

1. Define _bipolar disorder_ and specify what types of moods are typical of this disorder,

2. Describe what characterizes a manic episode and what cyclothymic disorder is.

3. Describe the course of bipolar disorder and state how prevalent it is.

4. Identify the factors that contribute to mood disorders.

Read the section "Bipolar Disorder: An Emotional Roller Coaster" and **write** *your answers to the following:*

1. (a) In contrast to major depression, bipolar disorder (previously called

   _____) almost always involves abnormal moods at both ends of the emotional spectrum; in most cases of bipolar disorder, the person experiences extreme mood swings.

   (b) Episodes of incapacitating _____ alternate with shorter periods of extreme euphoria called _____ episodes; for most people with the disorder, a(n) _____ episode immediately precedes or follows a bout with major _____ , with a small percentage of people experiencing only _____ episodes.

2. (a) _____ episodes typically begin suddenly and symptoms escalate rapidly; people sleep little, have boundless energy, and are uncharacteristically euphoric, expansive, and excited for several days or longer.

   (b) During a(n) _____ episode, the person's _____ is wildly inflated and he exudes supreme _____ that is reflected in grandiose (but often delusional) plans for obtaining wealth, power, and fame.

   (c) Words are spoken at a rapid rate and are often slurred as the _____ person tries to keep up with his own thought processes; attention is easily distracted by virtually anything, triggering a(n)

_____ , in which thoughts rapidly and loosely shift from topic to topic.

   (d) The ability to function during a(n)

   _____ episode is severely impaired; _____ is usually required, partly to protect people from the potential consequences of their own poor judgment and inappropriate behavior.

   (e) During _____ episodes, people can run up a mountain of bills, disappear for weeks at a time, become sexually promiscuous, or commit illegal acts; very commonly, the person becomes _____ or _____ abusive when others question his grandiose plans.

3. (a) Some people experience a milder but chronic form of bipolar disorder called

   _____ disorder.

   (b) In _____ disorder , people experience moderate but frequent mood swings for two years or longer; these mood swings are not severe enough to qualify as either _____ disorder or major

   _____ .

   (c) Often, people with _____ disorder are perceived as being extremely moody, unpredictable, and inconsistent.

4. (a) The onset of bipolar disorder typically occurs in the person's _____ ; the mood swings tend to start and stop much more abruptly than the mood changes of major depression, and the _____ and _____ episodes tend to be much shorter, lasting from a few days to a couple of months.

   (b) Annually, about _____ million Americans suffer from bipolar disorder, and, unlike major depression, there

   _____ (are/are no) sex differences in the rate at which bipolar disorder occurs.

(c) In the vast majority of cases, bipolar disorder is a(n) _____ mental disorder; a small percentage of the cases display _____ , experiencing four or five _____ or _____ episodes every year; more commonly bipolar disorder tends to recur every couple of years, especially when individuals stop taking _____ , a medication that helps control the disorder.

5. (a) There is ample indirect evidence from family, twin, and adoption studies that some people inherit a(n)

_____ , or a greater vulnerability, to develop mood disorders; researchers have consistently found that both major depression and bipolar disorder tend to run in families.

(b) Twin studies have shown that if one identical twin suffers from major depression or bipolar disorder, the other twin has about a(n) _____ percent chance of also developing the disorder; the same _____ percent shared risk rate has been found in studies of identical twins who were adopted and raised apart.

(c) There is a great deal of indirect evidence that implicates at least two important neurotransmitters, _____ and _____ , in major depression; antidepressant medications seem to lift the symptoms of depression by increasing the availability of _____ and _____ in the brain.

(d) Major depression is often triggered by _____ and _____ events, and exposure to these are the best predictors of major depression episodes; this is especially true for people who have experienced _____ episodes of depression and who have a family history of mood disorders.

Graphic Organizer 2

List the main symptoms of the mood disorders:

Major Depression	Bipolar Disorder
1.	1.
2.	2.
3.	3.
4.	
5.	
6.	
Dysthymic Disorder	**Cyclothymic Disorder**
1.	1.

The Dissociative Disorders: Fragmentation of the Self

Learning Objectives

When you have finished studying this section of the chapter, you should be able to:

1. Describe the dissociative experience and explain what dissociative amnesia and dissociative fugue are.
2. Define *dissociative identity disorder (DID)* and explain what causes the disorder.

Read the section "The Dissociative Disorders: Fragmentation of the Self" and **write** *your answers to the following:*

1. (a) A normal personality is one in which awareness, memory, and personal identity are _____ and _____ ; in contrast, a dissociative experience is one in which a person's awareness, memory, and personal identity become _____ or _____ .

   (b) Dissociative experiences _____ (are/are not) inherently pathological; in fact, they are quite _____ and completely _____ .

   (c) In some cultures, dramatic disruptions in an individual's sense of personal identity are perceived as _____ and even highly valued; for example, _____ is common in many cultures, typically within a religious context.

   (d) Another phenomenon that occurs in some cultures is a(n) _____ , in which the person loses her sense of personal identity or is unaware of her surroundings

   (e) _____ , or speaking in tongues, is common in some North American Christian churches and is another example of a dissociative possession state; the person is temporarily possessed by the Holy Spirit, who supposedly speaks through the individual.

   (f) As DSM-IV points out, dissociative _____ or _____ states _____ (are/are not) considered pathological if (1) they occur within the context of accepted cultural or religious practice; (2) they occur voluntarily; and (3) they don't cause distress or impair functioning.

2. (a) Dissociative experiences are not necessarily _____ ; but when a dissociative disorder occurs, the dissociative experiences are far more _____ and _____ , are more _____ , and severely disrupt everyday functioning.

   (b) _____ or recognition of familiar surroundings may be completely obstructed; _____ of pertinent personal information may be unavailable to consciousness; and _____ may be lost, confused, or fragmented.

   (c) Until recently, the dissociative disorders were thought to be extremely _____ ; however, there is increasing evidence that dissociative symptoms and dissociative disorders are far more _____ than researchers had believed.

3. (a) Dissociative _____ refers to the partial or total inability to recall important information that is not due to a medical condition, like an illness or injury, or to drug use.

   (b) Usually the person develops _____ for personal events and information rather than for general knowledge or skills; in most cases, dissociative _____ is a response to stress, trauma, or an extremely painful situation, such as combat, marital problems, or physical abuse.

(c) A closely related disorder is dissociative _____ ; outwardly the person appears normal, but, in fact, he has extensive _____ and is confused about his identity; he may suddenly and inexplicably travel away from his home, wander to other cities or countries, and in some cases adopt a completely new identity.

4. (a) Dissociative identity disorder (DID), formerly known as _____ disorder, involves extensive memory disruptions for personal information along with the presence of two or more distinct _____ or _____ within a single person.

   (b) Typically each _____ has its own name, and each will be experienced as if it has its own personal history and self-image; these alternative _____ , often called alters, may be of widely varying ages and different genders.

   (c) The number of alternative _____ can range from 2 to over a 100, but having _____ to _____ alters is most common.

5. (a) Alters are not really separate _____ but rather constitute a system of the mind; alters seem to embody different aspects of the individual's _____ that, for some reason, cannot be integrated into the primary _____ , and each holds memories, emotions, and motives that are not admissible to the individual's conscious mind.

   (b) At different times, different alters take control of the person's experience, thoughts, and behavior; typically, the primary _____ is _____ (aware/unaware) of the existence of the alternative _____ .

   (c) When under the control of one of the alters,

the person will have _____ (conscious/no conscious) knowledge or memory of her experiences; however, the alters may have knowledge of each other's existence and share memories, and sometimes the experiences of one alter are accessible to another alter but not vice versa.

   (d) Differences between the different _____ in visual functioning, allergies, brain function, and handedness have been reported, but many of these physiological differences have yet to be convincingly demonstrated under controlled conditions.

   (e) Symptoms of _____ and _____ problems for recent and childhood experiences are present in virtually all cases of DID; commonly, they are unable to _____ their behavior or whereabouts during specific time periods.

   (f) People with DID typically have numerous _____ and _____ problems as well as a chaotic personal history; headaches and other physical symptoms are common, as are physical symptoms for which no medical cause can be found.

   (g) Symptoms of major _____ , _____ , posttraumatic stress disorder, substance abuse, _____ disorders, and self-destructive behavior are also common; often, the DID patient has been diagnosed with a variety of other _____ disorders before the DID diagnosis is made.

6. (a) According to one explanation, DID represents an extreme form of dissociative _____ ; a very _____ (low/high) percentage of DID cases report having suffered extreme physical or sexual abuse in childhood—over _____ percent in most surveys.

(b) In order to cope with the trauma, the child _____ himself or herself from it, creating alternative _____ ; over time more alters are created to deal with the memories and emotions associated with intolerably painful experiences.

(c) Feelings of _____ ,

_____ , _____ , and guilt that are too powerful for the child to consciously integrate can be dissociated into these alternative _____ ; in effect, dissociation becomes a pathological _____ that the person uses to cope with overwhelming experiences.

(d) The dissociative _____ theory is difficult to test empirically, but a few researchers have provided independent evidence confirming the link between childhood trauma and frequency of dissociative experiences in adulthood.

7. Read the following and write the correct term in the space provided:

(a) Ursula is generally happy about her move to northern Canada six years ago, but at regular intervals since then she has suffered episodes of depression during the fall and winter months. Ursula is probably suffering from _____ disorder.

(b) Laura suffers from a mood disorder. Her therapist has taken a family history and found that Laura's mother and two sisters also suffer from the same problem. Although her therapist is aware that multiple factors may be involved in her problem, he is most likely to conclude that Laura may have a(n)

_____ predisposition for the disorder.

(c) Dr. Markoff has prescribed lithium for Sandro's mood disorder. It is most likely that Sandro suffers from _____ disorder.

(d) Nedzad has a chronic disorder involving moderate but frequent mood swings that are not severe enough to qualify as bipolar disorder or major depression. He is perceived as being very moody, unpredictable, and inconsistent, and taken together these symptoms may indicate

_____ disorder.

(e) Marion Einer, a fifth-grade schoolteacher in Jersey City, dissappeared a few days after her husband left her. One year later, she was discovered working as a waitress in a cocktail lounge in San Diego. Calling herself Faye Bartell, she claimed to have no recollection of her past life and insisted she had never been married. This example illustrates _____ .

(f) When Vanessa goes to a movie, she tends to become totally absorbed in the plot and loses all track of time and place; she is also often momentarily disoriented when she leaves the theater. This example illustrates a(n)

_____ .

(g) Karlson was one of five people who survived an airline disaster. He escaped from the burning plane with very few injuries but three of his friends were killed. Karlson is unable to recall any details from the time of the accident until a week later. Karlson has experienced _____ .

Review of Key Terms 2

mood disorders
major depression
dysthymic disorder
seasonal affective
    disorder (SAD)
bipolar disorder
manic episode
cyclothymic disorder
dissociative experience

spirit possession
trance state
glossolalia
dissociative disorders
dissociative amnesia
dissociative fugue
dissociative identity
    disorder (DID)

Matching Exercise

Match the appropriate term with its definition or description.

1. _____ A category of mental disorders in which significant and chronic disruption in mood is the predominant symptom, causing impaired cognitive, behavioral, and physical functioning.

2. _____ Formerly called multiple personality disorder; dissociative disorder involving extensive disruptions along with the presence of two or more distinct identities or "personalities."

3. _____ Often called manic depression; a mood disorder involving periods of incapacitating depression alternating with periods of extreme euphoria and excitement.

4. _____ A mood disorder in which episodes of depression typically recur during fall and winter and remit during spring and summer.

5. _____ A nonpathological dissociative experience, usually within a religious context, in which the occupant of the person's body is supposedly displaced by a "spirit" that takes control of the body, and the person often has no memory of the experience.

6. _____ A mood disorder characterized by extreme and persistent feelings of despondency, worthlessness, and hopelessness, causing impaired emotional, cognitive, behavioral, and physical functioning.

7. _____ A sudden, rapidly escalating emotional state characterized by extreme euphoria, excitement, physical energy, and rapid thoughts and speech.

8. _____ A break or disruption in consciousness during which awareness, memory, and personal identity become separated or divided.

True/False Test

Indicate whether each statement is true or false by placing T or F in the blank space next to each item.

1. ____ Dysthymic disorder is a milder but chronic form of bipolar disorder in which the person experiences moderate but frequent mood swings.

2. ____ A phenomenon that occurs in some cultures is a trance state, in which the person loses his sense of personal identity or is unaware of his surroundings.

3. ____ Dissociative fugue involves the inability to recall information but does not involve sudden, unexpected travel from home.

4. ____ Glossolalia, or speaking in tongues, is common in some North American Christian churches; it is a dissociative state in which the person is temporarily possessed by the Holy Spirit, who speaks through the individual in an unknown language.

5. ____ Dissociative amnesia involves sudden and unexpected travel away from home, extensive amnesia, and identity confusion.

6. ____ Cyclothymic disorder involves chronic, low-grade feelings of depression that produce subjective discomfort but do not seriously impair the ability to function.

7. ____ Dissociative disorders are a category of psychological disorders in which extreme and frequent disruptions of awareness, memory, and personal identity impair the ability to function.

> Check your answers and review any areas of weakness before going on to the next section.

Schizophrenia: A Different Reality
Learning Objectives

When you have finished studying this section of the chapter, you should be able to:

1. Define *schizophrenia* and list the major characteristics of the disorder.

2. Differentiate between positive and negative symptoms and identify the core symptoms of schizophrenia.

3. List the main subtypes of schizophrenia.

4. Describe the course of schizophrenia and state how prevalent the disorder is.

Read the section "Schizophrenia: A Different Reality" and **write** *your answers to the following:*

1. (a) Schizophrenia is a mental disorder that involves severely distorted

     _____ , _____ , and

     _____ processes; during a schizophrenic episode, people lose their grip on reality and experience an entirely different world that is often characterized by mental

     _____ , _____ ,

     and frustration.

   (b) Positive symptoms reflect an excess or distortion of normal functioning and include (1)

     _____ , or false beliefs; (2)

     _____ , or false perceptions; and (3) severely disorganized

     _____ processes, _____ ,

     and behavior.

   (c) Negative symptoms reflect a restriction or reduction of normal functioning, such as greatly reduced _____ ,

     _____ expressiveness, or production of _____ .

   (d) According to DSM-IV, schizophrenia is diagnosed when two or more of these characteristic symptoms are actively present for a(n)

     _____ or longer; usually schizophrenia also involves a longer personal history, typically _____ months or more, of odd behavior, beliefs, perceptual experiences, and other less severe signs of mental disturbance; there is enormous individual variation in the _____ ,

     _____ , and duration of schizophrenic symptoms.

2. (a) A delusion is a(n) _____ held

     _____ that persists in spite of contradictory evidence or appeals to reason; schizophrenic delusions are usually bizarre and farfetched and typically cause great

     _____ distress and inter-

   fere with _____ or

     _____ functioning.

   (b) Although the content of delusions is wide-ranging, delusions are almost always centered on the _____ who is

     _____ them; certain themes also tend to surface consistently.

   (c) In delusions of _____ , the delusional person believes that other people are constantly talking about her and that everything that happens is somehow related to her.

   (d) The basic theme of delusions of

     _____ is that the person is extremely important, powerful, or wealthy.

   (e) In delusions of _____ ,

     the basic theme is that others are plotting against or trying to harm the person or someone to whom the person is close.

   (f) Because people with schizophrenia find their delusions so convincing, the delusions can sometimes provoke _____

     or _____ behavior; in some instances, delusional thinking can lead to dangerous behaviors, such as the person who responds to his delusional ideas by hurting himself or attacking others.

3. (a) Hallucinations are _____ or

     _____ perceptions that seem vividly real; the hallucinations of schizophrenia are often _____ and

     _____ , such as hallucinated voices that continually tell a person what to do.

   (b) The most common hallucinations experienced in schizophrenia are

     _____ , followed by

     _____ , hallucinations; the most frequent form of _____ hallucination is hearing a voice or voices.

   (c) The content of hallucinations is often tied to

the person's _____ beliefs; if a
person harbors _____ of
_____ , hallucinated voices may
reinforce her grandiose ideas by communicating instructions from God or the angels;
if the person harbors _____ of
_____ , hallucinated
voices or images may be extremely frightening, threatening, or accusing.

(d) When a schizophrenic episode is
_____ , hallucinations can be
virtually impossible to distinguish from
objective reality; but when the symptoms
are _____ , the person may recognize that the hallucination is a product of
his own mind; in some cases of schizophrenia, the auditory hallucinations can last for
_____ or even _____ .

4. (a) People often report that during a schizophrenic episode sights, sounds, and other
sensations often feel _____ ;
along with these disturbances, the person
may experience severely disorganized
_____ ; it can be very difficult
to _____ , _____ ,
and integrate important information while
ignoring irrelevant information, and the person's mind drifts from topic to topic in an
unpredictable, illogical manner.

(b) Such disorganized _____ is also
often reflected in the person's
_____ ; ideas, words, and
images are sometimes strung together in
ways that seem completely nonsensical to
the listener.

5. (a) Excesses or distortions in normal functioning, such as _____ ,
_____ , and disrupted
_____ , reflect positive symp-
toms; in contrast, negative symptoms reflect
marked deficits or decreases in
_____ or _____
functioning.

(b) One commonly seen negative symptom is
referred to as _____ or
_____ ;
regardless of the situation, the person
responds in an emotionally _____
way.

(c) There is a greatly reduced or complete lack
of emotional _____ or
facial expression; few expressive
_____ are made, and the person's _____ is slow and monotonous, lacking normal vocal inflections.

(d) A closely related negative symptom is
_____ , in which there is greatly reduced production of _____ ;
verbal responses are limited to brief, empty
comments, and thus this symptom is also
referred to as poverty of _____ .

(e) _____ refers to the inability to
initiate or persist in even simple forms of
goal-directed behavior, such as dressing,
bathing, or engaging in social activities;
instead, the person seems to be completely
_____ , sometimes sitting for
hours at a time.

6. (a) The most common type of schizophrenia is
the _____ type, which is characterized by the presence of delusions, hallucinations, or both; however, the person shows
no _____ impairment, disorga-
nized _____ , or negative symptoms; instead, well-organized delusions of
persecution or grandeur are operating.

(b) The _____ type of schizophre-
nia, which is very rare, is marked by highly
disturbed movement or actions; these may
include bizarre _____ or grimaces, extremely agitated behavior, complete _____ , echoing words just
spoken by another person, or imitating the
_____ of others.

(c) The person will resist direction from others
and may also assume rigid _____

to resist being moved; _____
schizophrenia is often characterized by
another unusual symptom, called waxy flexibility; like a wax figure, the person can be
molded into any position and will hold that
position indefinitely.

(d) The prominent features of the
_____ type of schizophre-
nia are extremely disorganized behavior, disorganized speech, and flat affect; delusions
and hallucinations are sometimes present
but they are not well-organized and
integrated.

(e) A person with _____ type
of schizophrenia experiences delusions and
hallucinations that contain fragmented,
shifting themes; silliness, laughing, and gig-
gling may occur for no apparent reason and
the person's behavior is very peculiar; this
type of schizophrenia was formerly called
_____ schizophrenia, and
that term is still sometimes used.

(f) The label _____ type is
used when an individual displays a combination of positive and negative symptoms
that do not clearly fit the criteria for the
_____ , _____ , or
_____ types.

7. (a) Every year there are about
_____ new cases of schizophre-
nia in this country, and annually approximately _____ Americans are
treated for schizophrenia; about
_____ percent of the U.S. popu-
lation will experience at least one episode of
schizophrenia at some point in life.

(b) Worldwide, no society or culture is immune
to this mental disorder; although there is
some cultural variation in the rate, most
cultures correspond very closely to the

_____ percent rate of schizophrenia seen in the United States.

(c) The course of schizophrenia is marked by
enormous individual variability, but a few
global generalizations are possible; about
_____ of those who expe-
rience an episode of schizophrenia recover
completely and never experience another
episode, whereas another
_____ experience recur-
rent episodes of schizophrenia, but often
with only minimal impairment in the ability
to function.

(d) For the rest of those who have suffered an
episode of schizophrenia—_____
of the total—schizophrenia becomes a chronic mental illness, and the ability to function
normally in society may be severely
impaired; the people in this category face
the prospect of repeated
_____ and extended
treatment, which places a heavy emotional,
financial, and psychological burden on people with the disorder, their families, and
society.

Explaining Schizophrenia
Learning Objectives

*When you have finished studying this section of the
chapter, you should be able to:*

1. Identify the factors that have been implicated
   as possible contributors to the development of
   schizophrenia.

2. Describe the evidence that points to the
   involvement of genetic factors and brain
   abnormalities in the development of schizophrenia.

3. Specify the environmental factors that may contribute to the development of schizophrenia.

*Read the section "Explaining Schizophrenia" and
write your answers to the following:*

1. (a) Studies of _____ ,

    _____ , and _____

    individuals have firmly established that
    genetic factors play a significant role in
    many cases of schizophrenia.

   (b) First, _____ studies have con-
    sistently shown that schizophrenia tends to
    cluster in certain _____ ; sec-
    ond, _____ and

    _____ studies have consistently
    shown that the more closely related a person
    is to someone who has schizophrenia, the
    greater the risk that she will be diagnosed
    with the disorder at some point in her life-
    time; third, _____ studies have
    consistently shown that if either

    _____ parent of an adopted
    individual had schizophrenia, the adopted
    individual is at greater risk to develop schiz-
    ophrenia.

   (c) The strongest evidence that points to genetic
    involvement in schizophrenia—the

    _____ percent risk rate for a
    person whose identical twin has schizophre-
    nia—is the same evidence that underscores
    the importance of environmental factors.

2. (a) The idea that schizophrenia is the result of
    abnormal brain chemistry is supported
    largely by _____ (direct/indi-
    rect) evidence; according to the dopamine
    hypothesis, schizophrenia is related to
    _____ dopamine activity in the
    brain.

   (b) Two pieces of _____ evidence
    support this notion: first, antipsychotic
    drugs that reduce schizophrenic symptoms
    in many people _____ or
    _____ dopamine activity in the
    brain; second, drugs like amphetamines or
    cocaine that _____ dopamine
    activity in the brain can produce schizophre-

nia-like symptoms in normal adults and
increase symptoms in people who already
suffer from schizophrenia.

   (c) Although the dopamine hypothesis is com-
    pelling, there are inconsistencies; not all
    individuals who have schizophrenia experi-
    ence a reduction of symptoms in response to
    antipsychotic drugs that _____
    dopamine activity in the brain; and for
    many patients, these drugs reduce some but
    not all schizophrenic symptoms.

3. (a) Researchers have found that about

    _____ of the people with schizo-
    phrenia show some type of brain structure
    abnormality.

   (b) The most consistent finding has been the
    enlargement of the fluid-filled cavities called
    _____ located deep within the
    brain, but researchers are not sure how this
    might be related to schizophrenia.

   (c) _____ scans have revealed dif-
    ferences in brain activity between schizo-
    phrenic and normal individuals.

   (d) These findings _____
    (prove/do not prove) that schizophrenia is
    definitely caused by brain abnormalities;
    first, about _____ percent of the
    people suffering from schizophrenia do not
    show brain structure abnormalities; second,
    the evidence is _____ , and
    researchers are still investigating whether
    differences in brain structures and activity
    are the _____ or the
    _____ of schizophrenia; third,
    the kinds of brain abnormalities seen in
    schizophrenia are also seen in other mental
    disorders, and rather than specifically
    _____ schizophrenia, it's possi-
    ble that the brain abnormalities might con-
    tribute to mental disorders in general.

4. (a) One provocative theory is that schizophrenia

might be caused by exposure to an influenza _____ or other _____ infection during prenatal development or shortly after birth; such exposure is assumed to affect the developing brain, producing changes that make individuals more vulnerable to schizophrenia later in life.

(b) There is _____ (little/some) evidence to support the _____ infection theory; first, children whose mothers were exposed to a flu _____ during the second trimester of pregnancy _____ (do/do not) show an increased rate of schizophrenia; second, schizophrenia occurs _____ (more/less) often in people who were born in the winter and spring months, when upper respiratory infections are most common.

5. (a) Researchers have investigated such psychological factors as dysfunctional _____ , disturbed _____ communication styles, and critical or guilt-inducing _____ styles as possible contributors to schizophrenia; however, no single psychological factor seems to emerge consistently as causing schizophrenia; rather, it seems that those who are _____ predisposed to develop schizophrenia may be more vulnerable to the effects of disturbed _____ environments.

(b) Researchers have found that adopted children with schizophrenic _____ mothers have a much higher rate of schizophrenia than the children in a control group whose _____ mothers were not schizophrenic.

(c) However, this was true only when the children were raised in a psychologically disturbed adoptive home; when children with a(n) _____ background of schiz-

ophrenia were raised in a psychologically healthy adoptive family, they were no more likely to develop schizophrenia than control-group children.

(d) Although adopted children with no genetic history of schizophrenia were less vulnerable to the psychological stresses of a disturbed family environment, _____ percent of the control-group adoptees developed symptoms of a serious mental disorder if they were raised in a disturbed family environment.

(e) A healthy psychological environment may _____ a person's _____ vulnerability for schizophrenia; a psychologically unhealthy environment can act as a catalyst for the onset of schizophrenia, especially for those with a(n) _____ history of the disease.

(f) Thus far, no single _____ , _____ , or _____ factor has emerged as the causal agent in schizophrenia; nevertheless, in the last few years, new antipsychotic drugs have been developed that are much more effective in treating both the _____ and _____ symptoms of schizophrenia.

6. Read the following and write the correct term in the space provided:

(a) Franko and Alberto are identical twins. Franko has developed schizophrenia. The probability that Alberto will also develop schizophrenia is about _____ percent.

(b) Dr. Hansen is conducting research on the viral infection theory. He is likely to find that people born in the winter and spring months, when upper respiratory infections are most common, are _____ (more/less) likely to suffer from schizophrenia than those born at other times of the year.

(c) Derrick hears voices that tell him to be careful because he is being watched by aliens. Kirk believes that he is a famous rock star. Derrick suffers from

_____ and Kirk suffers

from _____ .

(d) Quincy falsely believes that others are plotting against him and are trying to kill him. He believes that these agents are putting poison in the hospital's coffee supply and will attack him if he ever tries to leave the ward. This example illustrates a positive symptom of schizophrenia called

_____ .

(e) Regardless of the situation she is in, Parminder responds in an emotionally flat way and she consistently shows a greatly reduced or complete lack of emotional responsiveness. She shows little in the way

of expressive gestures or facial expressions, and her speech is slow and monotonous, without normal vocal inflections. These schizophrenic symptoms indicate that Parminder suffers from _____ ,

or _____ .

(f) Mrs. Perez usually sits passively in a motionless stupor, but if the nurse moves her arms to a new position, she will stay in that position for a very long time. This symptom of catatonic schizophrenia is called

_____ .

(g) When Darcy was examined by his psychologist, she noted that he displayed some combination of positive and negative symptoms that did not clearly fit the criteria for

_____ , _____ ,

or _____ types of schizophrenia, so she diagnosed him as having an undifferentiated type.

Graphic Organizer 3

Write the main positive and negative symptoms of schizophrenia in the space provided.

Positive Symptoms	Negative Symptoms
1.	1.
2.	2.
3.	3.

Review of Key Terms 3

schizophrenia
positive symptoms
negative symptoms
delusion
delusions of reference
delusions of grandeur
delusions of persecution
hallucination
flat affect
alogia (poverty of
  speech)
avolition

paranoid type of
  schizophrenia
catatonic type of
  schizophrenia
waxy flexibility
disorganized type of
  schizophrenia
  (hebephrenic
  schizophrenia)
undifferentiated type of
  schizophrenia
dopamine hypothesis

Matching Exercise

Match the appropriate term with its definition or description.

1. _____ The view that schizophrenia is related to, and may be caused by, excess activity of the neurotransmitter dopamine in the brain.

2. _____ A mental disorder in which the ability to function is impaired by severely distorted beliefs, perceptions, and thought processes.

3. _____ A subtype of schizophrenia that is characterized by the presence of delusions, hallucinations, or both; the person shows virtually no cognitive impairment, disorganized behavior, or negative symptoms, but instead, well-organized delusions of persecution or grandeur are operating, and auditory hallucinations are often evident.

4. _____ An unusual symptom of catatonic schizophrenia in which the person can be molded into any position and will hold that position indefinitely.

5. _____ A commonly seen negative symptom of schizophrenia in which an individual consistently shows a dramatic reduction in emotional responsiveness and a lack of normal facial expression; few expressive gestures are made, and the person's speech is slow and monotonous, lacking normal vocal inflections.

6. _____ A falsely held belief that persists in spite of contradictory evidence.

7. _____ A delusion in which the person believes that other people are constantly talking about her or that everything that happens is somehow related to her; thus, the person grossly misinterprets or distorts the meaning of ordinary events.

8. _____ A false or distorted perception that seems vividly real to the person experiencing it.

9. _____ A label for a subtype of schizophrenia that is used when an individual displays some combination of positive and negative symptoms that do not clearly fit the criteria for the paranoid, catatonic, or disorganized type.

True/False Test

Indicate whether each item is true or false by placing T or F in the space next to each item.

1. ___ In schizophrenia, positive symptoms reflect defects or deficits in normal functioning and include flat effect, alogia, and avolition.

2. ___ Avolition refers to the inability to initiate or persist in even simple forms of goal-directed behaviors, such as dressing, bathing, or engaging in social activities.

3. ___ The catatonic type of schizophrenia is marked by highly disturbed movements or actions and may include bizarre postures or grimaces, waxy flexibility, extremely agitated behavior, complete immobility, echoing words spoken by others, and assuming rigid postures that resist being moved.

4. ___ Alogia, which is also referred to as poverty of speech, is used to describe the symptom where there is a greatly reduced production of speech.

5. ___ The basic theme of delusions of grandeur is that the person is extremely important, powerful, or wealthy.

6. ___ In schizophrenia, negative symptoms reflect excesses or distortions of normal functioning and include delusions, hallucinations, and disorganized thoughts and behaviors.

7. ___ In delusions of persecution, the basic theme is that others are plotting against or trying to harm the person or someone to whom the person is close.

8. ___ The prominent features of the disorganized type of schizophrenia are extremely disorganized behavior, disorganized speech, and flat affect; this subtype is sometimes called hebephrenic schizophrenia.

Check your answers and review any areas of weakness before going on to the next section.

Something to Think About

1. One of the most common misconceptions about mental, or psychological, disorders is that schizophrenia and multiple personality are the same thing. This myth is fostered by inaccurate portrayals and misinformation in the media. What are the important distinctions between these two disorders, and what would you say to someone who thought they were the same thing?

2. Most people are curious about mental, or psychological, disorders. It is not uncommon for students to recognize aspects of themselves in the descriptions they read and to wonder if they could end up suffering from some form of mental, or psychological, disorder. What is normal and what is abnormal? What are the chances of developing symptoms of psychopathology, and what causes it? How would you answer these questions?

Check your answers and review any areas of weakness before doing the progress tests.

Progress Test 1

Review the complete chapter (including Concept Reviews and the boxed inserts), review all your study notes, and then test yourself on the following progress test. Check your answers. If you make a mistake, review your notes, review the relevant section of the study guide, and, if necessary, go back and read the appropriate part of your textbook.

1. Phoebe believes that she is the president of the United States and thinks that her indecipherable scribblings are top-secret memos. Phoebe is most clearly suffering from a(n)
   - (a) delusion
   - (b) panic attack
   - (c) hallucination
   - (d) obsession

2. Phoebe is most likely to be diagnosed as suffering from the _____ symptoms of _____.
   - (a) positive; bipolar disorder
   - (b) positive; schizophrenia
   - (c) negative; bipolar disorder
   - (d) negative; schizophrenia

3. Dr. Koopman deals with people who suffer from a wide variety of problems that cause significant personal distress and impair their ability to function in one or more important areas of their lives. Like most people in his profession, Dr. Koopman uses the term *mental disorder* to describe these symptoms. Dr. Koopman is most likely a
   - (a) clinical psychologist
   - (b) psychiatrist
   - (c) social psychologist
   - (d) developmental psychologist

4. Mandy is a forty-five-year-old administrative assistant. Based on the National Comorbidity Survey (NCS), the chance that Mandy may have experienced the symptoms of a psychological disorder at some point in her life is about _____ percent.
   - (a) 10
   - (b) 50
   - (c) 80
   - (d) 100

5. Kaila often appears nervous and agitated. She frequently talks in a loud voice and giggles at almost everything she hears. Her behavior is most likely to be diagnosed as a psychological disorder if it
   - (a) is not caused by some biological dysfunction
   - (b) is the result of a genetic predisposition
   - (c) represents a significant departure from the prevailing social and cultural norms
   - (d) is caused by drugs or medication

6. Sidney, a college student, complains that he feels nervous and fearful most of the time but doesn't know why. He worries constantly about everything in his life, and if he manages to deal with one problem, he starts worrying about a dozen more things. Sidney most likely suffers from _____ disorder.
   - (a) generalized anxiety
   - (b) bipolar
   - (c) dissociative
   - (d) cyclothymic

7. Imogene, a third-grade teacher, sometimes experiences a pounding heart, rapid breathing, breathlessness, and a choking sensation. She breaks out in a sweat, starts to tremble, and experiences light-headedness and chills. These symptoms last for about ten minutes and are characteristic of
   - (a) a panic attack
   - (b) posttraumatic stress disorder (PTSD)
   - (c) dysthymic disorder
   - (d) cyclothymic disorder

8. Lucille suffers from dissociative identity disorder (DID). If she is like most people diagnosed with this disorder, she is likely to have experienced

    (a) extreme physical or sexual abuse in childhood
    (b) episodes when she believed she was a famous and powerful person
    (c) exposure to a viral infection during prenatal development or early infancy
    (d) excess dopamine in her brain during her childhood

9. Paula has been diagnosed with agoraphobia. Her symptoms include which of the following?

    (a) an extreme and irrational fear of experiencing a panic attack in a public place and being unable to escape or get help
    (b) a sudden, rapidly escalating emotional state characterized by extreme euphoria, excitement, physical energy, and rapid thoughts and speech
    (c) partial or total inability to recall important personal information
    (d) all of the above

10. Dr. Burstein explains the development of phobias in terms of basic learning principles. Which of the following are likely to be included in his explanation?

    (a) classical conditioning
    (b) operant condition
    (c) observational learning
    (d) all of the above may be involved in his explanation

11. Dr. Weinberg believes that phobias develop because humans are biologically prepared to acquire fears of certain animals and situations. Dr. Weinberg's position is most consistent with the _____ theory of phobias.

    (a) cognitive   (c) evolutionary
    (b) learning   (d) psychoanalytic

12. Jaime brushes her teeth 12 times every day. Each time, she uses exactly 35 strokes up and 35 strokes down and three different brands of toothpaste. Jaime suffers from a(n) _____ disorder.

    (a) obsessive-compulsive
    (b) panic
    (c) cyclothymic
    (d) bipolar

13. Kevin was working in a building when an explosion occurred, and although he escaped with relatively minor injuries, he can't stop thinking about all the dead and seriously injured people he saw. He has frequent nightmares about the event and feels guilt that he survived and many of his co-workers did not. Kevin's symptoms are indicative of

    (a) dissociative fugue
    (b) dysthymic disorder
    (c) cyclothymic disorder
    (d) posttraumatic stress disorder (PTSD)

14. Mrs. Landon has been diagnosed as suffering from major depression. Which of the following symptoms is she most likely to be experiencing?

    (a) feelings of guilt, worthlessness, inadequacy, emptiness, and hopelessness
    (b) awkward and slower than usual speech, movement, and gestures and frequent crying spells for no apparent reason
    (c) dull and sluggish thought processes and problems concentrating
    (d) loss of physical energy and vague aches and pains
    (e) all of the above

15. Karla suffers from a chronic, low-grade depression characterized by many of the symptoms of major depression but less intense; these problems started many years ago when both her parents were killed in a car accident. Karla is likely to be diagnosed as suffering from

    (a) dysthymic disorder
    (b) agoraphobia
    (c) cyclothymic disorder
    (d) dissociative amnesia

16. After living in Anchorage for a number of years, Jaunitta was diagnosed with seasonal affective disorder (SAD). Episodes of depression are most likely to occur

    (a) when she travels south to visit her family in Florida
    (b) during the fall and winter months
    (c) during the day but not at night
    (d) during the spring and summer months

17. After several weeks of feeling very apathetic and dissatisfied with his life, Elmiro has suddenly become extremely euphoric and full of energy. He talks so rapidly that he is hard to understand, sleeps very little, and has gone on

a number of very expensive shopping sprees. He gets very irritated when anyone tells him to take it easy and slow down. Elmiro is exhibiting all the signs of

(a) obsessive-compulsive disorder
(b) catatonic schizophrenia
(c) dissociative identity disorder (DID)
(d) bipolar disorder

18. During a religious ceremony in his local Christian church, Billy Joe suddenly starts speaking very rapidly in what appears to be a number of different languages and appears to be in a trancelike state. This form of dissociative experience is called _____ and is classified in DSM-IV as _____ .

(a) fugue state; pathological
(b) glossolalia; normal
(c) fugue state; normal
(d) glossolalia; pathological

19. According to the Application section, the best way to help prevent someone from committing suicide is to

(a) use some well-known platitudes like "every cloud has a silver lining"
(b) not let the person talk too much about what is bothering him because it will only make him more depressed
(c) suggest that seeking professional help would be a total waste of time and money in the present situation
(d) ask the person to delay his decision and encourage him to seek professional help

20. According to Critical Thinking Box 13.1, which of the following is true?

(a) People with mental disorders are generally portrayed with great accuracy in the media.
(b) The statistical risk of violent behavior associated with mental illness is far higher than the risks associated with being young, male, or poorly educated.
(c) The incidence of violent behavior among current or former mental patients is grossly exaggerated in media portrayals.
(d) The statistical risk of violent behavior is greater among people with catatonic schizophrenia than among those with any other mental disorder.

Progress Test 2

After you have checked your understanding of the material in Progress Test 1 and have done a complete chapter review with special focus on any areas of weakness, you are ready to assess your knowledge in Progress Test 2. Check your answers. If you make a mistake, review your notes, the relevant section of the study guide, and, if necessary, the appropriate part of your textbook.

1. Dr. Krane is involved in the scientific study of the origins, symptoms, and development of psychological disorders. Dr. Krane's specialty area is

(a) psychopathology
(b) personality
(c) perception
(d) psychosocioimmunology

2. Dr. Moretti believes that schizophrenia is the result of abnormal brain chemistry. Her views are consistent with the

(a) viral infection theory
(b) dopamine hypothesis
(c) genetic predisposition theory
(d) cognitive-behavioral theory

3. When dealing with patients, psychiatrists, psychologists, and other mental health professionals are likely to refer to _____ to determine the criteria for a particular diagnosis.

(a) pop psychology books
(b) standard medical textbooks
(c) DSM-IV
(d) astrology charts

4. Dr. Crewe believes that people with panic disorder tend to misinterpret the physical signs of arousal as catastrophic and dangerous, and this misinterpretation only adds to the problem by causing even more physiological arousal. Eventually they become conditioned to respond with fear to the physical symptoms of arousal, and repeated panic attacks lead to panic disorder. Dr. Crewe's explanation is most consistent with the _____ of panic disorder.

(a) social-cultural explanation
(b) biological theory
(c) cognitive-behavioral theory
(d) genetic predisposition explanation

5. Nima suffers from a type of schizophrenia that is marked by the presence of delusions, hallucinations, and delusions of grandeur but shows virtually no cognitive impairment, disorganized behavior, or negative symptoms. Nima suffers from _____-type schizophrenia.

(a) paranoid   (c) disorganized
(b) catatonic   (d) undifferentiated

6. Tara, a young married women, has wandered from her home to a distant city where she has completely forgotten her family and her identity. This example illustrates
   (a) undifferentiated-type schizophrenia
   (b) dissociative fugue
   (c) disorganized-type schizophrenia
   (d) dissociative amnesia

7. Vera has been diagnosed with cyclothymic disorder. Her symptoms are likely to include
   (a) moderate but frequent mood swings for two years or longer
   (b) chronic low-grade feelings of depression that produce subjective discomfort but do not seriously impair her ability to function
   (c) partial or total inability to recall important personal information
   (d) irrational fears of a specific object or situation
   (e) all of the above

8. Maury repeatedly checks to see if the stove is turned off and frequently turns around on his way to work to go back home to double check. This is an example of a(n)
   (a) delusion   (c) hallucination
   (b) obsession   (d) compulsion

9. Otis turned down a very highly paid job because it meant he would have to fly to the head office in Tokyo two or three times a year. He doesn't know why, but the thought of flying absolutely terrifies him. Otis may have
   (a) a type of schizophrenia called undifferentiated
   (b) a phobia
   (c) bipolar disorder
   (d) posttraumatic stress disorder (PTSD)

10. Every semester just before midterm exams, Lilly gets very anxious and worries about how she is going to do. To reduce her apprehension, she studies very hard. Lilly suffers from
    (a) anxiety disorder
    (b) free-floating disorder
    (c) panic disorder
    (d) obsessive-compulsive disorder
    (e) none of the above; her symptoms are quite normal

11. Jessica rarely leaves her home. She doesn't go shopping because she is frightened of having a panic attack and getting lost or trapped in a crowd. Jessica has symptoms that indicate she may have

(a) agoraphobia
(b) cyclothymic disorder
(c) posttraumatic stress disorder (PTSD)
(d) seasonal affective disorder (SAD)

12. Yvette usually stands motionless and will echo words just spoken to her. She resists directions from others and sometimes assumes a rigid posture to prevent people from moving her. These symptoms suggest that Yvette has a type of _____ called _____ type.
    (a) schizophrenia; catatonic
    (b) mood disorder; cyclothymic
    (c) schizophrenia; disorganized
    (d) mood disorder; systemic

13. Nester's sense of self-esteem is wildly inflated and he exudes supreme self-confidence. He has delusional, grandiose plans for obtaining wealth, power, and fame and is engaged in a frenzy of goal-directed activities that could cost thousands of dollars. This is an example of a(n)
    (a) manic episode   (c) social phobia
    (b) obsession   (d) hallucination

14. Brandy's doctor prescribed lithium for her symptoms, and as long as she keeps taking the medication, she feels fine. It is very likely that Brandy suffers from
    (a) schizophrenia
    (b) generalized anxiety disorder
    (c) bipolar disorder
    (d) dissociative identity disorder (DID)

15. Regardless of the situation he is in, Phillip responds in an emotionally flat manner and consistently shows greatly reduced lack of emotional responsiveness or facial expression. His speech is slow and monotonous, and he is unable to initiate even simple forms of goal-directed behavior, such as dressing, bathing, or engaging in social activities. Phillip is suffering from _____ and his symptoms are _____ .
    (a) schizophrenia; positive
    (b) anxiety disorder; positive
    (c) schizophrenia; negative
    (d) anxiety disorder; negative

16. Deidre suffers from frequent and unexpected panic attacks. Despite her apprehension about these episodes, Deidre functions fairly well in her job and has a relatively normal social life. Deidre is likely to be diagnosed with

(a) panic disorder
(b) social phobia
(c) bipolar disorder
(d) dissociative fugue

17. Perry has dropped out of college because of the extreme distress that being in social situations causes him. He is unemployed because he is unable to bring himself to take part in an interview. Perry has
(a) a type of schizophrenia called disorganized type
(b) a dissociative disorder
(c) generalized anxiety disorder
(d) social phobia

18. According to Critical Thinking Box 13.2, which of the following statements about DID is (are) true?
(a) Much of the skepticism about DID is related to the fact that the number of reported cases has decreased dramatically in the last two decades.
(b) Some psychologists suggest that DID patients are consciously or unconsciously faking the symptoms.
(c) Cross-cultural research has shown that the incidence of DID outside the United States is almost zero.
(d) Most psychologists believe that DID and schizophrenia are identical disorders.
(e) All of the above are true.

19. According to Culture and Human Behavior Box 13.3, which of the following is true?
(a) The content of schizophrenic hallucinations and delusions is virtually identical across cultures.
(b) People with a mental disorder who are not actively suffering from the symptoms of the disorder are twice as dangerous and violent as normal people.
(c) The content of schizophrenic hallucinations and delusions can vary tremendously from one culture to another.
(d) Schizophrenia is much more prevalent in North America than in any other part of the world.

20. According to the Application section, which of the following is false?
(a) Women outnumber men by 3 to 1 in the number of suicide attempts.
(b) Men outnumber women by 4 to 1 in suicide deaths.
(c) Over the last three decades, the suicide rate for adolescents has increased by about 200 percent, compared to a 17 percent increase for the general population.
(d) The lowest rate of suicide consistently occurs in the oldest segment of our population, among those aged sixty-five and above.

Answers

Introduction: Understanding Psychological Disorders

1. (a) is not; degree
   (b) origins, symptoms
   (c) strong social stigma; often reluctant

2. (a) psychologists; psychiatrists
   (b) behavioral; psychological; distress; function
   (c) *Diagnostic*; *Statistical*
   (d) 250; symptoms; criteria; diagnosis
   (e) language; guidelines

3. (a) any point in their lives; the previous 12 months
   (b) their lifetimes; the past 12 months
   (c) the previous year
   (d) awareness; stigma
   (e) most; 3 to 5
   (f) differed; higher; higher
   (g) anxiety; mood; dissociative; schizophrenia

Anxiety Disorders

1. (a) physical; tension, apprehension; adaptive; normal
   (b) physical; mental
   (c) maladaptive
   (d) irrational; exaggerated; nonexistent; uncontrollable; unrealistic; disruptive; interferes

2. (a) main
   (b) generalized; panic
   (c) phobias
   (d) posttraumatic stress
   (e) obsessive-compulsive

3. (a) global, persistent, chronic
   (b) dissipates; free-floating

4. (a) sudden; extreme; pounding; rapid
   (b) terror; ten
   (c) frequently; unexpectedly; frequency

5. (a) biological; psychological; biological; genetics
   (b) psychologically; panic-prone; physiological
   (c) cognitive-behavioral; apprehensive
   (d) conditioned; conditioned

6. (a) intense, irrational; panic attack
   (b) specific; irrational
   (c) mild; terror; anxiety
   (d) 10; specific; twice; specific

7. (a) situations
   (b) features; environment
   (c) injury, blood
   (d) animals; insects

8. (a) panic attack; panic attack; panic attack
   (b) most

9. (a) social; social; social
   (b) social; social; panic attack; social
   (c) social
   (d) social; social

10. (a) classical; conditioned; conditioned
    (b) operant; negative
    (c) observational; imitating

11. (a) biologically; disgust
    (b) repulsive; contamination

Posttraumatic Stress Disorder: Re-Experiencing the Trauma

1. (a) physical; psychological; horror; helplessness
   (b) military combat; disasters; assault
   (c) frequently; stimuli; situations; emotional; arousal; startled; sleep
   (d) more; an important; more; multiple traumas

2. (a) repetitive; obsessions; compulsions
   (b) repeated, intrusive, uncontrollable
   (c) repetitive; ritualistic
   (d) overt; covert; tension, anxiety

3. (a) either; both; terrible
   (b) similar; content
   (c) biological; serotonin
   (d) frontal; movement

4. (a) mental; psychological
   (b) normal
   (c) obsessive-compulsive
   (d) generalized anxiety
   (e) social phobia
   (f) posttraumatic stress
   (g) panic attacks

Graphic Organizer 1

General Anxiety Disorder
1. Persistent, chronic, unreasonable worry and anxiety.
2. General symptoms of anxiety, including persistent physical arousal.

Panic Disorder
1. Frequent and unexpected panic attacks, with no specific or identifiable trigger.

Phobias
1. Intense anxiety or panic attack triggered by a specific object or situation.

2. Persistent avoidance of the feared object or situation.

Obsessive-Compulsive Disorder

1. Anxiety caused by uncontrollable, persistent, recurring thoughts (obsessions) and/or

2. Anxiety caused by uncontrollable, persistent urges to perform certain actions (compulsions).

Posttraumatic Stress Disorder

1. Anxiety triggered by memories of a traumatic experience.

Matching Exercise 1

1. psychopathology
2. DSM-IV
3. obsessive-compulsive disorder
4. anxiety
5. phobia
6. posttraumatic stress disorder (PTSD)
7. agoraphobia
8. specific phobia

True/False Test 1

1. F	4. T	7. T
2. T	5. F	8. T
3. T	6. T	

Mood Disorders: Emotions Gone Awry

1. (a) criteria
   (b) serious, persistent; psychological; function

2. (a) two; external; negative; stressful
   (b) normal; several; two
   (c) suicide; suicidal; death
   (d) sleep; reduced

3. (a) dysthymic; chronic
   (b) dysthymic
   (c) dysthymic; double; dysthymic; dysthymic

4. (a) most; 12
   (b) twice; 4; 8
   (c) without; is not
   (d) half; increase; decreases
   (e) seasons; autumn; winter; fall; winter; women

Bipolar Disorder: An Emotional Roller Coaster

1. (a) manic depression
   (b) depression; manic; manic; depression; manic

2. (a) manic
   (b) manic; self-esteem; self-confidence
   (c) manic; flight of ideas
   (d) manic; hospitalization
   (e) manic; obnoxious; verbally

3. (a) cyclothymic
   (b) cyclothymic; bipolar; depression
   (c) cyclothymic

4. (a) early twenties; manic; depressive
   (b) 2; are no
   (c) recurring; rapid cycling; manic; depressive; lithium

5. (a) genetic predisposition
   (b) 70; 70
   (c) serotonin; norepinephrine; norepinephrine; serotonin
   (d) traumatic; stressful; previous

Graphic Organizer 2

Major Depression

1. Loss of interest or pleasure in almost all activities
2. Despondent mood, feelings of emptiness or worthlessness, or excessive guilt
3. Preoccupation with death or suicidal thoughts
4. Difficulty sleeping or excessive sleeping
5. Diminished ability to think, concentrate, or make decisions
6. Diminished appetite and significant weight loss

Bipolar Disorder

1. One or more manic episodes characterized by euphoria, high energy, grandiose ideas, flight of ideas, inappropriate self-confidence, and decreased need for sleep
2. Usually also characterized by one or more episodes of major depression
3. Possible rapid alternation between symptoms of mania and major depression

Dysthymic Disorder

1. Chronic, low-grade depressed feelings that are not severe enough to qualify as major depression

Cyclothymic Disorder

1. Moderate, recurring, up-and-down mood swings that are not severe enough to qualify as major depression or bipolar disorder

The Dissociative Disorders: Fragmentation of the Self

1. (a) associated; well integrated; separated; divided

(b) are not; common; normal
(c) normal; spirit possession
(d) trance state
(e) glossolalia
(f) possession; trance; are not

2. (a) abnormal; extreme; frequent; persistent
   (b) awareness; memories; identity
   (c) rare; common

3. (a) amnesia
   (b) amnesia; amnesia
   (c) fugue; amnesia

4. (a) multiple personality; identities; personalities
   (b) personality; personalities
   (c) personalities; 10; 15

5. (a) people; personality; personality
   (b) personality; unaware; personalities
   (c) no conscious
   (d) personalities
   (e) amnesia; memory; remember
   (f) psychiatric; psychological
   (g) depression, anxiety; sleep; psychological

6. (a) coping; high; 90
   (b) dissociates; personalities
   (c) anger, rage, fear; personalities; defense mechanism
   (d) coping

7. (a) seasonal affective
   (b) genetic
   (c) bipolar
   (d) cyclothymic
   (e) dissociative fugue
   (f) dissociative experience
   (g) dissociative amnesia

Matching Exercise 2

1. mood disorders
2. dissociative identity disorder (DID)
3. bipolar disorder
4. seasonal affective disorder (SAD)
5. spirit possession
6. major depression
7. manic episode
8. dissociative experience

True/False Test 2

1. F
2. T
3. F
4. T
5. F
6. F
7. T

Schizophrenia: A Different Reality

1. (a) beliefs, perceptions; thought; chaos, disorientation
   (b) delusions; hallucinations; thought; speech
   (c) motivation, emotional; speech
   (d) month; six; onset, intensity

2. (a) falsely; belief; psychological; social; occupational
   (b) person; experiencing
   (c) reference
   (d) grandeur
   (e) persecution
   (f) inappropriate, bizarre

3. (a) false; distorted; ongoing; persistent
   (b) auditory; visual; auditory
   (c) delusional; delusions; grandeur; delusions; persecution
   (d) severe; less severe; months; years

4. (a) distorted; thinking; concentrate, remember
   (b) thinking; speech

5. (a) delusions, hallucinations; sensation; behavior; emotional
   (b) flat affect; affective flattening; "flat"
   (c) responsiveness; gestures; speech
   (d) alogia; speech; speech
   (e) avolition; apathetic

6. (a) paranoid; cognitive; behavior
   (b) catatonic; postures; immobility; movements
   (c) postures; catatonic
   (d) disorganized
   (e) disorganized; hebephrenic
   (f) undifferentiated; paranoid, catatonic; disorganized

7. (a) 200,000; 1 million; 1
   (b) 1
   (c) one-quarter; one-quarter
   (d) one-half; hospitalizations

Explaining Schizophrenia

1. (a) families, twins; adopted
   (b) family; families; family; twin; adoption; biological
   (c) 50

2. (a) indirect; excessive
   (b) indirect; reduce; block; enhance
   (c) reduce

3. (a) half
   (b) ventricles
   (c) PET
   (d) do not prove; 50; correlational; cause; consequence; causing

4. (a) virus; viral
   (b) some; viral; virus; do; more

5. (a) parenting; family; parenting; genetically; family
   (b) biological; biological
   (c) genetic
   (d) 33
   (e) counteract; inherited; genetic
   (f) biological, psychological; social; positive; negative

6. (a) 50
   (b) more
   (c) hallucinations; delusions
   (d) delusions of persecution
   (e) flat affect; affective flattening
   (f) waxy flexibility
   (g) paranoid, catatonic; disorganized

Graphic Organizer 3

Positive Symptoms
1. delusions
2. hallucinations
3. disorganized thoughts and behavior

Negative Symptoms
1. flat effect
2. alogia (poverty of speech)
3. avolition

Matching Exercise 3

1. dopamine hypothesis
2. schizophrenia
3. paranoid type of schizophrenia
4. waxy flexibility
5. flat affect
6. delusion
7. delusions of reference
8. hallucination
9. undifferentiated type of schizophrenia

True/False Test 3

1. F   4. T   7. T
2. T   5. T   8. T
3. T   6. F

Something to Think About

1. Multiple personality disorder, now called dissociative identity disorder (DID), involves exten-
sive memory disruptions for personal information along with the presence of two or more distinct identities or personalities. Typically, each personality has its own name and each will be experienced as if it has its own personal history and self-image. These alternative personalities, or alters, may be of widely varying ages and different genders. When under the control of one of the alters, the person will have no conscious knowledge or memory of the experience. However, the alters may have knowledge of each other's existence and share memories. Sometimes the experiences of one alter are accessible to another alter, but not vice versa. From this description of the disorder, it is clear that symptoms of amnesia and memory problems are a central part of DID. In addition, people with DID have numerous psychiatric and physical symptoms as well as a chaotic personal history.

Contrast DID with a description of schizophrenia and the differences between the two disorders become apparent. Schizophrenia is a mental disorder that involves severely distorted beliefs, perceptions, and thought processes. During a schizophrenic episode, people lose their grip on reality. The positive symptoms of schizophrenia reflect an excess or distortion of normal functioning and include hallucinations, delusions, and severely disorganized thought processes, speech, and behavior. The negative symptoms reflect a restriction or reduction of normal functions and include flat affect, alogia (poverty of speech), and avolition, or the inability to initiate or persist in even simple forms of goal-directed behavior. There are four different subtypes of schizophrenia: paranoid type, catatonic type, disorganized type, and undifferentiated type. In addition, as noted in the textbook, the prevalence, course, and cause of DID are markedly different from those of schizophrenia.

2. The first thing to note is that the line that divides normal behavior and abnormal behavior is not clearly defined. In addition, it is affected by the social and cultural context in which the behavior occurs. Psychopathology is the scientific study of the origins, symptoms, and development of psychological disorders, and as you found out in this chapter, DSM-IV is the book that describes about 250 specific disorders, including their symptoms, the exact criteria that must be met to make a diagnosis, and the typical course of each mental disorder. The main categories of psychological disorders are

the anxiety disorders, mood disorders, dissociative disorders, and schizophrenia.

According to your textbook, the chance that someone will experience symptoms of psychological disorder some time in his or her lifetime is fifty-fifty. About one in three people will have experienced the symptoms of psychological disorder during the last year. However, about 80 percent of those people will not have sought professional help. The good news is that most people seem to weather the symptoms without becoming completely debilitated and without professional intervention. It is estimated that 3 to 5 percent of people have really serious symptoms that demand immediate treatment, and these people usually have developed several mental disorders over time, not just one disorder that suddenly appears. Women tend to have a higher prevalence of anxiety and depression, whereas men tend to have a higher prevalence of substance abuse disorders.

Nobody knows for sure what causes mental disorders. There is no shortage of theories, however. Biological and genetic factors have been implicated, and so have abnormalities in brain structure and chemical imbalances. Various environmental and social explanations have also been suggested. Research continues, and someday we may be closer to finding the cause or causes of these abnormalities.

Progress Test 1

1. a	8. a	15. a
2. b	9. a	16. b
3. b	10. d	17. d
4. b	11. c	18. b
5. c	12. a	19. d
6. a	13. d	20. c
7. a	14. e	

Progress Test 2

1. a	8. d	15. c
2. b	9. b	16. a
3. c	10. e	17. d
4. c	11. a	18. b
5. a	12. a	19. c
6. b	13. a	20. d
7. a	14. c	

Chapter 14   Therapies

OVERVIEW

Chapter 14 discusses how psychological disorders are treated with psychotherapies and biomedical therapies. Psychotherapy is based on the assumption that psychological factors play an important role in psychological disorders and symptoms, whereas the basic assumption of the biomedical therapies is that biological factors are involved.

Psychoanalysis, its basic assumptions, and the different techniques used in the psychoanalytic process are described. Short-term dynamic therapies are based on psychoanalytic ideas but are more problem focused and shorter than traditional psychoanalysis.

Client-centered therapy is used as the prime example of the humanistic approach to psychotherapy. The therapeutic approach taken is described, and the basic assumptions of this form of insight therapy are explored.

Behavior therapy is based on learning principles and assumes that maladaptive behaviors are learned. The techniques used to facilitate change are examined; they include procedures based on classical conditioning, such as counterconditioning, systematic desensitization, the bell and pad treatment, and aversive conditioning, and procedures based on operant conditioning, such as positive reinforcement, extinction, and token economies.

Cognitive therapies are explored next and include rational-emotive therapies and cognitive therapy. This approach assumes that psychological problems are caused by maladaptive patterns of thinking, and the various techniques used by both forms of cognitive therapy are described.

Group and family therapies are contrasted with individual therapy, and the advantages and benefits are examined. The effectiveness of psychotherapy is explored, and it is concluded that, in general, psychotherapy is better than no treatment at all and that no particular form of psychotherapy is superior to any other. Some therapies, however, are more effective than others for specific problems. The factors that are crucial to effective therapy are identified, and it is pointed out that most psychotherapists today identify their orientation as eclectic.

The biomedical therapies are discussed, and it is noted that the most common biomedical therapy is psychoactive medication. The nature of these drugs, their effects on the brain, the side effects associated with each, and the type of disorder they are prescribed for are presented. The main categories of drugs are the antipsychotics, the antianxiety medications, and the antidepressants. Lithium is prescribed for bipolar disorder, and electroconvulsive therapy (ECT) is used for treating severe depression.

Introduction: Psychotherapy and Biomedical Therapy

Learning Objectives

When you have finished studying this section of the chapter, you should be able to:

1. Define *psychotherapy* and list the types of problems that are treated.
2. Identify the basic assumptions common to all forms of psychotherapies.
3. Describe biomedical therapy and identify the assumption on which it is based.
4. Explain how psychotherapy and biomedical therapy differ.

*Read the section "Introduction: Psychotherapy and Biomedical Therapy" and **write** your answers to the following:*

1. (a) Many people seek help from mental health professionals because they are suffering from some form of _____ ; in addition, many people seek help in dealing with _____ relationships, such as an unhappy marriage, or in dealing with life's _____ , such as coping with the death of a loved one or adjusting to retirement.

   (b) Psychotherapy refers to the use of _____ techniques to treat _____ , _____ , and _____ problems; although there are many forms of psychotherapy, they all share the assumption that _____ factors play a significant role in a person's troubled _____ , _____ , and relationships.

   (c) Biomedical therapies involve the use of _____ or other _____ procedures to treat the symptoms associated with _____ disorders; these treatments are based on the assumption that the

symptoms of many _____ disorders involve _____ factors, such as abnormal brain chemistry.

   (d) There has been a steadily growing trend to combine biomedical therapy and psychotherapy in treating _____ disorders; traditionally, only licensed physicians, such as _____ , have been allowed to prescribe the different forms of biomedical therapy, but in recent years some clinical psychologists with additional training have been allowed to prescribe medications to treat _____ disorders.

   (e) The most influential approaches in psychotherapy are _____ , _____ , _____ , and _____ .

Psychoanalytic Therapy

Learning Objectives

When you have finished studying this section of the chapter, you should be able to:

1. Describe psychoanalysis and identify its founder and the theory on which it is based.
2. List the techniques that psychoanalysts use, and specify their purpose.
3. Explain the role that insight plays in psychoanalytic therapy.
4. Identify and describe the short-term dynamic therapies.

*Read the section "Psychoanalytic Therapy" and **write** your answers to the following:*

1. (a) Psychoanalysis is a form of psychotherapy originally developed by Sigmund Freud in the early 1900s and is based on his theory of _____ ; its assumptions and techniques _____ (are no longer/continue to be) influential today.

   (b) Freud stressed that _____ experiences lay the foundation for later personality development; when these experiences result in _____ conflicts and _____ urges, these emotionally charged memories are _____ , or pushed out of conscious awareness, but continue to influence a person's thoughts and behavior, including the dynamics of relationships with others.

(c) Psychoanalysis is designed to help unearth unconscious conflicts so that the patient attains _____ as to the real source of her problems; central to this process is the intense _____ that forms between the psychoanalyst and the patient in order to recognize and resolve the conflicts.

(d) Freud developed several _____ to coax a patient's unconscious conflicts to awareness.

2. (a) In the famous technique called _____ , the patient lies on a couch and spontaneously reports all _____ , _____ , and _____ .

(b) Blocks in _____ , such as an abrupt change in topic or sudden silences, may be signs of _____ , which is the patient's unconscious attempts to block the process of revealing _____ memories and conflicts.

(c) Another technique that Freud made famous is _____ interpretation; because psychological defenses are reduced during _____ , he believed that unconscious conflicts and repressed impulses were expressed symbolically in _____ .

(d) The analyst makes carefully timed _____ , explanations of the unconscious meaning of the patient's _____ , _____ , _____ , or _____ .

(e) One of the most important processes that occurs in the relationship between the patient and the psychoanalyst is called _____ ; this occurs when the patient unconsciously responds to the therapist as though the therapist were a significant person in the patient's life, often a parent, and this process is encouraged by the therapist's neutrality.

(f) All these psychoanalytic techniques are designed to help the patient see how _____ conflicts influence his current _____ and _____ ; once these kinds of _____ are achieved, the psychoanalyst helps the patient work through and resolve longstanding conflicts.

(g) On average, the traditional psychoanalyst sees the patient _____ or _____ times a week over the course of _____ years or longer.

3. (a) Today, _____ (few/many) psychotherapists practice traditional psychoanalysis lasting for years; people expect therapy to provide beneficial changes in a matter of _____ or _____ .

(b) Today, there are many different forms of short-term dynamic therapies that are based on traditional psychoanalytic notions and have many features in common: (1) therapeutic contact lasts for no more than _____ ; (2) the patient's problems are _____ assessed at the beginning of therapy; (3) the therapist and patient agree on _____ , _____ , and attainable goals; and (4) in the actual sessions, most psychodynamic therapists are more _____ than traditional psychoanalysts, actively engaging the patient in a dialogue.

(c) As in traditional psychoanalysis, the therapist uses _____ to help the patient recognize hidden _____ and _____ that may be occurring in important relationships in her life; therapy also focuses on helping the patient identify _____ resources she can use to cope with current difficulty as well as future problems.

(d) Traditional, lengthy psychoanalysis is _____ (frequently/seldom) practiced today, but Freud's basic assumptions and techniques _____ (are no longer/continue to be) influential.

4. Read the following and write the correct term in the space provided:

(a) During a session with her psychoanalyst, Felicity was asked to elaborate on her negative feelings about her husband. She responded by making a few wisecracks about men and then abruptly changed the subject. Her therapist would say she is engaging in _____ .

(b) When Felicity's therapist urges her to report all her spontaneous thoughts, mental images, and feelings, he is using the technique called _____ .

(c) When Felicity was asked to elaborate on a dream she had and talk about her feelings, she couldn't think of anything to say. This response is likely to be interpreted as a sign of _____ .

(d) Although her therapist has remained neutral and nonjudgmental throughout their sessions, Felicity is beginning to express feelings of hostility and anger toward him. This part of the psychoanalytic process is called _____ .

Review of Key Terms and Key Names 1

psychotherapy	resistance
biomedical therapies	dream interpretation
psychoanalysis	interpretation
Sigmund Freud	transference
insight	short-term dynamic
free association	therapies

Matching Exercise

Match the appropriate term/name with its definition or description.

1. _____ Austrian physician and founder of psychoanalysis who theorized that psychological symptoms are the result of unconscious and unresolved conflicts stemming from early childhood.

2. _____ The treatment of emotional, behavioral, and interpersonal problems through the use of psychological techniques designed to encourage understanding of problems and modify troubling feelings, behaviors, or relationships.

3. _____ A type of psychotherapy originated by Sigmund Freud in which free association, dream interpretation, and analysis of resistance and transference are used to explore repressed or unconscious impulses, anxieties, and internal conflicts.

4. _____ The use of medications, electroconvulsive therapy, or other medical treatment to treat the symptoms associated with psychological disorders.

5. _____ Psychotherapies that are based on traditional psychoanalytic notions in which therapeutic contact typically lasts for no more than a few months rather than years.

True/False Test

Indicate whether each statement is true or false by placing T or F in the blank space next to each item.

1. ____ Psychoanalysts believe that it is essential to move conflicts from the patient's unconscious to his or her conscious awareness; the process of recognizing and ultimately resolving these longstanding repressed conflicts is called insight.

2. ___ Transference is a technique used in psycho-analysis in which the psychoanalyst offers a carefully timed explanation of the patient's dreams, free associations, or behavior to facilitate the recognition of unconscious conflicts or motivations.

3. ___ In psychoanalysis, the patient's unconscious attempts to block the revelation of repressed memories and conflicts is called resistance.

4. ___ Dream interpretation is a technique used in psychoanalysis in which the content of dreams is analyzed for disguised or symbolic meanings.

5. ___ Free association is a technique used in psychoanalysis in which the patient spontaneously reports all thoughts, feelings, and mental images as they come to mind as a way of revealing unconscious thoughts and emotions.

6. ___ Interpretation refers to the process by which emotions and desires originally associated with a significant person in the patient's life, such as a parent, are unconsciously transferred to the psychoanalyst.

> Check your answers and review any areas of weakness before going on to the next section.

Humanistic Therapy
Learning Objectives

When you have finished studying this section of the chapter, you should be able to:

1. Identify the main humanistic therapy and the person who developed it.

2. Describe the conditions and techniques that are important in client-centered therapy.

3. Explain how client-centered therapy and psychoanalysis differ in terms of the role insight plays in each.

*Read the section "Humanistic Therapy" and **write** your answers to the following:*

1. (a) The humanistic perspective in psychology emphasizes human _____ , self-_____ , and freedom of _____ ; the most important factor in personality is the individual's _____ , _____ perception of him- or herself.

(b) Humanistic psychologists see people as being innately _____ and motivated by the need to grow _____ ; if people are raised in a genuinely accepting atmosphere and given freedom to make _____ , they will develop healthy self-concepts and strive to fulfill their unique _____ as human beings.

2. (a) Probably the most influential of the humanistic psychotherapies is _____ therapy, also called _____ therapy, developed by Carl Rogers.

(b) Rogers believed that the medical term *patient* implies that people in therapy are _____ and are seeking treatment from an all-knowing authority figure who can _____ them; instead of stressing the therapist's expertise or perceptions of the patient, _____ therapy emphasizes the _____ subjective perception of himself and his environment.

(c) The therapist must not _____ , make _____ , offer _____ , or pass judgment on the _____ thoughts or feelings; change must be chosen and directed by the _____ , and the therapist's role is to create the conditions that allow the _____ to direct the focus of therapy.

3. Rogers believed that three qualities of the therapist are critical in creating the therapeutic conditions that promote self-awareness, psychological growth, and self-directed change:

(a) _____ means that the therapist _____ and _____ shares her thoughts and feelings with the client; by modeling _____ , the therapist indirectly encourages the client to express his or her true feelings without _____ or pretention.

(b) The therapist must value, accept, and care for the client, whatever his problem or behavior, and Rogers called this quality

_____ ;

Rogers believed that a person develops psychological problems largely because he has consistently experienced only

_____ .

(c) The therapist must communicate

_____ by

_____ listening and reflecting the content and personal meaning of _____ being experienced by the client; in effect, the therapist creates a psychological mirror, reflecting the client's _____ and _____ as they exist in the client's private inner world, allowing him to explore and clarify them and to see himself and his problems more clearly.

(d) Rogers believed that when the therapeutic atmosphere contains _____ ,

_____ , and

_____ ,

change is more likely to occur; such conditions foster feelings of being psychologically safe, accepted, and valued and allow the client to move in the direction of _____ , which is the realization of his unique potentials and talents.

(e) Research has generally _____ (supported/not supported) Rogers' ideas of the therapeutic qualities needed for change; along with being influential in individual

psychotherapy, the client-centered approach has been applied to _____ counseling, _____ , education, _____ , and even community and international relations.

Behavior Therapy
Learning Objectives

When you have finished studying this section of the chapter, you should be able to:

1. Define *behavior therapy* and identify learning principles used to directly change problem behavior.
2. Explain how classical conditioning principles are used to treat specific problem behaviors.
3. Describe how operant conditioning principles are applied to modify problem behaviors.

*Read the section "Behavior Therapy" and **write** your answers to the following:*

1. (a) In sharp contrast to the therapies of Rogers and Freud, which assume that gaining insight into the source of the problem is sufficient to bring about desirable changes in behavior and emotions, the goal of behavior therapy is to _____ specific problem behaviors, not to change the entire _____ ; rather than focusing on the _____ , behavior therapists focus on _____ behavior.

(b) Behavior therapists assume that maladaptive behaviors are _____ , just as adaptive behaviors are; thus, the basic strategy in behavior therapy involves _____ maladaptive behaviors and _____ more adaptive behaviors in their place.

(c) Behavior therapists employ techniques that are based on the _____ principles of _____ conditioning, _____ conditioning, and _____ learning.

2. (a) John Watson _____ conditioned an infant called Little Albert to fear a tame laboratory rat by repeatedly pairing the rat with a loud clanging sound, and over time, Albert's conditioned fear _____ to other furry objects, including a fur coat, cotton, and a Santa Claus mask.

(b) Watson's research inspired one of his students, Mary Cover Jones, to explore ways of _____ conditioned fears; she used a procedure that has become known as _____ , which refers to the learning of a new conditioned response that is incompatible with a previously learned response.

(c) Jones's procedure involved gradually introducing the _____ stimulus and at the same time pairing it with a(n) _____ stimulus, such as food, that elicits a positive response that is incompatible with the original conditioned response; this procedure also _____ (increased/eliminated) fear of objects that were similar to the original feared stimulus.

(d) Along with _____ , Jones used _____ _____ techniques; she demonstrated that seeing others acting in a fearless manner encourages the fearful individual to _____ the behavior; for her pioneering efforts in the treatment of children's fears, Jones is widely regarded as the first behavior therapist.

3. (a) Systematic desensitization involves learning a new conditioned response (relaxation) that is _____ with or _____ the old conditioned response (fear and anxiety).

(b) First, the patient learns _____ ,

which involves successively _____ one muscle group after another until a deep state of _____ is achieved.

(c) Second, the therapist helps the patient construct a list of specific anxiety-provoking images associated with the feared stimulus, arranged in a(n) _____ from least to most anxiety provoking; the patient also creates a very relaxing _____ scene, such as walking on a beach on a sunny day.

(d) Third, while deeply relaxed, the patient imagines the least threatening scene in the _____ , and after he can maintain complete _____ while imagining this scene, he moves to the next.

(e) If the patient begins to feel anxiety or tension, he is guided back to imagining the previous scene or the _____ scene, and, if necessary, the therapist helps the patient relax again using the _____ technique.

(f) Over several sessions, the patient gradually works his way up the anxiety _____ , imagining each scene while maintaining complete _____ ; if the technique is successful, the feared situation no longer produces a _____ of fear and anxiety.

4. (a) Children who are bedwetters tend to be very _____ ; behavior therapists assume that bedwetting occurs because the child has not learned to _____ when his bladder is full.

(b) Therapy involves bell and pad treatment, which uses _____ conditioning to pair arousal with the sensation of a full bladder; when the child starts to wet the bed, a loud _____ goes off, waking the child, who then shuts off the alarm, uses the bathroom, changes the sheet, and resets the alarm.

(c) Over the course of a few weeks, the child's body becomes conditioned so that the sensations of a full bladder (the conditioned _____) triggers waking arousal (the desired conditioned _____); the bell and pad procedure is effective in about _____ percent of school-age children who have difficulties with bed-wetting.

5. (a) _____ conditioning, which is based on classical conditioning, involves repeatedly pairing an aversive or _____ stimulus with the occurrence of undesirable behavior such as drinking alcohol or smoking cigarettes; eventually, the alcohol or cigarette smoke produces a _____ conditioned response.

(b) _____ conditioning techniques have been used to treat alcohol addiction, sexual deviance, compulsive gambling, and overeating; for example, the medication Antabuse causes extreme _____ if alcohol is used, and mild electric shock has been used for other conditions such as sexual deviance.

(c) In general, _____ conditioning is _____ (very/not very) effective, and its use has been _____ in recent years.

6. (a) B. F. Skinner's operant conditioning model of learning is based on the simple principle that behavior is _____ and maintained by its _____ .

(b) Behavior therapists use a variety of techniques based on operant conditioning, including _____ reinforcement for desired behaviors and _____ ,

or nonreinforcement, of undesired behaviors.

(c) The token economy is an example of the use of operant conditioning techniques to modify the behavior of _____ ; a token economy is a very structured environment, a system for _____ desired behaviors through _____ reinforcement.

(d) Basically, tokens or points are awarded as _____ reinforcers for desirable behaviors and withheld or taken away for undesirable behaviors; the tokens can be exchanged for other _____ , such as special privileges or desirable items or activities.

(e) Token economies have been used in _____ , _____ , juvenile correction institutes, and _____ hospitals and have been effective even with severely disturbed patients who have been hospitalized for many years; the use of token economies has declined because of problems of implementation, time and training involved, and legal challenges related to withholding of privileges.

7. Read the following and write the correct term in the space provided:

(a) Dr. Soos does not analyze or interpret his clients' motives or problems. Instead, he believes that the client is in the best position to discover his or her own ways of effectively dealing with problems and that the role of the therapist is to provide the right conditions that foster self-awareness, psychological growth, and self-directed change. Dr. Soos is obviously a(n) _____ psychologist who uses _____ therapy.

(b) In an attempt to help her husband overcome his deep fear of traveling by sea, Mrs.

Bowman brings home travel brochures showing exotic destinations reached by cruise ships; she asks her husband to imagine both of them sitting in their deck chairs enjoying the warm sunshine and cool beverages, and at the same time she reassures him that these big ships are totally safe and comfortable and that he has nothing to worry about. Mrs. Bowman's efforts to reduce her husband's fear most closely resembles techniques used in _____ therapy.

(c) To help Trevor overcome his addiction to nicotine, Dr. Clarke asks him to smoke some cigarettes and at the same time administers electric shock to his arm. Dr. Clarke is using a technique called _____ conditioning.

(d) Retarded children in a group home are given plastic chips for making their beds, brushing their teeth, washing their hands, and being on time for meals. They are allowed to exchange these chips for candy, cookies, and activities like additional TV time. The group home is using a behavioral technique called

_____ .

(e) Eight-year-old Darryl has problems with bedwetting. His mother takes him to a behavior therapist who recommends a procedure that fixes the problem in a matter of weeks. The therapist most likely is using

_____ .

(f) Desiree told her therapist, "I feel so inadequate and useless and I can't seem to cope with even the smallest things in my life. What should I do?" Her therapist answered, "You are feeling very helpless about things in your life, and sometimes you feel unable to cope. Can you think where these feelings come from?" The therapist is using

_____ therapy and

appears to be communicating with

_____ .

Review of Key Terms and Key Names 2

humanistic perspective	systematic desensitization
client-centered therapy	progressive relaxation
Carl Rogers	control scene
genuineness	bell and pad treatment
unconditional positive regard	aversive conditioning
conditional acceptance	operant conditioning
empathic understanding	positive reinforcement
behavior therapy	extinction
Mary Cover Jones	token economy
counterconditioning	

Matching Exercise

Match the appropriate term/name with its definition or description.

1. _____ American psychologist who conducted the first clinical demonstrations of behavior therapy.

2. _____ A perspective in psychology that emphasizes human potential, self-awareness, and freedom of choice.

3. _____ A form of behavior therapy in which the therapeutic environment is structured to reward desired behaviors with tokens or points that may eventually be exchanged for tangible rewards.

4. _____ In client-centered therapy, a critical quality the therapist should possess that involves honestly and openly sharing his or her thoughts and feelings with the client.

5. _____ A type of psychotherapy that focuses on directly changing maladaptive behavior patterns by using basic learning principles and techniques; also called behavior modification.

6. _____ American psychologist who helped found humanistic psychology and developed client-centered therapy.

7. _____ The first step in systematic desensitization, which involves successively relaxing one muscle group after another until a deep state of relaxation is achieved.

8. _____ A behavior therapy technique used to treat nighttime bedwetting by conditioning arousal from sleep in response to body signals of a full bladder.

9. _____ A type of psychotherapy developed by humanist Carl Rogers in which the therapist is nondirective and reflective, and the client directs the focus of each therapy session; also called person-centered therapy.

10. _____ In behavior therapy, the term used to describe consequences such as praise, encouragement, social attention, and other rewards, that increase the probability of desired behaviors.

True/False Test

Indicate whether each statement is true or false by placing T or F in the blank space next to each item.

1. ____ Aversive conditioning is a behavior therapy technique based on classical conditioning that involves modifying behavior by conditioning a new response that is incompatible with a previously learned response.

2. ____ In client-centered therapy, empathic understanding involves active listening and reflecting the content and personal meaning of feelings being experienced by the client.

3. ____ Systematic desensitization is a type of behavior therapy in which phobic responses are reduced by pairing relaxation with a series of mental images or real-life situations that the person finds progressively more fear provoking; based on the principle of counterconditioning.

4. ____ The operant conditioning model is based on the principles that behavior is shaped and maintained by its consequences.

5. ____ In systematic desensitization, the therapist may have the client create a very relaxing scene, unrelated to the hierarchy of anxiety-provoking images, called a control scene.

6. ____ In client-centered therapy, unconditional positive regard is created when the therapist values, accepts, and cares for the client, whatever her problems or behaviors.

7. ____ In behavior therapy, when a behavior decreases because it no longer leads to a reinforcer, extinction has occurred.

8. ____ When a person has received acceptance by significant others only if she conforms to their expectations, she is said to have experienced conditional acceptance.

9. ____ Counterconditioning is a relatively ineffec-

tive type of behavior therapy that involves repeatedly pairing an aversive stimulus with occurrence of undesirable behaviors or thoughts.

> Check your answers and review any areas of weakness before going on to the next section.

Cognitive Therapies
Learning Objectives

When you have finished studying this section of the chapter, you should be able to:

1. Identify the assumptions that cognitive therapies are based on.

2. Describe rational-emotive therapy (RET) and identify the founder of this approach

3. Describe Beck's cognitive therapy and explain how it differs from rational-emotive therapy.

*Read the section "Cognitive Therapies" and **write** your answers to the following:*

1. (a) Cognitive therapies assume that most people blame unhappiness and problems on _____ events and situations, but the real cause of unhappiness is the way the person _____ about the events, not the events themselves.

   (b) Thus, the goal of therapy is to focus on the faulty patterns of _____ and then to _____ them to more adaptive, healthy patterns.

2. (a) _____ developed rational-emotive therapy (RET) because he believed that people's difficulties are caused by their faulty _____ and _____ beliefs; RET focuses on changing the patterns of _____ thinking that are believed to be the primary cause of the client's emotional distress and psychological problems.

   (b) In RET, psychological problems are

explained by the ABC model; when a(n) _____ event (A) occurs, it is the person's _____ (B) about the event that cause emotional _____ (C); this differs from the commonsense view that (A) causes (C).

(c) Identifying the core _____ beliefs that underlie personal distress is the first step in RET; the second step is for the therapist to vigorously _____ and _____ the _____ beliefs.

(d) The consequences of _____ beliefs are unhealthy negative emotions, such as extreme anger, despair, resentment, and feeling of worthlessness, which interfere with constructive attempts to change disturbing situations; according to RET, the result is _____ behaviors, _____ disorders, _____ , and other psychological problems.

(e) From the client's perspective, RET requires admitting her _____ beliefs and accepting the fact that those beliefs are _____ and unhealthy; in addition, the client must radically change her way of _____ and _____ to stressful events.

(f) According to RET, appropriate emotions are the consequences of _____ beliefs, and such _____ mental and emotional responses encourage people to work toward constructively changing or coping with difficult situations; RET has been shown to be generally _____ (effective/ineffective) in the treatment of _____ , _____ , and certain _____ disorders and in helping people overcome self-defeating behaviors.

3. (a) Aaron Beck's development of cognitive therapy (CT) grew out of his research on _____ ; he discovered that _____ people have an extremely negative view of the past, present, and future.

(b) Rather than realistically evaluating their situation, _____ patients have developed a negative _____ bias, consistently _____ their expectations in a negative way; these negative _____ are shaped by deep-seated, self-deprecating thoughts, and CT essentially focuses on correcting the _____ biases that underlie _____ and other psychological disorders.

(c) Like _____ , Beck believes that what people _____ creates their moods and emotions, and like RET, CT involves helping clients to identify faulty _____ and to replace unhealthy patterns of _____ with healthier ones.

(d) In contrast with RET's emphasis on _____ thinking, Beck believes that _____ and other psychological problems are caused by _____ thinking and _____ beliefs; the CT therapist encourages the client to _____ test the accuracy of his or her assumptions and beliefs.

4. (a) The first step in CT is to help the client learn to recognize and monitor _____ that occur without conscious effort or control; whether negative or positive, _____ can control your emotional and behavioral reactions to events.

(b) In the second step of CT, the therapist helps the client learn how to _____ test the reality of the _____ that are so upsetting.

(c) Initially, the CT therapist acts as a(n) _____ , showing the client how to evaluate the accuracy of _____ , and in this way hopes to eventually teach the client to do the same on her own; unlike the confrontational tactics used in RET, the CT therapist strives to create a therapy climate of _____ that encourages the client to contribute to the evaluation of the logic and accuracy of _____ .

(d) Beck's CT has been shown to be very _____ (ineffective/effective) in treating _____ and other psychological disorders, including _____ disorders, _____ disorders, PTSD, and relationship problems, and has been adapted to treat psychotic symptoms associated with schizophrenia.

Group and Family Therapy
Learning Objectives

When you have finished studying this section of the chapter, you should be able to:

1. Describe how group therapy works and list some of the key advantages of this approach.
2. Explain what family therapy is and differentiate between it and individual therapy.

*Read the section "Group and Family Therapy" and **write** your answers to the following:*

1. (a) _____ psychotherapy offers a personal relationship between a client and a therapist that is focused on a single client's problems, thoughts, and emotions; in contrast, group therapy involves one or more therapists working with several people _____ , and the group may be as small as three or four people or as large as ten or more people.

(b) Virtually any approach, whether _____ , _____ , _____ , or _____ , can be used in group therapy, and just about any problem that can be handled _____ can be dealt with in group therapy.

(c) Group therapy has a number of advantages over _____ psychotherapies: (1) group therapy is very _____ ; a single therapist can work simultaneously with several people; (2) rather than relying on the client's _____ _____ about how he relates to other people, the therapist can observe his _____ interactions with others; (3) the support and encouragement provided by the other group members may help a person feel less alone and understand that his problems are not _____ ; (4) group members may provide each other with helpful, practical _____ for solving common problems and can act as _____ for successfully overcoming difficulties; and (5) working within a group gives people an opportunity to try out new _____ in a safe, supportive environment.

(d) Group therapy is typically conducted by a mental health professional, whereas _____ groups and _____ groups are typically conducted by nonprofessionals.

2. (a) Family therapy operates on the premise that

the problem is not solely within the individual himself, but instead the focus is on the _____ ; the major goal of family therapy is to alter and improve the ongoing _____ among all family members, including important members of the extended family, such as grandparents and in-laws.

(b) Family therapy is based on the assumption that the family is a(n) _____ , an interdependent unit, not just a collection of separate individuals; the family is seen as a(n) _____ structure in which each member plays a unique role.

(c) Every family has certain unspoken _____ of interaction and communication that often revolve around issues such as which family members exercise _____ and how, who makes _____ , who keeps the _____ , and what kinds of alliances members have formed among themselves; as such issues are explored, unhealthy _____ of family interaction can be identified and replaced with new ones that promote the psychological health of the family as a unit.

(d) Family therapy is often used to _____ the effectiveness of individual psychotherapy, especially in cases where the client's problems reflect conflict and disturbances in the entire family _____ ; it is also indicated when there is conflict among family members.

(e) Many family therapists also provide _____ or _____ therapy with the goal of improving communication and problem-solving skills and increasing intimacy between the pair.

Evaluating the Effectiveness of Psychotherapy
Learning Objectives

When you have finished studying this section of the chapter, you should be able to:

1. Identify what meta-analysis has demonstrated about the general effectiveness of psychotherapy.
2. Explain whether psychotherapy is more effective than no treatment at all.
3. List the common factors that contribute to effective psychotherapy.
4. Define eclecticism and describe how this approach works.

Read the section "Evaluating the Effectiveness of Psychotherapy" and **write** *your answers to the following:*

1. (a) Most people with psychological problems _____ (seek/do not seek) help from mental health professionals; some cope with the help and support of _____ and _____ ; some people improve simply with the passage of time, a phenomenon called _____ .

(b) The basic strategy to investigate whether psychotherapy offers significant _____ is to compare people who _____ psychotherapy with a matched control group of people who _____ psychotherapy.

(c) To combine and interpret the results of a large number of studies, researchers have used a statistical technique called _____ ; this involves _____ the results of several studies into a single analysis, which can reveal overall trends in the data.

(d) When _____ is used to

summarize these studies, the researchers consistently arrive at the same conclusion: psychotherapy is significantly _____ (less/more) effective than no treatment; on the average, the person who completes psychotherapy treatment is

_____ (no better off/better off) than about _____ percent of those in the untreated control group.

(e) Approximately _____ percent of people _____ (show no/show) significant improvement by the eighth weekly session of psychotherapy, and by the end of six months, about _____ percent _____ (show no/show) significant improvement; these results suggest that psychotherapy _____ (is/is not) effective.

2. (a) It appears that _____ and _____ therapies are more successful than _____ therapies in helping people who are experiencing panic disorder, obsessive-compulsive disorder, and phobias; when meta-analysis techniques are used, a consistent finding is that, in general, there is _____ (a big/little or no) difference in the effectiveness of different psychotherapies.

(b) Researchers have identified a number of factors that are related to a positive therapy outcome: (1) Most important is a _____ relationship, characterized by mutual respect, trust, and hope, in which the therapist and the client form a(n) _____ alliance to actively try to achieve the same goals. (2) Certain _____ characteristics, such as warmth, sensitivity, responsiveness, being perceived as sincere and genuine, and actively helping people to understand and face their problems, are associated with suc-

cessful therapy; (3) effective therapists are also sensitive to the _____ differences that may exist between themselves and their clients; (4) _____ characteristics, such as level of motivation, commitment to therapy, active involvement in the process, along with openness, a willingness to change, expressiveness, and social maturity, all influence the likelihood of therapeutic success; (5) _____ circumstances, such as having supportive family members and having a stable living situation, can enhance the effectiveness of psychotherapy.

(c) None of these factors is _____ to any particular brand of psychotherapy; nevertheless, the _____ among psychotherapy techniques can be important; for therapy to be optimally effective, the individual should feel comfortable with both the therapist and the therapeutic techniques used by the therapist.

3. (a) Increasingly, a personalized approach to therapy is being facilitated by the movement of mental health toward _____ , which is the pragmatic and integrated use of diverse psychotherapeutic techniques; today therapists identify themselves as _____ more often than any other orientation.

(b) _____ psychotherapists carefully tailor the therapy approach to the problems and characteristics of the person seeking help; for example, a(n) _____ therapist might integrate insight-oriented techniques with specific behavioral techniques to help someone suffering from extreme shyness.

4. Read the following and write the correct term in the space provided:

(a) Dr. McGilvery wants to determine whether

psychotherapy is effective for particular psychological disorders. In attempting to analyze the results of numerous published studies on the issue, he should use a technique called _____ .

(b) Mike, a mental health professional, tries to tailor his therapeutic approach to the problems and characteristics of the person seeking help. Mike's pragmatic and integrated use of diverse psychotherapeutic techniques would classify him as a(n) _____ therapist.

(c) Dr. Samson believes that a key aspect of resolving some psychological problems is getting individuals to realize that others have problems similar to their own. To achieve this goal, _____ therapy could be useful.

(d) Jay's therapist attacks and openly criticizes the irrational and self-defeating ways of thinking that Jay engages in. Jay's therapist is most likely a(n) _____ therapist.

(e) Dr. Beaven tries to help her clients learn to recognize and monitor the automatic thoughts that occur without conscious effort or control, and she then encourages them to empirically test the reality of these thoughts. Dr. Beaven's approach is most consistent with _____ therapy.

(f) Dr. Sidhu believes that in order to understand psychological problems it is important to investigate interactions among family members within the context of a family system that is a dynamic structure with each member playing a unique role. Dr. Sidhu is most likely a(n) _____ therapist.

Graphic Organizer 1

Fill in each of the following with the correct information.

Type of Therapy	Founder	Source of Problems	Treatment Techniques	Goals of Therapy
Psychoanalysis				
Client-Centered Therapy				
Behavior Therapy				
Rational-Emotive Therapy				
Cognitive Therapy				

Review of Key Terms and Key Names 3

cognitive therapies
Albert Ellis
rational-emotive therapy
Aaron T. Beck
cognitive therapy
group therapy
self-help groups and
　support groups

family therapy
spontaneous remission
network therapy
Naikan therapy
eclecticism

Matching Exercise

Match the appropriate term/name with its definition or description.

1. _____ A form of psychotherapy that is based on the assumption that the family is a system and that treats the family as a unit.

2. _____ A group of psychotherapies that are based on the assumption that psychological problems are due to maladaptive patterns of thinking; treatment techniques focus on recognizing and altering these unhealthy thinking patterns.

3. _____ A type of cognitive therapy, developed by psychiatrist Aaron Beck, that focuses on changing the client's unrealistic beliefs.

4. _____ A form of psychotherapy that involves one or more therapists working simultaneously with a small group of clients.

5. _____ A type of cognitive therapy, developed by psychologist Albert Ellis, that focuses on changing the client's irrational beliefs.

6. _____ A phenomenon in which people eventually improve or recover from psychological symptoms simply with the passage of time.

True/False Test

Indicate whether each item is true or false by placing T or F in the space next to each item.

1. ___ Albert Ellis is the person who founded cognitive therapy (CT), which is a psychotherapy based on the assumption that depression and other psychological problems are caused by biased perceptions, distorted thinking, and inaccurate beliefs.

2. ___ Eclecticism is the pragmatic and integrated use of techniques from different psychotherapies.

3. ___ Network therapy is a Native American therapy that is conducted in the person's home and can involve as many as 70 members of the individual's community or tribe.

4. ___ Self-help groups and support groups deal with a wide array of psychological, medical, and behavioral problems through group processes and interactions that are typically organized and led by nonprofessionals.

5. ___ Aaron T. Beck is the person who founded the cognitive psychotherapy called rational-emotive therapy (RET), which emphasizes recognizing and changing irrational beliefs.

6. ___ Naikan therapy is a Japanese psychotherapy that encourages the client to meditate on what he has received from significant others, what he has done in return, and the problems that he has caused for these significant people.

> Check your answers and review any areas of weakness before going on to the next section.

Biomedical Therapies
Learning Objectives

When you have finished studying this section of the chapter, you should be able to:

1. Describe the approach taken by the biomedical approaches.

2. Identify the most important antipsychotic, antianxiety, and antidepressant medications, and explain how they achieve their effects.

3. List the disadvantages of using these medications.

4. Explain what lithium and ECT are and describe how they are used.

*Read the section "Biomedical Therapies" and **write** your answers to the following:*

1. (a) Today, the most common biomedical therapy is the use of

_____ ,

which are prescription drugs that alter mental functions and alleviate psychological symptoms; of all medical prescriptions written today, _____ percent are for medications used to affect mental processes.

(b) The synthetic version of an herb that has traditionally been used in India and Japan to treat diverse medical conditions, including psychotic symptoms associated with schizophrenia, is called _____ .

(c) In the 1950s French scientists demonstrated that the drug _____ diminished the psychotic symptoms commonly seen in schizophrenia; it is better known today by its trade name _____ and is still widely used to treat psychotic symptoms.

(d) Because _____ and _____ diminish the symptoms commonly seen in schizophrenia, they are called _____ medications.

(e) Both drugs work by reducing levels of the neurotransmitter _____ ; since the development of these early drugs, more than thirty other _____ medications, which also act on _____ receptors in the brain, have been developed.

(f) The first _____ effectively reduced the so-called positive symptoms of schizophrenia, such as _____ , _____ , and disordered thinking and contributed to the dramatic decrease in the number of patients in mental hospitals.

2. The early antipsychotic drugs had a number of drawbacks:

(a) They didn't actually _____ schizophrenia; psychotic symptoms often returned if a person stopped taking the medication.

(b) They were not very effective in eliminating the negative symptoms of schizophrenia, such as _____ withdrawal, _____ , _____ emotions, or lack of emotional expressiveness; in some cases, the drugs even made the negative symptoms worse.

(c) They often produced unwanted _____ , such as dry mouth, weight gain, constipation, sleepiness, and poor concentration.

(d) The fact that these early drugs *globally* altered brain levels of _____ altered normal motor movements and created a number of motor-related _____ , such as muscle tremors, rigid movement, a shuffling gait, and a masklike facial expression.

(e) The long-term use of these drugs causes a small percentage of people to develop a potentially irreversible motor disorder called _____ , which is characterized by severe, uncontrollable facial tics and grimaces, chewing movements, and other involuntary lip movements.

(f) A further problem is the _____ pattern of hospitalization, discharge, and rehospitalization; once the schizophrenic symptoms were stabilized by the drugs, the patients were discharged, but because of the unpleasant side effects, inadequate medical follow-up, or both, the patients eventually stopped taking the medication, and when the symptoms returned, they were rehospitalized.

3. (a) A new generation of antipsychotic drugs, called _____ antipsychotics, act differently on the brain than the older drugs; clozapine and risperidone affect levels of the neurotransmitter _____ as well as _____ in the brain.

(b) The _____ antipsychotics have

several advantages over the traditional antipsychotic drugs: (1) clozapine and risperidone are much less likely to cause _____-related side effects because they act on _____ receptors in the brain areas associated with psychotic symptoms; (2) they are also more effective than the older drugs in treating the _____ symptoms of schizophrenia; and (3) some patients who have not responded to any of the traditional _____ drugs improve after taking clozapine or risperidone.

4. (a) The best-known _____ drugs are benzodiazepines, which include the trade name drugs Valium and Xanax; they take effect rapidly and calm jittery feelings, relax muscles, and promote sleep by increasing the level of _____ , a neurotransmitter that inhibits the transmission of nerve impulses in the brain and slows brain activity.

   (b) The benzodiazepines have several potentially dangerous side effects: (1) they can reduce _____ , _____ , and _____ time; (2) their effects can be _____ when they are combined with alcohol and many other drugs, including over-the-counter antihistamines; and (3) benzodiazepines are physically _____ if taken in large quantities over a long period of time; if physical _____ occurs, the person must withdraw from the drug gradually, as abrupt withdrawal can produce life-threatening symptoms.

   (c) A newer _____ drug with the trade name Buspar has fewer _____ and lower risk of _____ and physical _____ ; its major drawback is

that it must be taken for two to three weeks before it takes effect.

5. (a) The medication used to treat _____ _____ disorder is lithium, a naturally occurring substance; it counteracts both _____ and _____ symptoms in patients with the disorder.

   (b) Lithium stops acute _____ episodes over the course of a week or two, and once they are under control, the long-term use of lithium can help prevent relapses into either _____ or _____ ; it is an effective treatment for most patients.

   (c) If the level of lithium is too low, _____ symptoms persist, and if the level is too high, symptoms of lithium _____ may occur.

   (d) How lithium works is a complete mystery, but some researchers have suggested that it somehow regulates _____ , evening out extremes of both _____ and _____ .

   (e) Recently, _____ has been treated with an anticonvulsant medicine, called Depakote.

6. (a) The antidepressant medications counteract the classic symptoms of depression, such as _____ , _____ , _____ , suicidal thoughts, difficulty _____ , and disruptions in _____ , energy, _____ , and sexuality.

   (b) The first generation of antidepressant drugs consists of _____ and _____ inhibitors, both of which affect multiple neurotransmitter pathways in the brain; evidence suggests that these drugs alleviate depression by increasing the availability of two key brain neurotransmitters, _____ and

_____ .

(c) In about _____ percent of depressed patients, these drugs effectively eliminate depressive symptoms, but they can also produce numerous _____ , such as weight gain, dizziness, and dry mouth and eyes, and, in combination with other chemicals found in many foods, can result in dangerously high blood pressure levels.

(d) The second generation of antidepressants includes trazadone and bupropion, and although chemically different from the first generation, they were generally _____ (more/no more) effective and had _____ (many/none) of the same side effects.

(e) When the selective _____ reuptake _____ (SSRIs) were introduced in 1987, the picture changed dramatically; rather than acting on multiple neurotransmitter pathways, the SSRIs affect the availability of a single neurotransmitter, _____ .

(f) The first SSRI to be released was fluoxetine, with the trade name _____ , and it was quickly followed by its chemical cousins, Zoloft and Paxil; these drugs tend to have _____ and _____ side effects but can cause headaches, nervousness, sleeping problems, loss of appetite, and sexual dysfunction.

7. (a) About _____ patients a year receive electroconvulsive therapy (ECT) as a medical treatment for severe _____ ; the procedure involves using a brief burst of electric current to induce a seizure in the brain, much like an epileptic seizure, but it is not known why inducing a convulsion relieves the symptoms of depression.

(b) ECT is a painless, relatively _____ medical procedure, usually performed in a hospital; the seizure lasts about a minute, and when the anesthesia wears off and the patient wakes up, he or she may be _____ and _____ .

(c) The patient may also experience temporary or permanent _____ loss for the events leading up to the treatment; to treat major _____ , a series of six to ten ECT treatments are usually spaced over a few weeks.

(d) ECT is _____ (a very/not a very) effective treatment for severe _____ with a slightly _____ (lower/higher) overall effectiveness rate than the antidepressant drugs; about _____ percent of depressed patients improve.

(e) ECT has potential dangers; serious _____ impairments can occur, such as extensive amnesia (memory loss) and disturbances in _____ and _____ abilities; it is also the most controversial medical treatment for psychological disorders, and not everyone agrees that it is either safe or effective.

8. Read the following and write the correct term in the space provided:

(a) For no apparent reason, Mrs. Bell has constant and persistent feelings of anxiety, nervousness, and apprehension that interfere with her ability to eat, sleep, and function. Her psychiatrist is most likely to prescribe a type of psychoactive medication called _____ medication.

(b) Mr. Millis still experiences intense feelings of despondency, hopelessness, dejection, and suicidal thoughts, despite extensive psychotherapy and months of psychoactive medication. Because of this lack of responsiveness, his doctor is likely to consider using _____ therapy.

(c) After being on antipsychotic medications for many years, Florence has developed a number of serious symptoms, such as severe, uncontrollable facial tics and grimaces, chewing movements, and other involuntary movements of the lips, jaw, and tongue. Florence suffers from

_____ .

(d) Dwayne has been diagnosed with bipolar disorder. His doctor is most likely to prescribe _____ .

(e) To treat her symptoms, which included hallucinations, delusions, and disordered thought processes, Debra's psychiatrist prescribed one of the atypical antipsychotic medications that affect the levels of the neurotransmitter serotonin as well as dopamine in the brain. He is likely to have prescribed either _____ or

_____ .

Graphic Organizer 2

List the credentials and qualifications of each of the following:

Clinical Psychologist	
Psychiatrist	
Psychoanalyst	
Psychiatric Social Worker	
Marriage and Family Therapists	
Psychiatric Nurse	

Review of Key Terms 4

psychoactive
  medications
antipsychotic
  medications
tardive dyskinesia
antianxiety medications

lithium
antidepressant
  medications
electroconvulsive
  therapy (ECT)
catharsis

Matching Exercise

Match the appropriate term with its definition or description.

1. _____ A naturally occurring substance that is used in the treatment of bipolar disorder.

2. _____ Prescription drugs that alter mental functions and alleviate psychological symptoms.

3. _____ A biomedical therapy used primarily in the treatment of depression that involves electrically inducing a brief brain seizure; also called shock therapy and electric shock therapy.

4. _____ Prescription drugs that are used to alleviate the symptoms of anxiety.

5. _____ Prescription drugs that are used to reduce the symptoms associated with depression.

6. _____ A potentially irreversible motor disorder that results from the long-term use of antipsychotic medications and is characterized by severe, uncontrollable facial tics and grimaces, chewing movements, and other involuntary movements of the lips, jaw, and tongue.

7. _____ Prescription drugs that are used to reduce psychotic symptoms; frequently used in the treatment of schizophrenia.

8. _____ The reduction of emotional and physical tension that occurs simply as a result of talking about one's psychological problems.

Check your answers and review any areas of weakness before going on to the next section.

Something to Think About

1. Many people suffer from fear and anxiety about things like going to the dentist or doctor, having job interviews, and taking exams. These kinds of fears are normal, and most people manage to cope with such anxiety-provoking situations. Other fears are more serious and may cause the person intense distress and interfere with his or her normal functioning in some way. Imagine a situation in which a friend or family member comes to you seeking help about how to overcome her fear of flying. Based on what you know about the behavior therapy technique of systematic desensitization, what might you say to this person?

2. Many people with psychological problems do not seek help from mental health professionals. There are many reasons for this. One reason may have to do with a lack of understanding about what to expect in psychotherapy. What are some of the important things a person should know about psychotherapy?

Check your answers and review any areas of weakness before doing the progress tests.

Progress Test 1

Review the complete chapter (including Concept Reviews and the boxed inserts), review all your study notes, and then test yourself on the following progress test. Check your answers. If you make a mistake, review your notes, review the relevant section of the study guide, and, if necessary, go back and read the appropriate part of your textbook.

1. Jacqueline's therapist wants to help her to become more aware of unresolved conflicts in her childhood, and he uses dream interpretation and free association to help in this process. The therapist's techniques and goals best reflect the primary aim of
   (a) psychoanalysis
   (b) client-centered therapy
   (c) behavior therapy
   (d) cognitive therapy

2. Tyler has been diagnosed with schizophrenia. His doctor is most likely to prescribe
   (a) electroconvulsive therapy
   (b) lithium
   (c) antipsychotic medication
   (d) antianxiety medication

3. Mrs. Alverz gives her third-grade students a silver sticker every time they get a perfect score on their weekly spelling test. At the end of the term students can exchange their stickers for prizes. Mrs. Alverz is using a strategy based on _____ conditioning called _____
   (a) classical; the bell and pad method
   (b) classical; the token economy
   (c) operant; the bell and pad method
   (d) operant; the token economy

4. Mr. MacKaskill has a serious drinking problem. In order to reduce his intake of alcohol, a behavior therapist might give Mr. MacKaskill a medication called Antabuse, which induces nausea whenever it is taken with alcohol. This behavioral technique is called
   (a) counterconditioning
   (b) systematic desensitization
   (c) aversive therapy
   (d) the token economy

5. For no obvious reason Mr. Henderson has recently begun to express feelings of annoyance, irritability, and anger toward his therapist, who has been consistently patient, concerned, and supportive. Freud would most likely consider Mr. Henderson's hostility toward his therapist to be an example of

   (a) insight   (c) aversion
   (b) counterconditioning   (d) transference

6. Aaron Beck is to _____ as Carl Rogers is to _____ .

   (a) cognitive therapy; rational-emotive therapy
   (b) behavior therapy; counterconditioning
   (c) client-centered therapy; psychoanalysis
   (d) cognitive therapy; client-centered therapy

7. Because of Rhian's persistent feelings of hopelessness, dejection, and guilt and her suicidal thoughts, her doctor prescribed a new drug that belongs to the group of _____ drugs called the selective serotonin reuptake inhibitors (SSRIs).

   (a) antianxiety
   (b) atypical antipsychotic
   (c) antidepressant
   (d) antipsychotic

8. Twenty-five-year-old Melissa told her therapist that she was worthless and unattractive because she didn't have a boyfriend and she was sure she was going to end up single and unloved. Her therapist said, "Your way of thinking is not only irrational but also totally stupid and absurd! You are worthless only if you *think* you are!" This statement would most likely be made by a _____ therapist.

   (a) behavioral
   (b) client-centered
   (c) rational-emotive
   (d) psychoanalytic
   (e) None of the above; no therapist would talk like that to a client

9. Gardner attends a local health clinic once a week where he is attempting to deal with some of his psychological problems by discussing them with five or six other people and two psychologists. Gardner is involved in

   (a) individual therapy
   (b) group therapy
   (c) a biomedical treatment program
   (d) a self-help group

10. Mr. Lansdon's intense feelings of despondency and helplessness are periodically interrupted by episodes in which he experiences excessive feelings of personal power and a grandiose optimism that he can change the world to fit his strange ideological beliefs. A biomedical therapist would most likely prescribe

    (a) electroconvulsive therapy
    (b) lithium
    (c) antipsychotic medications
    (d) antidepressant medications

11. Gabrielle's feelings of unhappiness, despondency, dejection, and hopelessness have become so extreme that she has attempted suicide. Which of the following treatments is likely to provide her with the quickest relief from her misery?

    (a) systematic desensitization
    (b) the bell and pad treatment
    (c) psychoanalysis
    (d) electroconvulsive therapy (ECT)

12. Because of his persistent psychological problems, Werner has been prescribed a benzodiazepine drug called Valium. It is most likely that Werner suffers from

    (a) bipolar disorder   (c) anxiety
    (b) schizophrenia   (d) depression

13. After a session with her therapist, in which she finally expressed all the anger and hostility she felt toward her parents and described the terrible guilt she felt about it, Charlene felt an enormous reduction in and relief from her emotional and physical tension. Charlene has probably experienced

    (a) resistance
    (b) catharsis
    (c) ECT
    (d) counterconditioning

14. Dr. Elson uses a therapeutic technique that involves modifying behavior by conditioning a new response that is incompatible with a previously learned undesired response. Dr. Elson is most likely a _____ therapist who is using _____ .

    (a) behavior; counterconditioning
    (b) cognitive; rational-emotive techniques
    (c) psychoanalytic; free association
    (d) biomedical; ECT

15. When Nelson asked his therapist what he should expect during their therapy sessions, his therapist said that the role of the therapist is to be nondirective and that she was there to provide unconditional positive regard in an open, honest way. Nelson's therapist is most likely a _____ therapist.
    (a) psychoanalytic   (c) cognitive
    (b) behavioral   (d) humanistic

16. Kathleen is on a committee at a community health care facility that has the task of determining which of the major forms of psychotherapy is most effective. After she reviews studies that used meta-analysis to assess the results of treatment outcomes, she is most likely to conclude that
    (a) behavior therapy is the single most effective therapy available
    (b) client-centered therapy has been consistently more effective than all the other forms of therapy
    (c) in general, there is little or no difference in the effectiveness of the different forms of psychotherapy
    (d) psychoanalysis works best for schizophrenia and cognitive therapy works best for phobias

17. The main difference between group therapy and self-help groups is that
    (a) self-help groups are usually organized and led by nonprofessionals
    (b) group therapy is typically much less expensive
    (c) self-help groups have a very low success rate compared to group therapy
    (d) group therapy usually follows a twelve-step approach, whereas self-help groups typically use a six-step approach

18. According to the Application section, which of the following is true?
    (a) Therapy is a collaborative effort.
    (b) Expect therapy to challenge how you think and act.
    (c) Your therapist will not become a substitute friend.
    (d) Your therapist will not make decisions for you.
    (e) All of the above are true.

19. Mashara goes to a therapist who specializes in a Japanese psychotherapy called Naikan therapy. According to Culture and Human Behavior Box 14.2, he is likely to be advised
    (a) that being self-absorbed is the surest path to psychological suffering
    (b) to focus on developing a sense of gratitude and obligation toward others instead of focusing on the self
    (c) to meditate on how he may have failed to meet the needs of others, rather than thinking about his own immediate needs
    (d) all of the above

20. According to Critical Thinking Box 14.3, which of the following is true?
    (a) Prozac helps seriously depressed people regain a normal level of functioning.
    (b) There is solid scientific evidence that Prozac can fundamentally alter and enhance functioning in every aspect of a normal person's life.
    (c) Prozac is an antipsychotic medication that alleviates the symptoms of schizophrenia.
    (d) Cosmetic pharmacology is now an accepted therapeutic approach used by most biomedical practitioners.

Progress Test 2

After you have checked your understanding of the material in Progress Test 1 and have done a complete chapter review with special focus on any areas of weakness, you are ready to assess your knowledge of Progress Test 2. Check your answers. If you make a mistake, review your notes, the relevant section of the study guide, and, if necessary, the appropriate part of your textbook.

1. Dr. Rassmunsen uses medication and other medical procedures, including electroconvulsive therapy, to treat the symptoms of psychological disorders. Dr. Rassmunsen's approach would most likely be classified as
    (a) cognitive therapy   (c) humanistic therapy
    (b) behavioral therapy   (d) biomedical therapy

2. Mr. Damson suffers from auditory hallucinations and falsely believes his co-workers are not only trying to steal his "secret inventions" but are also plotting to kill him. A biomedical therapist would most likely prescribe
    (a) electroconvulsive therapy
    (b) lithium
    (c) antipsychotic medications
    (d) antidepressant medications

3. Mervyn's therapist prescribed a medication that is classified as a selective serotonin reuptake inhibitor (SSRI) for his psychological symptoms. It is most likely that Mervyn suffers from
   (a) schizophrenia   (c) anxiety disorder
   (b) bipolar disorder   (d) depression

4. While giving a talk to students interested in graduate work in clinical psychology, Dr. Barton is asked what factors contribute most to effective psychotherapy. He is most likely to respond that
   (a) mutual respect, trust, and hope in the therapeutic situation are important factors
   (b) therapists who have warmth, sensitivity, sincerity, and genuineness are usually effective
   (c) clients who are motivated, expressive, and actively committed to therapy enhance the success of therapy
   (d) all of the above contribute to effective psychotherapy

5. Brian's therapist attempts to tailor the therapeutic approach to the problems and characteristics of the person seeking help and in doing so makes use of techniques from different psychotherapies. Brian's therapist would most likely be classified as a(n)
   (a) humanistic therapist
   (b) eclectic therapist
   (c) behavior therapist
   (d) cognitive therapist

6. When Freda told her therapist that she wanted to get his advice on what she should do about her relationship problems, he replied, "It sounds to me like you are experiencing some difficulties with you relationship. Is that right?" The therapist's response reflects the technique of
   (a) transference
   (b) free association
   (c) empathic understanding
   (d) counterconditioning

7. It is very probable that Freda's therapist is a _____ therapist.
   (a) cognitive   (c) behavior
   (b) psychoanalytic   (d) humanistic

8. When Greta's psychoanalyst asked her to elaborate on certain aspects of the dream she had,

she couldn't think of anything to say about it. Her lack of responsiveness is likely to be interpreted as
   (a) resistance
   (b) catharsis
   (c) transference
   (d) spontaneous remission

9. Dr. Whelan believes that people can overcome their problems if they learn to recognize and monitor their automatic thoughts and then try to empirically test the reality of these thoughts. Her approach is most consistent with
   (a) behavior therapy   (c) cognitive therapy
   (b) biomedical therapy   (d) psychoanalysis

10. A behavior therapist trains a child who is a frequent bedwetter to awake and use the bathroom by arranging for an alarm to sound every time he wets the bed. This technique is called _____ and illustrates the use of _____ conditioning.
    (a) aversive therapy; operant
    (b) the bell and pad treatment; classical
    (c) aversive therapy; classical
    (d) the bell and pad treatment; operant

11. For which of the following is Dr. Kelly most likely to prescribe a benzodiazepine drug called Valium?
    (a) Celia, who smokes three packs of cigarettes a day
    (b) Rachel, who suffers from nervous apprehension, intense anxiety, and an inability to relax
    (c) Garth, who irrationally believes that aliens are trying to steal his thoughts
    (d) Manuel, who fluctuates between extreme moods of euphoria and depression

12. Quentin has an irrational fear of flying. His therapist first teaches him to relax completely, then he asks him to come up with a list of anxiety-provoking images associated with flying. Finally, the therapist asks Quentin to close his eyes and imagine very clearly the least fearful scene on the list. Quentin's therapist is a _____ therapist using _____ .
    (a) behavior; systematic desensitization
    (b) cognitive; rational-emotive techniques
    (c) humanistic; emphatic understanding
    (d) psychoanalytic; free association

13. Jeneen is taking a prescription drug that contains a naturally occurring substance called lithium. It is most probable that she is suffering from
    (a) schizophrenia
    (b) bipolar disorder
    (c) chronic depression
    (d) anxiety disorder

14. Ursula is in a home for the mentally retarded and she is able to earn points for getting dressed, maintaining personal hygiene, and engaging in appropriate social interactions. These points can be exchanged for access to desirable items or special privileges. This example illustrates the use of
    (a) aversive conditioning
    (b) counterconditioning
    (c) systematic desensitization
    (d) a token economy

15. Seven-year-old Niall chews the ends of all his pens and pencils, so his mother paints them with a foul-tasting, but harmless, substance. After a few days of this treatment Niall stops chewing his pens and pencils. Niall's mother has used a form of
    (a) transference
    (b) counterconditioning
    (c) aversive therapy
    (d) electroconvulsive therapy

16. Which of the following individuals is most likely to benefit from a psychoactive drug that affects the level of the neurotransmitter dopamine in the brain?
    (a) Herman, who hears imaginary voices telling him that he is going to be abducted by aliens
    (b) Marcel, who is very nervous and anxious all the time
    (c) Carla, who feels sad, despondent, dejected, and worthless most of the time
    (d) Faith, who drinks at least a six-pack of beer every day

17. Harriet has asked her psychology professor whether psychotherapy is more effective than no therapy at all. If her professor is familiar with the meta-analytic studies on the topic, he is most likely to answer that
    (a) psychotherapy is no more effective than talking to a friend

    (b) it is not possible to measure the effectiveness of psychotherapy
    (c) psychotherapy harms more people than it helps
    (d) psychotherapy is significantly more effective than no treatment

18. Mr. Keiko, a middle-aged Japanese American, has been referred to a psychologist because he is displaying the classic symptoms of anxiety and depression. One problem that may occur with a Western-style therapist is that Mr. Keiko
    (a) may be reluctant to discuss personal, intimate details of his life with a stranger
    (b) may prefer to deal with a female rather than a male therapist
    (c) may believe that insight and awareness of all painful thoughts and feelings are necessary for mental health
    (d) all of the above

19. Self-help groups are discussed in the In Focus Box 14.1. Which of the following points is made?
    (a) Self-help groups are generally ineffective for the vast majority of psychological problems when compared with therapy provided by mental health professionals.
    (b) What self-help groups have in common is that all of them are organized and led by nonprofessionals
    (c) Compared to professional mental health services, self-help groups are much more likely to cause harm to the people involved.
    (d) What self-help groups have in common is that all of them are organized and led by professional mental health experts.

20. According to the Application section, which of the following is true of catharsis?
    (a) It produces long-term relief from most psychological disorders.
    (b) It is the cornerstone of the relationship between the therapist and the person seeking help.
    (c) It refers to the emotional relief that people experience from the simple act of talking about their problems.
    (d) It refers to the repression of anxiety-provoking emotions into the unconscious mind.

Answers

Introduction: Psychotherapy and Biomedical Therapy

1. (a) psychological disorder; troubled; transitions
   (b) psychological; emotional, behavioral; interpersonal; psychological; feelings, behaviors
   (c) medication; medical; psychological; psychological; biological
   (d) psychological; psychiatrists; psychological
   (e) psychoanalytic, humanistic, behavioral; cognitive

Psychoanalytic Therapy

1. (a) personality; continue to be
   (b) early childhood; unresolved; frustrated; repressed
   (c) insight; relationship
   (d) techniques

2. (a) free association; thoughts, mental images; feelings
   (b) free association; resistance; repressed
   (c) dream; sleep; dream images
   (d) interpretations; behavior; thoughts; feelings; dreams
   (e) transference
   (f) past; behavior; relationships; insights
   (g) four; five; four

3. (a) few; weeks; months
   (b) a few months; quickly; specific, concrete; directive
   (c) interpretations; feelings; transferences; psychological
   (d) seldom; continue to be

4. (a) resistance
   (b) free association
   (c) resistance
   (d) transference

Matching Exercise 1

1. Sigmund Freud
2. psychotherapy
3. interpretation
4. psychoanalysis
5. biomedical therapy
6. short-term dynamic therapies
7. transference

True/False Test 1

1. T   3. T   5. T
2. F   4. T   6. F

Humanistic Therapy

1. (a) potential; awareness; choice; conscious, subjective
   (b) good; psychologically; choices; potential

2. (a) client-centered; person-centered
   (b) sick; heal; client-centered; client's
   (c) direct; decisions; solutions; client's; client; client

3. (a) genuineness; honestly; openly; genuineness; defensiveness
   (b) unconditional positive regard; conditional acceptance
   (c) empathic understanding; actively; feelings; thoughts; feelings
   (d) genuineness, unconditional positive regard; empathic understanding; self-actualization
   (e) supported; marital; parenting; business

Behavior Therapy

1. (a) modify; personality; past; current
   (b) learned; unlearning; learning
   (c) learning; classical; operant; observational

2. (a) classically; generalized
   (b) reversing; counterconditioning
   (c) feared; pleasant; eliminated
   (d) counterconditioning; observational learning; imitate

3. (a) incompatible; inhibits
   (b) progressive relaxation; relaxing; relaxation
   (c) hierarchy; control
   (d) anxiety; hierarchy; relaxation
   (e) control; progressive relaxation
   (f) hierarchy; relaxation; conditioned response

4. (a) deep sleepers; wake up
   (b) classically; bell
   (c) stimulus; response; 75

5. (a) Aversive; unpleasant; distasteful
   (b) Aversive; nausea
   (c) aversive; not very; on the decline

6. (a) shaped; consequences
   (b) positive; extinction
   (c) groups of people; strengthening; positive
   (d) positive; reinforcers
   (e) prisons, classrooms; psychiatric

7. (a) humanistic; client-centered
   (b) behavior
   (c) aversive
   (d) the token economy
   (e) the bell and pad treatment
   (f) client-centered; empathic understanding

Matching Exercise 2

1. Mary Cover Jones
2. humanistic perspective
3. token economy
4. genuineness
5. behavior therapy
6. Carl Rogers
7. progressive relaxation
8. bell and pad treatment
9. client-centered therapy
10. positive reinforcement

True/False 2

1. F	4. T	7. T
2. T	5. T	8. T
3. T	6. T	9. F

Cognitive Therapies

1. (a) external; thinks
   (b) thinking; change

2. (a) Albert Ellis; expectations; irrational; irrational
   (b) activating; beliefs; consequences
   (c) irrational; dispute; challenge; irrational
   (d) irrational; self-defeating; anxiety; depression
   (e) irrational; irrational; interpreting; responding
   (f) rational; healthy; effective; depression, social phobia; anxiety

3. (a) depression; depressed
   (b) depressed; cognitive; distorting; perceptions; cognitive; depression
   (c) Ellis; think; thinking; thinking
   (d) irrational; depression; distorted; unrealistic; empirically

4. (a) automatic thoughts; automatic thoughts
   (b) empirically; automatic thoughts
   (c) model; automatic thoughts; collaboration; automatic thoughts
   (d) effective; depression; anxiety; eating

Group and Family Therapy

1. (a) individual; simultaneously
   (b) psychodynamic, client-centered, behavioral; cognitive; individually
   (c) individual; cost-effective; self-perceptions; actual; unique; advice; models; behaviors
   (d) self-help; support

2. (a) whole family; interaction
   (b) system; dynamic
   (c) rules; power; decisions; peace; patterns
   (d) enhance; system
   (e) marital; couple

Evaluating the Effectiveness of Psychotherapy

1. (a) do not seek; friends; family; spontaneous remission
   (b) benefits; enter or receive; do not receive
   (c) meta-analysis; pooling
   (d) meta-analysis; more; better off; 80
   (e) 50; show; 75; show; is

2. (a) cognitive; behavioral; insight-oriented; little or no
   (b) therapeutic; cooperative; therapist; cultural; client; external
   (c) specific; differences

3. (a) eclecticism; eclectic
   (b) eclectic; eclectic

4. (a) meta-analysis
   (b) eclectic
   (c) group
   (d) rational-emotive
   (e) cognitive
   (f) family

Graphic Organizer 1

Psychoanalysis:
Founder: Sigmund Freud
Source of Problems: Repressed, unconscious conflicts stemming from early childhood experiences
Treatment Techniques: Free association, analysis of dream content, interpretation, and transference
Goals of Therapy: To recognize, work through, and resolve longstanding conflicts

Client-Centered Therapy:
Founder: Carl Rogers
Source of Problems: Conditional acceptance and dependence that causes a person to develop a distorted self-concept and world view
Treatment Techniques: Nondirective therapy, with therapist displaying unconditional positive regard, genuineness, and empathic understanding
Goals of Therapy: To develop self-awareness, self-acceptance, and self-determination

Behavior Therapy:
Founder: Derived from the fundamental principles of learning
Source of Problems: Learned maladaptive behavior patterns

Treatment Techniques: Systematic desensitization, bell and pad treatment, aversive conditioning, positive reinforcement and extinction, token economy, observational learning
Goals of Therapy: To unlearn maladaptive behaviors and learn adaptive behaviors in their place

Rational-Emotive Therapy
Founder: Albert Ellis
Source of Problems: Irrational beliefs
Treatment Techniques: Very directive therapy: identifying, logically disputing, and challenging irrational beliefs
Goals of Therapy: To surrender irrational beliefs and absolutist demands

Cognitive Therapy:
Founder: Aaron T. Beck
Source of Problems: Unrealistic, distorted perceptions and interpretations of events due to cognitive biases
Treatment Techniques: Directive collaboration: teaching client to monitor automatic thoughts; testing accuracy of conclusions; correcting distorted thinking and perception
Goals of Therapy: To accurately and realistically perceive self, others, and external events

Matching Exercise 3

1. family therapy
2. cognitive therapies
3. cognitive therapy
4. group therapy
5. rational-emotive therapy
6. spontaneous remission

True/False Test 3

1. F	3. T	5. F
2. T	4. T	6. T

Biomedical Therapies

1. (a) psychoactive medications; 20
   (b) reserpine
   (c) chlorpromazine; Thorazine
   (d) reserpine; chlorpromazine; antipsychotic
   (e) dopamine; antipsychotic; dopamine
   (f) antipsychotics; hallucinations, delusions

2. (a) cure
   (b) social; apathy, flat
   (c) side effects
   (d) dopamine; side effects
   (e) tardive dyskinesia
   (f) "revolving-door"

3. (a) atypical; serotonin; dopamine
   (b) atypical; movement; dopamine; negative; antipsychotic

4. (a) antianxiety; GABA
   (b) coordination, alertness; reaction; intensified; addictive; dependency
   (c) antianxiety; side effects; dependency; addiction

5. (a) bipolar; manic; depressive
   (b) manic; mania; depression
   (c) manic; poisoning
   (d) neurotransmission; mania; depression
   (e) bipolar disorder

6. (a) hopelessness, guilt, dejection; concentrating; sleep; appetite
   (b) tricyclics; MAO; norepinephrine; serotonin
   (c) 75; side effects
   (d) no more; many
   (e) serotonin; inhibitors; serotonin
   (f) Prozac; fewer; milder

7. (a) 40,000; depression
   (b) quick; confused; disoriented
   (c) memory; depression
   (d) a very; depression; higher; 80
   (e) cognitive; language; verbal

8. (a) antianxiety
   (b) electroconvulsive
   (c) tardive dyskinesia
   (d) lithium
   (e) clozapine; risperidone

Graphic Organizer 2

Clinical Psychologist	Holds an academic doctorate (Ph.D., Psy.D., or Ed.D.) and is required to be licensed to practice. Has expertise in psychological testing, diagnosis, psychotherapy, research, and prevention of mental and emotional disorders. May work in private practice, hospitals, or community mental health centers.
Psychiatrist	Holds a medical degree (M.D. or D.O.) and is required to be licensed to practice. Has expertise in the diagnosis, treatment, and prevention of mental and emotional disorders. Often has training in psychotherapy. May prescribe medications, electroconvulsive therapy, or other medical procedures.
Psychoanalyst	Usually a psychiatrist or clinical psychologist who has received additional training in the specific techniques of psychoanalysis, the form of psychotherapy originated by Sigmund Freud.
Psychiatric Social Worker	Holds a master's degree in social work (M.S.W.). Training includes an internship in a social-service agency or mental health center. Most states require certification or licensure. May or may not have training in psychotherapy.
Marriage and Family Therapists	Usually hold a master's degree with extensive supervised experience in couple or family therapy. May also have training in individual therapy. Many states require licensure.
Psychiatric Nurse	Holds a R.N. degree and has selected psychiatry or mental health nursing as specialty area. Typically works on a hospital psychiatric unit or in a community mental health center. May or may not have training in psychotherapy.

Matching Exercise 4

1. lithium
2. psychoactive medications
3. electroconvulsive therapy (ECT)
4. antianxiety medications
5. antidepressant medications
6. tardive dyskinesia
7. antipsychotic medications
8. catharsis

Something to Think About

1. The first thing to tell someone with a phobia is that there are many different therapeutic approaches in psychology, such as psychoanalysis, client-centered therapy, cognitive therapy, and behavior therapy. It would be appropriate to briefly explain the differences between each of these approaches and to advise the person to seek professional help if she feels that her problem is severe. Having said that, you can then go on to describe an approach that has been relatively effective in dealing with phobias—systematic desensitization.

The first step in systematic desensitization is for the person to learn how to relax completely. The reason for this is that a state of complete relaxation is incompatible with being tense and anxious. The second step is to get the person to generate a hierarchy of feared situations associated with flying. For example, the most feared situation the person can imagine might be sitting on the plane when it is starting to take off and the least fearful might be hearing someone talking about flying. Once the person is totally relaxed, she can start imagining the least fearful situation in the hierarchy, and when she can do that for a number of times without tensing up, she can move to the next situation in the hierarchy, and so on. It is also usual for the person to create an unrelated, relaxing control scene, such as lying on the beach watching the waves roll in, which can be used to help her relax. Over a number of sessions, the person works her way up the hierarchy while maintaining complete relaxation, until eventually she can approach the real situation.

In practice, systematic desensitization is often combined with other techniques, such as counterconditioning (pairing pleasant associations, such as being able to get to exotic destinations, with the feared situation) and observational learning (using the real situation or a video), which involves watching other people being calm and relaxed in the anxiety-provoking situation.

2. First, people seek help from mental health professionals not only for psychological problems but also as an aid in dealing with troubled relationships, or coping with transitions in life, and other troubling situations. Second, there should be no stigma attached to getting help when it is needed. The prevalence of psychological disorders and similar types of problems is much higher than most people realize, so we all probably know someone who is or has been in therapy or perhaps needs to be. So, what should we expect from psychotherapy? The Application section gives some important guidelines about the therapist–client relationship and the psychotherapy process.

The cornerstone of psychotherapy is the relationship between the therapist and the person seeking help. This relationship is a collaborative endeavor where the client is actively involved in the therapeutic process. Therapy requires work not only during the therapy sessions but also outside them. So one should expect to be involved and active. In addition, people should not expect the therapist to make decisions for them. Virtually all forms of therapy are designed to increase a person's sense of responsibility, confidence, and mastery in dealing with life's problems. The therapist will help foster independence and encourage personal responsibility.

A therapist is not a substitute friend. Instead he or she is there to objectively and honestly respond to issues and problems and is more like a consultant than a friend. In addition, ethically and legally, everything that goes on in therapy is totally confidential. And under no circumstances does therapeutic intimacy include sexual intimacy.

A person should also expect therapy to challenge how he or she thinks and acts, and sometimes this can be a painful process. But becoming aware that changes are needed is a necessary step toward developing healthier forms of thinking and behavior. It is important, however, not to confuse insight with change. Just because people gain an understanding of the sources and nature of their psychological problems does not mean that they will automatically resolve these problems. Likewise, the catharsis that often results from therapy is not synonymous with change. With some effort and the help of the therapeutic process, one can move toward changing how one thinks, behaves, and reacts to other people, but this will not happen overnight.

Progress Test 1

1. a	8. c	15. d
2. c	9. b	16. c
3. d	10. b	17. a
4. c	11. d	18. e
5. d	12. c	19. b
6. d	13. b	20. a
7. c	14. a	

Progress Test 2

1. d	8. a	15. c
2. c	9. c	16. a
3. d	10. b	17. d
4. d	11. b	18. a
5. b	12. a	19. b
6. c	13. b	20. c
7. d	14. d	

Appendix   Statistics: Understanding Data

OVERVIEW   Appendix A introduces the topic of statistics and explains how and when various statistical techniques are used. Descriptive statistics are used to organize and summarize data in a meaningful way. Included in the discussion are frequency distributions, which can be presented as a table, histogram, or frequency polygon; measures of central tendency (mode, median, and mean); and measures of variability (range and standard deviation). The z scores are explained and the concept of the normal distribution is presented.

Correlation is defined, and the correlation coefficient is described. Both positive and negative correlations are illustrated, and it is noted that correlational research is restricted to prediction and cannot be used to identify cause-and-effect relationships. The scatter diagram can be used to graphically depict the relationship between two variables.

Inferential statistics are used to determine whether outcomes of a study can be generalized to a larger population, and they provide information about the probability of a particular result if only random factors are operating. It is pointed out that if this probability is small, the findings are said to be statistically significant.

Descriptive Statistics

Learning Objectives

When you have finished studying this section of the chapter, you should be able to:

1. Define *descriptive statistics* and state what they are used for.

2. Describe a frequency distribution, a histogram, and a frequency polygon and specify how they differ from each other.

3. Identify the three measures of central tendency and provide examples of each.

4. Identify two measures of variability, explain how the z score is derived, and describe the standard normal curve.

Read the section "Descriptive Statistics" and **write** *your answers to the following:*

1. (a) Descriptive statistics are used to _____ and _____ data in a meaningful way.

(b) A frequency distribution is a(n) _____ of how often various scores occur; _____ are set up and occurrences of each _____ are tallied to give the frequency of each.

(c) A histogram is a way of _____ representing a frequency distribution; it is like a bar chart with two special features: the bars are always _____ and they always _____

(d) A frequency polygon is a way of _____ representing a frequency distribution; in contrast to a histogram, a mark is made above each _____ at the point representing its frequency and these marks are then connected by _____

2. (a) A(n) _____ distribution is an asymmetrical distribution with more scores

piled up on one side of the distribution than on the other.

(b) In a(n) _____ distribution, most people have low scores; in a(n) _____ distribution, most people have high scores.

(c) A(n) _____ distribution is one in which scores fall equally on both halves of the graph; an example of a(n) _____ distribution is the normal curve.

3. (a) A measure of central tendency is a single _____ that presents some information about the center of a(n) _____ distribution.

(b) The mode is the score or category that occurs most _____ in a set of raw scores or in a(n) _____ distribution.

(c) The median is the score that falls in the _____ of a(n) _____ distribution; if the scores are arranged from lowest to highest, the median will have a(n) _____ number of scores on each side of it.

(d) A problem with the _____ and the _____ is that both measures reflect only one score in the distribution; the mean is the _____ of a set of scores in a distribution _____ by the number of scores and is usually the most representative measure of central tendency.

(e) Because each score in a distribution enters into its computation, the mean is particularly susceptible to _____ scores; any unusually _____ or _____ score will pull the mean in its direction.

4. (a) In addition to identifying the central tendency in a distribution, researchers may want to know how much scores in a distribution _____ from one another; a measure of _____ is a single number that presents information about the _____ of scores in a frequency distribution.

(b) A simple way to measure _____ is with the range, which is computed by subtracting the _____ score in a distribution from the _____ score; the range provides a limited amount of information because it depends on only the two most _____ scores in a distribution.

(c) The standard deviation is a measure of _____ that is expressed as the square root of the sum of the squared deviations around the mean divided by the number of scores in the distribution; the _____ the standard deviation, the more spread out are the scores in a distribution.

5. (a) Researchers can also describe the relative position of any individual score in a distribution by locating how far away from the mean the score is in terms of _____ units; a statistic called a _____ gives that information.

(b) To compute a(n) _____, subtract the mean from the score of interest (that is, calculate its deviation from the mean) and divide this quantity by the standard deviation; a positive _____ indicates that the score is _____ the mean, whereas a negative _____ shows that the score is _____ the mean.

(c) Some variables, such as height, weight, or IQ, if graphed for large numbers of people, fall into a characteristic pattern called the

_____

or the _____ ;

this distribution is symmetrical, and the

_____ , _____ , and

_____ fall exactly in the middle.

6. Read the following and write the correct term in the space provided:

(a) Professor Wilson calculated the mode, median, and mean of the scores from the midterm exam. These are descriptive statistics referred to as

_____

(b) Professor Wilson noticed that the most frequently occurring score was 73; this score is called the _____

(c) In order to determine how spread out the scores are, Professor Wilson subtracted the lowest score in the distribution from the highest. In this instance he has calculated a measure of _____ called the _____

(d) Next he subtracted the mean from each score in the distribution, squared each of these deviations, added them up, divided by the number of scores in the distribution, and finally took the square root of the number just calculated. Professor Wilson has calculated a measure of _____ called the_____

(e) Finally, Professor Wilson graphically represented the frequency distribution by placing a mark above each score at the point representing its frequency and then connecting these points with straight lines. This type of graph is called a(n)

_____

Review of Key Terms 1

descriptive statistics	histogram
frequency distribution	frequency polygon

skewed distribution	median
positively skewed distribution	mean
negatively skewed distribution	measure of variability
	range
symmetrical distribution	standard deviation
measure of central tendency	z score
mode	standard normal curve (standard normal distribution)

Matching Exercise

Match the appropriate term with its definition or description.

1. _____ A number, expressed in standard deviation units, that shows a score's deviation from the mean.

2. _____ Statistics used to organize and summarize data in a meaningful way.

3. _____ A symmetrical distribution forming a bell-shaped curve in which the mean, median, and mode are all equal and fall in the exact middle.

4. _____ A summary of how often various scores occur in a sample of scores. Score values are arranged in order of magnitude and the number of times each score occurs is recorded.

5. _____ A measure of variability; expressed as the square root of the sum of the squared deviations around the mean divided by the number of scores in the distribution.

6. _____ An asymmetrical distribution; more scores pile up on one side of the distribution than on the other.

7. _____ A single number that presents information about the spread of scores in a frequency distribution.

8. _____ A distribution in which the scores fall equally on both sides of the graph. The normal curve is an example.

9. _____ A measure of variability; the highest score in a distribution minus the lowest score.

True/False Test

Indicate whether each statement is true or false by placing T or F in the blank space next to each item.

1. ____ In a positively skewed distribution, most people have high scores.

2. ____ The mode is the most frequently occurring score in a distribution.

3. ____ A measure of central tendency is a single number that presents some information about the "center" of a frequency distribution.

4. ____ In a negatively skewed distribution, most people have low scores.

5. ____ A histogram is a way of graphically representing a frequency distribution where frequency is marked above each score category on the graph's horizontal axis and the marks are connected by straight lines.

6. ____ The mean is the sum of a set of scores in a distribution divided by the number of scores and is usually the most representative measure of central tendency.

7. ____ A frequency polygon is a way of graphically representing a frequency distribution and is a type of bar chart using vertical bars that touch.

8. ____ The median is the score that divides a frequency distribution exactly in half, so that the same number of scores lies on each side of it.

Check your answers and review any areas of weakness before going on to the next section.

Correlation and Inferential Statistics
Learning Objectives

When you have finished studying this section of the chapter, you should be able to:

1. Define *correlation*, explain what the correlation coefficient is, and describe how it is depicted graphically.

2. Describe how inferential statistics are used and explain what is meant by statistical significance.

3. Define *population* and explain why sampling is used.

*Read the sections "Correlation" and "Inferential Statistics" and **write** your answers to the following:*

1. (a) Correlation is the _____ between two variables and is assessed by a statistic called the correlation coefficient; this is a measure of the _____ and _____ of the relationship between two variables.

(b) To compute a correlation coefficient, the data from both variables of interest can be converted to _____ ; this is done so that data in different forms can be put into a standard scale.

(c) A correlation coefficient can range anywhere from _____ to _____ ; the exact number tells us about the _____ of the relationship being measured and its _____ .

(d) A number close to _____ indicates a strong relationship whereas a number close to _____ indicates a weak relationship; the sign (+ or −) of the correlation tells us about the relationship's _____ .

(e) A positive correlation coefficient means that as one variable _____ , the second variable tends to _____ ; a negative correlation coefficient indicates that as one variable _____ , the other tends to _____

2. (a) Plotting two variables together creates a _____ , or _____ , which is a graphic representation of the relationship between the two variables.

(b) A straight diagonal line starting in the lower left-hand corner of the graph and progressing to the upper right represents a perfect _____ correlation; a straight diagonal line starting in the upper left-hand corner of the graph and ending at the lower right-hand corner represents a perfect _____ correlation; when data points fall randomly with no general direction to them, a(n) _____ correlation is depicted.

(c) In addition to describing the relationship between two variables, correlation coefficients are useful for another purpose, _____ ; knowing a person's score on one of two related variables helps _____ what the person's score will be on the other variable.

(d) The one thing a correlation does not tell us is _____ ; the fact that two variables are highly correlated does not mean that one variable directly _____ the other; the only way to determine _____ and _____ is to conduct an experiment.

3. (a) Inferential statistics allow researchers to determine whether the outcome in a study is likely to be more than just a(n) _____ event and whether it can be legitimately _____ to a larger population.

(b) If the results of a study are more extreme than would be expected by _____ alone, we reject the idea that no _____ effect has occurred and conclude that the manipulation of the independent variable is the reason for the obtained results; when this happens, the results are

_____

(c) Generally, if the probability of obtaining a particular result if random factors alone are operating is less than _____ (5 chances out of 100), the results are considered

_____ ;

researchers who want to be even more sure set their probability value at _____ (1 chance out of a 100).

4. (a) A(n) _____ is a complete set of something—people, nonhuman animals,

objects, or events; because the entire _____ of interest usually cannot be studied, researchers select a subset of the population, called a(n) _____

5. Read the following and write the correct term in the space provided:

(a) Dr. Jabul discovers that the more education people have, the more money they tend to earn. Dr. Jabul has discovered a(n) _____ correlation.

(b) Based on his research, Dr. Jabul can use one variable to _____ the other but he cannot say that one variable _____ the other.

(c) When Professor Alphonse plotted his data on a scatter plot, he noticed that they clustered in a pattern that extends from the upper left-hand hand corner of the graph to the lower right-hand corner. This pattern suggests that the two variables are _____ related.

(d) When Kayla analyzed the correlational data for her psychology project, the correlation coefficient was +.07. Kayla can conclude that the two variables are _____ correlated.

(e) When researchers analyzed the data from their experiment, they found large differences between the control group and the experimental group that were not due to chance. They can conclude that the results are _____

(f) In order to discover how people feel about the level of service provided, the ABC company asks a randomly selected subset of their customers to fill in a brief questionnaire. ABC's customers represent the _____ and the subset surveyed is a(n) _____

Review of Key Terms 2

correlation
correlation coefficient
positive correlation
  coefficient
negative correlation
coefficient

scatter diagram (scatter
  plot)
inferential statistics
statistically significant
population
sample

Matching Exercise

Match the appropriate term with its definition or description.

1. _____ A graph that represents the relationship between two variables

2. _____ A measure of the magnitude and direction of the relationship (the correlation) between two variables; the closer the number is to +1 or −1, the stronger the relationship.

3. _____ Statistical techniques that allow researchers to determine whether the outcomes in a study are likely to be more than just chance events and whether they can be legitimately generalized to a larger population.

4. _____ A complete set of something—people, nonhuman animals, objects, or events.

5. _____ The relationship between two variables.

True/False Test

Indicate whether each statement is true or false by placing T or F in the blank space next to each item.

1. ___ Results can be considered statistically significant if the probability of obtaining them, if chance factors alone are operating, is less than .05 (5 chances out of 100).

2. ___ A positive correlation coefficient indicates that as one variable increases, the other tends to decrease.

3. ___ A sample is a subset of a population.

4. ___ A negative correlation coefficient indicates that as one variable increases, the other tends to increase.

> Check your answers and review any areas of weakness before doing the progress tests.

Progress Test 1

Review the complete chapter, review all your study notes, and then test yourself on the following progress test. Check your answers. If you make a mistake, review your notes, review the relevant section of the study guide, and, if necessary, go back and read the appropriate part of your textbook.

1. Professor Admunson used a scatter diagram to depict the relationship between her students' high school GPA and their first-year GPA in college. She noticed that the data points clustered in a pattern that extend from the lower left-hand hand corner of the graph to the upper right-hand corner. This pattern suggests that the two variables _____
   (a) are negatively correlated
   (b) have no relationship
   (c) are positively correlated
   (d) have a cause-and-effect relationship

2. A measure of variability is to _____ as a measure of central tendency is to _____
   (a) mode; median
   (b) correlation; scatter plot
   (c) standard deviation; mean
   (d) histogram; frequency polygon

3. One student in the class got an extremely low score of 10 out of 100 on a test. Which measure of central tendency is most affected by this low score.
   (a) mean   (c) median
   (b) mode   (d) range

4. Following the final exam, Professor Farrar calculated a number of statistics and noticed that the standard deviation was extremely small. This indicates that
   (a) the scores on the exam were clustered around the mean and not spread out
   (b) the distribution was skewed
   (c) the scores had a great deal of variability and were not clustered around the mean.
   (d) there were very few students in her class

5. Mrs. Kodiak has seven children aged 3, 5, 8, 9, 12, 15, and 15. The median age of her children is
   (a) 9   (c) 12
   (b) 15   (d) 67

6. When the results of an experiment were examined and the appropriate statistics calculated, the researchers concluded that the probability of obtaining these results, if random factors alone were operating, was less than .01. The results are
   (a) statistically significant
   (b) probably due to chance
   (c) statistically insignificant
   (d) skewed

7. For his class presentation, Liam prepared a graph that depicted a frequency distribution with vertical bars that touched each other. Liam has constructed a
   (a) scatter diagram
   (b) frequency polygon
   (c) histogram
   (d) standard deviation

8. Liam's graph is a symmetrical distribution with an equal amount of scores on each side of the graph. It is very likely that
   (a) the mean is larger than the median
   (b) the mode is larger than the mean
   (c) the mean, mode, and median have the same value
   (d) the median is larger than the mode

9. When researchers calculated the correlation coefficients for two different sets of data, they discovered that set A had a negative correlation of –.85 and set B had a positive correlation of +.62. They can conclude that
   (a) set A has a stronger correlation than set B
   (b) set A has a weaker correlation than set B
   (c) set B has a stronger correlation than set A
   (d) both (b) and (c)

10. When Gary calculated the mean, median, and mode of the data in his frequency distribution, he was using
    (a) inferential statistics
    (b) correlational statistics
    (c) descriptive statistics
    (d) measures of variability

Progress Test 2

After you have checked your understanding of the material in Progress Test 1 and have done a complete chapter review with special focus on any areas of weakness, you are ready to assess your knowledge of Progress Test 2. Check your answers. If you make a mistake, review your notes, the relevant section of the study guide, and, if necessary, the appropriate part of your textbook.

1. In addition to calculating the range, Matthew also calculated the standard deviation for his frequency distribution of scores. Matthew is using
   (a) measures of variability
   (b) inferential statistics
   (c) measures of central tendency
   (d) correlational statistics

2. When Professor Kitahara finished marking the final exams, he plotted the results on a graph by marking the frequency above each score category on the horizontal axis and then connected the marks using straight lines. Professor Kitahara has constructed a
   (a) frequency distribution
   (b) histogram
   (c) frequency polygon
   (d) scatter diagram

3. Professor Kitahara observed that the graph was a symmetrical distribution that resembled a bell-shaped curve and that the mean, median, and mode were all equal. A student who scored better than 84 percent of the other students in this distribution would have a *z* score of
   (a) +1   (c) +.84
   (b) –1   (d) –.84

4. Hanna has a grade point average of 3.5. What measure of central tendency was used to calculate this statistic?
   (a) the median
   (b) the standard deviation
   (c) the mode
   (d) the mean

5. In her research Dr. Simiak found that the more credit cards people have, the less money they have in their savings accounts. Dr. Simiak has found a _____ correlation between the number of credit cards owned and savings.
   (a) positive   (c) negative
   (b) zero   (d) skewed

6. Range is to mode as _____ is to _____
   (a) correlation; scatter diagram
   (b) median; mode
   (c) correlation coefficient; *z* score
   (d) variability; central tendency

7. Fydor compared two frequency distributions and noticed that in the first distribution most people had low scores and in the second distribution most people had high scores. The first distribution is _____ and the second distribution is _____

   (a) positively skewed; negatively skewed
   (b) symmetrical; normal
   (c) negatively skewed; positively skewed
   (d) a polygon; a histogram

8. When Tyborg calculated the mean and standard deviation for a set of scores, he found that the mean was 55 out of a 100 and the standard deviation was 15. If the scores are normally distributed, Tyborg can conclude that approximately 68 percent of the scores are between

   (a) 40 and 70   (c) 55 and 70
   (b) 25 and 85   (d) 40 and 55

9. In the above example, a student with a z score of −1 would have a score of

   (a) 55   (c) 70
   (b) 40   (d) 25

10. During the past month Karianne read 8 books, Kyle read 2 books, Phylis read 4 books, and Phillip read 6 books. The mean number of books read by this group is

   (a) 5   (c) 8
   (b) 20   (d) 6

Answers

Descriptive Statistics

1. (a) organize; summarize
   (b) summary; categories; category
   (c) graphically; vertical; touch
   (d) graphically; score category; straight lines

2. (a) skewed
   (b) positively skewed; negatively skewed
   (c) symmetrical; symmetrical

3. (a) number; frequency
   (b) frequently; frequency
   (c) middle; frequency; equal
   (d) mode; median; sum; divided
   (e) extreme; high; low

4. (a) differ; variability; spread
   (b) variability; lowest; highest; extreme
   (c) variability; larger

5. (a) standard deviation; z score
   (b) z score; z score; above; z score; below
   (c) standard normal curve; standard normal distribution; mean, median; mode

6. (a) measures of central tendency
   (b) mode
   (c) variability; range
   (d) variability; standard deviation
   (e) frequency polygon

Matching Exercise 1

1. z score
2. descriptive statistics
3. standard normal curve (standard normal distribution)
4. frequency distribution
5. standard deviation
6. skewed distribution
7. measure of variability
8. symmetrical distribution
9. range

True/False Test 1

1. F	4. F	7. F
2. T	5. F	8. T
3. T	6. T	

Correlation and Inferential Statistics

1. (a) relationship; magnitude; direction
   (b) z scores
   (c) −1; +1; magnitude; direction
   (d) 1; 0; direction
   (e) increases; increase; increases; decrease

2. (a) scatter diagram; scatter plot
   (b) positive; negative; zero
   (c) prediction; predict
   (d) causation; causes; cause; effect

3. (a) chance; generalized
   (b) chance; real; statistically significant
   (c) .05; statistically significant; .01

4. (a) population; population; sample

5. (a) positive
   (b) predict; causes
   (c) negatively
   (d) not
   (e) statistically significant
   (f) population; sample

Matching Exercise 2

1. scatter diagram (scatter plot)
2. correlation coefficient
3. inferential statistics
4. population
5. correlation

True/False Test 2

1. T	3. T
2. F	4. F

Progress Test 1

1. c	5. a	9. a
2. c	6. a	10. c
3. a	7. c	
4. a	8. c	

Progress Test 2

1. a	5. c	9. b
2. c	6. d	10. a
3. a	7. a	
4. d	8. a	